WHITE TERROR

Also by Allen W. Trelease

INDIAN AFFAIRS IN COLONIAL NEW YORK:
THE SEVENTEENTH CENTURY

WHITE TERROR

THE KU KLUX KLAN CONSPIRACY AND SOUTHERN RECONSTRUCTION

by Allen W. Trelease

HARPER & ROW, PUBLISHERS

NEW YORK, EVANSTON, AND LONDON

1817

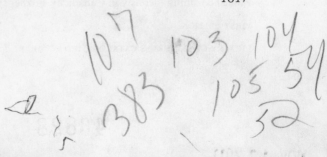

An Urban Affairs book under the general editorship of Kenneth B. Clark. The Urban Affairs Series is cosponsored by the Metropolitan Applied Research Center, Inc., and Harper & Row.

To Marcia E. Trelease

Contents

Illustrations

(Following page 272)

PORTRAITS

General Nathan Bedford Forrest, Grand Wizard of the Ku Klux Klan
Ryland Randolph, editor and Klansman of Tuscaloosa, Alabama
Governor William G. (Parson) Brownlow of Tennessee

PORTRAITS

Governor William W. Holden of North Carolina
Governor Powell Clayton of Arkansas
Attorney General Amos T. Akerman
Senator John Scott of Pennsylvania

Preface

Booker T. Washington once said that the white man could never hold the black man in a ditch without getting in the ditch with him. The Ku Klux Klan was a perfect illustration of that proposition. Beginning as a social fraternity devoted to playing pranks, it was soon transformed into a terrorist organization aiming at the preservation of white supremacy. And in the context of Reconstruction politics after 1867, it became a counter-revolutionary device to combat the Republican party and Congressional Reconstruction policy in the South. For more than four years it whipped, shot, hanged, robbed, raped, and otherwise outraged Negroes and Republicans across the South in the name of preserving white civilization.

The Klan could not have launched this career, much less persisted in it for so long, without widespread public support in the areas where it flourished. The Ku Klux were not simply desperadoes whom society abhorred but could not control. If some persons felt that way, there were as many others who joined the organization and gave it willing aid and comfort. Finally there was the large element—perhaps a majority—who were both repelled and attracted by the Klan. Sympathizing with its objectives, they deplored its methods. But more important than their private thoughts were their public actions. Such persons feared Klan retaliation upon themselves if they opposed its course; even more, perhaps, they feared to be accused of treason to the South and the white race. In effect the Klan wrapped itself in the Stars and Bars, recited the racist litanies which had been devised to justify Negro slavery, threatened death to unbelievers, and thereby rendered itself unassailable by orthodox Southerners. Willingly or unwillingly, they entered into a conspiracy to protect the Klan and advance its works.

The roots of this conspiracy ran so deep that, wherever it extended, the traditional system of local justice was undermined and subverted. In most places the reign of terror exceeded the power even of state governments to control, and federal intervention was required to bring it to a close. Even then the spirit which had animated it carried on and soon triumphed by other means, more humane in some respects as well as more effective.

In speaking of the Ku Klux *conspiracy* I recur to a term which Republicans used at the time, but which later became unfashionable and eventually archaic. If they gave it a more precisely political meaning than I, the distinction is only a relative one. The pages that follow attempt to explain the background and causes of the conspiracy, its violent career in the states where it took hold, and the agonizing process of stamping it out, involving men and measures at every level of government. This story is central to the history of Reconstruction after the Civil War. The Ku Klux terror colored nearly every aspect of Southern life and politics, often far beyond the immediate range of terrorist activity. It was therefore central to the formulation and implementation of Reconstruction policy in Washington.

My attitude toward the Ku Klux terror is in keeping with that of most recent historians of the Reconstruction period; it is impossible any longer to embrace the opposite view which for so long celebrated the Ku Klux Klan and its civilizing mission in the South. If I differ with my contemporaries at all in this respect, I suspect that the distinction arises from the heightened awareness of the magnitude and power of the Ku Klux conspiracy which this study has engendered. It has put the plight of Southern Republicans in clearer perspective and brought Republican men and measures into a still more favorable light than is customary. By the same token it has revealed still further the degrading effects of racism in societies which fall prey to that virus.

Inevitably I have incurred more debts for assistance than I can either repay or adequately acknowledge. Members of my family, friends, colleagues, librarians, and archivists from Boston to Austin all had a part in creating this book, though a few may conceivably wish to deny responsibility when they have seen it. More particularly, I am heavily obligated to the American Council of Learned Societies for a grant-in-aid, and to Wells College and the University of North Carolina at Greensboro for both money and time which were essential to its completion. I must express further gratitude to a contemporary South which welcomes the latter-day carpetbagger and permits him to join in criticizing certain uglinesses of the past which still cast shadows on the land but which are visibly and surely passing away.

ALLEN W. TRELEASE

Greensboro, North Carolina

... ...

Radical Reconstruction: The Reluctant Revolution

Compared with Reconstruction, no period better exemplifies historian Ulrich B. Phillips' dictum of forty years ago that the "central theme of Southern history" was a determination always to keep the section "a white man's country."[1]* Hardly an issue arose that did not involve the race question directly or indirectly and that was not fought out largely on that ground. The Louisiana Democratic party platform of 1865 proclaimed: "That we hold this to be a Government of white people, made and to be perpetuated for the exclusive benefit of the white race; and . . . that people of African descent cannot be considered as citizens of the United States, and that there can, in no event, nor under any circumstances, be any equality between the white and other races."[2] The same view was expressed by Alexander H. Stephens of Georgia, recent vice-president of the Confederacy: "Equality does not exist between blacks and whites. The one race is by nature inferior in many respects, physically and mentally, to the other. This should be received as a fixed invincible fact in all dealings with the subject. It is useless to war against the decrees of nature in attempting to make things equal which the Creator has made unequal; the wise,

* Source Notes begin on page 423.

humane, and philosophic statesman will deal with facts as he finds them."[3]

Few persons were as perceptive or candid as George Washington Cable, the New Orleans writer, who pointed out in the 1880's that Negroes had never advocated black supremacy during Reconstruction; their goal was equality.[4] Most Southern whites were unwilling to concede—even unable to comprehend—that freedom for the Negro could mean the same thing as freedom for them. Slaveholders could part with slavery as an economic institution—even welcome its passing in many cases—but to see the ex-slave compete for lands, jobs, and profits, to see him enter the professions and hold political power—that was quite another matter. Although pater-nalistic ties often survived, some of the old sentimental attachment to Negro dependents and concern for their welfare—and the corresponding devotion and obedience of the slaves—passed away with the severing of legal bonds. According to a Georgia Republican whose family had owned slaves before the war, white men did not look upon the Negro as they formerly had.

Before, they considered him as a gentle animal that they would take care of for his services; at least that was my feeling . . . and I think it was the feeling generally among the people where I was raised. Now, in place of that kindly feeling of the master, there is a feeling of bitterness—a feeling that the negro is a sort of instinctive enemy of ours. And I do not think that feeling leaves the mind in a condition to treat him as kindly as the white man would be treated under similar circumstances.[5]

After promoting for a generation and more the idea of innate Negro inferiority in order to justify slavery, Southerners could hardly be expected suddenly to abandon it with the coming of emancipation, especially in the wake of military defeat.[6] The newly freed slave, regarded as occupying an intermediate stage between humanity and the lower orders of animal life, fell into a niche already prepared for him—that of the ante-bellum free Negro. As such, he was not a citizen and had no civil or political rights except those which the white community deemed proper to confer.[7] "He still served, we still ruled," as Cable pointed out a few years later; "all need of holding him in private bondage was disproved. . . . Emancipation had destroyed private, but it had not disturbed public, subjugation. The ex-slave was not a free man; he was only a free Negro."[8] In effect Negroes were now the slaves of every white man. As subordination and discipline had been enforced by the lash before, it continued to be so now, but without the restraining influence of the slaveholder's self-interest. "The pecuniary value which the individual negro formerly represented having disappeared," Carl Schurz reported in 1865, "the maiming and killing of colored men seems to be looked upon by many as one of those venial offenses which must be forgiven to the outraged feelings of a wronged and robbed people." Most whites, he said, appeared to believe that Negroes existed for the special purpose of providing for their needs.[9] If Schurz exaggerated, the history of the Ku Klux Klan will show that he did not do so very much. Certainly whipping and corporal punishment were regarded as the white man's right and duty, emancipation or no emancipation; organized regulators or vigilantes took up this task with the advent of emancipation, and the Klan further institutionalized the practice.[10]

Negroes often suffered by their liberation.

As a slave [a Mississippi official pointed out in 1871], the negro was protected on account of his value; humanity went hand in hand with the interest of the owner to secure his protection, to prevent his being overworked, underfed, insufficiently clothed, or abused, or neglected when sick. But as a free man, he was deprived of all the protection which had been given to him by his value as property; he was reduced to something like the condition of a stray dog.[11]

For all the talk of white suffering during the Reconstruction era, it was the black man who experienced the greatest deprivation and mistreatment, first and last. But it was a rare freedman who regretted emancipation; stories to the contrary could almost invariably be traced to white men's rationalizations of slavery.

Negroes wanted the same freedom that white men enjoyed, with equal prerogatives and opportunities. The educated black minority emphasized civil and political rights more than the masses, who called most of all for land and schools. In an agrarian society, the only kind most of them knew, landownership was associated with freedom, respectability, and the good life. It was almost universally desired by Southern blacks, as it was by landless peasants the world over.[12] Give us our land and we can take care of ourselves, said a group of South Carolina Negroes to a Northern journalist in 1865; without land the old masters can hire us or starve us as they please.[13] A major failure of Reconstruction was that, except for a favored few, they never got it. Not only did they lack money or credit, but the government made no substantial effort to help them obtain it. Whites in many areas refused to sell, lease, or even rent land to Negroes when they did not have the means to buy, and often actively conspired to keep them from acquiring it. Negro landownership would have enhanced the economic and social well-being of the entire section, but it smacked too much of equality and independence. Some Negroes who did acquire farms of their own were driven off by mobs or the Ku Klux Klan. A Negro state senator in Florida believed that there was a general understanding among whites to deprive blacks of a great part of the income and property they had rightfully acquired. In many places this was correct.[14]

The desire for education was reflected in the avidity with which blacks of all ages took advantage of the limited schooling made available to them immediately after the war. Knowledge and literacy too were associated with freedom. Some of this enthusiasm was transitory, particularly among the elders, but parents continued to send their children to schools, where they existed, and to cry for their establishment where they did not.

Although a minority of Negroes moved to town—occasionally driven there by white terrorism—the overwhelming majority stayed on the land as wage laborers and sharecroppers. There was little motivation to work harder than they had under slavery. Many whites repeated the stock attitudes regarding Negro character: they were lazy, irresponsible, wasteful, and careless of property; they procrastinated, lacked forethought or perseverance, and derived no satisfaction from a job well done; they engaged in petty thievery and had no sense whatever of right and wrong or truth and falsehood. These characterizations were valid in varying measure—the natural defense mechanisms generated by a life of slavery. One well-disposed Northerner trying to cope with a Georgia cotton plantation reiterated nearly all of these traits from experience with his own laborers, but pointed out that the one thing which seemed to overcome Negro heedlessness was the desire to own their own land.[15] Native Southerners admitted, however, that Negroes were performing far better than they had had any reason to expect at emancipation. A few proclaimed Negro labor the best in the world. The truth seems to be that, after a brief exultation with the idea of freedom, Negroes realized that their position was hardly changed; they continued to live and work much as they had before.[16]

But white men generally agreed on the Negroes' good behavior after the war, and it was for many a matter of pleasant surprise; they had assumed that slavery alone could keep the blacks in good order. Most freedmen were as submissive and deferential to white men as before the war. The great majority were totally dependent upon white favor for a livelihood, and self-interest dictated subservience as a matter of second nature. If some aggressive souls—usually a minority of younger Negroes and other free spirits—talked back or refused to give up the sidewalk, this "insolence" was rare.[17] Seldom were Negroes willing to stand up to a white man and resist or defy him to his face; those who did automatically incurred the wrath of the white community, and risked their lives.[18] Concerted resistance was almost never successful and was apt to prove fatal. Whites were more numerous in most areas, and better armed. More important, they were used to commanding and the blacks to obeying. Next to poverty and economic dependence, this was the freedman's greatest handicap in asserting real freedom during the Reconstruction era.

When Negroes did strike back or defy the master race it was more often the product of impetuosity and extreme aggravation than forethought and planning. Whites commonly ascribed Negro violence, whether directed against them or (more often) among the blacks themselves, as the product of a congenitally passionate nature. The blacks were like children, it was said, who flared up without thought of consequences and then almost as quickly subsided.[19] Negroes seemingly committed fewer murders than whites in proportion to their number, and most of these were crimes of passion in which other Negroes were the victims. Certainly black men were more often the victims than the perpetrators of interracial violence.

A partial exception to the rule of Negro passivity was the crime of arson. The fires almost invariably occurred at night, with barns, gin houses, and other outbuildings the chief targets, and the culprits were seldom discovered. This was, in fact, one of the few relatively safe ways Negroes had of evening the score with white men. Incendiarism sometimes accompanied or followed outbreaks of white terrorism, although the fire victims were not always those guilty of the terror. Whites frequently imagined incendiary plots when there were none, just as they had long imagined servile insurrections.

But the chief crime complained of was petty thievery. Most thefts occurred after dark, with no witnesses, and it was almost impossible to discover the culprits. Cotton and corn were stolen from the fields, hams were abducted from smokehouses, tools and equipment disappeared from sheds and barns. Occasionally cows, sheep, and hogs were stolen and slaughtered. Some planters who had raised their own meat supplies before the war now gave up trying to keep livestock. Negro larceny, too, was a legacy of slavery: a poverty-stricken people, systematically denied the fruits of their own labor and having no property of their own to consider sacred, appropriated what they needed to make life more livable.[20]

In slavery times planters had customarily disciplined their own slaves without recourse to the law and without attracting much public attention, and, though Negro thievery was a legal offense, recognizable by the courts, habit and a reluctance to haul Negroes into the courts like white men, with all the attendant delays and expenses, encouraged a continuation of arbitrary and extralegal punishments.[21]

It has been the accepted view that wealthy, cultured whites, including the larger ex-slaveholders, cherished a kindlier feeling toward Negroes and exhibited less race hatred than their lower-class brethren.[22] Close investigation, however, uncovers so many exceptions that the truth or usefulness of the belief is open to question. Invariably coming from upper-class sources, it is possibly a self-gratifying myth. Many planters and their sons now cheated or browbeat the freedmen, as they had their slaves. John Dollard, a modern sociologist, reports recent evidence that the greatest hostility springs from neither the highest- nor lowest-class whites, but from middle-class whites striving to improve their formerly lower-class positions. They, rather than the poorest whites, are said to resent Negroes owning property or holding jobs that might otherwise belong to white men.[23] But, during Reconstruction, white men of all classes shared in the persecution of Negroes.

Of course, there were innumerable examples of upper-class white paternalism too. Some of it sprang from personal friendship or general benevolence. But much of it arose from the general belief in Negro childishness and irresponsibility. As Benjamin H. Hill of Georgia pointed out, white judges and juries sometimes were overly lenient to Negro criminals in cases between blacks, punishing them less severely than their offenses merited, on the ground that they were not really as accountable for their shortcomings as white people.[24]

It is an open question whether Southern patricians were more or less enthusiastic about Negro schooling than their lower-class neighbors. Many in both classes thought that education would make the freedmen better citizens; others opposed education on the grounds that it was irrelevant to their proper place in society, and might even spoil blacks for their true vocation in the cotton field. It was also expensive. Some men in every class opposed all public education on principle, even for whites; some argued that public schools might desegregate and lead to racial mixing. In Mississippi hostility to public schools constituted a major tenet of the Ku Klux Klan, but it stimulated white terrorism in nearly every other state, as well.[25]

Whites of every class united in opposition to what they called social equality—a completely integrated society—as leading inevitably to intermarriage and degeneration of the white race. In that event, a South Carolinian declared, "we shall become a race of mulattoes . . . another Mexico; we shall be ruled out from the family of white nations. . . . It is a matter of life and death with the Southern people to keep their blood pure."[26] A Republican of Georgia pointed out, "If you talk about equality, they at once conclude that you must take the negro into your parlor or into your bed—everywhere that you would take your wife. They seem to be diseased upon that subject. They do not seem to consider that he is merely to be equal before the law, but take it, I suppose designedly, to mean equality in the broadest sense; and hence they stir themselves up and lash themselves into a fury about it."[27]

Emancipation increased the Southern white rape complex because freedom presumably stimulated the Negro's innate passion for white women and removed external restraints. This was the supreme taboo, which evoked white supremacy in its most virulent form. Whether or not Negro rape of white women actually increased during Reconstruction, it certainly was not widespread; more important was the fact that whites *thought* it was on the increase.[28] The only penalty sufficient to deter the tendency was violent and speedy death—lynching without the delay and dignity of formal trial. The Fayetteville (Tennessee) *Observer* echoed widespread opinion when it condoned the lynching of an alleged Negro rapist in 1868: "The community said amen to the act—it was just and right. We know not who did it, whether Ku Klux or the immediate neighbors, but we feel that they were only the instruments of Divine vengeance in carrying out His holy and immutable decrees."[29] Here too the Ku Klux Klan helped to institutionalize a practice which preceded and long outlived it.

The physical and psychological necessities of keeping Negroes in subordination led to the wildest inconsistencies of attitude and expression. On the one hand the black man was best fitted by nature and temperament for a life of servility and happiest in his carefree dependence on white protectors. On the other hand he was only a degree removed from the wild beasts of the jungle, and the most constant surveillance was needed to keep him from bursting the bonds of discipline and turning upon his friends and protectors in a bloody insurrection. The first theory was necessary to rationalize slavery and the ensuing peonage, but as it never fully squared with the facts, the second argument served to justify necessary repressive measures. Both reinforced Negro subordinance.

Eternal vigilance is the price of despotism or white supremacy as well as of liberty. White men were never fully convinced by their own claims of affection for those they held in subjection, or by the accompanying belief that they were the Negroes' best friends, and they expected, at least subconsciously, that the blacks would react to slavery or white supremacy just as they liked to think *they* would if the shoe were on the other foot. This fear thus led to further aggression against the blacks in order to forestall any rebelliousness. Whenever Negroes did show evidence of discontent, whites were apt to react with disproportionate severity, regarding it as a symptom of greater discontent than the facts warranted. "I have heard planters complain very earnestly of the insubordinate spirit of their colored laborers," Carl Schurz reported in 1865, "because they remonstrated against the practice of corporal punishment. This was looked upon as a symptom of an impending insurrection." Investigation seldom revealed any basis for this fear; in fact there was reason to believe that rumors of a Negro rising were sometimes spread deliberately for the purpose of justifying tighter controls as a matter of general policy.[30]

Before the war, as Clement Eaton points out, "The Southern people suffered at times and in certain sections from a pathological fear of their slaves, not at all justified by the actual danger." Fears of a Negro insurrection, assuming the dimensions of a "black terror," had periodically rocked the section. They were stimulated by a very few actual slave revolts—the last was Nat Turner's in 1831—and rumors of countless others which the newspapers sedulously spread and exaggerated. In these periods of imagined crisis the courts were often ignored and mobs of vigilantes reigned supreme. Both Negroes and whites were terrorized and even lynched on the slightest suspicion of knowledge of or complicity in some rumored plot. Usually the fears were more or less localized, but others became general, as in 1856 when it was feared that the slaves would stage a mass uprising during the Christmas holidays.[31]

Such fears continued during the war and redoubled in the wake of Emancipation. In 1865 a general rising was again anticipated at Christmastime. Governor Humphreys of Mississippi called out the state militia and ordered it to patrol the roads and search Negro cabins for arms. This it did, in some cases with great brutality. Much the same thing happened in South Carolina and other states. Investigation revealed no evidence whatever to justify the panic, but fear recurred in 1866 and again in 1867. The advent of Radical Reconstruction in 1868 led to enhanced anxiety, which continued sporadically for years. Almost invariably the newspapers played a major role in spreading the terror. Over the years thousands of innocent Negroes were harassed, tortured, or dealt the extreme penalty. In this respect too the Ku Klux Klan for a time institutionalized a white vigilantism which long preceded and followed it. There was often no basis whatever for the fear; even the most peaceable Negro gatherings for political and other legal purposes were assumed to be incendiary conspiracies.[32] On occasion, however, white terrorism itself drove desperate freedmen to organize militarily for their own protection, or else Republican state governments mustered Negro and white militia for that purpose.

Louis F. Post, a onetime South Carolina carpetbagger, pointed out many years ago that it was a figment of the Southern white man's imagination that he knew the Negro better than anyone else and was even his best friend. Negroes had learned under slavery the " 'might of make believe,' that defence of the defenceless always and everywhere. . . ."[33] The truth was that Negroes often made the best of their inferior status, having no real alternative. Whites used their apparent acceptance as evidence of contentment, and whatever signs of dissatisfaction arose were ascribed to the influence of outside agitators (carpetbaggers during Reconstruction) rather than any deep-seated or general discontent.[34] Although the Southerner may have known the Negro as a slave, he did not know him as a man. The misconception, which endured for generations, probably arose from a need to rationalize white supremacy. It led to constant surprise and disillusionment over Negro behavior, which then had to be explained in terms of Negro ignorance and ingratitude as well as the machinations of outside agitators.

Northern Reconstruction policy evolved against this background of myths and realities. Again, the race question was crucial. The North began fighting the Civil War to defeat secession and ended by abolishing slavery as well. Emancipation brought the unavoidable problem of defining the freedmen's status. Northern Democrats generally shared the racial views of the white South and sanctioned the most minimal adjustments required by the ending of legal servitude. This was also the tendency of Abraham Lincoln and of Andrew Johnson afterward. Most Republicans fell between this conservatism and the Radicals' advocacy of full legal and political equality at war's end, but they were gradually driven toward egalitarianism by the course of events between 1865 and 1867. And as theirs was the majority party in the North, that drift determined federal government policy.

Lincoln had assumed the right to reorganize the South and guide her back into the Union, largely on his own authority as commander in chief. During the war, therefore, he sponsored new Loyal or Unionist state governments in Virginia, Tennessee, Louisiana, and Arkansas.[35] Following Appomattox and Lincoln's death, Andrew Johnson took advantage of a Congressional recess to organize the remaining seven states of the late Confederacy. Seemingly all that remained was for Congress to seat the Senators and Representatives chosen under these governments. But Congress delayed and ultimately refused to do so.[36]

While the Lincoln and Johnson regimes were dominated in the South by men who had taken a back seat in the secession movement, or opposed it altogether, and who accepted the end of slavery as a price of military defeat, they subscribed as a matter of course to the view that white men must continue to rule in the South. To this end they enacted a series of Black Codes in 1865 and 1866 which clearly and deliberately relegated the Negro to a second-class citizenship. No state extended the right to vote to black men, even to the few who might be educated or well-to-do. Nor was any hope extended for equality someday in the future.[37]

When new horizons did open up for the Negro, as they soon did, it was because of the Republican majority in Congress. Just as the war closed, Congress created a Bureau of Refugees, Freedmen, and Abandoned Lands, attached to the Army, primarily to care for the newly freed black population. The Freedmen's Bureau, as it was called, always suffered from inadequate funds and personnel to perform the tasks assigned it, but the services it did provide were indispensable. Under the direction of General O. O. Howard it distributed food and clothing to those of both races who needed them, protected Negroes against the most blatant forms of exploitation and mistreatment, arranged labor contracts with employers, and attempted with some success to enforce these contracts against infractions on either side. It established hospitals, schools, and colleges for its black charges with the cooperation of Northern charitable agencies.[38]

The Bureau represented an unprecedented extension of federal authority, regulating the economic, social, and legal affairs of individual persons within the respective states. Intended as an emergency device to cope with wartime and immediate postwar conditions, it was due to expire a year after the war ended. But the needs it was created to meet showed no sign of disappearing. Negroes were continually subjected to exploitation, discrimination, and outright violence, which they were powerless to combat alone. The new state governments not only failed to protect them or to assume the educational and other responsibilities of the Freedmen's Bureau, but their Black Codes actually perpetuated many of the hallmarks of slavery. So far as the Northern war effort had become a crusade to free the slaves, the victory seemed in danger of becoming undone. Thus the Republicans pushed through Congress in July 1866, over President Johnson's veto, a law continuing the Bureau for two years more.

In the same spirit were the Civil Rights Act and its sequel, the Fourteenth Amendment, which the Republican majority enacted over the President's objections in April and June of 1866. The former measure defined United States citizenship to include Negroes and extended to them the basic civil rights to sue and to testify in the courts, to hold and convey property, and most importantly, to enjoy equal benefit of the laws with white people. The Fourteenth Amendment, which was ratified and went into effect in 1868, incorporated the provisions of the Civil Rights Act into the Constitution; it also set forth a program for Southern Reconstruction which represented a compromise between the quick restoration favored by the white South and President Johnson and the stricter requirements (such as Negro suffrage) advocated by Radical Republicans.

The compromise was not acceptable to either the white South or Andrew Johnson. Among the Southern states, only Tennessee approved the amendment (because her government was in the control of Unionists), whereupon Congress promptly seated its Senators and Representatives. But without the support of other Southern states the amendment's ratification was impossible, and moderate Republicans saw their efforts going down to defeat. Rather than accept this, and armed with an overwhelming popular mandate in the 1866 Congressional elections, they adopted the more radical device of Negro suffrage to enable Negroes and Southern Unionists to defend themselves. The three Reconstruction Acts of 1867 declared the Johnson governments to be temporary and provided for new ones to be organized under military supervision in every Southern state except Tennessee. Mandatory Negro suffrage was coupled with temporary and partial rebel disfranchisement, and the new governments were required to ratify the Fourteenth Amendment before Congress would readmit them.

Implementing the new "Radical Reconstruction" policy occupied the greater part of 1867 and early 1868; in a few states delays prevented a full organization until 1870. Voters were registered and constitutional conventions were elected and convened; the work was then submitted to the voters, at which time state officials were also elected. These governments had hardly begun operation before Congress took additional steps to safeguard its handiwork. Negro suffrage existed in the South only by virtue of Congressional legislation, which could later be repealed. To prevent that, perhaps also to win some additional votes in the Northern states which had not yet enfranchised their black populations, and also because they had come to believe in impartial suffrage, the Republicans now wrote this policy into the Constitution via the Fifteenth Amendment. It was finally ratified and became effective in 1870.[39] The amendment did not prevent informal disfranchisement by terrorist means or otherwise, and this kind of activity (partly by the Ku Klux Klan) led to further legislation in 1870 and 1871 to enforce Negro rights. Republicans failed in their ill-starred attempt to gain immediate control of the executive branch in Washington by impeaching Andrew Johnson; but the same result was attained soon afterward by the election of General Ulysses S. Grant in November 1868.

In every Southern state the Republican party organized in support of Congressional Reconstruction and won control of the new state governments as they came into being. The majority of Southern whites bitterly opposed the policy from the beginning. Their political voice was the Democratic party, which assumed the name Conservative in several states in order to attract the many former Whigs who were also opposed. Throughout the period, Democrats were strong enough to control hundreds of county and local governments; eventually they took over each of the states as well, bringing Reconstruction to a close. Although most Southern Republicans were politically unconventional only in their acceptance of the Reconstruction Acts and Negro suffrage, Democrats labeled them all Radicals, and the term stuck. The party and the governments it organized were composed of three elements—Negroes, carpetbaggers, and scalawags—the diabolical trinity of Conservative mythology.

A basic assumption behind the Reconstruction Acts was that the Negro freedmen would support Congressional Reconstruction and would vote for the party which had freed them and granted them civil rights and the ballot. The assumption proved sound, for Negroes backed the Republican party overwhelmingly as long as they had the chance to do so. In fact they provided the bulk of the Republican electorate; in most states white supporters were more important for their leadership than for their numbers. No matter how dependent the freedmen were upon their former masters, or how much they continued to trust and confide in them as individuals, only a tiny minority of Uncle Toms willingly cast their ballots for the party of white supremacy.[40]

Negroes were elected to office in every state, leading Conservatives in moments of bitter abandon to characterize the whole policy as one of "Negro rule," an accusation made partly for political effect but also arising from the common conviction that racial sovereignty was indivisible. If whites did not rule blacks, it must therefore be the other way around.[41] The charge of Negro rule was absurd, for blacks never held office in proportion to their total number and they rarely held the most prominent posts. This situation resulted in part from the race prejudice which white Republicans shared, or which they sought to appease in nominating attractive party slates. But equally important was the plain fact that slavery was a poor training ground for the responsibilities of public office. The quality of those Negro officeholders high and low who did pass the barrier was not notably better or worse than that of white men who held comparable posts at that time, before, or later. Some, especially in the lower levels, were illiterate, but so were some of their white counterparts of both parties. Incompetent and illiterate officials did not begin or end with Reconstruction, nor were they typical of that period.[42]

The so-called carpetbaggers—Northerners who settled in the South during and after the war and affiliated with the Republican party—were only a tiny minority numerically. They had great influence, however, particularly in the deep South where the Negro population was heavy and there was no significant native white Republican element to provide leadership. The term "carpetbagger" was another canard. These men supposedly descended on the South like a swarm of locusts, bringing no more than they could carry in a carpetbag; their purpose was to prey on the defenseless region through political manipulation of the gullible freedmen. Actually most of these persons moved South by 1866, well before Radical Reconstruction was conceived or the Republican party was even organized in most of the South. Some were stationed there by the Army or Freedmen's Bureau, but most moved South for the same reasons of economic betterment that led greater numbers to go West. When the Republican party was organized and new governments were in process of formation these men filled a need for educated and occasionally experienced leadership. In fact, they usually raised the caliber of Radical government rather than lowering it. Of course their motives, abilities, and accomplishments ran the usual human scale; along with the incompetent or corrupt there were honest and highly able men whom posterity would have celebrated under other circumstances. Active Republicans required a tough skin and often great physical courage to withstand the social ostracism, economic boycott, verbal abuse, character assassination, and physical violence to which they were commonly subjected by Southern whites. In a few cases at least, this courage was inspired by a high degree of dedication. "That I should have taken a political office seems almost inexplicable," wrote General Adelbert Ames a quarter-century after he had been forced out of the governorship of Mississippi:

My explanation may seen ludicrous now, but then, it seemed to me that I had a Mission with a large M. Because of my [earlier] course as Military Governor, the colored men of the State had confidence in me and I was convinced that I could help to guide them successfully, keep men of doubtful integrity from control, and the more certainly accomplish what was every patriots' [*sic*] wish, the enfranchisement of the colored men and the pacification of the country.[43]

Men of Northern origin were to be found in local and subordinate offices here and there, and they served conspicuously in Congress, as governors, and in other high offices.[44]

The native white Republicans—scalawags to their enemies—were drawn from every walk of Southern life. Some had been Democrats and others were Whigs before the war. A few had served the Confederacy in conspicuous fashion, but most were wartime Unionists; the more uncompromising their Unionism had been, the more apt they were to embrace the Republican party afterward. Although they could be found, at least as isolated examples, throughout the South, most white Republican voters were concentrated in the hilly and mountainous regions where slavery had gained little foothold. The Appalachian highlands from western Virginia to northern Alabama and the Ozark Mountains of Arkansas were the major strongholds of white Republicanism during Reconstruction and for generations afterward.[45] The term "scalawag" was of course another form of political abuse; the personal character of Southern Republicans did not suffer by comparison with their accusers. Many joined the Republican party because it was the Unionist party and it opposed the planter interest as they themselves had done for years. Most of them shared in some measure the racial views common to the white South, and this helped make the Republican coalition unstable, but for the most part they lived in regions where the Negro was hardly more of a factor locally than in the North. In such places they commonly filled all of the political offices and supplied nearly all of the Republican votes. At the state level, particularly in the upper South, they filled many of the higher offices as well. A few members of the ante-bellum ruling class, usually ex-Whigs who had not been enthusiastic secessionists, also joined the Republican party, hoping to hold it to a moderate course and exercise a paternalistic rein on the Negroes while profiting by their strength at the polls. Such men carried great prestige and were given some of the highest offices in an effort to make the party more appealing to the white population generally, but the number of these converts was small. Governor James L. Alcorn of Mississippi belonged to this class, as did former Governors Lewis E. Parsons of Alabama and James L. Orr of South Carolina.[46]

In terms of ideology, Republicans were clearly the democratic party of the Reconstruction South. Unquestionably there was an element of political expediency involved in the raising of Negroes to civil equality with white men, but a great many believed in it as a matter of principle. The Charleston *Daily Republican,* a voice of moderation and a critic of corruption and ineptitude within the party in South Carolina, attacked Democratic predictions that white men must at some near day control the state again.

Such talk is as wickedly idle as for colored men to say that their race shall have complete control. It is not to be a matter of race at all. It is to be a matter of citizenship, in which colored and white are to have their rights and their due share of power; not because they are white, not because they are colored, but because they are American citizens. By-and-by we shall stop talking of the color of a man in relation to citizenship and power, and shall look at his wealth of mind and soul.[47]

Radicalism was also aimed less spectacularly at raising the status of poorer whites. Within limits the Republican party was a poor man's party which sought to obliterate racial lines as much as popular prejudice made it politically safe to do. Democrats defeated the effort, as they later did when the Populists tried it, by crying "nigger"; most Southern whites placed white supremacy above all other issues.

Many public offices which had been appointive were now made elective, sometimes at the cost of efficiency. In some states, but not all, more home rule was extended, making local government more responsive to local wishes and less subject to central control. Property qualifications for office-holding, where they still existed in 1867, were removed. Legislatures were reapportioned to provide more equal representation, although Negro counties in some states were slighted. By far the most important democratic extension was the granting of Negro suffrage. This had been required by the Reconstruction Acts, and it was incorporated in all the new constitutions.

The only exception to universal manhood suffrage lay in the partial and temporary disfranchisement of ex-Confederates. This provision had been written into the Reconstruction Acts to help ensure further that the new state governments would be organized by Unionists, but state law governed the matter thereafter. Where disfranchisement survived as a significant factor—in Tennessee and Arkansas—Republicans felt themselves outnumbered and regarded it as a continuing necessity to keep the former rebels and the Democratic party from taking control. However dubious this policy may have been in those states, a free and unfettered majority rule permitted Republican victories in most states, and disfranchisement was abandoned either at once or very soon. Much the same was true of eligibility for public office, which was more nearly determined by federal law. By 1872 Congress had removed the disqualifications of all but a relative handful of ex-Confederate leaders.[48] The Radical governments made no effort to outlaw the Conservative opposition or create a dictatorship. On the contrary, they were too lenient in enforcing law and order against those who used force to overthrow them.

There was corruption, electoral as well as financial, in nearly every state during the period of Republican control. Conservatives at the time succeeded in pinning on the Radical regimes a blanket charge of dishonesty which has never worn off, but the actual picture was not so simple. Corruption was rampant throughout the country after the war, and Democrats North and South were about as guilty as Republicans. The Tweed Ring in New York City supposedly stole more than all Southern politicans combined, if only because New York had more to steal. Within the South corruption varied widely from state to state. It flourished most in South Carolina, where it had been comparatively unknown, and in Louisiana, where it was endemic. In South Carolina the Republicans at least partially cleaned their own house under Governor Chamberlain after 1874. In Louisiana both parties were corrupt and remained so for generations. In Mississippi an honest Republican administration gave way to less honest Democratic regimes after 1875. During the period of Republican control, moreover, minority Democratic officials were sometimes as venal as their Republican counterparts, and Democratic businessmen sometimes offered the bribes that Republicans accepted. In the matter of electoral, as opposed to fiscal, corruption generalization is easier. Republicans were occasionally guilty of manipulating election returns, but these practices paled in comparison with the massive campaigns of fraud and intimidation, symbolized by the Ku Klux Klan, with which Democrats sought to return to power in nearly every state. It was largely owing to these methods that they did assume power in one state after another during the 1870's.[49]

The most visible Republican political machine was the Union (or Loyal) League. This Northern wartime patriotic society was carried South after the war, and with the advent of Radical Reconstruction it spread rapidly throughout the section. Organized as a secret society with oaths, ritual, and closed meetings, it drew its membership primarily from Negroes but from white Unionists in some localities as well. It was both a fraternal organization like the Grange and a branch of the Republican party. The League sponsored parades and barbecues and frequent meetings which served both a social and a political purpose. Speakers extolled patriotism and fidelity to the Union, adding that the Republican party was the champion of Unionism and the sponsor of Negro rights, appeals often coupled with bitter attacks on the Democratic opposition, who were accused of exploiting Negro labor and conspiring to restore slavery. Some League spokesmen called for the distribution of rebel lands among the freedmen whose labor had made them productive. They urged the blacks to assert their newly won legal rights and even on occasion to defend themselves by force when they were physically attacked. The League not only propagandized in behalf of the Republican party but helped to mobilize the voters, sometimes binding them by majority vote to support Republican nominees and then escorting them to the polls en masse to make sure they got there safely.

Like all political appeals, these exaggerated one party's virtues and the other's vices. The speakers sometimes promised more than they were able or willing to deliver, and the peonage to which Negroes were being subjected was not quite the same as slavery. But most of the appeals were justifiable and well within the bounds of acceptable political discourse. There is cause to regret that more of them were not carried out in practice. The Republican party had every right to win public support for its candidates and policies and to mobilize its voters as long as it operated peacefully and in conformance with democratic practices. There is almost no evidence to connect the League with aggressive violence or illegal activity of any kind. As a matter of fact it had a moderating effect more often than not, preaching a respect for democratic processes and obedience to the law even in the face of violence by the opposition.

Under the circumstances, however, it was dangerous to mobilize Negro support through the agency of a secret society whose full doings could not be known by outsiders. Given the psychopathic fear of Negro insurrection inherited from slavery days, and the explosive attitudes arising from Radical Reconstruction, the League's very existence was provocative and its secrecy unnecessarily so. Wild rumors circulated concerning what was said and done at its meetings; fears were hardly allayed by the sight of armed Negroes stationed outside to make sure that the uninitiated did not approach too close. The League provided, along with the carpetbagger and scalawag, a convenient scapegoat for every real or imagined evil of the day. Every Negro crime was attributed to the teaching and inspiration if not the direct order of this diabolical organization. And when the League was instrumental in producing Republican victories at the polls in 1867 and 1868, overturning the white establishment, Democrats almost universally denounced it as a subversive and inflammatory order which must be counteracted or broken up at any cost. The Union League therefore became a prime cause of white vigilantism in general and of the Ku Klux Klan in particular. The hostility it aroused became so great that Republicans generally disbanded the organization after the Presidential election of 1868.[50]

Radical egalitarianism for the Negro was primarily political and legal, but it also extended to economic and social matters. Republican governments repealed nearly all of the earlier laws requiring racial discrimination, and in some states it was specifically forbidden. A few states enacted laws to prevent racial segregation in railroad cars, theaters, restaurants, and hotels, but compliance was never complete and actual practice varied widely. It is mistaken to say that segregation did not begin until well after Reconstruction, although positive laws requiring it certainly were hostile to Republican policy.[51] Both constitutional and legal enactments guaranteed racial equality before the law.

The greatest and most enduring achievement of the Radical governments was the establishment of a functioning public school system for the first time in Southern history. As in politics, the greatest change lay in the fact that Negroes were included in the new dispensation. Building on the work of the Freedmen's Bureau and various charitable agencies before 1868, they created school systems which could not compare with most of those in the North, but which represented a great accomplishment in the light of Southern traditions and resources. Straitened finances and the difficulty of securing qualified teachers plagued the new school systems in every state. Economy was hampered further by the fact that almost everywhere separate schools were established for the two races—Negroes seldom demanded integrated facilities, which were opposed even by most white Republicans. Often churches or other buildings were converted to school purposes, and many schools were erected by groups of individuals on their own initiative, sometimes, in the case of Negro schools, with financial aid from interested whites. Local whites served as teachers of both white and Negro schools; literate Negroes also taught in Negro schools, as did white men and women from the North. Most who taught in Negro schools did so at the price of social ostracism and sometimes physical danger; they required a high degree of dedication and a high resistance to poverty, given the pay scales. The new state governments provided support for higher education for both races. In some cases this meant the creation of Negro colleges and universities, and in others it entailed efforts, largely unsuccessful, to desegregate existing institutions.[52]

New hospitals, orphanages, insane asylums, poorhouses, and other institutions were created, and older facilities enlarged. Jails and penitentiaries were built on a larger scale than before. Negro emancipation had rendered all of this necessary, for as slaves they had been under the wardship of their masters and rarely used public facilities. Moreover, the Radicals were somewhat readier than their predecessors to assume public responsibility for the welfare of citizens of both races, in many respects adopting attitudes and precedents which had been gaining headway in the North for a generation or more but which had lagged in the South.[53]

The Radical regimes generally shared the old Whig-Republican willingness to use government power to stimulate business activity and economic growth, especially in the field of transportation. As elsewhere in the country, the major beneficiaries of public aid were railroads, although a good deal of money was spent on roads, bridges, levees, and other public works. These projects were expensive, taken collectively, and some states assumed greater debts than the returns justified. Everywhere, North and South, politics and personal profiteering motivated some of these expenditures. For the most part, however, they were relatively sound, and in the South they decidedly enhanced the region's economic growth and prosperity. Some of the projects were essential to repair wartime deterioration and destruction.[54]

Radical governments did comparatively little to alter the conditions of labor or raise the incomes of citizens of either race; no governments did in nineteenth-century America. The Freedmen's Bureau continued most of its operations through 1868 and then gradually closed down because of Congressional nonsupport, suspending altogether in 1872. This was a misfortune, especially for the Negroes, as the state governments lacked the funds, personnel, and legal power to advise and protect them as effectively in relations with the white community. Even in Republican-controlled localities, the scales of justice were weighted against the impoverished freedmen. A number of states did enact laws, however, to protect persons against foreclosures of all their property for debt. These homestead exemptions were designed to appeal to both races, and some Democrats found them to be embarrassingly popular with poorer whites.[55]

One of the most cogent criticisms of Radical Reconstruction is that it failed to distribute land to the freedmen while it was giving them the ballot. Continuing economic dependence on the whites endangered every other right the Negro received. Some halting steps were taken by the federal government and the state of South Carolina to provide land to Negroes on easy terms, but they came to almost nothing, requiring as they did a social concern and an expenditure of tax money which most people in that generation did not have or were unwilling to make. At the same time, Southern whites were suspicious of Negro landownership and continued to discourage it, sometimes by outright violence. This was another service rendered by the Ku Klux Klan.[56]

The Radical governments spent more money and levied higher taxes than Southerners had been used to, as it was. But public needs were also unprecedented. Even the Johnson governments had raised taxes and expenditures to repair war damage, but left much yet to be done. The necessary new social services and especially the schools were extremely costly by previous governmental standards. When the aid extended to railroads is also added in, it is no wonder that both taxes and public debt rose unprecedentedly at every level of government. States, counties, and municipalities all raised what money they could and then mortgaged the future to meet immediate needs and finance improvements which required time to repay themselves. If debts occasionally climbed beyond a prudent level this was by no means universal; Democrats sometimes raised them further when they returned to power in the 1870's.

Even with these increases the Southern tax level remained considerably below that which prevailed in the North. The average tax rate in the eleven ex-Confederate states in 1870, including all state, county, town, and city taxes, was 1.57 per cent of assessed valuation; the comparable figure in all the remaining states was 2.03 per cent.[57] The Southern states were much poorer than the Northern, and less able to afford improvements and services; but this poverty was usually reflected in lower assessed valuations and hence a lower tax return at the same rate. Taxes levied by the Radical governments were extravagant only by comparison with the section's previous parsimonious standards.[58]

Equally controversial as the level of taxes and debts was the matter of who paid the taxes and who derived the benefits. Landowners, who had previously governed the South in their own interest, now found themselves bearing the major tax burden while the benefits went in large measure to businessmen and Negroes. Republican fiscal policies thus further infuriated the old ruling class and convinced them that civilization had given way to barbarism.

Republicans were often accused of partiality in law enforcement, winking at black criminality. Law enforcement was always difficult in the sparsely settled South, and lawlessness increased with the unsettled conditions that prevailed during and after the war. Negro criminality, chiefly petty theft, may well have grown temporarily, but it was always comparatively easy to convict Negro criminals when they were known. Republican officials (including Negroes) usually leaned over backward to demonstrate their impartiality in this respect. Republican governors were also accused of pardoning Negro criminals indiscriminately. This charge too was exaggerated if not wholly false. Whatever substance it may have had probably derived from the fact that some pardons were granted (after proper investigation) to redress the manifest injustices of many Southern courts against Negroes in interracial cases. White Conservatives often recommended such pardons in individual cases, but collectively it was easy to accuse the Radicals of yet another outrage against white civilization.[59]

Actually it was white men who committed most of the violence, and much of it was racially and politically inspired. When these overtones were not present, it was punished about as effectively, or ineffectively, in areas of Republican control as Democratic, and as was true in earlier and later periods of Southern history.[60] A great deal of violence was deliberate and organized, however, committed by mobs and by armed bands in and out of disguise. A disproportionate share was directed at Negroes and white Unionists, partly to avenge real or imaginary injuries arising from the war, partly to keep the Negro "in his place" economically and socially, and partly to overthrow the Republican party by intimidating, exiling, or assassinating its members. The Ku Klux Klan exemplified this kind of violence in the most spectacular way, but it extended far beyond the Klan. The greatest short-run deficiency of the Republican regimes—it would soon prove fatal—was their physical weakness. In the face of implacable white resistance they proved unable to preserve law and order, or their own existence, against attempts at violent overthrow. In certain parts of the South the authorities were almost paralyzed by organized lawlessness.

When conspiracies to obstruct justice assumed this dimension the only solution was armed force. Republican officials repeatedly called on the Army for help in suppressing combinations which they could not handle by the usual means, but the results were usually discouraging. In the first place, too many troops were mustered out of service too quickly amid the euphoric celebration of victory in 1865. Only 20,000 troops remained on duty in the South by the fall of 1867, and this number gradually fell to 6,000 by the fall of 1876; moreover, one-quarter to half of these were stationed in Texas, chiefly on frontier duty.[61] A much larger occupation force would have had trouble in maintaining order throughout the South. Furthermore, the traditional constitutional and legal safeguards against military power now sharply restricted the Army's peacekeeping potential. Its political and legal jurisdiction disappeared as soon as the new state governments were recognized by Congress. The military were limited thereafter to intervention only on application from, and in subordination to, the civil authorities. Where the latter did not act effectively, through incapacity, fear, or sympathy with the outlaws, the soldiers had little more than symbolic value.

For this reason most of the states organized militias, the traditional standby in times of emergency. But this weapon too was of doubtful value under the peculiar circumstances of Reconstruction. A militia composed in large part of the very white men who were engaged in lawlessness, or were sympathetic with it, seemed worse than useless. The only safe recruits were white Unionists and Negroes, but mobilizing these was equivalent to arming one political party against the other. The arming of Negroes in particular inflamed Conservatives and added fuel to the fire it was intended to quench. It summoned up the old fear of Negro insurrection and portended a race war which no Southern official was prepared to be responsible for. In the deep South, where white Republicans were few and far between, militia were seldom mobilized and they played a negligible peacekeeping role. Governors in the upper South organized white Unionist recruits, for the most part, to stamp out Democratic terrorism, a tactic that was relatively effective but highly dangerous politically, for it fed Conservative charges of military despotism.[62]

In the last analysis, Radical Reconstruction failed because the seed of biracial democracy which it planted fell on barren ground in the South, and the artificial nurture it received from the federal government was soon discontinued. Democracy has always required a high degree of popular homogeneity and consensus, a precondition which was altogether lacking in the South. Conservative opposition to Reconstruction was about as deeply felt as political opposition ever gets. As South Carolina whites expressed it in a protest to Congress in 1868:

Intelligence, virtue, and patriotism are to give place, in all elections, to ignorance, stupidity and vice. The superior race is to be made subservient to the inferior. . . . They who own no property are to levy taxes and make all appropriations. . . . The consequences will be, in effect, confiscation. The appropriations to support free schools for the education of the negro children, for the support of old negroes in the poor-houses, and the vicious in jails and penitentiary, together with a standing army of negro soldiers [the militia], will be crushing and utterly ruinous to the State. Every man's property will have to be sold to pay his taxes. . . . The white people of our State will never quietly submit to negro rule. . . . By moral agencies, by political organization, by every peaceful means left us, we will keep up this contest until we have regained the heritage of political control handed down to us by honored ancestry. That is a duty we owe to the land that is ours, to the graves that it contains, and to the race of which you and we are alike members—the proud Caucasian race, whose sovereignty on earth God has ordained. . . .[63]

Such views contrasted sharply with the vision of a biracial democracy quoted already from the Charleston *Daily Republican*.

Conservatives mercilessly pilloried the Negroes, carpetbaggers, and scalawags who staffed and supported the Republican regimes. The Democratic newspaper press—which far outstripped the Southern Republican press in numbers and circulation—played a vital role in stimulating and disseminating hatred of all things Radical. The wildest allegations and *ad hominem* arguments were at least half believed and unblushingly broadcast because they fit preconceived notions. Moreover, character assassination and slander were resorted to even when editors did not believe them, because they "served a good end" in discrediting the enemy. The Little Rock *Daily Arkansas Gazette,* for example, characterized the state constitutional convention of 1868 as "the most graceless and unconscionable gathering of abandoned, disreputable characters that has ever assembled in this state, outside of the penitentiary walls. . . . a foul gathering whose putridity stinks in the nostrils of all decency."[64] Altogether the whole tone of Southern government had been debased, Conservatives felt, and they proceeded to debase the tone of political discourse correspondingly. "So far as our State governments is [*sic*] concerned, we are in the hands of camp-followers, horse-holders, cooks, bottle-washers, and thieves," declared General James H. Clanton of Alabama. "We have passed out from the hands of the brave soldiers who overcame us, and are turned over to the tender mercies of squaws for torture. . . ."[65] Negroes were characterized as unfit to vote, much less hold office, and Democrats excoriated the federal and state enactments which had brought these things to pass. Few Southern Democrats in public life had any constructive proposal to make in behalf of the freedman. The whole thrust of their policy was to "put him back in his place" economically, socially, and politically. Some Conservatives disapproved in principle of universal manhood suffrage, even among whites, regarding it as a denial of character and intelligence in government and a threat to property; Negro suffrage was simply the ultimate outrage. An increasing number of so-called New Departure Democrats, like Benjamin H. Hill of Georgia, reluctantly accepted Negro suffrage as a *fait accompli* and hoped to control the black vote as they controlled black labor, but a majority rejected the idea out of hand and pledged themselves to repeal or nullify it at the earliest opportunity.[66]

To Conservatives, Republican affiliation was itself a sign of moral turpitude which only the flimsiest additional evidence sufficed to confirm. The laws of libel had no practical existence in that day, and such evidence was commonly embroidered or manufactured to suit the occasion.[67] Those Republicans who mingled socially with Negroes were morally depraved; those who refused to do so were hypocrites who betrayed their own political teachings. Those who came from the North were outlanders having no ties of knowledge or sympathy with the land and people they despoiled; those who were native to the South were traitors to their race and section and therefore equally unworthy of trust or confidence. Those who had owned slaves were now discovered to have treated them cruelly; those who had not owned them were the dregs of society who would never have risen to the surface in decent times. The greatest opprobrium was always heaped on those who associated most with the freedmen or who had substantial Negro followings.[68] Eric Hoffer has remarked that hatred requires a vivid and tangible devil.[69] Conservative Southern whites conjured them up by the hundreds.

But although Radical policies were condemned as a matter of course, Democrats in fact supported some of them unobtrusively. This was true of the exemption of homesteads from foreclosure, and also a great proportion of the railway expenditures. Opinion was divided on the subject of public schooling, especially for Negroes, but most Democrats accepted the policy and continued it when they later assumed power. Opposition was strongest in Mississippi, as noted earlier, but schools were unpopular with many rural people everywhere. The major complaints arose from the unprecedented cost of establishing and maintaining them and from the fact that Republicans sponsored the policy. Many persons objected less to Negro schools per se than to the Negro and Yankee teachers who staffed them. Most of these were advocates of racial equality, and some were quite militant about it. Hence Southerners resented them as they did the political carpetbaggers—outside agitators whose main purpose and effect was to alienate Negroes from the white population and make them less docile. H. C. Luce, a Northerner living in western North Carolina who had never engaged in politics at all, wrote of threats he received after establishing a school for local Negro children: "It is one of the perils of a Northern man residing in such a community that, however unexceptionable his conduct may be, if he is kind to the negroes and tries to help them, a report will very soon be put in circulation that he is inciting the negroes to revenge, and the chances are against him if he does not promptly and publicly convince his neighbors of their mistake in believing the report." Like countless teachers or sponsors of Negro schools across the South, Luce became a target of the Ku Klux Klan.[70]

In general, Conservatives advocated retrenchment and economy at the expense of many social services favored by the Radicals. Apart from white supremacy, their most popular and effective cry was for economy in government and lower taxes—a cry that often came from the heart as they compared present and past tax bills. The position of most Democrats on most issues was plainly reactionary. They appealed largely to a rural, agrarian, racist past which had become increasingly hostile to new ideas, and except for the most minimal accommodations required by the war's outcome they proposed to return to it. Later, after the Radicals had been swept aside, they were to become more enamored of the vision of an industrialized New South.

The bitterest opposition was always reserved for those Radical policies that portended racial equality. This was the supreme Radical sin.[71] Laws enacted for that purpose "have no binding force or moral sanction," the New Orleans *Times* declared in July 1868, "and will be disregarded and declared null and void as soon as the inalienable rights of the people are again recognized. . . . No privilege can be secured to the negro to which his white neighbors do not consent, and if he attempts to enforce privileges on the strength of carpetbag authority he will simply destroy his claims of future peace, and heap up wrath against the day of wrath."[72] Political and legal equality for the Negro was rendered all the more noxious by the common assumption that it would lead inevitably to social mixing. "[If] I sit side by side in the Senate House, or on the judicial bench, with a coloured man," one gentleman inquired indignantly, "how can I refuse to sit with him at the table? . . . If we have social equality we shall have intermarriage, and if we have intermarriage we shall degenerate; we shall become a race of mulattoes; . . . we shall be ruled out from the family of white nations."[73]

The Radical revolution, as some contemporaries on both sides regarded it, was only a halfway revolution. Within the South, Radical Reconstruction was clearly revolutionary in its overthrow of the old ruling class and above all in its establishment of political and legal equality for Negroes; hence the bitterness of the Conservative reaction. But economically and socially there was far less change, and most blacks remained a landless peasantry subject to manifold discrimination. In the larger national context, Radical Reconstruction reflected a revival of the old nationalistic constitutional doctrine of Hamilton and Marshall submerged by the state rights creed of Jefferson, Jackson, and their successors before 1860. The Radicals were not revolutionary by traditional American standards; if they appeared to be so it was chiefly because of the archaic social and political structure of the South. Nor did most of them regard themselves as revolutionaries. Southern Republicans, in trying to broaden their base of support at home, denied the charge and sought repeatedly to identify themselves with established political traditions. They claimed to stand for state rights within the higher national context and for the libertarian doctrines expressed in the Declaration of Independence. The Fourteenth and Fifteenth Amendments, the Reconstruction Acts, the civil rights legislation, and other related laws attempted to guarantee Negro rights and a loyal South within the accepted federal framework set forth in the Constitution. National authority and military rule were applied only partially and temporarily after 1865, and often reluctantly at that. The chief reliance in day-to-day government rested on the existing civil authorities. When the new state governments were formed after 1867, national and military control were withdrawn and the new regimes had to rely for their survival on customary legal institutions.

The experiment failed, and these regimes were overthrown in a few years because the ideas underlying them had become alien to the South during a generation or more of defending slavery, and because the Radicals' adherence to traditional forms weakened their resistance to attack. Radical regard for the civil liberties of ex-Confederates enabled the latter to sabotage the Reconstruction program almost from the start. Democrats had full access to the polls almost everywhere after 1868 and controlled hundreds of county and local governments throughout the period; they exercised the right to express themselves freely on every occasion, and they controlled the great majority of the section's newspapers. When they were charged with illegal activity and violence they had full access to the courts—in fact often dominated them. In such cases it was often impossible to get grand juries to indict, prosecutors to prosecute, or petit juries to convict, even if sheriffs were willing to arrest or judges to try them. This was even true in Republican-controlled localities. All of the safeguards for the accused in the Anglo-Saxon system of justice were mobilized to enforce the higher law of white supremacy. The Republicans themselves insisted upon certain limits to federal authority, and this was another source of weakness. Conservative violence against Negroes and Radicals involved crimes which had always fallen within state rather than federal jurisdiction, and as a result the federal government refused to intervene soon enough or strongly enough to check the terror effectively. Thus the Radicals were defeated within a few years by their very conservatism and unwillingness to employ more than halfway measures.[74]

Conservative resistance assumed many forms. In Alabama and Arkansas Conservatives tried to defeat the new constitution at the outset by boycotting the polls and denying the necessary majority of all registered voters. But Congress changed the requirement to a majority of the votes cast, and the boycott resulted instead in all but unanimously Republican state governments. Organized abstention was seldom repeated. In all but the most heavily Republican areas Democrats regularly contested local elections, winning power in many places within each state. In state elections they occasionally backed dissident Republican factions. This tactic regularly failed in South Carolina and Mississippi with their Negro Republican majorities, but in 1869 it succeeded in restoring Tennessee and Virginia to Conservative control, in the latter case before Radical Reconstruction had really begun. In two or three other states Democrats captured control after 1869 with comparatively little use of force or other illegal means. But once Democrats had gained control they seldom lost it; Alabama and North Carolina were the only states to elect Republican administrations after having previously gone Democratic, and it happened only once in those two states. Democratic victories occurred first and most easily in the localities and states with comparatively large white populations. In the heavily Negro deep South (and comparable localities elsewhere) the Republican party remained in power longer.

The greater the proportion of Negroes, obviously the more the Demo-

crats needed Negro votes to win elections. White patricians were confident
at first that the old paternal relationship would operate politically and that
Negroes would rally to the support of their old masters. In fact some of
them accepted if they did not welcome Negro suffrage as a means of
strengthening the old planter class against upstarts of both parties. A
brother of General Wade Hampton of South Carolina regretted only that
the blacks might become spoiled and unbalanced if whites came deferen-
tially to beg their votes.

> Beyond this, no harm would be done the South by negro suffrage. The old
> owners would cast the votes of their people almost as absolutely and securely as
> they cast their own. If Northern men expected in this way to build up a
> Northern party in the South, they were gravely mistaken. They would only be
> multiplying the power of the old and natural leaders of Southern politics by
> every vote given to a former slave. Heretofore such men had served their
> masters only in the fields; now they would do not less faithful service at the
> polls.[75]

To this end there was a great effort to win black voters to the party of
white supremacy, often with little or no effort to disguise that fundamental
characteristic. Nowhere did white underestimation of Negro intelligence
show itself more clearly. The revelation was both humorous and pathetic.
Political meetings were held, either separately for the two races or with
segregated seats for Negroes in the rear. At barbecues and picnics the
Negro guests ate either at separate tables or after the whites had finished.
Occasionally Democrats almost visibly held their noses as they nominated
an Uncle Tom for some minor public office.

Other Democrats weakened the strategy by refusing loudly to have any
part of it. "We proclaim that we are opposed to negro suffrage under any
circumstances, and stand ready to use all legitimate means to prevent its
present and future exercise," declared a Louisiana newspaper in 1868,
which claimed to speak for "an overwhelming majority of the enlightened
and liberal white people of the State. . . . Inducements to negroes to vote,
involving directly or indirectly a promise of future advancement, are pregnant with future disaster and disgrace. The Caucasian needs not to kneel to
any other race. It can stand on its own footing, and apparent expediency
presents but a poor, scurvy excuse for the sacrifice of its dignity."[76] Even
franker was Ryland Randolph, editor of the Tuscaloosa, Alabama, *Independent Monitor,* who prided himself on taking his racism straight:

> Let the negro alone. If he attends barbecues let his province be to wait on the
> tables and brush off flies. He befits the speaker's stand about as well as a skunk
> would suit a sofa. Let him squall aloud for Seymour and Blair [the Democratic
> national candidates in 1868] to his heart's content, for it is like a donkey

braying for his food. Hallooing for the white man's candidate should be regarded as declaring in favor of white supremacy—nothing more or less; and all negroes who thus, with docility, fall into traces, should be rewarded with plenty of work, porridge and kind treatment.[77]

Not surprisingly, the policy failed utterly, and "Sambo" continued obstinately and overwhelmingly to support the "renegades" and "outside agitators" in the Republican party. Many Democrats persisted in believing that the blacks would vote with them if only they were left alone by these elements; others recognized that some coercion would be required to achieve this result, carpetbaggers or no.

The most common type of coercion at first, which did not always wait for peaceful persuasion to have its day, was economic pressure. From one end of the South to the other white landlords threatened their Negro laborers with discharge if they cast Republican ballots. This movement was often well organized by state and local party agencies, and sometimes employers were themselves coerced into joining by threats of ostracism and boycott. This tactic worked somewhat better than simple persuasion among the Negroes, but it too proved disappointing. Although most Negroes depended upon white landowners for their livelihood, the reverse was also true; employers were too dependent upon Negro labor to follow through with these threats.

The last resort was physical intimidation and violence. These were not new to the South during Reconstruction. The Old South had emphasized individualism and self-reliance in personal relationships, but it also had demanded conformity of ideas. Nowhere in America was there a greater manifestation of that tyranny of the majority which Tocqueville set forth as a national characteristic in the 1830's. Intolerance was always greatest in the area of race relations. Slavery by 1860 had become a sacred institution, the rock upon which Southern civilization rested. Those who questioned or attacked it did so in the face of emphatic public displeasure and at great personal risk. There was no free speech on this or any other topic which threatened to subvert established ways. Men of every station sanctioned lynch law when it suited their purpose. Jefferson Davis once told a New York audience that Northern politicians who proclaimed a higher law than the Constitution, condemning slavery on moral grounds, *"should be tarred and feathered, and whipped. . . . The man who . . . preaches treason to the Constitution and the dictates of all human society, is a fit object for a Lynch law that would be higher than any he could urge."*[78] Newspapers condoned and even encouraged mob violence against the few hardy souls who spoke out against slavery. In following this course they reflected general community sentiment. Such persons were public enemies who could not safely be trusted to the delays and uncertainties of legal due process. They were tarred and feathered, run out of town, or lynched to avenge the feelings of an outraged community and to serve as a deterrent to others. Members of every social class were implicated in mob violence and vigilante activity. These extended even to the most settled regions, as in the periodic slave insurrection panics. The mob seldom tarried to investigate subtleties or facts hidden by surface appearances, and much innocent blood was shed.

Given these conditions and the predisposition to violence which grew alongside them, vigilantism became more or less institutionalized. Extralegal and semimilitary organizations were formed to supplement the state militias and sheriffs' posses which the law sanctioned. Slaves were kept under surveillance not only by their respective masters but by more or less legally sanctioned slave patrols. Every able-bodied man had the obligation periodically to join in nocturnal neighborhood patrols to make sure that black men were safely tucked in and not busy conspiring against the whites. These patrols did not exist everywhere or all the time, and they often lapsed into disuse, but they were an established institution to be revived when necessary.[79]

The war did nothing to lessen intolerance; by separating the population into Confederates and Unionists it increased the number of people to suspect and dislike. During and after the war—before Radical Reconstruction—Unionists suffered ostracism, proscription, and sometimes violence, except in the areas where they predominated. In Mobile in January 1866, for instance, a "Special Committee" sent letters to a number of Unionists notifying them to leave town on pain of death.[80]

The circumstances of Reconstruction increased in several ways the predisposition to violence. Many of the returning soldiers had a hard time readjusting to the tedium of small-town and farm life, and they swelled the ranks of a rowdy class which had always been present. Affluence was a rare commodity in the South, and this was certainly the case after the war, but subsistence was fairly easy. It required comparatively little work during most of the year simply to keep a small farm going, or even a larger plantation when Negroes performed the labor, and some whites aspired to no more. Every town had its quota of able-bodied men who made at least a part-time vocation of loafing around the streets or drinking away boredom in the local saloons. When excitement did not come unbidden they summoned it. Prewar standards of law and order deteriorated even further. All but the oldest and gentlest of men took to carrying guns wherever they went. The larger cities partially escaped this contagion, but town and country took on the air of a TV Western. Brawls and shooting affrays, lubricated with legal and bootleg whiskey, became matters of general regret and just as general occurrence. This was particularly true in Arkansas and

Texas, where the South merged with the Wild West, but it also applied to regions near the Atlantic Seaboard which had been settled for a century and more.[81]

A disproportionate amount of the violence was directed against blacks. Without the protection that their property value as slaves had once conferred, they became easier and safer targets for the pent-up fear, hatred, and derring-do of frustrated whites.[82] But this was only half of the problem. If Negroes had been feared even when they were subjected to the control of masters and prewar slave codes, they were infinitely more dangerous now that these controls were lifted. The possibility of an all-out race war was a matter of common speculation and concern throughout the Reconstruction period, just as the fear of slave revolts had tortured Southern minds earlier. If such a war came, white men were sure they could win it, but at what cost no one could tell. It had to be prevented by every means possible. White supremacy thus fostered a fear of Negro retaliation which in turn engendered a constant suspicion and even hatred of the black man. A former Mississippi Klansman justified violence as the only way of protecting white families against what he conceived to be "the threatened and rising arrogance of the negroes." Cruelty, seemingly beyond the gravity of the provocation, he said, was "justified by the fact that every little insolence, if left unnoticed, would be bragged about by its perpetrator and fellow observers to the other negroes. The news would spread with great rapidity, and there was no telling where it would end. . . . So when a leading negro would make himself particularly obnoxious . . . and was considered dangerous, he was selected as an example."[83] By this reasoning white men could and did commit the most brutal forms of aggression, convinced all the while that they were acting defensively.[84]

This aggression took every conceivable form, from individual assaults and minor street encounters through mob lynchings to pitched battles involving hundreds on either side. These attacks were seldom punished; it simply was not a punishable offense in the eyes of many whites to attack or even kill a Negro. Late in 1866 Freedmen's Bureau officials reported in detail the murders of 33 freedmen by whites since the war in Tennessee, 29 in Arkansas, 24 in South Carolina, 19 in Kentucky. In February 1867 General Joseph A. Mower reported 70 such murders in Louisiana, giving specific information; the actual total, he said, might have been twice that number. In addition he told of 210 cases of whipping, beating, and stabbing, almost all of them unpunished.[85] In the guise of preserving the peace, legally constituted militia of the Johnson governments commonly went about disarming Negroes and frequently committing violence in the process. This activity was not always sanctioned by higher authority, and some governors either disbanded the militia or curtailed their activity as a result. Then Congress, while passing the Reconstruction Acts in March 1867, ordered the disbandment of all Southern militia.[86] Once the new governments were organized, this ban was lifted.

The larger interracial collisions or riots increasingly showed signs of white organization and advance planning. The Negroes almost invariably suffered most of the casualties, but they were less responsible for initiating violence. Whites commonly believed otherwise, even when they consciously hurled the first stone or fired the first shot; for them the very fact of a League parade or a militia muster was an act of aggression that justified violence in self-defense. In many cases, however, whites deliberately covered their trail and sought to blame their antagonists for instigating hostilities. If this required the distortion of facts or outright lying, it was but another regrettable outgrowth of Negro emancipation. Sometimes one must level a few buildings to save the town from fire.

Many of the so-called riots came close to being massacres. Such was the case in Memphis between April 30 and May 2, 1866, when 46 Negroes were killed and more than 80 wounded as against one white man injured. So also in New Orleans the following July 30, when the toll was about 34 Negroes killed and more than 200 injured as against 4 white dead and 10 injured. Other riots which gained nationwide attention took place in Camilla, Georgia, in September 1868; Laurens, South Carolina, and Eutaw, Alabama, in October 1870; Meridian, Mississippi, in March 1871; Colfax, Louisiana, in April 1873; Vicksburg, Mississippi, in December 1874; Clinton, Mississippi, in September 1875; and Hamburg, South Carolina, in July 1876. Some of these affairs came up quickly and others were planned in advance. In each case the whites demonstrated superior organization and morale while the Negroes, whether caught off guard or not, were outmaneuvered, outgunned, and suffered far greater casualties. The purpose, and to a great degree the result, of these battles was to demoralize and intimidate the freedmen. Some, like Clinton and Vicksburg, were part of a larger campaign to carry elections by storm and thus return the Democratic party to power in the face of Negro Republican majorities which other methods had failed to sway.

The advent of Radical Reconstruction served to increase intolerance and violence as never before. The enfranchised blacks became more dangerous than ever. White Republicans, who took the place of both abolitionists and Unionists, were subjected to ostracism, boycott, threats, and physical attack. It was dangerous for them to campaign in many regions, or even to express their opinions openly. An Alabama Democrat conceded that "open-mouth" Republicans risked getting their mouths slapped. "That is a sort of privilege men in the West and South claim, slapping the mouth of a fellow who does not please them."[87] Newspapers and public opinion often condoned even the bloodiest outrages if they did not positively encourage them. In 1868 the same Louisiana paper already quoted remarked the murder of a Republican judge and sheriff in a neighboring parish:

Without directly condemning or approving the manner that the citizens . . . adopted to rid themselves of the presence and services of these northern emissaries of advanced political ideas, and of progressive social reforms, we are compelled to own that they have met the fate they deserved. . . . It is, indeed, unfortunate that . . . any portion of any community should be compelled to have recourse to measures of violence and blood to do away with lawless tyrants and wrong-doers in their midst. But who is to blame? . . . Assuredly not we people of the South, who have suffered wrongs beyond endurance. Radicalism and negroism, which in the South are one and the same thing, are alone to blame. . . . We can well pity a people forced to use such harsh means, but we have not the courage to blame them.[88]

Or as Floridians were quoted more succinctly as saying, "The damned Republican party has put niggers to rule us and we will not suffer it."[89]

The violence became more organized. In South Carolina white rifle clubs were organized, replacing the dissolved state militia. Eventually similar organizations would spring up in other states of the deep South, and they contributed importantly to the final overthrow of Reconstruction. But the more immediate source of harassment for Negroes and white Republicans throughout the South was the secret societies epitomized by the Ku Klux Klan. During the war and for a time afterward certain areas, especially the upper South and the western borderlands, were infested by bands of partisan guerrillas who respected neither life nor property. The postwar secret societies resembled these bushwhackers in some respects, but unlike them they usually operated after dark and in disguise. Furthermore, they often rode at least nominally in behalf of a higher and nobler end, the preservation of white supremacy. They were in fact the offspring of the old vigilante tradition and the ante-bellum slave patrol; there was a striking resemblance to both parents.[90] Some groups were composed of poorer whites whose object was to drive Negro tenants off the better land where they had been settled as slaves, so as to move in themselves. Whatever their motives, their victims were predominantly Negroes and white Unionists.

A Freedmen's Bureau official reported in March 1866 that in some counties of Kentucky "there are organized bands of men called 'rangers,' 'moderators,' 'nigger killers,' who have driven the freedmen entirely out of certain sections, and begin at last to threaten and intimidate Union white men."[91] A Bureau official in Mississippi reported: "The fear of a class of citizens calling themselves regulators, in some localities, is so great that peaceable citizens who are disposed to restore order and quiet are afraid to give the necessary information to secure the punishment of these men.

. . . These regulators shoot freedmen without provocation, drive them from plantations without pay, and commit other crimes."[92] Similar reports came from almost every Southern state for two years after the war.[93]

Some of these groups were sufficiently organized to adopt a certain ceremony and ritual in their proceedings, and to bear such names as (in Alabama) the Black Cavalry and the Men of Justice. Most of them lost their separate identity (at least to outsiders) in 1868 when the Ku Klux Klan became famous. But they generally carried on as before, and one, the Knights of the White Camellia in Louisiana and elsewhere, was large enough to be famous in its own name. Still other societies continued to form in 1868 and afterward, all more or less local in character. Even the Ku Klux Klan was so decentralized that it is hardly proper to refer to it in the singular number. But its name attracted so much attention that common usage after 1868 made it synonymous with all nocturnal regulators, regardless of what they called themselves.

The overriding purpose of the Ku Klux movement, no matter how decentralized, was the maintenance or restoration of white supremacy in every walk of life. In the minds of many men, the most urgent reason for resorting to vigilante activity was to check any incipient Negro rising. There was a great inclination after 1867 to overlook the earlier fears of this sort and the vigilantism arising from them, and to ascribe the dangers solely to Radical Reconstruction. Other men regarded the Klan primarily as an agency to deter and punish Negro crime, a function which the authorities— especially if they were Republicans—allegedly could not or would not do. But even when they admitted that the courts were ready and willing to punish Negro crime, many whites were reluctant to abandon the old and convenient methods of control which the Klan continued to supply. "I suppose these men who belong to this organization do not wish to take the trouble of having the matter investigated in court when they can attend to it so easily," an Alabamian explained.[94] Legal prosecutions required time, trouble, and money which white men should not have to spend in disciplining Negroes. Still other Democrats ascribed the Klan movement to high taxes, corrupt officials, or other deficiencies of the Republican regimes. Most Klansmen exhibited little knowledge or interest in such problems, however, and their raiding of Negro cabins did nothing to rectify them. The Klan was accepted widely as an extralegal defense against the Union League, which Conservatives mistook for a Negro terrorist organization.

Economic and social objectives too preceded Radical Reconstruction. Klansmen sometimes disciplined recalcitrant Negro laborers whose employers could not or would not do so themselves. (Some slaveholders had been helped in the same way.) This activity was commonly defended as a means of keeping Negro labor docile and on the job, but in fact it did much more to drive off labor and disrupt economic life. It was on this point that many landowners eventually became disenchanted with the Klan, whether they dared express their feeling or not. Similarly, the Klan in some places inherited the function of driving off Negro laborers in favor of poor whites. It prevented Negroes from owning or even renting land of their own in some areas. As a device for keeping blacks within their proper social bounds, the Klan lynched Negro men who cohabited with white women and frequently punished these women too, as well as white prostitutes who took Negro customers. It punished Negro assertions of social equality and real or imaginary insolence. It conducted a vendetta against the teachers of Negro schools.

The one really new ingredient of regulator activity after 1867 was political opposition to the Radicals. And so far as the Klan loomed larger than the earlier vigilante groups, this was undoubtedly the reason. Only now did upper-class elements and Conservative political leaders take much interest in the idea. In many places some took over Klan leadership, at least temporarily. The Klan became in effect a terrorist arm of the Democratic party, whether the party leaders as a whole liked it or not.

It is impossible to separate Klan activities and purposes into exclusive categories or to measure accurately their respective importance. But the Klan movement reached its fullest dimensions only with the advent of Negro suffrage, first in Tennessee and then in the South at large. Moreover, the testimony of its victims points to the intimidation and punishment of Republican voters and officeholders as its central purpose. Klansmen repeatedly attacked Negroes for no other stated offense than voting, or intending to vote, the Republican ticket. Their repeated admonition was to either vote the Democratic ticket or stay at home. Furthermore, the Klan made a special target of officeholders and other persons within its reach who exercised political influence in behalf of the Republican party. In some states and many localities, after Democratic persuasion and economic pressure had failed to sway Negro voters, terrorism represented the only remaining way of seizing political control.

Few Democrats were willing to admit the Klan's political character and purpose, at least until long afterward, and Northern Democrats joined them in denying the obvious.[95] Negro suffrage, the main political impetus to Klan activity, was the law of the land after 1867, and Democrats could hardly justify the Klan as a device to overthrow it without convicting themselves of rebellion and inviting dire retribution by the federal government. They were placed in the awkward position of having to pay lip service to the central evil of Radicalism while attacking it only indirectly or obliquely. Hence part of the undue emphasis they placed on malfeasance among carpetbag and scalawag officials and high taxes in explaining the

Klan. Perhaps the easiest solution was the common one of pretending that the Klan had no political bearing at all. Republicans, on the other hand, eager to secure federal intervention for their own self-protection, were inclined to exaggerate the Klan's political bearing and overlook its other objectives.[96]

The Ku Klux Klan was a mass movement of many sides, but nearly all of them slanted toward white supremacy. (Perhaps the major exception to this rule was in some mountain counties of Georgia, North Carolina, and other states, where the Klan protected moonshiners.) It grew naturally out of the folk beliefs and practices of the old South, compounded by the topsy-turvy conditions of Reconstruction. It provided a collective means to do a job that many Conservatives felt needed to be done. As an organization, it freed its members to commit atrocities which many of them would have shrunk from as individuals:

There is no telling to what extremes of cruelty and ruthlessness a man will go when he is freed from the fears, hesitations, doubts and the vague stirrings of decency that go with individual judgment. When we lose our individual independence in the corporateness of a mass movement, we find a new freedom—freedom to hate, bully, lie, torture, murder and betray without shame and remorse.[97]

This is a fitting characterization of the Klan in action, stripped of the heroic imagery with which apologists then and later obscured it.

Part I

KLAN BEGINNINGS IN
TENNESSEE, 1866–1868

CHAPTER I

The Birth and Transformation of the Ku Klux Klan, 1866–1867

The mysteries of the Ku Klux Klan begin at its birth. This event, it is agreed, took place in the law office of Judge Thomas M. Jones at Pulaski, Tennessee. The date is not so clear. In later years, when the founders were willing to admit their paternity and talk about it, memories had dimmed and details had become elusive. The most probable time was an evening in May or early June 1866.[1] All of the six founders were young Confederate veterans, "hungering and thirsting" for amusement, as one of them later put it, after the excitements of wartime had given way to the tedium of small-town life. They were Captain John C. Lester, Major James R. Crowe, John B. Kennedy, Calvin Jones (son of the judge), Richard R. Reed, and Frank O. McCord. All came of good families and were well educated by the standards of the time and place. In later years some entered the professions, some were active in church affairs, and most were by any standard useful and public-spirited citizens. Lester (like Jones and Reed) became a lawyer and was a member of the Tennessee legislature when his book, the first full account of the Klan's origins, appeared. The files of the local newspaper indicate that he was active in trying to raise funds for a reopening of Giles College in Pulaski and for the creation of a fire company after part of the town was burned in the summer of 1867; he was joined in this latter venture by McCord, then local editor and later editor-in-chief of the weekly Pulaski *Citizen,* the county's only newspaper.

The organization of the new society took place at successive meetings, with the membership growing to eight or ten almost at the outset. Two committees were chosen, one to select a name and the other a set of rules and ritual. They devised the name first, settling upon "Ku Klux Klan" because of its novelty, its alliterative content, and its uncertain meaning. They wanted to attract attention without specifically asking for it. The name did attract attention and baffled outsiders for years to come; less predictably, it probably mystified most of the later members too, as the order spread across the South, developed new roots, and lost all contact with its origins. Quite likely, as Lester and Wilson suggest, the name itself had something to do with the order's survival and expansion. It had a growth potential lacking in such names as (to use Stanley Horn's example) the Merry Six or the Pulaski Social Club.

As it was later explained, the derivation of the name was comparatively simple. "Ku Klux" was merely a corruption of the Greek word *kuklos*, meaning circle or band; "Klan" was redundant but it added to the alliteration. This was an age of classical learning, and Greek was a staple part of the liberal arts curriculum. The proliferating academic and social fraternities in American colleges (beginning with Phi Beta Kappa in 1776) had drawn heavily on Greek in devising names and rituals, and in the South perhaps the most familiar of these organizations was the social fraternity Kuklos Adelphon or "old Kappa Alpha," founded at the University of North Carolina in 1812. By midcentury it had spread throughout the South, not only to college campuses but to cities and towns where there were college alumni to keep it up. The society began to dissolve in the 1850's and disappeared altogether after the Civil War, but most educated Southerners in 1866 were familiar with it, including surely the founders of the Ku Klux Klan. One of the founders indicated that the Klan's ritual, at least, was closely patterned after that of a widespread college fraternity, and Kuklos Adelphon almost certainly provided the model.[2]

Having started with a mysterious name, it seemed natural to adopt an organization and ritual to match. The officers consisted of a Grand Cyclops or president, a Grand Magi or vice-president, a Grand Turk or marshal, a Grand Exchequer or treasurer, and two Lictors or guardians of the meeting place. This last was designated the Den. Members were required to maintain absolute secrecy regarding the order and all persons connected with it. Their existence should come to the attention of outsiders solely through their public appearances in disguise. The Klan's regalia usually consisted at the outset of a white mask with holes for eyes and nose, a high conical cardboard hat which made the wearer seem taller, and a long flowing robe. No special color was prescribed, and individual fancy was given free rein, with extravagant results. In fact some members adopted an entirely different costume consisting of "Spanish jackets and wide trowsers [*sic*], with cap and feathers." When appearing together in public, members communicated with each other by means of small child's whistles, using a code of signals. Although the first Klansmen sometimes attended fairs and social gatherings in this manner, their main amusement until the novelty wore off was initiating new recruits who were attracted by these public appearances.

The first meetings and initiations took place in Judge Jones' law office near the center of town. But the chance of interruption and discovery here was too great, and the Klan soon found new quarters. Just outside town there was an abandoned house which had been partially demolished by a cyclone in December 1865. Next to the ruins was a grove of barren, storm-lashed trees, adding to the desolate and haunted atmosphere of the place. In this environment the Klan held most of its meetings and initiated new members. The initiation ritual, patterned after Kuklos Adelphon's, was highly elaborate, while the actual process of induction combined much false solemnity with practical jokes and hazing. The whole process would be familiar to anyone who has gone through college fraternity initiations, formal and informal. The Klan tried to take in only those candidates who could safely be burdened with the responsibility of secrecy. There also was a moral test of sorts, excluding heavy drinkers among others. Frank McCord was elected the first Grand Cyclops.[3]

On one crucial point all the early members who later had anything to say about the matter were unanimous: the Klan was designed purely for amusement, and for some time after its founding it had no ulterior motive or effect. All the evidence supports this. The nonsensical initiation ceremony, the rules, and the ritual as we know them were largely irrelevant to the Klan's later activity and were in fact minimized by the generals, politicians, and vigilantes who took over the organization in 1867 and 1868. The disguises, secrecy, and general organization were relevant of course, but masquerading was popular at the time, and the rest was common to (and modeled after) other societies which were entirely peaceful. For several months at least there is no evidence that the Klan bullied or seriously tried to terrify anyone.

When vigilantism did become a serious business with the Klan a year later, outsiders reported the fact, and some of the Klan's founders began to regard their handiwork with mixed emotions. They shared the conservative views common to most white Southerners and Confederate veterans, and approved in general the later political and social goals of the Ku Klux Klan. They also approved, at least in retrospect, the milder forms of intimidation it undertook; indeed, some may have seen action themselves. But things got out of hand, and the more cautious among them grew alarmed. In April 1868 one of the six declared in an anonymous letter to the press:

It is to be lamented that the simple object of the original Ku-Kluxes should be so perverted as to become political and pernicious in its demonstrations. . . . If it has become a regular organization, with guerilla and "lynch-law" attributes, then better the Ku Klux had never been heard of, and the sooner such organization is dissolved the better for the country at large—especially for the South. *All* secret *political* orders, clubs, clans, or associations are pernicious in their tendencies, and every good man and sensible patriot should persistently express his disapprobation of them.[4]

This statement could hardly be interpreted otherwise than as an effort to head off the breathtaking Klan expansion throughout the South. Lester and Wilson's book of 1884 was less disapproving, but it was also defensive and at times almost apologetic in tone. So were some of the private opinions expressed by founders in letters written as late as 1912. Only Crowe and Kennedy lived long enough to see the Klan's career elevated to a folk epic in histories, novels, and motion pictures, and themselves celebrated as founding fathers. Both men betray an understandable pride of accomplishment under the circumstances, but Ku Kluxism contained much for which they felt obliged to deny responsibility, if not to apologize.[5]

Tennessee followed the same general course during Reconstruction as did the other Southern states. But unique characteristics of her own advanced the timetable, and she experienced the cycle of Republican control, Negro suffrage, Ku Klux violence, and Bourbon restoration sooner than her sisters. The major cause was the heavy Unionist population of east Tennessee. This mountainous region of small farms and few slaves had opposed secession in 1861 and remained a stronghold of militant loyalism throughout the war. No other Confederate state contained so large a loyalist community among the white population or, by the same token, so large or dependable a nucleus around which to rebuild a postwar state government acceptable to Congress and the national Republican party. Andrew Johnson, an east Tennesseean himself, had done a great deal to rally these Unionists during the war when he served as provisional governor under federal occupation. With his removal to Washington in 1865, the leadership of Tennessee Unionism fell to William G. (Parson) Brownlow, editor of the Knoxville *Whig* and one of the most abrasive and controversial personalities of the Reconstruction era. A former circuit-riding Methodist preacher, Brownlow was a political fundamentalist. Confederate gray was black treason, and he was no more ready to see Tennessee back in the hands of the rebels and secessionists who had once imprisoned him than in those of the Archfiend himself. In 1865 the Unionists reorganized the state and Brownlow became governor. For the next four years Unionist supremacy was the rock on which he built his administration. In December 1866 Congress seated Tennessee's Senators and Representatives, making her the first reconstructed of the Southern states.

At the very outset Brownlow and his supporters, who affiliated with the Republican party, had enacted a wholesale disfranchisement of ex-Confederates. Vindictiveness and a desire to punish treason had played a part in this, but the major cause lay in the fact that middle and west Tennessee, with most of the state's population, had heavily supported the Confederacy. Universal white manhood suffrage would have delivered the state to the rebels at once. But mass disfranchisement (of white men) was a drastic policy, counter to national traditions. Many Republicans accepted it only as a lesser evil, and no one supposed it would last very long. The longer it endured, in fact, the more unpopular it became; even in its presence there was an increasing possibility that Brownlow faced defeat in his forthcoming race for re-election in August 1867. A Conservative victory would mean a rebel victory. (Democrats in most Southern states temporarily adopted the label Conservative out of deference to the many ex-Whigs they enlisted in the battle against Radical Republicanism.) The obvious and only solution, to which the Republican party in Congress was being driven at the same time and for the same reasons, was Negro suffrage. Tennessee Unionists, including the dominant mountaineers, were white supremacists like almost everyone else, but in politics at least they were Unionists first. Only a few days before Congress passed the first Reconstruction Act Tennessee adopted a Negro suffrage law of its own late in February 1867. Republican enfranchisement of the freedmen was premised on the assumption that they would vote for the party which did it. This assumption was probable, but it could not be taken completely for granted, and the Republicans set to work that spring mobilizing the Negro vote. One of their chief instruments was the Union League, which was established throughout the state.[6]

Throughout the state, meanwhile, social and economic conditions made only a slow and uncertain recovery from the dislocations caused by civil war and defeat. This was especially true of middle and west Tennessee, where most of the white population regarded themselves as victims of oppression. They had lost their money, their slaves, and control of their government. As long as there was hope in the near future of regaining power and reordering society more to their liking through customary political means, most men were content to employ those means. But not all men. Moreover, the war had bred strife and hatred between neighbors who had chosen opposite sides. These conflicts did not die with the surrender, and for some people this was a time to settle old scores. In some countries there was hardly a semblance of law and order as bands of armed bushwhackers roamed at will and intimidated the local authorities. Much of this was simple brigandage, but the Unionist minority were particular targets of robbery and violence. (In parts of east Tennessee the roles were reversed.) An agent of the Freedmen's Bureau reported in October 1866 that a gang of outlaws was committing "numerous and revolting outrages" on the Unionists in Sumner and Robertson counties, north of Nashville. The victims were too few to offer resistance, and "the civil authorities either will not, or dare not attempt to bring the ruffians to justice."[7]

More often the proscription of Unionists assumed a less violent form, but it was still apt to be organized. The Nashville *Press and Times* (one of the chief Republican organs in the state) in July 1866 passed on a report that

in some portions of West Tennessee the rebels have formed a secret association, the object of which is to prevent the employment or patronage of Unionists in any capacity whatever, whether as day-laborers, clerks, book-keepers, teachers, physicians, lawyers or mechanics. In all cases rebels are to be employed, and the members of the association pledge themselves to starve out or drive out every Union man from that part of the country.[8]

As was to be expected, the Negro freedmen also received attention. Reports came from the southwestern corner of the state in November 1866 that bands of men were going the rounds of Negro cabins at night and seizing their guns, one of the tamer activities for which the Ku Klux Klan soon became famous.[9] For most white men the idea of free Negroes was unsettling enough, but the idea of free Negroes with guns raised again the old ante-bellum specter of a servile uprising, another Santo Domingo.

If Giles County, with Pulaski, was not the most lawless county in Tennessee in 1866 and 1867, it ranked high on the list. For this judgment we have the testimony not only of Captain George E. Judd, the conscientious and hard-pressed agent of the Freedmen's Bureau there, but also of McCord, local editor of the Pulaski *Citizen* and Grand Cyclops of the Ku Klux Klan. Their emphases and sources of concern were not quite the same, but together they portray a raucous, rowdy, and sometimes brutal atmosphere more in keeping with the stock Western cattle town than the placid village commemorated in pious histories of the Klan. Pulaski numbered 2,070 people, almost half of them Negroes, according to the 1870 census. The county, possessing relatively good soil and a high agricultural production, had been one of the more substantial slaveholding counties of the state before the war; in 1870 its population of 32,413 was 39 per cent Negro. Its plantations and farms raised cotton, tobacco, wheat, corn, and sheep.

The county was better endowed and more prosperous than some of its neighbors, but its race relations and the state of law and order were worse in the opinion of Captain Judd. In August 1866 he remarked an increasing bitterness against Yankees (including himself) and against the freedmen.

The people do all they can to degrade them [Negroes] and keep them down to what they see fit to call their proper place. The consequence is that the negroes do not do as well as they do in other places where I have been. A great many of them are indolent and vicious. They become so by having to fight their way against the abuse of the whites and from being cheated out of the proceeds of their labor. The idea of negroes getting justice before the magistrates of this county is perfectly absurd. They will hear the testimony of the blacks, but will give it no weight unless it happens to suit their purpose.[10]

When a Negro saloonkeeper in Pulaski hung out a sign in front of his establishment bearing the name Equal Rights, it was hauled down the same day, according to editor McCord, "by request of some of our young friends from the country."[11] Giles County was listed in September as one of four counties in middle Tennessee from which outrages against freedmen were most often reported. "There is certainly a gang of men in this county who are ready for anything desperate," Judd reported, but he said nothing of organized night riding, much less the disguises and weird antics of the Ku Klux Klan.[12]

A spirit of endemic lawlessness continued to pervade the county into 1867. Robbery and assault were so common in Pulaski, especially at night, that no man was safe on the streets alone after dark. The town was the scene of repeated rowdyism and shooting sprees on the part of young bloods who crowded the saloons. "Roughs collect in Pulaski from this and adjoining counties," Judd reported in January; "they have their own way here, threaten to kill and drag out all who disagree with them." McCord wrote in February that "chronic drunkenness and debauchery" had become so common that he wearied of reporting it. Nevertheless he chronicled another "riotous drunken jubilee," in which a mixed crowd of Negroes and whites had whooped, yelled, and shot off pistols on the streets from eight to twelve the previous Friday night. Although Negroes outnumbered whites on this occasion, they were more often victims than perpetrators of violence, and the small white Unionist element was subject to continual harassment and danger.

The responsibility for this state of affairs lay with the whole community. The "better element" complained loudly about the influx of desperadoes from outside, but for months made no effort to provide the police protection necessary to discourage them. The existing law officers were either incompetent or implicated in the violence themselves. Compounding the trouble was the typical double standard where Negroes were concerned. If

crimes against whites were seldom punished (unless committed by Negroes) crimes against the freedmen went wholly unnoticed. Local juries
were stacked against the Negro. "This is so notorious here," said Judd,
"that lawyers who have cases in hand for negroes dare not let them come
to trial but try to compromise, always with loss to the negro." A white boy
clearly guilty of murdering a Negro was acquitted. "The jury presumed a
justification, none being shown." Sheriff Bryant Peden was a fitting example of the county's ills. A racist of the lowest order, he publicly
maintained that the blacks were still slaves and offered ten dollars a head
for the interest of any ex-slaveholder in his former chattels. He boasted of
whipping his own Negroes whenever they required it, just as before the
war, and still listed them as property for tax purposes. All of this went over
well with many of his constituents, and so did his policy of law enforcement. The sheriff issued warrants with alacrity for Negroes suspected of
wrongdoing, but could hardly be forced to arrest a white man.[13]

It was in these circumstances that the Ku Klux Klan made its transition
from a social club to a band of regulators, self-dedicated to the curbing of
lawlessness and Unionism, and above all to keeping the Negro in his place.
Exactly when, how, and why this happened can only be inferred from very
fragmentary evidence, most of it provided by Lester and Wilson. Nearly all
of it comes from members who wrote long after the event. Their statements
usually lack detail, and some of their details, especially dates, are inaccurate.[14] But they are probably right in saying that the amusements which
preoccupied the original Klansmen lost their novelty and began to pall
about six weeks after the order was founded.

The Klan would probably have died out altogether in the summer of
1866 if the idea had not been picked up by young men from the country
who asked and received permission to organize new dens in their own
localities. (If this permission had been withheld they might well have gone
ahead and formed comparable societies anyway.)[15] This expansion signified no immediate change in Klan activity. In 1871 a man living in nearby
Alabama recalled having seen the Klan at a moonlight picnic near Pulaski
in the fall of 1866, shortly after he had first heard of them. They came out
of the woods wearing "rather a pretty and showy costume," consisting of
tall hats covered with spangles and stars, with long robes reaching nearly to
their feet. They joined the party, danced to the music, and talked with the
other guests, but disguised their voices. "It seemed to be a thing of
amusement," he said, and at that time, "I never heard anything in
connection with it as a political organization."[16] From the beginning the
newer dens diverged somewhat from the parent in details of organization
and ritual, but they shared the same basic character. Since they derived
their existence from the central den in Pulaski, it exercised a nominal

leadership over them, but no real control. In effect every den was free to act much as it pleased. At first there was no particular reason to limit that freedom, but gradually changes began to take place in the order's character, membership, and function which the founders in Pulaski had not contemplated.

It may be that the playing of practical jokes on each other broadened into playing them on outsiders, especially Negroes. Bullying Negroes was an established pastime with a sizable portion of Southern white manhood, and the inclination increased with Emancipation. It is also true that many Negroes took their new freedom literally and began to act more like white people: choosing their own employers, working or not working as the spirit moved them, expressing their opinions more freely, and not always giving up the sidewalk. Not only were they less servile, but many of them, poverty-stricken to the last degree and victims of generations of exploitation, engaged in petty thievery at the expense of those more favored than they. White men confronted by these trials had the precedent of the ante-bellum slave patrol before them. This institution was no longer possible on an open or official basis, but the need for it was apparently greater than ever. Thus duty and inclination combined to produce bands of postwar regulators or vigilantes throughout the South.

This apparently is what the Ku Klux Klan was coming to be by the spring of 1867. Its operations cannot have been very extensive or spectacular; the fact would have been reported if they were. A simple appearance with appropriate admonitions or threats may have been enough to cow all but the most daring among the colored population. Klansmen may not always have worn their disguises on these excursions, but the regalia would surely have enhanced their effect, whether or not the Negroes mistook them for ghosts. Lester and Wilson talk mostly of the Klan's impression on superstitious freedmen, but they may also suggest regulatory activity against the many lawless and rowdy whites who had made Pulaski their capital.[17] Crime does seem to have abated in the spring of 1867; at the time McCord seemed to ascribe it to a new constable, but the Klan may also have played a part.

Although they evidently approve this regulative activity in principle, Lester and Wilson report that "rash, imprudent and bad men had gotten into the order," and were beginning to commit acts of violence. The leaders in Pulaski became alarmed. Lacking means to control these excesses, some of them would have favored disbanding the order entirely, but "the tie that bound them together was too shadowy to be cut or untied," and this directive might not have been obeyed. It may well be that the founders "had evoked a spirit from 'the vasty deep' [which] would not down at their bidding." But simultaneously (although Lester and Wilson avoid saying so) a new object was coming into view, and at least some of the leaders did not want to disband.[18]

Probably Giles County was more typical than unique in the winter of 1866–1867. Reports of violence against Unionists and Negroes continued to reach Governor Brownlow's office from many places in middle and west Tennessee. The Ku Klux Klan had probably contributed very little of it, even in Giles County. Outrages were relatively scattered and unorganized, by no means as numerous as they would become a year later, when the Klan was in full swing. But at the time they seemed alarming enough. It was the governor's duty to preserve law and order if local authorities did or could not. Since Unionism itself was apparently under general attack, his responsibility was all the more clear. There may have been a third consideration; certainly it became obvious later. Negro suffrage was in process of enactment at just this time, and systematic intimidation of the freedmen could have disastrous results in the August elections. His own future, that of the Republican party, and the cause of Unionism in Tennessee were possibly at stake.

Brownlow was not one to temporize. On February 25 he issued a proclamation, couched in a vigorous prose style long familiar to readers of the Knoxville *Whig:* "I have no concessions to make to traitors, no compromises to offer to assassins and robbers; and if, in the sweep of coming events, retributive justice shall overtake the lawless and violent, their own temerity will have called it forth. The outrages enumerated *must* and SHALL cease." He announced his intention to organize the state militia and station it wherever needed.[19] As a stopgap measure he also requested federal troops from General George H. Thomas in Louisville.[20] The militia were organized during March and April, and meanwhile federal soldiers were stationed at various places, a squad arriving at Pulaski early in April. They were replaced in June by a small militia detachment which remained through the August election.[21] Similar arrangements were made elsewhere in the state.

The bitterness which existed between the Brownlow Unionists and the Conservative opposition, largely ex-Confederates, had few parallels in American history outside the Reconstruction South. Each side equated the other with utter darkness and felt it was fighting for its very life. The result was an inexorable series of actions and reactions which for a time portended another civil war. Brownlow had responded to Conservative violence against Negroes and Unionists by calling out the militia. The Conservatives, ignoring or denying the violence which some of their own number had set afoot, feared that he intended to perpetuate his control through military force and a massive manipulation of the Negro vote; hence they began to organize for their own defense. Seeing this, Brownlow feared another rebellion in the making and intensified his own activities. Given the depth of feeling and the initial premises of both sides, each reacted defensively and (so far as the leaders were concerned) with a certain amount of restraint.

Conservative organization in the spring of 1867 was chiefly political. It aimed at winning a portion of the Negro vote through an unstable and rather naïve combination of paternal kindness, logical argument, and threats of economic reprisal. But some prominent men—ex-Confederate officers for the most part—feared that this might not be enough. It is not surprising that such men responded to the state militia and the Union League in military or paramilitary terms; and as open military organization would have invited instant suppression by the United States Army if not the militia, it is natural that they organized secretly. What is surprising is the foolhardiness (or genius) they displayed in commandeering for their purpose the bizarre band of secret regulators around Pulaski who called themselves the Ku Klux Klan.

The details surrounding this event are even hazier than the Klan's history until this point. Lester and Wilson are very vague and give no names; they say the initiative was taken by the leaders of the Pulaski den, alarmed by the tendency to violence within the order. But if these young men had been motivated solely by that consideration they would probably have done all they could to disband the order and then dissociate themselves from it. They might even have done this publicly for greater effect, as their skirts were still clean. Instead they sought a tighter organization and made plans to turn over the whole concern to men of far greater prestige and authority whose influence extended throughout the state. Here lies the real beginning of the Ku Klux conspiracy of which the nation heard so much in the next five years.

It seems unlikely that Lester, McCord, and their colleagues were the first to hit upon the idea of adapting their Klan to the larger needs of Tennessee Conservatism. Perhaps they technically initiated the process by going for advice on their own problems to some local men of experience and discretion, or perhaps it was the other way around. Pulaski boasted at least two former generals in the Confederate army, John C. Brown and George W. Gordon. If Gordon was himself one of the earliest members of the Klan, as Stanley Horn says,[22] no communication problem existed; in any case it is generally accepted that both men participated in the reorganization and occupied high offices in the Klan afterward. Gordon was the younger; only thirty in 1866, he was the youngest brigadier general in the army at the war's close. He probably took the more active part in the Klan's inner workings, and is credited with writing the first Prescript, or constitution, at this time. Brown was the more important politically. The brother of an ante-bellum governor of the state, he was elected governor himself in 1870, symbolizing for Conservatives the "redemption" of the state from Republican control. Years later, as president of the Tennessee Coal and Iron Company, he would be one of the New South's major captains of industry. Quite possibly these two men made the contacts and helped plan the strategy which resulted in taking over and reorganizing the Klan.[23]

The reorganization took place at a meeting in the Maxwell House hotel in Nashville in the spring of 1867.[24] The meeting was officially called by the Grand Cyclops of the Pulaski den, who summoned delegates from all the dens of which he had knowledge. It is impossible to know how far the order had spread by this time, but probably not very far. The event, needless to say, was not written up in the newspapers, nor did the participants ever have much to say publicly about it afterward. Whether the prominent men who were interested participated directly or guided the activities from a distance, we do not know. Possibly many of them, including General Nathan Bedford Forrest, who would soon emerge as Grand Wizard of the Ku Klux Klan, had not yet associated themselves with the movement. Although the precise date of the meeting is unknown it likely occurred in April. On the third of that month ten visitors from Pulaski and Giles County checked in at various Nashville hotels—an unusually large number—according to the regular listing of hotel arrivals in the Nashville *Republican Banner*. Seven more checked in from Pulaski (including founder James R. Crowe) on the fifth, and another fourteen by the eleventh. A few days later the Conservative state convention met in Nashville to nominate candidates for the coming election. Every important Conservative in the state was in attendance or had an excuse for not coming. Whether this was the chosen occasion or not, it was an ideal opportunity for present and prospective Klansmen of every station and from all over the state to assist at the Klan's political rebirth. Frank McCord was a member of the Giles County delegation, but neither Brown nor Gordon was a delegate. Neither man is named in the *Banner*'s list of hotel arrivals during the days adjacent to the convention's session. One who was listed was General G. G. Dibrell, who became a Grand Titan of the Ku Klux Klan. Other men were present who might well have participated in the Klan meeting, but we have no evidence for singling out any of them. General Forrest was not listed either, and apparently was not initiated into the order until later.

The plan of organization, including a Prescript, had been prepared in advance of the meeting. The Prescript was apparently the work of General Gordon. Most of the document is concerned with administrative machinery; it says nothing about the purpose or function of the order, and except for its unique terminology and general air of mystery it could almost serve as constitution for a federation of labor unions or garden clubs. Rank-and-file members were denominated ghouls and were organized in dens as originally in Pulaski. Above them an elaborate superstructure was created, which looked to a vast expansion of the order beyond the state. Still at the head of each local den was the Grand Cyclops, now assisted by two Night Hawks; above them were the Grand Giant of the Province (county) and his four Goblins; the Grand Titan of the Dominion (congressional district) and his six Furies; the Grand Dragon of the Realm (state) and his eight Hydras; and at the top the Grand Wizard of the Empire and his ten Genii. The Empire was presumably the South, but perhaps hostility to the Radicals would know no sectional bounds. In addition to these officers there were the Grand Magi and Grand Monk, second and third in command of each den, respectively; the Grand Turk or executive officer of the Grand Cyclops; a Grand Sentinel and Grand Ensign in each den; and at all levels a Grand Scribe or secretary and Grand Exchequer or treasurer.

The Grand Cyclops and the other more important den officers were to be elected semiannually by the members of the den. At the higher levels, from Grand Wizard down to Grand Giant, officials were to be elected for two-year terms by a majority vote of their immediate subordinates. Thus the Grand Giant or county chief was elected by the various Grand Cyclops in his county, and the Grand Wizard by the several Grand Dragons or state commanders. A temporary exception was made in the case of the Grand Wizard; he was to serve initially for a three-year term beginning the first Monday in May 1867.

The Prescript sets forth the administrative duties of these officers in great detail. It resembles an army manual, and great deference is paid to the chain of command. Two judicial tribunals were provided for, a Council of Yahoos to try officers and a Council of Centaurs for common ghouls. There were also revenue provisions, including a one-dollar initiation fee and a ten-dollar fee for each copy of the Prescript issued to a den. (Actually, little money seems to have been exchanged in the Klan's subsequent experience; there was never any suggestion of the profiteering or extortion which marked the Klan of the 1920's.) Membership was restricted to those eighteen years of age or more who were recommended by a present member and who survived a screening of their antecedents and connections.

Members were required to take an oath of absolute secrecy concerning the order and those who belonged to it; betrayal of the secrets or purposes of the order would incur "the extreme penalty of the Law." This emphasis upon secrecy appears throughout the Prescript. The name of the organization is never given, and where it would normally appear asterisks are substituted. There was a specific provision that "the origin, designs, mysteries and ritual of this * shall never be written, but . . . shall be communicated orally." For purposes of communication among members there was a code by which to designate months, days, and hours. The months of the year were known by adjectives like Dismal, Dark, and Furious; hours of the day were similarly designated, and days of the week were named for colors. This code was later used primarily for public announcements of meetings, which appeared widely in the newspapers through the spring of 1868. There was also a reference to secret grips, signs, and passwords, but none were given.[25]

Sometime in 1868 a Revised and Amended Prescript appeared. The circumstances surrounding this revision are even cloudier than in the case of the original. It was the same basic document, with many mechanical clarifications and refinements which imply that the earlier version had not worked satisfactorily. Most of the changes are insignificant, but the revision was much more explicit in some respects, especially relative to the character and purpose of the order.[26] There is no reason to believe that the character and purpose had changed very much; rather the Klan had grown immensely in the interim and its leaders may have felt that a more elaborate and specific credo befitted its grandeur and might discourage simple vigilantism.

One of the most important additions was a series of ten questions which every incoming member had to answer satisfactorily. These tell a great deal which in the original edition was left unsaid. Members had to say whether they had ever belonged or subscribed to the principles of the Radical Republican party, the Loyal League, or the Grand Army of the Republic; whether they had served in the federal army during the war and fought against the South; whether they opposed Negro equality (both social and political) and favored a white man's government; whether they advocated re-enfranchising white Southerners; favored "Constitutional liberty, and a Government of equitable laws instead of a Government of violence and oppression"; favored "maintaining the Constitutional rights of the South"; and believed in "the inalienable right of self-preservation of the people against the exercise of arbitrary and unlicensed power."

Similarly, there was now a formal statement of character and purpose, whereas none had been given in the original: "This is an institution of Chivalry, Humanity, Mercy, and Patriotism; embodying in its genius and its principles all that is chivalric in conduct, noble in sentiment, generous in manhood, and patriotic in purpose." Its objects were "to protect the weak, the innocent, and the defenceless, from the indignities, wrongs, and outrages of the lawless, the violent, and the brutal"; to relieve and assist the injured, oppressed, suffering, and unfortunate, especially widows and orphans of Confederate soldiers; and to support the United States Constitution and constitutional laws.[27]

It would be hard to imagine a greater parody than this on the Ku Klux Klan as it actually operated. It frequently pandered to men's lowest instincts; it bullied or brutalized the poor, the weak, and the defenseless; it was often the embodiment of lawlessness and outrage; it did almost nothing to succor Confederate widows and orphans; and it set at defiance the Constitution and laws of the United States.

Much of this activity represented a departure from the objectives and methods sanctioned by the leaders; much of it did not. Their rhetoric in behalf of chivalry, humanity, mercy, and patriotism has to be read in the light of their crusade for white supremacy and Negro subordination. Their advocacy of "Constitutional liberty" and "equitable laws" was for white men only. Their support of the Constitution and constitutional laws was premised on a belief that the Fourteenth Amendment and the Reconstruction Acts were unconstitutional. Words had different meanings for the Ku Klux Klan, primarily because they did not conceive of the Negro as a man.

Those responsible for the Prescripts did not intend most of the bloodshed or brutality committed by their followers; indeed they repudiated much of it and tried in some measure to prevent or control it. They conceived themselves to be champions of a higher white culture and political order defending themselves against wanton political aggression. They also (perhaps first and foremost) regarded themselves as guardians of law and order against Negro criminality, whether it took the form of individual thievery or organized violence through the Union League. In some small measure they were right; there was some Negro criminality (though not through the Union League), and the Klan doubtless suppressed some of it by means of relatively nonviolent intimidation. But the Klan very soon lost even the semblance of nonviolence, and it committed far greater crimes, man for man, than did the people it purported to regulate. Its crusade against radicalism was even more misconceived. Where real misgovernment existed, the Klan seldom touched it. More typically the Klan was a reactionary and racist crusade against equal rights which sought to overthrow the most democratic society or government the South had yet known.

Its immediate enemy, however, was the Brownlow regime in Tennessee, a government concededly undemocratic in its wholesale disfranchisement of ex-Confederates. Moreover, Klansmen saw the rapidly forming Union Leagues as an imminent threat to their liberty and their physical safety; in this they were incorrect, although the League was an uncommonly effective political machine. They regarded Negro suffrage, accurately enough, as a

Republican political weapon directed at themselves, and thus doubly outrageous. Finally they saw the state militia as a device for cowing them into submission; in this too they were correct, but the submission sought was a submission to the public peace which they or their sympathizers had violated. To its leaders the Klan was a wholly defensive body of citizens who were regrettably driven underground in their defense of white civilization against Negro depredation and radical tyranny.

To Governor Brownlow the new Ku Klux Klan appeared as an aggressive, secret guerrilla army aimed at overthrowing Unionism and restoring an outlawed rebel regime by intimidation and violence. At this distance it is hard to deny that Brownlow had the stronger case. His worst crime comes to no more than a temporary political proscription of ex-Confederates for which an argument of political necessity can still be made. It is impossible, on the other hand, to grant the major premises of the Ku Klux leaders; if it were possible, they might be forgiven most of the "peaceable" night riding designed to keep the Negro in his place, but they are still left with a heritage of terror and bloodshed which they may not have intended but most surely set afoot. Until recently most historians of Reconstruction did in fact accept the Klan's premises rather than Brownlow's and made it palatable by ignoring, evading, or denying the greater substance of Klan activity.

The institutional mechanics set forth in the Prescripts proved too elaborate, too rigid and restrictive, for actual sustained use. The Klan never completely filled out the skeleton established for it. Most of the higher offices were filled only nominally if at all, and it is doubtful if the involved judicial procedure for trying members saw much service. The chain of command was often neglected and it seldom led very far upward. Most of the action and organization took place at the grass roots, with no more regard for the formalities of the Prescript than was convenient or necessary to the occasion. New members often failed to receive the careful screening prescribed; in fact some were drafted into the order against their will. The Prescript had also sought to ban alcoholic refreshment at meetings; but if truth be told, the hip flask became almost as fitting a symbol of the Ku Klux Klan in action as the revolver and hickory switch. The secret codes, grips, signs, and passwords had their day and for the most part passed away quickly like the original amusements in Pulaski. Together with the high-sounding rhetoric and elaborate organization they had little relevance for the real work at hand.

Klan partisans always objected that most of the departures from the forms and practices enjoined by the Prescript—or indeed any conduct of which they disapproved—were committed by false Ku Klux, men who used the name and disguise without authorization to accomplish their own selfish or sinister purposes. This argument is almost meaningless, for the Klan's continuing decentralization was so great that few dens outside Tennessee (and probably within it) had any meaningful affiliation with the parent order. If that kind of affiliation is to be the test of real Ku Klux, then there were very few of them. To ignore or dismiss most of the functioning units whom the world knew as Ku Klux is to present a very restricted view of the movement. The truth is that some Klansmen took a less restricted view than others of the order's proper function and there was little that the latter could do to stop them. It is highly arbitrary to designate one group as authentic and the other spurious.

Probably the best-kept part of the Prescript was its requirement of secrecy. In the interest of personal safety, if nothing else, most members kept the secrets of the order (including their own membership) to themselves. They began divulging information publicly only when the federal government (and one or two states) took steps to bring them to book; but that was a long time in coming. Another abiding characteristic, present from the beginning but unmentioned in the Prescripts, was the wearing of disguises. Like secrecy, it had a practical relevance to the Klan's real activities. There is good reason to believe that Klansmen occasionally operated out of disguise, serving as posses for friendly sheriffs and otherwise, but in most places this was exceptional if it occurred at all. In fact, if there is any line dividing Ku Klux bands from other armed bands of regulators it probably lies in the wearing of disguises together with a more continuing organization. In some cases it is impossible to draw such a line at all where Klansmanship shaded off imperceptibly into simple brigandage.

There never has been any serious doubt that the first and only Grand Wizard was General Nathan Bedford Forrest. He never admitted the fact in so many words, but his later statements to the press and to a Congressional committee in 1871 help to confirm the notion, which was almost universally shared by members and nonmembers alike. The only name advanced very often as an alternative is that of President Andrew Johnson, for which there is not a shred of evidence.[28] Forrest was eminently qualified for the post. He had been a dashing and strikingly successful cavalry leader during the war, one of the ablest field commanders in the Confederate army. Before that time he had been a planter and slave trader; afterward, like other Confederate generals, he went into railroad building and life insurance to recoup his depleted fortune. Although he lacked political experience, Forrest shared fully the Conservative doctrine of his peers and expressed it forcefully and often. A man of imagination, willing to take risks in what he conceived to be a noble cause, he had also a sense of discretion which usually (but not always) kept his militancy within bounds. He was, in short, a perfect embodiment of the Southern chivalric ideal and a perfect leader for the quixotic crusade projected by the Ku Klux Klan.

It is impossible to say when Forrest heard of the Klan and became attracted to it. Apparently absent from the Nashville meeting, he seems to have joined the order soon afterward and to have assumed command shortly after that, probably in May 1867. A circumstantial account of his joining was provided indirectly, years later, by Captain John W. Morton of Nashville, his wartime chief of artillery. Forrest came to Nashville one day and sought out Morton, who was Grand Cyclops of the newly formed den there, saying that he had heard of the order and wanted to learn more about it. Morton took him on a drive into the country and explained enough to make the general eager to join. Without further ado Morton administered the preliminary oath and they returned to town. That night, in Room 10 of the Maxwell House, Forrest was formally inducted, and shortly afterward was elected Grand Wizard.[29]

A good deal has been written about the Klan's further organization at the top levels, but most of it lacks substantiation and much of it is clearly fictitious. There was a tendency after a generation or so to sanctify the Klan along with the Lost Cause and to make it more widespread, more fully organized, more highly connected, and more noble than it actually was. The most prominent Bourbon and ex-Confederate leaders thus were identified at some time or another as leaders of the Klan in their respective states, thereby doing honor to both the Klan and themselves. Among these were Augustus H. Garland of Arkansas, Roger Q. Mills of Texas, Generals John T. Morgan and James H. Clanton of Alabama, General James Z. George of Mississippi, Zebulon Vance of North Carolina, General Wade Hampton of South Carolina, and General John B. Gordon of Georgia. Only in the last case is there much evidence to support the identification. Some of these men may have belonged to the order and occupied positions of nominal leadership for a time, but others, like Robert E. Lee, almost certainly did not.[30] By the same token, Father Abram J. Ryan, a former Catholic chaplain with the Confederate army and a widely read author of Confederate verse, was sometimes identified in later years as chaplain of the Klan, although no such office was mentioned in the Prescript. Whatever truth there may be in the claim, or in his reported attendance at Klan meetings, the priest's sentiments were fitting enough. He moved from a Knoxville pastorate early in 1868 to Augusta, Georgia, where he edited a rabidly anti-Yankee newspaper called the *Banner of the South*.[31] Similarly, General Albert Pike, editor of the Memphis *Appeal*, has been identified as the Klan's attorney general and as a collaborator in drawing up its ritual. The Prescript makes no provision for this office either. Pike may well have affiliated with the Klan, however. He was intrigued by secret societies and rituals, was a leading student and interpreter of Freemasonry, and sympathized with the Klan's stated objectives.[32]

Pike's Masonic connection suggests a further question as to whether some connection or correspondence may not have existed at least locally in parts of the South between the Klan and the Masonic order. There was probably no direct connection, but the two orders frequently and not surprisingly overlapped in membership. Both General John C. Brown and founder James R. Crowe later served as Masonic Grand Masters in Tennessee, and General George W. Gordon was also a Mason. There were six Masonic lodges in Giles County in 1868.[33] On several occasions elsewhere in the South intended victims of the Klan were able to escape whatever fate was in store for them by using the Masonic distress sign or some other token of their membership.[34] A Klansman of York County, South Carolina, indicated at least a strong similarity between the Masonic oath and hailing sign and those used by the Klan.in that vicinity. Although he denied that the two orders were being mixed there, the Klan may well have borrowed Masonic devices, much as it had originally drawn upon the name and ritual of Kuklos Adelphon.[35]

The Klan hardly extended beyond Tennessee and a few counties of north Alabama before 1868, and its organization was probably never as complete elsewhere as in the state of its birth. General Gordon probably became Grand Dragon of the state, although General Brown is also named as holding the post; both may have held it at different times.[36] Captain Morton is identified in a Klan document of June 1868 (printed many years later) as one of the Grand Wizard's Genii or councilors; as such he wrote out an order from the Grand Wizard appointing General G. G. Dibrell Deputy Grand Titan of the Third Dominion (congressional district) with power to complete the Klan organization in that region, east of Nashville.[37] Morton himself organized the Klan at Clarksville and perhaps elsewhere.[38] Another surviving document lists Colonel Joseph Fussell of Columbia as Grand Titan of the district containing Marshall and Maury counties, south of Nashville.[39] In 1909 Minor Meriwether, a St. Louis attorney, claimed to have been the Grand Scribe under Forrest, conducting the official correspondence in cipher.[40]

The basically defensive posture of the Klan's leadership in the spring and summer of 1867 is attested by their own later statements as well as the actual record of Klan activity at that time. Forrest himself consistently denied that the Klan ever meditated violence except in self-defense, and he seems to have disapproved of at least the grosser outrages which it later committed. A Democratic leader of Huntsville, Alabama, later recalled a conversation with Forrest in which the general justified the Klan chiefly with reference to affairs in Tennessee. "He said that Brownlow was drilling his negro militia all over up there, and bad white men, and they had organized for the protection of society in Tennessee."[41] In a newspaper interview of August 1868 and again before a Congressional committee in 1871 Forrest made the same defense, emphasizing allegedly unpunished Negro crime as well as politics and the Union League as the causes of Klan organization. He also claimed to have exerted himself from the outset to suppress Klan outrages, and eventually managed to disband it altogether for that reason. The general was a very reluctant witness, and his testimony is full of evasions and contradictions if not outright falsehoods, but there is no evidence to suggest that he contemplated more than relatively non-violent regulative activity among Negroes and an organization to resist what he regarded as a danger of forcible Republican aggression.[42]

Almost simultaneously with the Nashville meeting the Klan in Pulaski began to court publicity as never before. The *Citizen,* under McCord's editorship, gave its full cooperation. On March 29 it printed the nation's first Ku Klux notice, announcing a forthcoming meeting at "The Den," with a great show of ignorance and mystification as to what it was all about. McCord claimed that he had found the notice under his door one morning. The *Citizen* was a weekly paper, and almost every issue until late in June carried some further message from the Klan or an article purporting to wonder what it was and where it came from. On April 19 McCord described the invasion of his editorial sanctum one night by a strange figure whom he at once deduced to be

the Grand Turk of the Kuklux Klan. We laid hold of the shooting stick and at once placed ourself in a position of defence. Our visitor appeared to be about nine feet high, with a most hideous face, and wrapped in an elegant robe of black silk, which he kept closely folded about his person. He wore gloves the color of blood, and carried a magic wand in his hand with which he awed us into submission to any demand he might make. In a deep coarse voice he inquired if we were the editor. In a weak timid voice we said yes. We tried to say no, but a wave of his wand compelled us to tell the truth. (A wicked printer in the office suggests that we ought to have a wand waving over us all the time.) Whereupon the mysterious stranger placed his hand under his robe and handed us the communication given below, and without uttering another word bowed himself out.

The announcement itself implied strongly that many townspeople were more ignorant of the order than McCord, and were reacting to it unfavorably. The public, it said, should not jump at conclusions or condemn until condemnation was due. The order's secrecy was necessary to its purpose: "This is no joke either. This is cold, hard earnest. Time will fully develop the objects of the 'Kuklux Klan.' Until such development takes place 'the public' will please be patient." A week later the Klan claimed such an increase in members that its future meetings would have to be held at the "Rendezvous in the Forest." On May 28, after moving its meeting place again to ward off spies, it called a gathering to consult with representatives from four other dens, two of them in the county and the other two at Columbia and Franklin.

The purpose of this meeting was probably to plan for the Klan's first major public demonstration—a parade through Pulaski on the night of June 5 to mark the order's first anniversary. The event was well publicized in advance by handbills printed in the *Citizen* office and posted around town. At 10 P.M. the Klansmen appeared, about seventy-five in number and presumably representing several dens. Several hundred people were on hand to watch them, including a reporter for the *Citizen:*

> The crowd waited impatiently for their approach. A closer view discovered their banners and transparenc[i]es, with all manner of mottoes and devices, speers [*sic*], sabres, &c. The column was led by what we supposed to be the Grand Cyclops, who had on a flowing white robe, a white hat about eighteen inches high. He had a very venerable and benevolent looking face, and long silvery locks. He had an escort on each side of him, bearing brilliant transparencies. The master of the ceremonies was gorgiously [*sic*] caparisoned, and his "toot, toot, toot," on a very graveyard-ish sounding instrument, seemed to be perfectly understood by every ku kluxer. Next to the G. C. there followed two of the tallest men out of jail. One of them had on a robe of many colors, with a hideous mask, and a transparent hat, in which he carried a brilliant gas lamp, a box of matches and several other articles. It is said that he was discovered taking a bottle from a shelf in his hat, and that he and his companion took several social drinks together. The other one had on a blood red hat which was so tall that we never did see the top of it. They conversed in dutch, hebrew, or some other language which we couldn't comprehend. No two of them were dressed alike, all having on masks and some sort of fanciful costume.

In this fashion they marched up one street and down another, responding to toots of the leader's whistle. They returned to the town square, paraded around it several times, and then departed.[43]

The Nashville meeting seems to have been followed by an intensive organizing campaign, which first bore fruit in middle Tennessee. By early June the Klan had spread to such towns as Columbia, Franklin, and Shelbyville, as well as to Nashville, if Forrest was initiated there in May.[44] In July there were at least four dens in Giles County.[45] This growth in Tennessee continued well into 1868.

The spring and summer election campaign of 1867 was comparatively peaceful by Reconstruction standards and by comparison with the preceding winter months. The hand of the Klan was hardly to be seen at all. The Conservatives hoped to win over part of the Negro vote and carry the election fairly, or at least without terror. The prevalent notion among whites was that they understood the Negro best, were really his best friends, and that he would in the end vote with his former master. In Pulaski, as elsewhere, white employers encouraged their freedmen to attend Conservative rallies, and a few Conservative Negroes were brought forward as campaigners and fitting examples to follow. Whatever sentimental ties to the old master may have existed were strained, however, by his frequent threats to discharge any freedmen who were caught voting the Radical ticket. Most of the actual assaults and physical threats upon Negroes occurred in west Tennessee, where the Klan had not yet penetrated. Giles County was not entirely free of such activity, however, and a squad of militia arrived late in June; but Captain Judd's most serious complaint was threats of discharge. Small numbers of Klansmen made brief appearances in town but did little else.[46]

Whether or not the scattering of twelve militia companies (fewer than 900 men) around the state was responsible for this quietude, the Conservative press fairly teemed with its own accounts of militia outrages, ranging from robbery and assault to murder.[47] (Most of the militiamen were white, but Conservative papers liked to refer to them as "Brownlow's Negro militia.") General George H. Thomas, whose command included Tennessee, sent officers to investigate two such complaints, but they found nothing to justify the exaggerated press accounts. "Occasional rows, such as might be expected from a newly organized body of men, would occur, and would then be immediately seized upon by an unscrupulous set of newspaper demagogues, only too willing to misrepresent, if the opportunity were offered."[48]

The election passed very quietly and produced a resounding Republican victory. The Negroes voted overwhelmingly for that party, leaving Conservatives frustrated and bitter over the complete failure of their campaign strategy. From this time forward, intimidation of the freedmen became more systematic.

In Giles County the Republican vote was particularly top-heavy, with correspondingly serious aftereffects. Republicans were boycotted, ostracized, and threatened with bodily harm as never before. In his August report Captain Judd for the first time mentioned the Ku Klux Klan, characterizing it as a secret society organized to intimidate Union men.

This society is very numerous and seems to extend all over the country. They march about the streets nights thoroughly disguised and in uniform. . . . I am credibly informed that they are heavily armed. . . . I am sure they are capable of great mischief if they undertake [it]. Threats are continually made which keep the negroes up in arms all the time. . . . The best citizens here. . . . say this Kuklux Klan is got up by the young men merely for fun and that they never intend to interfere with anyone. This may all be true but I doubt it mightily. It is certainly a very extensive institution for a funny one.

Judd also reported a growing tendency to seize guns from the Negroes.[49] Similar accounts reached the desk of Governor Brownlow, coupled with a plea to retain the militia detachment in Pulaski.

The *Citizen,* reflecting frayed Conservative tempers, immediately ridiculed the idea that the Ku Klux Klan ever intended harm to anyone. And whoever asked for the militia to stay must be "some transient, low down, hog stealing, black-hearted, white-livered, pusilanimous villian [*sic*]" whom the militia were shielding from justice.[50] The newspaper showered similar bouquets upon the Union League, which until now had organized and held meetings without interruption. When members of the League began to receive threats from the Klan they came to meetings armed for protection. This in turn led to a congregation of armed whites who were disposed for a time to attack them. Although a conflict was averted, Conservatives were alarmed and outraged at the League's supposed presumption in gathering a body of armed Negroes. The *Citizen* called for an airtight economic and social boycott of Republican leaders, whom it held responsible. Captain Judd had been tolerated heretofore in his role as Freedmen's Bureau agent. But now he was accused of being the "Head Centre" of the nefarious Union League. As the result of a petticoat conspiracy among the ladies of Pulaski, he and his family found themselves ejected from their boardinghouse; unable to gain entry to another, they moved into his office. The most conspicuous of the white hoodlums who took it upon themselves to harass Republicans was young Alonzo Peden, son of the sheriff, who himself sported the badge of a deputy sheriff. Peden was a leader in the near-attack upon the League, and on another occasion he burst into a Republican-owned store while drunk and began abusing and threatening its proprietors. Although the actual violence arising from such incidents was small, the threats and turmoil resulted in a temporary reinforcement of the militia unit stationed in Pulaski at the same time they were being disbanded elsewhere.[51]

Even in Pulaski, however, there was little open manifestation of the Klan during the fall of 1867. When major public attention was first directed to it in December it was primarily in Columbia and Maury County, to the north. The Freedmen's Bureau agent there, H. A. Eastman, provides the earliest account of the Ku Klux engaged in what came to be their major avocation, night riding. "I think there is no doubt that their purpose is to annoy and intimidate the colored people, and perhaps to break up the loyal league." This activity extended into adjacent counties as well, he said, and caused "considerable uneasiness" among the freedmen.[52] Newspaper reactions clearly reflected the Klan's new political or quasi-political cast. The Republican *Press and Times* in Nashville castigated the night riders and charged them with killing a white man and beating a Negro;[53] the Conservative *Republican Banner,* on the other hand, claimed to know that the Klan consisted of "the most respectable young men of Giles and Maury Counties," who were above that kind of activity.[54] On Christmas morning the freedmen held a parade in Columbia, complete with fife and drums. Such events were apt to be noisy and boisterous, and irritated the whites no end. When a policeman demanded that they quiet their drums to avoid scaring horses and causing an accident, the Negroes at first complied, but later threatened to start again. At this point two red-robed Klansmen appeared, then rode off amid rumors that they had gone to fetch 300 more of their kind. The blacks now deemed it wise to disperse. The *Banner* reported that a bloody and bitter race riot was thus averted, as every white countenance showed a determination not to brook Negro resistance to the civil authorities.[55] It was episodes like this which would long recall the Klan to Southerners as a force for law and order.

These two Columbia Klansmen were referred to interchangeably as "Kuklux" and "palefaces." Columbia seems to have been the birthplace and headquarters of an Order of Pale Faces which spread throughout much of Tennessee by 1869. It was divided into Camps, of which there were thirty-four by October 1868, when it held a Grand Camp or state convention in Columbia. General Forrest in his Congressional testimony of 1871 first identified the Pale Faces with the Klan, and then distinguished between them. Although he admitted joining the Pale Faces in Memphis in 1867, he was never so explicit about his Klan membership.[56] Early in 1868 the two orders appeared together at a funeral in Columbia, but only the Klansmen were reported as disguised.[57] There was general confusion between the two societies among outsiders at least, and when a Nashville paper identified the Pale Faces as an auxiliary of the Ku Klux Klan the former emphatically denied the "soft impeachment." They were attached to no other order and were neither political nor sectarian in character; their purpose was charitable and to render mutual assistance in times of distress. Klansmen sometimes made the same claims but less convincingly. Whether the Pale Faces had a secret ritual or not, they were much less secretive about their organization and membership. The state convention in October 1868 was reported fully in the press, along with the names of its officers and members of its standing committees. It did engage in charitable or related work, for example, holding a ball in Nashville in December 1868 to raise money to reinter Confederate dead.[58] The two organizations were congenial, however; very likely their membership overlapped, and they may have had organizational ties as well in some localities.[59]

The first four months of 1868 saw a phenomenal expansion of the Ku Klux Klan, from half a dozen or so counties in middle Tennessee to every Southern state between the Potomac and the Rio Grande. Even in the state of its birth this expansion was remarkable. The Klan was organized in almost every county of the middle region, and by July it had virtually seized control of several. West Tennessee was only slightly less affected. The Klan tried to organize in Knoxville in March, but its only success in east Tennessee was brief and highly localized around Bristol, which had been a small island of Confederate sympathy during the war.[60] This growth surely satisfied the most visionary of the Klan's projectors, but only the most callous and irresponsible of them could have regarded their handiwork with much pride of accomplishment by midsummer. For all of their rhetorical chivalry, their devotion to law and order, and their defensive intent, they had launched a systematic crime wave which required a far holier cause than theirs to justify.

CHAPTER 2

Expansion and Violence in Tennessee, 1868

The best explanation for the Tennessee Klan's sudden descent into terror-ism early in 1868 is that it got out of control of its leaders. Such was its typical progress wherever it spread. Republicans thought that it was designed to sweep aside the Negro vote in the local elections which were scheduled throughout the state in March. Yet the elections came and went, and the terror continued. The Klan was not as narrowly political as this view assumed; whatever the intention of its founders, it fed on a race hatred which transcended politics. The terror was self-generating and indiscriminate save for the cardinal fact that Conservatives, black and white, were almost never touched. The victims were overwhelmingly Negro, and they suffered for every crime, real or imaginary, from murder and rape to defending themselves against attack and voting the Republican ticket. Every sign of manhood was an invitation to Ku Klux attack. In a few cases the victims did defend themselves with a measure of success, but usually they were caught off guard and utterly helpless as a dozen or more armed and hooded men arrived unannounced in the dead of night, battered down the door, and committed whatever violence it pleased them to inflict. Despite the high-sounding idealism of the Prescript, Klansmanship in practice was neither edifying nor inspirational; it was usually brutal and cowardly, for the odds were never even.

Maury was probably the banner Ku Klux county in Tennessee. The local Klan's tactics varied, but its members commonly traveled in small groups well after dark, each unit operating in a neighborhood where its members were not apt to be known. Thus there was probably some advance planning and organization, delimiting the respective spheres of operation, specifying persons to be raided, and guiding the attackers to their destinations. Total Klan membership in the county was several hundred. Approaching a Negro cabin, they sometimes stationed pickets to ward off any intruders before they called out the inhabitants or broke in and dragged them out. Men and older boys were the usual targets, although there were reports of abusing pregnant women and forcing children to wade in icy water. The normal punishment was a whipping or beating administered on the bare back with "hickories," sticks or small branches torn off a nearby tree. Many persons received several hundred lashes with these instruments, and one man reportedly got 900. The resulting scars were often permanent, and some victims were partially crippled. Others were shot, sometimes mortally. A Negro boy of twenty was taken out of his home in Columbia in July by fifty or sixty Klansmen who led him into the country and garroted him; then they tied a stone around his neck and dumped the body into the Duck River. Klansmen were not always sober in making their rounds, and, sober or not, typical raids were accompanied by a great deal of profanity and obscenity as well as indiscriminate physical abuse. The treatment was worse if the victims tried to resist.

Much of this activity was carried on without the advance knowledge of Klan leaders, even at the county level. Klansmen must therefore have enjoyed their work to engage in so much of it, but they also regarded themselves as purveyors of a rough justice. They accompanied their floggings with accusations of crime and other offenses which the victims had allegedly committed, and threatened even worse to come if they did not reform. The Klan administered 200 lashes on one Negro, Henry Fitzpatrick, and then returned another night and hanged him; the pretext was that he had set fire to two barns, although no proof or legal charge was ever brought against him. Perhaps the most common offense alleged—at least the one most often reported to the authorities by the victims themselves—was voting the Republican ticket or belonging to the Union League. The Klan was highly effective in bringing League activity to a standstill in Maury and other counties. A Negro veteran of the Union army, Clinton Drake, was reportedly taken from his house and hanged by a Ku Klux band who threatened to serve all Union veterans the same way. Almost every raid included a search for and confiscation of any guns left on the premises. At least 400 were seized in the county in February alone. Another objective of Klan raids was to warn the teachers of colored schools (who might themselves be of either race) to close up their schools and leave; a number of them did so.

A given band would frequently make several attacks in a night. This kind of raiding took place throughout the county, with only occasional periods of respite, from December 1867 until August 1868. H. A. Eastman, the Bureau agent, often received daily visits from Negroes who came in to his office in Columbia to report outrages upon them the night before. The freedmen were terrified, but also increasingly bitter as the months passed. Many slept out in the woods at night to avoid attack; others attempted resistance, singly or in groups, but resistance cost them more than submission, owing to the Klan's better organization and armament. Two hundred or more fled to Nashville and elsewhere, sacrificing most of their possessions and their share of the year's crop. They were safe in Nashville but utterly destitute, as there was little work for them, and they subsisted on the charity of the Freedmen's Bureau.[1]

Such were the workaday activities of the Maury County Klan. But there were special occasions too. Late in February a Negro named Walker robbed and murdered a young white man, John Bicknell, on a country road. Walker was later arrested and lodged in the Columbia jail. Although no one was so indiscreet as to announce it publicly, Bicknell apparently had belonged to both the Klan and the Pale Faces. Both societies made a serious occasion of his funeral, the Ku Klux attending in full regalia. At the cemetery the Pale Faces performed a "strange but solemn ceremony," according to a reverent newspaper account. Then, "after the last shovelful of earth had been thrown upon the freshly raised mound, the Kuklux, about twenty strong, kneeled around, and, raising their right hands toward Heaven, swore vengeance on the murderer of John Bicknell. They then rose slowly, mounted their horses[,] went off at a brisk gait southward and soon disappeared from the view of the awe-struck spectators." At 10 o'clock the following Monday night a lynch party of twenty Klansmen rode into Columbia and headed for the jail; less than five minutes later they were headed out of town again with Walker in tow. Two miles into the country, on the banks of the Duck River, they dismounted, untied their prisoner, and prepared for his execution. So far all had gone off without a hitch, as in one of Thomas Dixon's later novels of the Ku Klux Klan. But all of a sudden Walker bolted into the river and made his escape. The next day he was rearrested and returned to jail, where he reportedly confessed to Bicknell's murder. That night, to no one's surprise, the Klan made another appearance, at least sixty strong, secured Walker without a struggle, and took him back into the country. There, the next morning, his body was found hanging from the limb of a tree.[2]

Another major occasion took place on the night of July 4, when the Maury Klansmen, in concert with their brethren in other county towns around the state, planned a mass parade in Columbia. It was to be like the first anniversary parade in Pulaski, but much larger. And by virtue of its simultaneous enactment across the state, the event was intended to demonstrate to the faithful, to the freedmen, and to Governor Brownlow the power and majesty of the Ku Klux Klan. Taken as a whole, these demonstrations did have considerable effect on all the parties mentioned. But in Columbia things departed again from the plan. About midnight more than a hundred disguised horsemen rode in from the south, proceeded to the public square, and then moved to a point near the western edge of town. Here they joined at least 150 more Klansmen to set up a kind of field headquarters. What their subsequent plans were never became known. For weeks there had been rumors that black men around the county, made desperate by the terrorism to which they had been subjected for seven months, were planning some kind of retaliation.[3] Now it appeared that twenty or thirty Negroes, armed with shotguns and pistols which the Klan had overlooked, were lying in wait to attack the Ku Klux in their hour of triumph. They proceeded to do so. "With closed ranks and steady aim they fired a volley among their fantastically dressed enemy. Several [Klansmen] fell from their horses, uttering cries of pain. They immediately formed in line and charged upon the blacks who had fallen back to some old breastworks, where they received the charge with another volley, the best they had." Vastly outnumbered, the Negroes now retreated to the camp of an Army infantry company which had recently been sent to Columbia. The soldiers were at once called out to form in line. They too were badly outnumbered, but rather than risk the eventual consequences of attacking an Army detachment, the Ku Klux retired from the field. The Klan apparently suffered all the casualties, losing one man killed and three or four badly wounded.[4]

The Negroes almost always lost ultimately in their encounters with the Ku Klux Klan. The white community was thoroughly frightened at what it regarded as the advent of a general Negro uprising. The residents of Columbia organized, worked out an alarm signal, and amid mounting tension, waited for the black horde to descend. About 10 o'clock one night someone accidentally dropped a pistol on the pavement, causing it to discharge. "Immediately the Court House bell struck twice, cries of 'fall in' were heard, and from all quarters armed men sprang into the Square." They dispersed as soon as they learned the cause, but the young bloods organized a vigilance committee which patrolled the streets at night, almost hoping for an excuse to fall upon the Negroes and punish them for their temerity. Many of these vigilantes were likely Klansmen out of disguise, but in any case the Klan itself leaped into new activity. It systematically hunted down the offending blacks of July 4, catching and killing several while the rest fled to Nashville. By the middle of July at least three other Negroes were lynched, in one case by a party of 200 who rode into town and dragged the man from his home.[5]

There was no legal protection against the Ku Klux Klan wherever it became established. The civil authorities, like the general white public, were either in sympathy with the order or intimidated by it. During the lesser terror of a year before, when the governor had responded to pleas for help by calling out the militia, its very effectiveness had antagonized most of the white population. Far from tyrannizing over the Conservatives, the Republican legislature then tried to appease them by repealing the militia law altogether. Brownlow's only recourse when the present terror broke out, therefore, was to call for federal troops, which he sent to Columbia in April. In a signed editorial of April 15 in the Knoxville *Whig* he notified Maury County of the soldiers' impending arrival; they would be kept there, he announced, "until the disloyal, bushwhacking, jayhawking and murderous rebels learn lessons of moderation and acquire habits of decency." An infantry company did arrive, and the Klan lay low for about a month. But the soldiers' instructions—and this was general throughout the South once state governments had been reorganized and accepted by Congress—were to help enforce the laws only at the request and in cooperation with the local authorities. When these authorities did nothing, the troops were almost useless except as a symbol and a haven for refugees. This was the cause of their inactivity around Columbia on July 4 and afterward.

The local Klan leadership (whether prompted from above or not) did "learn lessons of moderation," but very imperfectly. In June the Grand Giant of the county undertook secretly to reorganize the Klan within his jurisdiction, hoping to weed out the disorderly members. He also issued a public decree which the Columbia *Herald* accommodated him by carrying in an extra edition. Admitting that parties in Klan disguise had often committed unlawful acts, he ordered this stopped and commanded members to destroy their regalia. A different disguise was contemplated as a result of the reorganization (which he did not mention), and this was to be worn only on his authority. The Klan is not organized "to whip and abuse negroes . . . radicals," or anyone else, he declared, "but to preserve law and order." It soon appeared that the more select members were being mobilized into a new and higher degree of Klansmanship called Ghouls. It was they, presumably, who gathered for the ill-fated Fourth of July parade, which was surely decreed by the Grand Giant on orders from above. Some of the later outrages in July involved so many men and required such extensive organization that it is hard to believe they were not sanctioned officially. If this is true, the leadership's disapproval of violence and its stand for law and order were not terribly impressive.[6]

In Pulaski and Giles County the Klan was under slightly better discipline. Its members duplicated most of the atrocities committed around Columbia, but they were fewer in number. Race relations continued to be bitter, with whites the major offender. In January a private quarrel between a white man and a freedman over a Negro girl erupted into a minor race riot. The white man fired on one of the Negro's friends in the street, whereupon eighteen young white men dashed out of their houses carrying double-barreled shotguns and pistols, and drew up in line in front of a store where several Negroes had gathered. The whites then charged, firing volleys into the store, and the blacks returned the fire as best they could. Older and wiser heads intervened to restore order, but not before at least one of the freedmen was killed and several others wounded. The whites, who included a John Kennedy, probably one of the Klan's "immortal six," suffered no injury.[7]

When outrages began to be committed by disguised parties, the Klan leadership acted to stop it. In February the Pulaski *Citizen* carried an official decree calling for the trial of all Klansmen guilty of wearing disguises outside their respective dens. It also disavowed any intention to "harm the poor African."[8] This order seems to have taken effect, for the night riding temporarily abated. When outrages recurred in April, they were confined chiefly to the northern part of the county and involved the usual attacks upon Negroes. Klansmen frequently rode through Pulaski at night creating commotion but little or no damage. On the night of June 29, however, about a hundred of them in full disguise rode into town and lynched a Negro confined for attempted rape. Taking him at gunpoint, they did not wait to get him out of town, but riddled him with bullets on one of the main streets and then departed. The body was left for an omnibus to run over soon afterward and for the public to observe the next morning. "We need not be understood as encouraging mob violence," the *Citizen* commented, "when we express the opinion that the fate of this black would-be raper was merited. While we would not like to have his execution resting upon our shoulders, yet if those who ministered speedy justice to the scoundrel are satisfied, we are, and shall not take the trouble to find out who they are. Let the black men of the community learn a lesson from this."[9]

Several days later the *Citizen* carried an order from the Grand Giant of Giles County forbidding Klansmen to commit "personal violence upon any citizen of this Province [county], regardless of color, without orders from these Head-quarters. . . . " At the same time he convened the Grand Council of Yahoos—also a rare event—to try the Grand Magi of one of the local dens for violating this order. These proceedings certainly did not result from the recent lynching, which the *Citizen* approved and the Klan leaders themselves had doubtless arranged. It arose rather from the host of beatings inflicted on unoffending Negroes or those guilty of "some trifling misdemeanor" which had created terror in the northern part of the county. The *Citizen* was to all intents and purposes the public voice of the local

Klan leadership. Now for the first time it openly condemned these activities, making clear at the same time that it approved the organization itself. "While we do not condemn all of the acts of the Kuklux Klan, yet there are many things done by them, or in their name and garb, which we do not hesitate to pronounce wrong, and which should be stopped by some means."[10]

The Fourth of July parade in Pulaski went off more smoothly than it did in Columbia. Well advertised in advance, its beginning was signaled about 11 P.M. by rockets shooting off in all directions over town. Three to four hundred Klansmen on horse and afoot converged slowly from several directions on the town square; both they and their horses were elaborately disguised. For about an hour they performed military maneuvers in the square and along the streets, in perfect order and without any word of command being uttered. Then they left as quietly as they came.[11]

All was not parading on the Fourth of July, however. The village of Cornersville, northeast of Pulaski, had been the center of Klan violence in recent months, and the Negroes there had begun organizing and drilling for their own defense. They also made threats against the Klan which members of the white community deemed unseemly. Not all of the crimes here had been committed in disguise, and the Negroes went so far as to capture some of the hoodlums involved. Until persuaded to release them, they intended to march them to Pulaski to stand trial. The *Citizen* was ready to condemn much of the oppression these freedmen had undergone, but their attempts to fight back were quite another matter. It identified the leading figure among the blacks (William Burk) as "a vicious and dangerous negro." On the night of July 4, the *Citizen* reported, Burk "was waited upon by some gentlemen, who approached him to talk the matter over in a civil way. He wouldn't listen to a word, but immediately commenced firing at the party. The gentlemen, who were said to be Kuklux, were compelled to shoot him down in self-defense." Every Negro who fought back was by definition vicious and dangerous, and the gentlemen callers were indeed, by other testimony, a Ku Klux raiding party, not heretofore known to call Negroes out of their houses after dark for polite conversation.[12]

Conditions were similar in most of the other counties to which the Ku Klux Klan spread in the spring of 1868. The same crimes were committed against the Negro population in particular, equally out of proportion to any offenses they might have committed. And as often as not, the only offenses alleged were voting for Brownlow, belonging to the Union League, or having served in the Union army. In Humphreys County, west of Nashville, some of the raiding was done by bands calling themselves Red Caps and Yellow Jackets, but they resembled the Ku Klux in other respects.[13]

The Klan and its defenders often claimed that it was not a political organization, but the evidence is conclusive that one of its major objectives was to decimate the Negro vote and thereby topple the Brownlow regime. There were repeated cases before the county elections in March of Klansmen threatening death to any Negroes who voted, as well as punishing them afterward for having done so.[14] In Marshall County in January they seized eight freedmen, marched them to an open field, and made them swear with upraised hands never to vote the Radical ticket on pain of death.[15]

There was a concerted effort as well to get rid of Republican officeholders, who in Tennessee at this point were invariably white men and almost always native Unionists. In fact one of the first signs that the Ku Klux had organized in any locality was a flurry of public or private notices to such officials, threatening death or destruction if they did not resign. Occasionally the Klan went further. In April Sheriff J. S. Webb of Rutherford County (Murfreesboro) was dragged from his home at midnight and threatened with a lynching unless he vacated his office. He did not resign and they did not return, but he slept out for a while afterward nevertheless. On other occasions they whipped his brother and called out the circuit court clerk but did not harm him.[16]

This county was almost completely in the grip of the Klan, which numbered 800 to 1,000 members. It paraded through town at will, often once or twice a week, and outrages upon Negroes occurred almost nightly. The blacks eventually stopped reporting these attacks to the Bureau agent in town after the Ku Klux threatened to kill anyone who did so. Republicans in office and out, black and white, exhibited courage merely in staying. The Bureau agent, J. K. Nelson, was subjected to such constant insult, harassment, and threats of violence that he regularly slept with a revolver under his pillow and other weapons close at hand.[17]

Fayetteville and Lincoln County were hardly better off. Here state senator William Wyatt, a man of sixty-five, was taken from his house at night by Klansmen who beat him over the head with pistols and left him unconscious. They also broke into the sheriff's house, but found him luckily or prudently absent. The Klan killed at least two men in Fayetteville and drove several Unionists from the county, besides the usual outrages upon Negroes.[18]

Much of the Klan's activity was purely racist in inspiration, with little or no political overtone. A farmer in Marshall County blandly announced to a Congressional committee that he had once invited the Ku Klux to his place to discipline a woman employee. They took her out and gave her sixty-five lashes with a leather strap; it did her good, he said, and he thanked them for it.[19] The search and seizure of Negroes' guns was general, as was the breaking up of colored schools and threatening or driving off their teachers.[20] On the night of July 4 the Bedford County Klan, instead of simply parading, galloped into Shelbyville about fifty strong, took two men from their homes and into the country, and whipped them. One was a Negro, James Franklin, who left the county by Klan invitation, and the other was J. C. Dunlap, a Northerner teaching in a Negro school. Dunlap had experienced every kind of indignity and social ostracism before receiving his 200 lashes this night, but a prominent Democrat now cared for his wounds, and his existence in general grew more tolerable. His treatment by the Klan seems to have helped turn local sentiment against the order.[21]

In contrast to these activities the Klan still claimed to be in part a philanthropic organization. The evidence to support the claim is very bare indeed, but apparently an order went out from the higher leadership in February to report cases of destitution among Confederate widows and orphans. At least twice, in Maury and Williamson counties, such persons were given money and other assistance.[22]

The Klan did a good deal of parading, which variously impressed both friend and foe. The most general occasion was the Fourth of July, and in most places it went off smoothly. In Murfreesboro 200 Klansmen improved the occasion by requiring a white man to return to the wife he had deserted. At Tullahoma they appeared at a ball, performed practical jokes, and then amused themselves on the way home by frightening Negroes. Democratic newspapers had a good time reporting or inventing Ku Klux high jinks. On this occasion, it was said, "the Nashville train passed by and one of [the Klansmen] was cut off from the band. 'Who will care for mother now?' he ejaculated and jumped over the passenger car to join his comrades."[23]

Sometimes the parading had an immediate political purpose, as in Nashville on the night of March 5, just prior to the county elections. The parade was announced in advance and the entire police force was mobilized to attack the Ku Klux when they made their appearance. At least thirty did appear; their parade was short-lived, but they managed to get away without a fight.[24] Nashville was not a country village to be ridden over roughshod. Very few outrages occurred within the city, and it had become a haven for Negro refugees from all over middle Tennessee. But the Klan was organized here, and it managed at least one lynching; in fact the job had to be done twice, as with Walker in Columbia, because the victim, a white man accused of murder, escaped from the Klan the first time.[25]

Memphis boasted a more active Klan organization, but it too was a place of refuge for Negroes from the surrounding countryside. (Soon afterward it would become an asylum for Ku Klux themselves, fleeing Governor Powell Clayton's Arkansas militia.) The Klan appears not to have organized, or at least surfaced, in Memphis before March 1868, despite General Forrest's residence there. For some days before the first notice of its presence appeared, on March 11, the Conservative Memphis *Avalanche* prepared the way with informative articles on the order's progress in other parts of the state; when the local organization was announced the *Avalanche* provided welcoming editorials.[26] The Klan committed little or no violence in the city; instead, it (or some organization like it bearing the unexplained initials "R.R.R.") tried to organize a boycott against Radical business houses.[27] During the summer it paraded through the city on several nights, apparently without incident.[28]

Actually there were several Klans or Klan-like organizations in the city. One offbeat society calling itself the Supreme Cyclopean Council was immediately staked out by the metropolitan police, who arrested about twenty members on the night of April 6 as they emerged from their den at Hernando and Beale streets. Captured with them were their disguises and constitution. The members regarded themselves as Ku Klux, but their constitution was an earthier and less sophisticated document than the Nashville Prescript. There was a committee on assassination, for instance, and members were required to swear that "should I ever . . . betray a secret, or a member of the Brotherhood . . . I hope that all the social relations which I now enjoy may be sundered, that honesty in the men or virtue in the females may not be known in my family and generation, and that all who own my name shall be branded as dogs and harlots." Or, on receiving orders from one's superiors, "should I be even in the embraces of my wife, I will leave her to obey them."

The Republican Memphis *Post* was jubilant at this exposé and reported every detail. The two pro-Klan Conservative papers diverged in their reactions. General Pike's *Appeal* waxed indignant at this naked and shameless outrage in breaking up a peaceful meeting while the *Avalanche* (for whom the exposed Grand Cyclops had recently worked as a reporter) preferred ridicule and obfuscation: the police had picked up a bunch of innocent boys who "were simply members of baseball clubs and a serenading glee club." A third Conservative paper, the *Bulletin*, was as emphatic an opponent of the Klan and its works as any Republican paper.[29]

Klan apologists often justified or excused the intimidation of Negroes on the ground that Radical government was corrupt or inefficient and no other means existed to prevent and punish Negro crime. In the sense that it was hard to identify and impractical to prosecute those who committed petty thievery, there may have been some basis for this view; night riding may conceivably have diminished these offenses, but at the cost of infinitely greater crimes on the part of the regulators. In the case of substantial

Negro crime, however, this defense reflected a blindness to the facts and a callous indifference to Negro rights and feelings which was perennially the ugliest aspect of Southern life. Even during Radical Reconstruction the legal system, like most other institutions, was stacked against the Negro. Conservative accounts to the contrary notwithstanding, there was seldom much trouble in arresting Negro offenders, bringing them to trial, or securing their conviction if guilty; in fact it was often too easy. Republican officials were usually as scrupulous as Democrats in punishing Negro crime, if only to prove their impartiality to the bitter and hypersensitive white community. The real problem, on the contrary, was in punishing white men for even the grossest offenses against Negroes; it became infinitely greater when the Ku Klux Klan was involved. The difficulty of identifying disguised attackers, great as it was, amounted to nothing compared with the problem of bringing them to book when they were perfectly well known. Dominant white opinion either supported the Klan or was afraid to oppose it; more frequently the two feelings ran concurrently among most individuals. Thus it was almost impossible to get a sheriff to arrest, a grand jury to indict, a district attorney to prosecute, witnesses to testify against, or a petit jury to convict Ku Klux criminals. Here it was that the legal system broke down and the Klan—far from upholding law and order—actually made it a mockery.

The hopelessness of the Negroes' position in a hostile white society and the futility of resisting the Klan were epitomized in the case of Bob Anderson, a veteran of two and a half years in the Union army, who lived five miles from Nashville. After several nights of marauding in the neighborhood, a Ku Klux band returned to his house on the night of March 17 and demanded admission. When he refused, they got a rail and began battering at the door, shooting into the house at the same time. Anderson poked a shotgun out one of the windows and fired back. One of the attackers fell mortally wounded and the others fled, scattering parts of their regalia in their haste to get away. The dead Ku Klux was unmasked and identified as a young man of the neighborhood. The next morning forty or fifty white men, including the deceased's brother, came and took Anderson and some of his friends into custody. The Negroes were soon released, but were ordered to leave the vicinity within twenty-four hours. They had no choice but to comply, and joined the hundreds of other Negro refugees collecting in Nashville, seemingly without hope of redress. According to Anderson's landlord, state supreme court justice H. H. Harrison, he had borne a good character and was hard-working and industrious.[30]

Negroes were somewhat better off where white Republicans were numerous and well enough organized to help them face down the Klan. In Wayne County, near Pulaski, sixty to a hundred Negroes were employed at a newly opened mine. Local whites wanted the jobs themselves and scared off some of the freedmen with threats that the Ku Klux would come after them. But the bolder Negroes obtained guns, organized a company, and began drilling nightly on the highway. This raised the vision of Santo Domingo, and whites redoubled their threats of a Ku Kluxing if they did not stop. In response the Negroes, joined by white Unionists, prepared for an attack. On August 15 about sixty Klansmen in full disguise appeared at the mine, where their leader told the blacks that the Klan meant them no harm; he insisted, however, that they stop drilling. The Negroes agreed and promised to store their guns. As the Ku Klux returned toward Waynesboro, the county seat, they were met by the sheriff, who brashly demanded their revolvers. When they refused he fired at them and then retreated hastily into town, still firing, with the Klan in hot pursuit. The sheriff took refuge in the jail, around which a stockade had been built for just such an occasion. As the Klansmen approached the stockade, seven or eight men inside opened fire. The Ku Klux returned the fire but soon withdrew after four of their men were shot from their horses. Fearing that they would return with reinforcements, the sheriff rapidly organized a posse of fifty-three men to resist a further attack.

At this point Lieutenant Colonel J. W. Gelray, a trouble shooter sent by the Army, arrived and assumed the role of peacemaker. He induced some of the sheriff's supporters to accompany him to the town of Clifton, where they met R. A. Allison, the acknowledged head of the county Klan. A pact was drawn up by which Allison promised to use his influence to support the law and the county officials, and the Klan would lay aside its disguises and raid no more. The sheriff promised in turn to disband his posse and take no further measures against the Klan. All parties, including the Negroes involved earlier, kept their agreements.[31] This happy ending was all too rare. Wayne County was a land of relatively poor soil and few large plantations. In consequence there were fewer Negroes, fewer Klans, and fewer outrages than in many of the other counties around. And as was often the case in poorer Southern counties, there were more Unionists and Republicans among the white small-farmer class. The sheriff (like Governor Brownlow on a larger scale with east Tennessee) had white men as well as Negroes on whom he could rely to resist the Klan. With the white population divided, a confrontation with the Ku Klux did not necessarily bring to mind the horrors of a race war in which every white man automatically went with his own kind.[32]

As time passed, white public opinion began very gradually to turn against the Klan, or more accurately, against its terrorist tactics. Most Conservatives approved the Klan's efforts to make the Negroes more docile, and they welcomed the prospect of fewer Negro and Republican votes at the next election. But common humanity rebelled against its grosser outrages, and employers resented the demoralization or exile of the black labor force which sometimes followed. Since they too had cause to fear the Klan's power, their disapproval was at first very hesitantly expressed. For some people the prospect of organized Negro resistance provided the greatest incentive to speak out against the Klan's reign of terror. If any panic equaled that of a Negro community on hearing that the Ku Klux were coming, it was that of a white community on hearing that the blacks were organizing into armed companies and drilling. White men were confident of winning ultimately in a war of the races, but visions passed across the mind of bands of maddened black men running amuck in the interim, sacking and burning towns, ravishing women, and indiscriminately shooting down persons of every age and description. This was the ultimate horror, and therefore the reaction to any signs of organization or arming among the blacks was immediate and emphatic.

Younger bloods and the reckless of all ages responded by trying to crush Negro resistance through greater repression and terror. Rank-and-file Klansmen, who belonged to this class, responded in this fashion through the organization, as in the murder of William Burk at Cornersville, although the leadership was sometimes more conservative. This kind of reaction also took the form of patrolling the streets, as in Columbia, or a mass turnout of armed whites without disguise. Such gatherings assumed an air of legality if the sheriff or other officials could be prevailed upon to designate them as posses or sanction them otherwise. This was easiest where the officials were Democrats.

Older men, including the members of the white power structure, increasingly spoke and acted for greater moderation. They tried to check violence for its own sake and also to remove the cause of Negro organization. Their statements were almost always couched in conciliatory terms, for these men had prestige and standing in the community which they stood to lose if they got too far ahead of public opinion. As usual, it is hard to say whether such leaders were really leading or reflecting and mobilizing a public sentiment already in formation. Yet it called for a certain amount of courage to criticize the Klan even by indirection, or to take in and care for a Yankee schoolteacher whom the community had ostracized and the Ku Klux had just whipped and ordered to leave.

One common device by which community leaders in that day mobilized public opinion was the public meeting, in which speeches were made and resolutions adopted on any subject of general interest. Few such meetings were held in behalf of law and order in the spring of 1868, but they became increasingly common as sentiment began to turn against the terror. Sometimes, at the beginning, federal officials were able to break the ice by encouraging the "best citizens" to call such meetings. The Democratic press began to cooperate through its editorials and selection of news coverage, playing down some of its earlier incitement to violence. In deprecating lawlessness, moderates almost never attacked the Ku Klux Klan; in fact most of them (like the Pulaski *Citizen*) approved of the order as originally contemplated in 1867. When they mentioned the Klan at all it was usually to blame the violence on outsiders masquerading as Klansmen, or at most a few bad men who had got into the order and were acting without their leaders' authorization.

Within the Klan the leaders often held the same position; of course they were sometimes the very same men. These leaders were in a difficult position, no less real for their having brought it on themselves. As public opinion began to turn against Klan violence, there was a danger that it might repudiate the organization itself unless it cleaned its own house. The longer violence continued, moreover, the greater the danger of forcible intervention by the state and federal governments, with incalculable results. Finally, the leaders too feared the consequences of organized Negro resistance, which the terror increasingly fostered.

The terrorists themselves, the rank-and-file Klansmen, may be excused for a measure of confusion. The leaders were themselves directly responsible for some of the violence, especially the more spectacular whippings and lynchings involving up to a hundred or more members. Ordinary Klansmen who wanted only to go out and whip a few Negroes may have found it hard to draw a logical distinction between these activities. Similarly, there was a fine line between threatening the blacks (which the leaders approved) and carrying out the threats (which presumably they often did not). The leaders were unable to make these distinctions clear, much less to enforce them. Their power was much greater in theory than in practice, and their orders were often disregarded.

When orders conveyed through the normal chain of command proved ineffective, the leadership used other means; they publicized their orders in the Conservative newspapers, along with statements that the Klan had higher and nobler ends in view than whipping Negroes. One such communication appeared as early as February 8, 1868, in the Nashville *Republican Banner,* threatening condign punishment for those who committed evil in Ku Klux disguise. It was widely copied in the Conservative press.[33] Even more authoritative was a directive from the Grand Dragon of the state (presumably General Gordon) which appeared in the same paper on July 17. His order was precipitated by information that the blacks in several counties had begun to organize into military companies under such names as the Whangs, Wide Awakes, and Black K.K.'s. The Grand Dragon commanded them to desist and disband immediately, and nearby

Klans were instructed to enforce this order "at any cost." The Klan, he explained, was "a *protective* organization. It proposes to *execute* law . . . and to protect all good men, whether white or black, from the outrages and atrocities of bad men of both colors. . . ." Bad white men (Republicans) had instilled in the minds of Negroes the idea that the Klan was their enemy, and had encouraged them to organize against it. They must stop. As to outrages by bands of disguised white men, these are committed by impostors, he said, who will be dealt with by the real Klan.

It is reported that these impostors have frightened and in some instances whipped negroes without any cause or provocation whatever. This is wrong! wrong! wrong! And it is denounced by this Klan, as it must be by all good and humane men. The Klan now, as in the past, is prohibited from doing these things, and they are requested to prohibit others from doing them and to protect all good, peaceful, well-disposed and law-abiding men, whether white or black.[34]

The Grand Dragon must have known as well as anyone that bona fide members were responsible for much of the violence. But in covering up for the Klan he sought also to reform it.

If orders to cease violence were unavailing, as often they were, Klan leaders on a few occasions resorted to the organization's own judicial tribunals to punish offenders like the Grand Magi in Giles County. General Forrest revealed (and later denied) that three Klansmen in Tennessee had suffered death for refusal to obey such orders.[35] No one can know how often (if at all) this penalty was invoked, but it could not have happened often without the fact being better known. In another case Forrest reportedly sent "a few of his old followers in the army" to arrest some disguised night riders in Madison County who were rendering the Ku Klux name odious.[36] Maury County, finally, may not have been the only place in Tennessee where the leaders attempted to reorganize the Klan, weeding out the "bad men" and retaining the good; certainly this happened in other states. None of these actions, it must be said, was successful over a large area or for very long by the summer of 1868. The action of the Wayne County Klan in leaving off raiding—imposed on it by the strength of its enemies—was the exception rather than the rule.

Negro resistance was sporadic and ineffective, and the Klan appeared to reign supreme throughout much of Tennessee. General W. P. Carlin, state commander of the Freedmen's Bureau, reported in July that

complaints are continually coming in of outrages committed by the Ku Klux Klan. The colored people are leaving their homes, and are fleeing to the towns and large cities for protection. They say that it is impossible for them to work during the day and keep watch during the night, which is necessary for them to do, in order to save their lives. Unless something is done immediately, by the

Governor, to protect the colored citizens of the country, the cities will be flooded by poor, helpless creatures, who will have to be supported by the State, or United States Government. It is impossible for me to advise the poor creatures, who are continually reporting to me.

The Ku Klux organization is so extensive, and so well organized and armed, that it is beyond the power of any one to exert any moral influence over them. Powder and ball is the only thing that will put them down.[37]

Governor Brownlow had long since come to the same conclusion. In February the legislature had passed a weak substitute for the repealed militia law, enabling sheriffs to employ persons from other counties if necessary to put down uprisings. But since most of the sheriffs either feared the Klan or sympathized with it, this law was a dead letter.[38] In March and April Brownlow procured small detachments of federal troops for Sumner and Maury counties. In June he received a telegram from Congressman Samuel M. Arnell reporting that Ku Klux had just searched a railroad train for him, "pistols and rope in hand," and asking for troops to fight it out with the Klan once and for all. The governor applied to General Thomas for soldiers to be stationed in six counties, only to be told that there were not enough men available.[39]

This left Brownlow with the alternatives of submission or getting additional powers to cope with the Klan himself. Given his background and personality, submission was unthinkable; the rebels must be brought to heel. He called a special session of the legislature for July 27 and demanded that "these organized bands of assassins and robbers be declared outlaws by special legislation, and punished with death wherever found." He also asked for a new militia law.[40] The legislature complied in both cases, after conducting an investigation of its own into Klan activities during the preceding months. The evidence it collected amply documented its conclusion that a campaign of systematic terrorism had enveloped much of the state, that not a single person had been legally punished for the hundreds or thousands of crimes committed, and that only the most drastic measures would bring the terror to a close short of a full surrender to the terrorists.[41]

On September 10 the two measures Brownlow had asked for were enacted. The first provided a minimum penalty of $500 and five years in the penitentiary for anyone belonging to, siding with, or encouraging any secret organization that "prowled" by day or night, in or out of disguise, "for the purpose of disturbing the peace, or alarming the peaceable citizens" of the state. This penalty also applied to anyone advising resistance to the laws or anyone who threatened or intimidated a voter. Henceforth no one could hold office or serve on a jury without swearing his innocence of these offenses, and lesser penalties were provided for officials and communities who willfully or negligently failed to enforce the law. Victims of Ku Klux attacks were authorized to kill their assailants and, failing that, to sue them for damages up to $10,000. The new militia law empowered the governor to organize a state guard and send it into any county where ten Union men certified that the law could not be enforced and citizens protected without military aid. He was further authorized to declare martial law in such counties, but this power was so hedged about with conditions as to be virtually meaningless.[42] Brownlow's resolute policy against the Klan proved effective as long as Conservatives thought that he intended to use the militia. This was true even before the requested laws were enacted. By the end of July, partly as a result of intervention by the "best citizens," Ku Klux activity had abated so much that Captain Judd, now in charge of Freedmen's Bureau operations in most of middle Tennessee, advised the Negro refugees in Nashville to return to their homes.[43] Conservative leaders were desperate at the prospect of another militia campaign. Ignoring or denying its cause, they regarded it as an attempt by Brownlow to carry the November Presidential and Congressional election by storm; and they feared that undisciplined militiamen, especially Negroes, would precipitate a conflict with the white community which could lead to the most serious consequences.[44] Of course, as Brownlow hoped, the militia would also disrupt their own plans for intimidating Republican voters and carrying the election themselves. To avoid this multiple catastrophe several former Confederate officers took the unprecedented step of calling on Brownlow at his home in Knoxville just prior to the legislature's assembling. They included John C. Brown and others who were either members of the Ku Klux Klan or able to influence it. Implicitly admitting this influence, they promised that the Klan would cease further activity in return for Brownlow's guarantee of "protection to the people,"[45] by which they meant chiefly not resorting to the militia.

On August 1, thirteen ex-Confederate generals met in Nashville and publicly renewed this offer before the legislature. The assemblage included Nathan Bedford Forrest, John C. Brown, George W. Gordon, and G. G. Dibrell, Klansmen all, and the others may have been members as well. They utterly disclaimed any intention for themselves or any society of which they were aware to overthrow the state government or do anything else by violent means. Hence there was no need for a militia. But as Republicans apprehended danger from ex-Confederates, they pledged themselves, as far as they were able, to "maintain the peace and order of the State . . . to uphold and support the laws, and aid in their execution. . . ." In return they hoped for a removal of political disabilities as the chief cause of Conservative discontent.[46]

Brownlow distrusted the rebel leaders as much as they distrusted him.

He was prepared to go partway with them, but neither side was ready to sacrifice its ultimate weapons. On the Republican side both the Ku Klux bill and the militia bill were pushed through as originally planned; moreover, the governor declared that he would sooner be quartered than make concessions on the suffrage under present circumstances. But negotiations were opened at the same time to secure federal troops instead of militia for the disturbed parts of the state. Federal soldiers were less frightening to the Conservatives (although they denied the need for any troops at all) and less expensive to the state; they were better disciplined and less subject to local passions and pressures. Owing to the legal restrictions on their peace-keeping activity, they were also apt to be less effective against the Klan, as events in Maury County had already demonstrated. But the Republicans too wished to avoid any armed conflict arising from the militia if they could end the terror in some other way. A legislative committee called on Andrew Johnson at the White House the day after the two bills had passed into law. They made perfectly clear (as Brownlow had from the outset) that the militia was intended as a last remedy in case federal troops were not available. Johnson, a Tennessee Unionist who by now had passed for all practical purposes into the Conservative camp, agreed promptly to the request for troops. Within a few weeks an Army regiment was on its way to Tennessee, where the soldiers were scattered in more than twenty communities, including Pulaski, Columbia, Murfreesboro, and Shelbyville.[47]

Five days after the White House conference Brownlow issued a proclamation calling for militia companies to be organized and assembled in Nashville, ready for emergency. But whether the militia would be called into actual service depended on the people themselves:

> I earnestly hope that there will be no occasion to call out these troops . . . but if, unhappily . . . I am compelled to put down armed marauders by force, I propose to meet them with such numbers and in such manner as the exigency shall demand, whatever may be the consequences. I will not be deterred from the discharge of my duty herein by threats of violence from rebel speakers or rebel newspapers, nor by any other means of intimidation.

To allay any white fears of race warfare, he added that he would rely first and foremost upon white Unionist recruits from east Tennessee.[48]

"Rebel threats" had already come from the furious and outmaneuvered Conservatives, who in the end did less than Brownlow to keep the bargain they had offered in Nashville. While the militia bill was still pending in the legislature, General Forrest publicly declared that if Brownlow called out the militia and it committed outrages, his government would be swept out of existence. The Ku Klux Klan had 550,000 members across the South and more than 40,000 in Tennessee alone, he announced in an exuberant newspaper interview on August 28. They were organized throughout the state, and if the necessity arose he could mobilize them in five days, ready for the field. In such an event, "I have no powder to burn killing negroes. I intend to kill the radicals. . . . There is not a radical leader in this town [Memphis] but is a marked man, and if a trouble should break out, none of them would be left alive."[49]

For the time being, Conservatives confined themselves to threats, waiting to see what the governor would do. Their leaders called public meetings and deprecated violence. In Pulaski, for instance, Generals Brown and Gordon told a large gathering on August 3 about their recent conference in Nashville, and "urged upon all good citizens the necessity of living in strict subordination to existing laws, and of pursuing such a course as will tend to restore perfect peace and harmony throughout the State."[50] The Klan continued to ride about, and murdered a Negro and a white storekeeper in Franklin, south of Nashville; but in general the number of outrages, which had dropped off late in July, remained relatively low during August and September.[51] It was in August that Grand Cyclops (or Giant) Allison made his agreement with the sheriff and left off raiding in Wayne County, and Forrest reportedly sent men to arrest night riders in Madison County. Only as the November election approached and Brownlow seemed content to leave matters in the hands of federal soldiers, who were legally impotent to do much good, did the Klan renew its campaign of terror.

Part II

EXPANSION THROUGHOUT THE SOUTH, SPRING AND SUMMER, 1868

CHAPTER 3

Organization and Expansion

However striking the Klan's emergence in Tennessee may have been, it was dwarfed by the order's spectacular expansion throughout the South during the spring and summer of 1868. The Ku Klux virus infected at least briefly every state of the former Confederacy, plus Kentucky. Most of this expansion—certainly its visible signs—took place almost at once in March and April, at a time when Radical state governments were being organized under the Congressional Reconstruction Acts of 1867. The timing alone is evidence of political inspiration, and Klan activities quickly confirmed it. But as in Tennessee, the Klan's purpose was political in the broadest sense. It sprang up in opposition to every aspect of Radical Reconstruction: the whole idea of racial equality or "Negro domination," as white Southerners chose to regard it, economic and social as well as narrowly political.

Quite possibly the earliest organizing activity outside of Tennessee occurred before the end of 1867. Fragmentary evidence suggests that this may have been true in northern Alabama and Mississippi and in North Carolina. In most cases this evidence represents recollections of members who were testifying several years later, and except in northern Alabama there was no public manifestation of Klan activity before March 1868.

It was widely believed that General Forrest was directly or indirectly involved in the Klan's spread, and circumstantial evidence tends to support the idea. He admitted in his Congressional testimony of 1871 that he was

49

receiving fifty to a hundred letters a day from persons throughout the South in 1867 and 1868, and had a private secretary busy writing full time. All that he would say of this correspondence was that he persistently urged people to avoid acts of violence, which accords with his idea of the Klan as a defensive organization designed to meet Radical aggression if it should come.[1] Furthermore, Forrest was president of the Selma, Marion, and Memphis Railroad at this time, and actively promoted its construction in northern and eastern Mississippi and western Alabama. He repeatedly traveled through this region in quest of support from leading citizens and local officials as well as popular backing for railway bond issues,[2] and he was also engaged in life insurance work during part of this time, giving a pretext if not necessity for more extensive travel.

We cannot trace all his comings and goings, but he was in Atlanta and Columbus, Georgia, only days before the Klan emerged in those places in March 1868. Some local Klans reportedly got their original charters from emissaries of Forrest or the Pulaski organization, or else sent their own emissaries to him at Memphis for this purpose. In most cases these reports come at second or third hand, and only appeared years later, after the Klan had assumed a romantic aura for Southern whites. They tended to magnify the degree of unity and organization it possessed, thus enhancing its dignity. Nevertheless some organizational links apparently did exist, at least at the beginning and in some places, with the parent order in Tennessee.

The easiest means of spreading the organization, and doubtless the most obvious to Forrest and other military men, was to confer personally with Confederate officers in the several states—men comparable to him in character, standing, outlook, and experience. Forrest and his associates in Tennessee naturally had a broad acquaintance with men in this stamp, who might well be interested in organizing a secret semimilitary society for the purpose of protecting Southern white society against the impending horrors of Radical Reconstruction. Established political leaders were less apt to have the requisite ability and experience for this purpose; nor were they as apt to be interested. Having built their careers on public service within the established legal and political framework, they were likely to suspect the Klan as too drastic and dangerous a departure from accepted practice. If trusted Confederate officers could be persuaded to serve as Grand Dragons and Grand Titans in their respective states, they could then undertake the formation of county and local units in their jurisdictions. Doubtless much of the early Klan expansion took this form, both inside and outside Tennessee, operating from the top downward. The evidence is fragmentary and untrustworthy, but some of the organizational activity in Georgia and the Carolinas appears to have followed this pattern, and it may have been true elsewhere.

At the same time it appears that many local Klans organized on their own responsibility and either established a connection with higher authorities later or never bothered to form such a tie at all. A former Texas Klansman reported many years later that his unit formed on its own responsibility after reading newspaper articles detailing Klan activities farther east, and that it never affiliated with any outside organization.[3] This was true in many other states as well, and quite likely most Klans throughout the South were local organizations inspired by reports of Klans in other areas but not organically connected with them. Some groups resembled the Ku Klux Klan in many particulars but bore a different name and obviously were not affiliated with General Forrest or the Tennessee Ku Klux. This was true, for instance, of the Knights of the White Camellia in Louisiana, Alabama, and elsewhere, the Young Men's Democratic Clubs of Florida, and the Knights of the Rising Sun at Jefferson, Texas.

These societies had their own organizational patterns, with more or less cohesion, but among all of them local control was predominant. Seldom did officials above the county level exercise much authority, where they existed at all. It was common for members in one locality to operate in neighboring areas, cooperating with adjacent organizations, but power almost invariably lay at the local level. For this reason and owing to diverse origins, organizational and operational details varied markedly from place to place. The general tendency, as in Tennessee, was to slough off elaborate rituals and complex organization as time passed and experience proved them irrelevant to the jobs at hand. Many klans began on a highly informal and *ad hoc* basis and remained so until they passed out of existence.

Klan membership throughout the South resembled that in Tennessee; it was drawn from every rank and class of white society. The traditional view held that the Klan was originally organized in the various states by men of rank, position, and balanced judgment, whose objectives and methods were above reproach, but inevitably less desirable elements found their way into the order and brought about its degeneration into violence.[4] This view is only half true. The maintenance of white supremacy, and the old order generally, was a cause in which white men of all classes felt an interest. All classes had been united in defense of slavery before the war, occasionally joining in patrol or vigilante activity for that purpose, and they had jointly fought a war to preserve the institution. The only native whites who stood out in significant numbers against the Klan were the Republicans, largely unconditional Unionists, who were mostly to be found in restricted areas like the Appalachian highlands and the Ozarks.

Most male Democrats therefore were potential Ku Kluxes. Some refused to join because of scruples, to be sure, but the chief barriers to larger membership were age and the lack of opportunity or necessity. In many parts of the South local conditions rendered the Klan unnecessary or unwise. Unquestionably the great majority of Klansmen were young men who were physically able to perform the night riding and who found the work attractive. "I believe that very frequently young men—boys and youth—are deluded into this thing by its novelty and mystery and secrecy," the attorney general of Mississippi testified in 1871; "there is a sort of a charm in this respect to young men, and they go into it frequently without realizing the extent of their wrong-doing."[5] The Klan was an adventure, a way to escape the tedium of rural life. It was also a patriotic venture which, like military service in wartime, often had the esteem and support of public opinion. These appeals know no economic or class barrier. Charles Stearns, a Republican of Northern birth who maintained a cotton plantation in Columbia County, Georgia, had several years' experience contending with the Ku Klux spirit there. The Klan, he said, was composed of men who "are neither better nor worse, than the average of the population; but simply young men, with plenty of leisure on their hands, and with a great love of adventure in their souls, and intensely rebel in their proclivities." Their original intention was to oppose Radicalism and "the great bug-bear of the Southern people . . . *negro domination.*" And in the process they could enjoy the "rare sport" of "frightening the darkies by their ghostly appearance."[6]

Older men and those with standing in the community quite likely played a greater part in Klan organization than in its subsequent actions. Many of them fell away in time, especially as violence increased, but some were to be found in the order until the bitter end, encouraging and shielding violence where they did not actively participate in it. Captain J. Banks Lyle, a state legislator and the principal of a boys' academy, was the active leader of the Klan in Spartanburg County, South Carolina, at a time when it was committing acts of unparalleled brutality; he eventually fled the state to evade arrest. Frederick N. Strudwick, a lawyer of Orange County, North Carolina, commanded a party of Klansmen whose purpose was to assassinate a Republican state senator; the latter had sponsored a law permitting the governor to proclaim a state of insurrection in areas of Klan terrorism. Strudwick failed in this attempt, but he was soon elected to the legislature, where he introduced successful motions to repeal the act in question and to impeach the governor for having used it.

Apologists from General Forrest onward have tried to distinguish between legitimate and illegitimate violence where the Klan was concerned, as well as between genuine and spurious Ku Klux. These distinctions are impossible to maintain. As historian John Hope Franklin points out, there is little difference in fact between "the 'lawful' violence of the Klan and the 'unlawful' violence of the disreputable element" whom apologists want to repudiate. "The assassination of an Alabama judge by the Klan should be no different in the eyes of the law from the murder of Negro would-be voters by hoodlums. In the final analysis, the 'respectable' organization remains a prime instigator of the use of violence as a counter-reconstruction measure."[7] Similarly, the informal and local organization which characterized the Klan in most places makes it futile to try to distinguish between real and counterfeit Ku Klux. This distinction became a stock defense on the part of Klan apologists; virtually all of the violence was committed, they say, either by degenerate elements who infiltrated the Klan or by persons who claimed to be Ku Klux but had no right to the name. What, then, was a real Ku Klux? If some tangible affiliation with the organization in Pulaski or Memphis is to be the test of bona fide Ku Klux, there were very few indeed of the genuine article, and the distinction becomes meaningless. Nevertheless, this defense was offered almost ritualistically, sometimes unconsciously in company with its own refutation. Charles W. Ramsdell, the historian of Reconstruction in Texas, for example, differentiates between true and false Ku Klux there while explaining that the Texas Klans were locally inspired, with no apparent general organization or affiliation at all.[8]

The local option concerning regalia and disguises which prevailed in Tennessee held true everywhere. Some groups did little more to avoid recognition than darken their faces with lampblack and turn their coats inside out. But more elaborate disguises were the general rule. These usually consisted of a long robe reaching from head to ankles and a cap or hood with a mask attached which covered the face. Very often the horses were also disguised with a covering which enveloped the animals down to their lower legs. Colors varied, with white being perhaps the most common because of its ghostly effect and the ease with which bedsheets could be converted to this use, but many Klans preferred black, which could not be seen at night. Others chose red, brown, or yellow. In some localities individual members designed their own regalia and no two looked exactly alike.

The headpieces offered the greatest scope for imagination, and these differed considerably. Many were conical in shape, but some were nearly flat. They often featured horns, beards, and occasionally long red flannel tongues. Probably the originality of these costumes declined as the novelty faded and members realized that Negroes were not mistaking them for ghosts. The need for portability also encouraged simple designs. Members usually donned their disguises at some secluded place and later removed them before returning home. The most practical costumes were those which could be folded into a small bundle and tucked into a saddlebag. Regalia were usually made by wives or other female relatives of the wearers, but some women either volunteered or were asked to make numbers of them as a sort of patriotic service.[9]

Almost every aspect of Klan activity in Tennessee was repeated as the movement spread to other states. The earliest operations were commonly peaceful enough so far as overt physical activity was concerned, but they were intentionally menacing, and it was not usually very long before they degenerated into crude violence.

The first news of local Klan organization often came in the form of written notices, mysteriously posted one night in prominent places around town, or printed in the local Democratic newspaper, or sent through the mail. These sometimes consisted of meaningless phrases redolent of ghosts and the graveyard, but they often carried more pointed warnings. Negroes and white Republicans generally, and prominent ones in particular, were notified to watch their conduct, or resign their offices, or leave the county. Ku Klux notices were distributed so widely and were so unprecedented in their character that they assumed the nature and dimension of a new art form early in 1868. It was obvious that their authors frequently expended no little time and ingenuity in their composition. The following flamboyant example appeared in the Tuscaloosa, Alabama, *Independent Monitor,* whose editor was the moving spirit behind the Klan there and the probable author of this communication:

Ku-Klux
Serpent's Den—Death's Retreat—
Hollow Tomb—Misery Cave of the
Great Ku-Klux Klan, No. 1,000

General Orders No. 1

Make Ready! make ready! make ready!!!
The mighty Hobgoblins of the Confederate dead in Hell-a-
Bulloo assembled!
Revenge! Revenge!
Be secret, be cautious, be terrible!
By special grant, Hell freezes over for your passage. Offended ghosts, put on your skates, and cross over to mother earth!
Work! Work!! work!!!
Double, double, toil and trouble;
Fire burn and Cauldron bubble.
Ye white men who stick to black, soulless beasts! the time arrives for you to part. Z.Y.X.W.V.U., and so, from Omega to Alpha.
Cool it with a baboon's blood
Then the charm is firm and good.
Ye niggers who stick to low White—Begone, Begone, Begone!
The world turns round—the thirteenth hour approacheth.
S. one two and three—*beware!* White and yellow,

J. and T——— P——— and L——— begone. — The handwriting on the wall warns you!

> From the murderer's gibbet, throw
> Into the flame. Come high or low.

By order of the Great

BLUFUSTIN,

G.S.   K.K.K.

A true copy.

PETERLOO

P.S.   K.K.K.[10]

The following notice, posted on walls about town one night, introduced the Klan to Montgomery, Alabama:

HORRIBLE SEPULCHRE, BLOODY MOON, CLOUDY MOON, LAST HOUR. Special Order

No. 1,

Shrouded Brotherhood of Montgomery Division No. 71.

The Great High Giant commands you. The dark and dismal hour will soon be. Some live to-day, to-morrow DIE. Be ye ready. The whetted sword—the bullet red and the rights are ours. Dare not wear the holy garb of our mystic brotherhood, save in quest of blood. Mark well our friends. Let the guilty beware!! In the dark caves, in the mountain recesses, everywhere our brotherhood appears. Traitors, beware!

By order of

Great Grand Cyclops, G.C.T.

SAMIVEL, G.S.[11]

Other notices were directed more pointedly at specific individuals, like the following, addressed to Riley Kinman, the sheriff-elect of Jackson County, Arkansas:

We have come! We are here! Beware! Take heed! When the black cat is gliding under the shadows of darkness, and the death watch ticks at the lone hour of night, then we, the pale riders, are abroad. Speak in whispers and we hear you. Dream as you sleep in the inmost recesses of your house, and, hovering over your beds, we gather your sleeping thoughts, while our daggers are at your throat. Ravisher of liberties of the people for whom we died and yet live, begone ere it is too late[.] Unholy blacks, cursed of God, take warning and fly. Twice has the Sacred Serpent hissed. When again his voice is heard your doom is sealed. Beware! Take heed! . . . To be executed by White Death and Rattling Skeleton, at 10 to-night. K.K.K.[12]

The burning of crosses, an ancient practice in the Scottish highlands, apparently was first introduced to America by Thomas Dixon, a turn-of-the-century novelist and preacher. His 1905 novel *The Clansman* and its film version, *The Birth of a Nation,* did more than anything else to foster the

Klan legend as a part of heroic Southern folklore. If the real Klan did not burn crosses it did comparable things; individuals it disliked not only received warning notices but sometimes woke up in the morning to find gallows or miniature coffins placed in front of their houses.

Klansmen developed a small repertory of practical jokes which they performed to amuse themselves and the white public, and to frighten the supposedly gullible blacks. Occasionally ghostlike creatures ranging up to twelve feet in height were seen walking the streets or riding through the countryside. This effect was created by means of a framework resting on a man's shoulders, the whole covered with a gown or robe and surmounted by a false head made from a gourd or pumpkin, sometimes carved like a jack-o'-lantern, with a candle burning inside. The head was commonly fastened to the end of a pole; when the pole was raised it appeared as if the specter's neck were stretching.[13] Sometimes a Klansman so outfitted would approach a Negro and ask him to hold his head for a minute as a favor. When the allegedly quaking Negro complied, the Ku Klux would either gallop off or, more economically, wait a moment, reclaim and replace his head with profuse thanks, and then depart. Related to this was the false hand trick: a Klansman would offer to shake a Negro's hand, but he extended in reality a false hand on the end of a stick hidden within the sleeve of his robe. When the Negro dutifully grabbed the hand the Klansman withdrew his own arm and galloped away, leaving the false hand in the grasp of the astonished black.

The most common trick, judging from the number of times it was described, involved the apparent drinking of vast quantities of water by ghostly Klansmen who claimed not to have had a drink since dying on some Civil War battlefield. The following story, copied by an Arkansas newspaper from one in Tennessee, reported the alleged appearance of such a Ku Klux spirit before a "rustic darkey" near Pulaski, Tennessee:

He was mounted on a snow-white horse and clad in a mantle as ghostly as that of the White Crook, with the representation on the back of a skull and cross bones, and underneath, in blood-red characters, the Latin inscription: 'In Hoc Signo.' —His visor was drawn down and his helmet was not lit up—for it was early candle light. He approached the negro, who was dipping water at a spring, and asked for a drink of water in such an unearthly whisper, that the poor African had hardly strength to lift even a gourd of water—yet, this he essayed to do without daring to lift his eyes upon the horrid specter. The spirit majestically waved the gourd away, and said: "It is not enough, hand up the bucket." Sambo lifted the bucket filled to the brim with water. With quickened ear he plainly heard each distinct swallow as the "swallows homeward flew," coursing each other down the dead warrior's throat. Then the bucket was returned, and, *mirabile dictu!* there was not a drop of water in it. "Goddle mitey, mars, did you drink all dat?" "I-i-i-i-i did," was the sonorous response. "I have been dead ever since the battle of Chickamau-au-au-ga, and have never drank water since; therefore is the spirit d——d thirsty. Hand up another bucket." "De Lord help my sole," exclaimed Africa, "den, marster, you had better git down and drink outer de spring," and with that he flung down the bucket and gourd and fled on the wings of evening, while Ku Klux quietly drew out of his chest a gum-elastic bottle of the capacity of several gallons, emptied the water out of it that had been artificially swallowed, returned the vessel to his shirt bosom, and rode off into the night.[14]

Similar tales were repeated by Democratic newspapers from Virginia to Texas in 1868 and by old Klansmen and Klan historians for years to come. In some cases the teller acknowledged that he was passing on someone else's story, and in others it was recounted as a unique event that had taken place locally.

These tricks enjoyed only a brief vogue; the novelty soon wore off and even the most gullible freedman was not apt to be taken in by very many of these performances. The stories, however, lived on and on, repeated and laughed over by generations of whites. They comprise one of the most cherished parts of the Klan saga. It was the supposed terror evoked among the blacks by these tricks which frightened them into good behavior and away from the polls; this in turn allegedly ensured the downfall of the Radicals and the return of good government to the South.

This legend was largely contrary to fact, however, and revealed more about the tellers than about the supposedly duped Negroes. The freedmen unquestionably were terrified by the Klan, but they feared ghosts in white sheets far less than they did the ruthlessness of the mortals they knew to be hiding in sheets while threatening or committing crimes of violence. Nearly all the accounts of Negro gullibility or superstition come from white men, and usually from Conservatives who either belonged to the Klan or sympathized with it. Moreover, they are usually related at least second hand and long after the event.[15]

By far the greatest body of firsthand evidence concerning contacts between Negroes and the Klan lies in the testimony of hundreds of freedmen before various Congressional and legislative committees in 1868–71. Some freedmen were probably taken in, if only momentarily, by the ghostly put-on. A Negro justice of the peace in De Soto Parish, Louisiana, indicated that some of the freedmen there didn't know at first whether the Klansmen were ghosts or not. "One man saw one of the Ku-Klux and thought he was a spirit, and raised his gun and was going to shoot at him when the man said, 'Look out; don't you shoot me, sir;' and then he knew he was a man. . . ."[16] Some Negroes, like Letty Mills of Walton County, Georgia, were ambiguous or noncommittal on the mortality of Klansmen.

"I heard of their shaking hands with people, and then leaving their hands in folks's hands; I heard of their drinking water, and of their going in and telling about their bursting out of tombs and rising from the dead. I kept feeling afraid all the time of the Ku-Klux." But she went on to say that she had also heard of their killing and whipping people. When they whipped her and her family she entertained no doubt of her attackers' mortality, and even identified one of them.[17] Most Negro witnesses never even suggested the possibility that Klansmen were ghosts. Of course all were testifying after the Klan's character had become manifest, and they may have feared that an admission of past belief would make them look foolish.[18]

Some Negro gullibility was deliberately fabricated for the white man's benefit. Solomon White, of Morehouse Parish, Louisiana, reported being told by whites that the Klan had risen from the dead. He also repeated a woman's account of a Klan visit to her house in which they asked for water, together with his own reaction to the story. According to his account, she "fetched them a bucketful of water. One of them took it and drank the whole bucketful, and called for another bucketful. The woman said, 'Why, you drink a great sight of water.' He said, 'Yes, old lady; and if you were dead and in hell as long as I was, you would drink a sight of water.' She was telling me about it," White continued. "I said, 'If a man goes to heaven, he would not want to come back, and if he goes to hell, he would not be allowed to come back.'" The Negroes never believed in the ghostly charade, he explained, but pretended to do so. "The colored people were afraid to say anything else for fear they might be dead themselves."[19] They knew by long experience what white folks wanted to hear, and it was a nice question as to who was hoodwinking whom.

The myth of superstitious Negro terror before the Klan represented in truth a prevailing white superstition about Negroes. It was largely false, but it nonetheless performed a valuable psychological service for white men. Reflecting and reinforcing the stereotype of Negro inferiority which was itself an article of faith and a buttress of white self-esteem, it carried on the game of one-upmanship which white supremacy always demanded.[20]

Pretending to be ghosts did not last long, and in many places the practical jokes were accompanied by violence from the beginning. The most fortunate places were those (like the state of Virginia) where public opinion or some other factor curbed lawlessness before it had a chance to develop. Elsewhere the threats of dire injury to carpetbaggers, scalawags, and Negroes became all too real. Before it ended, thousands of people— most of them innocent of any indictable offense—were subjected to beating, shooting, hanging, rape, or exile plus the loss of money, property, crops, and sometimes lives.

Nearly all of the violence was done at night by disguised parties of six to sixty or more men, although the average was probably nearer to a dozen. Although the Klan occasionally invaded towns, most of its work was done in the countryside. Members collected at a prearranged spot, donned their disguises, and set off for the night's work. The typical target was the small Negro sharecropper's cabin, specimens of which can still be seen in most parts of the rural South. Klansmen usually had all the advantages with them—darkness, disguise, superior numbers and armament, surprise, and the freedmen's ingrained fear of resisting white men. They usually encountered little opposition, therefore, when they rode up to an isolated cabin in the dead of night and either called out or dragged out its inmates. When they finished what they had come for, they moved on to the next destination. Often several such stops were made before the night riders called a halt, doffed their uniforms, and returned home.

The individual dens were organized in a multitude of ways. They ranged in size from fewer than a dozen to nearly a hundred members. The Grand Cyclops or chief (the former title was too grandiloquent for everyday use) was usually elected for a term of months or a year, but his authority depended on local regulations, custom, and the strength of his own personality. Large dens frequently had a council to advise the chief and share his responsibilities. Some missions required the full strength of the den, and occasionally two or more dens acting jointly, but most were performed by a small group chosen from the den by appointment, by ballot, or as volunteers. Sometimes the identity of these men was withheld from the other members, both for their own safety and to keep the others' skirts clean. Frequently the victims of meditated attacks were discussed and voted upon beforehand, although the leaders sometimes decided whom to raid and when. Many attacks were made more or less on the spur of the moment, however, as Klansmen rode by a place and decided to pay a call. Many others were spontaneous to the extent that they had received little if any prior sanction from the local leadership. Absolute power lodged in irresponsible hands was constantly abused.

Particularly important missions were sometimes decreed at the county level, but seldom any higher. The great majority of cases were handled entirely by the members of a single den. There were many cases of one den operating occasionally in another's territory, especially where the death penalty had been invoked. This practice was designed to prevent identification of the persons involved, and of course required prior arrangement between the dens. Although there are many individual examples of dens cooperating across county or even state lines, such cooperation seldom extended very far or involved many men.

Secrecy was always enjoined concerning Klan membership and activity, but people do talk. Frequently these matters became general knowledge in the community, even if sometimes in garbled or exaggerated form. Republicans and public officials were apt to be more in the dark than others, but in general many of the most pertinent details of the Ku Klux conspiracy were widely shared among the Southern white population. And what people did not know they could often guess fairly accurately.

Wherever the Klan spread, or even the news of its existence penetrated, it aroused the same curiosity as around Pulaski. In fact there was a minor Ku Klux sensation around the country, and especially in the South, in the spring of 1868. It was reflected in many ways. In Nashville "Ku Klux" and "Pale Face" juvenile baseball teams were organized, and a local theater staged a burlesque called the "Ku Klux Klan."[21] A music publisher there brought out a song entitled the "Kuklux Midnight's Roll Call." "The music and words sound ghostly," a notice stated.[22] The Ku Klux name was also applied to knives, paint, pills, a circus act, and a "Ku Klux Smoking Tobacco," containing the "spirits of a hundred faithful K.K.K.'s with an accurate and attractive full-length portrait of the 'Great Grand Cyclops' on the outside." Advertisers sometimes used the initials K.K.K. as a device to attract attention, no matter how irrelevant it was to the product they were selling.[23] Others parodied Ku Klux notices, like the editor of the Hartsville, Tennessee, *Vidette,* trying to collect his bills:

Head Q'rs Everywhere!! Dark of the Moon!! Heavy Times!!!
Halt and listen! Read and turn pale in the face!! Delinquent Subscribers hear your doom!!! Pay your Subscription! —The Vidette is looking for you! Death to Traitors!! Send the $3!?! Pay for your advertisements! Look out! Mule in the cellar! Dead man in the Loft!! —Guilty of Sedition if you don't send the Money!!!

By Order of Two Cyclopses. (Big Ones)[24]

A few Southern papers even incorporated Ku Klux into their own names in order to draw attention and identify themselves with militant Conservatism. These included the *Ku Klux Kaleidoscope* of Goldsboro, North Carolina, the *Ultra Ku Klux* in Jefferson, Texas, and the *Daily Kuklux Vedette* in Houston. None of these journals lasted very long.

At first the press, like the populace generally, was divided or uncertain in its conception of the Klan. Some regarded it with deadly earnestness as a semimilitary order designed to serve the holy cause of preventing or repelling Negro insurrection. Others saw it as a semicomical means of scaring gullible blacks into submission by practical jokes. For these people it was a fit subject—but never an object—of humor and satire. Much real or fancied humor circulated concerning the Klan, with the Negro serving very often as the butt of the jokes. Usually these involved some variation upon the Ku Klux pranks already referred to, but not always. One of the most original stories told of a visit by an Episcopal bishop to a small town in Georgia where Episcopalians were almost unknown, no bishop had ever been seen before, and where the Negroes were much disturbed by fear of the Klan. The bishop was to officiate at a small Baptist church where there was no anteroom in which to don his vestments. He therefore went out back of the church for this purpose, intending to walk around afterward and enter by the front door when properly clad. Back of the church was a graveyard, and he laid his robes across a tombstone while preparing to put them on. Once ready, he began to walk around toward the front of the church. A gust of wind came up and blew out his robes just as he arrived within view of a large crowd of Negroes standing nearby. They immediately let out a shout and took to their heels. For half an hour afterward there could be heard, receding in the distance, the cry, "Ku Klux! Ku Klux!"[25]

In this period, before syndicated press services had begun to report news in detail, newspapers provided what coverage they could of distant events by copying from each other, usually citing the source. In this fashion news and editorials concerning the Klan spread throughout the country during March and April 1868. Initially there was much curiosity—in Northern and Republican as well as Southern Democratic papers—concerning the Klan's origin, purpose, and character, as well as the meaning of its name. These obscure matters provided much food for speculation, sometimes serious but just as often not. According to one theory, voiced by the New York *Tribune,* the name came from the noise of a gun being cocked. But the *New York Times* observed that it resembled equally well the clucking of a satisfied hen. The Memphis *Appeal* offered another explanation for any who cared to believe it: the name was taken from an ancient Jewish text entitled *A True and Authenticated History of the Great Rebellion of the Hebrews against King Pharaoh, B.C.* In this work, it said, the name was spelled Cu Clux Clan, which is translated into English as The Straw Club. The name was supposedly derived from the fact that Pharaoh required his hod carriers to furnish their own straw, and also from the old Hebrew proverb, "Straws show which way the wind blows."[26] The Chicago *Republican* claimed that the order was named for a notorious Texas desperado of former days, Nal. K. Xulkuk, whose unceasing aim was to avenge real or fancied wrongs to himself, his followers, or his country. His name spelled backwards of course yields Kuklux Klan.[27]

The Klan's character and purpose were set forth similarly in a widely quoted article from the Richmond *Dispatch:*

The Ku-Klux klan are kalled upon to kastigate or kill any kullered kusses who may approve the konstitution being koncocted by the kontemptible karpetbaggers at the kapital. Each klan is kommanded by a karniverous kurnel, who kollects his komrades with kare and kaution kommensurate with the magnitude of the kause. Whenever konvened they must korrectly give four kountersigns. These are, kill the kullered kuss, klean out the karpet-baggers, krush the konvention, karry konservatism, konfusion to kongress, konfederates will konquer. Of course [*sic*] the klan kreates konsiderable konsternation among the kongoes and their kunning konductors, who kalculate that their kareer may be kut short by katastrophes. Kowardly kurs, they kan't komplain.[28]

The Richmond *Whig* advanced the thought that the Klan had originated among foreign merchants smuggling opium into China. One of its members there was an American, Humphrey Marshall, who allegedly organized the American branch at a meeting in Brown's Hotel in Richmond, never dreaming that it would later become an order to control Southern politics.[29] This story too was copied widely by Southern newspapers, and on reaching Tennessee it evoked a response from one of the real founders at Pulaski, who attempted to set the record straight if not to tell all.[30] At the same time the New York *Herald* carried a long article from a purportedly official Klan source, which it would not vouch for, indicating that the Klan had originated in Giles County, Tennessee, in August 1866. "The Ku-Klux Klan is . . . a secret political organization, the result of necessity, the sole object of which is to thwart radicalism, arrest negro domination in the South, negro equality in the North, perpetuate the Federal Union and preserve the Constitution as the fathers made it." After the passage of the Congressional Reconstruction laws, the informant continued, the Klan spread beyond Tennessee and even into the North and West, especially between November 1867 and April 1868, the time of writing. The contributor, who identified himself only as "Gabriel, G.G.T. & V.," obviously spoke with authority, despite his overoptimistic account of Northern and Western growth; but for outsiders who lived at a distance there was hardly more reason to believe this account than others.[31]

There is abundant evidence that the primary role in spreading the Ku-Klux Klan was played, not by General Forrest and his cohorts, but by the Southern Democratic newspaper press. It carried favorable news items concerning Klan activities in Tennessee and faithfully chronicled its appearance in other states, near and distant. Sometimes these events were reported straight, without comment or approbation, but often the Klan was treated as a fascinating and potentially useful agency to combat the evils of Radicalism and Negro ascendancy. Only a few Democratic papers opposed the idea from the beginning, whereas many openly or implicitly encouraged its growth and its organization locally. The Nashville *Gazette,* less subtle than some, remarked in April that the Klan seemed to thrive in Alabama despite efforts by the Army to curb it, "and niggers are disappearing . . . with a rapidity that gives color to the canibalistic [*sic*] threats of the shrouded Brethren. Run, nigger, run, or the Kuklux will catch you."[32] Besides mobilizing public opinion behind the Klan, the Democratic press supplied information concerning its organization and operations which helped interested readers to go out and do likewise.

This favorable coverage lasted until the Klan began to commit acts of violence and the authorities took steps to suppress it. Then Democratic editors became more cautious, either denying that outrages had been committed or pretending that the Klan was nothing but a hoax. The very same paper which in March reported the Klan's expansion and in April invited its readers to form dens themselves was sometimes claiming by June that the Ku Klux were only figments of disordered Republican imaginations. The next step was commonly to ignore the Klan altogether, completely eliminating any mention of it until much later, when state or federal actions to combat it assumed such proportions that the subject could no longer be evaded. At that point they denied most of the reported atrocities and excused or palliated the remainder. It is clear that Democrats sincerely refused to believe many reports of Ku Klux activity, regarding them as manufactured by the Republicans for political effect. But all too often Democratic papers knowingly suppressed or perverted the facts, partially for political effects of their own and partially to protect the good name of the community, state, and section. In this course they were encouraged and supported by the very public opinion which they were misinforming. Southern Democrats sympathized with the Klan, benefited by it, were intimidated by it, and were ashamed of it, often simultaneously. This was part of the psychological burden of white supremacy.

For the historian of the Klan, Democratic newspapers are an invaluable source of information during the initial organizing stage. From that time on, the Republican press assumes greater value. Southern Republican editors obviously wrote as outsiders. Quite naturally, they seldom retailed anecdotes about thirsty ghosts and superstitious blacks, regarding these as impolitic and often false, if not unfunny and in bad taste. From the start their curiosity concerning the order was mixed with apprehension and condemnation, for the Klan was patently directed against them. And once the Klan began to commit outrages, Republican papers reported them as fully as possible, together with appeals for law and order and for government action to suppress them. If they occasionally exaggerated the degree of terror, for effect or through misinformation, the fault was insignificant compared with the massive conspiracy to stifle the truth which the Democratic press engaged in.

The Ku Klux Klan was probably more widespread in the spring and summer of 1868 than at any time afterward. Virtually its entire career in many places, including the state of Virginia, was confined to this brief period. In general it was a time of greater organization and less violent activity than would be true later, somewhat like the year 1867 in Tennessee.

Across the South the Klan was more apt to appear in certain kinds of regions than in others. The least likely places were overwhelmingly white counties like those of east Tennessee and the Appalachian highlands generally, where white Republicans were plentiful. In similar counties nearer the coast Republicans of either race were usually too few to bother about and hence there was no need for Klan activity. The same tended to be true for opposite reasons in the Black Belt counties where Negroes outnumbered whites by at least three to one. Here the blacks were in such heavy preponderance that the Ku Klux themselves were in danger of being overwhelmed.[33] The Klan was organized in some of these counties in 1868, but discontinued its activity or disbanded in most of them when the initial warning notices and pretending to be ghosts proved ineffective. Viewed from another perspective, the Klan was least in evidence in counties where the Conservatives either possessed a safe majority already or were hopelessly outnumbered. By the same token, the Klan was apt to be strongest where the two parties or the two races were nearly equal, or where there was a white minority large enough to intimidate the freedmen.

Although true in broad terms, these generalizations are subject to many exceptions. Klan terrorism seized control of several white Appalachian counties, such as Chattooga in Georgia and Rutherford in North Carolina; it also held several Black Belt counties in its grip, like Warren in Georgia and Sumter and Greene in Alabama. There were also many counties which were relatively evenly divided where the Klan never made a significant showing. When "Klan counties" are plotted on a map they tend to fall into groups which defy clear-cut analysis based on racial or political alignments. Clearly the existence of a strong Klan organization in one county was apt to encourage organization and activity in adjacent counties. It is also fairly clear, although this is impossible to measure accurately, that the Klan pursued an active existence for a significant period of time in no more than a quarter of all Southern counties between 1867 and 1871.[34] In that quarter, however, it created a reign of terror which resembled and occasionally outstripped anything which had so far happened in Tennessee.

CHAPTER 4

The South Atlantic States

The first rush of enthusiasm for the Ku Klux idea even carried it momentarily to the national capital. Early in April 1868 Ku Klux warnings
showered upon Republicans of every station in Washington, from the
Negro who was warned to stick to his oyster business and forgo politics to
party leaders like Benjamin F. Butler, Benjamin F. Wade, and John A.
Logan. The first-named was told succinctly: "Butler, prepare to meet your
God! The avenger is upon your track! Hell is your portion! K.K.K." These
missives received great publicity, but few took them very seriously and they
soon stopped.[1]

The short-lived appearance of the Klan in Virginia in March and April
1868 is typical of its first manifestations throughout most of the South.
During the latter part of March the Conservative Richmond *Enquirer &
Examiner* undertook a deliberate campaign to acquaint its statewide
readers with the Klan and to encourage its spread throughout the state.
Speaking on March 26 of the order's recent introduction in Memphis, an
editorial announced:

It is now very evident that this "Ku-Klux-Klan" is not a meaningless Merry
Andrew organization, but that under its cap and bells it hides a purpose as
resolute, noble and heroic as that which Brutus concealed beneath the mask of
well-disembled [sic] idioticy [sic].

It is rapidly organizing wherever the insolent negro, the malignant white traitor to his race and the infamous squatter [carpetbagger] are plotting to make the South utterly unfit for the residence of the decent white man. It promises, we hope, to bring into the field for the defence of our lives, liberty and property hundreds of thousands of those heroic men who have been tried and indurated by the perils, dangers and sufferings of military service. It is, no doubt, an organization which is thoroughly loyal to the Federal constitution, but which will not permit the people of the South to become the victims of negro rule. It is purely defensive, and for the protection of the white race, and has been rendered necessary by the organization of thousands of secret negro leagues, whose members have been stimulated to carry out the work of disfranchisement of the whites by the promise of pillage and wholesale confiscation.

If such is the purpose and real object of the new secret society which is so rapidly increasing in numbers in Tennessee, Mississippi, Alabama, Georgia, North Carolina, and the other Southern States, it will arrest the progress of that secret negro conspiracy which has for its object the establishment of negro domination.

Secret societies would always be formed to protect liberty-loving people against despotism, the editorial continued. Wherever the Klan was forming, the Radicals were committing excesses; this was the case in Virginia too. "The sum of all their contemplated villainies is the Africanization of Virginia and the disfranchisement, outlawry and persecution of every Virginian who was not a base traitor to his section during the late civil war." The first duty of Virginians was therefore "to organize with such promptitude and stern resolution as to strike terror into the guilty souls of the secret negro societies and their delegates in the [state constitutional] 'Convention.' . . ." The Radicals must be taught that white men who had wrested their state from the Indians ("superior in every brave and manly quality" to the degraded Negro) and have reigned supreme there ever since, holding at bay for four years "the armies of a powerful government," will not submit to Negro and carpetbagger domination. The *Enquirer* favored an open organization if possible, but "if secret organizations, formed to sustain the constitution and to restore peace and order, and suppress violence, wrong and outrage, shall be preferred by the people of Virginia to any other, the lawless adventurers and vile emissaries who have kindled the baleful fires of incendiarism[,] negro hate, and a war of races in eight hundred secret oath-bound negro leagues in this State, will have no right to complain."

The next day the *Enquirer* announced that the Klan had made its appearance in Virginia, and the Radicals would "soon find that 'this is a White Man's State.'" On the twenty-eighth the paper reported KKK posters in Norfolk and told of the appearance in Richmond of a Ku Klux "skeleton" nine feet tall whom a Negro woman had seen drink nine horse-buckets of water. The skeleton was said to make nightly raids on peaceful sleeping people, entering their houses through keyholes. The newspaper also gave directions for those interested in viewing a nocturnal parade which the Richmond Klan was planning. On March 30 a supposedly humorous article threatened Republican leader James W. Hunnicutt with a possible Ku Klux visitation. The next day, in another attempt to combine humor with intimidation, the editor announced that Klansmen were appearing like locusts all over the state; churchyards were aswarm with them, their demand for shrouds had almost exhausted the state's supply of bleached cottons, and the terrified carpetbaggers were preparing to return to New England. The Richmond *Whig* added, for its part, that in the city alone Klan membership numbered 4,000, with 700 applicants waiting and two wards yet to be heard from.[2]

The Conservative press followed this tack for only two or three weeks. The supposed Klan murder of George W. Ashburn, a white Republican leader in Columbus, Georgia, on March 31, and General George G. Meade's efforts to suppress the organization there, had a cautionary effect on the Southern Democratic press generally. It was soon evident, moreover, that the Virginia Klans were not restricting themselves to innocent fun and games *en masque* either. A Northern lady teaching a Negro school near Williamsburg recorded that at first she and her friends thought the Klan intended to keep the Negroes from voting by playing practical jokes and pretending to be ghosts, but their antics ceased to be funny when they dragged a crippled New England missionary from his bed and flogged him.[3] Several agents of the Freedmen's Bureau reported a flurry of Ku Klux activity around the state in April, some of which went beyond the posting of notices and parading around in sheets after dark. Negroes were physically assaulted in Warrenton, and a white postmaster in Rockingham County was ordered to leave.[4]

In the wake of these events and the attention they brought, the *Enquirer* changed its tone. Despite a tongue-in-cheek editorial of April 24, saying that the Klan was expanding throughout the United States, it affected to believe by the middle of April that the organization was really only a myth which no one in his right mind took seriously. This was a common editorial position by that time. But in Virginia—alone among the Southern states—it soon became fact. Except for some outrages in June and December 1868 in mountainous Lee County at the southwestern tip of the state, almost no further Klan activity was reported in the Old Dominion.[5] This may be explained by the fact that Virginia never really passed under Republican control. The vote on her new constitution, which was held in most states in the spring of 1868, was deferred in Virginia's case until July 1869. By that time the state Republican party had split into conservative and radical factions and the former won with Democratic backing. Hence there was less political need felt for the Klan than the *Enquirer* at first believed. For this reason the leaders of Conservative opinion (including the newspapers) may have given the Ku Klux movement less encouragement or more active discouragement than in other states after April 1868.[6]

In North Carolina the Klan may have begun a little earlier, and it certainly lasted longer, than in Virginia. There is almost no direct evidence that the Klan was organized here before March 1868, but Hamilton C. Jones of Charlotte, identified by a number of Klansmen as a high-ranking official in the order, if not its Grand Dragon, was reported to have said that he had been a member since 1867.[7] A Klansman of York County, South Carolina, testified that he had joined the order in North Carolina in December 1867.[8] There are also two reports of activity by disguised bands in the western part of the state in the fall and winter of 1867–68, which may have been independent local ventures. They were reportedly engaged in illicit distilling and tobacco trading in one case, and in the other they raided white and Negro Republicans.[9]

At least three separate Klan-like orders existed in North Carolina; their precise relationship to one another was never fully explained, or even understood by their members. (Rank-and-file Klansmen everywhere, and often their officers as well, were apt to be ignorant of organizational matters and inner workings beyond their own immediate spheres of operation. This was owing partly to the deliberate policy of secrecy surrounding the order, partly to the difficulty of *sub rosa* communication over long distances, and partly to an ingrained provincialism which characterized the less educated rural populace everywhere.) The three orders were the White Brotherhood, the Constitutional Union Guard, and the Invisible Empire. This last designation was regarded fairly commonly across the South as a synonym for Ku Klux Klan, and some persons believed it to be the true official name of the order, with "Ku Klux Klan" adopted for public use only. The Prescripts of 1867 and 1868 used no name at all. Members in various parts of the South understood this to be deliberate, so that if they were officially queried concerning their membership in the Ku Klux Klan they could swear without perjury that they belonged to no order bearing that name.[10] This may well have been the idea of the organizers, although Klansmen in practice would seldom blink at perjury in clearing themselves and each other of criminal charges.

The names White Brotherhood and Constitutional Union Guard were confined almost entirely to North Carolina. In some places within the state they and the Invisible Empire may have existed successively, with the change reflecting a reorganization comparable to the Ku Klux Klan-Ghoul transition in Maury County, Tennessee. But in Alamance County, at least, the White Brotherhood and Constitutional Union Guard existed simultaneously in 1868 and 1869, with members of the former joining the latter when the White Brotherhood was supposedly dissolved.[11] The Invisible Empire apparently came last, and was primarily identified with the southwest part of the state in 1870 and 1871, after the other two orders (which operated to the north and east) seem to have disappeared. It was clearly related to the South Carolina organization of that name just across the state line. The main difficulty in distinguishing these orders arose from the fact that outsiders (and insiders, too, for public consumption) lumped them together as Ku Klux. And apart from organizational detail, there was little to distinguish them; the character of their operations, members, purposes, oaths, and rituals (so far as we know them) were similar, and sometimes their membership overlapped.[12] The Constitutional Union Guard called its local units klans, each having at its head a south commander, assisted by a west, a north, and an east commander, ranking in that order. The south commander of the oldest klan in a county was the county chief.[13] The operating units of the White Brotherhood were called camps, each being under a captain; he was at least nominally subject to a county chief who was also the captain of the senior camp.[14] There is no evidence of obedience to any higher officials in either order.[15]

Local units within the Invisible Empire were dens, as among the Tennessee Ku Klux, and there were county chiefs. But the title of Grand Giant seems not to have been applied to this office as it was in Tennessee or Georgia at least, nor is there much mention of Grand Titans or a Grand Dragon by that name. The state head of the Klan (presumably the Invisible Empire, though the matter is cloudy) was variously identified as Hamilton C. Jones and Colonel William L. Saunders. Saunders was associate editor of the Wilmington *Journal,* an outspoken Democratic paper which helped call the Klan into existence there in March 1868. He was also a scholar of sorts, as well as secretary of state of North Carolina for many years after Reconstruction, and edited the colonial records of the state for publication.[16] There is little evidence that Saunders or anyone else above the county level exerted much power over the Klan, but his connection with the order led to a summons by the Congressional investigators in 1871. Of hundreds of witnesses brought before that committee (including General Forrest), Saunders was the only one who flatly refused to answer the important questions put to him, pleading the Fifth Amendment.[17]

Whatever connection may have existed at the outset between any or all of these three orders and the Tennessee Klan headed by General Forrest, it amounted to little or nothing for practical purposes. Effective power seldom if ever extended above the county level, although the original organizing may have proceeded from above. It is sometimes stated that the North Carolina Klan was begun by an emissary from Forrest;[18] this may be true, but there is no solid evidence for it.

As in Virginia, the Klan was relatively nonviolent in its formative stages during the spring and summer of 1868. It reached Wilmington in March, reportedly organized there by Colonel Roger Moore, an ex-Confederate and member of the local gentry, who had gone to Raleigh for his own initiation. Ku Klux notices first appeared in the city on the night of the twenty-third. A few nights later a solitary horseman "of unusual size" and having the appearance of a skeleton made a rapid circuit of the Negro and white working-class neighborhoods, stopping at one house to drink four buckets of water; he claimed not to have had any water since dying at Fort Fisher, the nearby stronghold taken by the Federals in January 1865. Similar activities recurred until the state election on April 21. Although the Democratic press reported darkies fleeing in terror from these apparitions, the local Negroes patrolled the streets under arms on election eve. Republicans were in a large majority, and they carried the city by two to one; the Klan made no further appearance in Wilmington.[19]

By election time it had spread to other communities across the state, including Warrenton, Chapel Hill, and Salisbury. Although it played graveyard jokes, posted notices, and made threats, it was relatively nonviolent in these places.[20] Republicans nevertheless were apprehensive concerning the impact of these "rebel desperadoes" upon the Negroes, and on April 6 General E. R. S. Canby, commanding federal forces in the Carolinas, announced his intention to punish acts of violence by military courts if necessary, and to hold new elections wherever qualified electors were prevented from voting.[21] Such pronouncements would not deter the Ku Klux from violence in later times, but only the April elections would show them that the freedmen were not to be deterred by verbal threats and men posing as thirsty ghosts. When the Republicans carried these elections and swept into power, the Raleigh *Sentinel,* the chief conservative organ in the state, issued a thinly veiled call for more intensive Ku Klux organization.[22]

Conservative resistance took a more militant form in South Carolina than in most states at this time. As early as February 1868 ex-governor Benjamin F. Perry called on Southern whites to organize Democratic clubs and serve as unofficial guardians of the white man's peace in the face of the forthcoming Radical Reconstruction governments.[23] Most of the mobilization which took place was more traditional and less flamboyant in style than that of the Ku Klux Klan. But considerable Klan organization occurred, especially in the middle and upper counties, away from the coast. Democratic newspapers faithfully recorded its progress in other states and generally gave it a good bill of health.[24] There was a noticeable lack of enthusiasm, however. The Charleston *Mercury* argued early in April that the time for such organizations had not yet arrived; Southern whites were trying to prevent the need for secret societies by defeating the new constitutions at the polls. "But should they fail in their efforts, and negro governments be put over them, we doubt not that every city, town, village and neighborhood in the South will have combinations of the white population, to protect themselves against negro rule."[25]

The Klan's first appearance seems to have occurred in upcountry York County, where on March 30 it issued a call for its first meeting:

K.K.K. DEAD-MANS HOLLOW SOUTHERN DIV. Midnight, March 30. *General Order, No.* 1. REMEMBER the hour appointed by our Most Excellent Grand Captain-General. The dismal hour draws nigh for the meeting of our mystic Circle. The Shrouded-Knight will come with pick and spade; the Grand Chaplain will come with the ritual of the dead. The grave yawneth, the lightnings flash athwart the heavens, the thunders roll, but the Past Grand Knight of the Sepulcher [*sic*] will recoil not.

By order of the Great Grand Centaur SULEYMAN, G.G.S.

In printing this notice, the editor of the Conservative Yorkville *Enquirer* commented, "We believe no good can result from such organizations, and regret to hear of the K.K.K.'s in our midst."[26] He would not much longer have the freedom to make such remarks publicly; by the fall of 1871 the Klan had created such a reign of terror in York County as to attract national attention, military occupation, and a Presidential suspension of habeas corpus; military arrests supervised by the Attorney General and followed by trials and convictions in the federal courts would be required before order was restored and the Klan suppressed.

Elsewhere in the state, Klan organization and white mobilization generally followed the state elections in April, as the *Mercury* predicted. When Negro voters carried the new constitution and elected a solidly Republican state government, most of the Conservative press altered its tone. Newspapers either began to deny the Klan's responsibility for scattered outrages which were being reported or denied its existence altogether. Sometimes, inconsistently, they advanced both arguments simultaneously. On April 28 the Columbia *Phoenix* repeated a Ku Klux water-drinking story from Laurens County and maintained that the Klan was no worse than the Union League; two days later it denied that the Klan existed in South Carolina and equated its threatening letters with April Fools' jokes and comic Valentines. At the same time it resented Republican efforts to publicize and thereby make political capital of these harmless frivolities.

Far less typical was the Charleston *Daily News*. After a brief flirtation with the Ku Klux idea in March, it came out squarely against it in May. "The thoughtless young men" joining the Klan, it said, were furnishing "our enemies at the North" with ammunition in the form of outrage stories which simply fed the flames of Radicalism. Thus "no honorable and patriotic Southern man, who has the welfare of this people at heart, ought to sympathize with or countenance in any way this stupendous folly."[27]

The *News* associated the "Ku-Klux folly" with only "a few hair-brained youths," which was partially the case everywhere. If the solid Conservative leaders of South Carolina were any less involved in its origins than in other states, the difference was probably one of degree only, arising from their sponsorship of Democratic rifle clubs as a saner alternative. Whatever its sponsorship, Ku Klux organization took place quietly in various places around the state during the spring and summer.[28]

As in North Carolina, organizational lines and nomenclature are confused; and as everywhere, the evidence of what was actually happening is highly fragmentary. In upcountry Chester County an organization was formed calling itself the Chester Conservative Clan. In June it permitted ten residents of neighboring York County to organize a branch, perhaps in addition to the Klan already organized there in March. Moreover, one of the ten, a young Confederate veteran at Rock Hill named Iredell Jones, was soon to become Grand Scribe of the county's Ku Klux organization which bore the name of the Invisible Empire.[29] Most of this activity was locally inspired, but many years later R. J. Brunson, an early Klansman at Pulaski, told of traveling to South Carolina in July 1868, where during the next three months he organized several Ku Klux dens under the orders of General George W. Gordon.[30]

In most places the Klan confined itself that summer to pranks and threats. But Abbeville County (with neighboring Edgefield the most violent region of the state) experienced as early as June the kind of crimes which were rocking parts of Tennessee. The Negroes here reported almost nightly perambulations by bands of white-robed Klansmen, who whipped more than a dozen freedmen in one neighborhood, leading some of them to flee to Georgia, and drove off Nelson Joiner, a Negro member of the late constitutional convention, burning his house. Many other threats and outrages were committed, only some of which were attributed to disguised men. (In this county the Klan was later revealed to have performed some of its activities, including murder, in open daylight and without disguise.) These depredations were most conspicuous and systematic just prior to a local election in June, but they continued into the fall, when they assumed even greater proportions. Virtually no attempt was made by the local authorities to check, much less punish, these offenses, although a Negro accused of murdering another freedman was brought to book promptly enough. Amid reports in July that the Negroes were arming in self-defense (which proved to be false), the whites imported guns and made it a point to carry them.[31]

As a matter of fact, firearms were being surreptitiously imported throughout the state, and white men were plainly organizing into military companies and drilling. Conservative leaders probably placed more confidence in these unofficial white militia than in the weird Ku Klux Klan as a means of preserving white supremacy against the specter of Negro rule.

That specter seemed very real and pressing to most Conservatives. Unionism of the east Tennessee variety had been almost unknown in South Carolina, and the number of white Republicans was negligible. Party lines coincided with race lines to a degree unmatched anywhere except in Mississippi. Negroes constituted 60 per cent of the population and at least that proportion of the electorate. Thus the new state administration under Governor Robert K. Scott (formerly an Ohioan and lately in charge of the Freedmen's Bureau in the state) was almost totally dependent on Negro support. Conservatives had discovered in the April elections that the Negroes would vote solidly Republican, and that Ku Klux posters, warning letters, and nocturnal riding would not by themselves shake that allegiance. To restore white Conservative government would require extraordinary effort, therefore. Most of them did not yet plan a violent overthrow of the state government; the certainty of federal intervention precluded such frontal measures. There were still untried possibilities in the field of voter coercion and intimidation as well as the nonviolent attempts to split the Negro vote which were later tried in 1870. But the prospect of Negro domination—which far surpassed in white imaginations anything that actually came to pass—was so disturbing as to warrant defensive armament and organization. Hence the formation of Democratic clubs and rifle clubs.

The new state government could hardly regard them as defensive, however, particularly in the wake of the summer's outrages. Governor Scott lacked any real power to cope with these organizations if they chose to resist, but he issued a proclamation on August 31, ordering their disbandment and condemning (though he lacked the power to forbid) the importation of firearms.[32] The legislature also responded to widespread lawlessness in the upcountry by creating a state constabulary. It consisted of a chief constable in Columbia with deputies in every county who were to enforce the laws and repress disorder in conjunction with local authorities.[33] The constabulary was organized, but it did little to check forcible white resistance to Radical Reconstruction, whether this operated through the Ku Klux Klan or otherwise.

In Georgia there is good evidence that at least in certain parts of the state the process of organizing the Ku Klux began at the top and proceeded downward toward the grass roots during the spring and summer of 1868.

As in other states, most of the leaders involved were relatively young ex-Confederates, brigadier generals and below, who had not been active politically before the war. But the military prominence they achieved by 1865 paved their way to political careers afterward. There is circumstantial evidence, moreover, linking General Forrest with the Klan's beginnings in Georgia. The first public notice of the order's existence in the state appeared in the Conservative Atlanta *Intelligencer* on March 14, when Forrest was visiting the city, ostensibly on insurance business. From that time onward there were increasing evidences of Klan organization around the state. Also in the insurance business was General John B. Gordon of Atlanta, the Conservative candidate for governor in the forthcoming April elections; Gordon came to be almost universally regarded as Grand Dragon of the Klan in Georgia.[34]

Three years later, in testifying before the Congressional investigating committee, Gordon was as evasive as Forrest. He admitted that he had joined early in 1868 a secret organization that was formed throughout the state and probably beyond it for the purpose of protecting society against Negro depredation and the supposed dangers of the Union League. He would name neither the organization nor the gentlemen (some of the "very best" and wealthiest citizens of the state) who approached him to join, but he admitted that they had offered him the position of state commander. "I said very emphatically that upon that line I could be called on if it was necessary." But, Gordon explained, no general emergency ever arose to require completing the organization that far, and the position apparently was not formally filled. At the same time, however, he maintained that if the order had ever engaged in illegal activity he would have been in a position to know it. Despite his denial of any political purpose in the society, Gordon claimed that it was discontinued, so far as he and his associates were informed, soon after his defeat for governor in April. Its members, he said, were ex-Confederate soldiers and Democrats, good men and true who could be relied upon to act sanely and maintain discipline. The organization was most important at the county level and below, where it existed to prevent or quell any disturbances which might arise locally or as part of a general Negro rising. It held no regular meetings to his knowledge and committed no outrages. Its members, the general declared, were in reality the Negroes' best friends, the kindest of their former masters, those most apt to give them money in times of hardship. Gordon was extremely reluctant to give names, but did admit under pressure that other men who might have information concerning the order were General Alfred H. Colquitt (who like Gordon later served as governor and United States Senator), General G. T. Anderson, and perhaps Generals A. R. Lawton and Ambrose R. Wright.[35]

Gordon's disavowal of political intent has to be taken with great reservation. The danger of a Negro rising about which he and his colleagues were so apprehensive was attributable primarily, he said, to the carpetbaggers— "outside agitators" in modern parlance—who stirred up Negro dreams of equality and organized the blacks into Union Leagues. The enemy to be combated, therefore, was the Republican party, certainly a political orientation if the word has meaning. Like the Tennessee generals, Gordon and his friends intended more than they would admit to publicly. Nevertheless, their aim to keep the Negro in his place was partially defensive and non-political from their point of view; to them secret Negro leagues were almost synonymous with insurrection, and they themselves were organizing a force for law and order.

It is impossible, however, to maintain Gordon's denial of any Klan outrages, except on some technicality; even during the few months he admitted to being affiliated with the order the Ashburn murder in March has to be explained away. Altogether the Georgia Klan was responsible for countless crimes between 1868 and 1871. Possibly Gordon and his friends left the order by the summer of 1868, but the Klan went riding on, and he could hardly have been ignorant of the fact. The most charitable interpretation of his denial that he served as state chief of the Klan is that he acted in that capacity during the initial organizational stage without being formally inducted. It is also impossible to credit, except on some technicality, the statement that he knew none of the subordinate officials.

It was widely understood—and we have direct evidence to support it—that General Dudley M. DuBose was Grand Titan of the fifth congressional district in eastern Georgia, which included the most violent Klan counties in the state. He himself organized the Klan in Wilkes County, his home, and commissioned leaders in other counties.[36] Thirty-four years old in 1868, DuBose was elected to Congress from that district two years later in a campaign assisted by the Klan. He was a son-in-law of Robert Toombs, the ante-bellum Senator and wartime Confederate cabinet member. Toombs himself inveighed loudly against Radicalism and undoubtedly sympathized with the Klan, but he had no traceable connection with it. Many years later John C. Reed told of having established the order in Oglethorpe County shortly after the April election, on the direct solicitation of DuBose, who had just assumed the Titanship. Reed believed, though he did not know, that Gordon was Grand Dragon of the state, acting under Forrest. But most of the organization above DuBose's level, he said, was fanciful and functioned little if at all, which agrees with Gordon and the evidence available today.

As Grand Giant of Oglethorpe County, Reed picked the best den commanders he could find, and in conjunction with them the rank-and-file members. He organized dens in nearly all of the county's twelve militia districts, with more than one den in the largest districts. They usually numbered only ten to twenty members, disciplined Confederate veterans for the most part, who owned good horses. This organizational activity apparently continued through the summer, and they did not commence operations until their uniforms were ready shortly before the November Presidential election. Writing forty years after the event, Reed no longer feared criminal prosecution and admitted freely that their aims were chiefly political. They intended to defeat the Republican party through intimidating Negro voters; but they acted also as regulators to keep the black man in his place socially. The over-all objective, said Reed, was to help save the South from Africanization.[37]

Few Klansmen were so willing to tell their stories in later years, and our knowledge of the organization and inner workings of the order elsewhere must rest primarily on fragmentary external evidence. The Klan issued its typical notices in the spring of 1868 in Columbus, Macon, Savannah, and Milledgeville, as well as in Atlanta.[38]

The most notable case of violence was the Ashburn murder in Columbus on March 31. This was the first Ku Klux outrage to be reported outside of Tennessee, and it gained nationwide publicity. The Klan was only about a week old in Columbus, and as elsewhere it had announced its arrival by posting threats and warnings on the doors of local Republicans. One of these posters carried a coffin with the name of George W. Ashburn, one of the most effective Republican organizers in the vicinity, who had just returned from attending the constitutional convention in Atlanta. Although he had taken a moderate position in the convention relative to the treatment of ex-Confederates, Ashburn was a vigorous and outspoken Reconstructionist, with a large following among the freedmen. He was the kind of Republican whom Conservative whites most detested and found it easiest to defame. He was in fact the embodiment of the stock Reconstruction scalawag: a nobody before the war who, for reasons no one bothered to understand, fled to join the Union army during the conflict and became a leader and organizer of Negroes afterward. Fellow Republicans found Ashburn likable, self-reliant, and utterly (perhaps immoderately) devoted to the Reconstruction cause. But despite his Negro following, white Conservatives affected to believe that even the freedmen regarded him "as a man utterly destitute of principle," in the words of Democratic leader Benjamin H. Hill, "and a man of very low morals." They also discovered to their own satisfaction that as a prewar plantation overseer he had been notoriously cruel to Negroes.

Ashburn was separated from his wife and lived alone. On his return from Atlanta all the white boardinghouses in Columbus agreed not to take him in, and the hotel would accept him only if he ate his meals in his own room. After a fruitless search for other accommodations, he finally rented a room in a house owned by a Negro woman. His fellow tenants were of both races and one white girl bore a dubious character; thus it was easy to maintain after his death that Ashburn had inhabited "a negro brothel of the lowest order." Ben Hill even recalled in 1871 that Ashburn was cohabiting with a married Negro woman at the time of his death. Although most of the character assassination followed the murder and was designed to palliate and rationalize it, Conservatives obviously feared and hated Ashburn enough to ostracize and kill him in the first place.

Shortly after midnight on the night of March 30, between thirty and forty disguised men broke into the house. Five of them made their way to his room, where they shot and killed him. Klan apologists differed in their accounts of the matter, all being careful to disavow any direct knowledge. Some held that the invaders' purpose had been simply to warn him off, but that he had pulled a gun, forcing them to shoot him in self-defense. None of them attributed the crime, in public at least, to the Ku Klux Klan. As the Columbus *Sun* put it, that was a "wholly imaginary organization," although it had been real enough to the *Sun* a week before when reporting its arrival in Columbus. Moreover, the suggestion "that respectable white men should as a body plan murder" was cast aside as unworthy of a moment's credence. Some persons accused federal soldiers of the crime, but most preferred to believe with the *Sun* that Ashburn had been assassinated by fellow Republicans, black or white, on account of factional rivalry within the party.[39]

Reserving all their abuse for Ashburn and his fellow Republicans, Conservatives betrayed no anxiety to test the validity of their theories concerning his killers. The local coroner's jury contented itself with finding that Ashburn had died at the hands of persons unknown, and the matter would have ended here but for the intervention of General Meade and the military authorities.[40] The murder was obviously the product of advance organization and planning, and witnesses noted that the attackers' clothing, so far as it appeared beneath their disguises, would seem to identify them as members of "the better class of citizens."[41] A few days later the military arrested thirteen persons; three were Negroes, but most of the others were young men of social standing in the community. One was chairman of the local Democratic executive committee, and two others were candidates for local office. They were soon released under bond, which more than 400 persons had raised by subscription. After several weeks the accused were taken to Atlanta (where witnesses would be less subject to intimidation) to stand trial before a military commission. White Georgians assumed without question, publicly at least, that these upstanding young men were innocent victims of military despotism. But whether they were technically guilty or not, the accused were regarded as symbols of the Conservative cause in general, and had to be defended. Dragging them from their homes to stand trial in a distant city was branded as outrageous, and their temporary confinement in cramped cells was denounced as barbarous; the victor of Gettysburg was referred to in the Democratic press as Torquemada Meade. The whole procedure, Conservatives charged, was undertaken for political effect; but they themselves issued a distorted version of the affair, entitled *Radical Rule: Military Outrage in Georgia,* as a Democratic campaign document before the November Presidential election. Actually both parties were interested in the case: the prosecution included Joseph E. Brown, Confederate governor of the state and soon to be its Republican chief justice, while Alexander H. Stephens, late vice-president of the Confederacy, served for the defense.

Two men (one an Army sergeant) provided the most striking testimony in the case. They stated that they had been hired by local Conservative leaders to join the attacking party and were among the four or five who actually committed the murder while the leaders remained outside Ashburn's room. A Negro witness testified that one of these leaders referred to the group at the time as Ku Klux. Happily for the defense, the military trial coincided with the organization of the new state government and its acceptance by Congress. With military courts now superseded, General Meade on July 21 ordered the trial to cease and turned over its records to the civil authorities. The climate of opinion in Columbus being what it was, the local authorities took some perfunctory actions and dropped the matter. No one was ever punished for Ashburn's murder; on the other hand, the Klan made little or no further appearance in Columbus.[42]

General Meade's first reaction to the Ashburn murder and to Ku Klux terrorism in general was an order on April 4 warning against any further attempts at intimidation, whether by newspaper, mail, or public notices. Military and civil authorities in Georgia, Florida, and Alabama (the states comprising his jurisdiction) were instructed to arrest and prosecute anyone issuing or circulating such threats, including newspaper editors who printed them. At the same time he called on all good citizens to avoid inflammatory statements and preserve the peace.[43]

There is evidence that the highest Klan leadership in Georgia shared Meade's unhappiness with the direction of Ku Klux activity. Conservative newspapers carried an order, purportedly from this source, issued even before the Ashburn murder, rebuking what it termed unauthorized persons for using the Ku Klux name to publish threatening effusions in the newspapers. The Klan, it proclaimed almost desperately, was a peaceful and defensive order; the statement disavowed terrorism and ascribed such activity to a few unprincipled men both inside and outside the order.[44]

Notwithstanding these coinciding orders from generals of the blue and gray, Georgia Klansmen continued to carry out modest local campaigns of intimidation. And the Ashburn case was not the only example of physical violence.[45] It was this continued activity, no doubt, which prompted General Gordon to sever his connection with the order soon after the election and to pretend that it had no existence thereafter. Actually the Klan appears to have spread as a result of the Conservatives' electoral defeat, especially in General DuBose's section of eastern Georgia. Although John C. Reed confined its activity in Oglethorpe County to organization under a measure of discipline, he admits that his men were getting impatient to see action before they finally started operations in the fall. The Klan appeared in nearby Columbia County almost simultaneously, and wasted less time before committing depredations on the local Negroes. One Klansman identified on such a raid was George Stoball, who thereby helped propel himself into the state legislature.[46] Depredations by armed bands also occurred in the spring and summer of 1868 in Elbert and Twiggs counties.[47] Although Governor Bullock ordered inquiries to be made of these activities and forwarded information to the military, nothing effective was done either to prevent or to punish them.

Ku Klux activity came to Florida in April and May 1868. As in other states, its first manifestations preceded the state election, which in Florida's case came in May, but most of the organizing followed the Republican victory and the advent of the Reconstruction regime. The most prevalent organization was not even nominally affiliated with the Tennessee Ku Klux and did not use its name; rather it bore the euphemistic title of the Young Men's Democratic Club. This society differed in no important respect from the Klan, except that it did not typically operate in disguise. Beginning apparently at Tallahassee shortly after the election, it soon had branches throughout the state. Its members were drawn from all classes, and Joseph John Williams of Tallahassee, one of its leaders, testified in 1871 that in his county of Leon it included some three to four hundred men, amounting to half of the total Democratic vote. Williams himself had owned three hundred slaves before the war and later served nine terms in the legislature. There was little organization above the county level, and certainly no effective higher control.

In this state too there was comparatively little overt violence during the initial months, and in many areas the organization never became violent. Most members regarded it as a defense against the almost universally anticipated Negro risings which never materialized. What violence did take place was attributable to a small minority. Every local club had, or at least the constitution provided for, a secret "committee of observation and safety," which seems to have supervised most of the active operations. It consisted of the club's president and two vice-presidents, plus five other "discreet, active, energetic members" whose identity and activities were not to be known by the rank and file. However, the constitution provided that the committee in each club should divide up all the adult whites in its territory into fifties, and these into tens, each under a chief. Every chief of the tens was to compile a political dossier for each white and colored voter in his jurisdiction.[48]

Had this organization and information been completed it would have facilitated Democratic control of the Negro population and the electoral process throughout the state. But as everywhere, the plans of the organizers were too ambitious ever to be fully realized. The Negroes never posed the threat which nervous whites at first anticipated, and too many whites in most parts of the state were either apathetic or opposed in principle to this kind of organization and activity. In the spring and summer of 1868 a few Republicans received Ku Klux warnings, and there were some attempts to intimidate Negroes, but these efforts were neither intensive nor widespread.[49]

CHAPTER 5

Alabama, Mississippi, and Kentucky

Alabama was probably the first state to which the Ku Klux spread outside of Tennessee, in 1867. The Alabama Klans may also have borne a closer affiliation with the parent organization than those at a greater distance, but even here the connection was minimal. Here too the organization was more widespread in its initial stage than it was to be in its later, more violent days, and the greatest organizational spurt followed rather than preceded the state election which ratified the new Radical constitution and initiated a Republican state government. In Alabama, the first state to hold such an election in pursuance of the Congressional Reconstruction acts, this took place on February 4, 1868.

Secret organizations of a temporary and local character preceded the Ku Klux movement in parts of the state, and may sometimes have merged with it. In some places, like Montgomery, Mobile, and Talladega, the Klan made virtually its only appearance in the spring of 1868, manifested by the familiar warnings and newspaper notices.[1] In others it embarked at once upon strenuous regulative activity among the freedmen. A Negro witness before the Congressional investigating committee of 1871 recalled a band of regulators in Pickens County in 1866, called "night owls," who went around like ante-bellum patrollers, punishing Negroes whose landlords had complained of them.[2] Many years later Judge A. E. Caffee of Tuskegee recalled that an order there, to which he belonged, had organized as the

81

Knights of the White Carnation within a few months of the end of the war. They too were night riders who punished Negroes for real or fancied offenses, and were headed, he said, by General Cullen A. Battle, whom other evidence points to as a leader of the more militant local white population. Whether or not this organization really belonged to the much larger Knights of the White Camellia, which existed in Alabama, Caffee said it later merged into the Ku Klux Klan.[3] Negroes around Tuskegee were to experience a good deal of white aggression in 1868 and later, but little or none of it took the form of organized night riding.[4] Farther north a white Republican in mountainous Blount County began receiving Ku Klux warnings in November 1867. One of these, he said, came from the county probate judge, who admitted his membership in the order.[5]

As in South Carolina, much of the forcible resistance to "Negro rule" lay outside of the Ku Klux and comparable organizations. The Republican Montgomery *State Sentinel* reported in January that prominent "rebels" were receiving boxes of arms for use by newly forming Conservative clubs around the state. A week after the election it reported that armed men had kept Negroes from the polls in several counties.[6]

Coinciding with the Klan's rapid expansion in Alabama, which began in March, was a visit to the state early that month by General Forrest, purportedly on the same insurance business which took him next to Atlanta and Columbus, Georgia.[7] By April, if not earlier, there were Klans in existence around Huntsville, Athens, Tuscumbia, and at other points in the Tennessee Valley counties of north Alabama. Although they were most remarkable for their public notices and other signs of organizing activity, they had already begun committing depredations on the freedmen.[8]

Much of the organizational activity at this time involved another order altogether. The Knights of the White Camellia had originated in Louisiana in May 1867, and most of its membership and activity were confined to that state. But it penetrated as far as the western Alabama Black Belt by 1868, the year of its maximum growth.[9] The Klan existed in some of these counties too, and it is sometimes impossible to distinguish the two societies. Ordinarily the KWC was a less violent organization with a larger membership and did not assume disguises to the same degree as the Klan. Its members may have been a cut higher socially than the Ku Klux, and it was better disciplined, but their purposes were essentially the same. P. J. Glover, a planter in Marengo County, later testified that he had joined the KWC there in 1867, and that it had been introduced from Sumter County. The original organizer in that part of the state, he had been told, was a prominent (but unnamed) Democrat of Selma.[10]

The KWC also organized in nearby Perry and Monroe counties, which never saw much violence of the Ku Klux variety. A large proportion of the white men belonged, and its leaders included some of the "best citizens." Dr. G. P. L. Reid of Marion claimed more than thirty years later that in Perry County a thousand men could have been mobilized on four hours' notice. They engaged in nonviolent terrorism, sending threatening notices to Republican officeholders, riding about the countryside after dark, or posting themselves silently but conspicuously in squads along the roads where Negroes passed while returning home from League meetings. Law officers, even judges, belonged to the order, and no jury could be drawn without including a majority who were members. Most of the active work was carried out by an inner circle without the knowledge of the others.[11] The story was much the same in Monroe County, where Thomas Chalmers McCorvey recalled systematically intimidating (but not beating) blacks who had achieved a local prominence in the Republican party. The method used on some occasions was to ride in disguise, sixty-five or seventy strong, to the Negro's house and circle it three times, uttering only an occasional groan.[12]

Hale County, also in the western Black Belt, had a more active and more violent organization, apparently Ku Klux rather than White Camellia.[13] Its formation probably corresponded closely to Klan expansion elsewhere. John L. Hunnicutt many years later recalled proudly that in 1868 as an eighteen-year-old student at Greensboro, the county seat, he and four other college boys staged the first Ku Klux raid in the county. They had no organization as yet, but were supplied with horses by several prominent Democrats. Their main target was a Northern teacher of a Negro school, but they also "raided three Negro quarters in regular old style" while looking for him. On finding their man, they threatened to whip him; instead of doing so, however, they warned him to leave the county within twenty-four hours, which he did. The boys were not very careful about concealing their identity, and the local judge charged the grand jury to indict them, so as to discourage further raiding. But since the foreman of the grand jury was one of those who had supplied them with horses, no indictments were forthcoming. Following this, and at the request of "some of the best citizens," Hunnicutt formally organized the first Ku Klux den.[14] Its public notices began to appear in Greensboro in March, and the local Freedmen's Bureau agent first noted their nocturnal perambulations that month.[15] It was probably the Ku Klux who tried to burn down the courthouse on March 21, a day after they had done so successfully in neighboring Greene County. (Hunnicutt and his colleagues had got organizational assistance in Greene County.) The Klan visited Greensboro on a number of occasions, eluding arrest whenever it was attempted. They disrupted the local Union League; intimidated the judge, William T. Blackford, into temporarily recanting his Republicanism; tried to drive out two

Jewish storekeepers whom they accused of overcharging; and liberated two supposed murderers who were in transit under guard.[16]

The Greene County Klan this spring, apart from destroying the court-house, posted the usual threats, beat and drove off the teacher of a Negro school, and rifled the office of the Freedmen's Bureau agent before driving him away too.[17] Here for a change the offenders did not all get off scot-free. Troops were sent, who arrested several of the teacher's assailants; these were convicted by a military commission (before the state was readmitted) and sent to the Dry Tortugas, off the Florida coast.[18] The Ku Klux also formed, and engaged in at least minor activity, in other western Black Belt counties such as Wilcox, Marengo, Pickens, and Sumter.[19]

One of the first Klans to form was that in Tuscaloosa County, between October and December 1867. Its organizer, leader, and source of greatest inspiration was Ryland Randolph, editor of the Tuscaloosa *Independent Monitor*. Randolph was a prototype of the Southern race baiters who came to power in the 1890's; like the most successful of these, he had a quick wit, a sharp tongue and facile pen, a passion for controversy, and an instinct for identifying with and mobilizing the basest instincts of his constituency. But he lived a generation too soon to realize his greatest potential; Northern public opinion, the federal government, and the Republican party in 1868 were concerned to uphold at least minimal rights for the Southern Negro, and responsible Democrats had to live with this fact. The vulgarity of Randolph's diatribes in the *Monitor* and his penchant for street brawling embarrassed patrician Conservatives almost as much as they infuriated Republicans. Although he capitalized on his local following to win a seat in the legislature, state Democratic leaders felt obliged to disown him in 1868 for fear of having themselves and the national Democratic party convicted of guilt by association. Nevertheless this local career illustrates how much a talented demagogue can affect the character of a community.

When Randolph bought the *Monitor* and moved to Tuscaloosa in October 1867 the white population was divided in its attitude toward Radical Reconstruction and how to meet it. The upper portion of the county contained many Unionists who were prepared to cooperate with the new regime. Opposition sentiment was widespread but not yet crystallized until Randolph accomplished it by means of his newspaper and the Ku Klux Klan.[20] His motivation was frankly racist; the *Monitor* carried at its masthead the motto "White Man—Right or Wrong—Still the White Man!" In December 1867 he called editorially for organized armed resistance to prevent ratification of the Radical constitution. That document represented Negro rule and would open the way for buck Negroes to marry our daughters, he said.[21] The Klan made its first appearance on December 30, when amid much hilarity it rode into town and carried Randolph off into mock captivity. Soon he became county leader. Many years later he explained that the Klan was organized locally with knowledge of the Tennessee Klan but having no connection with it. Only later, he explained, did he acquire a copy of the Klan Prescript, which came through the mail from Memphis. There were about sixty members in his den, two of whom were later elected to the legislature. They met about once a week to discuss the doings of people they regarded as offensive. If a majority voted to punish such persons it was subsequently done, although they deemed it sufficient sometimes merely to post warning notices.[22]

These missives began to appear in March 1868, after Randolph called editorially for every community to organize a Ku Klux Klan. Its "peculiar service," he explained, "should be the condign cleansing of neighborhoods of all human impurities. Only by such means can good understanding and feeling be inculcated and preserved between the races, whose interests are not necessarily antagonistic."[23] In pursuit of this objective the Klan dragged Allen A. Williams, a Negro state legislator, from his home and beat him.[24] Other prominent freedmen were also "thrashed in the regular *ante bellum* style," as Randolph wrote in 1901, "until their unnatural nigger-pride had a tumble, and humbleness to the white man reigned supreme."[25] Randolph further contributed to race adjustment by street fighting on his own, which he was able to recall boastfully many years afterward. On one occasion he aided a white man fighting two Negroes, and stabbed one of them. Later he claimed to have stood off single-handedly a crowd of one or two hundred freedmen intent on killing him, despite pleas from his friends that he leave town temporarily for his own safety.

I was determined to settle the matter of race supremacy right there and then. . . . I raised my gun as if to fire and, alone, started towards the crowd. The way that crowd of darkies scattered and scampered away was "a caution," as the saying is; indeed, so great was the "skeedaddle" that even I could not resist the temptation of laughing; and, to make the fun more complete, I sighted my gun at the fleeing mob. Then there was not only running but actual "hollering"; and in less than five minutes not a negro was to be seen on the streets.[26]

These episodes early in 1868 made Randolph a local hero, especially when they brought his arrest by the military. A public meeting passed resolutions of sympathy and protest over his incarceration. Doubtless many persons endorsed Randolph's own estimate of the situation: "Radical, nigger-worshipping vagabonds are protected by military authority, while the gentlemen of the land are persecuted by the same."[27] The tyranny was incomplete, however; a military tribunal in Selma acquitted Randolph and he returned to a hero's welcome in Tuscaloosa, which his newspaper reported in full and fond detail. Two miles from the city he was met by several gentlemen in an open carriage who escorted him into town. Here a delegation of ladies decked the horses with flowers "and literally bombarded him with numberless boquets [sic] of exquisite taste and beauty." As his carriage passed through the streets, the church bells tolled their welcome, ladies waved handkerchiefs from balconies, and showered him with more bouquets. On alighting, "he was greeted with cheers by the assembled crowd, and welcomed in an appropriate speech from the Rev. W. H. Armstrong, of the Methodist Church, a man eminent alike for his talent, piety and patriotism."[28]

Randolph gloried in his role as the symbol of Tuscaloosa's defiance of Radical Reconstruction; it spurred him on to renewed activity. He engaged in street brawls with editors of the *Reconstructionist,* the struggling Republican paper in town, and he wrote editorials singling out individual Republicans of both races as fit victims of the Ku Klux Klan. Shortly after his return an article congratulated Tuscaloosa on the number of persons who had been driven out of town in recent weeks; it named and defamed eight of them, including two teachers of Negro schools.[29] In June he threatened that if the military did not crack down on the Union League, which he characterized as a "nigger K.K.K.," the real K.K.K. might be tempted to do so.[30] In August, after two more arrests and brief exiles, he reported the appearance of a large Ku Klux party on the University of Alabama campus, which had the misfortune to be located under his watchful eye. (The new state government had reorganized the university under Republican trustees, and Randolph with his Klan would soon make a shambles of it.) A week later he commented editorially on "an incendiary buck-nigger" of Tuscaloosa who had written a letter to the *Sentinel,* the Republican newspaper in Montgomery; this man, the *Monitor* threatened, "is certainly a candidate before the Ku Klux Klan for *grave* honors. Doubtless, his name will, if he keeps on scribbling, appear in the City Sexton's report, ere long." In the following issue Randolph suggested a Ku Kluxing for a local Negro who had been accused of theft, as well as for the justice of the peace who had discharged him.[31]

Randolph's greatest triumph (or his worst defeat) resulted from a woodcut which appeared in the *Monitor* on September 1 and won him nationwide attention. It portrayed two men hanging from a tree limb after a mule labeled "KKK" has walked out from under them. One of the figures bears a carpetbag labeled "Ohio," the former home of the newly appointed university president. The picture, according to the inscription beneath, "represents the fate in store for those great pests of Southern society—the carpet-bagger and scalawag—if found in Dixie's land after the break of day on the 4th of March next." Room was also left on the branch, it was pointed out, for any obnoxious Republican Negro who might be found.[32] It was after Republican newspapers had publicized this cut in the North that Randolph found himself repudiated as a political liability by his own party leaders.[33] He bore these rebuffs manfully, tried to explain away the cartoon, and kept his editorial pen in check until after the November election.[34]

Tuscaloosa Republicans, for their part, were completely outclassed by Randolph and his Klansmen. When Mayor Woodruff called on all citizens to take personal responsibility for keeping the peace and reporting violaters to the authorities, the *Monitor* refused to carry his appeal and abused him instead. Republican pleas to Governor William H. Smith for protection brought little relief. Federal troops were sent for a time, but without the active cooperation of law officers (who were subservient to the Klan if not in sympathy with it) they accomplished little good.[35]

The Klan was even more active in some of the northern counties during the summer of 1868. In Decatur it paraded through the streets without let or hindrance, and demanded that the editor of the Decatur *Republican* leave town within three days on pain of death. It committed depredations almost nightly in the surrounding countryside, murdering at least one Negro.[36] Around Moulton, Klansmen hanged one Negro and whipped another to death, while driving away all the Northern men in the locality and threatening similar treatment to Republicans generally.[37] Similar activities were reported from Colbert and Lauderdale counties.[38]

Except for the Greene County men who were sent to the Dry Tortugas, Klansmen did much as they pleased, with little opposition. General O. L. Shepherd, the federal commander in the state under Meade, echoed his superior's general order against the Klan with one of his own on April 4. It held local officials accountable to the military for preserving order, suppressing this "iniquitous organization," and arresting and punishing its members wherever found. It also forbade the issuance and circulation of Klan notices by newspapers or other means.[39] The chief effect of this order was to drive the Klan further underground; Ku Klux notices appeared less often in the press and on the streets, but Klan activity continued. Ryland Randolph was only a degree or two more brash than other editors in his incitements to violence and encouragement of Ku Klux organization.

What authority General Shepherd possessed to enforce his order disappeared soon afterward with the organization of the new state government and the supersedure of military by civil authority. Public opinion and local officials either sympathized with the Klan or were intimidated into silence and inactivity. The few persons who spoke out openly, like Mayor Woodruff of Tuscaloosa, were relatively powerless and took their lives into their hands. Republicans privately appealed to Governor Smith for aid, or more practically requested permission to form militia companies in self-defense.[40] This permission was seldom if ever forthcoming. The governor, an Alabamian of many years' residence who had embraced the federal cause in 1862, was sincere enough in his sympathy for Ku Klux victims and in his repeated appeals for law and order. But he was deathly afraid of taking drastic steps of the Brownlow variety to attain it, for fear of turning white opinion against the new state government. Majority white opinion was already alienated beyond redemption, however, and by appeasing the Ku Klux he served mainly to antagonize fellow Republicans. The federal troops he obtained for troubled localities were only a temporary deterrent to the Klan where they had any effect at all, because they were now limited to service as auxiliaries to the local authorities. Lacking a white Republican area comparable in size and strength to east Tennessee, his reliance for militarism would have had to be almost entirely with the black population. To arm the Negroes against a large proportion of the white population would surely have embittered race relations far more than was already the case, and precipitated a race conflict of incalculable consequences. Governor Smith naturally, and probably wisely, refused to risk such a conflagration. Like other deep South governors in these circumstances in the months and years to come, he refused to organize a militia, and the Klan in Alabama continued to grow almost unchecked.[41]

In Mississippi the Klan appeared at about the same time and in about the same manner as elsewhere, but there was less occasion for it to become active in 1868. When the new constitution went before the voters in June they rejected it, largely because it provided for disfranchising ex-Confederates. Thus a new state government was delayed until after a second vote in November 1869. General Forrest visited Mississippi several times during this period, and it was widely believed that he had a hand in some of the Klan's early organization, especially in the northern counties.[42] There was the usual spate of Ku Klux notices and warnings around the state in March and April.[43] A number of secret societies appeared, a few of them before the end of 1867, bearing such names as the Knights of the Black Cross (in Franklin County), Heggie's Scouts (in Holmes, Carroll, and Montgomery counties), and the Washington Brothers (in Leake County).[44]

Many of these organizations, including some who called themselves Ku Klux, died out after a few weeks or months and were never heard from again. But at the beginning they received the usual encouragement from the Democratic press. The Jackson *Clarion,* for instance, carefully denying knowledge of the Klan, nevertheless urged "the young men of Mississippi" in April to organize clubs and vigilance committees preparatory to the June elections.[45] These societies were scattered throughout the state, in cities as well as rural areas, in the heavily Negro delta and in white counties. Members sometimes galloped about after dark to amuse themselves and intimidate the freedmen, but for the most part they committed little violence. What few military arrests were made among these persons apparently came to nothing.[46]

Dr. William M. Compton, a Democratic newspaper editor at Holly Springs and an organizer and Grand Giant of the Klan in Marshall County, made an unusual transition; by 1871 he was in Jackson as editor of the Republican Jackson *Leader* and also as superintendent of the state insane asylum.[47]

Kentucky was the only state outside the former Confederacy where the Klan found any significant lodgment. There was little or no political need for the Klan statewide, since Kentucky never underwent Radical Reconstruction. Negroes did not vote until the Fifteenth Amendment imposed impartial suffrage on the state in 1870, and not until 1872 were they permitted to testify in cases involving white men. The Democratic party remained in full control of the state throughout the Reconstruction period. Perhaps for this reason there was even less evidence of higher organization or central direction in Klan affairs than was true elsewhere. But local Klans (or groups very much like them) were active sporadically in various parts of the state well into the 1870's, longer than in any other state.

Bands of armed regulators operated in Kentucky as in other Southern states before 1868. Much of this was simple banditry, but often it had political overtones, arising from the war. Kentucky had been rent internally as perhaps no other state was, occasionally dividing families and households, but more often settlements and neighborhoods, against themselves. The state supplied more men to the Union army than to the Confederate, but the preponderance of sentiment varied from one region to another. In many areas mutual depredations which began in wartime continued long after the surrender at Appomattox. Whether the Confederate partisans were a rowdier element than the Unionists, or whether the war's outcome placated the Union element while infuriating the rebels, the fact remains that the ex-rebels were more aggressive and were responsible for much the greater share of postwar violence. Unionists, especially those who joined the Republican party, were usually on the defensive. And as everywhere, the Negro freedmen, who were least able to defend themselves, were probably the most victimized. The motives for attacking them were economic and social in 1868, for the blacks had no political status to subvert.[48]

It is a bit arbitrary to begin calling the regulators Ku Klux in 1868, but their activities increased and the name came into general usage that year. Moreover, these bands clearly derived some of their inspiration and character in 1868 and afterward from the Klans of Tennessee. The state Freedmen's Bureau chief reported in April that bands of armed men were operating around Danville, in the center of the state, committing outrages on Negroes with the apparent support of the white community. A similar band operated in disguise in Meade County, on the Ohio River; at Bowling Green a teacher of a Negro school received a Ku Klux notice to leave town within five days. A Klan also was believed to have formed in this month at Henderson, across the Ohio from Evansville, Indiana. The Bureau agent there reported in June that he had seen them himself in gangs of sixty.[49] In Owen County, northeast of Louisville, a band of about forty men beat up a Unionist clergyman in May and forced him to leave.[50]

The Bluegrass region of central Kentucky was destined to be the worst part of the state, but at least scattered Ku Klux activity was reported from every region except the eastern mountains. This area, like adjacent east Tennessee, was Unionist country and dangerous ground for the Ku Klux Klan. Frankfort, the state capital, was located in the most infected region; a newspaper there reported in August that an organized band of regulators had been operating for a year in Anderson and several other counties just to the south. Its victims were almost exclusively Negroes and Union men, the latter being threatened with death if they did not leave.[51]

Many Democrats sanctioned this activity. A Garrard County woman, in a family letter, described the Ku Klux Klan there as "a band of invisible, nocturnal Regulators who keep the negroes straight. They manage to cause a good deal of terror in our region," she added dispassionately.[52] At Warsaw, on the Ohio River, the judge left town rather than try a number of men who had been arrested for parading through the streets one night, firing into Negro houses and into a building in which the freedmen were holding a religious service. After the Klan had broken up a religious meeting at Henderson the city council imposed a twenty-dollar fine on anyone appearing in disguise on a public thoroughfare. But the Klan responded through the local newspaper, denying the council's right to interfere with them. Few persons came to the council's support, and its members found themselves a laughingstock.[53]

Systematic terrorism also prevailed that summer in southwestern Kentucky, from Bowling Green to the Mississippi River. Klansmen issued warnings and erected gallows near the homes of Union men.[54] In many cases their threats were followed by physical attacks or exile, and occasionally murder. Union army veterans were singled out especially. The United States marshal for Kentucky, a wartime army major, was assassinated at Russellville in June after repeated threats from the Klan; he was the fifth Union man to be killed there in recent months. Soon afterward a Union veteran in Simpson County was riddled with bullets by Klansmen who called him out of his house at night; they also seriously wounded his wife when she ran to his assistance. Another Union veteran was taken from his house and murdered by Klansmen a week after they had poisoned his horses and mules by way of warning. Near Bowling Green they burned down some buildings in a Shaker community, with a loss of more than $250,000, in an effort to drive the residents away. By September masked bands were reported to be holding sway throughout the western end of the state. In some places the black population almost disappeared, most of them fleeing across the Ohio River for safety. White Unionists armed in self-defense and small parties of troops were sent to protect them, but they were badly outnumbered and the initiative (along with public opinion in this area) lay with their enemies.[55]

State as well as local authorities were usually unwilling or unable to redress the balance. This is not to say that the state government was in league with the Ku Klux; such was distinctly not the case. But just as the existence of a Democratic state government did not confer automatic immunity to the Ku Klux virus, it was no more effective than Republican governments in bringing the disease under control.

CHAPTER 6

The Trans-Mississippi States

The Ku Klux Klan and its organizational kinfolk were still more violent in the trans-Mississippi states than they were farther east. Substantial areas of Louisiana and Arkansas were hardly more than a generation removed from frontier conditions. This was emphatically true of Texas, in much of which the Comanche threat was still a living reality. Populations were less rooted than in the East, behavior was less settled, and institutions for the preservation of law and order were newer, weaker, and less regarded. In such an environment the Ku Klux Klan could more easily realize its full potential.

In Louisiana it existed side by side with the Knights of the White Camellia. The KWC was by far the more widespread and the more placid; its members were more numerous in the state, and generally more respectable in their social antecedents. They were also readier to admit the existence, purpose, and activities of their order despite its injunction of secrecy. The Ku Klux, or local vigilantes using that name, existed chiefly in the Florida parishes above New Orleans and in the northern parishes near the Arkansas line. By contrast the KWC, existing throughout the state, was strongest in the south. Democratic clubs which shared some of the same characteristics also existed widely in the state. Overlapping membership in these orders and the secrecy in which the Klan especially was shrouded usually make it impossible to distinguish them clearly. All were committed to the success of the Democratic party and the retention of white supremacy. How far they were willing to go in fulfilling this commitment was determined by many local factors, such as public sentiment, organizational discipline in the respective orders, and the character of the membership.

The White Camellias antedated the Klan in Louisiana. Their order was founded in May 1867 by Colonel Alcibiade DeBlanc in St. Mary Parish, in the French Creole section west of New Orleans.[1] It was organized formally in New Orleans immediately thereafter and spread subsequently throughout the state and into the Alabama Black Belt to the east, Arkansas to the north, and Houston and perhaps central Texas to the west. Most of this expansion, even within the state, apparently took place in two stages, the spring of 1868, as Radical Reconstruction was getting under way, and the fall, prior to the Presidential election.[2] By the latter time in many parishes it claimed half or more of the adult white male population as members. The KWC was typically better organized than the Ku Klux, and under better discipline. Its name was seldom associated with acts of violence, and by 1869 many of its members freely admitted their membership and discussed their limited activities within the order. Officers identified themselves as such before legislative and Congressional committees, and revealed a great deal concerning the order's membership, organization, and purposes. As with Klansmen, they insisted upon their peaceful and defensive intentions, primarily to combat a feared Negro uprising; but apparently they had less evidence of contrary activities to hide and less to fear from criminal prosecution should the laws ever be enforced. Reckless young men within the order occasionally committed outrages, but many members, on the other hand, became disenchanted with the order and dropped out after a short time because of its lack of militancy.[3] Men who admitted membership and positions of rank in the KWC included newspaper editors, physicians, lawyers, law enforcement officers, state senators, and even a few former officers in the Union army now resident in the state. In New Orleans and elsewhere the KWC regularly announced their meetings in the newspapers, beginning in March 1868.[4]

Like the early Klan in Tennessee, the KWC had an elaborate secret ritual and initiation ceremony, together with signs, grips, and passwords.[5] It was avowedly racist in purpose. The Charge to Initiates proclaimed that the order's

main and fundamental object is the MAINTENANCE OF THE SUPREMACY OF THE WHITE RACE in this Republic. History and physiology teach us that we belong to a race which nature has endowed with an evident superiority over all other races, and that the Maker, in thus elevating us above the common standard of human creation, has intended to give us over inferior races, a dominion from which no human laws can permanently derogate. . . .

And it is a remarkable fact that as a race of men is more remote from the Caucasian and approaches nearer to the black African, the more fatally that stamp of inferiority is affixed to its sons, and irrevocably dooms them to eternal imperfectibility and degradation.

Prospective members therefore were required to swear that they believed in white supremacy, that they had not married and never would marry a woman of another race, that they would do all in their power to prevent Negroes from taking part in politics, and that they would always vote against Negroes or white men "attached to negro principles." They were also sworn to obey the orders of their superiors and to protect a fellow member at the peril of their lives.[6] Members often claimed that a major purpose of the order was to prevent miscegenation and the mongrelization of the white race through intermarriage. There was no ready answer when a skeptical Congressman asked if such an organization was really necessary to prevent members from marrying or cohabiting with Negro women.

The organization of the White Camellias was similar to that of the Klan, although the nomenclature was less bizarre. The society's name was taken, of course, from the snow-white bloom of the Southern flowering shrub. The constitution was adopted at a convention in New Orleans by June 1868. According to this document individual members were organized into Councils whose enrollment might vary from five up to several hundred members. Each Council had a Commander, Lieutenant Commander, Guard, Secretary, and Treasurer, all elected for a term of one year. Councils were ordinarily designated by number in each parish, in the order of their establishment. They were divided and subdivided into Circles of fifty members and Groups of ten, if membership was large enough. When two or more Councils existed in a parish they elected delegates to a Central Council which met periodically at the parish seat under an Eminent Commander, Eminent Lieutenant Commander, etc. The Central Councils in turn sent delegates to a Grand Council for the state which was to meet at New Orleans under a Grand Commander, etc. There was also provision for a Supreme Council whenever five states had organized Grand Councils, but that point was probably never reached. No one ever publicly claimed to know who the Grand Commander for Louisiana was, but most of the speculation rested upon the founder, Colonel DeBlanc.[7] Most members and officers who testified later concerning the organization claimed (probably truthfully) that they were ignorant of its personnel and activities beyond their own neighboring localities. Higher officials in the order may have exercised no more power than in the Ku Klux Klan, although the relative peacefulness of the KWC may indicate a greater degree of discipline coming from above.

The Ku Klux Klan seems to have made its first appearances in Louisiana, as elsewhere, in March and April 1868. The Democratic press as usual played an important part in encouraging the organization, at least until the military authorities began to issue orders against it in other states.[8] There was little organized violence of a political character until shortly before the election, which occurred in April, and then it was restricted to a comparatively few places, chiefly in the northern part of the state. A Negro candidate for the legislature in Ouachita Parish was murdered just before the election, and in Claiborne parties of armed men perambulated the parish with notebooks and pencils, warning the blacks not to vote for the constitution and the Radical ticket on pain of death. They were also at the polls on election day, intimidating would-be Negro voters.[9] Elsewhere pre-election activity usually consisted of parading the streets and affixing warning notices on the doors of prominent Republicans. Alexandria offered the rare case of a sheriff and a posse of two hundred club-wielding Negroes putting the Klan to flight during one of these excursions.[10]

Radical victory in the state election brought increased violence and a more extensive organization among both the Ku Klux and the White Camellias. This activity continued through the summer and increased still further with the approach of the Presidential election in November.[11]

Virtually the whole state was affected, but conditions remained worst in the northern parishes. In Union Negroes were discharged by their employers after voting for the constitution, and whites began issuing "protection papers" promising immunity from attack to those freedmen who joined Democratic clubs or otherwise disavowed Republican political activity.[12] Beginning in May and continuing through the summer there were repeated reports of armed white bands—generally regarded as Ku Klux—committing systematic outrages, including many murders, on Negroes in Jackson, Morehouse, Richland, Bossier, Caddo, Franklin, and St. Landry parishes.[13] The same was true of Bienville Parish, where an active Negro Republican was dragged from his home, shot, and beheaded. The recent Republican candidate for sheriff there, a white man named Honneus, was shot and beaten; unlike most such cases, this one led to arrests if not convictions, and one of those charged was a Democratic candidate for the legislature.[14]

In Claiborne Parish William R. Meadows, a Negro member of the recent constitutional convention, was murdered by persons unknown on May 6, and W. Jasper Blackburn, the newly elected Republican Congressman from that district, delayed returning home from a trip to New Orleans when his life was openly threatened. The Klan warned the local Freedmen's Bureau agent to leave, and disguised bands prowled the countryside at night, outraging Negroes in their homes. Some were shot at as they worked in the fields, and even a few white men were afraid to cultivate their farms. A white man was whipped in Homer, the parish seat, on July 8. Then an organized mob destroyed the office of Blackburn's newspaper, the Homer *Iliad*. This title exaggerated the journal's worth and fame, but it was the only effective Republican voice in that part of the state.

The Negroes and white Republicans of Claiborne endured this terror for months. Local authorities were either indisposed or powerless to combat it, and the sheriff reported that there were parts of the parish where he dared not go because of threats on his life. Before its temporary demise the *Iliad* demanded to know why such activities were resorted to or tolerated. "Will any one point out to us a white Union man or a freedman who has harmed or offered violence to any one? Then why are these men dogged and hunted down to the death? Has justice fled this land? Is there no reason left?" Blackburn reported that every citizen he met on the street condemned the outrages, but if they were sincere the violence would end. In fact, he said, a majority of the white population condoned them. After the destruction of his paper a Republican pointed out that the terror was clearly organized and premeditated; it was politically inspired and most persons knew who was responsible. "These acts are not committed by persons of low standing in society, but by the sons of our wealthiest citizens, and the fathers look on with a smile of approval." At least at the beginning local whites in the parish seem to have shared the common hysterical fear that Negro and Republican organization presaged some kind of black revolt. But the terror continued after that fear abated, and political motivation was obvious from the fact that the victims were all Republicans.[15]

In New Orleans there was much less violence than upstate, but plenty of evidence of organization. Ten days after his election as governor Henry Clay Warmoth received a notice from the "Bloody Knights Klu [*sic*] Klux Klan," with the message: "Villain Beware Your doom is sealed—*Death* now awaites [*sic*] you."[16] More important, regular notices of KWC meetings began appearing in the New Orleans *Times* on May 1, and by the end of the month four Councils thus revealed their existence within the city. On June 30, the day before the new legislature was scheduled to assemble in New Orleans, a Democratic paper carried a notice for all KWC members to meet at their respective places. The next morning groups of armed men gathered at the Mechanics' Institute, where the legislature was due to meet, but police and federal troops surrounded the building and arrested some of the men, allowing the lawmakers to proceed with their organization.[17] Republicans remained in a state of alarm, however, as the cryptic announcements of KWC meetings continued to appear in the Democratic press. The New Orleans *Republican* quoted a "prominent Catholic priest" as saying that if the Republicans or any respectable and peace-loving citizens knew what he did, their hair would turn gray. " 'Ten thousand men can be drawn together at the tap of a bell,' said he; 'men organized in secret for purposes of assassination and murder, whose places of rendez-vous are in all parts of the city, and whose plans are terrible.' " On August 5 a priest was reported as saying that the Democrats were planning a massacre of leading Radicals in about two weeks and would stage a row among a small number of Negroes to serve as provocation. No such outbreak occurred at that time, but the idea bore a certain resemblance to riots which did take place in September and October. In reporting these rumors the *Republican* noted that the Democrats consistently opposed organizing a state militia or special constabulary or any strengthening of the police to prevent such events from coming to pass.[18]

The Democratic press in Louisiana played its familiar role as Klan apologist. In the spring it reported the order's expansion and carried stories of miraculous hooded apparitions, water drinking, and other high jinks, along with pointed warnings to Radicals.[19] But as atrocities came to be reported in the Republican papers, it began viewing the Ku Klux as a colossal hoax, or at least grossly exaggerated. As early as May 16 the New Orleans *Times* denied the existence of any such order, except as rural pranksters practiced foolish jokes on the freedmen "to keep them from stealing chickens and pigs in the night. . . . To this, and this alone, is due the existence of the frightful myth, the Ku Klux Klan." The *Picayune* agreed, quoting proverbs for the edification of frightened Republicans: "The wicked flee when no man pursueth," and "Guilty conscience is its own accuser." In August, after Governor Warmoth had reported 150 murders in a span of six weeks, the *Times* branded this "a willful Radical fabrication." It conceded that "disturbances have taken place in one or two of the interior parishes," but "staid communities of the North" had experienced disturbances equally violent and bloody. In a facetious story about bloody enormities committed by disguised men in the Teche country it specified by describing a raid upon a hen roost. But on August 13 the *Times* called seriously on Democrats to avoid violence which would give the Republicans an excuse to call in troops before the Presidential election.[20]

In the same fashion the Shreveport *South-Western,* which had virtually welcomed the Klan with open arms in April, was denying a reign of terror or even a widespread Ku Klux organization in that part of the state by the end of May. It deprecated the destruction of the Homer *Iliad* in July only because the Radicals would use this for political capital—unless, of course, the Radicals did the job themselves for that purpose. Almost by invitation a later issue carried a communication from Homer announcing that there was indeed much suspicion locally that the Republicans had pretended to destroy their own newspaper office. The composing stone had been broken, but it was still usable; the type had been pied and scattered about the office, but was recovered; damage to the press didn't amount to a dollar, and persons close to editor Blackburn were heard to say that the affair would put $5,000 or $10,000 in his pocket.[21] No further explanation or substantiation of this Republican plot was offered, but the story was there for Democrats who wanted to believe it. When Blackburn's office was mobbed and destroyed a second time in November the story was not revived; instead the Democratic paper in Homer had to defend itself for printing a supplement to the *Iliad,* carrying advertisements for which Blackburn was obligated by contract.[22]

The new government of Louisiana was beset by crisis at its inception. Hostile secret societies composed of the wealthiest and most respectable elements of the population were organizing against it throughout the state; armed mobs were trying with some success to intimidate it in New Orleans and were creating a reign of terror among Negroes and white Republicans in the northern parishes. Like the other deep South states, Louisiana had no large white loyalist element on which to rely for protection. The legislature authorized Governor Warmoth to organize a militia, but he declined to do so.[23] It would amount to arming one political party against the other, he explained, and he might have added more pertinently, arming the blacks against a white population which was already in a state of panic and near-rebellion over the specter of a Negro rising. The only immediate remedy for Ku Klux and other terrorism was more federal troops, especially after Warmoth failed to get a state constabulary or police force created. At the end of July he sent a special envoy to Washington armed with a formal legislative request for troops and a letter to President Johnson. This message described the state of affairs in Louisiana and revealed much of the nature, extent, and purposes of the KWC organization, which Warmoth had managed (by use of detectives) to penetrate in considerable measure. The alternative to troops, he said, would be confusion, disaster, and ruin to the state.[24] The next three or four months, culminating in the November elections, would go far to bear out his prophecy.

The Klan came to Arkansas too in March and April 1868. The Democratic press, and especially the *Arkansas Gazette* in Little Rock, paved its way with attacks on Radicalism and the Union League and with glowing accounts of the terror which the Klan was inspiring among Radicals in Tennessee. A *Gazette* article of March 18 dilated on the horrors of Brownlow's despotism in the Volunteer State and the attempts there "to enforce the political and social equality of the African." The Ku Klux Klan, it explained, "by taking advantage of the well-known superstitious fears of the negro," was effectively disrupting the Union League; but

we are inclined to regard this effect . . . as only an incident, and that the Klan is bent upon a much more earnest purpose than keeping the negro loyal leaguers close to home after night fall. . . . We take it . . . that this organization proposes something towards the ultimate relief of the state, and when the proper time comes the members will be prepared for a concentrated movement in the right direction.

Ordinarily, the *Gazette* continued, it deplored secret political organizations. But circumstances alter cases. "The radical party throughout the south is a sworn secret organization, and owing to this it has been able to manipulate the ignorant and superstitious negroes and vote them as one man." Democrats certainly were justified, therefore, in fighting this kind of fire with fire of their own. "It has always been and ever will be that where despotism bears cruel sway men will unite themselves for resistance to it and be prepared to avail themselves of opportunities that may offer to overthrow it. The state that is afflicted with the rule of its *canaille* must expect to be disturbed by conflicts." The necessity of secret organizations would disappear only when "a free and just government of the white race" was restored to Tennessee and the South. More immediately, the *Gazette* implied that adoption of the proposed Radical constitution of Arkansas would invite the organization of the Ku Klux Klan there too.[25]

That is what happened. After a campaign in which Democrats were accused of terrorism and Republicans of fraud, the constitution was carried and Republicans were elected to office in overwhelming numbers. The Klan made its first appearance in the state a few days later. Its notices were posted on street corners in Little Rock on April 2, stating that the order had just been established there and openly announcing a meeting that night "at their Grotto, on Beaver Avenue." Similar notices appeared soon afterward in Pine Bluff and Batesville.[26] In Batesville the Democratic *North Arkansas Times* had paved the way with attacks on the Loyal Leagues and an enthusiastic announcement of Ku Klux progress. In presenting the first local Klan notice (which was virtually unintelligible) the editor commented, "The perusal of the document makes one's blood run cold. We shut our eyes as we put it in type."[27]

Like many other Conservative papers at the time of the Klan's introduction, the *Times* was unsure how to handle the subject. After another week the editor had second thoughts. Printing both the ritual of the Union League and a Brownlow editorial from the Knoxville *Whig* attacking the Ku Klux Klan, he now deprecated secret political societies in general, pointing out that historically such organizations had been penetrated by "bad men" and perverted to their own "selfish and ambitious purposes." Although he had earlier taken the Klan seriously enough to report its activities in Tennessee and to imply strongly that it might be a blessing to Arkansas, he now claimed to know nothing of the organization,

save a few ridiculous notices and manifestoes, which we supposed were intended as mere burlesques. But we meet with those who profess to believe there is such an organization, and who insist that there is a necessity for it; that it has become necessary to fight the devil with fire; that the radicals have their secret political societies, and to counteract their bad influences the people should fight them with their own weapons. We do not acknowledge that mode of reasoning as sound. If it is wrong for the radicals to have secret political societies, it is equally wrong for the conservatives to have them. We see no reason why a good, peaceable and orderly citizen should connect himself with any such organizations.[28]

Conversions of this sort were not common. The *Gazette* declared on May 15, "There is no evidence that the Klan has a member within the borders of our state," but next day it carried a notice of a Klan meeting in Little Rock.[29]

The Klan continued to spread, reaching Fort Smith by April 23[30] and Arkadelphia a month later. An Arkadelphia newspaper reported mysterious skeletal apparitions there, ranging from three to twelve feet high, dressed in black or white. One appeared to be using a human backbone as a walking stick, others were seen carrying their heads in their hands, and some inevitably were thirsty, drinking a barrel of rain water and five buckets from the well. So far they had done no damage and made no threats.[31] Before the end of May, General C. H. Smith, the federal commander in Arkansas, reported: "The Ku Klux Klan serve their mysterious notices and make their midnight rounds" throughout much of the state.[32]

As usual, little is known of Klan organization, especially at the upper levels. One John McCauley of Searcy confessed in 1870 to having joined the Klan there in April 1868; the den had just been organized, and he understood it to be the first in the state. The Klan was characterized to him at the time as a political and military organization opposed to the new Reconstruction regime and devoted to doing justice (as they conceived it), even if this meant killing some people. The Grand Giant of the county was Colonel Jacob Frolich, editor of the pro-Klan Searcy *Record*. His superior, the Grand Titan of that congressional district, was General Dandridge McRae. As McRae's adjutant general, McCauley helped to organize other dens in White, Jackson, and Independence counties, northeast of Little Rock. Operating activities of McCauley's den were discussed by the members first, and if the death penalty was recommended it was referred to the Grand Cyclops and a committee of five for decision. If the decision was made to kill someone, a party was delegated to do the job and the identity of these persons might not be known to the members as a whole.[33]

McCauley believed that there was no state chief in Arkansas, although General Robert Glenn Shaver of Jackson County claimed many years later to have held that position. Both McCauley and Shaver recognized General

Forrest as Grand Wizard. McCauley believed the Klan to have numbered 7,000 in his congressional district, while Shaver, by no means a reliable witness when he was interviewed by a newspaper reporter in 1911, boasted that he had 15,000 armed men in Arkansas ready to assemble at his call. Shaver claimed to have initiated a number of persons, such as telegraph operators, whose services would have been invaluable in case of emergency. In similar fashion he referred to secret monthly meetings of the Grand Dragons, or state commanders, in Memphis, at which Klan policies were prepared and activities directed. He recalled mobilizing an army of 2,000 to 10,000 men near Little Rock on one occasion, for the purpose of capturing "the legislature, the supreme court and the entire carpetbag government. I had my foot in the stirrup; in another moment I'd have been in the saddle and away. Just in time to stop us there came a message from Gen. Forrest ordering a postponement of the movement and calling me to Memphis." There is not a particle of evidence to substantiate this story, and it is incredible that a moblization of several thousand men should have gone unnoticed at the time. But by 1911 the Klan had entered the realm of legend, and people said and believed what they wanted to say and believe about it.[34]

The Knights of the White Camellia also existed in southern Arkansas and in Little Rock, but they were either totally inactive or their doings were never credited to them by name.[35]

The Klan's actual work was more prosaic and more sordid than General Shaver's romantic recollection. As elsewhere, it consisted essentially of threats and small-scale violence. The latter was usually directed against Negroes and consequently gained less publicity and evoked rather less indignation than when the victims were white Republicans. In Woodruff County a Negro named Blufkins, imprisoned for vagrancy, was taken from jail and hanged by the Klan in May, while a Negro man and woman were taken from their home and each whipped 200 lashes. Their employer was accused of participating in the attack because he feared they were about to leave his employ.[36] Conditions grew progressively worse through the summer, with the southern and southwestern counties perhaps exhibiting the greatest lawlessness. (These counties were adjacent to the most troubled regions in both Louisiana and Texas.) In August Ku Klux bands were reported patrolling the southern part of Bradley County every night, riding up to the homes of peaceable citizens and shooting into them promiscuously. At the same time Union men of Columbia County were fleeing to the woods to evade prowling bands of armed men. A legislator from this county wrote Governor Powell Clayton on August 29 that ten Negroes had been murdered in the past twenty days, and men refused the sheriff's summons to join a posse to pursue the criminals. Civil law, he said, was utterly unable to cope with the situation. Lewisville, Lafayette County, was another center of terrorism. Seven blacks and one white Unionist were reported murdered within four miles of town on a single day in August, and the total was said to be twenty within a ten-mile radius between July 14 and August 28. One man, positively identified by a Negro woman as the person who had killed her husband in cold blood, rode into town at the head of an armed squad of twenty-five men and surrendered himself for a preliminary hearing; his followers proceded to swear alibis for him, securing his discharge; when the decision was announced they raised a cheer and rode off together. Altogether, it was said, fifty to seventy-five persons of both races in that county were either living in the woods or had been driven away entirely.[37]

In Crittenden County, at the opposite corner of the state and adjacent to Memphis, the Klan was as highly organized as anywhere in Arkansas. According to Captain E. G. Barker, the local Freedmen's Bureau agent, it consisted of about ninety men, well armed, who intended to take over the county by systematic assassination of the leading Republicans. By the end of August they had shot and wounded Barker himself and a leading Negro.[38] In later months Crittenden would prove to be the most persistent center of Klan activity in Arkansas. In neighboring Mississippi County "a gang of lawless desperadoes" who may or may not have been Klansmen murdered Dr. A. M. Johnson, a member of the legislature, on August 26. They also killed six freedmen by September 20, to say nothing of others assaulted, wounded, and driven from their homes. Up to that point, the county officials had been prevented by the terror from even taking office.[39] In Independence County twenty-five disguised men made a nocturnal raid on some Negroes who had just been mustered into the militia, driving them from their houses and shooting at them.[40] And in White County John McCauley's Searcy Klan murdered one Ban Humphries, a Negro Republican leader, and attempted to kill state senator Stephen Wheeler. In the Humphries case the Democratic press tried to blame the Loyal League for the crime, trumping up a motive to suit the case.[41]

When it became obvious that the local authorities could not cope with the situation, federal troops were called for. General Smith wrote as early as May that he was doing what he could with the forces at his disposal. "Troops are stationed at 23 different points in the State, but even that number of stations fails to cover all the ground." His only suggestion was to institute martial law.[42] When the soldiers made arrests for Ku Klux activity they exposed themselves to a barrage of criticism from Democratic newspapers, and their very arrival in a community was often resented by local citizens.[43] And once the new state government was recognized in Washington the military lost jurisdiction and was limited to providing such aid as local authorities requested.

For this reason Republicans looked forward to the establishment of a state guard or militia as soon as the new government was organized. The very existence of a militia might be beneficial, the Little Rock *Republican* observed, even if it was not used.[44] In his inaugural address and first legislative message, early in July, Governor Powell Clayton advanced this as one of the first and most pressing items of business; once a militia was provided for, he gave notice of his intention to use it if necessary.[45] The legislature promptly complied, and thus armed, the governor proceeded at once to organize a volunteer militia, beginning in the troubled southwestern region, where a cavalry regiment consisting of ten white and two Negro companies was ready for action by August 27.[46] On that date he issued a proclamation calling attention to depredations committed on Conway, Perry, and Columbia counties by bands of armed men who had over-powered the civil authorities and driven citizens from their homes; he referred also to murders and attempted murders in other counties where conditions were as bad or worse. After calling on all citizens to keep the peace and armed bands to disperse, Clayton announced his intention to enroll and organize a reserve militia as well, and to use every power at his disposal to restore order.[47] Unlike the deep South governors, he had a substantial body of white Union men on whom he could rely for military duty. Such men were to be found throughout most of the state, but particularly in the Ozark region of northwest Arkansas.

Mobilization proceeded throughout the state. Democrats, who chose to ignore the multiplying atrocities which had led to this policy, furiously accused the governor of establishing a military despotism. They employed both the carrot and the stick in efforts to reverse the policy. A militia captain at Augusta, northeast of Little Rock, reported that when he was enrolling men two leading Democrats had come to him with an offer to be personally responsible to the civil authorities for peace and order, if he would discontinue organizing the militia. Otherwise they would resist his activity and take physical reprisals on every militiaman he enrolled.[48] Threats and violence actually increased in intensity around the state as the fall election campaign approached. Governor Clayton continued to enroll the militia, but for the present made no effort to employ it.

Difficult as conditions were in Louisiana and Arkansas, those states were almost subdued by comparison with Texas—or large parts of it. Individual violence and mob violence, organized and unorganized, premeditated and unpremeditated, had been endemic in the Lone Star State for years. General Philip Sheridan, who commanded here in 1867, declared that if he owned both Texas and Hell he would rent out Texas and move to Hell.

The homicide rate, already high, went up sharply with the advent of Radical Reconstruction, leading the state constitutional convention to create a special committee to investigate lawlessness and violence. Apart from innumerable assaults with intent to kill, rapes, robberies, whippings of freedmen, and other crimes of violence, it reported that up to July 1, 1868, on the basis of incomplete reports, 1,035 homicides had been committed since the end of the war; one-third of these were inflicted in 1867 and another third in the first six months of 1868. Although whites outnumbered Negroes in Texas by about three to one, nearly half of the victims were freedmen. So far as the perpetrators of these murders were identified by race, whites had committed 833 of them and Negroes only 58.

Of course many of these killings grew out of private quarrels or were committed for purposes of robbery, often by bandits who infested the highways in some areas. Many others, however, had racial and political causes. As the two races were about equally armed, man for man, the committee argued that purely personal altercations between Negroes and whites would have resulted in a more nearly equal mortality, while the extreme poverty of the freedmen rendered it unlikely that many of them were killed as robbery victims. Moreover, there was evidence that a very large proportion of the whites murdered were Union men, and that bands of ex-rebels were organized in several sections of the state for the specific purpose of intimidating if not killing white Unionists and freedmen.

The number of prosecutions for these crimes was negligible, and only one legal execution had taken place, that of a Negro in Harris County. In twenty-five or thirty counties, the committee reported, these combinations of lawless men were too strong for the civil authorities to handle, and openly defied them. County officials themselves were implicated in violence in some places, one sheriff being identified as the leader of a band of desperadoes who had committed numerous outrages, including murder, on loyal whites and blacks in his county. Most of the local officials throughout the state were at this point Conservatives who had been elected in 1866 or appointed by a Conservative governor prior to July 1867. The committee (itself strongly Republican) accused the courts and law enforcement officials of simply refusing to proceed against ex-Confederates for offenses against loyalists and freedmen, who consequently abandoned any hope of legal justice. And even where law officers tried to do their duty they were not sustained by public opinion; one Republican sheriff who called upon citizens to help him make arrests was refused and told to "Call on your nigger friends."[49]

The committee's report was highly political in character, but it could hardly have been otherwise. Conservatives in many parts of the state were clearly implicated in a terrorist campaign aimed at Negroes and white Republicans. The Democratic press often participated or led the way, encouraging violence in cases of high excitement or wherever there was political advantage to be gained by it. The Houston *Telegraph* on July 14 specifically referred to Judge Charles Caldwell and Morgan C. Hamilton, Radical leaders, as fitting objects of lynch law: "We say it solemnly, such men ought to die."[50]

The major findings of the committee are amply substantiated by outside evidence in addition to that which it compiled itself. The Freedmen's Bureau agent in Trinity County reported of his jurisdiction in April 1868: "The whole community is armed and every man ready to kill his neighbour, or commence a war of extermination against all enemies, fancied or real. The Civil Authorities are really *afraid* to act. Life and property is not secure. The evil disposed rule by intimidation."[51] Four years later a United States district attorney recalled: "In 1868, almost the entire State was a hell on earth, and in the northern half of the State hardly a white man, who was obnoxious on account of his politics, escaped being driven from his home, or suffering persecution of some kind. As for the freed people, they were robbed, outraged, and intimidated systematically, almost everywhere, except in some of the larger towns garrisoned by United States troops."[52] Part of the committee's evidence was of the most direct kind possible. Its chairman, Justice Charles Caldwell of the state supreme court, was (rather improperly) an active Republican who more than once fled Democratic mobs to save his life. One example his committee cited was probably based on an episode at Marshall, in northeast Texas, in December 1867, when a Democratic mob led by the sheriff and chief of police disrupted a Republican meeting Caldwell was attending and forced him to take refuge with the local Army garrison.[53]

The Ku Klux Klan did not create these conditions, nor was it responsible for most of the crime. Rather it was an added ingredient which helped to give the violence its increasingly political flavor. One of the Klan's first recorded appearances was at Marshall, in April 1868. A local Democratic newspaper had already given favorable attention to its doings in Tennessee and had noted its arrival at Shreveport, Louisiana, only forty miles away. The editor claimed to know nothing about the Klan's organization or purpose, but he had a good opinion of it nonetheless. "From the demonstrations that it has made elsewhere, we are compelled to confess that it is widespread and powerful, and arbitrates to itself the swift and terrible punishment of crime. It will doubtless develop itself as occasion demands."[54] The order spread quickly to many parts of the state, reaching (among other places) Paris, Columbus, Palestine, and Navasota by the end of April, Clarksville and Bryan in May, and Bell County, between Austin and Waco, by June.[55] South Texas—San Antonio and below—was the only substantial part of the state as then inhabited which the Klan did not reach; most of the territory west of Austin was still Indian country.

Republicans living along the Comanche frontier were perhaps safer than

those farther east. Some Texas Klansmen confined themselves to masquerading as ghosts and drinking quantities of water, but many others did
not.[56] Their debut at Clarksville was marked by an attack on a Negro
school party.[57] Members at Columbus, between Austin and Houston, told
in later years of their work in hanging a native white man and a "big
octoroon from up North" who were preaching racial equality. This den
operated in both Fayette and Colorado counties, with the members from
one county performing nocturnal duties in the other.[58] At Millican in
Brazos County, Negroes fired into a party of about fifteen Ku Klux who
were marching through town to intimidate them. Fearing retaliation, the
freedmen formed a military company and began drilling. This alarmed the
white population, who asked the Freedmen's Bureau agent to stop it. He
did so after they promised to put an end to Ku Klux incursions. This truce
broke down a few weeks later, however, and interracial clashes continued,
with blacks suffering all the fatalities.[59]

Unquestionably the most lawless part of the state, and the area of
greatest Klan activity, was the northeastern section, adjacent to troubled
portions of Arkansas and Louisiana. Although the Klan had made one of
its first appearances in Marshall, that town possessed a small Army garrison
and soon became a haven for refugees from all over the region. Captain T.
M. K. Smith, the Bureau agent in Marshall, reported in June that Klan
depredations at Gilmer, in Upshur County, had driven the blacks there into
sleeping in the woods at night. Most of the white community was implicated at least indirectly in Ku Klux activity, he said, and the situation was
not much different in other counties. "Freedmen flying for their lives are
continually coming to this place, having been driven from their homes and
forced to give up their crops, and leave their families to the tender mercies
of these lawless ruffians. Titus, Panola, Rusk, and Upshur [counties] have
all been represented." In most cases the victims gave political motives for
the attacks,[60] but Smith discovered an apparent arrangement by which the
Ku Klux drove freedmen from their homes and crops at the request of
planters, enabling the latter "to reap the fruits of their labor." In several
instances, he added, the blacks "have been fearfully mutilated, and in many
cases shot at repeatedly." The Red River counties were repeatedly invaded
by armed desperadoes, who "kill negroes from the pure love of killing."[61]

Many of these bands operated without disguise and could not fairly be
described as Ku Klux, although it was often a fine line distinguishing them.
One of the most dangerous was the notorious Bickerstaff gang, who dealt
in general banditry but specialized in horse stealing. This gang virtually
took over Hopkins County and its town of Sulphur Springs in July, attacking and robbing an Army wagon train in broad daylight within sight of
town. Although they operated against all likely victims, most of those they
murdered were freedmen and Unionists.[62]

Bad as conditions were in northeast Texas generally, the worst trouble spot of all was Jefferson and surrounding Marion County, just north of Marshall and near the Louisiana line. With several thousand people, Jefferson in 1868 was the metropolis of northeast Texas. It lay on a tributary of the Red River, marking for practical purposes the head of navigation on that stream, and was thus a marketing center for a very large area.[63] A New York *Tribune* correspondent described it as a frontier town in 1869, with few redeeming features: "The *tout ensemble* of the place is anything but agreeable. The streets are not paved, and are always knee-deep with mud, except when the dust sweeps through them in blinding clouds. The city has almost ten thousand inhabitants, several churches, a rum shop every few doors, gambling hells in abundance, and many other abodes of vice, but no common schools."[64]

The region around Jefferson was rich agriculturally, and a little more than half of the county's population consisted of recently emancipated slaves. The white minority were distinctly unhappy at the implications of Radical Reconstruction; they were particularly nervous about the Union League, at whose meetings the most incendiary doctrines were supposedly preached to the gullible freedmen. By February 1868 Negroes were in fact attending League meetings under arms, in violation of municipal law, perhaps because of prior threats by the whites. As everywhere, this practice redoubled white fears, and one of the local Democratic papers even called for troops to prevent a collision.[65] At the end of April a new newspaper appeared, called the *Ultra Ku Klux,* but this was a publicity trick which failed to win over many subscribers, and the paper soon died.[66]

Just when the local equivalent of the Ku Klux first organized in Jefferson is unknown. But by the end of June the constitutional convention's committee on lawlessness reported that "bands of armed whites" were traversing Marion County, "forcibly robbing the freedmen of their arms and committing other outrages upon them."[67] Whites coupled violence with other common devices to immobilize the freedmen politically. They organized a Conservative Club of Marion County and induced Negroes to join by offering them certificates guaranteeing protection against violence as well as "a preference in all cases where employment is to be given or favors bestowed by members of the Club or Conservative party." Club members voted at the same time neither to employ Radicals nor to patronize anyone who did.[68] These carrot-and-stick tactics were effective with a limited number of freedmen. In August the *Jimplecute* (the chief Conservative organ in Jefferson) carried a card signed by fifty-seven Negroes, announcing that their interests and those of their children required that they "stick to their old-time friends, the white people of the South"; if they voted at all, therefore, they would vote Democratic.[69]

The community was on edge, with Republicans and especially Negroes in an advanced state of intimidation, while Democrats feared that every Negro gathering portended another Santo Domingo. All this came to a head when the Republicans held a celebration on the Fourth of July. A white Democrat attended the gathering and became involved in a shooting affray. At least 300 whites quickly assembled and took possession of the city, armed with shotguns and six-shooters. Some picketed the roads leading into town and others stationed themselves in the streets, while squads of horsemen rode about arresting or shooting Negroes and threatening to hang any white Republicans they found. The latter saved themselves by hiding, but many blacks were rounded up and jailed on a charge of inciting insurrection.[70] This crisis passed, but the pre-existing terror continued, with Negroes being outraged and killed.

The city officials in Jefferson were all Democrats (chosen before Negro suffrage) and, like the white population generally, in sympathy with much of the white terrorism. Governor Elisha Pease, a Republican whom the military had appointed to office in 1867, thus found himself bombarded with pleas for help from persecuted loyalists there, and he accordingly requested troops to prevent any further shootdowns.[71] What Texas required at this time was cavalry detachments stationed in perhaps half the county seats in the state, as well as facing the Indians. But there were no more than 5,000 troops stationed in Texas, three-quarters of whom were on frontier duty,[72] and most of those available for occupation work were infantry. When troops finally did arrive in Jefferson, therefore, they were infantry, and they had almost no effect outside the city. Squads of eight or ten Klansmen continued to prowl the countryside *en masque* almost every night.[73] Most of the Klansmen lived in the city, where they were described as primarily the "young drinking and reckless men about town." Their identity was generally known by "respectable citizens," who encouraged and approved of them. They held their meetings in town without any obstruction (since these were not of themselves illegal), and the meetings were even reported in the newspapers. The organization to which they belonged was a local one, with no apparent relationship outside the area. These Knights of the Rising Sun, as they called themselves, would continue to see activity well into the fall of 1868.[74]

Local and independent organization of this character was probably typical in the state. W. D. Wood, a former Klansman in Leon County, wrote later in life that his group had formed independently of any other, based on newspaper descriptions of the Klan in other states. Eight or ten men thus associated on their own initiative in order to repress Negro lawlessness, real or imaginary, which they claimed was causing great annoyance and alarm to white women and children. Wood did not know whether the Ku Klux proper, under General Forrest, ever penetrated Texas at all.[75] Later mythmakers ascribed a greater organization to the Klan than it ever possessed and named the future Senator Roger Q. Mills as the state commander,[76] but there is no evidence to support this claim, or even to link any of the Texas Klans with outside groups. The Knights of the White Camellia organized in Houston and perhaps elsewhere in the state. As in New Orleans, they advertised their meetings in the newspapers—this was in 1869—but they seem not to have engaged in violence.[77]

News of the Ku Klux Klan and its activity was not long in reaching the North. As early as April 7, 1868, New York lawyer George Templeton Strong recorded in his diary that the Klan seemed busy in various parts of the South. "The vocation of these chivalric creatures," he was already informed, "is to go about nocturnally in large parties, masked and disguised, shooting inconvenient niggers and uncomfortable Union men. Southern papers applaud and encourage them in a guarded and semi-ironical way."[78] The Northern press was only a degree less divided along party lines than the Southern in its attitude toward the Klan. Democratic papers repeatedly tended to extenuate or palliate Ku Klux activities. The New York *Herald,* one of the few papers of the time which sat on the fence politically, in this case followed the Democratic line of equating the Klan with the Union League. The League, it said, was just as pernicious; it committed outrages itself (which the *Herald* did not specify), and its Negro members aimed "to reduce the whites of the South to political vassalage." There should be no racial or class discrimination in the South, the *Herald* observed smugly, and it advised suppressing both organizations impartially.[79]

Republicans saw less parallel between the two orders and all but unanimously damned the Klan. As long as Southern states remained under Army jurisdiction they sanctioned military authority to suppress Klan terrorism. But once the military was superseded Republicans inclined to leave law enforcement to the new state governments. Murder, robbery, assault and battery, trespass, and other Klan activities were after all matters of state jurisdiction within our federal system, and even Radical Republicans saw limits to what the federal government might validly do to enforce state law. Only gradually did it appear that conditions in the South made it almost impossible for state and local authorities to cope with the Klan, thus rendering federal intervention imperative. Northern Democrats almost never came to this realization, lending their militant Southern brethren the support of silent acquiescence and often much more. Republicans seldom demanded federal intervention before the fall of 1868. By that time the nature and extent of the Ku Klux conspiracy were evident for all who cared to see.

Meanwhile Southern Republicans had to carry on as best they could. They obtained troops for some of the worst areas, but these soldiers brought only a marginal benefit. They often arrived too late, were too few in number, and were infantry when cavalry was required. Above all, they were legally impotent without the active cooperation of local authorities who either could not or would not act. In most of the Southern states these conditions were to grow much worse before they got better.

Part III

THE KLAN FAILS TO
ELECT A PRESIDENT, 1868

CHAPTER 7

The Southeast and Kentucky

The Presidential campaign of 1868 found the Democratic and Republican parties squarely opposed on the Southern question. The Republicans nominated General Grant, with Schuyler Colfax of Indiana as his running mate, and firmly endorsed the Congressional plan of Reconstruction. The platform went on to declare that the federal government had a duty to sustain the new state constitutions and prevent a return of "anarchy or military rule" in the South. The Democrats, on the other hand, called for immediate restoration of all Southern states, abolition of the Freedmen's Bureau, and no further federal regulations on suffrage. Concerning the treatment of ex-Confederates, the Democrats called for a full amnesty, while Republicans favored a removal of disqualifications only "in the same measure as the spirit of disloyalty will die out, and as may be consistent with the safety of the loyal people."[1] The Democratic candidates for President and Vice President were Governor Horatio Seymour of New York and Senator Frank Blair of Missouri.

The Ku Klux Klan played an important part in the campaign in most Southern states. Although its operations always included vigilante activity not directly concerned with the election, the political aspect was central. In the spring and summer the Klan had appeared in countless localities, urban and rural; now it tended to die out in the cities (Memphis and New Orleans were exceptions) but spread to new areas, chiefly in the small towns and countryside.[2]

In the South Atlantic states the Klan showed signs of increasing organization at the local level everywhere except Virginia. In North Carolina the White Brotherhood, the Invisible Empire, and the Constitutional Union Guard all expanded and acquired new members independently of one another. The Invisible Empire, affiliated with organizations in the neighboring South Carolina upcountry, spread through several counties west of Charlotte during the fall. At the same time the White Brotherhood expanded from Guilford to adjacent Alamance County in the upper Piedmont. In Alamance it developed alongside the Constitutional Union Guard, which was forming also in Sampson County far to the southeast.[3] There were reports of unspecified Ku Klux-type organization and activity in Wake, Moore, and Granville counties near the center of the state, and in Stokes County to the northwest.[4]

Locally prominent men took an active part in this movement, often to their later discomfiture. Apart from Hamilton C. Jones and William L. Saunders, mentioned earlier, John C. Gorman, later editor of the Raleigh *Telegram,* was later identified as an organizer of the White Brotherhood during the 1868 campaign. He and other leaders contemplated no violence, and very little was committed at that time; when it was, later, he and others dropped out.[5] At the same time many leaders did condone violence. One Democratic campaigner, in a speech at Oxford in October, promised to stop the Ku Klux if Republicans would dissolve the Union League; otherwise the Klan, which was beating and shooting Negroes in that vicinity, would go on.[6]

Nearly all members regarded the Klan (to use the generic term) as a secret political society in behalf of the Democratic party. Often they saw the deterrence or suppression of Negro crime, whether or not sponsored by the Union League, as another objective, but distinctly subsidiary. Surface appearances and observations of outsiders also pointed to the Klan movement as predominantly political. Most of the Klan's depredations at this time were apparently intended to deter their victims from voting, or supporting the Union League, or exerting their political influence in behalf of the Republican party. Apart from its outrages on Negroes around Oxford, the Klan rode through parts of Guilford County in October, calling persons from their homes in the night and threatening death to any who cast Republican ballots.[7] There were scattered reports of similar activity elsewhere before the election, and doubtless some of it went unreported.

At least as worrisome to Governor William W. Holden and the state administration was the news early in October that several hundred repeating rifles had been imported into the state and distributed to "Seymour and Blair Clubs" and "K.K.K.'s" around Wilmington, New Bern, and Charlotte.[8] Accordingly the governor issued a proclamation warning against any attempt to subvert the government or the civil rights of citizens by force.[9]

Despite the reports and warnings, terrorism failed to assume major proportions in the state this fall. Democrats made no effort at an armed insurrection, and the Klan played a very small role in the campaign. Partially for this reason, perhaps, North Carolina went Republican by a safe majority.

Ku Klux activity was greater in South Carolina, but it was restricted almost entirely to twelve northwestern counties in which the balance between races and parties was more equal than elsewhere in the state. A little of the terrorism was directed at white Republicans in the mountain districts of Oconee, Pickens, Greenville, and Spartanburg counties, but Negroes were the chief target. The earlier Klan organization in this part of the state was extended and intensified during the fall campaign. As elsewhere, there was some talk of defensive organization against a possible Negro rising—this stimulated a continuing growth of the rifle clubs and led them to import repeating rifles as in North Carolina—but the Klan itself was universally regarded as a Democratic political device. It was still impossible to draw a distinct line between the Klan, the rifle clubs, and Democratic clubs. A former Klansman in Abbeville County testified that the Democratic clubs there had secret committees which were in effect Ku Klux Klans. They did most of the work of intimidation and violence, sometimes in daylight and without disguise, and were affiliated with similar organizations that he knew of in Edgefield and Laurens counties.[10]

Whatever the degree of affiliation between these units, their operations were remarkably similar from one end of the region to the other. Beginning two or three weeks before the November 3 election, armed bands of disguised men rode through the countryside after dark, making the rounds of Negro cabins. Sometimes they fired shots into the houses as they rode by; at other places they called out the inmates and threatened them with the extreme penalty if they voted the Republican ticket. Those who possessed Republican ballots for distribution to voters on election day (following the general practice of the period) were sometimes raided and the ballots confiscated. In many cases the Klan administered beatings and in some they committed murder. This night riding was more intensive in some counties than in others, but it was most concentrated in the nights just preceding the election. Negroes in some areas took to the woods at night to avoid attack, and some fled the state. More prominent individuals were apt to find coffins marked K.K.K. deposited on their doorsteps, often with attached notes warning them to leave the county if they valued their lives. In addition, Republicans encountered a great deal of general harassment and intimidation on the streets as they went about their daily activities.[11]

In Abbeville, still the worst county in this respect, harassment extended to the political assassination of two legislators. One of these, James Martin, was a white man, but the more prominent was state senator B. F. Randolph of Orangeburg, a mulatto who had come south as chaplain to a Negro regiment in 1864, and later led in the establishment of both Negro schools and Union Leagues. Randolph had a large black following and was one of the ablest and most influential Republicans in the state.[12] He was gunned down on a railway station platform near Cokesbury on October 1 by three members of the Democratic secret committee, alias the Klan. The shooting took place in broad daylight in the presence of many witnesses, but the three were allowed to mount their horses and ride off undisturbed, leaving a supporting party behind to cover their retreat if that had been necessary. One of the murderers later confessed, saying, rightly or wrongly, that nearly all the Democrats in the county were Klansmen.[13] Moreover, Colonel D. Wyatt Aiken, the most prominent Democrat in the county and later a Congressman and leader of the South Carolina Grange movement, was perpetually instigating violence. He had previously counseled the Democrats of nearby Anderson County to dig Randolph's grave if he dared come in their midst.[14]

Efforts by the state government to counter the terrorism were too little and too late. The new state constabulary sent officers into the affected counties, and in October the chief constable tried to recruit thirty to fifty more in New York City. (He called for "desperate" types "that will bring a man if they are sent for him if they have to face the devil to get him.") But conditions demanded many more such men than he could recruit or find funds to pay for.[15] The legislature in September passed a law empowering the governor to use militia whenever unlawful assemblages or rebellion made it impossible to maintain order by normal means.[16] Although Governor Scott issued a proclamation two weeks before the election, threatening to call out the militia if necessary, that drastic resort might well have provoked more rebellion than it subdued.[17] Nearly all trustworthy militiamen would have had to be Negroes, and the state had no guns to compare with the Democratic clubs' new supply of Winchester repeating rifles. "It would have been folly," Scott later explained, "to have placed inexperienced and unarmed men against organized and disciplined ex-Confederate soldiers, armed with the most approved weapons known to modern warfare. . . ."[18] His only remaining alternative was to call for more federal troops, which he did at the end of September. As always, the Army had too few men available and operated under too great a legal handicap to perform the job adequately. The seven infantry companies distributed among as many upcountry counties in October provided almost no relief from Ku Klux activity outside of the towns in which they were stationed.[19]

As a result, there was little abatement of the terror. On election day, November 3, white Conservatives from Abbeville and Edgefield near the Georgia line to Rock Hill near the North Carolina border staged a concerted campaign to exclude Negroes forcibly from the polls. Large bodies of armed and belligerent men—Klansmen and members of the Democratic clubs—gathered in front of the polling places and remained there throughout the day. Thousands of Negroes who were brave enough to come out at all after the previous night riding were subjected to further threats and physically prevented from approaching the ballot boxes. The result was a remarkable political transformation. Democrats, who had lost most of these counties in the April state elections, now carried them for Seymour and elected two Congressmen. In Abbeville County less than a fifth of the registered Negroes cast ballots, in Anderson and Laurens counties about half.[20]

The Democratic press had remained silent as a ghost concerning the Ku Klux Klan and its activities. The Charleston *Daily News,* far from the conflict, continued its attacks on terrorism,[21] but other Democratic papers, like the Columbia *Phoenix,* reserved mention of the name Ku Klux Klan for crimes of violence committed by Negroes or Northerners. Republicans contested the outcome of the Congressional races, and months later formal investigations revealed facts sufficient to seat the Republican contenders.

The fall saw a scattering of Ku Klux activity around Georgia,[22] and there was a good deal of violence directed at Negroes and white Republicans which was not traceable to the Klan. The Freedmen's Bureau reported 142 major outrages in the state from August through October. This figure included 31 killings, 43 shootings, 5 stabbings, 55 beatings, and 8 whippings of 300 to 500 lashes apiece.[23] As with most such tabulations, it probably omitted a great number of equal or lesser assaults which were never reported or tabulated. The most spectacular incident was the so-called Camilla riot of September 19. A scheduled Republican rally had drawn a crowd of Negroes to that small south Georgia town, and as they mistrusted the local whites, many came armed. This in turn frightened the white townspeople, who formed an armed posse under the sheriff. Shooting broke out in very short order, initiated by a drunken white man, but after a few minutes the Negroes gave it up and fled into the nearby woods. The whites pursued them and according to some reports spent the rest of the day methodically hunting down and shooting black men. When it ended at least seven Negroes were dead and thirty or forty wounded, as against six white men slightly wounded.[24]

Most of the Ku Klux Klan activity was centered far away in the eastern part of the state (adjacent to the Abbeville-Edgefield part of South Carolina) where the greatest organization had occurred earlier in the year. In Oglethorpe County John C. Reed led his Klansmen on a nocturnal parade shortly before election day. Slowly and solemnly, he says, they passed and repassed through the most heavily Negro part of the county. Coming upon a Negro church while a service was being held inside, they circled the building, moaning loudly for water; according to Reed's account the worshipers rushed outside in a panic and fled. The Klan also stopped at white men's houses, where they were cheered as they announced through speaking trumpets that these dead Confederate soldiers would stay around until Negro and scalawag domination had passed from the land.[25] Reed made no mention of violence, and he claimed that this was the Klan's first demonstration, but at least two weeks earlier the local Freedmen's Bureau agent had reported a Negro taken from his bed at night and abused by the KKK.[26]

There was violence aplenty in other counties nearby. Virtually every night prior to the election the Klan rode out in parts of Richmond, Warren, Columbia, Lincoln, and Greene counties (if not others) searching for guns among the freedmen, whipping, and threatening death to any who voted Republican. Occasionally they refused to wait for that eventuality. In Warren, the worst county of all, they committed a number of murders and to all intents and purposes took over the county—a story to be told in a later chapter.[27]

The state government did almost nothing to combat this terrorism. In September Governor Rufus B. Bullock issued a proclamation, at the legislature's request, forbidding organization and drilling by unauthorized bands of armed men. He followed this with another, commanding sheriffs and other local officials to do their duty in maintaining the peace, but the few who seriously tried to do so, like Sheriff John C. Norris of Warren County, took their lives in their hands.[28] Otherwise the governor contented himself with calling for federal troops, some of whom were distributed in the affected area just before the election.

The soldiers had as little effect as usual. Election day saw companies of armed whites assembling around the polls, confiscating Republican ballots before they could be distributed and threatening violence to Negroes who insisted on the right to cast them. In Oglethorpe and probably elsewhere many of these were Klansmen out of disguise. In Columbia County they even intimidated the soldiers who had been sent there.[29] At many places throughout the state freedmen were simply muscled away from the polls, but in some localities they were forced to vote the Democratic ticket. The most common disfranchising device was to insist on Negroes' showing poll tax receipts, despite an attempt by Governor Bullock to suspend that requirement by proclamation. The results of this election were spectacular. In Reed's Oglethorpe County, where Governor Bullock had polled 1,144 votes in April, Grant's total was only 116, while the Democratic vote increased from 557 to 849; in Warren County the Republican vote fell from 1,124 to 188, and in Columbia County from 1,222 to 1. Twenty-two counties which had cast nearly 3,000 votes for Bullock now reported a total of only 87 for Grant, and in eleven counties he received no votes at all. By these means Georgia went for Seymour and Blair.[30]

In Florida the Young Men's Democratic Clubs and Klans (if they were distinguishable) continued to expand. A Ku Klux organization now formed in Jefferson and other counties east of Tallahassee. W. S. Simkins, a leader of this organization and much later a law professor at the University of Texas, indicated that they rode around after dark playing on Negro superstition, but committed no violence. This seems to have been true generally, but it is hard to determine the extent of violence. The Freedmen's Bureau reported at year's end that peace and order had prevailed throughout the state, and outrages upon freedmen were rarer than in most parts of the South. Neither the Bureau's annual report nor the Jacksonville *Florida Union,* the leading Republican organ in the state, made any mention of Klan activity in Florida during 1868.[31]

On the other hand, Negroes were killed as a result of organized violence in at least one county that fall.[32] As early as September 1, Governor Harrison Reed saw enough tumult, with mounting Conservative threats of intimidation, to call for additional troops to be posted in Tallahassee, Gainesville, Ocala, and Marianna. General Meade refused the request on grounds of insufficient need, but a month later, on the recommendation of Colonel John Sprague, the Florida commandant, six companies were distributed at various points from Jacksonville to Marianna. Despite their presence Sprague wrote on October 31 that Union men were cowed, civil authorities were afraid to enforce the law, and the state was on the verge of anarchy.[33] Whatever the cause of this violence, it had nothing to do with the November Presidential election. The Florida legislature had already enacted a law in August empowering it to choose the state's Presidential electors itself, without a popular choice. Democratic terrorism may have been one of the reasons for the drastic step; Republican dissension and the high cost of a popular election were also factors.[34]

In early November, nevertheless, the Florida Klan managed to pull off its most famous exploit. The legislature had also passed a militia law in August, and the next month Governor Reed went personally to New York, where he bought 2,000 muskets and 40,000 rounds of ammunition.[35] By

November 5 these armaments were en route by train from Jacksonville to Tallahassee, guarded by a special detachment of federal soldiers. The Klan learned of the shipment and kept watch over it. According to later inside accounts every telegraph operator, brakeman, engineer, and conductor along the line either was a member of the order or cooperated with it. On the night of November 5 forty Klansmen were posted at each of three stations east of Tallahassee where the train was scheduled to make night-time stops. The plan was for the easternmost group to board the train at what is now Greenville and destroy the arms before reaching the next station; the other groups were held in reserve in case of failure. They were not needed, for the first contingent obtained keys to the locked freight cars from the conductor and quietly boarded the train without arousing the soldiers, who were riding in passenger coaches. By the time the train reached the next station (the engineer went slowly on purpose) the Klansmen had thrown the armaments overboard, scattering them along the tracks for several miles. They got off just before the train pulled into the next depot, then went back and methodically destroyed the guns and ammunition, finishing just before dawn. The loss seemingly was not discovered until the train reached Tallahassee. Although Colonel Sprague later identified the leader of the band as Captain John J. Dickison, a former Confederate guerrilla leader and commander of a band of regulators in that vicinity, no one was ever apprehended for the crime.[36]

In Alabama terrorism continued in most of the western and northern counties where it had been conspicuous earlier in the year. Sumter and Tuscaloosa were among the worst. Neither saw much organized night riding, but cases of intimidation and violence abounded. At Northport, adjacent to Tuscaloosa, a disguised party raided the home of a Negro on the night of September 10 and killed his wife as he was climbing up the chimney to safety. A flourishing Ku Klux class existed around Moore's Bridge, in the northwest corner of Tuscaloosa County. Two separate ambush attacks in this vicinity took the lives of a United States mail carrier, a Republican state legislator (M. P. Crossland), and a young man traveling with Crossland. In both cases the sheriff confessed himself totally powerless to catch the murderers; such men as were disposed to do anything at all in the matter were afraid to enter the surrounding swamps where the criminals lay in wait for any pursuers.[37] Ryland Randolph was less belligerent editorially for the time being, after his ill-advised newspaper cartoon and the resulting criticism from fellow Democrats, but shortly before the election he led a mob of twenty or more men who broke up a Republican rally which was being addressed by Senator Willard Warner and Congressman Charles Hays.[38]

In Sumter County the two races approached an armed conflict as Democrats sought to overthrow the heavy Negro Republican majority by force. Beginning in September, individual encounters took place almost daily, with Negroes suffering most of the casualties. After at least two freedmen had been killed, the blacks began attending Republican rallies and League meetings armed to the teeth; this led whites to increase their organization correspondingly. One such meeting broke up when a Negro drew a pistol and shot at a white man who had arisen to give the lie to the preceding speakers; one of the latter, Daniel Price, diverted the shot by hitting the freedman's arm as he fired. Price was one of the few white Republicans in the county, the acknowledged political leader of the Negro community, and was correspondingly hated by the whites. On October 2 a party of twenty-five to thirty men went to the home of Ben Brown, the Negro president of a Grant and Colfax club, and killed him after he had ignored warnings to discontinue meetings. Brown lived on the plantation of Dr. Gerard Choutteau, another white Republican, who now was subject to a virtual state of siege, with his life continually threatened; white men picketed the roads leading to his home, driving off anyone who sought to enter or leave the premises. The Republican state senator from the county was warned by friends that it was not safe for him to return home. Meanwhile former judge Henry Reavis was enrolling new members into the Ku Klux Klan at his law office in Gainesville.

The county was temporarily without a sheriff, and the other officials, including the Freedmen's Bureau agent, were either in sympathy with the terrorism or overawed by it. Legal inquiries into the Brown murder and other crimes were a farce. Negroes came in large numbers to Price, who was confined to the village of Livingston, the county seat, for fear of his life, asking if it was not time to start defending themselves. "It needs but a breath to start midnight murder by the wholesale," Price wrote to Governor William H. Smith on October 7. Like other white leaders of the Negroes whom Conservatives regarded as firebrands and the authors of all current misfortune, Price advised against retaliation in kind for fear of provoking even worse attack. "I have cautioned quietness[,] have told them that you [Smith] would protect them if possible, and begged of them to wait still further on the officers of the law." Meanwhile Price asked for a squad of federal troops to help make arrests and confine prisoners until a sheriff was chosen. "This state of things cannot long continue. Either we must have protection, or leave. . . . Troops could not do harm and they certainly will be the means of preventing a collision between the races. We have fallen upon evil times when an American citizen can not express his honest opinions without being in great danger of being murdered." No effective steps were taken, and the terror continued for many months. On election day whites blockaded the polls in some precincts, and according to Choutteau 500 Negroes were prevented from voting in his locality alone.[39]

In mountainous Blount and Calhoun counties, where there were many white Unionists, the Klan attacked and intimidated Republicans of both races. They also burned two white public schools which they regarded as manifestations of Radical government.[40]

The greatest Klan activity was in the Tennessee Valley counties of Madison, Limestone, Morgan, Colbert, Lawrence, and Lauderdale. Here night riding was practiced regularly throughout the fall and beyond. Bands of a dozen and more disguised men rode about regularly after dark, calling or dragging Negroes from their homes and threatening, robbing, beating, and occasionally killing them. Some white Republicans received the same treatment. Most of this activity followed a common pattern. Klansmen nearly always searched for and confiscated any guns they found; in a few localities they made a blanket requirement that Negroes deposit their guns at a certain place by an assigned date or face a whipping. Generally they quizzed their victims about their voting intentions at the forthcoming election. If a freedman answered that he planned to vote for Grant he was likely to be whipped; if he said he planned to vote for Seymour or else stay home he was more likely to get off with a warning and the loss of his gun. In some cases blacks were robbed of money, watches, and other possessions. If the Klan occasionally punished real or suspected personal transgressions, this too was incidental to the primary object of rendering the freedmen impotent politically and militarily. Politically active Negroes were singled out especially, and in Madison County the Klan blockaded the roads in October to keep blacks from coming in to Huntsville to register.[41]

In other ways too the Klan reflected its political purpose along with occasional regulative activity among the blacks. In Decatur it invaded the homes of Judge Charlton (a local Republican leader), the circuit court clerk, and a deputy sheriff and threatened their lives.[42] At Tuscumbia more than 150 Klansmen lynched three Negroes confined in jail for suspected arson.[43] At Athens small numbers of Klansmen would ride into town in daylight and socialize with passersby. On election day six or eight of them offered to help an Army lieutenant and his soldiers keep order if any disturbances arose.[44] But they were not always so gentlemanly; they made the usual nocturnal rounds, occasionally even forcing white victims to commit obscenities with Negroes.[45] In October they reportedly took two white Republican legislators, Senator B. Lentz and Representative R. E. Harris, from a train and whipped them.[46] Warned not to return to the legislature, the two men were reduced to writing to the governor for a military escort when the next session approached.[47] At the same time the newly elected local officials were afraid to assume office, being threatened with death by the Klan if they did so.[48]

"These bands are having a great effect, in inspiring a *nameless terror* among negroes, poor whites, and even others," a Republican editor wrote privately from Huntsville in October. "The mischief is taking place daily and nightly—nobody is found out, or arrested, or punished. The civil authority is seemingly powerless—the military does not act—and the thing goes on, and is getting worse daily."[49] Klansmen in full regalia had occasionally ridden through Huntsville in small numbers to "show the flag," with nothing done to or by them. On the night of October 31 they staged a much larger parade, 150 strong, in an effort to overawe a Republican meeting then taking place at the courthouse, and then rode out again. The Klansmen apparently took no direct part in the minor riot which broke out as they left, but their coming had created the supercharged atmosphere which made it possible. News of their approach had preceded them, and some of the Negroes had armed themselves, not knowing what to expect. When a freedman refused a white man's demand that he surrender his gun (as the Klan was leaving), both races began indiscriminate shooting which ended in two deaths and several persons wounded.[50]

The ensuing election in these counties went much as the Democrats had intended, although the terror was not quite extensive enough to prevent the state as a whole from going Republican. Governor Smith had continued to follow his earlier policy of moral appeals and reliance on federal troops. This was by now the typical course for Republican regimes in the deep South. The Alabama legislature too had provided a militia law in August as a matter of general policy, but acquiesced in the governor's hesitation to use it. In September it requested soldiers to maintain the peace during the coming campaign and dispatched a committee to go with Governor Smith to present the appeal to President Johnson in person. Although the governor somewhat diminished the force of the demand by minimizing the need for troops, he subsequently called on them a number of times.[51]

Republicans who had to face the terror day after day found Smith's policy inadequate. As time passed, they grew more and more exasperated and bitter toward their apparently do-nothing governor. Partially to appease their wrath, he called upon the legislature when it reassembled soon after the election to investigate the activities of disguised bands, especially in north Alabama, with the idea of enacting a law against them.[52] A committee went through the form of an investigation, interviewing about a dozen witnesses, and then issued a report affirming the existence of the Ku Klux Klan in many parts of the state and specifying some of its crimes. It called for stricter legislation to curb Klan activity, and even recommended martial law in several counties.[53] The legislature responded to the first request with two laws passed in December. The first forbade under heavy penalties the wearing of masks and disguises in public and the commission (in or out of disguise) of personal violence or the destruction of schools and other buildings. The second act tried to stimulate enforcement of the first. It penalized local officials for failing to do so and held their counties responsible for any personal damages occasioned by Klan or mob violence; but if offenders were tried and convicted the county was no longer liable to pay damages.[54] Stringent as they looked on paper, these laws were no more self-enforcing than the pre-existing laws against trespass, assault, and murder. The same factors deterred sheriffs, prosecutors, grand juries, and the general white public from taking them seriously.

Mississippi, like Virginia and Texas, was not yet readmitted to the Union by the end of 1868, owing to the defeat of the proposed constitution in June. Thus the state took no part in the Presidential election and there was less cause for Ku Klux activity. Klan organizations remained in existence, and some of them arose to new life in 1869 and later. But the second half of 1868 saw only scattered outrages of Negroes by disguised men, probably more for economic and social than political causes. Most of these were in the northern part of the state.[55]

In Kentucky, where Negroes could not yet vote, they continued to be subject to Ku Klux harassment. A common pretext for these raids was to disarm the Negroes, but in many cases they were driven from their homes, sometimes with the connivance of their landlords once the crops were in. There was a deliberate purpose, often specifically avowed, to drive them from the state altogether. Negro ministers and teachers, the leaders of the black community, were singled out particularly; by the same token, Negro churches and schools were favorite targets for Ku Klux attack. White Unionists received similar treatment and in much the same numbers. Countless persons of both races were forced into the towns for safety or to leave the state and take refuge in Ohio, Indiana, and Illinois. The terror increased with the approach of the November election and fell off somewhat thereafter, but it continued into 1869 and beyond. In Henderson and elsewhere there was deliberate intimidation of prospective Republican voters before the election, but most of the raiding had no more than an indirect connection with politics.[56]

Ku Klux outrages in Kentucky equaled those elsewhere in size, frequency, and brutality. A party of seventy-two mounted and disguised men took two men from the jail at Nicholasville and hanged them outside of town.[57] A Cincinnati newspaper correspondent wrote in July 1869 that within a twenty-mile radius of Harrodsburg alone more than twenty-five persons had been hung and probably a hundred severely lashed or otherwise outraged by regulators in the past two years.[58] In many cases the attackers were not disguised and did not call themselves Ku Klux, but they showed all the earmarks of comparable organization, and the distinction between them was a fine one.

The regions most affected were much the same as earlier in the year: the counties from Frankfort and Lexington southward nearly to the Tennessee border; Henderson and Union counties on the Ohio, across from southwestern Indiana; and the westernmost counties of the state adjacent to Tennessee, Missouri, and Illinois. But outrages were reported from other sections too.[59]

As in other states, the Klan had, and depended upon, widespread public support. Some of this fell away in time, as the terror got out of hand and reached persons whom the "better element" had not intended. There was seldom any problem in identifying the members of these bands; they were known to children on the street, as the Cincinnati reporter observed. Some of the regulators themselves were reported to be law-abiding men who had joined in the first place to rid their localities of outlaws. But after the vigilantes began to outdo all others in lawlessness these men were afraid to break their oaths and drop out.[60] Some victims of the terror fought back, occasionally inflicting casualties on the attackers. But when a group of Negroes near Stanford repelled a Ku Klux band, killing three of its members, they found themselves arrested for murder. They were protected by federal troops, however, and were subsequently acquitted.[61]

At Morganfield public opinion seems to have swung against the Klan in December 1868. After a number of outrages against Negroes in the vicinity, the sheriff arrested five supposed Klansmen, and citizens guarded the town nightly against attack.[62] There was little help from the state administration of Governor John W. Stevenson. A Democrat, he sincerely deplored the terror (which in any event was unnecessary to assure continued Democratic control of the state), but he claimed inability to combat it because of the legislature's refusal to pass a law on the subject. Stevenson would later be forced to take action, but few officials at any level were eager to defy public opinion or endanger their own lives by interceding effectively against the Klan.

A few efforts were made to bring about concerted action by the Southern states against the Ku Klux terror. On September 2, Governor Reed of Florida suggested a Southern governors' conference to consider means of coping with it. This idea appealed to the Republican national committee, which hoped that a public exposure of Democratic terrorism would help elect General Grant. The committee asked Governor Holden of North

Carolina to call such a meeting, but it never came to pass.[63] Late in October another Republican committee in Washington called upon the Southern governors to invoke martial law, using federal troops.[64] This policy had very sandy legal foundations, however. In practice it boiled down to the stationing of troops in the most lawless places, as was already being done.

CHAPTER 8

Louisiana

The Presidential campaign of 1868 marked the climax of Ku Klux activity in Louisiana. Between the Klan and the Knights of the White Camellia, Democratic secret societies increased their membership and penetrated virtually the entire state. In addition there was a chain of less secret Democratic clubs, some of them called the Seymour Knights, organized specifically for this campaign. All of them dealt in intimidation and many of them in violence. Except in the southwest corner of the state and the heavily Negro Mississippi River parishes between New Orleans and the Arkansas line, the state witnessed a campaign of terrorism which ranged from night riding and threats of violence to systematic massacres of black men. Even the bloodiest crimes were frequently condoned and sometimes committed by leading figures in the white community—lawyers, doctors, editors, even sheriffs and other officeholders in parishes which had gone Democratic in the April state elections.

It remained impossible to distinguish fully between the various organizations. In the southern half of the state the KWC by November embraced a majority of the white male population in some parishes. The Seymour Knights or other Democratic clubs also enrolled many members in this part of the state, and there were occasional reports of Ku Klux organization as well. These orders may all have existed simultaneously, but often the names were used interchangeably; the situation was further confused by the common tendency to use the term Ku Klux generically to cover all of them. Although many KWC Councils were nonviolent and sometimes completely inactive, it is unsafe to acquit any of the organizations of complicity in the widespread violence which did occur.

Whatever their specific affiliations, white men organized militarily in large numbers in several of the predominantly Creole parishes west of New Orleans. By November the KWC alone contained ten Councils and 700 members in St. Mary Parish, according to one of its leaders, Daniel Dennett, editor of the *Planter's Banner* in Franklin. Here, as in neighboring St. Martin, Lafayette, and Vermilion parishes, bands of armed men beginning in September regularly patrolled country roads on horseback and town streets on foot, and made the rounds of Negro cabins. Sometimes they wore disguises and operated after dark, but more often they traveled without concealment and in broad daylight.

Although they sometimes argued the danger of a Negro uprising as the pretext for these activities, the whole operation was obviously and almost exclusively political. Republicans of both races were systematically threatened with death; a few were killed and others were forced to flee. Negroes were sometimes issued "protection papers" if they promised to vote the Democratic ticket. Republican meetings were either broken up or prevented in advance, and it became impossible to express Republican views in public. Republican leaders received special attention. On October 17 Sheriff Henry H. Pope (a former U.S. Army colonel) and Judge Valentine Chase of St. Mary Parish were publicly assassinated in Franklin by a band of armed men, and Pope's successor was run off just before the election. In some localities patrolling continued through election day, preventing Negroes from reaching the polls. By such means the Republican vote was drastically cut—to the vanishing point in some places. The similarity of action from one parish to another was so great that Democrats must have been following a common plan even if they did not actively cooperate across parish lines.[1]

In St. Landry Parish the KWC attained a membership of about 3,000, and there was also an active contingent of Seymour Knights.[2] Well before the election political and racial tensions here developed to the point that almost any incident could set off an explosion. The Seymour Knights contributed largely to this tension; they also triggered the explosion and participated heavily in the bloodshed which followed. On September 28 three Knights went to a Negro school in Opelousas taught by one Emerson Bentley. Bentley, a precocious eighteen-year-old, doubled as English language editor of the bilingual St. Landry *Progress,* a Republican newspaper. Because he refused to retract a recent political article he had written for the paper, the men assaulted him in front of his students, administering a stiff beating. When the Negroes heard of this they began to assemble under arms. Bentley and other friends prevailed on them to disperse, but they were too late. Inflamed at the thought of Negroes daring to gather in such a fashion, the whites, now mobilized, took over the town and sent out patrols to disarm the blacks and capture their leaders. (Given the magnificent degree of organization they displayed, it is possible that they planned the affair from the beginning.) François D'Avy, the parish Republican leader, was shot at while sleeping in his bed, but escaped, as did Bentley and most of the other leaders. However, the French editor of the *Progress,* named Durand, was captured, and his press destroyed.

Democrats and Republicans differed as to who fired the first shots and why, but there was substantial agreement on other details. The whites informed the Negroes generally that they would kill any who refused to surrender their arms, and during the next three days or more they combed the countryside, shooting any blacks they saw with guns in their hands. The blacks were completely demoralized and offered almost no resistance. By the time it ended, the whites had killed up to two hundred of them while suffering only a few wounds among themselves. The Negroes, as a jubilant Democrat put it, had learned a "wholesome lesson"; on election day they were herded to the polls to vote for Seymour and Blair, who carried the parish unanimously.[3]

In parishes farther north there is more evidence of orthodox Ku Klux activity—night riding by bands of disguised men. Such was the case in Alexandria and Rapides Parish, although most of it followed rather than preceded the election. Here as elsewhere, members of the KWC claimed that their organization was entirely defensive and pacific; so far as they admitted to hearing and crediting reports of Ku Klux night riding, they insisted that the Klan was a separate order.[4] In October a band of men partially destroyed the office of a new Republican newspaper, the Rapides *Tribune,* only hours after its editor, Mayor William F. McLean of Alexandria, had brought the equipment from New Orleans. Undaunted, he returned to the metropolis for a new supply, which arrived on November 15. That night the office was sacked once more, with brickbats being heaved at McLean for good measure. Meanwhile the Klan held demonstrations and attacked other Republicans too. According to the New Orleans *Republican,* Klansmen paraded the streets of Alexandria several nights a week, mounted and fully disguised. "These nocturnal parades are enlivened by calls on the District and Parish Judge[s] and other parties obnoxious to them, storming their houses, and making night hideous by unearthly groans, yells, cat-calls, and whatever else their fancies suggest, to provoke some hostile demonstration which they can resent, of course in pure self-defense, by massacreing the offending victim."[5] There was no confrontation or massacre as in Opelousas, however.

In Winn Parish Klan raids caused many blacks to flee for safety to

Natchitoches.[6] Democrats in Sabine Parish on the Texas border explained the Klan there as a group of thirty or forty young men who had organized to run out horse and cattle thieves; but some of them turned sour and began doing the same things themselves. Republicans pointed out that they also terrorized Negroes, who came to the polls in squads on election day and voted the Democratic ticket.[7]

The northern part of the state had been the worst region earlier in the year, and it remained a strong contender now. At least ten parishes, extending from the Texas line almost to the Mississippi River, were wholly or partially overrun by night riders whose activities ran the gamut from parading the streets and pretending to be ghosts to whipping and murder. In this region too the terror followed a common pattern which could not have been accidental. In addition, planters threatened to discharge Negro tenants who voted Republican, Democratic clubs issued them protection papers, and a mob sacked the office of the Homer *Iliad* a second time. Nearly all of this was politically inspired, even the outrages which continued some weeks after the election. No Republican tickets at all were cast in Jackson Parish and only one each in Union, Morehouse, Caddo, and Bossier; the foolhardy black who was responsible for the Republican vote in Caddo paid for it with his life.

Both Caddo and Bossier witnessed a brief open season on Negroes comparable to the Opelousas affair. It was reported that in the course of a month at least twenty-five or thirty Negro bodies floated down the Red River past Shreveport. The number killed in Caddo Parish in October alone probably exceeded forty-two, according to a legislative committee. Whites in Bossier, including some of the leading planters, systematically hunted down and slew impersonally and indiscriminately 162 blacks, ignoring the plea of a United States marshal to be permitted to go out with a few troops to arrest any suspected Negro criminals.[8]

Considerable organization and activity took place also in the three Florida parishes of St. Helena, St. Tammany, and Washington, north of New Orleans. Bands of disguised men rode about nightly before the election, impressing Negroes by their presence and threatening death to any who voted Republican. The few white Republicans often found Ku Klux notices posted on their doors, promising the same fate. At Franklinton in Washington Parish hooded Klansmen raided the homes of three Negro Republicans late in October, beat one of them, and destroyed Republican ballots in their possession. A band of at least sixty rode through town on five successive nights preceding the election. In these parishes few Negroes had the hardihood to go to the polls at all on election day. Those who did were frequently prevented from voting, but in Franklinton armed men herded blacks to the polls and made them cast Democratic ballots under drawn pistols; no Republican votes were cast in that parish. Blacks who voted Democratic were given certificates to that effect, or protection papers, signed by Robert Babington. He was a merchant, postmaster, chairman of the Democratic central committee, acknowledged member of the KWC, and unacknowledged but reputed secretary of the local Ku Klux Klan; he was also identified as one of the town's hooded invaders.[9]

In St. Helena Parish the Klan burned two Negro churches and a schoolhouse, the last of which whites cooperated to rebuild. Several Negroes were killed during the night riding, and in some districts most of the freedmen lay out at night to avoid being caught. On the night of October 29 about forty Klansmen rode into the town of Tangipahoa (then in St. Helena); they were "completely disguised, having their faces masked with skulls, and white caps about three feet long on their heads, and their horses covered with white sheets." General J. Hale Sypher, the Republican Congressman from this district, was due to speak there, and they rode around town calling for him. Not finding him, they went to the home of John Kemp, the parish coroner, who was a literate, capable, and very active Negro Republican. They broke down Kemp's door, dragged him from the house, and shot him to death. Before leaving they beat his wife and seized his papers, which may have contained incriminating evidence. During the night they visited the homes of several other freedmen, wounding two of them and robbing a third. They also called on two white Republicans, who managed to escape, and robbed a store of money and whiskey. The same band was said to have carried off another Negro from Franklinton, which was only a few miles away and also within their sphere of operations. On November 2, election eve, they visited the board of election supervisors and warned them not to distribute any Republican ballots.

The Kemp murder, with everything else, seems to have created so much resentment among the black population that whites became more apprehensive than usual about a Negro rising. Accordingly they organized still further, and some of them spent half a dozen nights on horseback patrolling the roads. The White Camellias were widely organized here, and some of the patrollers belonged to that order, but others did not. The blacks did not assert themselves, and thus there was neither an armed collision nor a general massacre. Very few Negroes voted on election day.[10]

New Orleans was a major exception to the rule that Southern cities remained free of terrorist activity. The KWC grew rapidly here during the fall, reaching probably 15,000 members by November. (The adult white male population of the city in 1870 was about 32,000.) These were organized into about fifteen Councils, three of them in suburban Algiers and Jefferson Parish. As elsewhere, many prominent whites belonged to the order and led it. Other groups sprang up alongside the KWC Councils, but the Wide Awake Club and the Innocents were distinct and more specifically attuned to the election campaign. Whereas the KWC kept up its organization after the election, as it had long preceded it, the Wide Awakes and Innocents disappeared from view in November. In addition there were apparently some vigilante societies which arose briefly during the campaign, unaffiliated with other groups. After these distinctions are made, however, the fact remains that all of these organizations were composed of white men who met frequently, drilled occasionally, held parades and demonstrations, patrolled the streets under arms, and were intensely concerned to see the Democratic party win the election and white supremacy restored. Their membership frequently overlapped. They differed from orthodox Ku Klux mainly in the fact that they did not use that name or operate in disguise. KWC Councils continued to announce their meetings in the New Orleans *Times*.[11]

The Negroes who comprised most of the Republican rank and file in New Orleans had also organized into clubs. They too carried weapons much of the time and occasionally drilled in the streets. For the most part they confined themselves to peaceful (if noisy) parades and demonstrations; by no means wholly guiltless of aggressive action, they nevertheless fought on the defensive most of the time. In the troubled days of that fall they were far less sinning than sinned against. Those who disagreed with this appraisal were usually those who regarded Negro political activity and especially Negroes under arms as in themselves a sufficient provocation to white violence. There is strong reason to suspect that many of the outbreaks which Negroes technically initiated were in fact deliberately provoked by white men as a pretext for massive retaliation of their own. Here too whites were deeply afraid of potential Negro violence, convinced of the necessity of curbing it by at least the threat of superior firepower on their part, and supremely confident of their own ability to prevail if it broke out. In the end it was usually trigger-happy whites who precipitated violence as a species of preventive warfare.

Rioting first erupted on September 22, when Democrats fired into a Republican political procession. According to previous instruction, the Negroes making up the procession began to disperse, but members of the Democratic clubs followed and attacked them. Although the fighting was short-lived and the casualties light, the attack bore the appearance of advance planning, and Democratic leaders seemed reluctant to have it end. When the fighting was almost over, the chairman of the parish Democratic committee went to the city hall and tried to sound the general fire alarm in order "to call out the citizens to put down this riot." As the New Orleans *Republican* pointed out, all this bore a strong resemblance to the great collision of July 1866. Democrats now as then referred to it as a Negro riot and called for force if necessary to overthrow Republican rule.[12] Three days later, after a number of encounters between Negroes and whites in suburban St. Bernard Parish, armed whites took control there and began methodically driving out white Republicans and shooting down troublesome Negroes. This lasted four days, at the end of which time at least thirty-eight persons had lost their lives.[13]

Tension grew steadily in the city, and whites stepped up their organization. Residents of the eleventh ward met on September 29 to form a "white man's volunteer Police" to help protect the community "in case of an outbreak by the negro Radical organizations. . . . " A special committee was authorized to spend up to $500 for guns for those who did not own and could not afford to buy any.[14] By the middle of October the city was an armed camp. Probably the most belligerent group was the Innocents Club, composed of about 1,200 workingmen—fruit venders, oyster sellers, market men, and others drawn from the French, Spanish, Italian, Portuguese, Maltese, and Anglo-Saxon communities of this the most heterogeneous place in the South. According to their president, Pascalis Labarre (who was later a Democratic city official), their name derived from a republican club in Sicily. It certainly was not descriptive in the present case. Labarre's public claim that the Innocents almost invariably acted peaceably was belied by a fellow Democrat who privately characterized them as "cut throats, thugs, assassins & the vilest characters in the city."[15] By most accounts the Innocents were involved in a great part of the rowdyism which occurred more or less continually until election day.

The KWC was hardly less active, if a bit more sedate. It established an alarm signal to be sounded on the church bells throughout the city—one tap, then two taps rapidly, then one tap—to mobilize its forces in case of a Negro uprising or other emergency. According to a detective who penetrated the organization and reported to Governor Warmoth, at least one Council organized ten patrols of ten men each, to meet nightly and hold themselves in readiness for any eventuality. Presumably other Councils acted similarly.

One project of the Democratic clubs—and probably the White Camellias too—was to break up the metropolitan police force. This body had been taken over and reorganized by Governor Warmoth under a six-member board headed by Lieutenant Governor Oscar Dunn. Conservatives resented the action because it meant Republican instead of Democratic control, and because Dunn and half of his colleagues were Negroes. The board appointed 243 white men and 130 blacks to the force. According to General Lovel H. Rousseau, the federal commander, most of these men were unreliable; whites refused to obey them and they were known to run away from trouble, he said. Whatever the extent of their deficiencies, it gave whites additional motive for supplanting them and organizing independently to police the city.[16]

On October 23 trouble broke out in suburban Jefferson Parish across the river, which also lay within the metropolitan police jurisdiction. The KWC there seems deliberately to have provoked Negroes to attack them, providing an excuse for massive retaliation of their own. Then, for more than a week, bands of armed whites patrolled the town of Gretna in particular, driving out the police (even in the face of a company of U.S. infantry sent to maintain order) and attempting to break up the Loyal Leagues or Republican clubs. They searched Negroes for guns, robbed them of money and other valuables, shot at them, and drove many into the swamps. Negro casualties totaled at least five dead, nine shot, and thirty-three otherwise maltreated. At the same time the blacks were threatened with a general massacre if they voted Republican on November 3. The whites got help from Algiers next door and from New Orleans. Each KWC Council in the city was ordered to detail twenty men for patrol duty in Jefferson Parish until the conflict with the metropolitan police was over. The whites in Algiers conducted a similar campaign of their own. According to one of Warmoth's detectives who belonged to the KWC Council there, its members and the Wide Awakes killed seven Negroes by October 25.[17]

On the night of October 24 the Democratic clubs escalated their operations in New Orleans proper. They started with another unprovoked attack on a Republican street procession, this time killing and wounding a number of Negroes. Then they invaded and sacked Republican club headquarters around the city and searched the homes of prominent Republicans. Policemen were ambushed and shot while on duty, and an armed mob besieged the metropolitan police headquarters, demanding its submission. The next day the Innocents Club announced a march for the coming evening, 2,500 strong, through the city's main Negro districts.

At this point Governor Warmoth notified General Rousseau that the civil authorities in the three metropolitan parishes had lost control, and asked the Army to take over. With telegraphed approval from Washington, Rousseau acceded and made General J. B. Steedman interim superintendent of police. Democrats had succeeded in overthrowing the metropolitan police, but this substitution was not precisely to their liking. They now offered to help police the city, an offer which if accepted would confer an air of legality on their operations. Rousseau declined and issued instead an order forbidding further street demonstrations. But the Democratic clubs paid little attention; in fact their rioting continued unabated every night until after the election. Voter registrars were favorite targets for attack, but black men in general suffered nearly all the casualties. At least sixty-three persons were killed, and many Negroes fled or went into hiding. General Rousseau had only 550 men available for duty, fewer than the Democratic clubs had in the streets every night. The latter ignored the troops rather than defying them. One nervous officer, however, advised that the general "would be as much justified in retiring with his troops as he would before an enemy of superior force."[18]

General Edward Hatch, the Freedmen's Bureau chief in Louisiana, reported of the entire state at the end of October: "Since the Bureau has been organized no such outrages and murders were ever before perpetrated, both as regards the number and character of them, as have been enacted during the past thirty days. Although my report is dark with these atrocities, still I can safely say that hundreds of instances are not yet reported and a great many never will be."[19] A Congressional committee later enumerated 1,081 persons killed, 135 shot, and 507 otherwise outraged in the state between the April and November elections, most of them shortly before the latter.[20] This represented for all practical purposes a deliberate campaign of terror by the white population against the black throughout most of the state. The civil authorities everywhere were incapable of contending with it. Governor Warmoth was widely criticized by other Republicans for not organizing the militia and using it as Brownlow had done in Tennessee, or as Governor Clayton was presently doing in Arkansas.[21] But Louisiana was not Tennessee or Arkansas, and Negro militiamen would likely have inspired still greater black casualties.

With few exceptions the Democratic press throughout the state ignored or glossed over the terror, except to defend the major outbreaks as cases of self-defense against wild and dangerous Negroes. Some papers actively encouraged the terror, like the *Courier of the Teche* in St. Martin Parish, whose editor later fled under a charge of complicity in the assassination of a state senator. So far as they noticed the KKK and the KWC at all, they tended to deny the existence of the one and to defend the other as a purely peaceful and defensive political order based on the Union League.[22]

Intimidation and violence reached such proportions throughout most of the state that Warmoth and the Republican leadership finally advised Negroes not to try to vote at all if they could not do so safely. It is impossible to determine how widely this message circulated or how much effect it had in contributing to the outcome. In any event a comparison of the vote Warmoth himself had received in April with General Grant's vote in November is striking. In those parishes where little or no violence occurred, the Republican vote was nearly the same in both elections. Elsewhere seven parishes, which cast 4,707 votes for Warmoth in the spring, gave no votes at all to Grant; eight others, with a Republican vote of 5,520 in April, gave 10 votes to Grant in November; twenty-one parishes cast 26,814 for Warmoth and only 501 for Grant; New Orleans cast but 276 votes for Grant. The whole state cast 61,152 for the Republican ticket in April and 34,859 in November. The Democrats, on the other hand, received 43,739 votes in April and 88,225 in November.[23]

Having carried the state for Seymour and Blair, its major objective, the terror fell off sharply after the election. The KWC carried on as an organization, continuing to hold meetings with decreasing frequency through the spring of 1869. There was some talk in its Councils of overthrowing the now-restored metropolitan police again, and even the state government, but this project was left for a later time and later organizations. There was also talk of reorganizing the KWC itself, especially in December after a Republican newspaper exposed its ritual, passwords, and signals. A state convention of the order met in New Orleans in January 1869 and changed these elements—some of the Councils appear to have begun calling themselves Caucasian Clubs at this time—but the KWC seems to have lapsed or disbanded in the summer of 1869. At that time investigations by Congressional and state legislative committees further exposed its organization and operations to public view.[24] The Ku Klux organizations upstate seem to have gone the same way. A new order called the '76 Association was founded sometime in 1869 with a high-toned membership that included Generals Braxton Bragg and Simon Bolivar Buckner, but it seems never to have been active.[25] There was little further night riding of the Ku Klux variety in Louisiana, but organized mob violence of the kind which proved so effective in 1868 was revived in 1872. As carried out by the White Leagues it finally achieved the overthrow of the state government in 1877.[26]

CHAPTER 9

Texas: The Knights of the Rising Sun

Large parts of Texas remained close to anarchy through 1868. Much of this was politically inspired despite the fact that the state was not yet reconstructed and took no part in the national election. In theory the Army was freer to take a direct hand in maintaining order than was true in the states which had been readmitted, but the shortage of troops available for this duty considerably lessened that advantage. At least twenty counties were involved in the Ku Klux terror, from Houston north to the Red River. In Houston itself Klan activity was limited to the holding of monthly meetings in a gymnasium and posting notices on lampposts, but in other places there was considerable violence.[1]

By mid-September disguised bands had committed several murders in Trinity County, where two lawyers and both justices of the peace in the town of Sumter were well known as Klansmen. Not only did the crimes go unpunished, but Conservatives used them to force a majority of the Negroes to swear allegiance to the Democratic party; in return they received the familiar protection papers supposedly guaranteeing them against further outrage. "Any one in this community opposed to the Grand Cyclops and his imps is in danger of his life," wrote a local Republican in November. In Washington County the Klan sent warning notices to Republicans and committed at least one murder. As late as January 1869 masked parties were active around Palestine, shaving heads, whipping, and shooting

137

among the black population, as well as burning down their houses. The military arrested five or six men for these offenses, but the Klan continued to make the rounds of Negroes' and Union men's houses, confiscating both guns and money.[2] Early in November General J. J. Reynolds, military commander in the state, declared in a widely quoted report that "civil law east of the Trinity river is almost a dead letter" by virtue of the activities of Ku Klux Klans and similar organizations. Republicans had been publicly slated for assassination and forced to flee their homes, while the murder of Negroes was too common to keep track of. These lawless bands, he said, were "evidently countenanced, or at least not discouraged, by a majority of the white people in the counties where [they] are most numerous. They could not otherwise exist." These statements did not endear the general to Conservative Texans, but they were substantially true.[3]

The worst region of all, as to both Klan activity and general banditry, remained northeast Texas. A correspondent of the Cincinnati *Commercial* wrote from Sulphur Springs early in January 1869:

Armed bands of banditti, thieves, cut-throats and assassins infest the country; they prowl around houses, they call men out and shoot or hang them, they attack travellers upon the road, they seem almost everywhere present, and are ever intent upon mischief. You cannot pick up a paper without reading of murders, assassinations and robbery. . . . And yet not the fourth part of the truth has been told; not one act in ten is reported. Go where you will, and you will hear of fresh murders and violence. . . . The civil authority is powerless— the military insufficient in number, while hell has transferred its capital from pandemonium to Jefferson, and the devil is holding high carnival in Gilmer, Tyler, Canton, Quitman, Boston, Marshall and other places in Texas.[4]

Judge Hardin Hart wrote Governor Pease in September to say that on account of "a regularly organized band which has overrun the country" he could not hold court in Grayson, Fannin, and Hunt counties without a military escort.[5]

Much of this difficulty was attributable to outlaw gangs like those of Ben Bickerstaff and Cullen Baker, but even their activities were often racially and politically inspired, with Negroes and Union men the chief sufferers.[6] Army officers and soldiers reported that most of the population at Sulphur Springs was organized into Ku Klux clubs affiliated with the Democratic party and some of the outlaws called themselves Ku Klux Rangers.[7] At Clarksville a band of young men calling themselves Ku Klux broke up a Negro school and forced the teacher to flee the state.[8]

White Conservatives around Paris at first took advantage of Klan depredations among Negroes by issuing protection papers to those who agreed to join the Democratic party. But the marauding reached such proportions that many freedmen fled their homes and jobs, leaving the crops untended.

When a body of Klansmen came into town early in September, apparently to disarm more blacks, some of the leading citizens warned them to stop. The freedmen were not misbehaving, they said, and if they needed disarming at a later time the local people would take care of it themselves. Still the raiding continued, and after a sheriff's posse failed to catch the culprits the farmers in one neighborhood banded together to oppose them by force. (Since the Klan had become sacred among Democrats, these men claimed that the raiding was done by an unauthorized group using its name. They carefully denied any idea of opposing the Klan itself.) Even this tactic was ineffective so far as the county as a whole was concerned, and the terror continued at least into November. The Freedmen's Bureau agent, Colonel DeWitt C. Brown, was driven away from his own farm thirty miles from Paris and took refuge in town. There he was subjected to constant threats of assassination by Klansmen or their sympathizers. From where he stood the Klan seemed to be in almost total command.[9]

The Bureau agent at Marshall (like his predecessor in the summer) suspected that the planters themselves were implicated in much of the terrorism. By driving Negroes from their homes just before harvest time the Klan enabled many landowners to collect the crop without having to pay the laborers' share.[10]

Jefferson and Marion County remained the center of Ku Klux terrorism, as the Cincinnati reporter pointed out. A garrison of twenty-six men under Major James Curtis did little to deter violence. Bands of hooded men continued to make nocturnal depredations on Negroes in the surrounding countryside during September and October as they had for weeks past. "Whipping the freedmen, robbing them of their arms, driving them off plantations, and murdering whole families are of daily, and nightly occurrence," wrote the local Bureau agent at the end of October, "all done by disguised parties whom no one can testify to. The civil authorities never budge an inch to try and discover these midnight marauders and apparently a perfect apathy exists throughout the whole community regarding the general state of society. Nothing but martial law can save this section as it is at present. . . ." Inside town, Republicans hardly dared go outdoors at night, and for several weeks the county judge, who was afraid to go home even in the daytime, slept at the Army post. The local Democratic newspapers, including the *Ultra Ku Klux,* encouraged the terror by vying with one another in the ferocity of their denunciations of Republicans.[11]

Major Curtis confirmed this state of affairs in a report to General Reynolds:

Since my arrival at this Post . . . [in mid-September] I have carefully observed the temper of the people and studied their intentions. I am constrained to say that neither are pacific. The amount of unblushing fraud and outrage perpetrated upon the negroes is hardly to be believed unless witnessed. Citizens who are esteemed respectable do not hesitate to take every unfair advantage. My office is daily visited by large numbers of unfortunates who have had money owing them, which they have been unable to obtain. The moral sense of the community appears blunted and gray headed apologists for such men as Baker and Bickerstaff can be met on all the street corners. . . . The right of franchise in this section is a farce. Numbers of negroes have been killed for daring to be Radicals, and their houses have so often been broken into by their Ku Klux neighbors in search of arms that they are now pretty well defenceless. The civil officers *cannot* and *will* not punish these outrages. Cavalry armed with double barrelled shotguns would soon scour the country and these desperadoes be met on their own ground. They do not fear the arms that the troops now have, for they shoot from behind hedges and fences or at night and then run. No more notice is taken here of the death of a Radical negro than of a mad dog. A democratic negro however, who was shot the other day by another of his stripe, was followed to his grave through the streets of this city by a long procession in carriages, on horseback, and on foot. I saw some of the most aristocratic and respectable white men in this city in the procession.[12]

On the same night that Curtis wrote, the new Grand Officers of the Knights of the Rising Sun were installed in the presence of a crowd of 1,200 or 1,500 persons. "The town was beautifully illuminated," a newspaper reported, "and the Seymour Knights and the Lone Star Club turned out in full uniform, with transparencies and burners, in honor of the occasion." Sworn in as Grand Commander for the ensuing twelve months was Colonel William P. Saufley, who doubled as chairman of the Marion County Democratic executive committee. Following the installation "able and patriotic speeches" were delivered by several notables, including a Democratic Negro.[13]

As usual, the most hated Republican was the one who had the greatest Negro following. This was Captain George W. Smith, a young Union army veteran from New York who had settled in Jefferson as a merchant at the end of the war. His business failed, but the advent of Radical Reconstruction opened the prospect of a successful political career; at the age of twenty-four Smith was elected to the state constitutional convention by the suffrage of the Negro majority around Jefferson. At the convention, according to a perhaps overflattering posthumous account, he was recognized as one of the abler members. "In his daily life he was correct, almost austere. He never drank, smoked, chewed, nor used profane language." However, "he was odious as a negro leader, as a radical, as a man who could not be cowed, nor scared away." Smith may also have alienated his fellow townspeople by the strenuous efforts he made to collect debts they owed him. Even a few native Republicans like Judge Charles Caldwell, who was scarcely more popular with Conservatives, refused to speak from the same platform with him. As his admirer pointed out, Smith "was ostracized and his life often threatened. But he refused to be scared. He sued some of his debtors and went to live with colored people." One day, as he returned from a session of the convention, his carpetbag—perhaps symbolically—was stolen, its contents rifled, and a list of them published in a local newspaper.

The beginning of the end for Smith came on the night of October 3, after he and Anderson Wright, a Negro, had spoken at a Republican meeting. As he opened the door of a Negro cabin to enter, Smith was fired upon by four men outside including Colonel Richard P. Crump, one of Jefferson's leading gentry. Smith drew his revolver and returned the fire, wounding two of the assailants and driving them away. He then went to Major Curtis at the Army post. Here Crump, with the chief of police and others, soon arrived bearing a warrant for his arrest on a charge of assault. The attackers' original intention to kill Smith now assumed greater urgency because he and several Negroes present had recognized their assailants. Smith objected strenuously to their efforts to get custody of him, protesting that it was equivalent to signing his death warrant. Nevertheless Curtis turned him over to the civil authorities on their assurance of his safety. Smith was taken off to jail and a small civilian guard was posted around it. The major was uneasy, however, and requested reinforcements from his superior, but they were refused.

The next day there were signs in Jefferson of an assembling of the Knights of the Rising Sun. Hoping to head off a lynching, Curtis dispatched sixteen soldiers (the greater part of his command) to help guard the jail. At 9 P.M., finally, a signal was sounded—a series of strokes on a bell at the place where the Knights held their meetings. About seventy members now mobilized under the command of Colonel Saufley and proceeded to march in formation toward the jail; they were in disguise and many carried torches. The jail building lay in an enclosed yard where at that time four black men were confined for a variety of petty offenses. One of the prisoners was Anderson Wright, and apparently the real reason for their being there was that they had witnessed the previous night's attempt to murder Smith; they may even have been fellow targets at that time. When the Knights reached this enclosure they burst through it with a shout and overpowered the guard, commanded by a young Army lieutenant. The invaders then turned to the Negro prisoners and dragged them into some adjoining woods. Wright and a second man, Cornelius Turner, managed to escape from them, although Wright was wounded; the other two prisoners were shot nearly to pieces. As soon as Major Curtis heard the shooting and firing he came running with his remaining soldiers; but they too were quickly overpowered. Repeatedly the major himself tried to prevent the mob from entering the jail building in which Smith was confined, only to be dragged away from the door each time. They had no trouble unlocking the door, for city marshal Silas Nance, who possessed the key, was one of the conspirators.

At first Smith tried to hold the door shut against their entry. Eventually failing at this, he caught the foremost man, pulled him into the room, and somehow killed him. "It is common talk in Jefferson now," wrote a former Bureau agent some months later, "that Capt. Smith killed the first man who entered—that the Knights of the Rising Sun afterward buried him secretly with their funeral rites, and it was hushed up, he being a man from a distance. It is an established fact that one Gray, a strong man, who ventured into the open door, was so beaten by Capt. Smith that he cried, 'Pull me out! He's killing me!' and he was dragged out backward by the leg." All this took place in such darkness that the Knights could not see their victim. Some of them now went outside and held torches up to the small barred window of Smith's cell. By this light they were able to shoot him four times. "The door was burst open and the crowd surged in upon him as he fell, and then, man after man, as they filed around fired into the dying body. This refinement of barbarity was continued while he writhed and after his limbs had ceased to quiver, that each one might participate in the triumph."[14]

Once the mob had finished its work at the jail it broke up into squads which began patrolling the town and searching for other Republican leaders. County Judge Campbell had anticipated trouble earlier in the evening and taken refuge as usual at Major Curtis' headquarters. Judge Caldwell was hated second only to Smith after his well-publicized report as chairman of the constitutional convention's committee on lawlessness. Hearing the shooting around the jail, he fled from his home into the woods. In a few moments twenty-five or thirty Knights appeared at the house, looking for him. Some of the party were for killing him, and they spent two hours vainly trying to learn his whereabouts from his fifteen-year-old son, who refused to tell. Another band went to the house of G. H. Slaughter, also a member of the convention, but he too escaped.

The next day the few remaining white Republicans in town were warned by friends of a widely expressed desire to make a "clean sweep" of them. Most of them stayed at the Haywood House hotel the following night under a military guard. Meanwhile the KRS scoured the city looking for dangerous Negroes, including those who knew too much about the preceding events for anyone's safety. When Major Curtis confessed that the only protection he could give the white Republicans was a military escort out of town, most of them decided to leave. At this point some civic leaders, alarmed at the probable effects to the town and themselves of such an exodus under these circumstances, urged them to stay and offered their protection. But the Republicans recalled the pledge to Smith and departed as quickly as they could, some openly and others furtively to avoid ambush.[15]

White Conservatives saw these events—or at least their background and causes—in quite another light. They regarded Smith as "a dangerous, unprincipled carpet-bagger" who "lived almost entirely with negroes, on terms of perfect equality." Whether there was evidence for it or not, they found it easy to believe further that this "cohabitation" was accompanied by "the most unbridled and groveling licentiousness"; according to one account he walked the streets with Negroes in a state of near-nudity. For at least eighteen months he had thus "outraged the moral sentiment of the city of Jefferson," defying the whites to do anything about it and threatening a race war if they tried. This might have been overlooked if he had not tried repeatedly to precipitate such a collision. As head of the Union League he delivered inflammatory speeches and organized the blacks into armed mobs who committed assaults and robberies and threatened to burn the town. When part of the city did go up in flames earlier in the year Smith was held responsible. Overlooking the well-attested white terrorism which had prevailed in the city and county for months, a Democratic newspaper claimed that all had been peace and quiet during Smith's absence at the constitutional convention. But on his return he resumed his incendiary course and made it necessary for the whites to arm in self-defense.

According to Conservatives the initial shooting affray on the night of October 3 was precipitated by a group of armed Negroes with Smith at their head. They opened fire on Crump and his friends while the latter were on their way to protect a white man whom Smith had threatened to attack. Democrats did not dwell overlong on the ensuing lynching, nor did they bother to explain the killing of the Negro prisoners. In fact the affair was made deliberately mysterious and a bit romantic in their telling. According to the Jefferson *Times,* both the soldiers and the civilians on guard at the jail characterized the lynch party as "entirely sober and apparently well disciplined." (One of the party later testified in court that at least some of them had put on their disguises while drinking at a local saloon.) "After the accomplishment of their object," the *Times* continued, "they all retired as quietly and mysteriously as they came—none knowing who they were or from whence they came." (This assertion, it turned out, was more hopeful than factual.)

The *Times* deplored such proceedings in general, it assured its readers, but in this case lynching "had become . . . an unavoidable necessity. The sanctity of home, the peace and safety of society, the prosperity of the country, and the security of life itself demanded the removal of so base a villain." A month later it declared: "Every community in the South will do well to relieve themselves [sic] of their surplus Geo. Smiths, and others of like ilk, as Jefferson rid herself of hers. This is not a healthy locality for such incendiaries, and no town in the South should be." Democratic papers made much of Judge Caldwell's refusal to appear publicly with Smith— which was probably inspired by his Negro associations. They claimed that Smith's fellow Republicans were also glad to have him out of the way, and noted that the local citizens had assured them of protection. But there was no mention of the riotous search and the threats upon their lives which produced that offer, nor of their flight from the city anyway.[16]

The Smith affair raises problems of fact and interpretation which appeared in almost every Ku Klux raid across the South. Most were not so fully examined or reported as this, but even here it is impossible to know certainly where the truth lay. Republican and Democratic accounts differed diametrically on almost every particular, and both were colored by considerations of political and personal interest. But enough detailed and impartial evidence survives to sustain the Republican case on most counts. Negro and Republican testimony concerning the actual events in October is confirmed by members of the KRS who turned state's evidence when they were later brought to trial. Smith's prior activities and his personal character are less clear. Republicans all agreed later that he was almost puritanical in his moral code and that he was hated because of his unquestioned social associations and political influence with the blacks. He never counseled violence or issued threats to burn the town, they insisted; on the contrary, the only time he ever headed a Negro crowd was when he brought a number of them to help extinguish the fire which he was falsely accused of starting.[17]

As elsewhere in the South, the logic of some of the charges against Smith is not convincing. Whites had a majority in the city and blacks in the county. Theoretically each could gain by racial violence, offsetting its minority status. But Conservatives always had the advantage in such confrontations. They were repeatedly guilty of intimidating the freedmen, and in case of an open collision everyone (including Republicans) knew they could win hands down. Democrats were certainly sincere in their personal and political detestation of Smith; almost as certainly they were sincere in their fears of his political activity and what it might lead to. From their viewpoint an open consorter with and leader of Negroes was capable of anything. It was easy therefore to believe the worst and attribute the basest motives without clear evidence. If some Negroes did threaten to burn the town—often this was a threat to retaliate for preceding white terrorism—it was easy to overlook the real cause and attribute the idea to Smith. The next step, involving hypocrisy and deliberate falsehood in some cases, was to charge him with specific expressions and activities which no other source substantiates and which the logic of the situation makes improbable. Men who practiced or condoned terrorism and murder in what they conceived to be a just cause would not shrink from character assassination in the same cause.

Interestingly enough, most of the character assassination—in Smith's case and generally—followed rather than preceded Ku Klux attacks. This did not arise primarily from a feeling of greater freedom or safety once the victim was no longer around to defend himself; some victims, unlike Smith, lived to speak out in their own behalf.[18] Accusations after the fact were intended rather to rationalize and win public approval of the attack once it had occurred; since these raids were the product of at least semisecret conspiracy there was less need to win public approval beforehand. Sometimes such accusations were partially true, no doubt, and it was never easy for persons at a distance to judge them; often it is no easier now. Democrats tended to believe and Republicans to reject them as a matter of course. The *Daily Austin Republican* was typical of Radical papers in its reaction to Democratic newspaper slurs against Smith after his death: "We have read your lying sheets for the last *eighteen* months, and this is the first time you have made any such charges. . . ." It was surely justified in charging the Democratic editors of Texas with being accessories after the fact in Smith's murder.[19]

The military authorities had done almost nothing to stop KRS terrorism among the Negroes before Smith's murder, and this violence continued for at least two months afterward. Similar conditions prevailed widely, and there were too few troops—especially cavalry—to patrol every lawless county. But the murder of a white man, particularly one of Smith's prominence and in such a fashion, aroused officials to unwonted activity. The Army recalled Major Curtis and sent Colonel H. G. Malloy to Jefferson as provisional mayor with orders to discover and bring to justice the murderers of Smith and the two freedmen killed with him. More troops were also sent, amounting ultimately to nine companies of infantry and four of cavalry. With their help Malloy arrested four of Jefferson's leading men on December 5. Colonel W. P. Saufley, whom witnesses identified as the organizer of the lynching, would have been a fifth, but he left town the day before on business, a Democratic newspaper explained, apparently unaware that he was wanted. (This business was to take him into the Cherokee Indian Nation and perhaps as far as New York, detaining him so long that the authorities never succeeded in apprehending him.) That night the KRS held an emergency meeting and about twenty men left town for parts unknown while others prepared to follow.

General George P. Buell arrived soon afterward as commandant, and under his direction the arrests continued for months, reaching thirty-seven by early April. They included by common repute some of the best as well as the worst citizens of Jefferson. Detectives were sent as far as New York to round up suspects who had scattered in all directions. One of the last to leave was General H. P. Mabry, a former judge and a KRS leader who was serving as one of the counsel for the defense. When a soldier revealed that one of the prisoners had turned state's evidence and identified Mabry as a leader in the lynching, he abruptly fled to Canada.[20]

The authorities took great pains to recover Anderson Wright and Cornelius Turner, the Negro survivors of the lynching, whose testimony would be vital in the forthcoming trials. After locating Wright, General Buell sent him with an Army officer to find Turner, who had escaped to New Orleans. They traveled part of the way by steamboat and at one point, when the officer was momentarily occupied elsewhere, Wright was set upon by four men. He saved himself by jumping overboard and made his way to a nearby Army post, whence he was brought back to Jefferson. Buell then sent a detective after Turner, who eventually was located, and both men later testified at the trial.

The intention of the authorities was to try the suspects before a military commission, as they were virtually sure of acquittal in the civil courts. Defense counsel (who consisted ultimately of eleven lawyers—nearly the whole Jefferson bar) made every effort to have the case transferred; two of them even went to Washington to appeal personally to Secretary of War Schofield, but he refused to interfere. R. W. Loughery, the editor of both the Jefferson *Times* and the *Texas Republican* in Marshall, appealed to the court of public opinion. His editorials screamed indignation at the "terrible and revolting ordeal through which a refined, hospitable, and intelligent people are passing, under radical rule," continually subject to the indignity and danger of midnight arrest. He also sent requests to Washington and to Northern newspapers for intercession against Jefferson's military despotism. The prisoners, he said, were subject to brutal and inhuman treatment. Loughery's *ex parte* statement of the facts created a momentary ripple but no reversal of policy. In reality the prisoners were treated quite adequately and were confined in two buildings enclosed by a stockade. Buell released a few of them on bond, but refused to do so in most cases for the obvious reason that they would have followed their brothers in flight. Although they seem to have been denied visitors at first, this rule was lifted and friends regularly brought them extra food and delicacies. The number of visitors had to be limited, however, because most of the white community regarded them as martyrs and crowded to the prison to show their support.

After many delays the members of the military commission arrived in May and the trial got under way; it continued into September. Although it proved somewhat more effective than the civil courts in punishing Ku Klux criminals, this tribunal was a far cry from the military despotism depicted by its hysterical opponents. The defense counsel presented their case fully and freely. Before long it was obvious that they would produce witnesses to swear alibis for most or all of the defendants. Given a general public conspiracy of this magnitude, and the oaths of KRS members to protect each other, this was easy to do; and given the dependence of the prosecution by contrast on Negro witnesses whose credibility white men (including Army officers) were accustomed to discounting, the tactic was all too effective. The results were mixed. At least fourteen persons arrested at one time or another never went on trial, either for lack of evidence or because they turned state's evidence. Seventeen others were tried and acquitted, apparently in most cases because of sworn statements by friends that they were not present at the time of the lynching. Only six were convicted. Three of these were sentenced to life terms, and three to a term of four years each in the Huntsville penitentiary. General Reynolds refused to accept the acquittal of Colonel Crump and three others, but they were released from custody anyway, and the matter was not raised again. Witnesses who had risked their lives by testifying against the terrorists were given help in leaving the state, while most of the defendants returned to their homes and occupations. The arrests and trials did bring peace to Jefferson, however. The Knights of the Rising Sun rode no more, and the new freedom for Radicals was symbolized in August by the appearance of a Republican newspaper.[21]

Relative tranquillity came to northeast Texas generally during the early part of 1869. Some Republicans attributed this to the election of General Grant, but that event brought no such result to other parts of the South. Both Ben Bickerstaff and Cullen Baker were killed and their gangs dispersed, which certainly helped.[22] The example of military action in Jefferson likely played a part; it was accompanied by an increase of military activity throughout the region as troops were shifted here from the frontier and other portions of the state.[23] Immediately after the Smith lynching in October, General Reynolds ordered all civil and military officials to "arrest, on the spot any person wearing a mask or otherwise disguised."[24] Arrests did increase, but it was probably owing less to this order than to the more efficient concentration of troops. In December the Bureau agent in Jefferson had cavalry (for a change) to send out after men accused of Ku Klux outrages in Upshur County.[25] Between October 1868 and September 1869 fifty-nine cases were tried before military commissions in Texas, chiefly involving murder or aggravated assault; they resulted in twenty-nine convictions.[26] This record was almost breathtaking by comparison with that of the civil courts.

The Texas crime rate remained high after 1868. Organized Ku Klux activity declined markedly, but it continued in sporadic fashion around the state for several years.[27] A new state government was elected in November

1869 and organized early the next year under Republican Governor E. J. Davis. In his first annual message, in April 1870, Davis called attention to the depredations of disguised bands. To cope with them he asked the legislature to create both a state police and a militia, and to invest him with the power of martial law.[28] In June and July the legislature responded affirmatively on each count. The state police consisted of a mounted force of fewer than 200 men under the state adjutant general; in addition, all county sheriffs and their deputies and all local marshals and constables were considered to be part of the state police and subject to its orders. In November 1871 a law against armed and disguised persons followed.[29] Between July 1870 and December 1871 the state police arrested 4,580 persons, 829 of them for murder or attempted murder. Hundreds of other criminals probably fled the state to evade arrest. This activity, coupled with occasional use of the governor's martial law powers in troubled localities, seems to have diminished lawlessness by early 1872. There still remained the usual problems of prosecuting or convicting Ku Klux offenders, however, and very few seem to have been punished legally.[30]

CHAPTER 10

The Arkansas Militia vs.
the Ku Klux Klan

The months of September and October 1868 saw a continuation of the systematic terrorism which had enveloped large parts of Arkansas that summer. In the view of General C. H. Smith, the federal commandant, this represented a concerted effort to overthrow the new state government and was not geared specifically to the fall election campaign.[1] It is difficult to know exactly what the Ku Klux intended, or to what degree they followed a statewide plan. As always, many Negroes and Unionists were attacked for economic, social, or purely personal reasons. In some counties Klansmen disarmed Republicans of both races, on general principle and to prevent the organization of militia companies. Most of the specifically political terrorism was aimed at local officials rather than at the state government itself. Despite the boasting of General Robert Glenn Shaver many years later that he had had a Ku Klux army of several thousand in the field ready to ride on Little Rock and topple the state government,[2] no attack of this nature ever impended. Much of the terrorism this fall aimed at disrupting voter registration and intimidating prospective Republican voters. In addition, Arkansas was one of the few states which significantly disfranchised ex-Confederates, and terrorists tried to force registrars to enroll such persons.

The areas most affected continued to be the southern and northeastern counties, where lawless bands had existed since before the war.[3] Least affected were the heavily Negro counties of the southeast and the strongly Unionist west and northwest. The proportion of Negroes and Unionists alone was not decisive, however; one of the strongest Klan counties—Crittenden, across the river from Memphis—was about 80 per cent Negro. (In Phillips County, three-quarters black, a flurry of Klan raids to disarm freedmen on plantations near Helena ended in September, soon after white public opinion condemned it through a public meeting and the local Democratic newspaper.) [4]

To the south, around Monticello, Klan activity was largely political in motivation. A band of about fifteen disguised men took Deputy Sheriff William Dollar from his home one night in October and tied a rope to his neck. They tied a Negro, Fred Reeves, to the other end, led them about 300 yards from the house, and shot them to death. Then they entwined the two bodies together in an embrace and left them in the road, where they remained as an object of attraction to the curious for two days. [5] There was no further activity until just before the election, when disguised bands rode through town, took two Negro preachers (who were known as Republican leaders) from their homes, and whipped them; one man received 400 lashes. White Republican leaders in Monticello were threatened with assassination, and several county officials declared themselves Democrats to avoid that fate. Throughout the county Negroes were threatened with death if they voted Republican, and on election day nearly all of those who came to the polls cast Democratic ballots. The result was 1,292 votes for Seymour and 33 for Grant. This did not entirely stop the marauding, for one man who refused to vote was taken out and whipped, and another Negro minister was carried off from his home. [6]

The chairman of the Lafayette County voters' registration board reported to Governor Clayton in mid-October that he had just fled that county for his life. Since the latter part of August, he said, "there was an organization formed of from one to two hundred men, for the avowed object of killing Union men, of both colors, who would not join democratic clubs and vote their ticket. Some ten to fifteen colored men were shot down for this cause, and I had reliable information that if I attempted to register [any voters] I would be assassinated." Other county officials either fled too or refused to take office. [7]

The same conditions prevailed in Little River, Hempstead, and Sevier counties in the southwest corner of the state, where the Cullen Baker gang and other desperadoes duplicated or even exceeded Ku Klux activity, so far as they were distinguishable. In Little River County the United States revenue assessor and the Freedmen's Bureau agent were murdered, the sheriff was shot in the arm, one freedman was killed, and another was wounded, all near the appropriately named village of Rocky Comfort. When a Negro militia detachment was raised to go after the murderers, it was confronted by an assemblage of 300 armed whites who forced it to surrender and give up its arms. Thereafter Negroes were shot down in cold blood and Negro women were raped, with scarcely a hand raised to prevent it.[8]

L. G. L. Steel of Sevier County wrote Governor Clayton three days after the election, reporting that he and another Republican, Mat Locke, had been hiding out in the woods for more than a month. "We are daily advised that we are in imminent danger, but to-day I leave my camp. Mr. Locke will leave for Little Rock. I have not the means to go." The sheriff was similarly threatened, he said, but had apparently "caved," and was permitted to remain at home unmolested. Other Republicans who might have helped Steel "are alarmed to see me appear at their houses. I am one of the marked ones. . . . I bless God that I am a republican, but regret that I live in a government that gives me no protection. It is probable that I will be in eternity when you receive this letter." Steel survived, but as late as March 1869 he continued to complain of desperadoes infesting the county.[9]

In the northern counties where Negroes were few and white Unionists at least a substantial minority, Ku Klux activity was very limited. It usually represented a continuation of the partisan warfare between Unionists and Confederates which had begun in 1861. The only Ku Klux raids of any importance in the Ozark region occurred in September in Boone (then part of Carroll) County. A band of Klansmen raided a small Negro settlement and ordered the residents to leave the state. Most of them did so the next day, abandoning their crops and many of their possessions. One man refused, however, and the Klan returned and killed him. Although they threatened all Radicals and militiamen in the vicinity too, the sheriff went after them with a posse of eighty militiamen. He failed to capture anyone, but the Ku Klux made no further appearance.[10]

In Fulton County, farther east along the Missouri border, Negroes were not involved and the Rebel-Unionist conflict assumed greater proportions. After a long period in which the Union minority was subjected to mounting threats and intimidation, the Democrats in September formed a club which looked very much to outsiders like a Ku Klux den. The Republican sheriff, E. W. Spear, responded by raising a company of state guards or militia who began patrolling the county. On September 19, as Captain Simpson Mason was riding down a road with half a dozen men, apparently engaged in this duty, they were fired upon from ambush and Mason was killed.[11] Suspicion rested on the Ku Klux and especially their reputed leader, Colonel N. H. Tracy, one of the county's most substantial farmers. Sheriff Spear then assembled a posse of about thirty men, probably state guards, who went out and arrested several of Tracy's followers. Tracy himself went into hiding and eventually fled the county.

At the same time, the Ku Klux began raiding. They warned Union men to stay home and law officers to resign their positions if they didn't want to share Mason's fate. The Unionists now appealed for help to Colonel William Monks of Missouri, who had operated as a Unionist partisan chief here during and immediately after the war. Monks had also been a friend of Mason's, and he responded by bringing a force of about seventy-five armed men from Missouri. Reaching Fulton County about September 25, they reinforced a detachment of local militia who had commandeered Colonel Tracy's farm and were fortifying themselves in expectation of a Ku Klux attack. Monks and his Missourians were now sworn into the Arkansas militia by Sheriff Spear. Under his authority they arrested several more persons for complicity in Mason's murder and took over those already in custody. All but four of the prisoners were soon released. According to Democratic accounts, however, they were subjected to threats and torture to extort information from them. This likely was true; Captain L. D. Bryant supposedly was hung by the neck until he admitted to holding a position of leadership in the Klan and revealed some of its organization and designs in that part of the state. He said that the Mason killing had been planned in advance, and identified Uriah B. Bush (a fellow prisoner) and several others as part of the plot. Having told all this, Bryant was released and apparently went into hiding.

When Monks came on the scene the local Klan sent out couriers to adjacent counties, appealing for reinforcements to help capture the prisoners before he could put them to death. This message reached Batesville, more than thirty miles south, on Sunday the twenty-seventh; within hours a sizable body of men was under arms and on its way. At least 300 men converged on Salem, the Fulton County seat, that night, and when the army reached full strength the next day it numbered about 700 men from at least five counties, fully armed and ready to do battle.[12] Their intention was to take the prisoners, by force if necessary, and turn them over to the civil authorities; the latter in turn would have to release them when the Klan produced alibis clearing them of Mason's murder. To lend a further air of legality to the proceedings they offered to be sworn as a posse under Sheriff Spear, but he declined.

Open warfare might have resulted but for the arrival of Judge Elisha Baxter, a Republican who would be elected governor in 1872. He averted a conflict by falling in, to all intents and purposes, with the Ku Klux plans. After consulting with both the Klan leaders and the sheriff he issued a writ of habeas corpus for the prisoners and sent a deputy sheriff to Monks's camp with a letter demanding that the men be turned over to him for trial. When the deputy added the further warning that the Ku Klux army would attack his small force if he refused, Monks surrendered his prisoners. That night he went back to Missouri with his men—as he later said, to recruit reinforcements—while the state guard company moved to a more defensible position.

The deputy sheriff started back toward Salem with the prisoners. But along the way he was stopped by a party of fifty armed men who took Uriah Bush away, carried him into the woods, and shot him to death. Sheriff Spear later said that these were Ku Klux, while Democrats alleged that they were Monks's men wearing paper caps and pretending to be Ku Klux. Of course Monks could have killed the prisoner long since if he had wanted to; apparently the Klan suspected, rightly or wrongly, that Bush had joined Captain Bryant in confessing what he knew of the order. When the other prisoners reached Salem no evidence against them was forthcoming, and Judge Baxter discharged them. Some of the Klansmen moved on to attack Monks's camp anyway, only to find it deserted. Most of them then dispersed and left the county, but local Klansmen resumed their raids, threatening death to Unionists who refused to leave, and especially to any who might try to make further arrests. Not long afterward someone found the body of Captain Bryant hanging from a tree, eaten away by buzzards.

In the middle of October Governor Clayton sent a detachment of state guards to Fulton, and soon afterward, at his request, Monks returned with three more companies of Missourians. They too were sworn into the militia, and their leader was commissioned a lieutenant colonel. The militia conducted a further investigation of the Klan and its activities, but Clayton advised the sheriff against any further arrests until after the November election. Meanwhile Union men still complained of having to seek refuge in the woods for fear of Rebel attacks.[13]

A little to the south, in those counties which had provided reinforcements for the Fulton County Klan, the Ku Klux were most active in opposing the recruitment of local militia. They intimidated Negroes into not joining, ambushed recruiters, and raided the homes of militiamen and Negroes, confiscating their weapons. This occasioned a brief battle in Woodruff County between Negroes and Ku Klux, in which one man was killed and several wounded on either side. A militia captain in Jackson County reported in November that he could muster in his command of 85 men at any time, but it would be pointless, since their guns had been taken from them. On election eve the Klan paraded through Jacksonport, perhaps 200 strong, and rode about through the countryside. This followed much previous intimidation, and most Negroes refused to vote on election day.[14]

Perhaps the worst terror in this part of the state occurred in Crittenden County, opposite Memphis. The Ku Klux there continued with impunity the patrolling and raiding which they had begun in the summer, and shot and hanged several persons during the latter part of October. The most publicized crime was the attempted murder of Captain E. G. Barker, a one-armed Union veteran who doubled as state senator and Bureau agent in the county. Barker was shot and seriously wounded by a party of Klansmen in August. The doctor who attended him obviously thought he was taking his own life in his hands by doing so. Captain E. M. Main, who succeeded Barker briefly as Bureau agent, reported that the terror became so intense that hundreds of freedmen were flocking to his plantation for protection. Main appealed for troops, and a few were sent late in October, but they accomplished almost nothing.[15]

The highest-ranking official to fall victim to the Ku Klux terror in any state was Congressman James M. Hinds of Little Rock, who was shot and killed from ambush in Monroe County on October 22. Hinds's companion, James Brooks, another future governor, was seriously wounded in the same attack as they were riding along a road on their way to fill a speaking engagement.[16]

According to reports received in the governor's office, more than 200 murders were committed in Arkansas during the three months prior to the November 3 election; to these must be added innumerable other crimes of violence.[17] Ku Klux raiding and the accompanying threats pervaded the state so thoroughly by November that no informed person of either race or party could fail to know in general what was happening, who was doing it, and why. The victims were without significant exception Negroes and white Union men; some were government officials, voting registrars, or members of the state guard, and virtually all were Republicans. If some of the outrages—especially in the southwest—were committed by desperadoes like the Cullen Baker gang, the greater part were the work of disguised bands generally known as Ku Klux Klans. Despite the fact that nearly all of these operations were local in character and inspiration, they were collectively the product of a Democratic conspiracy which embraced most of the state. Democratic newspapers and party leaders steadfastly ignored and occasionally denied altogether the existence of the Ku Klux Klan within the state. The major statewide Democratic organ, the *Arkansas Gazette* in Little Rock, set the tone by arguing that Republicans deliberately assumed disguises to beat and murder Negroes and to break up their own meetings in order to blame it upon unoffending Democrats. "They invited a carnival of blood that they might be sure of their spoils." And where white Democrats were undeniably responsible for shooting prominent Republicans the incidents were said not to be politically inspired and not countenanced by Democrats as a whole.[18]

It was obvious as early as August that local officials and ordinary civil processes were impotent to cope with the terror in most of the afflicted counties. Like other governors, Clayton tried to use detectives to penetrate the Klan, expose its secrets, and secure evidence that might be used to punish malefactors in court. These efforts failed until September, when a repentant Grand Cyclops came to him and told what he knew of the Klan in Independence and White counties, northeast of Little Rock. With this information Clayton was able to send a detective, Albert H. Parker, with enough mastery of the ritual and passwords to gain admittance to the den at Searcy in White County. His assignment was to discover the murderers of Negro leader Ban Humphries earlier in the year and those who had tried to kill state senator Stephen Wheeler. Clayton soon employed eleven other detectives on similar missions around the state, most of whom sent back useful reports. But he never heard from Parker again, and it was not until March 1870 that he discovered what had happened to him. At that time John McCauley confessed membership in the White County Klan and revealed that he had participated in Parker's murder in October 1868. When Parker failed to buy any cattle (his ostensible purpose in going to Searcy) the Klan grew suspicious and discovered his real mission. He was killed on order of the local hierarchy, including General Danridge McRae, the Grand Titan of that congressional district, and Colonel Jacob Frolich, newspaper editor and Grand Giant of the county; his body was thrown into an old well. After McCauley's revelation both McRae and Frolich fled, the former to Canada. In 1871 they returned to Arkansas to stand trial with several others, including the mayor of Searcy, for murder. Despite the testimony of McCauley and another participant who turned state's evidence, all were acquitted. The trial was a farce, and Clayton regretted that he had not declared martial law in the county at once and tried the suspects by military commission.[19]

It was clear that the Arkansas Klan intended to help carry the November elections for the Democratic party. Voter registration took place during several weeks prior to the election, and in many counties Klan terrorism disrupted the process. Clayton's immediate response was simply to withdraw registrars and set aside the registration (and hence the election) in the worst counties.[20] This might have frustrated the Klan's political objective, but it did nothing to protect the black and white Republicans who were on the firing line. Army troops continued to be sent to various points in the state, and probably they deterred violence somewhat in their immediate vicinity.[21] But for the average Republican in the hinterland the soldiers afforded little relief.

Clayton had served notice as early as July that he would call the militia into being and use it against the Ku Klux if necessary. The next month he began the process of organization, which continued into October. Doubtless he hoped that the bare existence of a militia subject to call would itself suffice to decrease terrorism, but often it had the opposite effect. The Klan harassed militia organizers, raided the homes of recruits, and confiscated their weapons. Wherever Union men were numerous and sufficiently well organized to sustain the local authorities, on the other hand, Clayton encouraged sheriffs to mobilize them as posses, and sometimes they were used to good effect. Thus the sheriff of Carroll County managed to quell the small-scale terror there, even if he failed to catch the criminals. In Fulton County, where the governor had to send in reinforcements from other counties and make use of Monks's Missouri volunteers, the policy contributed to a mutual escalation, but was ultimately successful. In Little River County, where the sheriff summoned a posse of predominantly Negro militia, it was overwhelmed by superior force and disarmed, leaving the terrorists in control. In many other counties the sheriffs were too powerless or too frightened to do more than write the governor for outside protection.

The militia were often less well armed and equipped than the Confederate veterans whom they might have to meet in the field. To increase the militia's firepower, therefore, Clayton sought guns and ammunition outside the state. He tried first to borrow guns from Illinois and other Northern states and, failing this, sent an agent to purchase them in New York. This man bought 4,000 rifles with ammunition and accessories for $15,282.59 and had them shipped as far as Memphis, where they arrived on October 5. The Democratic Memphis *Avalanche* learned of the shipment even before its arrival. The editor's indignation was boundless; these guns, he exclaimed, were "to be placed in the hands of the negroes of Arkansas . . . for the purpose of shooting down inoffensive citizens." He pronounced anathema upon the warehouse company which accepted them for temporary storage: "The vender of poison is as guilty as he who administers it, and the man who secretes, shelters and protects weapons intended for the hands of a wild, infuriated and insurrectionary mob of negroes, is as culpable as the peddler of poison, the receiver of stolen goods, the retailer of falsehoods, or the assassin who murders." He promised to keep "our friends in Arkansas" advised of the guns' destination, and to retain them in Memphis as long as possible; "but if the people of Arkansas quietly submit to their being distributed among negroes for their own destruction, they are unworthy of the life which these implements of death are intended to take. . . . Woe to the steamboat," he warned, "that prefers such freight as swords and guns to plows and pruning hooks." A few days later the *Avalanche* all but invited someone to destroy the guns before they could reach their destination.[22] As a result of this pressure neither of the steamboat lines going to Little Rock would accept the shipment, and it remained in storage until the state could charter a special boat.

The vessel it secured was the *Hesper,* a small steamboat captained by one Sam Houston, known with his brother as the only Republican steamboatmen on the Arkansas River. Houston came to Memphis, loaded his explosive cargo on October 15 amid great excitement in the city, and headed downriver. About twenty-five miles below the city he noticed a tugboat, the *Netty Jones,* rapidly overtaking him. Having plenty of reason to suspect an attack by this stronger and faster vessel, he deliberately ran aground on the Arkansas shore to avoid being rammed in midstream. The tugboat followed and came alongside. Until that moment no one had been in sight on the pursuing vessel. But the moment they touched, a whistle blew and sixty or seventy armed and masked men sprang up and began shooting wildly at the *Hesper.* Houston's crew of fifteen was in no mood to resist, and they promptly surrendered; the captain and his brother jumped ashore and scrambled up the bank as the Ku Klux fired after them. The Klansmen then boarded the *Hesper* while the *Netty Jones* took her in tow and headed back into the river. They seized the guns and apparently threw them overboard, although there were stories later that they kept at least part of them and even sent some down to the KWC in New Orleans. Then they turned the *Hesper* loose, allowing her to drift back to the Arkansas shore, where Houston reclaimed her. No one was injured except Houston's brother, who was wounded while making his escape.

The whole operation was obviously well organized and planned in advance. (According to a friendly account, "Several bottles and flasks of the fluid were seen circulating among the raiders, but no one was under its influence.") During the mission the Klansmen exchanged signals with land parties on at least one and perhaps both banks. Those on the eastern or Mississippi shore sent out skiffs which took the Klansmen ashore and back to a carefully preserved anonymity in Memphis. The attackers were apparently all from the city, and the raid was probably planned there. Governor Clayton had expected that the Arkansas Ku Klux might try to capture the arms, and he sent a hundred militia to board the ship at Helena for the trip up the Arkansas River. But as Houston later advised him, the Klan had intercepted every word in every dispatch the governor sent him. Captain Ford of the *Netty Jones* was probably in on the plot; his story that the Klansmen had overpowered him and commandeered his boat was not very convincing, and he was later arrested when he ventured into Arkansas.

Democratic newspapers reveled in the triumph. None attributed it to the Ku Klux Klan, however, since they refused to admit publicly that such an organization existed. In the words of the *Avalanche,* "No one knows who these mysterious beings are that have exhibited so much antipathy to guns and blunderbuses. Some are of the opinion that they are mermaids riding upon the back of a dolphin; others believe that they are angels of mercy who believe in Grant's motto, 'Let us have peace,' and that they have destroyed them in order to prevent murder, and to give peace to the people of Arkansas." But no Ku Klux outrage could be allowed to go by without at least a half-hearted effort to pin it on the Radicals: "Still a larger portion of our people believed that these guns were sent to Memphis by Radicals, to be destroyed by Radicals, in order to frighten the Northern people into the belief that another rebellion had bursted [sic] out in the South. . . . We know not, and care not, who it was that destroyed these weapons; but we do know that the party deserves the everlasting thanks of the people that they were intended to shoot and murder."[23]

Having lost his arms shipment, Governor Clayton now appealed to the Secretary of War, General John M. Schofield, for the use of federal guns stored in a government arsenal in Little Rock. Schofield deemed the matter important enough to raise at a Cabinet meeting on October 23, and supported Clayton's request. Both President Johnson and Navy Secretary Gideon Welles objected, however; Welles took the Conservative line that Clayton was a carpetbagger "who feared the people he professed to govern." There was no insurrection against the laws in Arkansas, he said, and Clayton's only purpose in asking for arms was to perpetuate rule by the "black and ignorant element" of the state over the "intelligent white population." Moreover, there was general reluctance in the Cabinet to release federal arms under these circumstances during the climax of a heated political campaign, and Secretary of State Seward prevailed with a compromise formula to send more federal troops to the state instead.[24]

In addition to these logistical problems, Clayton was as aware as anyone of the political hazard in using troops during an election campaign. Democrats would charge (as they did throughout the South whenever state or federal troops were employed before elections) that he had carried the voting by storm. For Clayton this consideration weighed even more heavily than the shortage of guns. On October 14, when he had every reason to believe that the guns in Memphis would soon be available, he nevertheless sent a circular to voter registrars around the state denying their requests for troops to ward off actual and threatened violence. "In view of the fact that an election is pending, and from motives of public policy, I do not wish to use a military force if it can be avoided. The whole principle of the ballot is a free expression of the public will, and the use of a military force, either at the registration or election, is not desirable." Counties where the laws could not be enforced would have to do without a registration or election.[25] By this means he would thwart the purpose of Democratic violence without incurring blame for using it himself—at least before the election. When the voting took place on November 3, fourteen counties did not participate, and the Republicans won a statewide majority of 3,000. The counties not represented in the total were for the most part those in which terrorism had been most endemic.[26]

Even before the election Clayton made it clear that he had not been intimidated and that a lack of guns had not been the major obstacle to military action against the Ku Klux. On November 1 he wrote each member of the legislature, telling of his intention to proclaim martial law in the most disturbed counties as soon as the election was over. On November 4 he issued a proclamation to that effect, applying to ten counties scattered around the state. These were not the only counties which had seen Ku Klux terrorism, but they were among the worst, and he threatened to extend martial law to others if they proved disorderly. Clayton blamed the Klan for much of the preceding violence and called upon all members of the order to withdraw from it.[27]

In resorting to martial law Clayton roused a storm of controversy which reverberated throughout the country. Democratic anger and abuse were predictable, but many of the governor's own followers advised against it and publicly voiced reservations after the step was taken. Foremost among these was the Little Rock *Republican,* the main party organ in the state, which had faithfully chronicled the reign of terror ever since April. Another new critic was General C. H. Smith, the federal commander in the state, who also admitted the preceding terrorism and had even suggested martial law himself within the past week as the only solution. The *Republican* associated the violence with the political campaign and expected it to subside after the election. Martial law, it said, was too drastic an expedient now that the crisis had probably passed.[28]

Clayton believed, however, that the terror extended beyond the current political campaign; it represented a concerted effort to overthrow the state government by threats and assassination, and would not disappear when the election was over. Something had to be done, if only symbolically, to sustain the power and reputation of the state government and to show that it, rather than the Ku Klux Klan, was the highest authority in Arkansas. The laws had been flaunted with impunity, and if defiance went unchecked and unpunished it could easily extend throughout the state until it overcame all resistance. He hoped that a show of military force, coupled with arrests and punishments, demonstrating the state's power and determination to protect its citizens against terrorism, would prove sufficient and that civil law could be restored and the militia disbanded within thirty days or so.[29]

The governor might simply have sent militia to the affected counties without declaring martial law, as he had done in Fulton County and as Brownlow had done in Tennessee in 1867. But this might have had no greater impact than sending federal troops. Even if it halted terrorism during the militia's stay it made no provision for punishing those who had committed violence, and the terror could be expected to resume after the militia left. The civil authorities would do little if anything to punish terrorists when they knew that the state guards would soon depart and leave them exposed to even greater Democratic wrath. Clayton's purpose was to break up the Ku Klux Klan and halt the terror permanently; martial law, involving military arrests and military trials, seemed the only answer.

Unfortunately, as the Little Rock *Republican* pointed out, the state constitution made no provision for martial law. The governor could call out the militia to enforce the laws in concert with the civil authorities, but there was no authorization for military trials. On the other hand, neither the Arkansas constitution nor the American legal system contemplated such a widespread conspiracy against law and order as the Ku Klux terror represented. As Lincoln had stretched the federal constitution to cope with a rebellion unforeseen by the founding fathers, and Congress stretched it further to deal with the rebellion's aftermath, so Clayton was prepared to do in Arkansas in 1868.

Martial law was justifiable long before the election, but the militia was not organized sufficiently to carry it out until September or October; by that time political considerations supposedly made it unwise. Meanwhile the terror increased, and when the governor did invoke martial law it was overdue. Clayton was not a dictator, and he did not misuse the power he now assumed. Martial law was withdrawn and the militia disbanded just as soon as it appeared safe to do so—even sooner than was safe in some counties, because of pressure within his own party.

Although the responsibility ultimately was his alone, Clayton required the support of the legislature for both political and financial reasons. After some astute diplomacy on his part, Republicans made a show of closing ranks behind him and he weathered the storm. The legislature met later in November and endorsed his policy unanimously, although there continued to be some grumbling behind the scenes.[30]

After a month there were signs that dissatisfaction might come into the open again and possibly result in a legislative curtailment of the campaign. Clayton had no desire to perpetuate it in any case, but this uneasiness on the part of fellow Republicans may have hastened its termination. Adjutant General Keyes Danforth wrote the militia commander in northeast Arkansas early in December, asking him to cease his operations within thirty days. "All we can do now is to show the rebels that we can march the militia through any county in the State whenever it is necessary. . . . You see we are likely not only to have to fight the rebels but the Legislature also."[31] The same policy, less resolutely pursued, would two years later land Governor Holden of North Carolina in a court of impeachment and result in his expulsion from office. Other governors, with smaller white Union elements from which to recruit an effective militia, lacked Clayton's options and remained relatively powerless in the face of the Ku Klux terror.

Clayton started by dividing the state into four military districts. The southwest was placed under the command of Robert F. Catterson, a Union brigadier general and presently a member of the state house of representatives. The southeastern district was entrusted to Colonel Samuel W. Mallory, a state senator. The northeastern commander was Brigadier General D. P. Upham, another legislator who had been the object of earlier Ku Klux threats. The northwest was least affected by the terror; no over-all commander was ever named and no general campaign was undertaken there, but militia units from that region composed a large part of the forces sent to other sections. The commanders of the other three districts were ordered on November 7 to occupy the counties in which martial law had been declared and to mobilize as many additional militia as they could, by conscription if necessary.[32] Clayton spent several anxious days wondering if the militia would actually respond to his call, but they did. About 2,000 men served in the campaign, chiefly white Unionists from the northern and western counties and Negroes in the south and east. In many of the operations they served together, but usually in separate companies.

As Clayton recalled, the state entered the campaign "without a gun or round of ammunition, without a single tent, wagon, horse, mule or [other] equipment, and without food or raiment with which to feed and clothe the men." All these things the men had to supply themselves at the outset and replenish by foraging or commandeering as they went along.[33] The militia had orders to give vouchers upon the state treasury for the animals, provisions, and equipment they took. In general they seem to have done so, but there were many exceptions. The later practice, moreover, was to honor only those vouchers held by "loyal" men, which usually meant Republicans. The intent was undoubtedly to put the financial burden on the localities and persons who had caused the trouble, but complete accuracy in that respect was obviously impossible.[34] Compensated seizures were probably necessary, but as practiced they unnecessarily increased Conservative hostility to the campaign as a whole.

On November 13 General Catterson took command of 360 mounted guardsmen who had assembled at Murfreesboro, ninety miles southwest of Little Rock. They encountered armed resistance almost immediately. Hearing that the prospective enemy had stored a supply of arms at the town of Center Point, a hundred militia were sent to seize them. The guards searched the town, seized all of the arms and ammunition they found, and commandeered horses, bridles, shoes, and other goods for their own use.

While the search was in progress they herded a number of residents into a nearby field to keep them under observation. Before they finished, news came that 500 men were gathering from four adjacent counties to oppose them. The militia now released their prisoners and retreated back toward the main base at Murfreesboro. Conservatives later claimed that this raid was their first notification of martial law; the counter assemblage, they said, consisted of men from the surrounding countryside who came in response to reports that the place was being sacked by lawless marauders.

The next morning Catterson and the main body of militia advanced on Center Point, absorbing the retreating detachment en route. Nearing the town, they encountered at least 400 men who were drawing up in line of battle to block their way. Catterson sent flankers off to the left and right, then resumed his advance. The defenders took cover in and among the houses and opened fire, but as soon as the flanking columns approached from different directions they were forced to withdraw and regroup behind a church. The main column of militia now rallied and charged this position, causing the enemy to scatter in disorder. This ended the Battle of Center Point, and with it all organized resistance in this part of the state. The militia lost one man killed and five wounded.

Catterson now made another, more thorough, search of the town, confiscating additional supplies. His men occupied one building from which a shot had been fired and discovered it to be the meeting place of the Ku Klux Klan, with disguises hanging about on the walls and a Confederate flag draped over an altar. Climbing through a trap door in the ceiling, they discovered several men in hiding, whom they arrested. (One of these was identified as John Crawford, a former Confederate major and later a defaulting Democratic state auditor.) About sixty other prisoners were taken under similar circumstances. Catterson sent some of them to Little Rock for trial or safekeeping. Clayton promptly returned them, however, with orders to try those who were charged with serious crimes before a military commission and to withhold punishment pending his approval.

From Center Point the militia moved west through Sevier County, then southward into Little River County. From here they doubled back eastward through Lafayette, Columbia, Union, and Ashley counties, along the Louisiana line. Along the way they searched for individuals who were suspected of major crimes in the preceding months. Most of these persons had fled before their arrival, but others were arrested and tried by military commission. Clayton's orders to Catterson were to "select the worst" for trial and punishment, letting the rest go. However, "All desperate characters that may fall into your hands, you had better deal with summarily." The governor soon abandoned his requirement that all convictions be sent for his approval before sentence was carried out. The number of executions was apparently small. Two persons were hanged in Little River County, one of them a murderer of the tax assessor and Bureau agent some weeks before. Seventeen other prisoners in that county were turned over to the civil authorities for trial, only to be discharged after martial law was lifted. Some members of the Cullen Baker gang were arrested; Baker himself eluded arrest but was killed soon afterward by a private citizen.[35]

The militia continued to seize provisions, which led furious Conservatives to brand them as marauders and robbers. Catterson discovered that some of the pillaging attributed to his command was in reality committed by small bands of freebooters who followed along in his wake. He gave angry citizens permission to shoot such men on sight.[36] A storekeeper in Ashley County accused the state guards of robbing him of a quantity of finger rings, cambric handkerchiefs, gold watches, fine laces, and the like. But according to Catterson they really took from him two cases of double-barreled shotguns, 1,400 pounds of buckshot, 15 kegs of powder, and 50,000 percussion caps.

The militia were also accused of torturing prisoners—even hanging some by the neck—to extract confessions. This charge was not refuted and may well have been true in a few cases. Negro militiamen who augmented the command were charged with raping white women, a story which horrified Democrats readily believed and circulated in exaggerated form across the country. In fact a small group of Negro guards did rob a Sevier County man's home while one of them assaulted his wife. Catterson promptly tried them by court-martial; on conviction, the assailant was shot and the others were dishonorably discharged.[37]

However valid the charges brought against them, the militia under Catterson accomplished their major objective of rooting out the terrorists who had infested southwest Arkansas. Conservatives in that region were more fearful of the militia than of the Ku Klux criminals they had earlier supported or condoned. They now sent delegations to Little Rock promising to maintain order and asking for the removal of martial law. In one county after another until early February Clayton granted these requests as soon as conditions appeared peaceful enough to justify it. At the same time he arranged with General Smith to post federal troops at least temporarily in the counties where martial law was lifted, to help deter further outbreaks.[38]

Colonel Mallory's campaign in the southeast was later in beginning and smaller in proportions. His force consisted at first of three companies of Negro militia recruited in Little Rock and Pine Bluff. They arrived at Monticello on November 30 and encountered no opposition. One Saturday night some of the men broke discipline, however, and engaged in indiscriminate shooting for a few minutes. They inflicted no casualties, but the next day 200 white men assembled and insisted on disarming them. At the same time a delegation of leading citizens from both parties went to Little Rock to assure Clayton of the community's peaceful intentions. Under the circumstances Clayton agreed to let them raise two companies of home militia on a nonpartisan basis to take over the occupation of the county. The Negro troops were then mustered out of service. On their way home they engaged in considerable plundering, thereby confirming the prejudices of the white community.

In December General Catterson moved into the southeastern district and joined Mallory at Monticello. The militia now made a number of arrests here, including one of the Klansmen who had murdered the deputy sheriff and the Negro in October. He was tried by military commission, convicted, and executed. Most of the other serious criminals fled the county. By these means one of the worst trouble spots in the state was rapidly pacified.

Catterson and Mallory returned to Little Rock on January 5 with their joint command of 450 men. They were met at the outskirts of the city by a military band and an official reception party headed by the governor. These conducted them in a triumphal procession through the streets to the state house, where they passed in final review. "A rougher looking band could scarcely be conceived," sniffed the *Gazette*, "heightened as it was in appearance by the dust and fatigue of a long march. They were dressed in citizens' clothes [as they had been throughout the campaign], with red flannel bands to their hats as a sort of distinguishing mark, mounted on anything that could be picked up, from a poor mule to a superb horse, and armed with pretty much every weapon known in civilized or uncivilized warfare." The troops were soon mustered out, and on February 6 the governor lifted martial law in the southeastern district. The militia did less in this district than in the southwest, but its very presence frightened Conservatives into assuming responsibility themselves to end the terror. This was the major result hoped for—and to a considerable degree attained—everywhere.[39]

In December Clayton extended martial law to Conway County, a short distance northwest of Little Rock, where an earlier pacification attempt on his part had failed. The Klan became active here in August, when a mob broke up the county court and disguised bands began systematically disarming, robbing, and driving persons from their homes. This was well before the general militia campaign was contemplated, and Clayton decided to go there in person and try to arrange an amicable settlement. Chartering the soon-to-be-famous steamboat *Hesper,* he took a number of prominent Democrats and Republicans with him. At Lewisburg (the chief town) he conferred with leading citizens and addressed a public meeting. Whites here had fallen prey to the familiar terror of Negro uprising and saw it confirmed in the organization of the militia. Clayton tried to set the fears at rest, appealed to all parties to obey the law, and promised to call out the militia only if the civil authorities could not maintain order. There were no further serious outbreaks before the election, although Clayton said he learned later that the Klan had intended to disarm the blacks and then intimidate them into either abstaining or voting the Democratic ticket in November. As it was, the Republicans carried the county.

Ku Klux raids resumed late in November, however, while the militia campaign was getting under way elsewhere in the state. Klansmen killed a Negro and set fire to a Republican-owned store in Lewisburg; the fire got out of control and burned about a third of the town. The county militia joined the sheriff as a posse and arrested three Klansmen, one of whom confessed to the recent crimes. Then he was shot and killed—the militia said he was trying to escape. It was an act of cold-blooded murder according to Conservatives. A local peace justice wrote Clayton that "Lawlessness, with all its horrors, reign[s] supreme here. . . . I do not try to maintain the authority and majesty of the law, for I am very well convinced that at least half of the people here are of the Ku-Klux order." On December 8 the governor imposed martial law and sent in 200 outside militia under Captain John J. Gibbons. A week later the Klan murdered an elderly Lewisburg merchant and burned his store too. Democratic accounts, through design or misinformation, immediately attributed these crimes to the militia, and they were copied by newspapers around the country. But local citizens testified otherwise, and a coroner's jury composed of Democrats named two culprits, at least one of them a Klansman. Both men fled the county along with many of their colleagues and neighbors. Some went to Memphis, which was becoming a major haven for Arkansas Klansmen.

By now the Klan had exhausted the tolerance of the local Democratic community. Terrorizing Negroes was one thing, but burning the town was quite another. The citizenry cooperated fully with the authorities, got permission to form their own militia company, and prevailed on the governor to lift martial law after two weeks. A small detachment of federal troops went in to replace the guards when they left.[40]

The militia campaign in the northeast had to wait several weeks because troops were not yet available. Meanwhile the Klan continued to ride in several counties as if no proclamation had been issued. The sheriff of Izard County, hitherto comparatively quiet, reported that the Ku Klux had organized 200 strong there. They were a menace to life and property and swore to whip the militia if it was brought out against them.[41]

Operations began early in December, when General D. P. Upham brought sixty state guards to Augusta, in Woodruff County. Other companies soon joined him, composed of mountaineers from the northern part of the state. On his arrival Upham confiscated all of the arms and ammunition he could find and also commandeered provisions. The next day he got word that at least 200 insurgents were mobilizing outside town under Colonel A. C. Pickett and were planning to attack. Upham responded by seizing fifteen hostages and threatening to destroy both them and the town if attacked. The citizens, with his blessing, now sent a delegation into the woods and persuaded Pickett and his men to disperse. The hostages were then released, except for a few who were wanted for previous crimes. Soon afterward another insurgent force gathered near Augusta, composed of men from other counties. Upham sent a detachment of troops which attacked and quickly routed them.

Like the other militia commanders, Upham found that many of the men suspected of terrorist activity had fled before his arrival. Nevertheless he made a number of arrests. One man was apprehended for supplying ammunition to the insurgents in the woods. Some of the prisoners were tried by military commission, and several were shot by firing squad.

Despite Conservative charges, it is unlikely that executions took place without even the pretense of a trial. But the raw recruits in Upham's command lacked military discipline at times, and residents had legitimate complaints. Some of the guards had been fired upon on their way to Augusta, and as a result they began plundering the town as soon as they arrived. Upham arrested them and returned the goods to their owners. When reports of wholesale plundering reached Little Rock the governor sent Adjutant General Danforth to investigate. Most of the charges, Danforth found, arose from the authorized confiscation of arms and provisions, for most of which the owners were entitled to reimbursement later.

More serious was the misconduct of Captain John H. Rosa, whom Upham left in command late in December while he himself moved on to other counties. Together with one or two fellow officers, Rosa proceeded to milk the residents of some $4,000 by arresting and then releasing them in return for ransom payments of up to $500. Others had to pay in order to save their property from confiscation. When the authorities caught up with his racketeering Rosa was arrested and sent to Little Rock to stand trial for blackmail.

Many of the leading citizens in Augusta got together as soon as possible to rally support for a return to law and order and civil government. The whole trouble had originated with a few irresponsibles, they said, and they pledged their influence in dispersing the remaining insurgents and maintaining order. In return they asked for the lifting of martial law and the removal of the militia. Much of their argument was made in good faith. But Clayton later recalled an interview he had at the time with a delegation who came to Little Rock. It was headed by Colonel Pickett, the recent insurgent leader, who opened by saying, "Governor, I know not how it is in other counties in the State, but we can assure you that there are no Ku Klux in Woodruff County." Clayton interrupted and pulled from his desk drawer a list of Woodruff County Klansmen which he had recently received from General Upham. He handed the paper to the colonel to look over, asking him to note that his own name headed the list. Before Pickett had a chance to reply, Clayton reprimanded his visitors for coming with lies on their lips. "If you will go back home, and in good faith disband the Ku Klux organization there, and furnish me with conclusive evidence that you have done so, and I have means of knowing whether you do or not, I will revoke martial law and restore the civil authorities there." After a speechless moment they agreed to do so. Years later, after one of the visitors, Colonel C. L. Gause, had been elected to Congress, he told Clayton that they had ribbed Pickett all the way home for failing to deliver the speech that he had prepared and read to them in advance. On December 19 a public meeting was held in Augusta at which 400 persons signed a pledge to assist the civil authorities in bringing all criminals to justice. Later, on Upham's recommendation, the governor suspended martial law in the county.[42]

Militia detachments also went to Craighead, Greene, and Mississippi counties in the northeast corner of the state, where the Klan had been active through November. Colonel Monks and his Missourians took charge of Mississippi County, where he had to discipline a subordinate for the same kind of activity Rosa had engaged in. In January Colonel Will Tisdale fought a skirmish with several hundred insurgents near Jonesboro, but they soon disbanded. Otherwise the campaign in these counties was uneventful, and martial law was soon suspended.[43]

A main trouble spot all along had been Crittenden County, opposite Memphis, although Clayton had not included it in his original proclamation. Bands of Ku Klux reportedly were busy around the county for many weeks prior to the election, killing, whipping, and intimidating prospective Negro voters. The situation hardly improved after the election. Late in November they took a Negro from his home and shot him; when a physician was asked to dress the wounds he refused to come and the man died the next day. His widow recognized the assailants as the same men who later sat on the coroner's jury pronouncing the verdict: "Killed by a gunshot by unknown parties." The sheriff himself was apparently a Klansman and participated in outrages. Democrats and Republicans alike, in fact, were so completely cowed by desperadoes that men hardly dared speak aloud in opposition to the terror. Republicans appealed repeatedly to the governor to extend martial law here. Local militiamen were subjected to constant threats and harassment. When the governor did proclaim martial law in December, implying that a militia occupation impended, white men repaired their guns and openly proclaimed their intention to repel the Yankee invader. Memphis Klansmen, on the pretext of going hunting, crossed the river to reinforce them.

Despite their preparations and bravado, the Crittenden Klansmen were caught off guard when the militia finally arrived. The first unit to reach Marion, the county seat, was a flying squad of cavalry who dashed into town shortly after Christmas and made several arrests before any resistance could form. On their heels were 400 infantry commanded by Colonel J. L. Watson of Helena. Two of his seven companies had been raised locally and the others were from nearby counties. All of the men and two of their lieutenants were Negroes, and they were possibly the best troops in the state service. Most had seen active service in the Union army, a fact which was not long in showing itself. Taking over the jail as headquarters, they made camp around it and then enclosed the whole with a ditch and an earthen rampart eight feet thick, topped with palisades. This in turn was ringed by an outer line of fortifications. As observers from Memphis carefully noted, it would require artillery to reduce these defenses.

The Ku Klux were not intimidated, however. Although the troops went abroad freely to hunt down suspects and forage for provisions in the daytime, they found themselves besieged in their fortifications after dark. Every night for about a week rebel parties drove in the pickets, and skirmishing took place reminiscent of events four and five years earlier. The siege lifted with the arrival of William Monks's cavalry on their way to Mississippi County.

As usual the militia were accused of indiscriminate plunder, but there was very little of this, and offenders were punished. One soldier was court-martialed and shot for robbing and killing a man in the country. Four others gained national publicity by raping two white women, for which offense they were tried, convicted, and dispatched by an all-Negro firing squad. In general the troops maintained good discipline; atrocities laid at their door by the Memphis Democratic press, and thence relayed around the country, were in some cases deliberate fabrications which local Democrats later disavowed. Governor Clayton made a special trip to the county late in January, partly to investigate these reports for himself, and he concluded that the militia had been as orderly as could possibly be expected under the circumstances. The federal commandant in Memphis sent over an officer who rendered the same judgment.

The militia made a number of arrests. Three or four men apprehended for complicity in the attempted Barker assassination earlier in the year were shot while attempting to escape. This seemed questionable on its face;

Clayton investigated it particularly and pronounced the explanation true. At least one man, charged with several murders, was executed after a military trial; he confessed to at least one of these crimes on the scaffold. Two others were standing trial at the time martial law was lifted, and their cases were turned over to the civil authorities. Among the others arrested was the Ku Klux sheriff, who was eventually released after submitting his resignation. By early February, after Clayton's visit, signs of organized insurgency had disappeared and the greater part of the militia were sent home. Colonel E. M. Main, a local resident, took over command, and Crittenden remained until March 21 the last county in the state under martial law.

Here, too, many or most of the criminals fled before they could be apprehended. Nearly all of the refugees seem to have congregated in Memphis, where they were supported in every way by the Ku Klux Klan and the Democratic establishment. In Conservative eyes they included some of the "very best citizens of Arkansas," the innocent victims of brutal Negro bandits. Within a week of the militia's arrival the refugees met in Memphis to decide how best to get them to withdraw. They arranged a public meeting on January 5 at Mound City, just across the river, which adopted resolutions deprecating abusive and inflammatory language against the militia. Armed with this olive twig, delegates from Mound City went to Colonel Watson to ask respectfully that his command take its leave. But Watson was still fighting off nocturnal Ku Klux attacks and had not yet arrested all the people he came to arrest. On his refusal the refugees and their Memphis allies again took thought of driving the militia away by force. Serious plans were apparently made to raise a force in Memphis for this purpose, and there were even reports that they wired General Grant in Washington to see what his reaction would be. But the President-elect is said to have replied that he would fully support the state authority, and the contemplated invasion was set aside. Again they turned to diplomacy. The attacks on the garrison at Marion broke off and the refugees began urging strongly that the prisoners presently in military custody be turned over for trial to the civil authorities in Crittenden. In anticipation of this happy event they engaged some of the best lawyers in Memphis for the defense. On January 20 Confederate General Gideon J. Pillow added his weight by sending a personal appeal to Governor Clayton for permission to hold another law and order meeting in Crittenden. He offered himself as a personal hostage against any further outbreak of violence.

Assurances of this sort were doubtless one reason for Clayton's personal inspection trip to Crittenden on January 26. Although he sent home most of the militia force, leaving only about fifty men on duty, the governor had no intention yet of lifting martial law. Many fugitives were still at large, and the ending of martial law would require turning over all prisoners to the civil courts, which were almost certain to discharge them. He had hopes of securing some of the refugees through extradition, and in that case wanted military courts available to try them. For whatever reason—conferences with some of the refugees or their friends, negotiations with the Memphis authorities about arrest and extradition, or simply the theater and city lights—Clayton seems to have spent more time in Memphis on this trip than across the river in Crittenden County. The visit entailed some personal risk, whether he knew it at the time or not. Years later a Memphis Klansman who turned Republican informed him that the Klan had held a meeting to consider his assassination, but finally rejected the proposal. One of the Memphis papers reported at the time that an attempt might be made on the governor's life on his return trip to Little Rock.

As long as Governor Brownlow held sway in Tennessee, Clayton could hope for extradition of some of the Arkansas refugees. In fact the Parson was preparing at this time to call out the Tennessee militia once more against the Ku Klux, and sympathized fully with Clayton's policy. He acceded readily, therefore, to Clayton's initial request for the extradition of Major Joshua F. Earle. Earle had been not only a leading figure in the visible Democratic party of Crittenden County, but the head of its Ku Klux Klan too according to sworn statements of members which were in Clayton's possession. News of Brownlow's action set off a further exodus of the Arkansas refugees, the Memphis *Appeal* urging them to flee to unreconstructed Kentucky. The Memphis police caught up with Major Earle on March 2, just as he was boarding a boat to leave. He offered resistance, but was overpowered and brought to the police station. On his person was a letter addressed to Colonel Main in Crittenden, informing him that the Ku Klux Klan had been ordered disbanded there and throughout Arkansas on January 29. Earle doubtless hoped that this news would hasten the end of martial law. The disbandment order purportedly emanated from a higher authority, but Earle's possession of it tended to confirm his own high rank within the organization.

The Earle arrest set off a near-panic among the Ku Klux and their partisans in Memphis. They mustered the best legal talent in the city to get him freed on a writ of habeas corpus, and they supplemented their legal case by intimidating the court and the Republican community generally. The effort was largely successful. Earle was freed on bond to appear before the civil courts in Crittenden County at a later date, which was tantamount to acquittal. Moreover, the Klan or its supporters seem to have persuaded Nashville not to extradite any more Arkansas Klansmen. Brownlow dealt a blow to anti-Klan efforts in both states by resigning the governorship on February 25 to enter the United States Senate. His successor, DeWitt C.

Senter, chose to conciliate the Klan rather than defy it. On March 21, 1869, Governor Clayton finally lifted martial law in Crittenden. Peace had been restored, the militia had arrested all the terrorists they could find in the county, and there was no longer any hope of capturing and trying the Memphis refugees by military commission.

The sequel showed once more how farcical it was to entrust Klansmen to the civil courts of a Ku Klux county. Of the two prisoners in military custody who were turned over to the local authorities on March 21, one was acquitted and the other never brought to trial despite strong evidence that they both were guilty of murder. Moreover, the militia were hardly disbanded when persons clamored to try Colonel Main and one of his subordinates, Captain A. J. Haynes, for murder in connection with actions they had performed in the line of duty. This never happened, but in July 1869 Captain Haynes was murdered on a street corner in Marion by a twenty-one-year-old gunslinger named Clarence Collier. Collier had been a Ku Klux, was involved in its earlier atrocities, including at least one murder, and had fled the county with the advent of martial law. When it was lifted he returned to settle old scores. Although a number of persons were standing around watching, Collier was left undisturbed as he shot Haynes in the back with a shotgun, then walked up and emptied his revolver into the body, retrieved his coat from a nearby restaurant, mounted his horse, and rode away. The Memphis *Public Ledger* rhapsodized over his heroism: "Gallant Clarence Collier! The blessings of an oppressed people go with you, and whenever the clouds lift you shall be known and honored throughout the lands [*sic*] as the William Tell of Crittenden County, Arkansas."[44]

Elsewhere in the state martial law had come to an end on February 6, three months after its institution. No other county was subjected to it for that long, however, since the militia did not take over most of the affected counties until late November or December and then withdrew as soon as conditions appeared to warrant it. The militia campaign was expensive, given Arkansas's financial resources; a Congressional committee later estimated the total cost at $300,000. In January 1871 some of the militia had not yet been paid and some persons had not been reimbursed for goods confiscated.[45]

There were scattered outbreaks of Klan activity after the militia left, but they were of short duration.[46] More typical of the campaign's aftermath were the public meetings held in many counties, in which residents pledged themselves to maintain law and order and to discourage inflammatory political activity. The governor made a tour of the southern counties and addressed several of these meetings. People turned out for them in large numbers, he said, and treated him with the utmost respect. "During the past three months," he reported to the legislature on March 21, "but five murders have been reported . . . while during the preceding four months nearly two hundred murders and attempted assassinations were reported."[47] When some of the desperadoes of Little River County who had fled from the militia returned in January, local militiamen (apparently with public backing) arrested them and put them in jail.[48]

Democrats publicly characterized the militia campaign as an unprovoked orgy of murder, plunder, and rapine imposed on an innocent and defenseless population. According to Republican accounts some Conservatives privately endorsed its effects in their own localities, but if so, these views got little circulation. Much of the specific criticism was directed at the militia's alleged plundering of private citizens in the course of living off the lands it occupied. Part of this resentment was justified, but Democratic outrage arose fully as much from the campaign's legitimate objectives and positive achievements. And Conservative critics often chose, like the Memphis *Appeal,* to ignore the fact that the militia was predominantly white:

The consequences of this act of the villain who calls himself governor of Arkansas, in arming these bands of negroes and sending them to murder and rob the peaceable inhabitants, are not only disastrous to the parties who suffer directly, but to the whole state. Just at the time when every hand is needed in the cotton fields this large force is drawn off and muskets thrust into their hands, that civil war, which is sure to follow, may rage throughout the state, to gratify "Governor" Clayton's hatred and fiendish thirst for blood.[49]

The innocent inevitably suffered from military operations along with the guilty, but a large proportion of the white population in these counties was implicated in the preceding violence and intimidation. The larger share of active criminals, however, suffered no more punishment than exile from their homes, and for many of these the banishment was short-lived.[50]

Approval of the governor's course came ultimately from many of those men who had recognized the need for some kind of action all along, but who advocated reliance on federal troops instead of the militia. General Smith and federal district judge Henry C. Caldwell in Little Rock both conceded afterward that Clayton's judgment had been better than their own. The governor also won praise from United States Supreme Court Justice Samuel F. Miller, who was doing circuit court duty in Arkansas during most of the militia campaign. General Grant was favorably disposed at the outset, but in December, after the newspapers began filling with militia outrage stories, he sent General Horace Porter of his staff to investigate personally. In January General Rousseau in New Orleans sent General R. B. Ayres on the same mission. Both officers sustained Clayton's policy.

Ayres found that militia outrages had been exaggerated in many cases and wholly fabricated in others. Such excesses as did occur, he said, were unavoidable accompaniments of all military operations and were far outweighed by the campaign's pacifying effect throughout the state. According to Porter, "The Governor is certainly a man of intelligence and nerve, and has labored under difficulties that would have deterred a less able officer."[51]

The Camden *Journal* provided a fair appraisal of the campaign in the southern counties, and its judgment applies as well throughout the state:

If we look at affairs as they existed in those counties *before* being visited by Gen. Catterson, and as they exist now, any man who loves order and deprecates indiscriminate murder, will be satisfied that the militia was a good institution in general. No one denies, or attempts to apologize for the wrongs committed by *individuals* belonging to the command. Many of them robbed innocent persons of their property, which was bad, and beyond the power of the officers to prevent; but we hope no good citizen will assert that the *stealing of property* was as great an evil as the shooting and hanging of men, for no other reason than their political opinions, as was common before Gen. Catterson went there. Those counties are now peaceable, quiet and law abiding.[52]

For all practical purposes the Klan ceased to exist in Arkansas early in 1869. In most cases, probably, it simply stopped functioning. But there were group resignations from the order at Jonesboro, and in other places the order was apparently disbanded. It was reported in November that the Ku Klux organization in Little Rock had decided to burn its records, discontinue its meetings, and send couriers throughout the state to halt all "assassination schemes" until further notice. This decision was made on November 5, the day after martial law was proclaimed. The reason given, however, was that the state authorities had penetrated the secrets of the order, making it necessary to consult the parent Grand Council in New Orleans. If the story is true it probably involved the Arkansas branch of the Knights of the White Camellia, but Clayton and other outsiders regarded the KWC and the KKK as identical.[53]

Two factors apart from the militia campaign may conceivably have influenced Ku Klux disbandment in the spring of 1869. The Klan leadership in Tennessee apparently disbanded at about this time, largely in response to conditions there. The generally accepted view is that General Forrest tried to apply this action to the South as a whole, and there are evidences of dissolution in northern Alabama too. Thus when Major Earle wrote in February or early March of an order disbanding the Klan in Crittenden County and throughout the state, it may have been promulgated on orders from Forrest. On the other hand, Forrest's disbandment order was generally ineffective outside of Tennessee. Most Klan leaders at a distance were not in communication with him, even indirectly, and doubt-less never heard of his order. Their activities were determined almost entirely by local considerations in their own states. This was likely the case in most of Arkansas.

Another motivation for disbandment may have lain in an act of the Arkansas legislature, passed on March 13, outlawing " 'The Knights of the White Camellia,' . . . more generally known as the Ku-Klux." This law was copied extensively from the one passed in Tennessee in September 1868, but was less severe in some respects. Members of this or any other society which engaged in violence or prowled the countryside in disguise who did not resign their membership within thirty days were subject to a fine of at least $500 and a prison term of from one to ten years. The law also penalized those who aided and abetted the Klan, and public officials who refused to prosecute its members. In Congressional debate in 1871 Representative O. P. Snyder of Arkansas stated that Governor Clayton had "obtained not only the constitution and by-laws of the Klan, but the names of its leaders and hundreds of their followers." He had "no less than six hundred affidavits on file" by 1871 of acknowledged Klansmen who came forward to purge themselves under the state law of March 1869.[54] This act was undoubtedly responsible for twenty-five Klansmen collectively and publicly resigning from the order in Jonesboro later that month. But actions of this sort were not widely reported. Few if any prosecutions were brought under the law, moreover, and similar enactments in other states had little effect in curbing the Klan.[55]

It seems very clear now as it did then that the militia campaign was directly responsible for disrupting the Klan and restoring peace throughout most of Arkansas. Governor Clayton's calculated risk had paid off. As a result he accomplished more than any other Southern governor in suppress-ing the Ku Klux conspiracy.

CHAPTER II

Tennessee: Abortive Martial Law and Disbandment

When the Presidential campaign opened, Governor Brownlow was holding in abeyance his threat to call out the militia in Tennessee. Ku Klux activity had diminished in recent months, and he relied on a regiment of federal troops, distributed in about twenty localities, to maintain order.

One of the towns playing host to a small garrison was Pulaski, the Klan's birthplace. Civic and Klan leaders here (who were substantially identical) had at length asserted themselves in favor of moderation and brought the terror to a stop during the summer. This spirit continued to prevail until just before the election. But then and especially on election eve, November 2, disguised bands again raided throughout the county. There is no evidence that the leaders discountenanced this activity; they likely ordered it. Men of both races were threatened with death if they voted Republican. Black men were promised protection papers and immunity from further outrage if they voted Democratic. One Negro was murdered, his body left hanging with a note attached, promising similar treatment to anyone who cut him down. Little actual violence was committed on election day itself, but the polls were surrounded in some places by gangs of threatening and abusive whites who made a rush at Negroes trying to vote. One Confederate veteran who cast a Republican ballot was seized by the crowd, put on a block, and offered for sale as a "white nigger." Under this pressure only 664 Negroes voted out of about 2,100 registered; some of these voted Democratic, receiving certificates or protection papers in return. Many of those who cast Republican ballots went to the polls in a body in order to defend themselves. When complaints were voiced about the acts of terrorism, the Pulaski *Citizen* dismissed some of them out of hand and completely ignored the rest. It characterized the resulting Democratic county victory (by about fifty votes) as a triumph of fair play; every man entitled to vote had been free to do so without molestation, it said, and bayonets had not compelled Negroes to vote the Radical ticket.[1]

The same conditions prevailed throughout much of middle Tennessee, and with the same results. In Lincoln and Franklin counties, east of Pulaski, the Klan seized white Republicans' guns before the elections as well as whipping Negroes and repeating the usual admonitions about voting. Here, too, the greatest activity was concentrated on the night of November 2, though it was by no means confined to that night. Both Negroes and whites later testified that they had voted the Democratic ticket the next day out of fear. Abraham Lillard, a legislator from Marshall County, reported that he and many of his Republican colleagues were afraid to return to their homes from Nashville. When they did return they sometimes felt it necessary to lie out in the woods to evade attack. According to the sheriff of Rutherford County, the arrival of troops a month before the election led the Klan to desist from night riding there, but did little to guarantee a free election. Negroes were still fearful of voting near their homes, and many came in to Murfreesboro for that purpose, as the law permitted. But once they got to town white men serving as special police prevented most of them from reaching the polls.[2]

The story was similar in parts of west Tennessee. The Klan relied on nonviolent intimidation in some counties, but elsewhere whippings were frequent and murders by no means unknown. In Weakley County drunken Klansmen burst in on the commissioner of registration while he and his family were at evening prayers. Rushing at him with drawn pistols, they demanded that he swear to a string of oaths which they read from a paper. They got into a dispute among themselves, however, began pushing and even shooting each other, and finally withdrew with a number of self-inflicted wounds.[3] One of the worst areas was in Shelby County, just outside Memphis. The city itself was bristling with Ku Klux (as Arkansas developments showed), but Negroes were not terrorized there and the city became a haven for refugees from the surrounding countryside.[4]

The Republicans carried Tennessee again in November by a two-to-one margin because of the continuing legal disfranchisement of ex-Confederates. But Grant's total was 18,000 fewer than Brownlow's in 1867. The effects of the Ku Klux Klan were strikingly reflected in returns from the counties where it had been most active. The Republican vote fell off in west Tennessee, dropped drastically in the middle region, and remained about the same in the east, where the terror had not penetrated. In Giles (Pulaski) and seven other counties of middle Tennessee the approximate Negro voting population was 18,293. Brownlow's vote for governor in August 1867 (which included white Republican ballots) was 17,712, but the vote for Grant in these counties was only 8,924. In Giles County the Republican vote fell from 1,879 to 561. In none of these counties did the Democratic vote rise very much. The political effects of the terror were nullified in large part by throwing out the votes of several counties, and the House of Representatives ultimately seated the Republican Congressional contender in this district after an investigation of Democratic campaign tactics.[5]

The terrorism diminished only slightly after the election. The Klan remained very much in evidence, with raids continuing in November and December, and in some cases as late as February 1869. In Shelby, Gibson, Tipton, and other counties of west Tennessee conditions actually grew worse after the election. Many outrages were economically or socially inspired, and won little support from the Conservative establishment. When the KKK severely whipped some Negro railroad construction workers for taking "white men's jobs," the Memphis *Avalanche* referred to them as "prowling vagabonds." (The *Avalanche* had so much sympathy for the labor contractor, a Confederate veteran who faced financial loss if his workers were driven off, that no compassion was left for the black men who suffered the beatings.)[6]

Some of the violence in middle Tennessee was still politically inspired. A Negro in Coffee County was whipped 200 lashes soon after the election for having voted Republican; several of his neighbors were similarly treated. A white county commissioner there lay out nights after receiving Ku Klux threats. When he relaxed this policy one night in January to get out of the cold, he was discovered, taken from his house, and beaten with "beech gads." The only reason his assailants gave was that he was a Radical.[7] A band of at least twenty-five Ku Klux galloped into Shelbyville one night early in January, shouting for "Dunlap and fried nigger meat." When Dunlap, a schoolteacher whom they had flogged on the Fourth of July, and some friends fired on them the Klansmen beat a hasty retreat, apparently suffering one fatality. Union men threatened that if either Dunlap or his school was attacked they would exact a comparable vengeance on prominent Rebels. Neither was harmed thereafter, but Negroes outside town continued to suffer from beatings and robbery.[8]

The blacks of Overton County routed a small Ku Klux band late in December, capturing three horses and as many shrouds. But several nights later at least a hundred undisguised white men returned to the scene and demanded the horses. The Negroes were badly outnumbered, and they agreed. Night riding continued, with the Klan both taking and receiving casualties. One night, after a Negro was killed in a raid, one of the attackers was himself found hanging from a tree, reportedly executed by the Klan for killing an innocent man. This action, if true, was not typical here or elsewhere. When the Ku Klux lost another member in raiding a Negro home, they renewed the attack, shot the offending black man to pieces, and according to a newspaper account, disemboweled him with knives. White men here were fully convinced that it was the blacks, not they, who threatened the peace of the community, and they determined to protect themselves. Some 200 men took over Livingston, the county seat, walking the streets with guns on their shoulders and disarming Union men.[9]

Even more newsworthy was the Barmore murder at Columbia. Governor Brownlow had hired Seymour Barmore, a former Treasury Department agent, as a detective to gather evidence about the Ku Klux Klan at Pulaski and elsewhere. During the fall he apparently worked his way into the order—or at least into the confidence of some of its members. But eventually they became suspicious and warned him off. Nevertheless he returned to Pulaski from his base in Nashville early in January. Whatever his real purpose, he went ostensibly to convey a Negro prisoner who was wanted in Pulaski for robbery. After the prisoner's trial (and perhaps after attending a Klan meeting as well) Barmore boarded a return train for Nashville on the night of January 11. The train crew and the telegraph operators along the way, it developed, were either Ku Klux members or collaborators. When the train stopped at Columbia after midnight, a dozen or more masked men boarded Barmore's car, overpowered him in a short struggle, and took him off the train. He was taken about four miles into the woods, hanged, and shot. Several weeks later his body was fished from the Duck River, by now a favorite repository for Ku Klux victims. Barmore is said to have had a full list of Pulaski Klansmen on his person, but how much information he had earlier conveyed to the authorities is unknown. After his death his effects included a full Ku Klux disguise of the sort worn in Pulaski.[10]

In and around Pulaski too the Klan remained active, attacking white Republican planters and driving off their black laborers. Members also boarded trains, warning certain crew members to quit their jobs. On the night of December 18 a Negro was taken from jail and lynched by disguised men.

As the violence continued, it became increasingly clear that white leaders (including those of the Klan) had again lost control of the movement they reanimated before the election. Conservative spokesmen began voicing displeasure at the trend of events. The Pulaski *Citizen,* still the mouthpiece of the Klan leadership, carried a letter early in December from an anonymous former admirer of the Klan, saying that raiding had gone too far. As elsewhere, this attitude was motivated less by sympathy for Negro and Radical victims than by resentment at poor whites whose use of the Klan organization unsettled the community and discouraged business. The leaders' own political objectives were no longer served by this activity. On Christmas eve the leaders sponsored a public meeting at Pulaski like that which had temporarily stopped Klan activity several months earlier. General John C. Brown and Frank McCord officiated, and speeches were delivered deprecating mob law. It now became safe and even fashionable to express these views publicly. Once again this technique virtually ended Ku Klux activity around Pulaski.[11]

The Conservative reaction to Klan violence spread across the state. Former governor Neill S. Brown, elder brother of General Brown of Pulaski, wrote a public letter which appeared widely in the press in the middle of January. Like the Pulaski leaders, he paid his compliments to the Klan's original purposes so far as he claimed to know them, and declared that many of the stories of Klan outrages were doubtless exaggerated. But, he said, the time for secret societies of regulators had now passed and Klan activity was unnecessary. It frightened away capital, discouraged immigration to the state, and frustrated the efforts of ex-Confederates to regain the vote.[12] Democratic newspapers in Nashville and elsewhere adopted the same line. Where outrages continued to be committed, the Conservative press began reporting them. Public meetings which were held in many counties adopted resolutions befitting the occasion. "We condemn in unmeasured terms," declared the people of Shelbyville, "the practice of an organization known as the Ku-klux Klan, or any set of men who assume disguise and prowl over the country, creating terror and excitement, or who write anonymous letters, or who are threatening innocent parties with retaliation; and we hereby pledge ourselves to use every persuasive and peaceable effort in our power to put down all lawlessness of whatever character, no matter who may be the perpetrators." There was no intimation, however, in these resolutions of any intent to ferret out and punish those who had committed violence in the past.[13]

On January 25 there followed a lengthy order from the Imperial Wizard, General Forrest, calling for the drastic curtailment of Klan activity. Bad men had entered the organization and perverted it from its original purposes, he declared, and public opinion had turned against masked societies. Therefore masks and disguises must be "entirely abolished and destroyed" in the presence of each Grand Cyclops. Any persons seen in disguise thereafter would be considered enemies of the Ku Klux Klan. All further demonstrations were forbidden unless ordered by a Grand Titan or higher authority. More specifically, Negroes were not to be disarmed unless they were arming and meeting for insurrectionary purposes; no one was to be whipped for any purpose or interfered with because of his political opinions; breaking into jails to abduct or execute inmates was forbidden; and members were not to send threatening letters in the name of the society or use it for personal gain. This order stated explicitly that it was not to be understood as a complete disbandment of the Klan; on the contrary, the organization should hold together more firmly than ever before to guard against any emergency.[14]

A Conservative revulsion against violence was only part of the reason behind these events. Republicans were calling increasingly for another militia campaign to restore order, and hopefully to root out the Klan for good. By January they were hailing Governor Clayton as the nemesis of Klan terrorism in Arkansas and a fit example for the "old hero" to follow in Tennessee. Brownlow (like Clayton) saw little use in calling out the militia again without giving it the power to try and punish criminals. The existing militia law was too weak in this respect, requiring the written request of many officials and private citizens before militia could be sent or martial law imposed in any county. On January 16 the legislature dropped these restrictions. It left it to the governor to decide on martial law and gave him full control over the use of militia.[15] Four days later Brownlow proclaimed that a reign of terror existed in middle and west Tennessee, and called on all good men to enlist in the state guards to put it down. He promised another proclamation as soon as possible designating the counties to be put under martial law.[16] Enlistments in the militia had lagged up to this time, but in the next month he collected 1,600 men, chiefly from east Tennessee.

Conservatives regarded martial law as the ultimate catastrophe. They believed the worst stories of militia atrocities in Arkansas, and they feared the same in Tennessee. Sympathizing with the terror if they were not guilty themselves, they recognized that martial law alone promised to bring the terrorists to book. The Memphis *Avalanche* threatened a popular uprising if Brownlow tried to emulate Clayton.[17] But the efforts of Arkansas Conservatives to resist the militia were hardly encouraging. By far the greatest reaction to Brownlow's proclamation was a redoubling of efforts to head off martial law by ending the Ku Klux terror. This was the purpose of Forrest's order on January 25, and of increasingly frequent newspaper editorials and public meetings attacking the Klan and appealing for law and order. Conservatives understandably exaggerated the degree to which terrorism was declining. They circulated petitions and sent delegations to Nashville insisting that militia were not necessary in their localities and pleading to be spared the horror of martial law. In Lincoln County (Fayetteville) Democratic leaders promised the Republicans that if the latter would keep the militia away they would try to stop the Klan. The Republicans agreed and joined in a bipartisan delegation to Nashville. Brownlow's response to such groups was that if the terror in fact stopped and serious efforts were made to apprehend past offenders, the militia would not be sent.[18] Democrats were willing enough to stop the terror, and continued to make progress in that direction.[19] But they did nothing to punish past offenders or ensure that the terror would not start over again on some future day when it pleased them to revive it.

It was not Brownlow's nature to forgive and forget—certainly not in these circumstances. He had bought peace cheaply in September only to see it evaporate in October when Conservatives found it expedient to renew the terror. Martial law, with all of its hardship, danger, and expense, seemed the only permanent remedy. Just as soon as he had recruited enough troops to carry out the policy, therefore, he invoked it by proclamation on February 20, designating nine counties in middle and west Tennessee.[20]

The governor delegated over-all command to General Joseph A. Cooper, who immediately ordered Lieutenant Colonel D. B. Gamble with five companies to Pulaski. Gamble's orders were to take command of Giles and three adjacent counties, to suspend civil law within them, try criminals by military court, and punish the guilty summarily. Tennessee benefited by Arkansas's experience in several respects. The state was able to supply its troops with many of their provisions and Gamble was ordered to draw on these as far as possible; any foraging was to be conducted under written order with certain safeguards for property owners. Soldiers found pillaging or marauding at the expense of peaceful citizens were subject to drumhead court-martial and immediate punishment. The troops were sent on February 24.[21]

It was precisely at this point that Brownlow resigned as governor to take a seat in the United States Senate. Perhaps he supposed that his successor, state senate president DeWitt C. Senter, would pursue the militia policy without change; if so, he miscalculated. In fact the new governor so modified the policy that it lost much of its meaning. Senter was a bona fide Republican who had supported Brownlow in the past and who was no more enamored of the Ku Klux. But he was less flamboyant by nature and much readier to meet the Conservatives halfway. On February 27, two days after taking office, he issued an order restoring civil law in the affected counties. The militia occupation continued, but the guards were restricted to aiding the civil authorities in the same fashion as federal troops. Under this limitation he soon sent militia to the other five counties named in

Brownlow's proclamation.[22] When delegations continued to arrive in Nashville denouncing the Ku Klux and asking to be spared the militia, he gave the same answer as Brownlow: arrests and prosecutions would speak more eloquently than even the noblest verbal declarations. The Nashville *Press and Times* could still remark in March, "that of all the organized bands which have put Union men to violent deaths in Middle Tennessee within the last twelve months, not a single criminal has been punished or even arrested."[23]

General John C. Brown and others from Pulaski came to Nashville on the governor's first day in office, asking him—in vain—to recall the militia sent there the day before.[24] When the state troops arrived in Pulaski they brought orders for the arrest of certain men who were already known to the authorities. Some of these they arrested before Governor Senter revoked martial law. When that order arrived, the prisoners were turned over to the civil authorities. This permitted General Brown and other Klansmen or fellow travelers to post bond for them and let them escape. Others fled before they could be arrested, repeating the exodus of Klansmen which had occurred in parts of Arkansas. Some of the refugees, like Frank McCord, a founding father of the order and editor of the Pulaski *Citizen,* returned as soon as the militia left. Others were like O. H. Crebbs, who settled in Texas and wrote back almost twenty years later, recalling "that memorable night that we scattered. About 40 of us going in different directions."[25]

The militia campaign was anticlimactic. Terrorism had generally abated by the time the troops were called out, although in a few counties it continued even in the presence of militia. Powerless to try criminals themselves, and with local officials unwilling to do so, there was little the militia could do. Democrats continued to call for their withdrawal, but the troops maintained good discipline and occasioned much less controversy than in Arkansas. In April the governor recalled five of the ten companies in service; the remaining five were disbanded by the end of June, permitting the last Ku Klux refugee who wanted to return to do so.[26] The major benefits of the campaign had been accomplished in anticipation of its start rather than by any direct services performed by the troops. No one was ever convicted of the preceding acts of terrorism.[27]

In August 1869 Tennesseeans held another gubernatorial election. Governor Senter ran for a full term to succeed himself, backed by Senator Brownlow. But party and factional lines became almost hopelessly confused as the Democrats also endorsed him, and the opposition was assumed by a more radical Republican, William B. Stokes. Deprived of most of the Radical vote, the governor handily won the election (as he had won Democratic backing in the first place) by disbanding the militia and restoring the vote to ex-Confederates. By the latter means Conservatives captured the legislature, and Radical Reconstruction came to an end in Tennessee, the state of its birth.[28]

Nearly every authority on the Ku Klux Klan agrees that sometime between January and August of 1869 the organization disbanded, so far at least as a formal order could bring that about. Evidence on the matter is so sketchy and contradictory that it is impossible to say exactly what did happen, or was intended. General Forrest himself claimed in 1871 to have suppressed the Klan, but he was exceedingly vague about the date and details.[29] Some have interpreted his order of January 25 as a disbandment in effect, despite its disavowal of that intention. Others say that a later order was issued, perhaps in March, but if so, that order has never come to light. There is even a tradition (without a shred of evidence) that disbandment resulted from a White House conference between General Forrest and General Grant immediately after the latter assumed the Presidency on March 4.[30]

The Republican Memphis *Post* (certainly not an inside authority) picked up rumors in February that the Klan was about to disband. In March it associated these rumors with the letter of Klansman Earle of Crittenden County, Arkansas, discovered at the time of his arrest. This spoke, apparently on high authority, of a Ku Klux disbandment in Arkansas, effective January 29, and the *Post* was inclined to give it broader application. An editorial of March 20 guessed that a large proportion of the order had already disbanded by that date.[31]

Lester and Wilson, writing many years later, credited General Forrest with issuing a disbandment order in March as a reaction to Brownlow's proclamation of martial law. It was supposed to embrace the entire Invisible Empire, they said, although they recognized that many Klansmen never learned of it. (Tennessee law after September 1868 forbade newspapers to carry Klan pronouncements, making it difficult to disseminate the order.) Nevertheless Lester and Wilson were too ready to assert that where the order was received it was promptly obeyed. Their summary of its contents, moreover, is so close to Forrest's January 25 order as to arouse suspicion that they confused the two.[32]

Another Klan source deserves respect, although it appeared forty years after the event. Minor Meriwether, the St. Louis attorney who claimed to have been Grand Scribe under Forrest, wrote in 1909 that Forrest had already resigned as Imperial Wizard when a convention of high Klan officials met in Nashville in February and dissolved the order. The reasons Meriwether assigned were that the order had achieved its original purpose and that bad men had got into it—similar to the reasons Forrest advanced in January.[33] Circumstantial support for this account lies in the rumors reaching the Memphis *Post* and the fact that Conservative leaders from around the state were indeed coming to Nashville in February, ostensibly to plead for withdrawal of the militia.

According to a third elderly Klansman—interviewed in 1930—the Memphis Klan received the disbandment order from Forrest ten days after the August election. This version was given in more detail than the others and also makes sense, for Conservatives then knew that they were on their way to control of the state and no longer needed the Klan politically.[34]

It is impossible to reconcile all of these accounts. But it is clear that the Conservative gentry of Tennessee renounced the Ku Klux Klan and severed their connection with it by the summer of 1869. Their peers in Arkansas, Texas, and northern Alabama were following the same course, as were the White Camellias in Louisiana. But in many places Conservatives would find the Klan a usable instrument for up to two years more. Forrest and other Tennessee Klan leaders probably intended their order (or orders) to apply beyond that state. In practice the members in every state acted independently, with a main eye to conditions at home. Even in Tennessee men in some localities would continue to don the Ku Klux garb and go raiding without the sanction of their betters.[35]

Night riding of this sort occurred late in August in Sumner, Wilson, and Rutherford, three adjacent counties east of Nashville. Masked raiders descended on Negroes primarily, but whites were also attacked. At least two persons were killed and others were whipped, raped, and robbed of guns; scores of Negroes abandoned their homes and crops to take refuge in Nashville. Democratic newspapers now joined in condemning the atrocities. "It is high time these masqueraders be unmasked and brought to justice," thundered the Pulaski *Citizen*. "All good citizens deprecate and condemn such acts." When Governor Senter had federal troops sent to the region both Democrats and Republicans applauded. Former Confederate congressman Henry S. Foote said that if necessary 500 men ought to escort the Negro refugees home to protect them, and he offered his legal services to prosecute the offenders.[36]

Early in September the Wilson County *Herald* at Lebanon copied a printed circular from the Ku Klux Klan which had been passed around in that county. Although it was headed with a dating formula unknown to the Klan Prescript and emanated from an equally unknown officer called the Grand Tycoon, the document seemed to speak with authority and reflect a broader policy:

Our mission on earth, to some extent is ended. Quiet and peace must be cast abroad in your land. Wherever possible, we have protected you from outrage and wrong. We will still lend a helping hand and the evil doers must remember that while we sleep we are not gone. . . . For the present, and we hope forever, we are done. When you see men, things or demons on your premises, claiming to be of me, shoot them down, for you may be certain that we are not there.[37]

This order may have represented a belated local confirmation of previous orders from above. At any rate the terrorism in that region came to an end.

Almost simultaneously there was a flurry of violence in Dyer and Weakley counties in the northwest corner of the state. A Negro was taken from jail and lynched; two Negro teachers and a minister were whipped; a county commissioner was threatened with hanging if he did not rescind a special railroad tax; and another white man was shot and killed, all by masked men.[38] Even at Pulaski, where the leadership was supposedly more firmly in control, about fifty disguised men galloped into town in December to rescue a barrel of whiskey which a federal revenue agent had confiscated.[39]

All told, the Klan probably appeared in fewer localities across the South in the latter part of 1868 (to say nothing of 1869) than it had in the preceding spring. But wherever it showed itself that autumn it tended to be more violent and more dangerous than before. It played a greater political role and had a larger impact on the fall campaign than it had on the earlier state elections. The terror it helped create was a major political factor at least locally in eight states. It decimated the Republican vote in many counties and threw Georgia and Louisiana into the Democratic column. More important, thousands of innocent persons lost their lives or property. In the three trans-Mississippi states—Louisiana, Texas, and Arkansas—the Klan virtually disappeared at the end of 1868. In Tennessee it fell off sharply at the same time with the loss of respectable Conservative patronage, and in Virginia it had already proved to be stillborn. But elsewhere the Klan rode on, all but oblivious to General Forrest and his orders—whatever they were.

Part IV

THE KLAN IN 1869
AND 1870

North Carolina: The Terror in Alamance

North Carolina had seen very little Klan action in 1868, and the Presidential election passed quietly. But trouble broke out almost immediately thereafter in several parts of the state. One such region centered in Lenoir and Jones counties in the east. It was the Constitutional Union Guard which flourished here in 1869, apparently introduced by an organizer from Raleigh. Its hundred or so members in Lenoir included a deputy sheriff and a lawyer, A. Munroe, of Kinston; the county chief was Jesse C. Kennedy, a well-to-do mill owner.[1] As represented to at least one prospective member, the CUG was an organization to put down robbery, but one of its major activities was stealing horses and sending them to other counties for sale. Most of these animals were taken from Negroes, partially to keep them from farming for themselves. The CUG also decreed a maximum wage for black laborers, and it forbade white men to work alongside them. Another function of the group was to safeguard the illicit still of one of its members, Henry Croom. The Klan supplied corn for the still, took whiskey in return, and held their regular meetings around it. There were political objectives to serve too, as in the flogging of a Negro Republican leader.[2]

The CUG also rescued its members from jail and engaged in arson, lynching, and political assassination. On the night of January 24, 1869, a party of CUG members, including lawyer Munroe, took five prisoners from the Kinston jail at gunpoint. Often, as in this case, they did not bother to disguise themselves beforehand. The prisoners (four of them Negroes awaiting trial for murder) were taken to a bridge outside town and killed.[3] On another occasion they liberated a Negro accomplice of their own who had been arrested for horse stealing. But this was only to kill him, out of fear that he would report them to the authorities. Two members performed the job and took away an ear as a proof of accomplishment.[4] One of the murderers was on another occasion freed from the jail himself by thirty-five or forty colleagues after being arrested for illicit distilling.[5]

The Lenoir County CUG maintained a close correspondence with those in Jones, Duplin, and other nearby counties. They followed the widespread practice of calling on neighboring units to perform some of the most dangerous assignments, and returned the courtesy themselves. Such was the case when the Jones County organization called on them to dispose of Sheriff O. R. Colgrove, a Northerner who had settled in Jones County with his brother after the war. The Colgroves and a few others constituted a new white Republican establishment in this largely black county, and by virtue of their Negro following held most of the local political offices. Colgrove was therefore an object of hatred among displaced Conservative whites. In addition, he had arrested members of the CUG. The Lenoir County organization had already signified a willingness to kill Colgrove if the Jones County members asked for it, and even raised a purse to reward the man who did it. As it turned out, nine or ten members performed the act, ambushing Colgrove as he rode down a country road on May 28. A Negro companion was also shot and killed. The CUG and its apologists rationalized the crime by alleging a New York prison record for Colgrove before his coming to North Carolina. Then they held a big barbecue to celebrate the event.

The terror in Jones and Lenoir counties intensified after the Colgrove murder. Other Republicans were threatened with the same fate, and Negroes apparently began striking back by burning the houses of the most conspicuous CUG members. Colgrove's brother (a state senator) and others called on Governor William W. Holden to send troops. "We cannot tell at night who will be living in the morning," he wrote.[6] At the same time another Republican leader, Colonel M. L. Shepard, organized several hundred freedmen into a militia detachment and armed them with state muskets.[7]

Governor Holden had already sent a detective, Captain L. H. Mowers, to Kinston to uncover evidence that might be used to prosecute the terrorists.[8] Early in June, after the Colgrove murder, he sent to Trenton, the Jones County seat, a company of twenty-five white militia from Raleigh. Their presence temporarily halted the violence, but threats and intimidation continued. The militia never left camp, and their only positive action was to disband the local Negro militia in order to placate Conservatives. When they returned to Raleigh after a month and a half the Republicans were no safer than before. Senator Colgrove and others left the county; Shepard, who remained, pleaded for the arrest of the terrorists and predicted his own assassination. "I am not generly [*sic*] a man easly [*sic*] backed down but this is a time when I find my self deserted by the leading men of our county and it is every man for himself. The col'd men I can trust with my life and them only," he wrote the governor, "they are true to their party." On August 16 Shepard's expectation was fulfilled; he was gunned down with one or two other men while working at his sawmill.[9]

After several months of investigation, detective Mowers at Kinston got three members of the CUG to turn state's evidence and furnish the names of their criminal confederates. On the night of August 23 he and the sheriff arrested eighteen members and sent them to the New Bern jail for safe-keeping. Several others were taken later, and a few managed to evade arrest. Subsequently about twenty-five men, including lawyer Munroe, Jesse Kennedy, and Henry Croom, were indicted for a variety of crimes including murder and were held for trial. In October Governor Holden called attention to continuing lawlessness in Lenoir and Jones counties and threatened to declare them in a state of insurrection. These actions effectively ended the terror in that vicinity.

Meanwhile the local community spared no effort to assist the prisoners. According to the prosecuting attorney, "quite a number of the prominent citizens of Lenoir Co. are secretly using their influence and money to prevent the conviction of any of these prisoners. . . ." At the same time he himself was subjected to personal threats. When the prosecution tried to hire an additional lawyer they found that the defense had already retained almost every attorney in the district.

Beset with Ku Klux outbreaks in several parts of the state, Holden attempted in late 1869 and early 1870 to restore order through a policy of conciliation and appeasement. As a result, the terror having subsided in Lenoir and Jones, he ordered the prisoners released. Although their cases technically were still pending as late as 1871, none of the criminals was punished.[10]

Editor Josiah Turner of the Raleigh *Sentinel*, the chief Democratic organ in North Carolina, took a prominent part in furthering, rationalizing, and covering up the Ku Klux conspiracy throughout the state. The *Sentinel's* first admission that the Klan actually existed, on April 29, was coupled with a charge that the Jones County murders were really committed by the Union League; members of that order, it asked people to believe, were busy killing one another in order to blame it on the Democrats. This was too absurd to repeat indefinitely, and the *Sentinel* soon contented itself with holding the Union League responsible for calling the Klan into existence in the first place.[11] In treating the Colgrove murder the Democratic press as a whole dwelt more on the alleged shortcomings of the victim than on the crime or its perpetrators. Governor Holden's Raleigh *Standard,* on the other hand, not only condemned the terrorism but deprecated threats by Negroes and Republicans to retaliate in kind. "This is all wrong. The law and the law alone has the power to punish the guilty. . . . Assassination should not be met with assassination, nor guilt with guilt."[12]

Meanwhile violence spread. The Ku Klux became active in Moore County, in the center of the state, late in 1868, and remained intermittently so for many months. Most cases of widespread or systematic arson in North Carolina seem to have been the work of Negroes retaliating against prior Ku Klux violence. But in Moore County the Klan itself burned down houses and barns in an effort to drive out Negroes and white Republicans. In one notable episode they shot a Negro woman and her five children and then burned the house down around them; according to a participant's later confession, one of the party "killed one of the children by kicking its brains out with the heel of his boot." In the fall of 1869 they branded one Jacob Starling in four or five places with the letters U.L., presumably for membership in the Union League. Both the sheriff and the superior court clerk appear to have been members of the Klan, and they did nothing to stop these proceedings.[13]

By January 1869 outrages were being reported from the counties of Chatham, Orange, Alamance, Caswell, and Rockingham, west and northwest of Raleigh. All of these would be scenes of recurrent Klan activity in 1869 and 1870, but Alamance eclipsed the rest. Most of the terror in this county was attributable to the White Brotherhood, although the CUG existed alongside it and later absorbed some of its members.

The White Brotherhood had been introduced in Alamance in 1868 by one Obed McMichael of next-door Guilford County, where it never assumed as large proportions. In October 1868 McMichael appointed Jacob A. Long, a young aspiring lawyer, as chief of Camp (or den) number 1. By virtue of that position he served also as county chief until his withdrawal in May or June 1869. About seven camps were formed in Alamance by the end of 1868.[14]

The Constitutional Union Guard was introduced from Chatham County in September 1868. The south commander (or chief) of its first klan, and therefore *de facto* county chief, was James A. J. Patterson. Only two klans were in existence by the end of the year, but in June court week of 1869 Patterson organized three more. This spurt of activity coincided with efforts by part of the White Brotherhood leadership to disband that order on account of the widespread violence it had committed. Hoping to slough off disorderly elements, some of the White Brotherhood leaders and members transferred to the CUG. They intended if possible to hold this order more nearly to their own relatively pacific idea of Ku Klux policy. The south commanders of the new CUG klans were Jacob Long and two other recent chiefs in the White Brotherhood. Despite this secession, the White Brotherhood carried on for another year, including the period of its greatest activity. In fact it continued to outnumber the CUG in membership. Both organizations remained in the field until the summer of 1870, when Governor Holden sent in militia to break them up.[15]

The local Freedmen's Bureau agent reported in mid-November 1868 that hundreds of families of poor colored people in both Alamance and Caswell counties were being thrown out of their homes and work for having voted in the recent election. By all the evidence this reflected "a preconcerted plan," with widespread community support.[16] Klan violence, not always political in inspiration, began about the same time.

One of the first victims was Caswell Holt, a Negro whom the Klan suspected of thievery. Calling him out of his house one night in December 1868, they hung him by the neck from a tree limb several times, raising him just enough that he had to stand on his tiptoes, trying to extort from him a confession of stealing. Failing to get this, they beat him severely, rubbed a rough stick up and down his raw back, and ordered him to leave within ten days. When he went to his former master to complain, the latter advised him to be quiet about the matter and intimated mysteriously that his attackers had risen from the dead. Holt refused to accept the ghost story since he had recognized twelve of his sixteen assailants. Instead of leaving as ordered, he went into Graham, the county seat, made formal complaint against the twelve, and had them arrested. He paid a lawyer ten bushels of corn to prosecute the cases, which the authorities should have done gratis. But when the accused came up for preliminary hearing Holt had no witnesses to support his identification. The defendants swore that they had been elsewhere on the night in question, and Republican magistrate Peter Harden had no alternative but to release them.

A year later the Ku Klux returned to Holt's house. They shot him through the bolted door, then broke in and roughed up his daughters while throwing his possessions outside. For several months afterward he was confined to his home with severe shoulder and chest wounds, and by that time he knew it was pointless to appeal to the law. In his case, too, stories were later circulated to justify the attacks: in addition to the earlier charges of stealing it was said that he had behaved indecently and exposed himself to white women and also boasted that he was not afraid of the Ku Klux. Some Klansmen had been for killing him outright, but county chief Jacob Long claimed credit for averting this.[17]

Alamance Republicans assumed that the first isolated raids were only the work of a few neighborhood boys on a tear. But as they continued, and suspects frustrated prosecution by furnishing alibis for one another, it became increasingly apparent that a widespread conspiracy was forming, directed against Negroes and white Republicans. (By this time the White Brotherhood alone numbered 600 to 700 members in Alamance.)[18] All remaining doubts disappeared with the Graham raid in March 1869. At about 10 or 11 P.M. at least forty Klansmen galloped into town in full disguise, yelling and shouting. As they passed through the streets they shot into the houses of several Negroes, including Wyatt Outlaw, the most prominent black man in the county. Coming to the house of lawyer Henry Badham (who had taken Caswell Holt's case) they left a note warning him and magistrate Harden against any further attempts to discover or prosecute Klansmen.[19]

If the raid was meant to intimidate officials, it was successful. Some of them candidly admitted that they had no desire to become martyrs and advised subsequent complainants to drop the subject. Klan outrages continued in the countryside with little official hindrance, therefore. In the same month Joseph Harvey, a Negro, was given 150 lashes on the bare back and his baby was clubbed to death.[20] On the other hand, a Negro woman wielded an ax with such proficiency against a Klansman breaking into her house that he retired to Texas after recovering enough to travel.[21] At a Union League meeting several blacks advocated a policy of retaliation in kind. Both Wyatt Outlaw and Mayor William R. Albright vigorously dissented, advising instead a reliance on the law and avoiding any conduct that would give a pretext for Ku Klux attacks.[22] They supplemented this barren counsel by sending for a company of militia, who came up from Raleigh but remained only a few days.[23]

Governor Holden, for his part, announced that he would punish the Alamance outlaws "if it should require a thousand men and all the arms in the State arsenal."[24] The militia helped to arrest several men during their short stay, but the prisoners produced the usual alibis and were never indicted by the grand jury.[25] On April 12 the state legislature enacted a law making it illegal to wear a disguise with intent to frighten or to commit trespass or violence while so attired.[26] In a proclamation of April 16 the governor declared his intention to enforce the act if necessary, but he first appealed to public opinion to suppress such activity before enforcement was necessary.[27]

Certain Klan leaders in fact did react to the new law and Holden's proclamation by discouraging further violence and even trying to disband the White Brotherhood. The Raleigh *Sentinel* undercut Holden's policy, however, by denying the existence of any disorder in Alamance and ridiculing his sending of "negro 'malish' " there. (In fact the militia were all white.)[28] The lawlessness in Alamance abated for several months, but the prisoners were not punished. White Republicans in particular began abandoning a party membership which subjected them to threats and violence with no hope of redress.[29]

Officials in Rockingham County to the northwest reported in May that disguised men had been whipping Negroes there for a month. When they called for a special court term to try the suspected criminals the local Democratic lawyers fought the idea, denying any need.[30] The court clerk kept an informal tally of outrages occurring in the county, which soon mounted to sixty-two. State Supreme Court Justice Thomas Settle, a local resident, described some of the cases which came to his attention. On one occasion a Negro man was forced by Klansmen to go through the motions of sexual intercourse with a Negro girl while they whipped him and forced her father to look on. In another case they forced a firebrand into the mouth of a Negro woman who had screamed murder as they drew a gun on her husband. Justice Settle himself (a Republican) acted as a magistrate to commit suspected offenders to trial. Democrats publicly defended or justified the Klan, however, and Judge Albion Tourgée of Greensboro was threatened with mob violence when he came to try the cases. (Tourgée's experience with the Klan and its supporters provided material for his famous Reconstruction novels, written a few years later.) Owing to alibis, the intimidation of witnesses, and like methods, none of the Klansmen was convicted. Here too Republicans became demoralized for a time. One of them attributed the terror to Conservative political leaders who had dominated the county from time immemorial and now resented their expulsion from power. In local elections in August the Democrats used Ku Klux tactics and carried four of seven townships. Despite those successes, the Rockingham Klan rather surprisingly broke up soon afterward. Former Governor David S. Reid, a local man and a Democrat, probably deserves the major credit for this development; it occurred soon after he joined Justice Settle and unequivocally denounced the Klan.[31]

In July the terror spread to Orange County, just east of Alamance.[32] The next month a party of 75 to 100 disguised men took two Negroes from the jail at Hillsborough and killed one of them. The prisoners had been arrested for burning barns; when the survivor came to trial later he was acquitted. The sheriff led a posse in pursuit of the culprits the next morning, but lost the trail at a fork in the road, one branch of which led into Alamance and the other toward Chatham. (The Klan was well organized and active in both counties.) Soon afterward the father and uncle of the lynched man were themselves taken from their homes at night and hanged from trees by twenty-five or thirty Alamance Klansmen. The body of one had a note pinned to it: "All barn-burners, all women offenders [sic], we Kuklux hang by the neck till they are dead, dead, dead." A fourth Negro was later hanged in this vicinity, charged with attempted rape of a white girl, although the sheriff, who knew him, considered the accusation false.[33]

No rapes were actually committed in the county, but whites were desperately afraid of them nonetheless. According to a Democrat who helped put down the Klan here, "The poorer classes in the community, women who carry blackberries, cherries, eggs, butter, and things of that sort to town to sell, were afraid to go to town by themselves . . . for fear of being insulted or ravished by negroes." Instead they formed large companies for mutual protection. This fear, he added, was what had brought the Klan into existence.[34] Whites at the same time betrayed an insouciant attitude toward the feelings and even the lives of black people: "An old negro came to town last week . . . [reported the *Hillsborough Recorder*] bringing something to eat to a son of his whom he said some disguised men had carried off . . . for the purpose—as they said—of putting him in jail at this place. It seems that his son had threatened to ravish a white woman. . . . But the ole man didn't find his boy here. We reckon he was 'lost.' "[35]

At Chapel Hill, a resident wrote to the governor in September, "It has become no unusual thing to see groups of 40 to 50 . . . Ku Klux rowdying up and down through the streets of this village at the late hour of twelve o'clock." They galloped around the state university campus, beat up Negroes, and drove white persons from their homes on the ground that they were an encumbrance on their families. A party of 75 to 100 took a man suspected of being a state detective from his hotel and whipped him. They also threatened death to a Negro Republican leader until he took an oath to support the Democratic party. Another group whipped and otherwise maltreated many inmates of the county poorhouse, most or all of them Negroes. Republicans felt helpless, the informant concluded; like many others in these circumstances, he asked the governor not to reveal his name lest the Ku Klux visit him next.[36]

Some of the victims left the county. A writer in the Raleigh *Standard* recorded a street scene there early in October:

Passing up Fayetteville street, Saturday night, our attention was drawn to a group of four or five women and children, gathered together under the light of a street lamp, quietly taking supper. They presented a discontented air, looked quite unhappy and equally dependant [sic]. We endeavored to find out something of their history and could only learn from one of them that they were going where there were no Ku Klux, and in search of their male friends who had been compelled to come to Raleigh, to save their own lives.

They would say only that they had come from "up the country," but the writer surmised that they may have been the families of three Orange County men who had fled to Raleigh because of Ku Klux maltreatment a few days earlier. On October 30 the *Standard* reported that: "The guard house of this city is filled with destitute people from Orange county, who have been driven from their homes by the Ku Klux. Some of these refugees are white and some are black. They represent the condition of affairs as fearful, and say they cannot stay at home unless something is done to check the murderous Ku Klux."[37]

Altogether the Klan murdered five Negroes in Orange County, apart from innumerable whippings, between the summer of 1869 and the spring of 1870. Several men were arrested at different times, but no one was ever tried for these crimes. The widow of one of the Negroes hanged for barn burning later protested her husband's innocence. She had recognized some of the attackers but dared not identify them for fear they would return upon her. When someone suggested that there were good men in the community who would have protected her, she replied simply, "The Lord knows who the good men were, I didn't."[38] If the Orange County Klan decreased Negro crime, as its apologists repeatedly claimed, it did so at great cost to the white crime rate. These apologists also repeated what was coming to be a familiar story across the South: unworthy elements eventually infiltrated the Klan, took control, and gave it a bad name. But in view of the hangings and whippings with which it began, and which these apologists tacitly approved, this story is hard to take very seriously.[39] Orange County Republicans besieged Governor Holden with requests for troops. Under existing laws he had no white militia readily available, and he was reluctant to send Negro militiamen; the most he could do was request a company of federal troops for Chapel Hill.[40]

Klan expansion, with accompanying violence, also occurred in counties to the southwest during the summer and fall of 1869. There was a small and intermittently active organization in Catawba County, which committed one murder and perhaps two dozen whippings between June 1869 and early 1871.[41] Lincoln, Gaston, and Cleveland counties saw greater activity. In addition to Klan outrages against the freedmen, Gaston County witnessed a rash of barn burnings late in 1869, attributed to the Negroes and the Union League. There is some confusion as to which activity began first, but they went hand in hand. In Lincoln and Gaston at least, there was a constant internal struggle in the Klan from autumn 1869 onward between a violent element and moderates who sanctioned no more than political intimidation. Moderates held most of the major offices and tried to reorganize or even disband the order in a generally failing effort to hold the rank and file in line. David Schenck, a Lincolnton attorney, joined the order in Gaston County in October 1868, when it was still quiescent. (It was the Invisible Empire in this region.) About Christmastime 1869, after the burnings (and beatings) began, he and some friends organized the Klan in Lincoln County, their own home, fearing the spread of Negro arson. Their purpose, Schenck insisted later, was purely defensive and nonviolent, although he never made clear just what he expected a nonviolent Klan to do. Within a month or so outrages began to occur against Negroes there too, whereupon Schenck and other moderates severed their ties with the organization. Subsequently he claimed to have disbanded three dens which had reportedly committed outrages. But other men took over the order, he said, and "it degenerated into a band of robbers, rioters, and lynch-law men, who deserve the severest punishment. . . ." What Schenck and others like him did not admit, although it is plain from the record and their own testimony, is that this element had been present virtually from the beginning, and they had tried to use it for their own political purposes, which were only a degree less criminal.

Men of public standing like Schenck could and did advocate law and order in general terms; but the terror was such that even they did not dare attack the Klan openly after they had broken with it, for fear of retaliation and injury to themselves. They became, like their counterparts in nearly every state, captives of the monster they had created. This situation lasted until the federal government intervened in 1871, over the bitter opposition of these very men. They were caught in an ideological and moral as well as a tactical dilemma: Schenck's diary, which survives, shows him to be a devoted white supremacist who felt that "the Anglo-Saxon and the African can never be equals . . . one or the other must fall." Despite considerable evidence before his eyes to the contrary, he equated the Negro with Barbarism and the white race with Civilization. Fundamentally he approved much of the Klan's vigilante activity, but feared its consequences in unsettling society. He was both attracted and repelled by the prospect of a "second 'Irrepressible Conflict' . . . which must sooner or later end in the extinction of the negro race." Views such as these help to explain why most Conservatives spoke out so softly against the Klan and why their voice of moderation had so little effect.[42]

Despite the Klan activity in Gaston and Lincoln, major attention in the fall of 1869 shifted back to Alamance. Here and in neighboring Caswell County there was a resurgence of violence so great as to lead ultimately to a direct confrontation between the state and the Ku Klux Klan. Most of the county officials in Alamance and Caswell were Democrats. In Alamance, not only was Sheriff Albert Murray a Democrat, but he, all of his deputies, and the county's representative in the legislature were members of the White Brotherhood. Nevertheless, the Republican party was strong in both counties, and elections were closely contested.[43] This fairly even division doubtless contributed to the high degree of Klan organization and activity. Republicans drew most of their strength as usual from the Negro population, but in Alamance especially a white Unionist minority was often inclined to vote Republican, and held the balance of power between the two parties; in Caswell the Negroes were in a majority. Political feelings ran so high that Democrats and Republicans hardly spoke to one another socially. It even divided families. Mayor William R. Albright of Graham, a Republican, declared that some of his own brothers would delight in his assassination. Two of them belonged to the Klan, he said, and a third sympathized with it but was too old and infirm to join; and all of his brothers-in-law were members along with his father-in-law. Albright doubtless exaggerated concerning his brothers' enmity. When his assassination was in fact actively debated within the order in 1869, one of them opposed going that far because several children would be left orphans; "but his back was broad enough and they ought to give him a few licks any how."[44]

As elsewhere, objectives of the Alamance Klan varied somewhat from time to time and from person to person. Evidence on this and other matters is especially plentiful here because of subsequent state and federal investigations. Most of the Klan leaders, whether of the White Brotherhood or the Constitutional Union Guard, belonged to the local establishment and were well regarded. They formed their societies both as political organizations to intimidate Republican voters and as regulative bodies to deter or punish Negro criminals. According to James E. Boyd, one of the first leaders to turn from the order and expose its secrets, the Klan was supposed "to ride around the country, and whip a little, and go about the houses of the negroes and tell them if they went to election they would meet them on the way."[45] The most politically sophisticated leaders often tried to underplay or deny the political purpose, fearing that state or federal intervention would more surely be invoked for this reason than the other. Leading Democrats at the state level (whether they belonged to the Klan or not) were usually at pains to deny any connection between their party and the Klan, but its political objective was obvious and many members made no effort to hide it. Although large numbers of people doubtless believed that the Klan was needed to suppress Negro crime, the argument was almost wholly baseless. Much of the law enforcement machinery in Alamance was in Democratic hands, and Republican officials usually bent over backward to appease white opinion by punishing Negro offenders. The only disguised marauders ever convicted in the local courts were several misguided black men who took a leaf from the Klan book and began preying on their neighbors. They were caught after the first night and were tried and convicted without the slightest obstacle or delay; ever afterward Democrats made much of the fact that the only "Ku Klux" ever caught and tried in the county turned out to be Negro Republicans.[46] Democrats also claimed that whenever Negro criminals were convicted in the courts Governor Holden pardoned them and turned them loose on society again. But this was a blanket charge, common throughout the South, and was seldom if ever substantiated; certainly this "evil" had no significance in Alamance County.

The rank-and-file Klansmen, judging by their later confessions, were less political in outlook than their leaders. The latter, in fact, sometimes tried to attract and hold members on other grounds. At one meeting Dr. John A. Moore, the county's legislator-Klansman, argued that the Klan "was a good thing for . . . poor men," and would help them "to protect [their] families from the darkies. . . ."[47] Many Klansmen also wanted to punish social transgressions. As one member put it, they were "to take Law in our own hands to whip any one we thought had done anything mean."[48] This kind of regulation was chiefly applied to Negroes, but occasionally they raided white persons too—wife beaters or women of easy morals—who did not conform to their standards of rectitude. The fact remains, however, that nearly all of the victims, black or white, were Republicans. It was never possible wholly to separate political from personal transgressions, especially among a white population which regarded Republican affiliation itself as a form of personal misconduct.

Ku Klux leaders themselves were by no means entirely innocent of murder and violence. Although they increasingly sought to discourage such crimes, they sometimes sanctioned and even participated in murders, particularly political assassinations. Often they differed among themselves as to how far the Klan should depart from mere intimidation and threats. The same disagreements took place further down. There were many scenes of wrangling in den meetings and in the meetings of den chiefs over the specific action to be taken in particular cases.

Supposedly all Klan affairs were secret, and discussions were limited to the closed meetings of the order. But in fact most of the Klan members and leaders were widely known in the community, even among Republicans and Negroes. Whenever an assassination or a major raid was under discussion, rumors of the matter leaked out and passed along the grapevine. Occasionally Conservatives, and even Klansmen, would pass on these reports or whisper generalized warnings to Republicans who were in danger of attack if the informants happened to disapprove of it themselves. Mayor Albright received many notices from friends and enemies alike that he was apt to be raided, although in his case moderate Klansmen managed to prevent it from happening.[49]

The White Brotherhood continued to exist in Alamance, despite the efforts of some of its leaders to disband and move over to the Constitutional Union Guard in June 1869. Old members dropped out or became inactive, but new ones were recruited as late as March 1870. Membership numbered 600 or 700 in that county, about half the number of white voters; the CUG had fewer than 100. A few members of the White Brotherhood had been threatened or tricked into joining, and occasionally a Republican affiliated in order to prevent raids upon himself or his family, but these cases were exceptional. Raiding was confined to a minority of activists, most of whom were in their twenties or younger. Many members were able to evade this duty, but persons of some standing occasionally participated. A Negro who was beaten in November 1869 identified a justice of the peace and a deputy sheriff among his five attackers. The deputy had already been arrested by the militia for Ku Klux activity earlier in the year.[50]

There were ten camps (or dens) of the White Brotherhood in Alamance, most or all of them in existence by the beginning of 1869. The CUG had five klans after acquiring seceders from the other order in June. These units were distributed fairly evenly around the county, one in every township in the case of the White Brotherhood. Although individual camps or klans met frequently, White Brotherhood county chief Jacob Long held only two full county meetings, both in the spring of 1869. These were discontinued, since they created too large a crowd and too much danger of detection. He reported to no higher authority, although individual camps "exchanged work" (as one chief put it) with other camps inside and outside the county. Long himself commanded camp number 1 in Graham, while Sheriff Albert Murray was chief of camp number 4, several miles north.[51]

Klan procedures varied from camp to camp and from one occasion to another. Some members testified that a raid had to be sanctioned in advance by vote of the camp, while others indicated that the chief's voice was decisive. Most raids were carried out by bands of from half a dozen up to twenty men, always after dark, and consisted of surprise attacks upon the homes of the victims. Pickets were often posted before they called out the occupants or broke in and dragged them out. Often one person did all the talking and tried to disguise his voice. Despite the disguises and other precautions, victims managed to identify a large number of their assailants. Confidence in their power and security often bred carelessness among the raiders, and precautions slipped. For Klansmen the main safeguard lay not in their secrecy but in their ability to thwart legal processes if they were identified. False alibis, the intimidation of witnesses and officials, and the manipulation of juries offered greater protection than robes and masks.[52]

The Alamance Klan began raiding again in September 1869 after several months of quiescence. One of the first attacks was on a white man at Haw

River who was beaten because he had voted in the August election.[53] Another white man was visited three times and warned to leave because he regularly patronized a backwoods bordello operated by one Mary Gappins and her daughter. The Klan warned her to leave, too, and reinforced the command by tearing her house down.[54] Sallie Holt, a competitor, was also raided. At her place two boys were driven off without harm, but one of her daughters was forced to expose herself while the Klansmen beat her private parts.[55]

One of the most highly publicized raids, reported around the country, was on Alonzo B. Corliss, a partially crippled Northerner who taught a Quaker-supported Negro school in Company Shops (now Burlington). On the night of November 26 several disguised men called him out of his house, dragged him to a nearby woods, and gave him about thirty lashes with a rawhide and hickory sticks. Then they shaved one side of his head, painted it black, and warned him to leave. Corliss tried to carry on with a small squad of soldiers provided by Governor Holden, but he was soon obliged to go when his landlord asked him to evacuate for fear of damage to the house and no one else would take him in. Corliss had four men arrested, three of whom later admitted the deed privately, but the authorities did nothing to prosecute them. Conservatives explained and justified the attack on several grounds. Corliss had formerly headed the Union League at Mebanesville nearby; he had brought a crippled Negro boy to church there one Sunday (for which he was expelled from the congregation); and he taught a Negro school.[56]

The great majority of the Klan's victims were blacks; they were attacked and beaten everywhere in the county for many reasons. The raiders explained on one occasion that they were simply out whipping Radicals that night. In December a disguised band attacked a Negro home in which about twenty persons were holding a frolic or party. They broke open the door, shot into the house, and then rushed in themselves, knocking over a woman who was holding a four-month-old baby in her arms. The baby fell to the floor, whereupon several Klansmen went over to it and put their feet on it, mashing it, as the father later described, without actually stamping on it. The child died a week later. Then they dragged three men outside and whipped them, not bothering to explain why.[57] On another raid Dr. Thomas Lutterloh, a physician, whipped a black man so severely that he died of the effects, according to the doctor's later private admission.[58] Still another Negro was whipped and then forced to mutilate his penis with a pocketknife; he too died of the effects.[59] More than one freedman was whipped and turned out of his house with his family at the behest of white men who wanted to farm the land themselves.[60] A Negro woman of about sixty was whipped after struggling with a white woman who tried to beat her granddaughter.[61] It was Alamance Klansmen who crossed over into Orange County and murdered the Negroes suspected of barn burning.

When there were murders to be committed in Alamance, the Orange County Klan returned the favor. Members from Chatham County helped out too, as in the Shoffner raid around Christmastime 1869. State senator T. M. Shoffner of Alamance, a Republican, introduced a bill late in 1869 authorizing the governor to suspend habeas corpus and to use militia to suppress lawlessness in counties such as his own where Ku Klux terrorism had overawed the civil authorities and raged out of control. Governor Holden was besieged with requests from harried Republicans around the state for military relief; as a result he had already been calling for such a measure, and probably inspired Shoffner's action.[62] The Klan was furious at the proposal (which eventually became law), and in late December or early January one or more of its units voted for Shoffner's assassination. Accordingly a party of sixty Orange and Chatham County men was organized under the leadership of Frederick N. Strudwick (who would soon be elected to the legislature from Orange). The plan was to assemble at a bridge near the Alamance-Orange line after dark and then ride to Shoffner's home, where he was spending the Christmas recess. They intended to take him from the house and hang him. Advance notice of the mission reached James E. Boyd and other Klan leaders who had been attempting for some time to brake the terror. When Boyd learned in Graham that the Klan was "going to suspend Shoffner's writ of habeas corpus" that very night, he conferred with Dr. Moore. That gentleman agreed rather reluctantly to head off the assassination party if possible by intercepting them and telling them that Shoffner had gone to Greensboro. He found Strudwick and his party near the point of rendezvous and conveyed this message. After some hesitation and doubt the men turned back disappointed and frustrated. Actually Moore's message was accurate and Shoffner had gone to Greensboro that day, but Moore did not know whether he had yet returned. He was taken by Captain Eli Euliss, a CUG leader but also a friend and neighbor of the senator's, who had learned of the plot too. In succeeding weeks Shoffner was subjected to additional threats. When the next legislative session came to a close he returned home, wound up his affairs, and moved to Indiana. He was a native of the county, a blacksmith by trade, who had always borne a good character.[63]

Almost simultaneous with the assassination attempt, Conservatives held a public meeting in Graham to protest Republican policies in general and the Shoffner bill in particular. Klansmen dominated the proceedings. Jacob Long, recent county chief of the White Brotherhood, served as secretary, and James Boyd was chairman of the resolutions committee. Dr. Moore and Boyd delivered speeches attacking the Shoffner bill, which was still pending before the legislature. The resolutions reported by Boyd's committee were all adopted unanimously. They condemned lawlessness in general terms, but reserved their real indignation for the proposed law to curb it. There were no disorders in Alamance which the civil law was not perfectly adequate to handle, they said. This bill, on the other hand, was a malignant measure which threatened to create strife and bloodshed among peace-loving citizens by punishing all for the wrongs of a few.[64]

The truth of course was quite the opposite. The Ku Klux terror was so all-encompassing that even members of the order like Boyd himself dared not speak openly against it.[65] A humbler member declared later, "I would have given anything to have got out of the organization, but could not get out without telling [about] it, and if I told I would have been killed. They told me if I told anything that I should hang to a limb."[66] For Republicans it was much worse. All of them felt a constant apprehension of nocturnal whippings or worse. Mayor Albright, like others, slept with weapons handy every night, and once had to draw a gun to prevent being attacked on the street.[67] Senator Shoffner was not the only Republican to leave altogether. Another effect of the terror was to break up the Union League early in 1870—one of the Klan's objectives all along.[68]

The only disguised men who were ever tried and convicted by the local courts were the Negroes who briefly imitated the Klan. That the sheriff and all his deputies were Klansmen naturally impeded the making of arrests, but paradoxically, that was not the major obstacle. At least twenty persons were in fact arrested for Ku Klux activity, only to be released for one reason or another. The very certainty of their discharge made it easier to arrest them. The prosecuting attorney in this district, Republican James R. Bulla, was far from enthusiastic about prosecuting Ku Klux cases, but few of them got as far as his desk. Klansmen were represented on almost every jury, including the grand jury which brought indictments, but even fewer cases reached it, and none at all got to a trial jury. Klansmen were so ready to swear false alibis in one another's behalf that most accused members were cleared by this means at preliminary hearings, before formal indictment or prosecution could occur. But the overriding barrier to justice was the conspiracy and terror which permeated the entire community. Half of the population was engaged in a tacit conspiracy to obstruct justice in such cases, motivated by sympathy for the Klan or fear of it, and usually both. Ordinarily law-abiding citizens simply looked away from the violence and pretended it did not exist, when they were not secretly applauding it. Coroner's juries found it infinitely easier and safer to rule "dead at the hands of persons unknown," when in fact they and everyone else had a good idea who was responsible. Trial magistrates accepted sworn alibis that they knew to be false and ruled that there was insufficient evidence to prosecute persons of whose guilt they were morally certain. The other half of the community—Negroes and Republicans—was intimidated and help-less. Many victims were afraid to identify their attackers for fear of worse to come, and witnesses declined to testify. Those who did make formal complaint, like Caswell Holt at the beginning of the terror, found that they had risked their lives for nothing; later victims were not encouraged by their example to follow suit. In all other respects the laws operated and the courts functioned as usual, but in Ku Klux cases the judicial process broke down completely.[69]

The first prominent murder victim in Alamance was Wyatt Outlaw, Graham town councilman, founder and president of the local Union League, and the foremost Negro in the county. According to a Conserva-tive fellow councilman Outlaw "was one of the most polite niggers you ever saw in your life. His deportment was quite gentlemanly. He bore a pretty fair character." Outlaw was murdered for racial and political reasons, although lame stories were invented after the event, including one that he had fired at the Klan when they rode through town a year earlier. This time at least seventy-five Klansmen (some of them from Orange County) rode into Graham on the night of February 26, 1870, howling and making ungodly noises. About twenty of them headed directly for Outlaw's house. After dragging him out they invaded another Negro home nearby, got several feet of cord from one of the beds, and headed for the square in the center of town. Here Outlaw was hung from the limb of a tree thirty yards from the courthouse door. Before leaving town the Klan dropped a note at Mayor Albright's gate threatening him with the same fate. No one interfered with them during the raid, nor did anyone dare even take down the body until 11 o'clock the next morning. Sheriff Murray did nothing to track the party, and in due time a coroner's jury handed in the usual verdict. As far as Conservatives were concerned, the case was closed.[70]

A sequel to the Outlaw murder was the killing about two weeks later of an intermittently insane Negro, William Puryear, who recognized and reported two of Outlaw's killers whom he saw returning to their homes the morning after the raid. Puryear was taken from his home at night, and two months later his body was discovered weighted down with stones in a mill pond. In his case the fabricators tried to pin the blame on other Negroes acting (so it was said) at the behest of his wife.[71]

The Outlaw murder created an uproar around the state. It came after more than a year of terrorism and perhaps a hundred whippings and other outrages in Alamance County.[72] Republicans loudly demanded troops to restore order and punish offenders. The longer redress was delayed the more bitter they became at the seeming negligence of the state government.

"It may be sport to you but it is death to us," one irate man wrote Governor Holden.[73] Conservatives, on the other hand, were desperate to avoid a military occupation, especially by state militia, now that the Shoffner Act was on the books. Their leaders called another public meeting in order to pass more resolutions against lawlessness. Doubtless many were sincere in wanting to mobilize public opinion in that direction, but the last thing they wanted was action to uncover the terrorists and bring them to justice. The major purpose of the meeting was to head off a military occupation by creating the impression in Raleigh that the public opposed outrages and intended to stop them. When troops arrived before it could be held, this purpose was frustrated, and they called the meeting off altogether.[74]

For Governor Holden the Outlaw murder climaxed a cumulating wave of terror around the state. By early 1870 reports of outrages were coming to him from nearly every direction. In the west there was continuing violence in Catawba, Lincoln, Gaston, and Cleveland counties, plus newly reported outrages in Iredell, Rowan, and Davie. (These last involved chiefly attacks on the teachers of Quaker-supported schools for Negroes.)[75] There was also sporadic violence in Moore County, closer at hand.[76] Southeast of Raleigh the Klan had recently broken up in Lenoir and Jones counties, only to become active in Sampson, Johnston, Wayne, and Harnett.[77] Within a few miles of the governor's office, in the western part of Wake County, the Klan had just begun riding and attacking both Negroes and white Republicans. Sheriff T. F. Lee one night watched about thirty Klansmen ride down a country road in formation, they and their horses disguised, while he hid by the side of the road.[78] In Chatham County, a little farther west, sporadic outrages which had occurred for a year seemed to increase late in 1869. Thirty Negroes from that county passed through Raleigh on December 21, refugees from the Ku Klux and bound for Chattanooga.[79] Outrages were still being reported from Orange County in December;[80] soon afterward, just to the north, they began for the first time in Person County and resumed in Caswell.[81] The Ku Klux terror seemed on the verge of engulfing the state, tearing apart the very fabric of society, as Holden later put it. In addition, the Republican party seemed headed for disaster in the legislative elections coming up in August.

The Raleigh *Sentinel* ignored the violence as long as it could and then implicitly justified it by condemning the victims instead of the perpetrators. It blamed every Negro crime, real or imaginary, on the Union League and explained the Klan as a natural and perhaps necessary response by outraged white men. Both organizations were to be deplored, wrote editor Turner on many occasions. Yet as late as October 1869 he could turn around and say, "We do not pretend to know the object and purposes of the Ku Klux; indeed, we do not know that there is such an organization; we have always doubted the existence of a general organization of that kind for political or other purposes."[82] When Chatham County Negroes shot a Klansman from ambush as he and several colleagues were returning from a raid, the *Sentinel* reported only that Union Leaguers had tried to murder a man who was "suspected of having been to a secret political meeting." The Klansman was in full regalia, much of which was captured and turned over to the authorities.[83]

Josiah Turner was in fact one of the most effective members of the Ku Klux conspiracy in North Carolina. He may not have been "King of the Ku Klux," as the Raleigh *Standard* dubbed him, and perhaps was not even a formal member. But in private conversation he cheered on the Klan as a superb electioneering device. His position was identical to that of highly placed Klansmen who wanted to use the order selectively for political purposes, but were embarrassed if not fearful at some of the other uses to which it was put. Only after the Outlaw murder appeared to have triggered a massive Republican response did the *Sentinel* come out with a forceful appeal to stop such crimes: "We call upon the Ku Klux to cease their lawless course; good men can't justify it."[84]

Other Democratic papers around the state were little more candid. The Weldon *News,* for instance, wrote in October that the Klan was a product of the fevered imagination of Holden's Raleigh *Standard,* invented "with a view of masking some damnable evil which his party would hurl upon an innocent people." Yet a little earlier the *News* had admitted the Klan's existence and commented on its activities in Lenoir County.[85] There were exceptions among the Conservative press—more of them as the atrocities multiplied—but they were never very numerous or conspicuous.

CHAPTER 13

North Carolina:
The Kirk-Holden War, 1870

The conspiracy was so widespread and local authorities were so heedless or helpless to contain it that Republicans threatened to fight back with guerrilla warfare of their own. The Greensboro *Register,* for example, called for an organization

designed expressly to Kuklux the K.K.K. . . . Let this organization be one vast vigilance committee. Where ever an outrage is committed by the K.K.K., let them meet, follow the track, and avenge the blood that has been shed before it is yet cold in the earth. Let them have such a show of trial as they give their victims and *no more!* . . . Let there be as many Ballard rifles in the hands of our men . . . as there are K.K. masks and *let them be used* whenever the *masks are brought out!* Let us fight fire with fire, and shed blood! . . . A dozen hangings will save a hundred murders![1]

Negroes in several counties turned to arson in retaliation, sometimes organizing for the purpose. Conservatives reacted to this in horror and found it convenient to ignore the cause.

Responsible Republicans like Governor Holden at first deprecated violent retaliation of every kind, while advocating self-defense. But by May 1870 patience had worn thin: "We tell the people of North Carolina to . . . load your guns and fire on these midnight assassins whenever they attack you," advised the *Standard.* "If they catch you at disadvantage, take your gun down next day, if you are not too badly whipped, and fight it out then. A shot or two in every county in this State will break up these bands of outlaws and murderers."[2] This counsel was less a solution than a measure of Republican desperation. It was the responsibility of the state—and ultimately the governor—to enforce the laws and prevent the state from lapsing into anarchy.

In October 1869 Holden issued a proclamation calling attention to "a feeling of insubordination and insurrection" in the counties of Lenoir, Jones, Orange, and Chatham. If conditions did not improve, he promised to declare a state of insurrection in those counties and use the full power of the state to restore order.[3] With that in mind he asked the legislature for a stronger militia law, enabling him to raise large numbers of white troops to send wherever they were needed. The legislature's response was the Shoffner Act of January 1870.[4]

For all of the controversy it aroused, this law conferred little more power than the governor already had. It enabled him to proclaim a state of insurrection in lawless counties and employ the militia to suppress disorders. But Holden already had power to call out the militia, and had used it in Alamance and Jones counties within the past year to arrest Ku Klux Klansmen. The legislature struck out before passage a section that would have empowered him to suspend the writ of habeas corpus; that power was specifically denied him by the state constitution in any event. Under the new law, therefore, the militia had no more power than it had before and the proclaiming of a "state of insurrection" was chiefly of psychological importance. It is true that in such a case the county involved could be assessed for the cost of the militia's expenses; this was a common feature of state Ku Klux laws of the period, but it seems to have been unfeasible politically, and seldom were these sections enforced. Another section of the Shoffner Act enabled judges and prosecutors to remove judicial cases to an adjoining county or district if they thought a fair trial could not be had where the crime was committed. This too was provided in other states but seldom used against Klansmen; a defendant had to be indicted by the grand jury before his case could be transferred, and few Klansmen were ever indicted. Moreover, the conspiracy was so widespread that the same obstacles to a fair trial were apt to apply in other counties as well.[5]

What the situation demanded as far as state action was concerned was full martial law of the Arkansas variety. Holden was bombarded with requests for this every day, but as already noted, the state constitution forbade even the supension of habeas corpus, much less military trials. To send in militia under these circumstances was not only troublesome and expensive, but possibly futile.[6] In Arkansas Clayton had deliberately exceeded his authority in proclaiming martial law, hoping for legislative support after the event. He thereby risked civil war, political defeat, and repudiation by the federal government. Brownlow had momentarily followed suit in Tennessee. But Holden's legal position was weaker than theirs, and he refused to go that far as long as there were other straws to grasp at.

For one thing, he continued to use the Army. On March 7, after the Outlaw murder, he proclaimed a state of insurrection in Alamance and had a detachment of forty U.S. soldiers sent there. But Holden had few illusions concerning their ability to break up the Ku Klux under existing laws. "We tell the [federal] government," his newspaper warned in October, "that unless it means to allow all that was accomplished by the war to be undone, that it must crush out the Ku Klux and those who aid them, or hell will be a place of rest and peace compared with the South."[7] Holden's greatest hope was an act of Congress empowering the President to suspend habeas corpus in the supposedly reconstructed states and to punish Ku Klux offenders by military tribunal. He sent appeals to this effect to President Grant and the North Carolina Congressional delegation in March 1870, shortly after his Alamance proclamation. Congress did not pass such a law, but if it had, the measure would have affected the Klan very little. Ku Klux outrages, consisting of assault and murder primarily, were state offenses, not punishable by federal law once a state had been reconstructed. Thus further Congressional legislation was needed making these offenses federal crimes, punishable in the federal courts or by the Army in extremity. In this respect Congress made a beginning with the Enforcement Act of May 31, 1870, but like all laws, it could apply only to offenses committed after its enactment. Holden was not a lawyer, and perhaps expected more immediate relief than either Congress or the President could provide. But his demand for federal legislation was sound. This was eventually forthcoming, but too late to help him.[8]

The governor's proclamation of insurrection gave no more authority to the soldiers who went to Alamance early in March than they had already. The most they could do was help the authorities make arrests, and Sheriff Albert Murray did not tax them in this respect. They established camps in Graham and Company Shops, providing some relief for the Republicans in those places, but the Klan still rode in the countryside. One night the troops "were up and under arms" in answer to an alarm, their commander reported, "praying that [the Klan] might come; but morning came and no Ku-Klux."[9]

In other counties this spring Holden adopted a different policy, actively appeasing Conservatives in hopes that they would end the terror themselves. Until February he had relied on generalized appeals for public support of the laws, coupled with threats if it did not materialize. He had repeatedly written to sheriffs asking them to investigate reported outrages and urging them to arrest and prosecute offenders. He had also employed detectives in troubled counties, whose revelations proved useless when offenders could not be brought to trial.[10] But on February 3 he took a new tack, appointing N. A. Ramsey of Chatham County as a special agent to halt the outrages there. Ramsey was a Democrat of standing in the county who had not been associated with the Klan. He accepted the commission, probably with some danger to himself, on the advice of friends who warned that otherwise Holden might send in militia. During the next few months Ramsey made speeches in about fifty places around the county; doubtless he also conferred with members of the Klan. In these meetings he seems to have held out the hope of amnesty for past offenses if they stopped raiding, and the likelihood of a military occupation if they did not. Outrages gradually abated in Chatham; perhaps they would have anyway, given the events in other nearby counties, but Ramsey claimed and probably deserved some credit for the improvement.[11]

In March Holden offered the same commission to Dr. Pride Jones in Orange County. Again it was accepted once prominent Conservatives in the county (including former governor William A. Graham) approved the idea. Jones too conveyed an offer of amnesty to the local Klan leaders, who promised in return to disband. They were weary of both the organization and the terror, and were relieved to bring both to a close without having to answer for past actions. When Jones informed the governor of his amnesty offer Holden refused to confirm it, saying that this power lay outside his jurisdiction as governor. But his answer was conciliatory, and whatever the understanding of the various parties may have been, outrages stopped, no arrests were made, and in April Jones reported that the local Klan had disbanded.[12]

Holden also contacted Thomas A. Donoho in Caswell County for this purpose. Donoho suggested another man, but as events worked out no one was appointed.[13] Conditions soon deteriorated to such a point in Caswell—as they had in Alamance—that Holden preferred to smash the local Klan rather than conciliate it. Negroes, who outnumbered whites, were the main victims of Klan activity. They were threatened, beaten, driven from the county, and one was killed, for the usual variety of reasons. Members of the Union League were singled out for special attention, as were Negro schoolteachers and locally prominent black men generally.[14]

One project of the Caswell Klan in February was to thwart the efforts of a Negro labor recruiter who was trying to enlist black laborers to go to Alabama.[15] It surely was no coincidence that General Nathan Bedford Forrest visited nearby Greensboro at this time, recruiting construction hands for two railroads he was building in Alabama. According to the

Greensboro *Patriot,* he induced "a large number of able-bodied blacks" to leave by offering higher wages than local employers were paying.[16] Republicans who blamed Forrest for instigating Ku Klux outrages at the time of his visit were probably wide of the mark. On the contrary, his agents were probably the objects of Klan resentment. It would have been the supreme irony if the late Imperial Wizard himself or his agents had fallen victim to Ku Klux attacks.[17]

Caswell Republicans repeatedly asked Holden for troops or else for guns with which to defend themselves. A few soldiers came for a time but accomplished nothing. Some Negroes took the law in their own hands and burned several barns, which likely stimulated further Klan outrages. The local Republican leaders seem to have consistently advised the freedmen against retaliation and warned the governor that more of it would occur if help was not forthcoming.[18] But Conservatives were sure that these were the very men inspiring the arson. Their wrath fell principally upon state senator John W. Stephens.

Of humble antecedents and barely literate, Stephens had been a wartime Unionist in Rockingham County before moving to Caswell. He joined the Republican party at its establishment and showed his willingness to work and associate with the Negroes on a basis of equality. As elsewhere in black counties, few white men met these specifications and Stephens became a natural candidate for party leadership. Like George W. Smith at Jefferson, Texas, he was a loyal friend of the Negro community and became the acknowledged Republican leader of the county. Within the context of equal Negro rights, however, Stephens was a political moderate. In 1868 he had told Conservative elders that if they would make the young whites behave he would pledge his life for the Negroes' behavior. He seems always to have advised against physical retaliation,[19] and in 1870 he offered to support a moderate Democrat for sheriff in order to allay mounting strife. Neither offer was taken, and extremism consistently dominated the other side.

Stephens' character and circumstances were reflected in a letter he wrote to Holden in 1868:

I wish to call your particular attention to the condition I have placed myself in by cuming out & standing up for the Republican party in this Co. & ask your support & protection in the matter. before I taken this stand (whitch I did becaus I thought it was rite & have never yet regreted and hope I never shall) I had money friends & credit for anything I wanted but now I have neither the trouth is that I have not means to buy what I actuly kneed for the support of my family. my creditors have pushed on me and taken everything that the law would allow & I can look to know source but the Republican party if thaire is any thing that you can do for me in this hour of kneed pleas let me know what it is.[20]

Because of his origins and associations Stephens was anathema to the white community. "It is an unfortunate circumstance for the welfare of the county, as well as for the interest of your party," Thomas A. Donoho wrote Holden in May 1870, "that the recognized exponent of the Republican party in the county, should be a person of the *antecedents* and *surroundings* of the member who represents the county in the State Senate."[21] Conservatives regarded him as a firebrand who preached violence to the Negroes at Union League meetings. On one occasion, it was reported and perhaps believed, he gave to each of twenty Negroes present a box of matches and told each one to burn a barn. An active Methodist, he was expelled from the church and socially ostracized because of his political course. Because of constant threats on his life, Stephens fortified his house in Yanceyville and carried a ten-shooter and two derringers around with him.[22]

On May 21 Caswell Democrats held their county convention at the courthouse in Yanceyville, where speeches were made and candidates nominated for the coming elections in August. Stephens attended as an observer, sitting impassively and taking notes while speakers berated him from the platform. At length he left the meeting, which was being held in the second-floor courtroom, and went downstairs in company with ex-sheriff Frank A. Wiley, a Democrat. It was Wiley whom Stephens had offered to support for that office again, and he now was seeking to learn his decision whether to run.

Unknown to Stephens, Wiley was either a Klansman or a fellow traveler, and was using this interview to lure him into a trap. The Klan had previously voted Stephens' assassination, and a number of its members were waiting around the courthouse. According to plan, Wiley persuaded Stephens to accompany him into a back room which was used to store firewood. As soon as he entered, Stephens was overpowered by several men who had been waiting for him. After a moment or two of irresolution one of them drew a rope around his neck and choked him while another stabbed him three times in the throat and chest. Whatever noise this created was drowned out by voices in the corridor and in the convention which continued overhead. Leaving Stephens' body on the woodpile, his attackers left the room, locked it behind them, and lost themselves in the crowd. They intended to move the body that night to a Negro schoolhouse where Republican meetings were often held, so as to cast suspicion on the Negroes. But this plan was foiled when the blacks, noting Stephens' disappearance and suspecting foul play, posted an armed guard around the building until it could be unlocked and searched the next morning.[23]

As soon as the murder was discovered the next day, the perpetrators attempted to throw blame on the Negroes anyway. A story was concocted that Stephens had quarreled with his black followers on many occasions and thus they had as much reason to kill him as any white men. The Ku Klux Klan did not even exist in the county, Democrats insisted. Wittingly or unwittingly the white community as a whole entered fully into the conspiracy, as did the *Sentinel* and other Democratic newspapers. The *Sentinel* carried a letter from Wiley saying that he had last seen Stephens in conversation with an unknown Negro. Later it declared editorially, "The evidence is becoming more palpable that the negroes killed him. It is known that most of the crimes committed in this State, have been done by disguised negroes and white Radical Ku Klux or League men." The fact that the murder room overlooked some Negro homes was said to be very significant, and the Hillsborough *Recorder* found a remarkable parallel between the manner of Stephens' death and the way some Negroes recently committed a murder in Hillsborough. The *Sentinel* even linked Governor Holden to the crime by suggesting that he had recently advised Caswell Negroes to "kill off" Stephens politically as a liability to the Republican party; the black men merely took him literally. In addition, Democrats embroidered upon certain slanders which had already been circulating against Stephens. The most notable of these, apart from his alleged incendiarism, were that he had killed his own mother and made it appear as an accident, and that he had been convicted as a common chicken thief before leaving Rockingham County in 1866.[24]

At the same time, hoping to avert a military occupation like that which followed Wyatt Outlaw's murder in Alamance, Democratic leaders called a public meeting to deprecate violence and murder. Speeches were made and resolutions adopted to this end, but in the process Stephens and the Republican party incurred about as much criticism as did violence and murder. The Democratic county platform, which two of the assassins helped write, also denounced violence as well as all secret organizations. The authorities went through the motions of an official inquiry into the crime. Several Negroes had seen Stephens conversing with Wiley and identified some of the other murderers as being near the storage room at about the time Stephens was last seen. Two witnesses even overheard a remark that Stephens "will be in hell before night." But no great effort was made to locate or examine these witnesses closely, and at least one found it expedient to leave the state. The coroner's jury therefore returned the usual verdict of death by persons unknown, and people were free privately to assign guilt where they wished. Three of the murderers, including Wiley, were arrested and then discharged for lack of evidence. Stephens' two brothers were pressured (as they later said) into issuing a statement prepared by ex-Congressman John Kerr of Yanceyville and carried in the *Sentinel,* commending the authorities for their zeal in trying to uncover the culprits; there was no reason at all, the statement declared, to suspect "certain prominent individuals," or indeed anyone else in Yanceyville, as some persons were suggesting.

As a matter of fact a considerable number of reasonably prominent men from around Yanceyville were implicated in the murder, either as participants or as accessories. Probably very few people in town could not at least guess who some of them were. Many facts in the case were developed after subsequent militia arrests, and some of the participants talked. A Republican legislator was able to reconstruct the crime with fair accuracy in 1873, as reported in the *New York Times.* Some of the participants were said to have confessed on their death beds years later, but authoritative revelation was deferred until 1935. In that year Captain John G. Lea died and the North Carolina Historical Commission released a long account of the murder which Lea had deposited in 1919 on condition that it be withheld during his lifetime. By his own account Lea had been the founder of the Caswell Klan, the organizer of the Stephens assassination, and one of those present in the murder room.[25]

In the aftermath of Stephens' murder Governor Holden learned that Wilson Carey, a Negro legislator and second-ranking Republican in Caswell, had fled the county in fear of his life. There was also continuing news of outrages in Lincoln, Cumberland, and Alamance counties. Holden issued yet another proclamation, offering rewards for those guilty of several specified murders, and telegraphed Senators Pool and Abbott in Washington that "prompt and decisive action by Congress is necessary." The *Standard* asked that militia be sent to Caswell.[26]

A few days after Holden sent off his telegram Congress passed its first Enforcement Act, but federal authorities took no perceptible steps to carry it out. In fact Republicans in Washington from President Grant on down were saying that the federal government had no business interfering actively in the states until they had exhausted their own resources. Holden had not used the militia to the full limit of his power, and the example of Clayton in Arkansas was held out as a fitting one to follow. As a matter of fact, Grant was reportedly criticizing both Holden and Governor Smith of Alabama for letting the Ku Klux take over their states. It was incumbent on the governor to act before that became literally true.

About June 8 Holden met in Raleigh with Senator John Pool and other prominent Republicans to decide on a policy. All the men present agreed that military force was needed and that federal troops had proved ineffective. The question then was whether the state militia would be limited to making arrests and turning over prisoners to the civil courts, or whether the governor should violate the state constitution by suspending habeas corpus and establishing military tribunals as in Arkansas. Pool, an exceedingly able man—Conservative historian J. G. de Roulhac Hamilton called him Holden's "evil genius"—reported the feeling in Washington that Holden had been excessively timid. Pool advocated stern measures. He later denied that he had proposed military courts, however, and it is unclear what decision on this point emerged from the meeting. One participant said they agreed that prisoners should be turned over to the civil courts, and that special prosecutors be assigned to accompany the militia and handle the cases. On the other hand Holden appointed a military commission in July to try prisoners, even making Mayor Albright of Graham a brigadier general to sit on it.

The next questions were how and where to raise troops for the campaign, and who should command them. Holden had always rejected the idea of Negro militia because he felt they enflamed white race prejudice; and white men recruited in most parts of the state would amount to little more than an army of Ku Klux raised to fight the Ku Klux. Moreover, white men drafted into the militia, whom he had used in small numbers already in Alamance and Jones counties, had proved inefficient. What he needed was dependable volunteers, and (as in Arkansas and Tennessee) recourse was had to the Unionist mountaineers. Over-all command was entrusted initially to Colonel William J. Clarke of New Bern.

Clarke was immediately sent off to Washington to obtain supplies from the federal government. President Grant and General Sherman (then acting Secretary of War) approved the plans and granted what was requested. (Sherman was obliged to secure a bond from Holden to pay for the supplies, but the money, he said, "will, in effect, be payable at the day of Judgment.") Soon afterward Holden transferred the command to Colonel George W. Kirk of Jonesboro, Tennessee, who had commanded a regiment of federal troops in the mountains of western North Carolina and east Tennessee during the war, and more recently led Brownlow's militia against the Ku Klux Klan in Tennessee. Late in June Holden himself went to Washington, conferred with the President, and received his blessings as well as the promise of additional federal troops to supplement the militia. Thus began the North Carolina militia campaign which its enemies dubbed the Kirk-Holden War.[27]

Holden and Kirk prepared a handbill over the colonel's name which was distributed through the mountains. It called on Union veterans to rally to their old commander and join the forces being raised to combat the Ku Klux Klan. This appeal, coupled with regular Army pay, induced about 600 men to sign up in late June and early July. By July 15 Kirk had brought about 200 of them to Company Shops in Alamance County, where they were formally inducted and the military court was appointed. Kirk went on to Raleigh and got from Holden a list of persons to arrest, based on information supplied by local Republicans. Meanwhile the governor had proclaimed a state of insurrection in Caswell too, and Kirk was ordered to occupy that county himself. Alamance remained in charge of his second-in-command, Lieutenant Colonel George B. Bergen, a New Jersey man chosen by Kirk on the basis of joint wartime service.[28]

A sizable minority of the troops were east Tennesseeans like their commander, a fact which Conservatives held forth as a great abuse. The men were not all war veterans by any means either, and ranged in age from fifteen or sixteen to sixty or seventy. Only a few were Negroes; they were employed chiefly as teamsters. Not surprisingly, the men were undisciplined and unsoldierly in many ways. They committed next to no depredations except raids on apple orchards and the like, but they were known to curse each other and their officers freely, and they were markedly disrespectful at times of suspected Ku Klux. The ladies and gentlemen of Yanceyville were offended to see one trooper strip bare at the town pump to wash himself and his clothes. At their first appearance, though they wore clothes, they made a ragged sight until uniforms were issued.[29]

Colonel Kirk himself was highly controversial because of his wartime activity. According to Conservatives he was a man of no principle or character, and had been no better than a desperado or jayhawker in the mountains. His present role did not recommend him to Conservatives either, for they were outraged at the whole militia campaign. Except for his prisoners, who generally testified to good treatment, Democrats portrayed him as a monster during this operation too. Even Republicans were divided over Kirk's wartime career, a minority echoing Conservatives and asking Holden to appoint someone else to command. Most Republicans agreed substantially with the view of a wartime associate who described Kirk as a terror to rebel outlaws but a man of high character who would mete out even-handed justice. His performance in 1870 bore out that evaluation.[30]

The arrests began immediately in both counties and proceeded for a week or two as squads went out into the country to pick up the men named in the governor's list. Many Klansmen anticipated this and either took to the woods or left the state on the militia's arrival. Jacob Long, sometime county chief of the White Brotherhood in Alamance, went to Arkansas. A few resisted arrest; Frank Wiley of Caswell was found working in his fields and had to be forcibly apprehended. Those arrested fell into every age bracket, social rank, and official position. They included the sheriffs of both counties, young lawyers like Long and James E. Boyd, and respected elders like ex-Congressman John Kerr. Most were small to middling farmers and not very old, reflecting the active membership of the Klan.

Leaders of the order were taken along with common members. Many perpetrators of Ku Klux atrocities were never identified, and many others were suspected on such slight evidence as to preclude arrest. These, with the members who fled, probably constituted a majority of those guilty of serious crime. But since the greatest activists participated in many outrages, some of them were picked up on the basis of only fragmentary knowledge.

The most highly publicized arrest—and certainly the most controversial —was that of Josiah Turner. He was picked up at his home in Orange County (outside the sphere of militia operations) by a militia detachment which brought him to Company Shops and eventually to Yanceyville. There he was confined for a time in the same courthouse room where John W. Stephens had been murdered. Holden seems to have sanctioned Turner's arrest beforehand, with some misgiving, because of his notorious encouragement of Klan activity throughout the state; but that consent was conditional on Turner's entering Alamance or Caswell counties. As it happened, Colonel Bergen ordered the arrest on his own responsibility, believing that Holden really wanted it done but lacked the nerve to order it explicitly. Kirk was wholly ignorant of the matter until Turner was brought in. The legal grounds for this arrest were highly questionable, and it provided lethal ammunition to Democrats who were charging that the whole campaign was no more than a vendetta by Holden against his personal and political enemies. Josiah Turner was unquestionably a part of the broader Ku Klux conspiracy which sought to undermine state and local authorities and win political power through intimidation and violence. Witnesses even testified that he had privately urged the Klan to ride in Negro neighborhoods before elections, but no one ever suggested that he participated in Ku Klux raids himself. Whatever his moral guilt, it is doubtful that he had committed any indictable offense. The same was perhaps true of John Kerr and certain others arrested, unless they were accessories to Stephens' murder and other crimes. Owing to the outcome of the militia campaign, the state never fully presented its evidence against many of the prisoners, and neither their guilt nor their innocence was satisfactorily established.[31]

Altogether, about 100 prisoners were arrested by military authority in the two counties, a few of whom were released almost immediately. There were too many to lodge in the two county jails, and some were confined elsewhere, as in the Caswell County courthouse. Some of the prisoners complained later that they were fed by friends and relatives during the confinement, rather than by the military. However widespread this may have been, there were few complaints of serious mistreatment. Suspected Ku Klux were treated roughly in many cases, but not brutally except as noted below. Some described Kirk as gruff and abrupt, but others regarded him as friendly within the limits imposed by his office of jailer. Josiah Turner ostentatiously rejected his overtures for a time, preferring the role of martyrdom, but later gave this up.

Bergen's record at Company Shops was not as good. Still in his twenties, he was too immature to handle the serious responsibility which Kirk had conferred on him. Although he denied it, there is good evidence that he partially hanged three prisoners and threatened their lives to extort information about Wyatt Outlaw's murderers. When Holden heard of this he issued orders immediately to stop mistreatment of the prisoners. There were complaints too that, like Captain Rosa in Arkansas, he had accepted money for not making certain arrests. Later, in August, Holden made no objection when Bergen himself was arrested and jailed in Raleigh. Bergen's indiscretions (to say the least) were magnified and broadcast to the world by the Conservative press as typical of the whole campaign. As with the Arkansas and Tennessee campaigns, readers of Democratic newspapers around the country got their most lasting impressions of the North Carolina campaign from the exaggerated tales of militia atrocities.[32]

Klan violence ceased in both Alamance and Caswell by the time the militia arrived. Conservatives claimed that the militia were therefore unnecessary, but there was every reason from past experience to believe otherwise. Klansmen were badly frightened by the militia's coming and ensuing arrests. Rank-and-file members who were innocent of gross offenses hastened to confess their membership and activities to Mayor Albright and other officials, who took down their sworn statements and the accumulation of evidence to use in the ensuing military trials of greater offenders.[33]

Some of the leading members, who for months had been trying to moderate the Klan's course if not to disband it altogether, saw this as the first safe opportunity to sever their own connection with the order and break it up. They hoped to buy immunity too, but were sincerely concerned to end the terror once and for all. The foremost among these was James E. Boyd, whom Alamance Democrats had already nominated as their candidate for the legislature. After making an individual confession of his own, Boyd prevailed on fifteen others (including camp and klan chiefs in both the White Brotherhood and the Constitutional Union Guard) to join him in formally renouncing their membership. This public statement implicated no others by name, but it called on all law-abiding men to follow their course. "Unless the crimes which have been committed by this organization can be put a stop to," they said, "and the organization itself entirely broken up, civil liberty and personal safety are at an end in this county and life and property and everything else will soon be at the mercy of an organized mob." When this document and the confessions of several other members were released to the press at the end of July they created a sensation locally and even nationally.[34]

The Alamance Klan—and apparently that in Caswell too—did break up as a result of the militia campaign. In the case of both the White Brotherhood and the Constitutional Union Guard the breakup seems to have taken the form of a general abandonment rather than formal dissolution. As late as February 1871 there was talk of a reorganization in Alamance through the medium of the Invisible Empire, the order which prevailed farther south. But this never caught on, and only a few scattered outrages were reported thereafter.[35]

After Boyd's action became public, several local Democrats came to him and privately expressed disgust at the party's involvement in terrorism.[36] Former governor Thomas Bragg, chairman of the Democratic state committee, had already written Klan leaders in Lincoln and Cleveland counties, urging them to disband the order because it was giving the party a bad name.[37] But this attitude was not typical. When Boyd subsequently testified publicly against other members of the order he was socially ostracized and his law practice evaporated. Even before his revelations were made public Josiah Turner declared that no man who broke a solemn oath of secrecy (like the Klan's) could be believed thereafter. The *Sentinel* cast slurs upon all those who were making disclosures, and minimized their truth or significance. At worst, it said, the crimes of the Ku Klux were no graver than those which it ascribed to the Union League. The *Sentinel* advised Democratic voters in the coming election not to credit the lies they were hearing from the Ku Klux traitors.[38] Democrats concentrated their greatest fury on Holden. He had magnified a few outrages for political capital, said the Greensboro *Patriot,* in order to justify martial law and personal dictatorship. "For cool, persistnet [*sic*], studied, planned and deliberate turpitude and perfidy we have never read its equal. . . ."[39]

The Conservative counterattack assumed legal form as well. As soon as the arrests began, suits were instituted before Chief Justice Richmond M. Pearson of the state supreme court to have a number of the prisoners released on writs of habeas corpus. This of course was the weak spot in Holden's legal position. Lacking the power to suspend the writ, his course at this point would normally have been to furnish sufficient evidence of the prisoners' guilt to justify Pearson in holding them for trial. Pearson was a veteran member of the court, a conservative Republican who had been elected chief justice with bipartisan support; he knew the background and causes of Holden's policy and sympathized with it. But without such evidence before him he had ordered the prisoners freed, and he notified the governor accordingly.

Holden, despairing of a fair trial in the civil courts, had resolved to try them by military commission. He therefore wrote Pearson a lengthy public letter on July 26, justifying his proclamations of insurrection and politely declining to surrender the prisoners. "As the Chief Executive I seek to restore, not to subvert, the judicial power. Your Honor has done your duty, and in perfect harmony with you I seek to do mine. . . . It would be mockery in me to declare that the civil authority was unable to protect the citizens against the insurgents, and then turn the insurgents over to the civil authority." In effect Holden suspended habeas corpus without saying so. The illogic lay not in his argument but in the state constitution which with one hand empowered him to call out the militia to suppress insurrection and with the other denied him one of the essential supports of that power. Pearson accepted the governor's answer gracefully. He ruled that his authority was now exhausted and he lacked power either to arrest the governor as requested by the prisoners or to force him to comply with a court order. It was not unlike the legal impasse between President Lincoln and Chief Justice Taney over habeas corpus cases during the war, except that Holden and Pearson may have had a personal understanding.[40]

Failing to get relief from the state's highest court, some of the prisoners repaired (through their attorneys) to the federal district court at Salisbury with a similar motion. They now claimed to have been denied liberty without due process of law, in violation of the new Fourteenth Amendment. Judge George W. Brooks also had no choice but to order the prisoners brought before him, together with whatever evidence the state had to bring against them. He too was ready to order them held for trial if the evidence was sufficient. But Holden was still insistent on military trials and planned to resist Brooks just as he had Pearson. He telegraphed President Grant to this effect on August 7, requesting the Army not to interfere. Holden doubtless believed on the basis of their prior consultation that the President was still behind him and would support him in this action. But Grant was placed in an awkward position. Judge Brooks's stand was legally correct, and Grant could hardly sanction state defiance of federal authority, even in such a case as this. The administration therefore upheld Brooks and advised Holden to yield.

The governor could only comply, and he abandoned his plan of holding military trials. (These had originally been scheduled for late July, as soon as possible after the arrests, but then were postponed until August 8 so as not to influence the state elections on August 4.)[41] He now ordered Kirk to have the prisoners taken before the two judges as they previously ordered. Accordingly one group went to Raleigh on August 18 to face Chief Justice Pearson; Kirk himself appeared before Judge Brooks in Salisbury on August 19 with the second group, which included Josiah Turner. Surprisingly, he presented no evidence whatever against them and left Brooks no choice but to release them. Conservatives raised a cheer throughout the state. Klansmen in Alamance suddenly stopped coming in to confess; some who had already made statements now regretted their haste and asked to withdraw them. Ironically, Ku Klux Klansmen were now free under a constitutional amendment which Republicans had enacted to protect the Negroes against just such aggressors as they.

Holden's plans were thrown into confusion by poor planning and his failure to anticipate federal intervention. Many persons, including Kirk, had worked around the clock taking the mass of confessions as they poured in and assembling the evidence to present at the ensuing trials. But too few skilled lawyers were assigned to this task. The evidence certainly was not ready to present to Pearson when he first asked for it on July 18, three days after the arrests began, even if Holden had intended to cooperate at that time. By August 19 this situation was no longer true for the prisoners sent to Raleigh, and it should not have been so for those at Salisbury. Yet Kirk's reason for not defending his case that day was that he had had no opportunity to bring witnesses or evidence. The reason assuredly was not that the state had no evidence at all, as Conservatives claimed, for some of it was offered soon afterward in Raleigh. Brooks was told later that the state made no defense because it denied his jurisdiction. All of this indicated major confusion.[42]

The state was better prepared with evidence against the prisoners it took to Raleigh. During the next two weeks Chief Justice Pearson and one or two of his colleagues heard at least eight cases, most of them involving several defendants. They were accused of participating in the Stephens murder in Caswell and a number of whippings and other outrages in Alamance. The justices credited the record of conspiracy and violence revealed by the state's witnesses, including Boyd and other former Klansmen, and bound over forty-nine of the defendants—nearly all of them—for trial in their respective counties at the next court term. These cases touched only a small fraction of the crimes which had been committed, and the defendants did not include many of those involved even in these crimes. (Frank Wiley was bound over in the Stephens murder, but Captain Lea was not, apparently for lack of evidence, although he had been arrested. None of the cases involved the Outlaw murder, most of the important participants in which had fled.)[43] The defendants were all released on bond. When the time came to try them the cases were quietly buried by the local authorities.[44] Except for the trouble involved in their month's imprisonment and facing preliminary charges, none of them was punished. If the terror had abated in Alamance and Caswell, the larger conspiracy remained.

Governor Holden disbanded the militia in September and lifted the state of insurrection in Alamance and Caswell in November. Federal troops remained there for a time—they had been passively present all along—but Republicans were again subjected to intimidation if not outright violence.[45]

Klansmen not only escaped punishment; they turned the law on their erstwhile prosecutors with a series of suits and harassments that drove some of them from the state as fugitives. No sooner had Kirk brought his prisoners to Raleigh than two of them sued him for false arrest. He was released on bond and returned to his command while other similar suits accumulated against him. In effect he became a refugee from process servers and sheriffs, protected only by his own soldiers. When they were mustered out, Kirk arranged to have a United States marshal arrest him and bring him to Raleigh under guard. Passing through Hillsborough en route, he narrowly escaped capture by the Orange County sheriff and a posse of thirty armed men; some of them were still hanging on the train as it pulled out of the station. Kirk remained in Raleigh until the federal case against him was thrown out. On December 1 he returned to his home in Tennessee, traveling secretly and by a circuitous route to avoid an armed mob which reportedly was waiting to intercept him at Greensboro.[46]

Holden himself was indicted in the state courts for having ordered military arrests. This harassment proceeded from grand juries which in the past had refused repeatedly to indict Ku Klux terrorists.[47] The cases were eventually dropped, but not before Holden himself was obliged to flee the state to avoid possible arrest.

Josiah Turner and other Democratic leaders had apparently planned on a massive night riding campaign around the state just before the August 4 election, in order to intimidate Negro voters.[48] Comparatively little of this actually took place, with the militia campaign then under way. Nevertheless the Republican vote fell off and the Democrats, without gaining appreciably over their 1868 showing, carried the state by 8,000 votes. With this victory went control of the next legislature, which met in November. Ten of the fifteen counties which switched into the Democratic column had seen appreciable Klan activity earlier, and only Alamance and Caswell in their portion of the state reported Republican majorities. The militia had patrolled both counties during the election and apparently guaranteed a fair vote. The new legislature threw out their returns, however, on the ground that the militia had imposed a Republican victory. In a special election in December, marked by the kind of tricks and intimidation that Negroes would face nearly everywhere after Reconstruction, the Democrats carried both counties.[49]

Governor Holden told the new legislature in November that the results of his militia campaign had been "in the highest degree fortunate and beneficial." The state government was sustained, he said, the Klan was broken up, and peaceful men were no longer molested because of their political opinions. Of course he overstated his case. He could hardly have been this sanguine privately about the prospects for peace and order.[50]

Throughout the militia campaign there had been sporadic outbreaks of

Klan activity in other parts of the state, and they continued afterward. In Lincoln County it was more than sporadic. A committee of Negroes wrote to the governor on May 11, reporting sixteen outrages since the end of March. A white Republican, citing specific cases of robbery, whipping, stabbing, shooting, and gang rape, put the Klansmen "on a par with the Indians of the plains." W. P. Bynum, the able and distinguished prosecutor of that district, wrote that he had tried repeatedly to bring offenders to book, but always met the same obstacles of complicity among some of the populace and fear among all.[51] Similar conditions existed in Rutherford, Cleveland, and Gaston counties, and in July Holden sent militia to all of these but Rutherford. Most of the men were local recruits, but a few were detached from Kirk's command. They accomplished little, and the terror in this region broke out anew a few months later.[52] Conditions in Cleveland and Rutherford became as bad as they had been in Alamance. The Klan would also ride again in late 1870 and early 1871 in Wake, Chatham, Harnett, and other counties in the center of the state.[53]

The militia campaign was at best a mixed success. Holden might have foreseen the legal obstacles which tripped him up, but he lacked any obvious means of avoiding them. Perhaps it was only luck which spared Governor Clayton the necessity of obeying a federal court order in Arkansas, reinforced by the administration in Washington, demanding the release of all prisoners or remanding them to the civil courts, which was the same thing. As it turned out, the greatest casualty of Holden's militia campaign was Holden himself.[54]

The new Democratic legislature met in November, determined to impeach the governor and remove him from office. The resolution of impeachment was fittingly introduced by Representative F. N. Strudwick of Orange, the would-be assassin of Senator Shoffner. The Klan occupied an influential place in the new legislature. House Speaker Thomas J. Jarvis was identified as a member by James Boyd and others, and Hamilton C. Jones of Mecklenburg County, a senate leader, was repeatedly named as one of the highest officials in the Invisible Empire. Novelist Thomas Dixon and others identified Dixon's uncle, Leroy McAfee of Cleveland County, as Grand Titan of that district and also an active participant in the impeachment proceedings. The Democratic majority as a whole made its sympathies with the Klan abundantly clear before the session was over.[55]

The trial took place between December 23, 1870, and March 22, 1871. There were eight articles of impeachment. The first two, general in character, accused Holden of violating the constitution by using militia to oppress the people on the pretext of putting down an imaginary insurrection. The other six charges elaborated on these, accusing him of exceeding his authority in raising the militia and making arrests. In reply the defense produced a tremendous volume of testimony chronicling in minute detail the state of affairs, especially in Alamance and Caswell, which led Holden to call out the militia. This testimony still comprises the largest body of information concerning the Klan in North Carolina up to that time. On the first two counts Holden was acquitted by a straight party vote, the Democrats lacking the requisite two-thirds senate majority. But several Republicans believed Holden to have technically exceeded his powers. At some risk of inconsistency they voted guilty on the specific charges and thereby secured his conviction. By a vote of 36 to 13 the senate then expelled him from office, on March 22.

As the New York *Tribune* put it, the senate

virtually acknowledged the propriety of Gov. Holden's proclamation declaring Alamance and other counties [*sic*] in a state of insurrection, by acquitting him of charges of illegally and unnecessarily instituting martial law therein; while it condemns him for the employment of militia in suppressing the insurrection and restoring order. In other words, he was right in declaring the rebellion but wrong in suppressing it. For this decision there could be no respect, even if the trial had been otherwise fairly and decently conducted.

The *New York Times,* which had condemned Holden in August, agreed with this estimate after hearing the causes of his action. The impeachment was politically inspired, of course, with the Democrats deriving their precedent from the trial of Andrew Johnson. Holden was the first state governor in American history to be convicted and removed from office on impeachment. Debarred from holding state office again and facing lawsuits for false arrest, he moved to Washington, D.C. But some years later when the dust had settled, he returned to Raleigh, where he spent the rest of his life and served as postmaster.[56]

Lieutenant Governor Tod R. Caldwell, who succeeded Holden, was also a Republican. But governors of North Carolina lacked the veto power, and Caldwell was powerless to keep the Democrats and the Klan from consolidating their victory. Even before the impeachment proceedings had ended, the legislature repealed the Shoffner Act and most of the militia law of 1868 under which Holden had acted. The legislature did pass a new measure outlawing membership in any secret political or military societies.[57] This clearly included the Klan as well as the Union League (which had already disappeared). The law reflected the view of Conservative leaders that the Klan had served its purpose and had better come to an end. But the Klan would not die, and Democrats made no serious attempt to invoke this or any other law against it. As the terror continued in parts of the state Governor Caldwell, with no militia powers left and Holden's example before him, confined himself perforce to moral appeals and the stationing of federal troops.

CHAPTER 14

Georgia and Florida: Warren County and the Conservative Conquest of Georgia

Nothing shows better the localized character of Klan activity than its lack of synchronism from one place to another. North Carolina experienced a surge of terrorism in 1869 and 1870, having had very little in 1868. South Carolina saw much of it in 1868, only to have the Klan virtually disappear until late 1870. In Georgia and Florida it continued to ride in many regions at a diminished rate in 1869 and then increased in 1870.

There were local exceptions even to these generalizations. Warren County, in Georgia's eastern Black Belt, descended much further into terrorism in 1869 than most Southern counties ever got. Its population, 10,545 in 1870, was 59 per cent Negro; the same proportion held among the 620 inhabitants of Warrenton, the county seat and largest town. Negro votes made the county safely Republican in a fair election, but no such elections were held after April 1868. As in other Black Belt counties the few white Republicans held the major offices and were anathema to the Conservative whites who had hitherto monopolized power and continued to possess most of the wealth and education. Such pressure was put on these Republicans that most of them embraced the Conservative side in time, thereby increasing the heat on those who held firm.

The center of controversy for more than two years was Sheriff John C. (Chap) Norris. Elected as a Republican, he was neither a party leader nor a conspicuous friend of the Negroes. Conservative hostility concentrated on him partly because of a desire to seize his office and the powers that went with it, and partly because of his dogged determination to enforce the law against terrorists. Norris had his share of human weaknesses and seems eventually to have succumbed to the lure of Conservative money. The battle of Southern Republicans against the Ku Klux Klan spawned few heroes, however, and Norris certainly deserves honorable mention among them. His life was constantly threatened, he was seriously wounded in an ambush attack, and more than once he was forced to flee the county, but he returned each time, and when troops were available and willing to help, he made arrests.

Norris was a native of the county, a boot and shoe maker before the war who became a Unionist and then a Republican. Elected sheriff in April 1868 along with the rest of the Republican ticket, he was prevented briefly from taking office by Conservative demands that he endorse Seymour and Blair as the price of their signing his bond. When he refused to do so the county's only newspaper, the bellicose *Georgia Clipper,* denounced in advance anyone who might come forward to stand his bond. State senator Joseph Adkins and other Republicans performed the service nevertheless, whereupon Conservatives (including General Robert Toombs, the Georgia statesman of bygone days, who lived in a nearby county) tried vainly to have the bond set aside on a legal technicality. At the same time erstwhile friends advised Norris that his life was in danger if he insisted on taking office. There was an organization, they said, that would not suffer Radicals to hold office. Norris heeded these threats only to the extent of asking General Meade to send troops. An officer came to investigate, but no troops were sent.[1]

Ku Klux violence began seriously in the summer of 1868. Night riding, with accompanying whippings and shootings, became an almost nightly occurrence, and the Klan murdered its first Negro in September. The next month a freedman died after receiving 900 lashes with saddle stirrups. The violence continued intermittently through 1869 and assumed a fairly set pattern. Although white people were occasionally attacked for social misdemeanors, the dominant motive was to keep the Negro in his place economically, socially, and politically. This embraced attacks on the handful of white Republicans who led or befriended the black majority. Many Negroes were driven off the land near harvest time, leaving the benefit of their year's work to the landlords. Warren Jones, an intelligent and enterprising black man, was exploited in this fashion. He was initially offered a half share of the crop he proposed to raise in the coming year. He went ahead, even hiring additional laborers, and made the crop, but after it was gathered the landowner told him he must stay and work for nothing. He was threatened with a Ku Kluxing if he complained, and eventually he fled to Atlanta without a cent to his name. Jones later testified that when the Negroes of his neighborhood erected a school, whites forbade it to meet unless they supported it themselves rather than out of tax money. Even Negro prayer meetings were broken up, he said. "They supposed the negroes would get together and talk politics, and in that way . . . find out too much to work for nothing. . . . They wanted us to know nothing but what they said; they supposed we would get too much sense if we talked together." The blacks were also warned never to hire out to another employer without first getting a pass from the man they lived with. Emancipation was not to get out of hand in Warren County.[2]

The terrorism increased with the approach of the Presidential election and was marked by general rowdyism as well as night riding in disguise.[3] The Freedmen's Bureau agent, R. C. Anthony, reported in September that only once had he seen a Negro create a disturbance on the streets of Warrenton; drunken whites, on the other hand, were constantly in evidence abusing Negroes and the handful of white Republicans. Sheriff Norris was repeatedly hounded. He stood almost alone in attempting to maintain order, Anthony said, even his friends fearing to risk their lives by supporting him. A major source of inspiration to the Ku Klux and the rowdy element generally was the *Clipper,* whose editor, Charles Wallace, was almost certainly one of the Klan's leaders. Only with the greatest reluctance did Conservatives permit a Republican rally to be held in the county, seemingly fearful that it might lead to a Negro insurrection. While this meeting was in progress—in a Negro church, the courthouse having been denied—scores of armed whites rode into town from different directions, many of them from neighboring counties. Local Democrats welcomed them with speeches in the courthouse, one of them waving a revolver in the air and declaring, "This is the law, and this shall rule the country." Although the Negroes were meeting quite peaceably in their church the whites became increasingly threatening and even got into a fracas among themselves. Fearing they would go to the Republican meeting and provoke a riot, Norris and Anthony persuaded the blacks to break up early and go home.[4] When troops finally came a few days before the election, they ended the rowdyism in town, but night riding continued. Conservatives carried the election through a combination of intimidation and refusal to let Negroes vote on grounds of nonpayment of taxes. These methods proved successful throughout much of the state.[5]

One of the black men whom the Klan singled out for attack was Perry Jeffers, who with his sons worked part of a plantation four miles from town. They were industrious, bore a good reputation according to their employer, and were making money. Jeffers refused to join the Democratic club before the election as he was bade to do, and announced that he would vote for Grant. On the night of November 1 a party of half a dozen Klansmen approached his log cabin and began shooting inside through the cracks in the wall. Jeffers had been warned to expect them and was ready. He and his sons returned the fire, killing one of the attackers and wounding at least three others. The Klansmen remounted their horses and beat a hasty retreat. The dead man turned out to be the son of a respectable farmer nearby; no inquest was held into his death, and he was buried after dark without fanfare. One of the wounded men was sent away quietly to recover, while a second passed off his disability as rheumatism.

Retaliation came four nights later when a company of fifty to a hundred hooded men returned to the house. Jeffers and four of his five sons had taken to the woods nearby and watched as the Klansmen entered to confront only Mrs. Jeffers and a fifth son who was crippled and bedridden. The family was mistaken in thinking that the helplessness of this pair would protect them. They were dragged outside, and the son was shot eleven times. The Klansmen then threw out the cabin's contents—furniture, feather mattresses, and all—making a pile of them in the yard. To this they added the boy's body and then set fire to the whole. Finally they seized the mother and with a length of bed cord hung her from a tree. As soon as they rode off, the woman was cut down; she survived but continued to bear the marks of her treatment.

Jeffers and his sons now followed their landlord's advice to leave, and came into Warrenton, abandoning a good cotton crop. Sheriff Norris and Bureau Agent Anthony put them in the jail for safety, where they stayed for several nights. Every night the Klan came into town, keeping them under surveillance. Meanwhile a coroner's jury held an inquest over the dead boy's remains. Known and suspected members of the Klan hovered around as the proceedings began. When it appeared that damaging evidence might be offered, the coroner was told to stop the inquest, and the jury returned a verdict of death at the hands of unknown parties.

It was only a matter of time before the Klan would attack Jeffers and his sons in the jail, and Norris advised them to go to South Carolina, traveling at night to escape detection. Anthony, however, advised going by train in the daytime on the theory that the Klan would not dare to attack them in broad daylight with witnesses all around. He was wrong. Anthony himself accompanied the Jefferses from Warrenton to the railway junction at Camak, four miles away, where they changed to an eastbound train for Augusta and South Carolina. He observed some Klansmen (undisguised but known or suspected to be such) at both the Warrenton and the Camak depots. Klansmen in fact watched the party all the way. A few of them boarded the train at Camak, and others at a station farther on. The father of the deceased Klansman was on board, carrying a double-barreled shotgun and telling people that he intended to shoot Jeffers. When the train stopped at Dearing, a station outside the county and about halfway to Augusta, half a dozen armed men converged on Jeffers and his four sons and took them off the train. One of the boys escaped and soon reached Augusta. The others were marched into the woods and shot. Their bodies were thrown into a well.[6]

No effort was made at the time to apprehend the killers, and Ku Klux raids continued. Agent Anthony was offered a job in the revenue service in Virginia and eagerly accepted. Both he and Norris had reported events to persons higher up, however, and Governor Bullock forwarded one of Norris's letters to General Meade with a request for cavalry. Instead the general sent an officer to investigate. The Freedmen's Bureau headquarters in Atlanta and Augusta both sent officers as well to investigate the murders at Dearing. They all encountered the usual situation: a public too implicated in the terror or too much intimidated by it to tell what they knew, much less to enforce the law against the offenders. At Dearing everyone was reticent about the Jeffers murders and most people were even prepared to deny that they had occurred. One of the officers was told that no one would be allowed to make inquiries on that subject among the local blacks. A Negro witness to the crime fled to Augusta and only there made an affidavit concerning what he had seen.[7]

Despite the findings of these investigators no troops were sent. One night in mid-December Norris himself was waylaid and shot from ambush outside his house. He was severely wounded in the legs, side, and arm. The attackers, who were partially disguised, ran away, but among them Norris recognized three Cody brothers. These were members of a once prosperous family which had been impoverished by the war. They were repeatedly involved in rowdyism and probably Klan activity. Norris was left partially crippled. On the advice of friends he decided not to press charges against the Codys, but he spurned advice to resign as sheriff.[8]

Norris had hardly recovered when another crisis arose in March 1869. It developed from a personal dispute between editor Charles Wallace and Dr. G. W. Darden, a physician who was a Republican but essentially nonpolitical. Wallace understood (correctly or not) that Darden had blackballed his application to join the Masons. As a result he published a card in his newspaper branding the doctor a scalawag, a coward, a liar, and a villain, and dared him to demand satisfaction. This quarrel had a political bearing only in that there was open season on Radicals among men of Wallace's stamp, and he believed Darden's hostility was politically inspired. Wallace, a Confederate veteran with five battle wounds, was a perfect caricature of the Southern chivalric ideal. A friend referred to him later as "a very gallant fellow, the very soul of honor. . . . rash, intemperate . . . excitable . . . dangerous when aroused." He had exhibited his valor in various street fights, killing a Negro in one and suffering grave knife wounds in another. He was the reputed leader of the local Klan, and according to Norris he admitted leading the party that burned the Jeffers boy and hanged his mother. Darden, it appeared, was a gentleman of the same school. Instead of challenging the editor to a duel, however, he simply posted himself in his office window with a double-barreled shotgun. When Wallace passed by on the street Darden shot him down and killed him.[9]

The sheriff was out in the country on business when the shooting took place. Almost immediately a threatening crowd of armed men formed at a saloon across from Darden's office, their favorite meeting place. When Norris returned, he sent an intermediary to E. H. Pottle, the leading lawyer in town, who had influence over the Ku Klux element, asking him to intercede before the crowd got out of hand. Pottle refused. By 5 o'clock the crowd had grown to about a hundred; they sent an envoy proposing that if Darden surrendered and went to jail, and if Norris gave them the key, they would let the law take its course. Norris and Darden felt they had little choice but to agree, although the sheriff did not disarm Darden as the mob had demanded. When the doctor left his office several of the men across the street advanced on him with drawn guns, but his wife and children surrounded him closely. Norris persuaded eight or ten of the town's oldest citizens to guard the jail to prevent a lynching, but James Cody, who had apparently led the crowd, threatened to kill anyone who approached the jail. Norris's life was in danger if he did not return home and stay there, he was told, but then the crowd demanded that he come back and search the prisoner for arms before they would permit him food. Norris refused to go, fearing that they would confine him too.

Between 8 and 9 o'clock that night the crowd began to don disguises, black gowns instead of their usual white ones. (They continued to wear black regalia thereafter.) A band demanded the jail key again. John Raley, the town marshal, who claimed to be acting under duress, searched Norris's house but found no key. The men tried in vain to beat in the jail's iron door, then ripped boards from a nearby building and set a fire around the door. They discovered Darden in a cell behind still another locked iron door, flourishing a pistol and threatening to shoot, but the choking cloud of smoke forced him finally to surrender. The men broke open the cell door with cold chisels, took Darden to his office, let him write a letter to his family, and made him drink a quart of whiskey. About 1 or 2 in the morning, they took him to the edge of town, apparently forced him to strip, and shot him repeatedly. The next morning the body was found riddled with bullet holes but fully clothed—the clothes bore no bullet holes at all.

The people of Warrenton professed to be entirely ignorant of the "mysterious beings" who had committed the lynching. The coroner's jury met and rendered the usual verdict.[10]

Norris took the train to Augusta the next day and reported the affair to the military commander, who disclaimed authority to send troops as Norris asked. The sheriff went to Atlanta and made the same request of Governor Bullock, but this also was fruitless, and for the next two months Norris remained as a refugee in Atlanta.[11]

The terror against Negroes continued in the countryside. At Barnett Station, on the edge of the county, a disguised band briefly took possession of a railroad train in February. On a Sunday night in March they reportedly beat eleven freedmen almost to death, shot and killed another, and four of them raped a sixteen-year-old girl.[12] Older citizens, like those who agreed to guard the jail before Darden's lynching, were disturbed at the continuing violence, but they blamed it on the authorities' alleged refusal to punish Negro crime in the first place, and any efforts they may have made to curb the terror were ineffectual.[13]

The most prominent victim in Warren County, state senator Joseph Adkins, was killed on May 10, 1869. After the adjournment of the legislature that spring, Adkins had gone with some of his colleagues to Washington to report on conditions in Georgia and ask for a restoration of military control. Norris and others advised him not to return afterward, as his life was repeatedly being threatened. After three weeks Adkins decided to risk going home. When he left the train at Dearing, the scene of the Jeffers murders, local toughs were waiting for him at the station. They confiscated the buggy that had come for him and forced him to proceed toward home on foot. Then they rode on ahead and ambushed him. Mrs. Adkins and her daughters later found him lying in the road. He lived long enough to identify at least one man who had risen up from the roadside and shot him.

The Adkinses refused publicly to identify the killer, but privately they told an Army officer that the senator had named Ellis Adams, one of the men at the Dearing depot. A year earlier Adkins himself had reported Adams to the authorities for stabbing a Negro and committing other outrages; it developed later that Adams and others at the station had been involved in the Jeffers murders too. Ellis Adams died in another shooting fray the following December.[14]

Although there were brief efforts to pin the crime on Negroes, Conservatives settled on another story which was harder to disprove. Apparently a clubfooted girl related to Ellis Adams had been befriended by the Adkins family some time earlier and had lived with them for a time. After the murder it was alleged that the senator had written her a letter expressing love and in effect trying to proposition her. The verbal altercation at the depot had arisen, people said, when one of the Adamses (Ellis or another) had expressed resentment of the letter. The murder, then, was a justifiable atonement by male relatives for an insult which no red-blooded man could allow to go unavenged. This story was retailed around the country, with elaborations. A Georgia correspondent informed the readers of the *New York Times* that Adkins was "a notorious debaucher. His negro *amours* are more numerous than the number of his years." According to the Shreveport, Louisiana, *South-Western* he "was a habitual inmate of negro brothels. . . . He was among the most degraded of the scalawags." Adkins' death, Democrats insisted, had nothing to do with politics.

Adkins, who was in his sixties, had been a preacher as well as a politician and farmer, a pious man who had led prayer meetings with his colleagues at the state constitutional convention and frequently visited prisons to pray with the inmates. His friends found the idea of his seducing a young girl ludicrous and, under the circumstances, infuriating; his wife and daughters repudiated it angrily. Adkins might well have written a letter to Miss Adams, indicating affection of some kind. Many leading Democrats claimed later to have read it—strange for a private matter that would normally have been kept quiet—but no one ever made it public and its contents were described only in the vaguest and most damaging terms. But whether it existed and whatever its contents, the letter effectively blackened Adkins' reputation all over the country—and with it, of course, the reputation of Southern Republicans in general.[15]

Adkins' murder nearly coincided with that of Dr. Benjamin Ayer, a legislator from Jefferson County who had also gone on the trip to Washington. Ayer, a man of at least seventy, had lost almost everything he owned during the war because of his Unionist sympathies. Like Adkins he had been elected to office by Negro voters and was totally ostracized by the white community. He too was shot down on the road near his home, allegedly by a Negro robber, but he had no family or friends capable of interceding in the matter and his case was never investigated very carefully. He was subject to the same kind of posthumous character assassination.[16]

In Warren County the Adkins murder, unlike that of Darden, brought a quick response from the commanding general in Atlanta, who was now General Alfred H. Terry. Two companies of infantry arrived three days later, on May 13, and established camp just outside Warrenton. Sheriff Norris returned on June 4. During his absence the Conservatives had declared his office vacant and installed in his place John Raley, the town marshal and a Ku Klux member or sympathizer. They refused to recognize Norris until he went to Atlanta once more and procured a special commission from Governor Bullock and General Terry; when he returned two more companies of soldiers came with him. Under military escort Norris now arrested six men who were suspected in either the Darden lynching or the earlier attack on Norris himself. They included the three Codys, John Raley, and A. I. Hartley, Wallace's successor as editor of the *Clipper*. Governor Bullock even sent the state attorney general, Henry P. Farrow, to prosecute the cases arising from these arrests. But when Farrow reached Warrenton the prisoners had been released on writs of habeas corpus by a local judge who had no authority to hear such cases; although they were under bond to stand trial, three days' observation convinced Farrow that no further steps would ever be taken to indict them or any of the other terrorists in the local courts. The terror was so complete, he reported to Bullock, that only martial law could bring it to a close. Norris wanted to override habeas corpus and other legal obstructions, but his view did not prevail. Moreover, a superior court judge now overruled the orders of Bullock and Terry and forbade him to serve as sheriff. Farrow and the local garrison commander persuaded Norris to leave the county again on the ground that he could accomplish nothing more under the circumstances and his life was in danger if he stayed. He returned to Atlanta with Farrow and a guard of soldiers on June 12.

Democrats represented the Army's arrival and the arrests as a species of tyranny stirred up by Governor Bullock for his own nefarious political purposes. According to the Augusta *Chronicle and Sentinel* the whole Ku Klux business in Georgia was a political fiction dreamed up by "Booby Bullock and his pimps in Atlanta." As it turned out, however, the episode reflected instead the governor's inability to secure the most elemental justice in a county where the Klan reigned supreme. Night riding did fall off, or even ceased altogether, for a time after the arrival of the troops. But the Ku Klux organization remained.[17]

Perhaps the most revealing statement of affairs in the county was provided by Curran Battle, a Conservative Warrenton lawyer, in a confidential interview with Governor Bullock in Atlanta on June 20. The active Ku Klux organization there, he said, numbered only fifty to a hundred men. But they were of such disreputable character that good citizens were intimidated and afraid to oppose them. Many good citizens, like himself, would be happy to see the Klan suppressed, but there were other supposedly law-abiding persons who supported the organization even if they did not belong to it. Perhaps two-thirds of the leading citizens acted in concert with the Klan, through either sympathy or fear. And there was an ocean of difference, Battle continued, between what was said about the Ku Klux in public and in private. "There are a great many men like myself, who do not dare to speak against the Kuklux for fear of being accused of sympathy with radicals." The organization could prove anything it wanted in court, and there was no chance of convicting any of its members. Battle would not think of testifying against anyone connected with the order. "To do that and go home and stay there five days—I would not do it for the whole state of Georgia."[18]

The Warren County grand jury met in October. Instead of indicting the men whom Norris had arrested in June it blasted the governor for refusing to enforce the law against Negro criminals. More specifically, it repeated the fiction that Bullock pardoned murderers and desperadoes by wholesale and turned them loose again upon the state. This in turn "had caused an outraged people to take the law into their own hands." The jury also protested against the continued presence of an Army garrison, designed only to overawe and intimidate the civil authorities.[19] Attorney General Farrow's appraisal was borne out.

Although systematic violence was worst in Warren County, it also existed in other counties. The legislature adopted a joint resolution on February 1, noting widespread reports of night riding in the eastern part of the state and voting to send a committee there to investigate.[20] Nothing came of this investigation, however, if in fact it was made at all.

In October 1869 Greene County Democrats offered Negro legislator Abram Colby $5,000 to resign his office. When he refused, about sixty-five Klansmen raided his house, dragged him into the woods, and beat him with sticks and leather belts for what he estimated to be three hours. Twenty-five men participated in the beating, taking turns; some of the last in line complained volubly when it looked as if they might be denied. Colby may not have received a thousand blows as he thought, but he was partly crippled in the attack and was left for dead. He had acquired a small plantation, but the Klan would not let him live on it in peace. Colby identified some of his attackers as among the leading professional men in the county while others, he said, "are not worth the bread they eat." Two were Democratic Negroes. The reason assigned for the attack was Colby's political influence with the black population; but one hundred of the blows were evoked by his having named a son for Foster Blodgett, a prominent Georgia Republican. Only afterward did Conservatives seek to explain the attack by saying that Colby had been living with his daughter as her husband.[21]

Three days after his interview with Curran Battle in June, Governor Bullock wrote General Terry that a reign of terror enveloped much of the state, directed fundamentally at the policy of Negro equality and those who tried to uphold it. Only two sheriffs in Georgia had dared to oppose this terror, he said: Sheriff Ruffin of Richmond County (Augusta), who was assassinated on election day in November, and Sheriff Norris of Warren

County, who was now crippled after an ambush attack and was a refugee from his home. The local authorities were powerless, Bullock continued, and he himself lacked the power to replace incompetent local officials, to organize a militia, or to declare martial law. He could not convene the legislature to correct these ills, or even have it petition the President to exercise military control, because that body, having expelled its Negro members in 1868, was no longer recognized by Congress and was in Conservative hands. Bullock had offered rewards for the apprehension of criminals, but to no avail. His powers were exhausted, and the Reconstruction policy of Congress had been nullified. Even General Terry, the governor reminded him, had exhausted his present powers by sending troops to the most troubled areas, with little effect. The only remedy left, he concluded, was a Presidential order restoring military supremacy in Georgia until further action by Congress.[22] This would enable the Army once more to make arrests and try persons by military commission.

Bullock's case was hard to refute, and General Terry made the same recommendation in August.[23] In fact the terror probably accomplished more in Georgia than in any other state to subvert the Republican party and Reconstruction. Bullock was even more helpless than other governors at this point because the conspirators had so far permeated the government as to control the legislature itself. He had already made these points in testimony before Congress, and at the beginning of 1870 Georgia was remanded to military control.

By the time this reversion took place there was less overt terrorism than earlier in the year. Conservatives had attained power at the local level throughout most of the state, and the reasons for terrorism were correspondingly diminished. Nevertheless General Terry hoped to punish as many offenders as possible. Lacking enough men to police the entire state, he decided to make an example of the eastern counties where disorders had been greatest. Thus Warren, Taliaferro, Wilkes, Lincoln, Columbia, Glascock, and Oglethorpe counties were organized into a military subdistrict, and troops were sent to occupy the most important points. The command was given to Major Jacob Kline, with headquarters at Barnett Station in Warren County.[24]

In mid-January 1870 John C. Norris was back in Warrenton with a new military commission as sheriff. Once more he set out with a military escort to arrest those he suspected of participating in past crimes. Some, like editor Hartley, anticipated his coming and escaped. Democrats referred to Norris's operations as a reign of terror. The Augusta *Chronicle and Sentinel* even announced that the Ku Klux Klan "does not now and never has existed in Georgia."[25]

Norris still favored a suspension of habeas corpus and perhaps military trials for his new prisoners, but no such order came down from Atlanta. As long as trials and convictions were a possibility the Conservatives of Warren County were badly frightened; they offered Norris $12,500 to leave the state and destroy all the incriminating evidence in his possession. Norris refused the bribe, and another offer of $5,000 was tendered to make no further arrests. By his own account Norris promised them only to confine his arrests to persons whom he believed guilty; but he accepted a note for $5,000 and later received four installments on it amounting to $3,250. It is unlikely that the donors considered this very limited promise worth that much money; Norris likely promised more than he later admitted, but it is also conceivable that the offer was intended from the beginning as a trap. Certainly the Conservatives used it as such.[26]

In any event, few persons were actually arrested, owing to lack of evidence, the flight of guilty parties, and whatever *sub rosa* agreements Norris or the military may have made. Late in March Norris took a file of soldiers to arrest one of the toughs in Dearing who was wanted in the Adkins murder, but the man was not to be found.[27] In April he thought he had enough evidence on several persons involved in the Darden murder to justify arresting them. But to avoid having to release them again and risk their subsequent flight, he went to Atlanta briefly and asked General Terry to suspend habeas corpus. The general refused but told him to go ahead with the arrests and report back. Norris found on his return that most of the parties had fled, and he was able to apprehend only one man, named Martin. Terry approved this action and ordered Major F. H. Torbett, the Warrenton commandant, to hold a preliminary examination.

After the hearing had run four days, Torbett told Norris if the case proceeded any further it would involve the whole community. E. H. Pottle, the attorney for the Ku Klux, Torbett said, was offering to submit pleas of guilty for Martin and four others in connection with the Darden lynching if Norris would make no further arrests in that case. Torbett, for reasons never adequately explained, virtually insisted that Norris accept the offer; to sweeten the deal he indicated that Norris would be eligible for $25,000 in reward money which Governor Bullock had offered for these men upon conviction. Norris again succumbed, and his final undoing rapidly followed. Now that the danger of further arrests was over, the Conservatives formally charged him with accepting the $5,000 bribe back in February. In quick order Torbett had him arrested, General Terry removed him as sheriff, and he was taken to Atlanta in irons to be tried by a military court. Eventually the case was dropped. Nor was the agreement in Warrenton kept; the Ku Klux prisoners were not convicted or punished and Norris received no reward money. To cap it all, once the bribery charge had been abandoned, the Warren County Ku Klux had Norris indicted for false arrest. He remained in Atlanta, and only a pardon from the governor spared him a forcible return to face trial and almost certain conviction.

Norris believed that Major Torbett had been manipulated by Pottle and the Ku Klux; certainly the sheriff himself had been. According to one of the officers there, Norris had begun shaking down local citizens, demanding money in return for immunity from arrest. When questioned about this he replied that some of the officers, including Major Kline at Barnett Station, were taking even larger bribes than he. Norris's conduct was certainly unethical and probably illegal. Yet the fact remains that for two years he displayed remarkable courage and persistence, trying harder to apprehend and bring Klan terrorists to justice than probably any other local official in the South. He shared no responsibility for the fact that these criminals were never punished. The primary blame lay with the Army officers and ultimately General Terry himself, who refused as a matter of policy to institute military trials.[28]

The Ku Klux organization in Warren County was never touched, and none of its members suffered more than temporary arrest or self-imposed exile to avoid arrest. The number of Negroes who fled the county to escape Ku Klux attack was probably much greater. Systematic violence, which had declined by the end of 1869, never markedly resumed. Conservatives emerged from the crisis in full control of the county and, despite the Negro majority, carried it by a wide margin in December 1870 and subsequent elections.[29]

In approximately twelve counties surrounding Warren Klan operations increased during 1870. Although this region largely coincided with Terry's military subdistrict the Klan was little hampered by Army intervention. The terrorism became particularly acute during the summer, and in many places continued beyond the legislative and Congressional elections which were held just before Christmas. Night riding occurred two or three times a week for months on end in some counties. Occasionally the Klan merely rode through black communities, but at other times it was guilty of murder and other atrocities.

The victims were nearly all blacks; there were few white Republicans to begin with in most of these counties, and almost none left by 1870. As usual the most prominent or influential persons, like legislators and school-teachers, were singled out, but a majority of victims were simple farm laborers or sharecroppers who were raided for the usual variety of political, social, and economic reasons. Many gave up sleeping at home and regularly took to the woods at night. Some fled to Atlanta, Augusta, or Athens, where they were relatively safe but often without means of support; at the same time they left behind a labor shortage in the country. "Every town in our State where there is any protection is overrun with colored people," said Alfred Richardson, a Negro legislator from Clarke County, who was himself a refugee in Athens. "Many of the farm hands are there; and there is a great mass of loafers who stand round town because they have got no work to do. Yet people's fields around in the country are running away with grass." Still other blacks, he added, were held to forced labor against their will on some plantations. Richardson himself was resented not only as a Republican leader and officeholder but as a partner in a grocery store, making more money than a Negro supposedly should. Blacks who were known as Democrats were almost never raided, and some became Democrats for that reason.[30]

The other major theater of Klan operations in Georgia was a group of about eight counties north of Atlanta. Significant Klan activity here began early in 1870. It was a mountainous area with a large white Republican minority. These people were attacked as well as the relatively small Negro population. In some places the Ku Klux helped guard moonshiners, but otherwise it followed about the same pattern as elsewhere. Probably the worst of these counties was isolated Chattooga, nestled in the mountains north of Rome and along the Alabama line. There was considerable correspondence between the Georgia Klans and those in northeastern Alabama, as between adjacent counties within the state.

If the South was rural, Chattooga County was extraordinarily so; its capital, Summerville, was a village of only 281 people. White Republicans and Negroes together constituted a slight majority of voters, but Democratic terrorism soon nullified this and many Republicans switched sides out of fear.[31] The Chattooga Klan did little but ride around until December 1869. When outrages began then, public opinion at first condemned them. A public meeting passed a resolution to that effect early in January 1870 and the Democratic Rome *Courier* agreed, attacking the Ku Klux Klan by name. (The associate editor of the *Courier* was young Henry W. Grady, the later well-known protagonist of the New South movement whose reactions to the Klan in this period fluctuated.)[32]

When one of these raids resulted in a murder a detachment of soldiers came up from Atlanta and arrested a man named Ackridge, lodging him temporarily in the county jail at Summerville. Many Democrats found this arrest to be more outrageous than the crimes which produced it, and public opinion gradually shifted toward the Klan. Its operations rapidly increased thereafter. Soon it dominated the community through the usual combination of fear and a felt need for racial-political solidarity against Negroes and Republicans. Many Democrats were desperate to release Ackridge, perhaps before he was forced into incriminating others. They first thought of freeing him by habeas corpus, but decided on direct action as speedier and more certain. Not long after the arrest a crowd gathered in town one night, amid much firing of guns, shouting of threats, and general disorder. At least 100 men donned disguises and marched on the home of superior court judge Kirby, a Republican, demanding that he order the soldiers to turn Ackridge loose. After they had kicked in the door and threatened to burn the house and take his life, Kirby gave in. He went to the jail in great fear and informed the lieutenant in command that a mob of 300 men was prepared to take the prisoner by force if he was not surrendered peaceably; in that case they would not be overly careful to spare the lives of any who opposed them. The thirty soldiers barricaded in the jail had already traded shots with the crowd. The young lieutenant went out to reconnoiter; after some hesitation he came to the same conclusion as Kirby and released the prisoner.

Ackridge left the county and was not pursued. Local Democrats later made a point of showing that part of the mob at least had come from Alabama. The *Courier* was still incensed by Ackridge's arrest but regretted the method of his release. This would give Governor Bullock more political ammunition to use against the people of Georgia: "Every evidence of the existence of the Ku Klux Klan is a strong help to the Radicals. The K.K.K. is the high horse with which they ride down the conquered Southrons. Let us starve this horse and then we can meet them on fairer terms."

The Ku Klux attack on a United States Army detail brought surprisingly few repercussions. The lieutenant was court-martialed and narrowly missed expulsion from the service. Additional troops were posted in Summerville amid rumors that they had a list of persons to arrest. Several potential suspects left for Alabama, but nothing happened to substantiate their fears. Governor Bullock removed Judge Kirby, and the local grand jury indicted two of the terrorists in March, but they were never convicted. The Chattooga Klan continued to raid with little restraint.[33]

Conservatives around the state still denied most of the terrorism and often the very existence of a Klan organization in Georgia. Violence was laughed off as boyish pranks or justified as well-merited punishment for social transgressions. Governor Bullock offered rewards for the apprehension of guilty parties and pleaded with local officials to enforce the law. He sent troops to some of the trouble spots, but almost no effort was made locally to prosecute the criminals, and none was convicted.[34]

The election campaign of 1870 (for members of the legislature and Congress) saw less night riding and systematic violence than there had been in the fall of 1868. For the most part Democrats relied on other techniques which had accompanied the night riding two years before and promised to serve them better in the future; some expressed an unwonted hostility to the Klan and its tactics, fearing that it would rock the boat and, by inviting retaliation, undo their present work. Still, the memory of earlier Ku Klux raids kept many Negroes from voting and stimulated others to cast Democratic ballots, especially in places where the blacks' own political leaders had been driven off. Governor Bullock and General Terry stationed troops around the state well before the election to prevent violence at the polls;[35] but in many counties the work of intimidation had already taken place and the soldiers found little to do on the three election days, December 20–22.

Elsewhere, white men crowded the polls to overawe the Negroes and prevent their voting. The tactic was often successful and the blacks gave way, but it led to a riot at Sparta in Hancock County, where Linton Stephens (Alexander's half brother) superintended the operation. Many of the whites involved were Klansmen out of disguise; such was the case in Oglethorpe County, where John C. Reed was in charge. Another Conservative tactic was to have election officials, predominantly Democratic in most counties, require evidence that prospective voters had paid their poll taxes before allowing them to cast ballots. As in 1868, this device, particularly when applied selectively against Negroes, was remarkably effective in reducing the Republican vote. The fact that the Republican legislature (its Negro members restored by military authority) had waived the poll tax requirement carried no more weight with many election officials than Governor Bullock's suspension of it in 1868. In a few counties Democrats increased their margin by forcing Negroes to cast Democratic ballots in large numbers, but this was not really necessary and was not generally done. The Democrats swept the election, carrying more than 80 per cent of the seats in the legislature and most of the Congressional seats. General Dudley DuBose, Grand Titan of the Ku Klux Klan, was elected to Congress in the eastern district where the intimidation was most complete.[36]

As in Warren County so in the state; General Terry permitted intimidation and terror to prevail by refusing to employ more than halfway measures against them. Unlike General Reynolds in Texas, he refused to try terrorists by military commission. Perhaps he feared a public reaction in the North and repudiation in Washington; if so it was further evidence that Radical Reconstruction foundered because it was not radical enough. Congress, instead of throwing out the December election returns, accepted them, seated the state's Senators and Representatives, and returned it to civil control. The new legislature was not scheduled to meet until November 1871; meanwhile Governor Bullock carried on as he had before, utterly helpless to stem the Democratic tide or protect the civil rights of Georgia Republicans.

By the end of 1870 Georgia Democrats had devised a system of intimidation which no longer required the grosser outrages of the Ku Klux Klan. As a matter of fact they have been denied their proper credit in this respect, in favor of Mississippians and others who simply developed the system further in the next few years. The Georgia Plan of 1870 came into general use throughout the South, but especially the deep South. If Virginia and Tennessee pointed the way for the upper South to overthrow Radical Reconstruction by reenfranchising white majorities, Georgia pioneered for the deep South in developing a more subtle and acceptable way of nullifying Negro majorities than the rustic terrorism of the Ku Klux Klan.

John C. Reed claimed years later that the Georgia Klan, having accomplished its great purpose in the campaign of 1870, was formally disbanded soon afterward.[37] He and others like him probably severed their connection then, just as General Gordon had done as early as the summer of 1868. But many Georgia Klansmen refused to accept their obsolescence and continued to ride in 1871. In some counties they did so on an unprecedented scale. Their activity was not as directly political as it sometimes had been, but it perpetuated the terror and cemented further the triumph of white supremacy under Democratic party auspices.

Ku Klux or regulator bands were active at least intermittently in about ten counties in Florida in 1869–70. The counties were not all contiguous, but most were near the northern boundary of the state. Some of the regulators were affiliated with the Young Men's Democratic Clubs, which continued to grow at least briefly after November 1868. On the other hand, some who had joined these orders in 1868 out of fear that a Negro uprising was then impending dropped out or became inactive after a few months. There was never a great deal of conventional Ku Klux night riding in Florida; members did not go in as much for disguises and other flummery. But they were about as violent as Klansmen anywhere. Active Republicans of both races were frequent targets of attack; Negroes were repeatedly assaulted or killed in attacks aimed, in particular, against Negro landownership; Florida possessed more available land than the other southeastern states, and its acquisition was somewhat easier. The Klan's impact in this respect cannot be measured, but it contributed to maintaining the blacks as landless tenants.[38]

Jackson County, lying adjacent to both Georgia and Alabama, was by far the worst county in the state, and one of the worst in the South. This "is where Satan has his seat," one Negro clergyman and politician put it; "he reigns in Jackson County."[39] Scores of murders took place here between the end of the war and late 1871, virtually none of them punished. The county had a record of lawlessness truly Texan in proportions, to which night riding in disguise and somewhat greater organization were added in 1869. It was never revealed just what kind of an organization existed here or how extensive it was. But undisguised hoodlums, belonging to the organization or not, were responsible for most of the crime. Nine-tenths of the victims were black—in general the most intelligent and industrious Negroes in the county. Residents attributed most of the trouble to a comparatively small number of men—youngsters of the "pistol-and-bowie-knife" chivalry—but they had influential leadership, and most people of whatever degree were afraid to risk their displeasure. By general testimony the leader was Colonel James P. Coker, a storeowner in Marianna (the county seat) and one of the county's wealthiest men. His son Billy, one of the main guns, was involved in many assaults and killings.[40]

The county had a substantial Negro, and hence Republican, majority. The foremost Republicans by 1869 were Congressman Charles M. Hamilton and state senator W. J. Purman. Both were twenty-nine-year-old Pennsylvanians who had come to Marianna in military service and remained after the war to serve successively as Freedmen's Bureau agents before going into politics. Conservatives were confident that both men taught the most Jacobin doctrines to their Negro followers. They therefore subjected the pair to the same abuse that men in that position encountered throughout the South. Hamilton went on to Washington in 1868, but Purman remained at Marianna between legislative sessions, an ever more obvious prospect for assassination. On the night of February 26, 1869, after attending a concert, he was shot from ambush as he walked homeward with a friend through a small park in the center of town. Purman was only wounded, but his companion, Dr. John Finlayson, the county clerk, was shot dead by the same bullet. Two days later, as Purman lay recovering, some of his Negro supporters came to visit him. They reported that 600 to 800 others had gathered around the town, intending to sack it in retaliation, but Purman persuaded them to abandon the idea. Although Governor Harrison Reed offered a $2,000 reward for Finlayson's murderer, no one ever collected it.[41]

The terror mounted during the remainder of the year. In the process Negroes took lives as well as lost them, and the county fell into near-anarchy. Purman fled in the spring, as did Negro legislator Emanuel Fortune after repeated warnings that his life was in danger.[42] In August two penitentiary guards were murdered while searching for men suspected of the Purman and Finlayson shooting. Another influential Negro whom whites regarded as dangerous was Calvin Rogers, the Marianna constable. On September 28 he was fired on from ambush as he accompanied a crowd of Negroes on a picnic. The shots missed Rogers but killed another man and a little boy in the crowd. The next day two more blacks were shot from ambush and badly wounded. Then, on the evening of October 1, Colonel James McClellan (an active Conservative politician) and his attractive daughter were shot as they sat on a hotel veranda; the colonel recovered, but his daughter was killed on the spot. With them was Colonel Coker, the Ku Klux leader, if that label is appropriate, who may have been the person aimed at in the darkness.

Before daybreak white men began gathering in Marianna, swearing to avenge this latest crime. They took over the county for at least a week under Coker's apparent leadership and committed many more crimes before they were finished. First they searched for Calvin Rogers and other blacks whom they suspected of the McClellan shootings. Two Negroes were apprehended and taken out of town; one was killed and the other escaped. Older men soon tried to stop or at least slow down the vigilantes' proceedings, but at a public meeting called to discuss the question the militant Coker faction prevailed. The hunt continued, and that same day young Billy Coker and others murdered in cold blood a black man, his wife, and their son and threw the bodies into an old lime-sink. Samuel Fleishman, a Jewish storekeeper who was regarded as unsound on the racial question, was notified to leave town. When he refused to do so, protesting that his family and everything he owned was in Marianna, he was forcibly escorted across the Alabama line and told not to return. Fleishman did try to return a few days later and was shot down on the road before he could reach home.[43]

The Republican state convention, meeting at this time in Tallahassee, took note of the terrorism in Jackson and several other counties and called on Governor Reed to proclaim martial law. The governor replied that he had none but Negro militia to send, and very little armament with which to equip them. Sending Negro militia, he added, would only put more fuel on the fire. Therefore he had to rely on the civil authorities and federal troops. Factional rivalry within the party had contributed to the convention's demand. It certainly figured in the governor's response, for he ended by blaming Purman and other party rivals for having stirred up the trouble in the first place. The arrival of troops and a newly appointed sheriff in Marianna late in October merely reduced the terrorism in Jackson County to its usual proportions.[44]

During the election campaign of 1870 there was an increase of systematic intimidation in the county, but comparatively little night riding in disguise. Purman and Hamilton ventured back to Marianna in September to address a Republican rally—the first time either of them had dared enter the county for more than a year. This absence was well advised, as their reception now confirmed. They were met by an armed mob, and after the rally armed men set up roadblocks outside town, intending to intercept them as they left. Hearing of this, Hamilton and Purman remained in town, where they were virtually besieged in a private house for several days. Sheriff Thomas West proposed raising a posse of 500 men to protect them, but Conservative elders, deferring to the young bucks, rejected the idea. Instead about ten of the older citizens offered to serve as hostages to escort the two Radicals out of the county. This offer was accepted, and Hamilton and Purman went to Tallahassee, by means of a circuitous route through

Georgia. The Marianna *Courier,* a fire-eating sheet which spoke for the Ku Klux element, branded this arrangement as a cowardly and dishonorable surrender to two infamous villains who had reduced the good citizens of Jackson County to slavery; a more fitting treatment, it implied, would have been lynching. The terrorist campaign was successful enough in Jackson County to decrease an 800 Republican majority in 1868 into a majority of only 14 in November 1870. One of the two Republican legislators chosen at this time was soon pressured into resigning and was replaced by a Democrat.[45]

Throughout north Florida that fall there were signs of increased Democratic organization for strong-arm purposes. Conservatives at least pretended to fear an armed Negro rising in some counties and organized in their Klans and Democratic Clubs to prevent or defeat it. But they also hoped to carry the election by storm themselves. At stake were the entire legislature, the lieutenant governorship, and Florida's lone seat in the House of Representatives. Although there was comparatively little night riding by hooded bands, there was plenty of action by armed bands operating without disguise. The whites made it known that they were organized and prepared for trouble. There was much correspondence between county organizations for mutual help in case of need, as well as with groups across the line in Georgia. Governor Reed made it appear that he might actually call out militia to combat the terror, but Conservatives paid no further attention to this threat than to accuse him of trying to bulldoze the electorate himself.

At Lake City, perhaps the most disorderly place outside Jackson County, armed bands rode in and out of town repeatedly during the summer and fall, shooting and making threats. In October they seized the sheriff and forced him to resign. On election day (November 8) they rode into town again, disrupting a Negro parade and driving many blacks out of town without voting. The Jefferson County Klan, just east of Tallahassee, expected trouble on election day and got the services of scores of armed Georgians, who came down for the better part of the day. The same things happened on a smaller scale in other counties, with the result that many blacks did not vote and the election came out a near-tie. Republicans claimed victory by narrow margins and retained a bare control of the legislature, but Democrats eventually won the two major offices at stake by decision of the state supreme court and the House of Representatives in Washington, respectively, when the terms were nearly over. This was more than they deserved, for most of their winnings were the product of overt terrorism. Neither Governor Reed's mild measures nor those of the few federal troops stationed in Florida made much impression on the terrorists, who continued to operate well into 1871.[46]

Alabama: Terrorism in the Western Black Belt

With the possible exception of North Carolina, Alabama saw more widespread and virulent Ku Klux activity in 1869 and 1870 than any other state. There were two major theaters of activity, which together embraced half of the state. The first consisted of several western counties, especially Greene and Sumter in the Black Belt and Tuscaloosa and Fayette just above them. The second and larger area contained the entire northern end of the state from Mississippi to Georgia and most of the mountain counties lying east of present-day Birmingham. Some of these adjoined the troubled region of northwest Georgia.

Unlike North Carolina, the Klan had been active throughout most of this area in 1868 and merely continued or intensified its operations after the Presidential election. When the legislature assembled in November 1868, following the election, it established a committee at Governor William H. Smith's suggestion to investigate Klan activity in the state. The brief hearings that followed confirmed what was already well known: an organized Ku Klux Klan was systematically terrorizing Negroes and Republicans in large parts of the state, and existing laws were inadequate to combat it. The committee called for additional legislation, but in the case of five counties (Madison, Lauderdale, Butler, Tuscaloosa, and Pickens) it recommended martial law as the only remedy.[1] Two laws were passed late in December, similar to the enactments of other states. The first provided heavy penalties for wearing masks or disguises, and especially for committing violence or destroying a church or school while so attired. Anyone killing or wounding a person so engaged and attired was exempted from punishment, and local officials who failed to prosecute such offenders were liable to a fine and removal from office. The second act entitled Ku Klux victims or their next of kin to recover damages from the county whenever the offenders were not prosecuted and convicted.[2] Both laws were virtual dead letters from the day of their enactment; the courts simply did not function in Ku Klux cases. A few Negroes were tried and convicted of committing crimes in disguise, illustrating the double standard of justice. When a plaintiff in Mobile was actually awarded damages in a lower court, the state supreme court reversed the decision.[3]

There is good evidence that Klan leaders, in north Alabama at least, tried to disband the organization in the spring or summer of 1869, probably taking their cue from Tennessee. But the results were less noticeable here; night riding and violence were unabated. The major effect of the "disbandment" was to give Klan apologists an excuse for saying that subsequent outrages were the work of spurious Ku Klux. The White Camellias in the Black Belt very likely lapsed at this time if they did not disband formally, and there is almost no reference to that order after 1868.[4]

Among the western counties Sumter, on the Mississippi line near Meridian, witnessed the most sustained terrorism, continuing that which had marked the Presidential campaign. Gerard Choutteau, the Republican planter who had organized a Negro Grant and Colfax Club and then saw its president murdered, still lived under constant harassment. On November 14, 1868, a man rode by his house and fired five shots into the yard where his children were playing. The next night men shot off guns around the house all night long, terrifying his family further. Less than a month later they returned one night during the absence of Choutteau and his immediate family, drove his mother-in-law out of the house, and burned it with all of its contents and eight or ten bales of cotton. They whipped four Negroes on the plantation and warned them to leave the county or be killed. The new sheriff, A. W. Dillard, was afraid to go into that part of the county, much less arrest any of the men responsible, who apparently did not bother with disguises. Moving into Livingston, the county seat, Choutteau was continually badgered and threatened—and his house was shot at—by the younger chivalry, including some men he managed to get indicted for previous attacks. In May 1869 the same men murdered two Negroes and gravely wounded a third, then fled into Mississippi. Choutteau appealed to Governor Smith for protection, but the only response was advice to proceed against the sheriff for dereliction of duty. When the sheriff, the mayor of Livingston, and the county solicitor urged Smith to send a detective to catch the offenders before the Negroes rose up in righteous wrath, the governor complied, but there is no evidence that the detective accomplished anything.[5]

Elections were held in Alabama in August 1869, including the choice of Congressmen. The preceding disorders in Sumter County may have been partially geared to this campaign, but they were not so widespread as to prevent the re-election of Republican Congressman Charles Hays in this heavily Negro constituency. Troops were sent to Livingston just before the election and were withdrawn soon afterward.

A few nights later, on August 12, the Ku Klux came to town and attacked Choutteau's house in force. This time they killed a white man, John Coblentz, who had been staying there nights to help protect the place; the Klan lost one of its own members, a man from neighboring Marengo County. On the same raid they attacked and seriously wounded Negro legislator George W. Houston at his home. Coblentz was the fifth man killed by nocturnal bands in the county in six months, Houston claimed the next day, the others being Negroes. Houston too appealed to the governor for protection before the blacks rose up and redressed their wrongs forcibly. The sheriff was powerless, he said, and most of the local whites were either involved with the Klan or tolerant of it. "If you can't send soldiers here *permanently* and a good strong force, for Gods sake dont say anything about it at all, for loud sounding proclamations to the Sheriff isn't [*sic*] worth the paper on which you write them." Two days later, after tracing the attackers as far as the Marengo County line, whence they apparently had come, Sheriff Dillard confessed his inability to deal with the situation and resigned.[6]

The Conservative Livingston *Journal* typically denounced the victims rather than the crime. Choutteau's "incendiary conduct for many months past had filled the public mind with apprehensions of danger." As for Coblentz, he would still be alive if he had stayed home and minded his own business instead of serving as Choutteau's watchdog. Choutteau's crime—shared by Houston and Daniel Price, the foremost white Radical in the county—had been to dupe ignorant Negroes into following them, thereby sowing mistrust between the races. More specifically, they had organized the blacks militarily as well as politically:

Gangs of from 25 to 75 negroes have night after night, for weeks in succession, been kept under arms in thickly populated neighborhoods. Armed gangs of the kind mentioned have held secret [Union League] meetings in this town, and continued in session until mid-night. Parties of armed negroes have marched through the county . . . in broad daylight, at the *order* of one man— their object being left for the public to conjecture. Threats have been made to reduce our town to ashes, if our citizens did not conduct themselves as the self-constituted commanders prescribed.

"Ignorant, pliant negroes" had been summoned from their work in the fields to attend political meetings and had been bound by oath to support only the Republican party. The result was that Sumter County, where white men owned 999/1,000 of the property and paid a proportionate share of the taxes, was represented in the legislature by three illiterate Negroes. The only persons who had been outraged, the editor said, were conspicuous actors or promoters of this policy of oppression.[7]

From the Republican standpoint the Negro meetings represented legitimate political activity, fully within the law. Armed patrols and incendiary threats followed rather than preceded the first outrages, although they doubtless had a mutually and cumulatively antagonizing effect. And it is quite true that George Houston for one reacted to the attack upon his home—wounding his son as well as himself—by exclaiming that he would like to see the whole country go up in flames. He quickly apologized for the statement, citing the circumstances and defying anyone to point to a single act of lawlessness he had ever committed or advised. He even counseled his friends not to retaliate in kind after the attack.[8] His statement, however, led the town marshal to institute patrols of his own for several nights following, every able-bodied white man in town being required to serve. Although some blacks in the county continued to meet and drill under arms they did not rise en masse. Instead Houston fled to Montgomery as soon as he was able, and did not return.[9]

Choutteau left the state altogether. In October Governor Smith received a letter from Governor John M. Palmer of Illinois, saying that Choutteau had turned up in Springfield in a destitute condition, asking for help. When Palmer queried Choutteau's record and standing in Alabama, Smith's reply told at least as much about himself and conservative Republicanism in the South as it did about Choutteau. There were decided Republicans in Sumter County who got along well with their fellow citizens, Smith said, but Choutteau was a Frenchman and "perhaps not sufficiently acquainted with our institutions of government, to comprehend the true American theory of differences of political opinion. I presume that it may be safely stated that he was not as tolerant toward people who differed from him as is contemplated by our free government." Further, although his motives were probably worthy, he was ignorant of "the true relation between the blacks and whites in the South," leading him to seek an unwise influence "with a certain class of freedmen." In spite of this discouraging evaluation, Palmer lent Choutteau money from time to time in return for a mortgage to his plantation.[10]

Actually, as Choutteau had earlier made known to Smith, he was a native of Louisiana who had been resident in Alabama for fifteen years; he was a former slaveholder who had supported the Confederacy but accepted Reconstruction afterward. If he had shown a striking reversal of attitudes by joining the Republican party and organizing Negroes in behalf of it and Governor Smith, the latter's position was hardly less remarkable. The governor was a native Georgian long resident in Alabama who possessed conventional racial views; his wartime Unionism and political ambition had led him to become a Republican and to acquire the governorship by Negro votes. But once elected he in effect relegated most of his supporters to a second-class citizenship; it was wrong to terrorize Negroes, but it was also wrong to treat them as equals. Choutteau, in truth, was a victim rather than an instigator of intolerance, who discouraged retaliatory violence against the terrorists.

Smith refused to institute martial law in Sumter as he was asked by some Republicans, but he sent more troops who stayed until October, and he eventually appointed a new sheriff.[11] Daniel Price, the only prominent Radical left in the county, continued to receive threatening letters.[12] The troops may again have exerted a moderating influence,[13] but before the year was out, the Klan invaded Livingston once more, this time to release a white man accused of murdering a Negro. As in the Choutteau-Houston raid, they probably came from outside the county, perhaps from Mississippi.[14]

A lull followed in Sumter during the first half of 1870, but conditions worsened again with the approach of that year's political campaign. In June a white planter was shot while trying to defend a Negro tenant against night riders.[15] Houston was advised for his own safety not to return to the county, and Congressman Charles Hays urged the governor to send troops again, to stay until after the election.[16]

The troops did not come, however, and late in July racial and political friction at Belmont in the eastern part of the county precipitated a major crisis. A Republican rally was broken up and other aggressions were committed by whites. Negroes in the vicinity then organized into armed bands, about 200 strong, prepared to defend themselves and perhaps seek revenge. Some threatened to burn the town, according to Sheriff A. E. Moore, and a number of its inhabitants fled. Armed white men now began assembling from all over the county and from adjoining counties to confront the blacks. At least part of these were Klansmen, sufficiently organized to answer promptly a call for assistance. Responsible men on both sides at this point were anxious for troops to come and head off an explosion. Governor Smith tried to procure them, but none were available. In their absence Sheriff Moore was pressured into accepting the armed whites as a posse. For three or four days they combed the countryside, seeking to break up organized Negro bands and capture their leaders. At one point fifty armed men arrived from Meridian, Mississippi, to help, but matters were well in hand and they returned home the next day. The "posse" made the rounds of Negro cabins and attacked the inmates while making arrests. One Negro so attacked killed a white man. Eventually and with great effort Sheriff Moore persuaded the armed blacks to disperse and then got his posse to disband likewise. He later arrested a Negro and lodged him in jail, where he remained for almost a year. In September 1871, as the date of the Negro's trial finally approached, a Ku Klux band took him out of jail and lynched him. Many whites were disgruntled at the inconclusive outcome of the disturbance in 1870 and regarded it as a missed opportunity to clean out the Radicals and reduce the blacks to submission once and for all.[17]

Only two weeks later they were confirmed in this view when a Republican county convention reportedly threatened to attract hundreds of Negroes to Livingston, armed to the teeth and ready to renew the battle. One dispatch had 100 armed blacks passing through the village of Gainesville in the north end of the county, headed toward Livingston. More were coming from other directions, it was said, on orders from Congressman Hays, who was supposed to address the meeting. Fearful whites telegraphed to Greene County and to Meridian for reinforcements, which arrived as quickly and amply as before. About noon on August 13 the sheriff and 200 men rode off in the direction of Gainesville, intending to head off the black army. They actually encountered about forty Negroes on their way to the meeting, some of them carrying guns. These they disarmed and dispersed after considerable argument. Negroes coming from other directions also turned back, and in consequence the convention did not meet. Conservatives felt that under the circumstances they had acted with great restraint, although some admitted later that the blacks had probably intended no trouble. The minority of blacks who carried guns probably did so as a natural defensive reaction to recent events in the county. Hays denied having ordered any Negroes to come to the meeting, armed or unarmed, and knew nothing of the alarm until it was over. He and other Republicans were convinced that Democrats had deliberately manufactured the crisis for political purposes. Recent events supported Hays's view that the Negroes were too cowed by white authority to initiate a conflict themselves. But he underestimated the degree to which whites misunderstood and genuinely feared the black population, and the way rumors magnified in the telling. The fact was that white Democrats, who came and went as they pleased, often armed to the teeth, were unready to concede as much to black Republicans.[18]

Five days later, on the night of August 18, a band of armed whites shot and killed the Reverend Richard Burke, one of the county's three Negro legislators, at his home in Gainesville. The attackers were undisguised and unrecognized by several witnesses; as in every other notable Ku Klux attack in Sumter County they appear to have come from a distance, probably outside the county. The Livingston *Journal* palliated the murder by tagging Burke as a ringleader in the Republicans' projected bloodbath of August 13, but other whites (including his former owner) had only praise for his character and deportment.[19] Soon afterward Daniel Price, the last active white Republican in the county, left with his family for Meridian, where he would encounter equal troubles.[20] Republicans tried to reschedule their county convention for August 27, but this evoked so many threats that it was again postponed.[21] Troops finally arrived on August 31, and the convention was apparently held—at least nominations were made—before their departure a month later.[22]

Greene County, just east of Sumter, was comparatively quiet in 1869 except for some violence associated with the August election.[23] This calm disappeared early in 1870, when seven murders were committed within three months, Negro schools were burned, and their teachers either forced to stop or driven away altogether. Most of this took place around the village of Union in the northern part of the county. The handful of white Republican officials were subjected to the familiar threats and harassment; the local newspaper explicitly called for their displacement by the ballot box if possible and by the cartridge box if necessary.

The casualties were all among poor and obscure freedmen until the end of March. On the night of the thirty-first a band of thirty or forty disguised men galloped into the county seat of Eutaw and headed for the hotel, where county solicitor Alexander Boyd was living. They went inside, got him out of bed, and shot him several times, fatally. Then they left the hotel, rode around the courthouse square yelling, and departed into the night. Boyd had filled much the same role here as Daniel Price in Sumter or George W. Smith in Jefferson, Texas, or John W. Stephens in Caswell County, North Carolina—a white Republican who associated politically at least with the local Negroes and gained influence and power correspondingly. It is also likely that as county prosecutor he had learned enough about the local Klan to make him doubly dangerous. On the same night that he was killed another band murdered a locally prominent Negro Republican, Jim Martin, near Union. The sheriff made no real effort to discover the culprits in either crime.

Governor Smith immediately sent for troops. He also sent a special agent, John A. Minnis, to ferret out the criminals if possible and prosecute them. Minnis—later a United States attorney and federal prosecutor of the Ku Klux—made a thorough investigation. He discovered that a Klan organization unquestionably existed in the county, but that the Boyd murder was probably done by members from outside acting in collusion with them. Persons in the northern end of the county reported that armed men had crossed the Sipsey River, coming from either Pickens or Tuscaloosa County, before the crime, and returned the same way afterward. The Martin murder, on the other hand, was apparently done by the same local Klansmen who had been committing outrages in that vicinity for three months. One of them was wounded during the attack, and his identity was well known. When the grand jury met later, it declared that Boyd's killers, coming from a distance, could not be discovered, and it virtually ignored the Martin killing. Minnis concluded that there was not the slightest chance of punishing such crimes in the local courts. It was even dangerous there for a man to know very much about the Klan.

The "best citizens" of the county were in the familiar quandary. They disapproved, or only half-approved, of Klan violence and wanted to stop it. But they did not want soldiers to be sent or any action taken to expose, much less inflict penalties on, local people. Republicans on their part were fast losing any confidence they might have had that Governor Smith would provide effective relief. Soldiers did little good; they embittered the whites, and conditions often got worse after they left. Some Republicans advocated martial law or at least the organization of a white militia company to be on hand for emergencies. But others, reflecting that its membership might duplicate the Klan's, thought this expedient worse than none. Soldiers did come for a while, and conditions quieted temporarily. Much of the blame for Ku Klux activity and general violence rested with the local newspaper, the Eutaw *Whig & Observer*. Bitterly intolerant of Radicalism and all its works, the *Whig* at least indirectly encouraged the terror in almost every issue.[24]

There was nothing indirect about Ryland Randolph and his Tuscaloosa *Independent Monitor*. When the Presidential campaign was over, Randolph threw off the garb of moderation which he had donned in the furor over his cartoon advocating the lynching of carpetbaggers and scalawags. Once again his bigotry and his genius for invective won him widespread attention and no small share of personal trouble. In February 1869 he attacked Henry A. Wise of Virginia, who had just thanked God publicly for the late war because it enabled the South to get rid of the "wickedness of slavery." Wise was crazy, Randolph declared; he himself would thank God for another war if it re-established slavery. Any former slaveholder who rejoiced at the loss of his property was a fool, a falsifier, or a madman.

Aside from this selfish view, slavery was a God-send for the negro race. Negroes, as bondsmen, were happier, more sleek and greasy-looking, and better clothed, than they are now. We never hear the ringing horse-laughs, the picking of banjoes, beating of tamborines, and knocking of feet against puncheon-floors, that formerly marked their *sans souci* existence. Instead thereof, they may be heard to grumble, in squads, collected in fence-corners; and may be seen with ashy faces, grum countenances, and squalid appearance generally.[25]

Randolph not only approved the lynching of Negroes accused of rape; they should be burned at the stake after as many blacks as possible had been rounded up to watch. The *Monitor* took such exception to a state supreme court decision that it publicly questioned the sanity of Chief Justice E. Woolsey Peck, a local resident. If he were truly insane, wrote Randolph, "for the safety of justice, he should be locked up in the State Lunatic Asylum. . . . If not, for the benefit of decent society, he deserves to be Ku-Kluxed." As a result of this sally one of Peck's friends challenged Randolph to a duel. He went to Memphis to fight it, but third parties intervened at the last minute and patched up the quarrel.[26]

Beginning in 1868, Randolph conducted a vendetta against the University of Alabama, located in Tuscaloosa and newly reorganized by the Republican state government. Academic freedom and the virtue of conducting a university without political intervention were ideas equally exotic to Randolph and the Republicans who attempted to remake that institution. The constitution of 1867 placed the university (with the public school system) under an elected state board of education which served as its regents. This body was dominated by Republicans, and it appointed a president and faculty who were as conspicuous for party fealty as for learning. The new president was the Reverend A. S. Lakin, a Northern Methodist clergyman who had come to the state in 1865. Northern and Southern Methodists had divided over slavery before the war, and Lakin was one of many missionaries sent down after the conflict to win converts—especially Negroes—to the Northern Methodist church fold. He was to experience bitter hostility and physical danger in both of his undertakings. When Lakin came to Tuscaloosa in the summer of 1868 to assume his post, accompanied by Dr. N. B. Cloud, the state superintendent of education, he was welcomed by a screaming and groaning mob who strongly intimated that his life was in danger. It was this visit that inspired Randolph's famous woodcut—Lakin representing the Ohio carpetbagger and Cloud the scalawag. (Whatever Lakin's qualifications, Cloud had won renown before the war as an agricultural reformer and editor.) Lakin left immediately and did not return.

The new faculty and student body experienced similar harassment, incited or encouraged by the *Monitor*. Some of the faculty were Northerners by birth, and in the eyes of Randolph all were to be despised as either carpetbaggers or scalawags for having accepted appointments from the present administration. Some critics raised pertinent questions about professional competence in a few cases, but Randolph was more concerned with their doctrinal purity. The university opened in April 1869. In the absence of Lakin or a permanent successor J. D. F. Richards served as acting president. A native of Vermont, Richards had been an active Republican, serving as state senator and sheriff of Wilcox County in the Black Belt. Until 1871, when the university closed again in defeat, the student body gradually dwindled from an initial thirty members to none at all, largely the work of Randolph and the Tuscaloosa Ku Klux, although a statewide Conservative boycott was also responsible. Randolph's course could hardly have been more violent if the regents had enrolled Negro students and faculty; in fact he made it appear as if this were imminent.[27]

The *Monitor,* joined by residents of the town, waged an incessant campaign of vilification against Richards and the faculty and persuaded many would-be students to return home. Even before his arrival the *Monitor* reminded its readers that Richards as a state senator had recommended martial law for Tuscaloosa and other counties; this information was especially directed, the paper said, to the "Sipsey Swampers," denizens of the county's major Ku Klux hangout. Another woodcut portrayed the new president embracing a gorilla which it helpfully identified as the son of a Tuscaloosa Negro legislator and allegedly a prospective student. "Richards is, undoubtedly, a great scamp. . . . He is the best subject for Ku-Klux treatment we have ever seen." He and his new colleagues, Randolph warned in January, "cannot be comfortably fixed in Tuskaloosa. We advise them in time." If they and any prospective students were so foolish or depraved as to insist on coming they could expect to hear from the Ku Klux Klan. "A man from Moore's Bridge [near the Sipsey Swamp] called to see us . . . ," Randolph announced soon afterward, "and swore that it was the purpose of the Ku-Kluxing people of his neighborhood to dissipate the bogus Faculty soon after their arrival." In March the *Monitor* printed a dramatic sketch of a column's length, a farce in two scenes. Featuring an illiterate university faculty, "nigger students," and the Ku Klux Klan, it ended with students and faculty on the run after glimpsing the Ku Klux in the distance.

When Conservatives elsewhere in the state failed to match Randolph's enthusiasm in this crusade he complained indignantly at having to do battle single-handedly. "Every democratic newspaper should have come to the aid of the *Monitor,* in its efforts at breaking down an institution that all agree is a disgrace to the State. . . . Had each county paper exposed the hideousness of this institution of ignorance, and the infamy of the besotted Faculty, there would have been no respectable students sent here."[28]

Based on Randolph's evidence, the "besotted" portion of the faculty consisted of Professor Vernon H. Vaughan. The editor claimed to have served briefly with Vaughan during the war, and branded him as incompetent, an "absorber of whisky," and a "perfect jackass."[29] He too merited a woodcut, along with a news item stating that he had been drunk in the streets a few days before and had to be helped home by a friend.[30] Other faculty members received less specific attention, but all were socially ostracized in the community. After the university opened in April and other papers failed to support him with equal fervor, Randolph's attention shifted to other matters.

The quarrel with Vaughan seems to have continued privately, however, and a year later it exploded in the street. In March 1870 the Republican *Alabama State Journal* in Montgomery carried a letter from Vaughan that Randolph found abusive. He went out looking for that gentleman on April 1, armed with a revolver and bowie knife. Hearing that Vaughan was on his way into town with some friends, heavily armed, he waited on the street, talking to an acquaintance. One of Vaughan's friends was William A. Smith, a student at the university and a nephew of Governor Smith; Randolph had also attacked him editorially. As Randolph was conversing, young Smith crossed the street and deliberately bumped into him while walking past. The editor promptly struck him in the face. Smith drew a pistol and fired point blank. The wound was superficial, and Randolph drew his own gun, whereupon the two men emptied their revolvers at each other, only a few steps apart. The marksmanship was so poor on both sides that they did no further damage to each other, but one of Smith's shots killed an old man standing behind Randolph. The editor drew his bowie knife. Smith ran, firing twice over his shoulder, and this second shot took effect, entering Randolph's leg above the knee, and ended the brawl.

Smith was promptly arrested for murdering the old man. Vaughan had been across the street the whole time, but he was arrested too on a charge of instigating the affray. They spent almost a month in jail, while the Klan periodically threatened their lives and bullied Vaughan's family. He was eventually released, and soon afterward Smith escaped with the help of friends and fled to Illinois. In July Vaughan was named by President Grant as Secretary of Utah Territory.[31]

Randolph came out less well, for his wounded leg had to be amputated. He resumed his editorial course, but minus some of the old fire. The few remaining students at the university were subjected to a campaign of intimidation intended to drive them away. On one occasion several Ku Klux notices were found pinned to a campus door with a dagger. The notices to two of these students, David Smith, a son of the governor, and Charles Munsell, whose father was a well-known editor and publisher in Albany, New York, went as follows:

David Smith: You have received one notice from us, and this shall be our last. You nor no other d———d son of a d———d radical traitor shall stay at our university. Leave here in less than ten days, for in that time we will visit the place and it will not be well for you to be found out there. The State is ours and so shall our university be.

Charles Muncel [*sic*]: You had better get back where you came from. We don't want any d———d Yank at our colleges. In less than ten days we will come to see if you obey our warning. If not, look out for hell, for d———n you, we will show you that you shall not stay, you nor no one else, in that college. This is your first notice; let it be your last.

These warnings were effective and the students left. When the university reopened later in 1871 it was under less partisan influence and with greater public support. It continued thereafter under both Democratic and Republican state administrations.[32]

Far more lethal was the off-campus lawlessness of the Ku Klux or Sipsey Swamp boys, who issued from that den in the western part of the county and committed mayhem for miles around. Late in April 1869 they took up as their own a minor quarrel between two whites and two Negroes, and set out to chastise and drive off the black men. The latter were on guard, however, and killed one of the attackers. The next day the gang returned and burned all the Negro houses on that plantation. For two or three days they combed the countryside and rode through town, allegedly for the purpose of arresting refractory Negroes. In the process they killed two freedmen, wounded others, and suffered another death themselves. One day they paid a call on Randolph, their spiritual leader, at his office; having nothing better to say of this visit, the *Monitor* explained facetiously that they were Loyal Leaguers come to tar and feather the editor, who escaped by slipping out the back door and hiding in an empty barrel. Sheriff T. P. Lewis made no effort to arrest or hinder these desperadoes. He alleged inability, which was probably true, and arrested instead one of the wounded Negroes. Several nights later the Klan rode into town and lynched the black man near the courthouse.

The *Monitor* had nothing to say about these depredations apart from a brief, and unprecedented, plea not to lynch Negroes who were innocent of violence. When certain blacks appealed to the governor for troops to end the terror, however, Randolph branded them public enemies and promised to publish their names as soon as he could learn them. Local Radicals, he thundered, ought to be kept as hostages for any good men and true who might suffer military arrest.[33]

Of course the governor did not resort to martial law, although he sent for troops, who arrived a month later. More importantly, he sent two personal emissaries (including Colonel D. L. Dalton, his private secretary and alter ego) to Tuscaloosa to investigate, compose differences, and if possible get local officials to enforce the laws. After talking to many persons, they concluded (with only moderate exaggeration) that Ryland Randolph had inspired most of the trouble in Tuscaloosa and that nine-tenths of the Democrats privately condemned him as an extremist. They also found the sheriff and county solicitor to be incompetent and persuaded them to resign. On the recommendation of leading citizens of both parties J. J. Pegues, a moderate Democrat, was appointed sheriff in the hope that somehow he could win enough popular backing to end the violence. At least 700 persons signed a law-and-order pledge (including some of the ringleaders in lawlessness), but no one seriously expected any of the Klansmen to be tried or convicted for past offenses. In fact many of the signers subscribed merely in a vain attempt to prevent troops from coming. Their fear on this ground was a little surprising.[34]

Despite the pledges and the presence of troops in town, armed bands continued to roam the county at will. At least four murders were committed by the end of June, besides countless other outrages. One Jacob Miller, a mason living near the Sipsey Swamp, wrote the governor that his son had been taken off by eight men with a rope more than a week before and had not been seen since. Several days later he wrote again to say that his son's body had been discovered—in the North River beneath a rock which required five men to lift. Was there any protection for Union men, he demanded to know. Receiving no satisfactory answer, he wrote back repeatedly in July and August, asking the same question and reporting that the atrocities continued. One letter enclosed a petition from Union men of the vicinity demanding action to stop Klan depredations. President Richards of the university and Mayor Woodruff of Tuscaloosa wrote the governor in equally emphatic terms. When Democrats petitioned to have the soldiers removed, these two asked not only the governor but the President and the Secretary of War to have them retained and to invest them with powers of martial law. Republicans complained that Sheriff Pegues did little or nothing to enforce the law, and Governor Smith sent repeated injunctions to him to do so, accompanied by offers of reward for apprehension of the criminals. The sheriff replied that he was investigating crimes as diligently as he could, but no one, victims and witnesses alike, dared make formal complaints; there was no courtworthy evidence on which he could proceed. Meanwhile, he said, the soldiers could accomplish nothing and merely embittered the lawless element still further.[35]

By the end of June even Ryland Randolph had had enough. "It is now time, we are free to announce, for murders and assassinations to cease." The *Monitor* affirmed its support of Sheriff Pegues and his efforts to restore order, even hoping that he could uncover the murderers of young Miller.

Randolph was elected to the legislature again in August in a light voter turnout. The violence was not particularly geared to that event, however, and continued afterward. Finally in September several men were arrested for serious crimes and bound over for trial. The *Monitor* conceded that if they were guilty they should be punished; but as it happened, the case against them rested on Negro testimony and therefore was highly dubious. "We contend . . . that negro oaths are insufficient to establish a Southern white man's guilt. There exists a degree of cowardly, instinctive hatred, on the part of the tailless baboon race, for the whites, that can never be gotten rid of till the race itself shall be gotten rid of." A week later the paper facetiously noted the appearance of a great comet in Tuscaloosa and Greene counties, the tail of which dropped down one night and burned three or four Negro schoolhouses. "The antics of the tail of this wonderful comet have completely demoralized free-nigger education in these counties; for negroes are so superstitious that they believe it to be a warning for them to stick, hereafter to 'de shovel and de hoe,' and let their dirty-backed primers go." As for Ku Klux outrages, they were the work of carpetbag incendiaries who outraged and robbed Negroes for their own political and personal profit. The Ku Klux Klans, said the *Monitor,* had long since ceased to exist.[36]

Republican complaints of Klan activity around Tuscaloosa declined in August, partially because of the futility of complaining. The arrests in September brought no court convictions, but they may have contributed to the falling off of Klan activity which occurred in the fall. Otherwise the atmosphere was unchanged. General S. W. Crawford, who commanded in Alabama under General Terry, visited Tuscaloosa in January 1870 and reported his findings: "The whole civil system is poisoned to the core. Fear seems to have possessed executive men and intimidation [seems] to control the avenues of Justice." The soldiers stationed there were helpless to do any good, given the incompetence or fear of local officials, he said, and might as well be withdrawn. When General Terry forwarded this assessment to Governor Smith, suggesting that the soldiers could better be used elsewhere, the governor assented.[37]

Meanwhile Randolph gratuitously involved himself in a public dispute with no less a personage than General Forrest. The general had been traversing western Alabama regularly, meeting with local politicians and civic leaders to drum up financial support for his railroad. He found it necessary and therefore possible to work with men of both parties, in and out of office, especially since many of these counties were under Republican control. One such man was Judge William T. Blackford of Hale County, just south of Tuscaloosa, whom local Democrats had long been trying to drive from office. Randolph not only found Forrest's association with Blackford "disgraceful and disgusting," but he proclaimed it to the world. The general responded in kind with a long letter to the *Alabama State Journal,* the Republican organ in Montgomery. No man with a reputable war record would have thought to level such an attack, he declared, and certainly Randolph's record did not justify it. Ever since the war this man had been a source of strife and discord:

His course as an editor has been constantly injurious, not to the Republicans, but to the Democratic party, and the true interests of the people of Alabama. . . . Unlike the editor of the *Monitor,* my object has been to bring peace to the country, and prosperity to the people; to soften down the prejudices of men of both parties; and in the development of the great material interests of the country, to smoothen the asperities engendered by the war, and efface alike the marks and the memories of strife.[38]

Thus General Forrest, his Ku Klux days behind him, stood forth as the embodiment of the New South—cooperative, conciliatory, and bent on the enrichment of the newly united nation; Randolph and his kind were reactionaries and boat-rockers. It was not only Republicans, therefore, who applauded when Randolph was expelled from the legislature soon afterward for a vicious racial diatribe against one of his Negro colleagues.

But he was not yet chastened. In March he attacked another Conservative hero, General John C. Breckinridge of Kentucky, for having denounced the Ku Klux Klan. Apparently forgetting that by his own account the Ku Klux no longer existed, Randolph expressed a hope that "those patriotic men . . . may live to perform their good deeds long after all the repentant rebels and renegades [*sic*] have disappeared from the stage of life." And when the county tax assessor in Tuscaloosa displeased the *Monitor* it threatened him with a Ku Kluxing if he did not leave first. "The vile creature should not be permitted to hold office till the going down of another sun."[39]

The old ways were hard to drop, but after his traumatic experience with young Smith in April, Randolph subsided. By the same token Klan activity around Tuscaloosa tapered off further in the spring of 1870. Local members probably took part in the Boyd murder at Eutaw late in March, but the terror at home clearly diminished—and, as it turned out, permanently.[40]

CHAPTER 16

Alabama: The Northern Counties, and the 1870 Campaign

In 1871, when a Congressional committee looked into the matter, one witness after another testified that the Klan had disbanded in northern Alabama in the spring or summer of 1869. In fact notices were posted and published in the newspapers to that effect at the time—as early as February 1869 in Lauderdale County.[1]

Yet night riding and outrages by disguised bands continued long afterward. These were attributed to "home-made Ku Klux" who belonged to a lower social plane; they were less well organized and less politically motivated. Many or most raids, it was claimed, resulted from private quarrels and plain robbery. All this was true within limits, but Negroes and Republicans still comprised the vast majority of victims. The terror extended to at least fifteen counties in the northern and eastern parts of the state, embracing the entire Tennessee Valley and most of the eastern mountain region below it. The Klan had organized throughout this area in 1868, playing a significant part in the November election in some counties. But night riding and related violence actually increased after the election and throughout the first half of 1869; they declined again after the August 1869 elections, only to resume in the spring of 1870. A. S. Lakin and other Northern Methodist missionaries reported that they and their congregations were repeatedly subjected to threats and nocturnal attacks. Negro schools and churches (especially of that denomination) were favorite targets. So were active Republicans and Republican officeholders who had managed to survive 1868.[2]

The following letter from a Republican in Florence is typical of dozens that reached Governor Smith's office:

> Our county is full of Ku Klux they are going about at night, much to the terror of many citizens—on last Saturday night week our town was visited by the Ku Klux to the number of 150 or more—they killed one negro in our town whipped another and lectured several others they awoke me up at my privat residence at 11 oclock at night to lecture me for what they asserted they heard I said about them—What the negro was killed for God only knows—Several persons have been killed in the County in a misterious way—in a word terrorism and anarchy reins [sic] in this County. . . .[3]

In Lawrence County eight Klansmen were actually arrested in June 1869, after they had hanged a man and taken to roaming the countryside in disguise, burning houses and appropriating their contents. While in jail three of them turned state's evidence. A few days before the trial was slated to begin, a band of disguised men released the prisoners and executed those who had confessed. Three men, however, were rearrested, tried, convicted, and sentenced to jail terms—one of the very few cases of its kind in the South. Because the county jail was obviously unsafe they were transferred to the one at Athens in Limestone County. But on July 14 another disguised band released them there.[4] In Jackson County Klan depredations against James D. Weir, a British subject, brought protests from the British minister in Washington and Secretary of State Hamilton Fish.[5]

The reign of terror in Madison County (Huntsville) was continuous from before the Presidential election until after the Congressional election in August. Early in January 1869 thirty-two disguised men rode into Huntsville after midnight, looking for two white Republican legislators who had just returned home from Montgomery. The two were warned in time and went into hiding. The Klan also broke into the home of a Northern man, abused his family, and took him out into the country where they threatened to hang him, but ended by warning him to leave within thirty days. Then they returned to town to visit a bawdy house before dispersing. State senator J. D. Sibley, one of their intended victims, reported from the nearby Army post (where he had taken refuge) that the Ku Klux had apparently blockaded every road out of town to intercept him if he tried to escape.[6]

Here too the Negroes bore the main burden of attack. By May the perambulations of disguised bands were a weekly occurrence in the countryside around Huntsville. It became even worse in June and July, as the election approached. "Acts of violence are becoming so common in this county that no man is safe," wrote Judge Lewis M. Douglas, "and is all for the purpose of intimidating the colored people so that they will not vote at this election." They were whipped, robbed of guns, and warned to stay home on election day; a few were killed. Many crimes went unreported out of fear.

Not only were victims and witnesses afraid to testify or make formal complaint, but Sheriff Joseph P. Doyle did even less than usual to curb the violence. When prodded by Republicans to take action he demurred, "I have nobody to protect me." In fact General S. W. Crawford, the Army commandant in Alabama, made his headquarters in Huntsville and troops were always on hand (although they were infantry and of little use in catching Ku Klux on the hoof). Doyle did ask for soldiers on one occasion and was encouraged by both the general and Governor Smith to get horses for them to ride, but his enthusiasm was not equal to the task of finding them. Of course, as Doyle probably knew, the most exemplary valor and determination on his part could not have secured the conviction of any prisoners he might have taken. Apart from the conviction in Lawrence County it was the same everywhere; braver or more dedicated sheriffs accomplished little more. The prosecutor and judge in Morgan County engaged in active collusion to frustrate the prosecution of Klansmen arrested by the sheriff there for brutally assaulting a Negro.

Almost every report of outrages reaching the governor was coupled with an appeal for martial law or decisive action of any kind from Montgomery. Otherwise, his correspondents warned, Republicans would have to flee the state for their lives and would also lose the coming elections. As time passed and no effective response was made to these appeals, they became more insistent and bitter. The *Alabama State Journal* in Montgomery joined in with a pointed comparison to the Arkansas militia campaign, then under way. John H. Wager, a Freedman's Bureau agent, bluntly told the governor that he talked big and accomplished little. "If for nothing else[,] for the sake of humanity awake and let the men . . . by whom you were elected [see] that your promises and oaths are more than vain and that you have not sold out to the other side. I have defended you as long as I can. . . . " The next day Wager wrote again to report angrily that 300 Ku Klux had invaded Huntsville the night before, boasting of their invincibility. To prove it they roamed the streets at will, hunting for Union men and driving Negroes from their Saturday night worship services. There will be a day of reckoning, said Wager, for officeholders who have failed in their responsibilities.[7]

It would be unfair to say that Governor Smith did nothing in reply to the anguished appeals and occasional threats with which he was bombarded. As always, he requested and got troops for some of the worst areas.[8] He wrote repeatedly to sheriffs and other local officials, requesting and even demanding that they enforce the laws.[9] But the futility of these measures must have become as obvious to him as it was to his correspondents. In writing Secretary of State Fish after the Weir affair in April 1869, he pointed to the state's anti-Klan laws of December 1868 and reported that they were having "a most salutary effect." As he surely knew, terrorism was then on the increase. It is impossible to measure the Klan's effects on the August elections, but in some counties at least, intimidation obviously decreased the Republican vote.[10] Smith turned a deaf ear to suggestions that he organize a militia and put down the Ku Klux as Clayton was doing in Arkansas. And he refused when white Republicans of DeKalb County, including the circuit judge, asked permission to organize a militia company of their own to arrest disguised marauders. Such a company would be composed largely or wholly of Republicans, he explained, and thus would irritate rather than tranquilize the difficulties there.[11]

Republican criticism reached such proportions that Smith felt obliged to defend himself before the legislature when it assembled in the fall. He conceded that lawlessness was prevalent throughout much of the state, but insisted that the primary responsibility for controlling it lay with the sheriffs and other local officials. There was no evidence of organized resistance to arrests when sheriffs had set out to make them, he said. And even if there were, troops had been shifted around the state, often at his request, with orders to help local officials whenever they asked for it. This help had almost never been requested. It was pointless, therefore, to organize a state militia for the same purpose. Martial law—the ultimate weapon—was hardly appropriate when sheriffs had not used the powers they already possessed and the courts were open and functioning. Under the state constitution, moreover, the power to suspend habeas corpus lay with the legislature rather than with the governor. That body wisely had not used this power, he said, but even if it did there was no constitutional authority whatever to establish military courts. If a militia were organized and habeas corpus suspended—the maximum steps permitted under the constitution—the prisoners it arrested would still have to be turned over to the civil courts for trial.

Smith's predicament was all too familiar. His argument was legally and logically correct except for its refusal to recognize the fundamental incompetence of local authorities to deal with systematic terrorism. Whether blindly or willfully, he underestimated the dimensions of the conspiracy, and "passed the buck" back again to those who were looking to him for relief. Certainly he refused to entertain the idea of organizing a largely black army to keep white men in line. Practically speaking, it is almost certain that no preponderantly black militia could have imposed law and order on the white population of Alabama or any other state in 1869. For the deep South especially, the only real remedy lay with the federal government.

However sound Smith's argument may have been logically and legally, it was morally and politically weak. Smith was a far different personality type from Clayton, Brownlow, and even Holden. Wholly conventional in outlook, he lacked the energy or imagination to depart from orthodox ways and to cope with extraordinary problems. He was a weak executive, almost wholly lacking in crowd appeal. By taking the course of least resistance to combat the terror he was doing what came naturally. Unfortunately for himself, he gave a public impression of not caring particularly about the sufferings of his fellow Republicans, and especially the blacks. This was untrue, despite his obvious race prejudice. But conceiving himself powerless to cope with the terror, he found it convenient to minimize its seriousness and thus further exculpate himself. "This is no time for usurpations, or the exercise of arbitrary power," he told the legislature. "The time honored bulwarks of civil liberty must be sacredly observed, even if in their observance there be exceptional cases of individual hardships." "There is neither war nor rebellion in Alabama," he said; the state was in profound peace, and the initiation of military law by the governor would be "a palpable assumption of unwarranted power."[12] When persons in Calhoun County told him that no grand jury there would ever indict people guilty of outrages, he replied that he was unwilling to believe that badly of the county and its people.[13] It was this attitude which enraged fellow Republicans who had to dodge the lash, halter, and bullets of roving Ku Klux gangs.

Although the incidence of terrorism had declined in some areas by the time Smith addressed the legislature, it continued or increased in others. Mountainous Blount County was among the latter. The Ku Klux organization there reportedly dated from November 1867, and night riding had been sporadic ever since. But it became worse late in 1869 and 1870. In one section raids took place regularly twice a week. Here a substantial white Republican population contributed more victims than did Negroes. Deviant Methodism ranked with deviant politics as a cause of Ku Klux raids, although personal and family feuds, often arising from the war, were also involved. Racism was present too, in the suppression of Negro schools and churches. Both blacks and whites were whipped, disarmed, driven from their homes, and occasionally murdered. Hardly any black men voted after 1868. One witness estimated the Ku Klux membership in the county at 300, and bands of up to 75 were occasionally seen at one time. Together with their sympathizers they controlled the judicial apparatus of the county, and efforts to punish them legally always failed. When it appeared early in 1870 that troops might be sent, the outrages declined, only to resume when that prospect disappeared.[14]

Similar conditions prevailed in adjoining Morgan County. (The present Cullman County, between them, was not yet created; it contained some of the most troubled areas.) In the fall of 1869 Isaac M. Berry of Blount County and Judge Charlton of Morgan formed an anti–Ku Klux organization, even recruiting a few disenchanted Klansmen who gave them useful information. Under Berry's command a party of these regulators went, openly and without disguise, to the homes of several Klansmen in Morgan County and warned them to stay home in the future. The tactic was effective, Berry later testified, ending the terrorism in that neighborhood.[15] Such was not true in the rest of that county, however; General Crawford characterized it as having lapsed into anarchy.[16] By the beginning of 1870 it was a virtual battleground between two armed bands. The larger, numbering about sixty, was roughly identifiable with the Klan and enjoyed substantial public support; the other consisted of only about eight men, apparently Unionists or Republicans. The former, at least, operated in disguise much of the time. An Army officer reported after an investigation that political, personal, and family feuds were so blended and mixed here that it was impossible to say where one began and the other ended. He enumerated six murders since the beginning of the year, culminating in the assassination of Judge Charlton on March 18. Charlton was the foremost Republican in the county and was actively trying to suppress the disguised parties. Soon after his death the smaller band was driven from the county, leaving the other in control. Disguised men invaded the circuit court clerk's office and took away incriminating records. The list of murders soon climbed to twelve.

Sheriff H. G. Thomas was caught in the middle. Warned not to visit the upper end of the county if he valued his life, he came to General Crawford at Huntsville under cover of night, saying that he could no longer perform the duties of his office. But the general encouraged him to return, and he reported a month later that things had quieted down after some of the gunmen fled. On April 23 a public meeting was held to debate the question of calling for troops. The meeting voted against them, and none were sent. The violence nevertheless declined, as it did generally this spring in the Tennessee Valley counties.[17]

It was not so in several of the eastern counties.[18] Klansmen in this region often collaborated with their brethren across the line in Georgia; it was probably Cherokee County members who rescued Ackridge from the soldiers in Summerville, Georgia, early in the year. In Macon County (Tuskegee) there was organized white intimidation, openly led by the gentry rather than conventional night riding.[19]

In 1870 many Republicans renewed their requests to be allowed to organize militia companies. This policy was advanced to the governor more than once by General Crawford, especially after the Charlton and Boyd murders in March.[20] Under this urging and the pressure of events, Smith embarked in April on what he described as "a vigorous and determined policy" to stop violence and bring offenders to justice. He issued a proclamation singling out the counties of Greene, Morgan, and Tuscaloosa as particularly disorderly and requiring special attention. In each he proposed to organize a company of militia for active service as soon as responsible citizens there requested it and consented to raise and command the troops. He reiterated his inability to proclaim martial law, but threatened if lawlessness continued to call a special session of the legislature to impose a tax on any county where extraordinary expenses were required to restore law and order. Not included in the proclamation, but part of the new policy, was a further intention to appoint special attorneys to conduct searching criminal investigations in the most troubled counties. If necessary they were to summon every man and woman in the county as witnesses to testify to everything they knew. Smith sent John A. Minnis in this capacity to ferret out the murderers of Boyd and other malefactors in Greene County, and perhaps Tuscaloosa as well. He asked D. C. Humphreys and David P. Lewis (a later governor) to perform the same office in Morgan County, but they appear not to have served.[21]

When Minnis went to Greene County, as already discussed, he found the conspiracy and fear so tight that it was impossible to make any headway with prosecutions in the local courts. Moreover, no one regarded as worthy and competent could be found who was willing (or brave) enough to organize a militia company there. The consensus of Republicans, Minnis reported, was that the governor should organize a regiment at Montgomery, composed of white men if possible, train it, and hold it ready to send wherever emergencies arose. It was thought that if state troops were sent to lawless places and quartered at the expense of the county it might have a more salutary effect in deterring crime than sending federal troops, who accomplished little and spent money wherever they went. Furthermore, federal troops were apt to be removed before the need for them had disappeared. This was all very well, but how the governor was to find a regiment of dependable and willing white men around Montgomery Minnis did not say. Smith was contemplating some kind of militia, however, and in July he wrote President Grant asking to borrow guns from the federal government.[22]

The first militia company actually to be authorized was in Fayette County, north of Greene and Tuscaloosa. This county had not figured much in Klan doings before, but in April 1870, just as Smith was trying to implement his new policy, news came of widespread outrages there. The Klan had begun whipping and otherwise maltreating Negroes at different points in the county, including the region near Tuscaloosa's Sipsey Swamp. Five Negroes and a white man were brutally murdered. And during the circuit court term a disguised band marched through Fayetteville after dark in an effort to intimidate the court. Under these circumstances white Union men asked and were granted permission in June to form a militia company. They delayed doing so until November, however. Meanwhile some of them formed a less official band of anti–Ku Klux regulators, called Mossy-backs, which led to several months of sporadic guerrilla warfare. Unlike their counterparts in Morgan County, the Mossy-backs were numerous enough to sustain themselves and were not driven from the county. Nevertheless the Klan, with about 200 members, kept the initiative and continued to commit outrages, mostly against the unorganized Negroes.

Sheriff F. M. Treadway, a Confederate veteran, sided with the Mossy-backs, as did a few others of similar background, because the Klan was obviously the lawless element in the county. The substantial white Unionist population in Fayette, with this organization, gave Treadway a power for law and order which few deep South sheriffs possessed. He occasionally used them as well as soldiers to form posses, and arrested twenty Klansmen, including two chiefs, at different times between July and October. The Klan was so shaken by these arrests, especially in October when three members confessed and turned state's evidence, that some of its members promised to disband and commit no more outrages. Others refused to honor the agreement, however, and the violence continued. When the prisoners came to trial, witnesses against them were intimidated into silence and the cases had to be dropped. A major problem was that many white Conservatives who no longer sympathized with the Klan, especially after the October schism, still resented the Unionist and Republican character of the opposition. Rather than commit treason to the Democratic party, their Confederate past, and other related loyalties, they either remained silent or continued to vent their hostility to the sheriff and his Mossy-back supporters. Without martial law, Treadway reported, it seemed pointless to make any further arrests. The Mossy-backs having failed as an effective means of suppressing the Ku Klux, Unionists went ahead in November to organize a local militia, but the terror persisted.

John A. Minnis went to Fayette in 1871 and asked the obvious question: With so many men, so well organized, with the power of law on your side, why can't you put down this terrorism? The Union men replied, "To do that we must do as they do—disguise and kill." Sheriff Treadway explained, "When I gather my posse, I could command the posse, and I could depend upon them; but as soon as I get home, I meet my wife crying, saying that they have been there shooting into the house. When we scatter to our houses, we do not know at what time we are to be shot down; and living with our lives in our hands in this way, we have become disheartened, and do not know what to do."[23]

In July 1870 still another opportunity arose to test Governor Smith's limping policy of Klan suppression. In Calhoun County, in the northeast, at least three different dens had been active for months, whipping blacks and threatening white Republicans, especially county officers. Negroes were forced to stay at some farms against their will and were driven away from others. Klansmen also took exception to Northern employees of the Selma, Rome and Dalton Railroad, which ran through the county, and threatened to run them off and burn their buildings. Around the neighboring villages of Patona and Cross Plains it was estimated that two-thirds of the young men were implicated in Klan activity.[24]

On July 11 this erupted into a major crime, winning national attention. A white youth in Cross Plains precipitated a racial conflict by picking a fight with a Negro boy. The black was not satisfied with the outcome of the fight and rounded up eight or ten friends who got guns and came looking for the white boy. They spotted him, with several friends, just as Sunday evening church service had ended and many people were on the street returning home. Oblivious to these persons, the Negroes began firing at the white boys from a distance, and bullets whistled over and among the crowd. Nobody was hurt, but most of the white people assumed that the blacks had wantonly fired into the crowd. White men returned the fire and soon chased them away, but several Negroes were overheard threatening to return and burn the town.

The whites now organized to repel the expected attack, and if possible head it off. They obtained the names of the Negroes and the next day managed to arrest three of them. Someone identified William C. Luke, a white Canadian who taught a Negro school at Patona, as one of the aggressor party, and he was arrested too. Luke, it developed, had not been with them and had even warned them beforehand not to go, but he was unpopular with the white community as a race mixer. A preliminary hearing was begun immediately to determine whether the four prisoners should be held for trial. Luke was the nearest substitute they had for a defense attorney. As night came on, the hearing was recessed until the next day. In the absence of a jail the prisoners were taken under guard to the front porch of a new store building to spend the night. A fifth prisoner—another Negro—was added to the company for helping a further suspect to escape.

About midnight fifty or sixty Klansmen converged on Cross Plains from different directions, fully disguised. After some inquiry they found the building where the prisoners were being kept and quickly overpowered the guard. They took all five men a short distance out of town and hanged them. Several miles away they captured another Negro who had been with the blacks in town the night before and executed him too.[25]

As soon as he heard of these murders Governor Smith sent state supreme court justice Thomas M. Peters to investigate and hold a preliminary hearing of those responsible. Smith appointed former governor Lewis Parsons as a special prosecutor in behalf of the state and secured a detachment of federal troops whom General Crawford brought personally. The governor even visited the scene himself for a time. For all of its fanfare and stellar cast, the judicial proceeding at Cross Plains led nowhere. The hearing dragged on for two months, and well over a hundred witnesses were examined. Nine men were arrested on suspicion of taking part in the lynchings. Their names were turned over to the county grand jury in October with the evidence which had been amassed, but that body ignored them. It chose instead to indict another Negro whom the whites had passed over in July.[26]

Altogether Smith's policy for combating the Ku Klux Klan turned out a complete failure. Only two "searching investigations" took place, which produced no indictments. No militia were organized until November, and then in only one county. Ku Klux outrages went on as before.

In November 1870 Alabama elected her governor, legislature, and members of Congress. Many Republicans, especially the more radical wing led by Senator George Spencer, were angry at Governor Smith's failure to cope with Klan terrorism. Notwithstanding their hostility, he was renominated for a second term.[27] The Democrats chose Robert B. Lindsay, a Tuscumbia lawyer and a party moderate with no known Klan associations. The ensuing campaign was comparable to those in other states; night riding and organized terrorism were less marked in most counties than they had been in months past. This was especially true in northern Alabama, where the Klan had become inactive the previous spring. Generally the Democrats who engaged in intimidation relied on the previous terrorism, coupled with threats and occasional mob violence.[28]

Around Tuskegee, where the Klan seems to have remained under patrician leadership to a remarkable degree, intimidation was as systematic as anywhere but remained largely free of night riding in disguise. Legislator James H. Alston, the foremost Negro Republican, was run out of the county in June by a Klan (or Klan-like) organization commanded by General Cullen A. Battle, his former master. Later, a white Republican was ambushed and a Negro church was attacked, with two fatalities, by whites who mistakenly believed that Alston had returned to conduct a Republican meeting there. Other Negro leaders either fled or were convicted of imaginary crimes and sentenced to the chain gang; they had been given this choice of alternatives. Nearly every Negro church and school in the county was burned prior to the election. The local Democratic paper, the Tuskegee *News,* attributed some of the outrages to Republicans; others it glossed over or totally ignored. White leaders made it a policy to send several observers to every Republican meeting in the guise of "special police"—a widespread practice in slavery times. Despite all these efforts by Conservatives, they were not quite enough to overcome the large Negro Republican majority in the county; nevertheless the Republican margin was much reduced.[29]

Overt terrorism was most prevalent in several of the western counties where the Klan had already been active. "I believe that last fall it would have cost a republican his life to have gone alone and without protection to some portions of Greene, Sumter, Tuscaloosa, and Pickens Counties, and made republican speeches," one of them reported in 1871.[30] Of the counties named, Sumter and Greene were by far the worst. Sumter entered the campaign fresh from the Belmont riot, the insurrectionary scare at Livingtson, and the Negro hunts which followed them in August. In Greene County a Republican leader, Guilford Coleman—one of only two Negroes who could be prevailed upon to attend the recent district and state conventions from that county because of the terror—was taken from his home in September by the Ku Klux, who murdered him and mutilated his body almost beyond recognition. Another Negro leader was killed soon afterward. Meanwhile the Klan rode through parts of both counties, often in broad daylight, whipping Negroes on the various plantations.[31] They were threatened with even worse if they voted the Radical ticket in November, and it was indicated generally that outrages would intensify if the Republicans won. On the other hand, Conservatives promised, a Democratic victory would bring more efficient law enforcement and an end to violence.[32]

The climax of the campaign in both counties came late in October. Congressman Charles Hays, the Republican leader in this part of the state, was the recipient of so many threats that he refused to risk his life trying to campaign alone in either county. Yet this area, with its large Negro majority, was potentially the strongest Republican district in Alabama and possibly essential in carrying the state. It might be political suicide to neglect it. "I thought if Governor Smith came here," Hays later recalled, "and [former] Governor Parsons, and other men of distinction in our party, that probably their speeches might be tolerated." To this end he secured the services of Smith, Parsons, and Senator Willard Warner, and scheduled Republican meetings at Livingston and Eutaw on October 24 and 25.

The Livingston meeting was held in front of the courthouse, with the speakers standing on the steps facing the crowd below, largely Negro. As soon as Governor Smith, the first speaker, began his talk a dozen or more armed whites pushed their way to the front of the crowd. Their leader stationed himself only a few feet from the governor and stood there throughout the speech, brandishing a large knife. Smith pretended not to notice him and finished his speech. The other speakers took their turns, except Hays, who was afraid that any attempt by him would provoke a riot. Every speech was interrupted with jeers, catcalls, and insulting or abusive questions. There was every indication that the bravoes were looking for some provocation to attack, and the speakers were careful not to provide it.[33]

When Smith and his colleagues went on to Eutaw that night, some of the pistol-and-bowie-knife crowd shared the same train. Others collected from different directions the next day. By the time of the meeting some 160 armed and belligerent white men—mostly young—were gathered beside the courthouse with 2,000 blacks. The number of whites was enlarged when a Democratic rally, held on the opposite side of the building, adjourned while the Republican meeting was still in progress. Warner and Parsons spoke first, receiving the same kind of treatment they had got the day before. Then Hays was called upon to say something, and he climbed onto the small table which was serving as a platform. He had hardly stood up when one of the hoodlums nearby pulled him to the ground. At the same time someone fired a gun. Some Democrats said later that the first shot came from Hays himself, others said from Negroes coming to his assistance; on the other hand, Republicans testified that the armed whites began the firing, apparently according to a prearranged plan. The blacks had been orderly up to this point, as they had in Livingston, and whites did most of the firing because they carried most of the armament. As usual the Negroes suffered most if not all of the casualties. Even Democrats held that white men standing around the edge of the crowd and in the courthouse windows overhead tried to stampede the Negroes with gunfire directed first overhead and then into the crowd itself. They achieved this purpose, wounding about fifty-four blacks in the process, four of them mortally. No more than two whites, if that many, were wounded. Some of the freedmen rallied in their flight and began to march back, armed with poles, fence palings, and any other available weapons. But before they reached the courthouse square again, they were stopped by soldiers lined up across the street to block their way. The troops, stationed at Eutaw for some time past, had remained in their camp at the edge of town until the firing began. The Eutaw riot ended according to the usual pattern, with several Negroes and no whites under arrest for committing acts of violence. The next

Head Quarters "Klu Klux"
Blood! Blood!! Blood!!!
First Quarter Bloody Moon
April 27, 1868

To H. C. Warmoth

Villain Beware! Your doom
is sealed — Death now awaites you. The
Midnight Owl Screames.

Revenge! Revenge!! Revenge!!!

Klu Klux Klan

By Order of Grand Giant

Bloody Knights

Klu Klux Klan

Prepare Death now awaits you

Ku Klux warning to Governor Henry Clay Warmoth of Louisiana, April, 1868 (Southern Historical Collection, University of North Carolina, Chapel Hill, North Carolina)

Ku Klux warning, Alabama, 1871 *(Ku Klux Report)*

"Dam Your Soul. The Horrible *Sepulchre* and Bloody Moon has at last arrived. Some live to-day to-morrow "*Die.*" We the undersigned understand through our Grand "*Cyclops*" that you have recommended a big Black Nigger for Male agent on our rail rode; wel, sir, Jest you understand in time if he gets on the rode you can make up your mind to pull rope. If you have any thing to say in regard to the Matter, meet the Grand Cyclops and Conclave at Den No. 4 at 12 o'clock midnight, Oct. 1st, 1871.

"When you are in Calera we warn you to hold your tongue and not speak so much with your mouth or otherwise you will be taken on surprise and led out by the Klan and learnt to stretch hemp. Beware. Beware. Beware. Beware.

(Signed)   "PHILLIP ISENBAUM.
                              "*Grand Cyclops.*
                        "JOHN BANKSTOWN.
                        "ESAU DAVES.
                        "MARCUS THOMAS.
                        "BLOODY BONES.

"You know who. And all others of the Klan."

North Carolina Klansmen with captive (Stanley Horn, *Invisible Empire*, 1939)

Soldiers in captured Ku Klux
uniforms from Huntsville,
Alabama *(Harper's Weekly,*
December 19, 1868)

Captured Mississippi Klansmen (*Harper's Weekly,* January 27, 1872)

"Hang, curs, hang! * * * * * Their complexion is perfect gallows. Stand fast, good fate, to their hanging! * * * * * If they be not born to be hanged, our case is miserable."

Cartoon by Ryland Randolph in the Tuscaloosa (Alabama) *Independent Monitor (Ku Klux Report)*

GENERAL GRANT.—"Who has been Mutilating this Tree?"
KU-KLUX.—"Mr. President, I can not tell a lie—that Nigger done it."

Anti-Klan cartoon by Bellew (*Harper's Weekly*, April 29, 1871)

York County Jail, Yorkville, South Carolina (a later view), where Klansmen were imprisoned, 1871-1872 (J. K. Williams, *Vogues in Villainy,* University of South Carolina Press, 1950)

Union County Jail, Union, South Carolina, scene of two major Ku Klux Klan raids in 1871 (J. K. Williams, *Vogues in Villainy,* University of South Carolina Press, 1950)

Maxwell House, Nashville, Tennessee, where Klan was supposedly reorganized in 1867 (Tennessee State Library and Archives)

Caswell County Courthouse, Yanceyville, North Carolina, where John W. Stephens was murdered and Klansmen were imprisoned by the militia in 1870 (North Carolina Collection, University of North Carolina, Chapel Hill, North Carolina)

Ryland Randolph

General Nathan Bedford Forrest

Governor William G. (Parson) Brownlow

Top left, General Nathan Bedford Forrest, Grand Wizard of the Ku Klux Klan. (John A. Wyeth, *That Devil Forrest,* Harper & Row, 1959). Top right, Ryland Randolph, editor and Klansman of Tuscaloosa, Alabama. (J. C. Lester and Daniel L. Wilson, *Ku Klux Klan: Its Origin, Growth and Disbandment,* Reprint House International, Fleming Edition, 1905). Bottom, Governor William G. (Parson) Brownlow of Tennessee, first major foe of the Ku Klux Klan. (William G. Brownlow, *Sketches of the Rise, Progress and Decline of Secession,* Da Capo Plenum Publishers, Second Edition, 1968)

Governor William W. Holden

Governor Powell Clayton

Attorney General Amos T. Akerman

Senator John Scott

Top left, Governor William W. Holden of North Carolina, the Ku Klux Klan's highest-ranking victim. (North Carolina Collection, University of North Carolina, Chapel Hill, North Carolina). Top right, Governor Powell Clayton of Arkansas, the Ku Klux Klan's most potent enemy. (Arkansas History Commission). Bottom left, Attorney General Amos T. Akerman, the Ku Klux Klan's Chief Prosecutor in 1871. (*Harper's Weekly*, July 16, 1870). Bottom right, Senator John Scott of Pennsylvania, Chairman of the Congressional Ku Klux Klan Investigating Committee of 1871 (*Harper's Weekly*, February 13, 1869) morning the Sumter County boys returned home on the train, boasting that "they had been to Eutaw and cleaned out the damned Radicals."[34]

General Crawford cooperated fully in stationing troops wherever the state administration felt they were necessary. Not only did the soldiers not sweep Republicans into office by force or intimidation—the customary Conservative charge throughout the Reconstruction period—but they did comparatively little to offset Democratic terrorism. There was no visible correlation between the presence of troops and the election outcome around the state.[35] Their most likely contribution was to prevent violence on election day, November 8, which passed quietly enough almost everywhere. But for Conservatives this was no longer necessary. Hundreds and perhaps thousands of Negroes voted Democratic either through persuasion or prior threats; still greater numbers did not vote at all. This was most conspicuous in the black counties of Sumter, Greene, and Macon. In two or three Sumter precincts no Republican votes were cast at all, despite a Negro preponderance and Republican majorities in previous elections. Greene County went Democratic by 35 votes, compared with a 2,000 majority for Grant in 1868. Sumter Democrats were more thorough, winning by more than 600 votes compared with a 1,000-vote loss in 1868. In all three of these counties fewer votes were cast than in 1868 despite a statewide increase in 1870. Because of quieter conditions elsewhere in his district Hays was returned to Congress by 1,800 votes, much reduced from his margin of 12,000 in 1869.[36] Noting the Democratic majority in Greene County and recalling the Eutaw riot, Ryland Randolph observed that "a row occasionally does no little good."[37]

Alabama Republicans were correct in their prior assessment of the importance of these counties. The state went Democratic by roughly 1,400 votes in a total of 150,000 votes cast. Republicans polled more votes statewide than they had two years earlier, but this was conspicuously not the case in some counties, including Sumter, Greene, and Macon. Had there been a full and free election in these counties Republicans might not have won the 10,000 majority they later estimated, but they would surely have upset Lindsay's margin with many votes to spare.[38] For this reason Smith refused to give up his office, and for two or three weeks Alabama had two rival governors. Smith was not sustained by the courts, however, and finally retired. Although the Democrats also won a majority in the lower house of the legislature, the senate remained Republican. Alabama Conservatives were not as thorough statewide as those of Georgia.

CHAPTER 17

Mississippi, Tennessee, and Kentucky

Having rejected a Radical constitution in June 1868, Mississippi remained under military jurisdiction for another year and a half. Late in 1869 the voters approved the same constitution, now shorn of disfranchising clauses, and elected a Republican state government. James L. Alcorn, a substantial delta planter and former slaveholder, was paradoxically the new Republican governor. He had been prominent in the Whig party before the war, opposed secession until it became an established fact, and then supported the Confederacy. Alcorn accepted Reconstruction in 1867 as a matter of expediency and helped organize the state Republican party. His administration took office early in 1870 and was quickly recognized by Congress.

The Ku Klux Klan had played a minor role in Mississippi in 1868. This continued to be true throughout the military administration, but night riding and related violence increased markedly in 1870. The state as a whole was not involved in this, however; most of the Klan activity was confined to about a dozen counties in the northern and eastern parts of the state.

One of the few scenes of significant Klan activity during the military regime in 1869 was Panola County, in the north. Five dens were distributed more or less evenly around the county, with a total membership of at least 150. They engaged in the usual acts of intimidation and violence against Negroes and white Republicans, although members later attributed most of the violence to outsiders. The military authorities sent troops, who arrested several men in February and March and sent them to Vicksburg for trial. When the officer in command indicated that this was only the beginning, there was public consternation; tension mounted further when an armed skirmish took place between soldiers and disguised men. As a result a public meeting was held—one of the largest on record according to the local paper—and resolutions deprecating the lawlessness were passed. Outrages may have diminished thereafter, but in the fall the Klan engaged in another armed clash, this time with a sheriff's posse. The authorities seem to have won that engagement, and soon afterward the local Klan disbanded.[1]

There was also a sporadically active organization in Alcorn and Tishomingo counties in the northeast corner of the state. In March 1870 a hundred or more men in full disguise reportedly broke into the jail at Jacinto and lynched two inmates, one Negro and one white. The former was literally shot to pieces, and the latter was mutilated and then hanged.[2]

The only general election held in Mississippi between June 1868 and November 1871 was the constitutional ratification vote and election of a state government in November 1869. Thus there was less occasion or need than in most states for the Klan to engage in overt political activity. Moreover, the fall campaign in 1869 was freer of night riding and organized voter intimidation than the contest in 1868, when the Klan was only beginning to form. The most directly political Klan operations lay in intimidating Republican officeholders to drive them from office, as well as Republican leaders in general to disrupt the party. In Lauderdale County, Klansmen (or armed white marauders) killed two Negro members of the county board of supervisors at different times in 1870. Both men were active in mobilizing Negroes to fight off white predators.[3] But while this took place, it was by no means general, even in the counties of greatest activity.

Most Klan operations were designed to keep the Negro in his place socially and economically. The organization was used to regulate Negro labor as nearly in the ante-bellum fashion as circumstances allowed. Black men were Ku Kluxed to drive them off one man's land and onto the land of someone else;[4] or they were Ku Kluxed for leaving when the landlord wanted them to stay. Some of the first outrages in Noxubee County, in November 1870, were committed against Negro renters of land, presumably on the theory that they should remain wage laborers or sharecroppers.[5] Most often they were beaten or killed for legal infractions which white men could not or would not punish at law, or for social infractions which were not illegal at all. A black man charged with rape was almost invariably lynched by disguised parties before he could be brought to trial. To be charged with the murder of a white man was almost as certain to bring lynching. Even theft was occasionally punished in this manner, as with the Negro riddled with bullets at Jacinto. Three Negro women of Noxubee County were visited on the same night and whipped for living as mistresses (in the guise of housekeepers) of as many bachelor or widowed planters. Almost every whipping or beating sprang from at least the accusation of some minor wrongdoing, ranging from larceny to impertinence. Some Negroes were beaten and a few were killed for speaking out openly against the Klan or threatening to resist it. Among white victims, one of the greatest offenses was to teach in a Negro school. Scores of public schools (including a few white ones) were closed down or destroyed, and as many teachers of both races were forced to stop or were exiled or beaten; but much the greater part of the Klan's campaign against public education came in 1871.

There is no obvious reason why most of the Klan operations in Mississippi should have been limited to seven adjoining counties (Monroe, Chickasaw, Lowndes, Noxubee, Winston, Kemper, and Lauderdale) on the eastern border of the state.[6] They lay adjacent to Alabama counties where the Klan was active, and there was a great deal of cooperation across the state line between counties on either side. But Ku Klux activity did not extend very far westward into Mississippi counties which were just as close on that side. Nor did all of these counties share identical characteristics; Lauderdale and Noxubee especially were rich plantation counties with Negro majorities—an extension of the Alabama Black Belt—while some of the most troubled areas of Winston, Monroe, and Lowndes had poor soils and white majorities. Monroe County, with its town of Aberdeen, was bisected from north to south by the Tombigbee River; the more fertile and prosperous western half was relatively free of violence while the poorer whites in the eastern half made life a hell for their racial and political opponents. Many of the raiders here came over from adjacent Sanford (now Lamar) County, Alabama, but there was almost no record of Klan activity in that county itself. Of course this same challenge to logical analysis existed in every state.

The same difficulties existed in Mississippi as elsewhere in punishing Ku Klux criminals. The military officials in 1869 usually depended on sheriffs and other local officials for the maintenance of law and order, just as if the civil law were supreme. Nevertheless, military trials were always a possibility and law enforcement was somewhat better in this period than it later became. Of the counties named above, Kemper was probably the most peaceful, and much of the credit belonged to Sheriff W. W. Chisolm. After night riding and violence broke out early in 1869 he used soldiers to make arrests. Several men were taken off by the military to face trial, and although they were later released it was only after they had experienced great inconvenience and considerable apprehension. Others left the county before they could be taken. This action strengthened the sheriff personally and the idea of law and order generally among some of the more influential Conservatives; henceforth they cooperated to hold Klan activity to a minimum. On several occasions groups of rowdies came over from Alabama to reinforce the local boys in whatever trouble they cared to start. Once, when they lay in wait for Chisolm near his home, he collected a posse and chased them back into Sumter County, where such rebuffs did not occur. They had come under the impression that they would get general white support, but when they found this lacking they stopped coming. Such examples were rare, however, and after the military gave way to civil control the familiar pattern of frustrated prosecutions became universal.[7] (Several years later Chisolm himself was assassinated.)

While running for the governor's office in November 1869, Alcorn pledged that "society should no longer be governed by the pistol and the Bowie knife" if he was elected. On assuming office he took steps to sustain this promise, asking the legislature for drastic measures to combat the Klan. His demands bore fruit in three laws, passed in April and July 1870. The first appropriated a secret service fund of $50,000 to enable him to hire detectives, employ counsel, and otherwise bring terrorists to book. The second law provided for organizing a militia, and the third (resembling earlier statutes of Alabama and other states) outlawed the wearing of disguises in public and "prowling or traveling" in that attire.[8]

For a long time Democratic newspapers played their usual role, encouraging, ignoring, or rationalizing Klan activity. When they did admit that violence was taking place the admission was usually coupled with denials that any general organization was at work or that political motives were involved. By the spring of 1870 a number of papers were ready to denounce the violence. Said the Macon *Beacon,* located in one of the most Klan-ridden counties:

These midnight banditti are doing more to thwart the peace and prosperity of our country than a wise legislation of years can counteract. Our people should personally endeavor to remove these foul ulcers that now and then break out where bad blood exists, and apply remedies that will finally restore these diseased parts to healthy action. . . . It should be made disreputable to aid or countenance such outrages, and the very perpetrators will then pause and look back with horror on the deeds of darkness which they have blindly committed.[9]

Most Conservative papers were not so opposed to Ku Klux lawlessness as to support the governor's plans for ending it, however. The Jackson *Clarion,* perhaps the leading Democratic organ in the state, bitterly opposed Alcorn's secret service fund. It was based on the "slanderous assumption" that the people of Mississippi were remiss in keeping the peace. Actually, declared the *Clarion,* it was a political slush fund to feather the nests of deserving Radicals and a means by which they could hunt down their political foes.[10] No assessment of the measure or its author could have been more inappropriate.

Alcorn used the $50,000 at his disposal strictly for the purpose of enforcing the anti–Ku Klux law. He created a secret service department which, by fall, was employing about seven detectives. They went to counties that were plagued with disorders, conducted investigations, and sent back reports of their findings. By this means Alcorn obtained a list of Klansmen around the state, a copy of which he deposited in a Memphis bank vault with orders to publish if anything happened to him. Armed with this information, he communicated with leading members in an effort to get them to disband and held a stormy interview with one of them in Jackson. He offered rewards of up to $5,000 for evidence leading to the conviction of offenders. Yet almost nothing happened. If his threats brought about any Klan disbandments there is no record of it. There were few prosecutions under the new law, and no convictions. The violence actually increased.[11]

Even in Tennessee, where the Klan supposedly disbanded in 1869, it by no means disappeared. Night riding and outrages on Negroes continued to take place in the middle and western sections of the state. In December 1869 William Jones, an Obion County planter, gathered his Negro laborers into his own house for their mutual defense after repeated Klan attacks. When the marauders returned they were met by gunfire which killed one member and wounded others. Now the authorities finally acted by arresting Jones and several of the blacks. As they were being taken to jail the Ku Klux attacked the party and shot five of the blacks, two of them fatally. The others were rearrested and lodged in jail, while Jones fled to Nashville. That city and Memphis remained havens for Negro refugees from the Ku Klux, as in days gone by. Klansmen were subjected to no prosecution worthy of mention.[12]

The new Conservative legislature shared the general upper-class white revulsion at this violence and regarded it as senseless. One of the lawmakers' first actions was to repeal the Republican laws against the Klan, including Governor Brownlow's militia law, which were anathema to good Democrats. But in January 1870 they passed a new one of their own outlawing the activities of masked or disguised persons, even providing the death penalty in some cases. Governor Senter was not impressed. In a special message he pointed out that the major problem was to enforce the laws already in existence against murder, assault, and the like. When he asked for authority to use military force for this purpose the legislature lost most of its enthusiasm for law and order. The new statute was no better enforced than the others, and the governor called for additional federal troops. Many Republicans, including Brownlow, urged the remanding of Tennessee to federal control, like Georgia. Senter was not among these, but he did go to Washington in April 1870 and told Congress that the Klan was still powerful enough to require suppression by the federal government. The Conservative presiding officers of the state senate and house of representatives also went to Washington, hoping to head off Congressional legislation on the subject altogether.[13] Congress did pass its first "force bill" this spring, aimed at Southern terrorists, but the executive branch did almost nothing to enforce it for another year.

Meanwhile conditions deteriorated in parts of Tennessee as in other states. The worst area in the fall of 1870 consisted of half a dozen or more counties east and southeast of Nashville. In October the circuit judge charged the Putnam County grand jury to look into Klan activities and crack down on them. That night the Ku Klux paraded through town in open defiance of the court, and the next night a riot took place in which two Union men were beaten and driven from town. Lynchings and murders were reported from Manchester, Murfreesboro, and elsewhere. Governor Senter's efforts to invoke the Democrats' January Ku Klux law by offering rewards for the arrest of terrorists were unavailing. The worst of this activity took place before the fall election, but some of it continued afterward. In November, with the blessing and in some cases the active help of the Ku Klux Klan, Tennessee Democrats elected their candidate for governor under a new Conservative constitution. He was General John C. Brown of Pulaski, once a godfather of the Klan.[14]

The Tennessee Ku Klux had long since declared their independence of General Brown, and at least scattered outrages continued in 1871. In March a convention of blacks formally complained of continuing attacks on Negro schools, and the sheriff of Rutherford County was arrested by federal authorities for taking part in a Ku Klux raid.[15] Many Democrats continued to speak out against the Klan, and this gradually had its effect in reducing terrorism. Conservatives near Nashville formed a continuing posse to help the sheriff arrest Ku Klux, and they called on Democrats all over the state to do likewise.[16] Carroll County, west Tennessee, contributed in May what was apparently the first case in the state of a Klansman's being convicted of Ku Kluxing by a local jury.[17] In October a public meeting was held in Winchester following a Klan lynching of three Negroes. Conservative leader A. S. Colyar spoke, strongly condemning such crimes and warning that they could lead to drastic federal intervention. Following the meeting seventy-five men joined the sheriff as a posse and rode off after the maskers.[18] The Ku Klux threat, as a widespread phenomenon, pretty much disappeared in Tennessee by the end of 1871, although scattered outrages by masked men would take place for some years to come.

The marauding by disguised bands against Negroes and Unionists in Kentucky continued through 1869 and well beyond. The Bluegrass region and central Kentucky remained the most disorderly. In January, Klansmen—or so they frequently called themselves—paraded peacefully through Nicholasville while others kidnapped a stagecoach driver from his hotel in Harrodsburg. Still others invaded Georgetown one evening and, disregarding crowds of people, broke into the home of a Negro, shot him several times, and left. In March they whipped a man in Stanford and suffered a fatality in Jessamine County when a prospective victim fired back. In April they lynched a Negro in Garrard County. In June they attacked the home of a Union veteran in Lincoln County; finding him away, they whipped his wife and burned down the house. In July, Wayne County regulators were reportedly holding their own courts, supplanting the regular ones.[19]

Occasionally federal troops were sent to troubled places, with minimal effect. Far more unusual was the actual trial and conviction of two Webster County Klansmen in the federal court in Paducah late in March. They were sentenced to a year in prison and a fifty-dollar fine.[20] But whatever impact this may have had in Webster County, it hardly created a ripple elsewhere.

Many Democrats continued openly to defend or excuse the Klan. The Paris *Kentuckian* credited it with cleaning up the morals of Jessamine County, and the Stanford *Dispatch* justified its activity in Lincoln County.[21]

This attitude did not extend to the Democratic state administration of Governor John W. Stevenson. In August, after Marion County regulators took a man from his home near Lebanon and hanged him, three companies of Louisville militia were mobilized, sent to Lebanon, and distributed around the county. A fourth company was ordered to the village of Crab Orchard in Lincoln County, where federal soldiers had gone in June. The local newspapers in these counties opposed the militia campaign, but many Democrats joined Republicans in supporting it. After a few weeks the infantry companies in Marion County were returned to Louisville in favor of a company of cavalry, which remained until the middle of October. There was no suggestion of martial law; in fact the troops were specifically ordered to make arrests only in cooperation with the local authorities. They were under the same restraints, therefore, as federal troops. State adjutant general Frank Wolford, who was in over-all command, later claimed that the militia had had a very salutary effect. As far as Marion

County was concerned he was apparently correct, but no Klansmen were tried or convicted.[22]

Elsewhere the regulators went on as if the militia had no existence. Richmond and Madison County were the main scene of activity in late 1869 and early 1870. Negroes and white Unionists were whipped, shot, or hanged by armed gangs who sometimes numbered more than fifty. In February they committed two lynchings on successive nights, hanging a prisoner whom they took from the jail at Richmond on Friday and repeating the performance on Saturday at Winchester in adjoining Clark County. The first victim was left hanging with a $5 greenback attached for funeral expenses.[23] The terror embraced many counties, from above Lexington and Frankfort southward and eastward to the mountains. Angry Republicans in Booneville wrote President Grant to send a regiment of Negro troops, "and let them subsist off of those rich Rebel Ku Klux and hunt down and punish those midnight assassins. . . . "[24]

Republican anger was to be expected; more complicated was the ambivalent reaction of many Democrats who also disapproved the terrorism. Their inner conflict was best reflected, perhaps, in the coverage and editorials of the Louisville *Courier-Journal,* by far the most influential Democratic paper in the state. For many months the *Courier-Journal* carried occasional stories of violence by the regulators, with little or no editorial comment. Editor Henry Watterson had been a wartime aid to General Forrest and remained sympathetic to the goals of those Confederate officers who took over the Tennessee Klan in 1867. But as the terror dragged on, without any clear political purpose, he began in 1870 to criticize it with increasing vehemence. There was no connection, he said, between the real Ku Klux Klan, which had never existed outside Tennessee, and the bandits now infesting parts of Kentucky. Any tie between them and the Democratic party was a figment of Republican imaginations, working overtime to advance the interests of their party. Ex-Confederates and Democrats, claimed Watterson, were victims of these predators equally with Negroes and white Republicans. This opinion was demonstrably untrue, but the *Courier-Journal* stuck to it tenaciously. And so far as it was compatible with meaningful action to root out the terrorists, they had no more effective foe than this powerful newspaper. When John C. Breckinridge forcefully denounced them in March as idiots or villains—the denunciation which Ryland Randolph resented in Alabama—the *Courier-Journal* backed him. A month later, after describing three murders by regulators in Lincoln and Garrard counties, the paper demanded that the men responsible be hunted down and punished.[25]

Yet the terror continued. It was in 1870 that the Fifteenth Amendment brought Negro suffrage to Kentucky. Its first test was local elections throughout the state on August 1, followed by the Congressional elections in November. As early as May, disguised men began visiting Negro homes just a few miles from Frankfort, the state capital, threatening the occupants with death if they voted in the August elections.[26] But they were also out to seize guns, and in general the nature of Klan activity changed very little. On August 1 Democrats prevented some Negroes from voting by various means, but in most places the Republican vote went up in rough proportion to the size of the local Negro population. In some places this brought Republicans into office for the first time, although the state as a whole remained Democratic.[27]

Both the federal and the state governments tried to combat the terrorism, although the efforts of neither can be described as massive. General Eli H. Murray, the United States marshal in Louisville, sent deputies with soldiers to a number of counties to arrest Klansmen and moonshiners. (As in other states, the two were sometimes identical.) This duty was often as hazardous for the hunters as the hunted, but a number of arrests were made under the new Enforcement Act. Klansmen around Harrodsburg threatened to hang the United States commissioner and other Republicans if they made any effort to prosecute Democrats who took part in an election day riot there. In general the arrests around the state seem not to have led far.[28]

State action was no more effective. In August, after Negroes had apparently committed systematic arson in a rural area near Frankfort and Ku Klux depredations were widespread, Governor Stevenson issued a proclamation offering rewards for the apprehension of the culprits.[29] Some sixteen militia companies were organized in 1870, as compared with only six prior to that time. On several occasions these were briefly called into service, but still under the same restrictions and with about the same results as federal troops throughout the South. When a Ku Klux band invaded the town of Versailles one night in August and killed two Negroes, there was fear that a general riot might ensue. Two or three militia companies sped to the scene and perhaps were instrumental in keeping the peace. The company at Frankfort was called out several times to cope with actual and potential disorders in and around the city. The militia accomplished nothing in catching or suppressing the Ku Klux, however, and after his previous experience Adjutant General Wolford advised the governor not to use them again generally for that purpose. But he left standing orders for militia commanders to proceed on their own initiative against lawless bands who appeared in or near their localities. Wolford never suggested martial law as a remedy, and he doubtless knew it would not have been adopted if he had. Apart from raising the possibility of a permanent state police force, he left it to the legislature to devise a solution. Governor Stevenson did the same.[30]

If the raiding fell off in one place it picked up in another. By fall rural Franklin County, around Frankfort, was as hard hit as any place. Negroes were the targets, and a number of them moved into town for safety. The Republican vote in the rural precincts fell off in November.[31] Generally the November elections went as those in August had, and most of the night riding was not specifically geared to the campaign. Late in September a disguised band rode into the town of Lancaster and abducted a Republican named Hicks from his home. Some of Hicks's friends gathered and went off in pursuit, overtaking them a mile from town. They fired on the masked men, who promptly scattered, leaving Hicks and some of their horses behind. Democrats later tried to make it appear that the Radicals themselves had captured Hicks in order to alarm the Negroes against the Klan and keep them in the Republican fold.[32]

Such propaganda was not uncommon. The Richmond *Register* blamed recent outrages in that long-troubled vicinity on the Republicans, who supposedly attacked one another for political profit.[33] The Lexington *Gazette,* obviously out of touch with the local paper, reported one of these same outrages—the murder of a Negro preacher named Williams—as a bona fide Ku Klux act, and therefore probably justifiable: "We have not heard the reasons for the lawless act, but if Williams was not a bad character it is the first instance when the Ku Klux were mistaken."[34]

It would take a head count to verify or refute the *Courier-Journal's* contention that most Kentucky Democrats did not wink at the Ku Klux and regard them as allies. That paper was not alone, but it faced plenty of intramural hostility when it assailed the Klan. Its attacks were often indistinguishable in fervor from those in the Republican press: "This thing of serving notices of exile upon Kentuckians at will, and hanging or shooting, at midnight and in their own door-yards, men who stand convicted of no crime, is a burning disgrace to the State, a positive injury to every interest cherished by her people." If the state government cannot control the evil, editor Watterson continued in November, public opinion should be mobilized against it. The longer this is put off, the harder it will be. The next day the paper applauded an announcement—which proved to be exaggerated—that the federal government was going to crack down militarily on the Kentucky Ku Klux.[35]

At this point Watterson drew back. Only two days later he accused Republicans of sending for more troops to serve their own partisan ends. The Klan was not an agency of the Democratic party, he said, despite Republican accusations to the contrary. Ordinarily all persons should welcome the arrival of soldiers to restore order, but the Radicals were using them to feather their own nest. By December 9 the paper deplored the sending of troops and declared that the state could handle the problem itself. In fact the *Courier-Journal* had got too far ahead of Democratic opinion and had to retreat before it lost its party standing. So it was with many Southern Democrats, who found the inner resources to protest the terrorism but dared not embrace the forceful measures necessary to end it. The connection between the Klan and the party was closer than they may have realized at first, or would ever admit.[36]

Part V

THE CULMINATION OF
THE KU KLUX TERROR, 1871

CHAPTER 18

Mississippi: The Campaign Against Schools

Klan activity in Mississippi, which had increased during 1870, reached its climax in the spring of 1871. Violence then fell off sharply when federal arrests began in June. Virtually all of this activity was still limited to a row of counties one or two deep, extending down the Alabama border as far as Meridian.

Much of the terror was politically inspired. In Tippah County, Klansmen lined up seventy Negroes employed on one plantation and announced that if they heard of anyone voting the Republican ticket they would "lick the last one of them." Politically active or prominent Negroes were singled out for special attention as usual. Several such persons in Monroe County were whipped until they promised to vote the Democratic ticket. Jack Dupree, the president of a Negro Republican club there, was beaten severely, then taken to a wood several miles away, beaten again, and disemboweled. Several active Negro Republicans were murdered in Alcorn and Noxubee counties. A few white Republicans were also beaten, and one, a magistrate in Noxubee County, was killed by persons firing through the window of his house. Mayor Lacey of Aberdeen was driven away by a Klansman who told him in the guise of friendship that the Ku Klux were out to kill him.[1]

Nearly all of this took place many months before the state election was held in November. Klansmen were threatening to take an active part in the fall campaign, but by the time it got under way some of them had been

287

arrested and most were lying low. Night riding and other acts of intimidation took place on only a small scale that fall and played very little part in the campaign.[2]

The Klan was also a device for controlling and exploiting Negro labor in various ways. In Noxubee County it voted to whip all the blacks on one plantation for laziness or improper work. In Lowndes County it beat a man for not keeping stove wood in the kitchen; his employer was in the attacking party. Freedmen were also beaten for moving from one employer to another without getting the former's permission. In Tippah County the marauders wanted to drive Negroes from better lands so as to settle there themselves. In nearby Alcorn County they tried to drive away Negro laborers on the Gulf and Ohio Railroad, probably for a similiar reason. Economically as well as politically, the black man who showed the greatest initiative and independence was the most liable to suffer attack. In Noxubee and Winston counties there was a concerted effort by the Klan to drive off or despoil Negroes who owned or even rented the land they worked, and a white man who sold land to Negroes was threatened with death. Some of this activity was undertaken by whites who had an immediate interest in the outcome, but just as often it sprang from the general conviction that Negroes had no more right to economic independence than any other kind, and white men had a God-given right to enjoy the fruits of Negro labor. Most blacks submitted to these efforts to perpetuate slavery; a few fought back, but the most common course of resistance was simply to move away. An emigration meeting was held in Aberdeen, and many blacks departed singly or in groups for Louisiana and elsewhere to escape the terror. One effect of Klan activity, therefore, was to create a severe labor shortage in much of the area.[3]

Most Ku Klux depredations were designed to punish legal or social infractions by the freedmen. Any Negro accused of killing or raping a white person was almost sure to be lynched, sometimes before he could be got to jail. These offenses were exceedingly rare—far more Negroes were killed or raped by whites than vice versa, and with little or no punishment—but when they did occur whites rose up in righteous indignation and the Klan imposed exemplary punishment for the good of society. Disguised parties lynched Negroes in Tishomingo, Winston, Lowndes, and Oktibbeha counties, in the last two cases taking the victims from law officers on their way to jail. Whippings for lesser offenses became so common as to excite little notice. Blacks were taken out and beaten for being too outspoken, for thievery, or for contesting their rights. One was whipped for failing to raise his hat, another for having sued a white man. But having arrogated to itself the power of chastising black men, and receiving public acquiescence if not favor as a result, the Klan proceeded to regulate white men's lives too.

Prominent and respected Conservatives were immune from vigilante attack no matter what they did (as were the few Democratic Negroes), but poorer and more insignificant whites were visited without much regard to political leaning. Thus a white man in Noxubee was briefly hung by the neck two or three times to extort a confession of theft; one in Lowndes was run off for alleged improprieties with a step-aunt; another was driven away as the result of a land dispute; and a third was warned to stop posting religious and Masonic tracts by the roadside. Northern Methodist preachers were driven away as they were in Alabama.[4]

It was not always possible to distinguish between Klan operations and those of the community at large. A case in point was that of a Northern Methodist minister at Starkville, named McLachlan. A Scotsman by birth, and educated at Oberlin, he preached to the Negroes in Starkville and taught a Negro school before the state education system came into being. At one point in 1870 McLachlan received a Ku Klux notice to leave, but the white community, to its credit, called a public meeting which endorsed his activity and condemned the effort to drive him away. Later McLachlan organized a cooperative store; the freedmen were stockholders and paid him to manage it. The store proved to be successful, which may have occasioned some jealousy in the community. But it was also alleged then or later that he accepted stolen cotton at the store; no evidence was brought forth to support this accusation, and it may have been fabricated. McLachlan was not molested until the Ku Klux movement reached its peak in the spring of 1871.

A Negro had shot and killed one of the Klansmen who were riding and whipping through his neighborhood. He in turn was arrested for murder, and as law officers were taking him in to jail they were ambushed and the black man killed. One evening at this time white townspeople were alarmed to see a number of armed Negroes going into McLachlan's store; the old fears of a Negro insurrection arose again. Actually the stockholders customarily met there on this night every week, and during the current terror some carried guns. When they left awhile later and scattered to their homes in the country, some whites, assuming that they must be going to recruit more men for the insurrection, organized a patrol. The next morning they searched the store and found seven guns, only four of them usable. They tried to arrest McLachlan, but the mayor had no charge to prefer against him and ordered him released. Rumors of an insurrection continued to multiply all that day. Sheriff Homer C. Powers organized some of the soberer men to stand guard that night. They stationed themselves in the outskirts and turned back crowds of armed whites who came to help repel the Negroes.

While they were at the edge of town a dozen disguised men marched up to McLachlan's store in military order. The sheriff's men rushed back and stopped them from breaking in the door. The attackers warned McLachlan that they would return next night. A large delegation of citizens waited upon McLachlan in the morning. The town was in a turmoil, they said, because of him. For his own good he should leave the county. Sheriff Powers refused to be a party to this transaction but agreed to give him safe conduct if he decided to go. Hearing rumors of more violent plans and fearing that the sheriff himself was part of a general conspiracy against him, McLachlan slipped away quietly with the help of some Negro friends. The blacks were permitted to carry on their store, but at least one was driven away by the Ku Klux. McLachlan returned to Starkville some weeks later with a United States marshal to make arrests. The sheriff cooperated and later testified for the prosecution. Colonel H. L. Muldrow, the organizer and leader of the local Klan, served as defense attorney, but the cases never came to trial. McLachlan left, and many years later Klansmen recalled with pride how they had rid their county of the infamous carpet-bagger.[5]

Of much greater proportions was the Meridian riot of March 1871. Winning national attention, it contributed importantly to the belated actions of Congress that spring against Southern violence. The riot was the culmination of several weeks' racial and political strife. Many Negroes had fled to Meridian from the terrorism in Klan-ridden Sumter and Greene counties, Alabama, only a few miles to the east, where riots had occurred the previous August with the Democrats' forcible capture of the counties in November. Among the refugees was Daniel Price, the white Republican leader at Livingston, Alabama, who left there in August to teach a Negro school in Meridian. Price associated primarily with blacks as he had before, and again became a trusted leader and spokesman. Something of a Black Belt prototype of the Northern big-city machine politician, he found jobs in and around Meridian for many of the Negro refugees who followed him.

White Alabamians found that their terrorism had created a labor shortage, and they made great efforts to draw the refugees back. Before the year was out, Negroes near Meridan were organizing militarily to fight off predatory white gangs who crossed the state line to kidnap them. Several times in January or February 1871 Adam Kennard, a Negro Union Leaguer-turned-Democrat, came over as a Sumter County deputy sheriff to arrest and return certain Negro refugees, on criminal charges or, as in most cases, on charges of violating labor contracts by running away. At least once Kennard was accompanied by armed whites who forcibly captured and wounded a man they were seeking. They had no legal authority in Mississippi, but never bothered with the formalities of extradition; in effect they were kidnappers.

On one of Kennard's February trips, when he stayed overnight in Meridian, his lodging house was attacked by about a dozen disguised men who took him out and beat him, Ku Klux fashion. Kennard said later they were Negroes except for Daniel Price, whom he identified specifically. Price bitterly denied the accusation, but white Conservatives were quick to seize the opening and had Price arrested under Mississippi's anti-Ku Klux law of 1870. On the day set for the preliminary hearing Kennard reappeared with a dozen or more white armed Alabamians, calling for Price's blood. The Negroes referred to these men as Ku Klux, which they likely were; and even respectable Meridian Conservatives regarded them as desperadoes. Price's hearing was postponed to avoid a possible riot, but the men accidentally found three Negro refugees, captured and beat them, and sent them back to Alabama on the first train. Other trips to Meridian were made for this same purpose; the marauders generally came on the 11 P.M. train and returned on another at about 3 in the morning. Some were men known as activists in the Sumter County terror of a few months before. One Republican said they were supported by only a handful of embittered Democrats whom the process of Reconstruction had displaced from power. Respectable Meridians of both parties condemned these invasions but did little or nothing to stop them.

Price's hearing was again deferred amid reports that he had threatened to call on the black community for armed assistance if held for trial. It was his contention that he had been framed and was unlikely to receive a fair trial. Many agreed with him. In fear that a racial confrontation was imminent, Republican Mayor William Sturgis secured a squad of soldiers from Governor Alcorn, but they left after only a few days. The sheriff, city marshal, and certain other prominent men of both parties urged Price to leave for the sake of peace and his own safety, and he finally did, fleeing Meridian just as he had fled Livingston earlier. Mayor Sturgis and many black men were angry at his failure to stand firm, and Sturgis instituted proceedings against a number of prominent Meridians, charging that they had invited the Alabamians over to provoke a riot. Sturgis, a Northerner, was already unpopular with Conservatives, and they now bent every effort to drive him away too. This partisan movement was part of a statewide Conservative drive to force the resignation of local Republican office-holders—municipal elections had never been held, and these officials were still serving by appointment of Governor Alcorn or his predecessors. There were no valid charges against Sturgis personally or his conduct in office, but even some fellow Republicans urged him to resign for the sake of harmony. When he refused to do so, they asked the governor to remove him. Sturgis sent a delegation of Negro leaders to Alcorn to counter this move and to complain of the continuing raids from Alabama.

The delegation, led by William Dennis and Warren Tyler, a teacher with Price in the local Negro school, got no satisfaction from Governor Alcorn; his policy had been conciliation with the Conservatives. They called a public meeting on March 4 to report their failure. Without the governor's protection, Dennis, Tyler, and Negro legislator Aaron Moore told the predominantly Negro gathering, the black men had no alternative but armed resistance to the raiders, accepting whatever help they could get from the white community. The blacks paraded through the streets with fife and drum to demonstrate their determination to resist white terrorism. Conservatives saw this as a form of black terrorism directed against them, a prelude to Negro insurrection. That evening a fire broke out near a store operated by Mayor Sturgis and his brother. Each race believed it was started by the other as an act of provocation. Armed Negroes from the surrounding countryside began to arrive in town in the belief that the long-expected racial confrontation had begun. If the whites wanted war, they said, let it come. Whites also mobilized, and there were many scattered acts of violence, including an attempt on Dennis's life, but instead of killing him white leaders jailed him for making incendiary speeches. As so often before, the Negroes backed down and no general battle took place. This happened on Saturday night; by Monday morning Tyler and Moore were in jail on similar charges.

Also on Monday, the whites held a public meeting of their own. It was a cardinal doctrine that blacks never asserted themselves in this fashion without instigation by agitators, especially white men, who exploited their ignorance and emotionalism, and with Price gone and the three leading Negroes in jail, Mayor Sturgis was regarded as the chief remaining threat to the peace of the community. The public meeting was, in effect, part of a white *coup d'état,* aimed at seizing control of the city. Resolutions demanded the removal of Sturgis and other Republicans from office; the mayor would have a specified number of hours to leave town. They called for the appointment of new officials to disarm the blacks and break up their organizations and appointed a committee of public safety to take over the policing of the county under nominal command of the sheriff. The men from Alabama had been secretly called upon to help, and scores came by train to finish the work they had begun several weeks earlier. Some of these men were professional rioters by now, veterans of Belmont, Livingston, Eutaw, and other engagements in both Alabama and Mississippi.

During the afternoon of March 6, a preliminary hearing was held for Dennis, Tyler, and Moore. The courtroom was filled with armed men, determined to see that these troublemakers got their due. When Tyler at one point proposed to call for witnesses to impeach the testimony of a white man, James Brantley, the latter advanced on him with an upraised stick.

Suddenly a shot rang out and the courtroom instantly became a pandemonium. Judge Bramlette, the presiding officer, and two Negro spectators were killed in the melee; others, including Tyler, were wounded. Friends tried to hide Tyler in a nearby store, but armed men (many of them Alabamians) went in search of him, discovered his hiding place, and riddled him with bullets. Dennis also was wounded, captured, and taken supposedly in protective custody. That night his guard conveniently withdrew, permitting an armed party to come in and cut his throat. Democrats later claimed that Tyler had fired the first shot, perhaps at Brantley but probably at Judge Bramlette himself; Republicans dismissed the charge as absurd.

The white mob, organized into companies or posses under the nominal control of the sheriff, took over the town, searching from house to house for leaders of the black community and confiscating weapons. The blacks, demoralized and outgunned, hid in anticipation of a general onslaught. Three more were arrested, jailed, and lynched before the night was out. Mayor Sturgis fled the city amid reports that they were coming after him. The search then centered on Aaron Moore, who had escaped being killed by playing possum in the courtroom. During the night organized white parties, using preconcerted whistle signals, searched his home and burned it along with a Negro church nearby. (Presumably they were Alabamians, for they seem to have mistaken this church for another in which Moore had preached and Negro political meetings had customarily been held.) Some whites commandeered a train, taking it fifty miles toward Jackson in hopes of capturing Moore, but he reached Jackson and safety after making his way through the woods and swamps on foot. Other Negroes were shot down and mutilated during the several days' hunt. Eastbound trains carried crowds of armed white men out of Meridian on Tuesday morning, depositing them at stations as far away as Eutaw, Alabama.

Whites had accomplished their major objective by cowing the Negro population and destroying its leadership. Six men only were later bound over for trial on charges of unlawful assembly, intent to kill, and assault, but when the grand jury met in April it refused to indict them. One Alabamian was later convicted of raping a Negro woman during the riot. The state legislature investigated the affair, but it was powerless to do more than publish its findings. The Congressional Ku Klux investigating committee also looked into the riot quite minutely with the same result.[6]

If the Mississippi Klans won any distinction for novelty it resulted from their crusade against public schools. Democratic leaders had verbally opposed the school system from its inception, and the farmers, especially in the eastern counties, carried their strictures into action, using the Klan as their vehicle. Even some white schools suffered in this "taxpayers' protest" against the newfangled ideas and costs of Radical Reconstruction, but

Negro education was the primary target. If it was a matter of debate whether hard-pressed white farmers should have to pay taxes to send their own and their white neighbors' children to school, it was outrageous to pay school taxes for black cottonpickers.

The school system, like most other Radical innovations, had come later to Mississippi because of her delay in reorganization and readmission. Established in 1870, its tangible results in the form of buildings, personnel, and higher taxes became visible only late that year and in 1871. By the standards of any other time and place the cost of this rudimentary program would have been thought insignificant. In fact many or most of the school buildings in use had been constructed by Negroes themselves at private expense or were churches being used for that purpose. These were burned or torn down in large numbers, and an even greater number of teachers of both races and parties were called upon by bands of disguised nocturnal visitors. Some received warnings to stop teaching, others were whipped or driven away or both, and a few were killed. In Winston County, where eleven schools were broken up in 1871, not one Negro school was left in operation. In Monroe County twenty-six were closed and A. P. Huggins, the county superintendent, was whipped by the Klan. His testimony and that of Miss Sarah E. Allen, an Illinoisan who had been sent down to teach by the American Missionary Association, were two of the highlights in the Congressional Ku Klux hearings of 1871 concerning Mississippi. (An Army lieutenant reportedly took Huggins' blood-stained nightshirt to Washington and presented it to Ben Butler, the Massachusetts Congressman. When Butler used the garment to illustrate a Congressional speech on Southern outrages, the memorable phrase "waving the bloody shirt" came into usage.)[7] A teacher in Aberdeen, who was also a member of the county school board, was required to close his school and have nothing more to do with the board; but they offered to help him collect tuition money if he reopened it as a private school. The same distinction between public and private schools was made in other counties. Most of these actions occurred in the spring and ultimately failed. White public opinion turned against them by the end of the year and came to support the growing school system, for both races. In fact, most of the funds for public schools came from a head tax which Negroes paid along with whites.[8]

Some teachers refused to heed Ku Klux warnings and went ahead with their schools, occasionally to be dealt with more severely a second time. An extraordinary case of opposition was provided by Robert W. Flournoy, the superintendent in Pontotoc County. Flournoy was himself one of the most improbable types to be found in the Reconstruction South. The offspring of an aristocratic and impeccably Conservative Georgia family, he had moved to Mississippi in 1856. After opposing secession he raised a company of men for the Confederacy and took it to Virginia. He then resigned because of Unionist feelings and returned home for the duration. With the advent of Radical Reconstruction he joined the Republican party and began editing a newspaper at Pontotoc called the *Equal Rights*. It was perhaps the most radical paper in the state in its advocacy of what the name proclaimed. His own personal preference was for integrated schools, Flournoy admitted to the Congressional investigating committee, but such views were rare and he had not insisted on them. As county superintendent he established fifty-two white and twelve Negro schools (whites were in a large majority there) by May 1871. In hiring teachers he paid no attention to party affiliation, but when the subject was later raised he checked and found that only eleven of sixty-four were Republicans.

Soon after the schools began in Pontotoc, teachers reported that the Klan had been around; some complied with its warnings. Flournoy had not deigned to notice earlier Klan attacks upon Negroes, but he now wrote a series of articles in his paper attacking this campaign against the schools. The Ku Klux came after him on the night of May 12. Flournoy was awakened after midnight by two friends who had overheard the Klansmen asking directions to his house. As they rode through the streets they made a peculiar whistling noise, occasionally mentioned by witnesses in other states as well. Flournoy dressed hastily and hurried to round up friends. About eight came out, including Judge Austin Pollard and a deputy sheriff, and they encountered the Ku Klux on the street. Pollard advanced alone and unarmed toward the Klansmen, who numbered about thirty, and demanded that they surrender. They declined and one fired a shot. Flournoy and the others now opened fire until the Ku Klux turned and fled. A wounded Klansman was found lying on the ground; he died about two hours later, after admitting that they had come to kill Flournoy.

The Pontotoc County Klan regarded this as a lost battle, not the end of the war. The men who had come to Flournoy's help continued to patrol the streets at night, but the Klan never returned. These patrollers (most of them Democrats) soon discovered that they were the objects of widespread public disapproval. Most of the white power structure sympathized with the Klan, and a local Democratic newspaper tried to pass off the invaders as a group of young masqueraders out for amusement. The author repudiated this article a few days later, however, saying that he had written it merely to allay the excitement of the rowdy element in town. A public meeting a week after the incident condemned lawlessness, but this had become almost a ritual procedure to forestall official retribution. In November the county elected as sheriff the Grand Cyclops of the local Klan, named Tom Saddler, who had led the ill-fated raid on Flournoy. A public subscription was raised to erect a monument over the grave of the man who had died in town.[9]

Klan membership in Mississippi—as across the South—was broadly based economically and socially. Witnesses from some counties identified the members with the poorer white class; those from other counties said they were largely the sons of middling and well-to-do planters. Most of those later indicted in the federal district court were between eighteen and thirty-five years old, with a high proportion of unmarried men. Two-thirds, according to a grand jury member, were relatively well off by the standards of the time and place.

There was an interesting distribution of Klan activity within the Ku Klux counties. Persons from several counties, both pro- and anti-Klan, indicated that the Ku Klux were most numerous and most lethal in the poorer sections, where Negroes were comparatively less numerous. Elsewhere in these counties the Klan may have existed but it was less active. Older and more prominent men gave it essential support, whether or not they were members, even through the period of bloodiest excesses; if they had any misgivings they seldom expressed them publicly.[10]

Leadership within the organization more clearly belonged to the professional and planter class which had governed the region before the Radicals displaced them politically, but their economic and social power was hardly affected. The old ruling class undoubtedly divided over the Klan here as elsewhere. Many "first citizens" privately condemned the organization and its excesses by 1871, but others continued to hold positions of leadership. General Samuel J. Gholson, for instance, was almost universally identified in 1871 as the Klan's chieftain in Monroe County and perhaps beyond it. A federal judge for many years before the war and speaker of the assembly in 1865, he consistently ignored, excused, or defended Klan activities as the case demanded, and he served as defense counsel for local Klansmen in federal court. The similar case of Colonel H. L. Muldrow in Oktibbeha County has already been mentioned. It is likely that Klan membership and leadership helped launch a number of political careers in the Democratic party. This was probably true of the new sheriff of Pontotoc and also the sheriff of Alcorn County, who was strongly suspected of Klansmanship.[11]

Monroe County claims the rare distinction of having Negro Ku Klux— not initiated members, to be sure, but hangers-on who participated in raids. Apparently there were five such men; three were forced to go along against their wills (two of them later turning state's evidence against their captors), and two were Democratic Negroes who went voluntarily.[12] When victims identified some of their attackers as black men it gave Conservative newspapers like the Aberdeen *Examiner* an opportunity to brand the whole

Ku Klux movement there as a Negro affair. Nevertheless, they continued to defend the Klan and opposed all efforts to suppress it.[13]

Despite its increasing violence, or perhaps because of it, there was greater newspaper support for Klan activity in the spring of 1871 than ever before. The Aberdeen *Examiner* declared in March, at the height of the terror: "Notwithstanding the commission of some deeds that cannot be generally commended, we believe that they have done much to improve the morals and conditions of the county. We are forced to confess our belief that the good people of the county, of both races, are all the better off for the frequent rides of these mysterious troopers."[14] The Columbus *Index* had such respect for Ku Klux prowess that it could hardly credit the account it received of the Flournoy raid in Pontotoc.

Flournoy was not captured. For the Ku Klux this was a very badly managed affair, and there is something so at variance with the usual daring and success of the mysterious brotherhood, that we cannot but receive the account with some grains of allowance. We are opposed to lawlessness, but we could have heard of the hanging of this ungodly wretch with a very great degree of fortitude, consoling ourselves with the conviction that "his loss was Mississippi's gain."[15]

The Jackson *Clarion* had implicitly sanctioned Klan intimidation of Negro voters before the election of June 1868. After that date it maintained almost absolute silence on the subject. Any reader who relied wholly on that paper for information had no idea that outrages were occurring in Mississippi. Only when these could be pinned on Negroes or Republicans was the matter ever broached or the name Ku Klux Klan employed. It must have come as a surprise to *Clarion* readers in March 1871 to learn belatedly that combinations of armed men were possibly committing acts of violence in the eastern counties. The paper made this concession while seconding the stalwart efforts of Governor Alcorn to prevent more federal troops from being sent to the state. If any violent or extralegal measures had been resorted to, the *Clarion* explained, it was purely a defense against the corrupt, incompetent, and vicious government Mississippians had been subjected to. Now that the governor promised to reform these abuses to stave off another army of occupation it behooved all Mississippians to give him a fair chance. For this reason the paper appealed to the alleged terrorists to stop. It denied any knowledge of "Ku Klux combinations," however. "If they really exist we could not recommend their disbandment so long as the Loyal League conspiracies whose operations they must have been designed to circumvent, are in full blast." (The Loyal League had all but disappeared by this time.) Once having admitted the possibility of a

Ku Klux organization in Mississippi, the *Clarion* henceforth was a little freer in referring to it. After only a week it knew enough of the order to compare its members with William Tell in their opposition to tyranny.[16]

The *Clarion's* appeal for a suspension of violence had little immediate effect on the workaday Klansmen in the field. But so far as outward manifestations could serve as a measure of public opinion, it gradually mobilized against violence as one outrage followed another in April and May. Public meetings were held to condemn them, or at least to call for a stop.[17] It was never very clear whether these expressions reflected genuine revulsion at the violence or a desire to stem the flight of Negro labor or, as with the *Clarion*, an effort to forestall federal action. At any rate the most effective force in ending the terror was the reality of federal arrests in June and July.

There is evidence that considerable reorganization took place, or at least was attempted, in the Mississippi Klans in 1871; it may have begun earlier. The movement was well under way when E. P. Jacobson, a United States district attorney, reported it to Washington early in August. A new Democratic secret society was forming in the state, he said, "which must resemble in its purposes somewhat the 'Ku Klux' organization as originally instituted. Its purposes are political and do not embrace any violation of the letter of the law. . . . It is intended through this organization, to form a 'white man's party,' with an eventual prospect of a 'white man's government.' "[18] The reorganization extended to at least eight eastern counties, probably more. It took different names and forms, with at least four new societies organized in that region.

The most widespread took the anomalous title of the Robinson Club, or the Jack Robinsons. Henry Clark, a federal detective in northern Mississippi, testified in November 1871 that the Robinson Club (he called it the Robertson Family) had recently been formed to carry the state election that month. The order, numbering 1,200 to 1,500 members, he said, originated in Pontotoc County and was headed by the new sheriff there, Tom Saddler, whose Ku Klux antecedents were well known. According to Clark and others, the order had spread into Tippah, Chickasaw, and Monroe counties. Two Monroe County historians wrote that the Robinsons existed alongside the Ku Klux Klan there, one saying it was affiliated with the Klan and the other mentioning a third organization called the Johnsons. Clark reported that the "Robertsons" in Pontotoc had forced nearly all the merchants there to join, threatening a boycott otherwise. He knew of no night riding, nor is there clear evidence from other counties on this point. Outsiders found it difficult to distinguish between the various secret societies, but it is likely that the newer ones arose from a desire to achieve political results with less bloodshed—as Jacobson said, to restore their original idea of the Ku Klux Klan.[19]

Other groups formed or in existence in 1871 were the White Rose society in Noxubee County, the Native Sons of the South in Noxubee and Lowndes, and the Seventy-Six society in Lowndes, Monroe, and Kemper. The White Rose was an earlier group of regulators which may have predated the Klan but existed for a time alongside it.[20] The Native Sons of the South was organized in Lowndes County in the summer or fall of 1871 with a direct eye to the coming election. It was in fact a negative copy of the Union League; both races were admitted, and it advocated, on paper at least, protection of the rights of all men without regard to race or color. Membership, oaths, and rituals were supposedly secret, but members wore distinctive caps and badges at public functions. The organization was clearly in behalf of the Democratic party, without saying so; members pledged themselves on oath to support only native Southerners for office. "You all know what it was," a member admitted to the Congressional investigating committee; "we wanted to vote the freedmen; we were honest in it." By election time the order had several hundred members in Lowndes County and also extended into Noxubee. It seems to have had little effect on the election and disappeared afterward.[21] Less is known of the Seventy-Six society. It was also a secret political organization in behalf of the Democratic party, apparently with an exclusively white clientele. Formed in 1871, it had an estimated 300 members in November in Monroe County, where it existed alongside the Ku Klux, the Robinsons, and the Johnsons.[22] None of these orders (with the possible exception of the Robinsons) appears to have amounted to much, nor do they seem to have outlasted the Ku Klux movement in 1871 or 1872.

Governor Alcorn had spent the latter part of 1870 in futile attempts to prosecute Ku Klux terrorists under the state law passed that summer. Early the next year he pressed for further legislation: a law raising the maximum rewards he could offer to $25,000; another taxing bowie knives and pistols and prohibiting the carrying of concealed weapons; a third permitting the removal of trials to other counties; and authorization to raise a regiment of cavalry. He removed some sheriffs whom he regarded as derelict in their duty and threatened to activate the militia in disordered counties.

But by this time Alcorn's policies had become enmeshed in intraparty factionalism and he lost the support of the legislature. Like Smith in Alabama he was a Republican moderate who had attempted from the beginning to conciliate the Conservatives in order to avoid the deathly racial and partisan hatred that had marred the progress of Reconstruction in nearly every state. He had appointed moderate Democrats to office in many counties, and within his own party had favored fellow white moderates over Negroes and their Radical allies. The tactic failed on almost every count, for Democrats refused to be placated and a majority of Republicans came to regard him as a trimmer if not a traitor to the ideals of the new era. Alcorn had been more active and had shown greater ingenuity in pursuing the Ku Klux than Smith had evidenced in Alabama, but he encountered even greater difficulty within his own party.

The state senate passed his change of venue bill in March 1871, but the lower house rejected it. Moreover, the legislature refused to renew the secret service fund of 1870 and he had to stop employing detectives. Alcorn's measures were blocked by an unlikely coalition of Democrats and Radical Republicans. The former disapproved his activities as a matter of course, and the latter, despairing of any effective state action to suppress the Ku Klux terror, turned their hopes and pleas to Washington.

The Radical leader in this controversy was General Adelbert Ames. A career officer from Maine who came to Mississippi with the Army, Ames was appointed military governor in July 1868, when the sitting Conservative governor was removed from office. Until Alcorn and the new civil administration superseded him early in 1870, Ames acted vigorously and with fair success in checking Ku Klux activity; at least so it seemed in retrospect as the terror mounted in 1870 and 1871. Ames never felt at home in Mississippi, but he was thoroughly committed to the Reconstruction experiment and particularly the advancement of the state's black majority. He won and deserved their confidence, and this brought him a seat in the United States Senate when Mississippi was readmitted to the Union. Like Governor Smith's Republican critics in Alabama, Ames and his followers were probably as angered by Alcorn's public posture and rhetoric as by his specific failings in controlling terrorism. The governor's determination not to offend Mississippi Conservatives led him to minimize the extent of disorders just as they did. When Radicals pointed to the growing terror and the state's inability to control it, Alcorn belied the obvious facts and even the reports of his own secret service department in denying the existence of organized Ku Klux activity. The violence was comparatively insignificant, he insisted; it was confined to a small portion of the state, and well within its power to control. When Radicals demanded federal intervention he did everything he could to prevent it, for fear of antagonizing the white population further. Meanwhile Republicans continued to be flayed and murdered in the eastern counties. The Radicals' refusal to enact Alcorn's recommendations, which were desirable if not very likely to prove effective, was a minor blunder, for it enabled the governor to blame them for his inability to restore order. This dispute dragged on for many months, even after the federal Ku Klux Act in April and Alcorn's departure from the governorship in November had rendered it obsolete. A cardinal test of Radical orthodoxy—in Mississippi as elsewhere—was one's readiness to recognize Democratic terrorism and to suppress it by every possible means.[23]

Alabama, Florida, and Kentucky

Many Alabama Democrats had promised that outrages would fall off if they won the state elections in November 1870. Within limits this happened, but armed and disguised bands continued to traverse much of the state in 1871. The western counties, adjoining the lawless part of Mississippi, were the worst afflicted. The white toughs of Sumter and Greene counties, who repeatedly invaded Meridian, Mississippi, and its environs during the spring, continued to make occasional forays against local Negroes. In Sumter, Zeke High, a black man, was lynched in September after spending almost a year in jail for killing a marauder who had invaded his home during the 1870 riots.[1]

In Choctaw County, just to the south, outrages against the black population broke out for the first time on a significant scale late in 1870 and continued into 1872. Several Negroes were murdered, many were whipped, and some of their churches and schools were burned. Robert Fullerlove, a locally prominent Negro who had acquired 400 acres of land, was coerced into signing a card pledging to support the Democratic party. Although he was promised immunity from further Ku Klux attacks for doing so, the marauders kept coming, and he and his family slept out in the woods almost every night from April to October. In the latter month, having received a subpoena to appear before the Congressional investigating subcommittee in Livingston, he claimed to have been beaten by two white men while going there to testify. With many other blacks in this county, he considered moving to Kansas to escape the terror.[2]

Similarly in Pickens County, just north of Sumter and Greene, Klan violence reached a new height just after the fall election of 1870. A number of Negroes were taken out and whipped for voting the Radical ticket in defiance of prior warnings. Ordered to leave the county by Christmas, they crossed into Mississippi, where local blacks were talking of flight to Louisiana and points still farther west. White Republicans in Pickens were also whipped and driven away.[3]

In Greene and Sumter, the heartland of Klan activity in western Alabama, the most notable Klan operations were directed against Negro and Republican railroad workers, especially railway mail agents. The Klan issued warnings against any Negro employees on the east-west trains that ran from Selma through Livingston to Meridian; they took Negro firemen off the trains and whipped them, and threatened the same to the engineer who brought them. In the latter part of 1870 Frank Diggs, a Negro mail agent on this run, was shot and killed while his train was stopped at Kewaunee, just inside the Mississippi line. His successor, John Coleman, a white man, was accosted by disguised Klansmen at the same place in February 1871, at the time when the crisis around Meridian was reaching its peak and Klansmen were riding the trains with great frequency; they notified him to stay east of Sumter County henceforth. Mail agents were employees of the federal government, and they received their jobs through political patronage. Coleman and others whom the Klan objected to were Republicans who had received their appointments through Congressman Charles Hays. In Coleman's case, he had also taught in a Negro school and was accused of intimacy with a Negro woman. The Klan's campaign was effective, for Coleman transferred to a different route, a conductor they objected to resigned, and another mail agent gave up his job and publicly recanted his Republicanism.[4]

The Klan was also involved in a Conservative plan to drive out local Republican officeholders. Having won the governorship and partial control of the legislature by strong-arm methods in November 1870, Democrats in this part of the state were eager to make a clean sweep. Governor Lindsay had the power to fill many of the vacancies that might be created, and local Democrats could handle the rest. This campaign had little to do with the capacity or conduct of the individual officials involved. Judge Luther R. Smith, whose circuit embraced several of these counties, was the prime target largely because of his honesty and diligence in trying to bring terrorists to book. None of his efforts bore fruit, but Klansmen and fellow travelers resented him nonetheless. A Sumter County mass meeting on February 18 proclaimed its devotion to law and order and then declared

that Smith could not enforce the laws "on account of his being so un-
acceptable to the people." It was essential, they said, to have a judge who
possessed the confidence of the people. If he refused this call to resign, the
Livingston *Journal* added, he would lay himself open to the suspicion of
"valueing [*sic*] his paltry salary above the public interest." Democrats in
Choctaw County, Smith's home, held a similar meeting and posted notices
in the courthouse announcing that he could not hold court there. When
threats of assassination did not work either, a band of fifteen or twenty
disguised men raided his plantation one night and in his absence set fire to
a cotton gin and other structures.[5]

Smith and a few other officials refused to bow to this pressure, but others
were subject to even harsher treatment and succumbed. The probate judge
in Choctaw County finally resigned in May, after he received three Ku
Klux notices, after shots pierced his office windows, and after he was shot
and wounded from ambush on the road. The sheriff and tax collector of
this county had already quit.[6] In Eutaw, two prominent Republicans were
attacked on the street and badly beaten in separate incidents. One victim,
Pierce Burton, the editor of the Demopolis *Southern Republican* and
recently the party's candidate for lieutenant governor, was thought to be
permanently injured. He had already undergone the rigors of campaigning
in Livingston and Eutaw the previous fall; after returning home to Demopolis and receiving a notice from the "Knights of the Black Cross" to
leave within fifteen days or face death, he moved from the state.[7]

Militant Democrats had been trying for years to get rid of William T.
Blackford, the probate judge in Hale County. They pointed out that Blackford was a heavy drinker, but they could find little to criticize in the way he
performed his office; rather he was an active politician who effectively
mobilized the county's black majority behind the Republican party. That
he lasted as long as he did was attributable to his political and personal
moderation. At one point he had abjured the Republican party under pressure, but soon returned to the fold. He consistently cultivated moderate
Democrats, especially the "best citizens," getting appointments for them
from Governor Smith's administration and managing to work harmoni-
ously with them. In this spirit, he accompanied General Forrest on his
railway promotion campaigns. At the same time Blackford kept his Negro
following, and Republicans kept control of the county. When he advised
Negroes from the stump to fight force with force, some whites accused him
of trying to foment insurrection. The burning of several gin houses in the
fall of 1870 seemed to confirm this view. The Klan lynched a Negro
suspect whom they took from law officers who had him in custody; there
were no more burnings after this, but Blackford remained. The advent of a
Democratic governor early in 1871 encouraged many Democrats to try to

oust Blackford. Ku Klux depredations on the black population increased.

One night in the middle of January, sixty or seventy disguised men rode into Greensboro, the county seat. Blackford got word of their coming and escaped to the woods. The Klansmen ransacked the house and went on to release one of their colleagues from jail. They were traced the next morning as far as the Black Warrior River, the boundary with Greene County. (Hale County Klansmen were probably responsible for an unsuccessful attempt to release a prisoner from the Perry County jail in Marion at about the same time.) Soon afterward, when a Selma newspaper carried an article saying that they had liberated an accused horse thief, one of the party wrote an outraged letter branding this a malicious falsehood. The man had been confined merely for killing a Negro and taking a Yankee's horse in order to escape from a "court of injustice" like Blackford's. Their main purpose, moreover, he said, had been "catching and giving Mr. Blackford what he lawfully deserves and will get before the 1st day of March." The writer signed himself, and presumably identified the order whose honor he had restored, with the initials "K.W.C."; the Knights of the White Camellia had organized in this region in 1868, but its name seldom appeared after that time.

Nathan Bedford Forrest arrived in Greensboro soon after the raid, and Blackford asked for his protection. The general gave him a highly confidential and vastly impressive account of the size, prowess, and methods of the Ku Klux Klan; like most of Forrest's pronouncements, it did not suffer from understatement. He urged the judge to resign, indicating that it was hopeless to remain and try to breast the tide. Greensboro's "best citizens" cooperated by banding together to buy their erstwhile friend's property; he was able to leave in March without sacrificing everything.[8]

Sporadic outrages continued in most of the counties of northern Alabama —both the mountain region with its large minority of white Republicans and the Tennessee Valley. For the most part there was less of this activity than in 1869 or 1870, and it was less markedly political in motivation. Much of it was no more than simple robbery by men who had learned that disguised bands could do anything with impunity. The sheriff of Limestone County estimated in October that nineteen-twentieths of the lawlessness there, including night riding, was connected with illicit distilleries. In Jefferson County, where Birmingham came into being this year, some of the marauding was reportedly committed by mountain Republicans upon others of their kind. Klansmen from St. Clair and Etowah counties in May commandeered a train and took it to the town of Attalla, where they beat a number of Negroes; they forced the train crew to take them back, dropping them off at stations along the way. The Tuscaloosa Klan drove off the last remaining students from the university early in 1871 by means of warning notices; outrages also occurred, but they were on a smaller scale than in previous years.[9]

In Fayette County, where Unionist Mossy-backs had engaged the Klan in guerrilla warfare and the sheriff had arrested Ku Klux terrorists in 1870, the terrorists swept aside all resistance and virtually took over in 1871. Klansmen continued to whip Republicans of both races; they paraded through the countryside in broad daylight, defying the sheriff, the Mossy-backs, and the newly organized local militia, which seems never to have been used. They attained this power because the forces of law and order, who far outnumbered them, were unwilling or unable to match them in acts of terrorism. In February, hooded Klansmen rode into Fayetteville, entered the courthouse, removed their disguises, and, with others who joined them, held a convention to nominate candidates for county offices. The depredations continued through most of the year. In one case a band of thirty men visited a plantation, drove off the Negro men, and raped the women, including one nearly seventy years old. Two Klansmen in full disguise rode through Fayetteville during the spring court term, to the cheers of many onlookers; at the fall term both the judge and the grand jury received Ku Klux warning notices. Crowds of disguised men constantly rode past Sheriff Treadway's house two miles out of town, cursing, shooting, and threatening his life. He moved to a remote part of the county and turned over his official business to a deputy. Less than a month later the deputy was forced to quit. The grand jury, instead of prosecuting the terrorists, indicted Treadway and members of his former posse on a variety of nuisance charges brought by Klansmen to make him resign. One indictment, for petty larceny, arose from the confiscation of two Ku Klux disguises. Instead of resigning, Treadway appealed to John A. Minnis, now the United States attorney for this district, who came with a squad of soldiers and prevented his probable conviction. Minnis himself got warrants for a number of the terrorists; most of them fled, but two were arrested and taken to Huntsville for trial in federal court.[10]

The counties of Coosa, Tallapoosa, and Randolph, northeast of Montgomery, were another scene of activity in 1871. In Tallapoosa at least, the Black Cavalry had formed soon after the war as a regulative body which disciplined the blacks and drove some of them away. Eventually it was supplanted by the Ku Klux Klan, but the terrorism did not reach widely noticeable proportions until the end of 1870. Bands of disguised men visited plantations around Nixburg in Coosa County after the November elections. They systematically called out the Negroes and demanded to know how they had voted and intended to vote in the future. Those who answered Republican were whipped, shot, or hanged, depending on the whim of the attackers and how the victims behaved themselves. The

Klansmen burned a Negro church at the same time. These raids continued into the summer of 1871, becoming somewhat less political as time passed. One proclaimed objective was to prevent Negro laborers from congregating on the larger plantations where the pay was better. Some of the raids were designed to force blacks to work for smaller farmers at lesser wages, and some were intended to drive them away altogether. Two districts of Tallapoosa County had lost virtually their entire Negro population by the fall of 1871, causing a severe labor shortage. Many planters were furious at the Klan but dared not protest openly for fear of being attacked themselves; one who did had his house burned down. The Negroes as usual suffered most. Some refugees had to leave their families behind. They went to Montgomery and tried to find work while getting reports from home of neighboring whites dividing up their crops and other possessions. One such victim, Smith Watley, got District Attorney Minnis to prosecute some of his attackers in federal court. Despite an abundance of corroborative testimony, all of the men he identified produced witnesses to swear that they were somewhere else on the night he was beaten, and all were discharged without ever coming to trial.[11]

By 1871, Democrats and Republicans alike were saying that the Klan had deteriorated in its membership since 1868 and 1869. The night riders were "the lowest-down, meanest characters that we have got among us," declared a Tallapoosa County planter. They included renters, small landowners, and some with no visible occupation at all, he said. Many Democrats, unwilling to repudiate the Ku Klux idea, added that the present marauders were spurious Ku Klux, composed only of the rowdy, drinking element. It is true, too, that there was no longer any riding about the country in disguise simply to overawe the blacks by their presence. On the other hand, the atrocities committed in 1871 differed little from those of 1868 and 1869, except that they were more frequent in those years. In general, the more politically motivated Klan operations were at any time and place, the more upper-class elements were apt to be involved. They were apparently involved in the Klan-supported efforts to drive out Republican officeholders, but for the most part the political purpose receded in 1871 after Democrats returned to power in much of the state. [12]

Respectable Conservatives expressed a growing impatience with Klan excesses in several ways. Democratic witnesses before the Congressional investigating committee were often far from candid concerning the order, but many freely denounced the continuing outrages more outspokenly than before, in rare cases even applauding legal efforts to control or punish them. The Livingston *Journal,* part and parcel of the Ku Klux conspiracy until it achieved its political objective in November 1870, now called attention to the promises of law and order if the Democrats won the election. These pledges were made in good faith, it declared, and order must be restored without regard to "the color or standing of offenders." Sumter County was not going to be stripped of its labor force, the paper warned, by "mid-night marauders" who had only private ends to serve. The Greensboro *Beacon,* a more moderate paper and less implicated in earlier terrorism, went much further in blaming the Democratic press generally for fomenting violence. "So grossly personal and abusive have many of them been in their political discussions, that a portion of their readers have come to look upon it as not only no crime, but a patriotic duty, to do personal violence to those who render themselves obnoxious by their political opinions." It called on young men of education to organize for the purpose of repelling lawless bands and helping the authorities to arrest them.[13] The *Beacon's* criticism reached to the heart of the Ku Klux conspiracy and was exceptional among Democratic newspapers.

Public meetings also condemned violence more frequently than before, and in a few cases whites took up arms to repel the terrorists by force. The organizers of these efforts were sometimes former Klan members and leaders. This was true in Athens and Limestone County, where citizens organized to repel undisguised toughs who descended on the town to release some prisoners from jail. Later a public meeting appointed a special police force to put down lawlessness in each beat or precinct of the county, and the former officers of the local Klan publicly condemned anyone (members or not) who continued to go raiding.[14] The terrorism in Sumter County created a serious labor shortage despite the Livingston *Journal's* warnings. The Meridian, Mississippi, riot in March was occasioned partly by the efforts of the Alabamians to bring back Negro refugees. By fall forty or fifty Sumter County planters had organized an armed patrol which called on suspected night riders at their homes and warned them to stop. One family of poor whites was ordered to leave altogether after they whipped and tried to drive away the Negroes on a neighboring plantation.[15] In Fayette County former Klansmen who had disbanded by agreement with the authorities in 1870 were bitter against those who continued to raid and were eager to put them down.

But such opposition was still the exception rather than the rule among Democrats. The ladies of Greene County held a tableau to raise money for the defense of prisoners indicted for participating in the Eutaw riot.[16] When leading citizens of Randolph County began organizing a public meeting to condemn recent outrages there, they received Ku Klux warnings and abandoned the effort.[17] General James H. Clanton, the Democratic state chairman, privately advised individual Democrats to use their influence to put down violence; but at the same time he served as defense counsel for accused terrorists and steadfastly denied in public that the

outrages represented any more than occasional cases of juvenile delin-
quency.[18] Most Democrats asserted that no regular or continuing Ku Klux
organization existed in their counties, or in the state if they were statewide
figures, and they denied even more vehemently that the disguised bands
were politically motivated. Even those few who advocated prosecuting the
terrorists grew furious at the thought of federal intervention for this
purpose. Any who openly favored the Enforcement Acts of 1870 and 1871
virtually lost their Democratic standing.

Democratic newspapers continued to ignore violence more than they
condemned it. In May a bipartisan federal grand jury in Montgomery drew
attention to the "frequent and outrageous violations of law" which had
taken place. It called on all citizens to bring the offenders to justice, but
made no indictments itself because the witnesses it examined were unable
to identify their attackers. Despite the fact that it absolved the great
majority of citizens of any complicity in these crimes, the jury was
castigated by Democratic journals for slandering the people of Alabama.
District Attorney Minnis, who initiated the cases, was accused of manu-
facturing them for political effect.[19]

Governor Robert Lindsay followed the Democratic party line in minimizing the degree of Ku Klux organization and its political motivation. He
told the Congressional committee in June that no one in Alabama had been
whipped for two or three years past on account of political principle or to
deter Negroes from voting. Republicans who continued to point out the
prevalence of terrorism and appealed for federal intervention, he declared
in a legislative message in January, were "selfish, restless, and aspiring
men" who would destroy the state to serve their own political ambitions.
No matter how anxious Lindsay was to ignore or deny violence, he in no
sense condoned or connived at it. In January he instructed the solictor of
Coosa County to prosecute members of the lawless bands who were
committing outrages there, and he warned local officials around the state
that he would hold them legally accountable for neglecting this duty.[20]

The continuing violence was increasingly regarded as a political liability,
a source of embarrassment, and even of danger by moderate Democrats
like Lindsay. This was especially true now that Democrats were in power
and the Klan no longer served a useful political purpose. On at least two
occasions Congressman Joseph H. Sloss (a friend and political ally of
Lindsay's) wrote from Washington, calling the governor's attention to Ku
Klux outrages in different parts of the state which had been reported in the
national capital. "I . . . urge upon you the great necessity for prompt and
decided action . . . to put down all such outrages. It is simply impossible
for us here to relieve our people from the villainous charges which are
being hourly made against them by partisans, for political purposes, while

such conduct is permitted in any part of the State, no matter by whom perpetrated."

What Sloss feared was the sending of more federal troops to Alabama, possibly with extraordinary powers like those soon to be invoked in South Carolina. As a matter of fact the number of troops in Alabama dwindled by October to three companies, one stationed at Huntsville and two at Mobile, where they were not needed.[21] Few Republicans bothered to request Lindsay for troops as they had Governor Smith, and he seems to have made no use of them. Local officials made no greater effort to punish terrorists under Lindsay than they had before. The really marked decline of violence which occurred in the summer and fall of 1871 resulted from the growing public disapproval, coupled with an increase in federal prosecutions.

The Klan remained active in half a dozen Florida counties in 1871, tapering off here too during the summer and fall. At Gainesville several Klansmen held a mock trial in which they sentenced Republican state senator L. G. Dennis to be hanged. They included the scions of some of the town's leading families, and Dennis had them arrested for disturbing the peace. They were acquitted, whereupon they returned the same night and assaulted the mayor in the courthouse yard. Besides other attacks of this nature, they occasionally shot into houses and Republican meetings.[22] In Columbia County state senator E. G. Johnson received a notice to resign if he wanted to live. This order resulted, the notice said, from "sober deliberation in brotherhoods," and Johnson was warned to keep the notification secret. Believing that it was the work of a local lawyer who had earlier advised him to leave the Republican party, Johnson published the notice in the newspaper. Despite warning shots fired into his home, he also defied the order to resign. In testifying before the Congressional committee, Johnson described eight killings in the county since the fall of 1868—seven of the victims Negroes and the eighth a white Republican legislator—aside from whippings, house burnings, and other acts of terrorism. The sheriff had already resigned under pressure in 1870, and there was an assassination attempt on the town marshal at Lake City. Two or three hundred Negroes, Johnson said, had fled the county to escape the terror.[23] If any elements of the Conservative population disapproved of this activity, they were less conspicuous and influential than the ones who fostered and defended it.[24]

Nevertheless, it was Marianna and Jackson County where Satan retained his headquarters. Marcellus L. Stearns, speaker of the state house of representatives and destined to be governor in a few years, described this as the only county "entirely and effectually in the hands of a mob." The number of terrorists apparently remained small, but they reigned supreme with the backing of Colonel James P. Coker and other Conservative leaders. Sometimes they operated in disguise and sometimes not. Close to 100 persons, and possibly more, were murdered in this county from the end of the war through 1871; this was many more than in all other counties combined. About nine-tenths of those murdered were Negroes. As elsewhere, the most active or influential persons—the natural leaders of the Negro community—were the most apt to fall. Sheriff Thomas West, a white man, finally resigned in March 1871 after repeated threats and at least one physical assault on the street.

The only Republican official left, county clerk John Q. Dickinson, was assassinated less than a month later. A native Vermonter who had succeeded Hamilton and Purman in the Freedmen's Bureau here, Dickinson was commonly regarded as the foremost Republican in west Florida. This was not wholly the product of elimination. Republicans all spoke of him in superlative terms, and he was conceded a character, ability, and importance far beyond what was generally looked for in a county clerk. His friends, many of them Army acquaintances, held a memorial service at the Gramercy Park Hotel in New York, in which he was characterized as a man of refinement, culture, and distinction. Dickinson had been subjected to constant threats and occasionally physical abuse. Colonel Coker once knocked off his hat and spat in his face. For many months he kept a private journal of the terror, which was found among his effects, and he wrote friends that he expected to be killed at any time; but he refused to run away. Dickinson was shot down on the night of April 3 in the public square, only a few yards from where his predecessor, Dr. Finlayson, had been murdered in 1869.

Democrats generally were relieved at the dispatch of the last carpet-bagger and sanctioned the deed with the usual posthumous character assassination. Dickinson had been shot, they said, by an outraged Negro husband whose wife he had kept. They also accused him of trading in tax-delinquent property, and he was allegedly killed at the behest of a man with whom he had quarreled in this connection. A Negro associate believed that Dickinson had indeed bought up some land in tax sales and owned about 2,000 acres at the time of his death, but he also lent money to people to pay their taxes. As usual, the truth of these matters was never clarified. Democrats did not mention in this connection their own systematic efforts to drive Republicans from office. In Florida county officials were appointed by the governor, who was still Harrison Reed, a Republican. But Jackson County Democrats, having disposed of nearly all possible Republican officeholders and confident of their ability to dispose of any others, nominated a slate of Democrats after Dickinson's death and presented it to the governor for ratification.[25]

Nor did the terror stop here. Black men continued to be called out of their homes at night and whipped or shot. Running out of conspicuous targets at home, Jackson County toughs went into neighboring counties, offering to assassinate anyone the local whites wanted out of the way. In March one ambushed and killed a state legislator in Calhoun County, just to the south. These gangsters were well known, and it was widely recognized that they were being subsidized by Conservatives higher up. It was no secret either that Colonel Coker in Marianna was the ringleader. They encountered no obstacles. Unlike many other communities, there was no evidence of growing indignation at the violence, much less any effort to check it.

Governor Reed regarded himself as helpless to stem the terror in Jackson County or elsewhere, and he did even less than at the outset in 1868. In June a state convention of Negro Methodists urged all the blacks in Jackson County to leave and offered to help find them homes elsewhere. In November the Republican state chairman appealed to President Grant for martial law, presenting evidence of more than a dozen Negroes murdered since Dickinson's death in April. A detachment of twenty soldiers arrived on December 7, and four days later Colonel Coker was arrested and taken to Tallahassee for trial under the federal Enforcement Acts. After a year's delay the case was dropped. But this action, along with more militant federal activity in other states, brought the terror to a close in Jackson County and Florida generally. The Republican state chairman had appealed for martial law (which was not invoked) to assure a free vote in a special legislative election scheduled for December 19. On that day the Negro majority in Jackson County elected two Republicans by a wide margin, with no reports of violence or intimidation.[26]

The regulators or Ku Klux Klans of Kentucky remained active throughout 1871. Many parts of the state were involved, but the most consistent and aggravated lawlessness still occurred in a wide swath of territory extending from the Ohio River between Louisville and Cincinnati down almost to the Tennessee line and into the mountains of southeast Kentucky. Lexington and Frankfort, the state capital, lay in the heart of this region, more normally known for its bluegrass, thoroughbred horses, and bourbon whiskey.

During January the Republican Frankfort *Commonwealth* angrily reported a succession of outrages which came to its attention, some of them uncomfortably close to home. On the night of January 7 the Ku Klux shot and killed a Negro near Lexington, and a white man was shot and whipped by a band near Shelbyville. About the same time, Klansmen visited some Negro cabins at Stamping Ground, a few miles northeast of Frankfort. The blacks resisted, killing one of the attackers; he turned out to be a schoolteacher in Henry County, toward which the rest of the band retreated. Soon afterward a Negro church was burned. In another neighborhood near Frankfort, Klansmen forced two Negroes to lie in the ice until their clothes were stiff, then sent them home with a warning to leave the county with their families. The Ku Klux also robbed them of a watch and $30. Many blacks—some of them landowners—fled into the capital for safety. The *Commonwealth* estimated their number at 300. Near Lexington blacks retaliated by burning several farm buildings.[27]

Kentucky Klansmen resented Negro postal route agents as much as did those in Alabama. W. H. Gibson had been appointed agent on the Louisville and Lexington Railroad, which ran through one of the most heavily Klan-infested regions. When the train on which he was working pulled into the North Benson depot on January 26, a small reception committee was on hand. According to the station master, one of the committee threatened to shoot the mail agent. His friends disarmed him, but he grappled with Gibson in the mail car. The next day a white agent made the trip in Gibson's place, and at nearly every station crowds of angry and disappointed whites demanded to know where Gibson was. In the substitute agent's opinion, Gibson would require a guard of soldiers to make the trip again.[28]

The government did provide a guard of ten soldiers, who traveled with Gibson for a month. But when rumors arose that the train would be attacked by enough men to overpower the guard, mail service was simply discontinued on this route. The cities of Louisville, Frankfort, and Lexington, which were responsible for most of the mail and little or none of the violence, bore the brunt, as Democrats pointed out, while the Ku Klux along the way hardly received or sent a letter a year and were largely unaffected. In addition, the government ordered a regiment of troops to Kentucky from the West.[29]

Another Ku Klux escapade contributed to this federal interest. A man named Scroggins escaped indictment by the Frankfort grand jury on the charge of murdering a Negro. He was almost certainly guilty, but the case against him rested largely on Negro testimony, which Kentucky courts still did not recognize. A United States deputy marshal promptly arrested him on federal charges. Until the marshal was ready to take him to Louisville, where the federal court sat, Scroggins remained in the Frankfort jail, and on the night of February 24 a masked party of about seventy-five men entered town and forced the jailer to release his prisoner.[30]

This raid took place in the state capital at a time when the legislature was in session, pondering what measures if any to take against the Ku Klux Klan. Governor John W. Stevenson had called attention to the chronic lawlessness in his regular message early in January. He was helpless to call out the militia, he said, or even to offer rewards for the arrest of these marauders unless requested to do so by local officials. Only the legislature could strengthen his hand by giving him greater discretionary emergency power. Stevenson also suggested both a state police and a reorganization of the militia, but he did not mention martial law.[31] After the North Benson affair, the governor sent a special message reiterating his plea for legislative action.[32]

The Louisville *Courier-Journal* consistently seconded the governor, in fact far exceeded him in denouncing mob violence and demanding its suppression. Day after day, week after week, editor Henry Watterson needled the legislature about its dilatoriness. He was supported by most of the other Democratic papers in the state, but not by all. Republicans also agreed, but they were in a hopeless minority and had little influence in shaping policy. Both the *Courier-Journal* and the Hopkinsville *New Era* complained of the criticism they received from other Democratic organs accusing them of treason to the party. Typical of these was the Lexington *Gazette,* which declared that nine-tenths of the country people approved of the Klan, including many who publicly opposed it. This would continue, the *Gazette* observed, until the people had security, but it failed to indicate what kind of security the Klan provided in Democratic Kentucky.[33] When state judges charged grand juries to investigate Ku Klux crimes and indict their perpetrators, they were met with a shrug and a yawn.[34] Many Democrats, like others farther south, in truth regarded the Klan as an ally.

By early March a Ku Klux bill had passed the state senate, but only after senators had struck out a $25,000 secret service fund for the governor and another provision admitting Negro testimony in Ku Klux cases. The house refused to pass any bill at all. When the legislature adjourned in March the *Courier-Journal* was scathing in its appraisal:

We need not speak of its vacillation as to negro testimony. Reason has long ago exhausted the argument on that subject. But what shall we say of its treatment of the Ku Klux bill? It piddled from first to last, and dared not act. Its timidity served to encourage violence, which increased its audacity. Outlawry went on unchallenged under its very elbow. It paid no attention to the North Benson affair. . . . It did not so much as rebuke the raid upon Frankfort.

Moreover, the legislature's inaction embarrassed the state in Washington.

When Mr. Sherman taunts us with having done nothing, and bases his argument in favor of Federal interference on the fact that we have done nothing, we are dumb. The idle gabble that the Ku Klux are all Radicals in disguise is even weaker than the silly platitude that there is no such thing as the Ku Klux at all. If the Ku Klux are Radicals, the more reason to put them down. If there is no such order, there is outlawry which calls for extraordinary appliances. These appliances our Governor recommended. The press urged them. But the Legislature stood with a cigar in its mouth and a champagne glass in its hand, and would do nothing.[35]

Many Kentucky Democrats continued to oppose all efforts to suppress the Ku Klux, especially if it involved intervention by the federal government. Governor Stevenson resigned in February to enter the United States Senate, and at once found himself embroiled in debate on the federal Ku Klux bill then pending. With no seeming hesitation he adhered to his party's universal position that there was no general Ku Klux conspiracy and that the Klan had no political bearing save as the Radicals invented it. The new Senator went far to belie some of his most notable pronouncements as governor. He conceded in his maiden speech on March 18 that there had been occasional acts of violence in Kentucky, and he had taken steps to suppress them; but in his three and a half years as governor there had been no more than a dozen such cases of violence, all confined to one locality; there was no evidence that they sprang from a secret organization of political character. The whole thrust of Stevenson's speech was to minimize the nature and extent of the Ku Klux disease and thereby avert federal legislation.[36]

As soon as Stevenson's remarks became known in Kentucky, Republicans hastened to refute them by pointing to the record, including his own statements as governor. G. C. Wharton, the federal district attorney, in a public letter, said that Ku Klux intimidation was well known around the state and had even affected the federal grand jury.[37] A meeting of Negroes living in and around Frankfort drew up an itemized list of 116 outrages by organized bands in Kentucky since November 1867, culminating in the February 1871 jail delivery in the state capital. The situation, they said, cried out for federal legislation.[38] The Frankfort *Commonwealth* listed eighty-one murders and seventy shootings or whippings during Stevenson's governorship, as opposed to the minute figure given by him.[39] A correspondent of the Cincinnati *Gazette* wrote: "Were all the Ku Klux arrested and brought to trial, among them would be found sheriffs, magistrates, jurors, and legislators, and it may be clerks and judges. In some counties it would be found that the Ku Klux and their friends comprise more than half of the influential and voting population."[40]

All Democrats opposed to the Klan were embarrassed by the Republican demands for Congressional action. Unlike Stevenson, the *Courier-Journal* did not reverse itself and deny the Klan terrorism, but it said that states could and should handle the problem themselves; the Kentucky Ku Klux were of concern only to Kentucky; the central government had no business in matters of this sort. Federal laws do not serve the aim of long-range peace, whereas state laws do; those Republicans who called for troops were bent on promoting strife rather than peace. Part of Editor Watterson's anger with the recent legislature sprang from the very fact that its dereliction (to use his word) had gone far to nullify this argument; but he adhered to it nonetheless.[41]

Meanwhile the Klan continued to ride, and the *Courier-Journal* continued to report it. Most of the outrages were familiar: a jail rescue by 75 to 100 disguised men at Winchester, a white man lynched in Stanton, Negro and white men whipped and a Negro schoolteacher notified to stop teaching near Lexington, a white man near Frankfort notified by masked visitors to pay a debt he allegedly owed. But there were some variations: a white Democrat was whipped in Owen County, and the jailer there turned back a lynch party without surrendering his prisoner.[42] In Madison County, if reports were true, Republicans banded together briefly to Ku Klux a Negro and two whites for having voted the Democratic ticket.[43] In Estill County, southeast of Lexington, a Klan became active in the spring and rode roughshod through the community for months. It rescued a man from jail, whipped a woman for criticizing the organization publicly, whipped a trustee of Berea College for associating with Negroes, and reportedly murdered three men at the time of local elections in May. It also caused 400 miners of both races to stop working for the Red River Iron Company, closing down its operations in the county. Repeatedly identified as leader of the Ku Klux here was state senator Harrison Cockrill, whose Klan jurisdiction was said to include four counties. According to a recanting member, the order was aimed at driving both Negroes and Unionists from desirable lands and jobs; the mining company incurred its ire by coming in from Ohio and hiring blacks.[44]

Some of this information came to light as the result of federal arrests and prosecutions, which began in July. Unlike their counterparts farther south, federal officials in Kentucky had been making at least sporadic efforts to punish Ku Klux terrorists from the beginning. Their arrests had led to very few convictions and seemingly had little effect in ending the terror. A Shelby County Klansman who confessed and turned state's evidence was hanged by his fellow members in February after he was released on bond.[45] Nevertheless the authorities increased their efforts in 1871, with greater encouragement from Washington. At the same time troops were distributed around the state, and they sometimes helped in making arrests. More than a dozen arrests were made at different times in July and August in Estill County.[46]

State elections were held on August 7, and in Frankfort this occasioned a race riot. Federal troops were stationed here, but instead of using them the mayor called out the local militia company to restore order. During the hostilities two whites were killed and several of both races were wounded. A Negro was charged with firing the first shot and was confined to jail. Almost immediately rumors began to circulate about a plan to lynch the prisoner that night. During the evening most of the militiamen absented themselves without leave, and finally the commander dismissed the few who remained, at their request. To no one's great surprise, a mob of thirty-five to forty men later materialized, demanding and gaining entrance to the jail. They took out two Negro prisoners, the one arrested during the riot and another held for rape, and hanged them a half mile away.

Local officials did almost nothing to discover or punish the criminals (some of whom did not bother to disguise themselves), but six weeks later federal authorities arrested three men and brought them to Louisville to stand trial. Despite a battery of high-powered defense counsel, including former governor Thomas E. Bramlette, two of the three were bound over for trial after a preliminary hearing.[47] In another federal case, in October, four Jessamine County men (including a Negro) were convicted of Ku Kluxing a black man the previous winter.[48]

These prosecutions undoubtedly slowed down the incidence of Ku Klux activity through the state by the end of 1871. But the Klan continued to ride, around Frankfort especially.[49] When the new legislature assembled in December, Governor Preston H. Leslie called attention to the problem and renewed his predecessor's appeal for legislation facilitating the capture and punishment of offenders.[50] Not until 1873 did the legislature respond.

CHAPTER 20

Georgia

If Klan operations in Georgia were less extensive in 1871 than formerly, as some persons believed, they were certainly reported more fully. Despite Democratic capture of the legislature in December 1870, night riding and terrorism continued on a large scale through the following summer and in some cases beyond. Most of the activity was centered, as formerly, in two large areas: eight or nine counties in the northwest corner of the state and about seventeen counties extending from Atlanta eastward to the South Carolina line. Masked bands were active in at least two northeastern counties also, and they were reported in scattered localities farther south. In most of these places the activity represented a continuation of earlier operations. Nocturnal depredations on Negroes and white Republicans were so common as to excite little comment beyond gross quantitative estimates.

No Southern governor was accused more often of abusing his pardoning power in behalf of Negro criminals than Governor Rufus Bullock of Georgia. This was advanced as a major justification of the Ku Klux Klan. Bullock was so beset with Democratic criticism on this score that in July he had a list of executive pardons for the past four years compiled and published in the Atlanta *New Era*. By this account he had issued 41 pardons for murder, 25 of which were granted before trial; most of the latter arose from prewar indictments which the authorities had not prosecuted, often because of the death or disappearance of witnesses. There were 31 pardons for manslaughter, 66 for various kinds of assault, 172 for burglary, robbery, or larceny, 5 for arson, and several others for miscellaneous crimes. Nearly all of these cases involved convicts who had served part of their sentences and would have been released on parole if such a system had existed. They were recommended by prison authorities on grounds of good conduct or physical disability. Nearly all came at the solicitation of respectable citizens in the convicts' home communities, the great majority of them Democrats. In many cases they were also recommended by the superior court judges. The governor had no motive or purpose in releasing criminals upon the public; it was not demanded by the Negroes, the Republicans, or anyone else, and many appeals for pardon were rejected. This charge was as empty as those that the courts would not punish Negro criminals.[1]

As in other states, Klan raiding was less political in motivation by 1871. There was a dearth of elections this year, and the earlier terrorism had decimated Republican officeholders in the most affected counties. In Putnam County a special legislative election was required after the murder of Abram Turner, a Negro elected in December 1870. The new election, featuring a minor race riot, produced a Democratic victory.[2] Another black legislator, Abram Colby of Greene County, who had been whipped almost to death in 1869, was forced by renewed terrorism to remain most of the time in Atlanta. In fact it appeared that he was being kept away deliberately to provide a pretext for declaring his seat vacant on the ground of nonresidence when the legislature reconvened in November. "They Ku-Klux my house every time I go home," Colby reported. "I have not staid there more than one night this year; I had to stay in the woods. . . . "[3]

In Haralson County, on the Alabama line, the Klan helped influence a legislative by-election. The county was almost evenly divided politically, with a small Negro and a large white Republican element slightly outnumbering Democrats in a fair election. The legislative election in December 1870 had produced a tie vote, necessitating a special election which was held on October 4, 1871, about a month before the new legislature was slated to convene. Meanwhile Negroes and white Republicans in two districts of the county were subjected to sporadic attacks throughout most of the year. The motives behind specific raids were mixed, and personal transgressions were alleged more often than not. Two or three Negro women were whipped on one occasion to make them stay at home; a Negro man was killed in May for consorting with white women; persons of both races were whipped for alleged stealing; a number of Negroes were attacked for attending school; and guns were confiscated. Many Negroes regularly took to the woods at night to escape attack. The sheriff, circuit judge, and all witnesses to Ku Klux activity were threatened with death if they tried to prosecute offenders. As usual Democrats were almost never molested, no matter what their private lives. The attackers came from the immediate locality in many cases, and in others they came over from adjacent sections of Polk County and Cleburne County, Alabama. Two Ku Klux dens drew their members from both sides of the state line and operated regularly in both states. Their organization and the designation of their officers corresponded closely to those set forth in the Tennessee Klan Prescript. Local Democratic leaders encouraged the violence if they did not actually participate in it, and one of the Klan leaders (Daniel Head) was father of the Democratic legislative candidate. The raids increased with the approach of the October election. The Republican vote fell sharply in the two districts where terrorism prevailed, enabling the Democrats to win by a margin of almost fifty votes.[4]

Elsewhere Klan activity was aimed more exclusively at keeping the black man in his place economically and socially. Hundreds were whipped and a number killed in the counties east of Atlanta in a continuation of the violence which had reached major proportions by 1870. Actual and prospective victims continued to flee to Atlanta and other cities, losing their crops and most of their possessions in the process. In the three adjacent counties of Gwinnett, Walton, and Jackson the Klan expanded its organization and operations far beyond the level of previous years. Three dens reportedly existed in each county, those in Gwinnett numbering 75 to 100 members apiece. Members of all these dens raided frequently in the other two counties. In some districts they raided regularly once a week and even posted notices beforehand that they were coming. In Walton the Klan announced in March that it would tolerate no Negro schools and threatened to whip anyone who sent a child to school. They burned the books belonging to one teacher and "said they would just dare any other nigger to have a book in his house." In Gwinnett a white planter told of the Ku Klux coming to his house one night in May and making him show the way to the houses of certain Negro tenants whom they accused of misconduct; he was directed to hold their horses while they went from cabin to cabin beating the occupants and destroying their guns. A proper air of servility was insisted upon. "The colored people dare not dress up themselves and fix up, like they thought anything of themselves, for fear they would whip us," reported one woman who was whipped in March and again in October. "I have been humble and obedient to them, a heap more so than I was to my master, who raised me; and that is the way they serve us."[5] William Felker, a country storekeeper and moonshiner repeatedly identified as a leader of Ku Klux raids in Walton County, gave helpful advice to his own Negro employees, as one of them testified: "He told me how to do. He said if I always raised my hat to the people when I passed, and was always polite to them, I would not be bothered."[6]

Once the Klan had begun disciplining the freedmen, one step led to another, beyond the members' original expectations. White planters who protested against raids on their Negro hands were threatened and even attacked; as a result almost none dared to speak out. An exception was J. R. Holliday of Jackson County. When the Klan began interfering with his tenants in April or May and they came to him saying that they were afraid to stay any longer, Holliday threatened to prosecute the neighborhood boys who were responsible. After this, business fell off at Holliday's mill and he became the object of threats and malicious gossip, some of which aimed at alienating him from his wife and her family. One night in July, after prior warnings, the Ku Klux descended on his home, twenty or thirty strong. They broke into his house, and Holliday engaged them single-handedly in a furious knife and gun battle that raged from room to room in the darkness. He claimed to have killed at least two of the attackers and wounded several others before escaping outside. Holliday had thirteen men arrested for this attack, and subsequently his mill and cotton gin were burned and all the Negro laborers were driven off.[7] In Gwinnett County disguised men burned down the courthouse in September, destroying nearly all the county records including the evidence against a dozen recently arrested Klansmen.[8]

In the Black Belt counties to the south and east, night riding and other Klan activity diminished after the Democratic victories in December 1870. Warren County, the worst in the state during 1869 and 1870, was peaceful in 1871. In a few counties, however, night riding reached unprecedented levels.[9] W. H. Harrison, a Negro legislator defeated in an election day riot in Hancock County, reported to the Congressional investigating committee in November that he still lay out in the woods about one night in three to avoid the Ku Klux.[10]

The case of Scipio Eager in Washington County was typical of scores or hundreds of Negroes. According to his testimony before the committee, about a hundred fully disguised Ku Klux—the number perhaps was less, but no one was in a position to count them carefully—came one night in April to the house where he lived with his parents, brothers, and children. The Klansmen announced that they were going to kill everyone who hadn't voted the Democratic ticket according to prior instructions. One of Eager's brothers, moreover, was accused of being "too big a man" because he could read and write and had talked of starting a Negro school. When this brother now tried to escape from them he was riddled with bullets and buckshot, and he died the next day. Eager himself was taken to the woods a half mile distant, his hands tied behind his back. Then: "They took off every rag of clothes I had, and laid me down on the ground, and some stood on my head and some on my feet. I can't tell how many men whipped me at once. They went out and got great big long brushes, as big as these chair-posts, and they whipped them all into frassels. There are welts on me now [six months later]. After they quit whipping me, they told me to go home. . . . I tried to run, and some threw rocks at me, and some said, 'Shoot him;' but they did not." Several Klansmen returned in July and searched the house, but Eager had been hiding out every night since the first attack, and they missed him. This time they had dogs with them, "what they call 'nigger-hounds;' such as they had in old slavery times." Eager, keeping a safe distance, trailed some of them home and saw them take off their disguises. After this, he said, "I did not know what to do. I was just like a rabbit when the dogs are after him; I had to do anything that I could to try and save my life." He ended by fleeing to Atlanta, leaving behind a blind father, a helpless mother, and a house full of children with no means of support.[11]

In Morgan County the climax of the terror came with the lynching in September of Charles Clarke, a Negro who had been jailed on a charge of raping a white woman. Local blacks, anticipating such an effort, banded together to guard the jail the first night after Clarke's confinement. The next day they disbanded after assurances from the mayor (who had been elected as a Republican) that such precautions were unnecessary. The following night, however, a party of Klansmen rode into town and tried to break open the jail, but for some reason they gave up the attempt. Three nights after that, at least fifty men entered town. This time they performed the mission they had come for, and they did so with the obvious connivance of the mayor and other officials. A Negro witness to the transaction, who testified before the Congressional committee in October, was forced by threats on his life to flee the county immediately after his return home. In this county too a Negro legislator who had survived the rigors of the 1870 campaign was subjected to continuing threats of imminent death.[12]

Lynchings were reported from several counties. On the night of January 14 a disguised band rode into Louisville, Jefferson County, demanded keys from the jailer, and took out nine Negro prisoners. Outside of town the Ku Klux cropped the ears of seven, who had been convicted of various misdemeanors, and turned them loose along with an eighth man. The ninth, awaiting trial for arson, was taken back to jail, where they shot and killed him. Although Judge H. D. D. Twiggs called a special court term to deal with the raid and the grand jury condemned it, they managed to condemn Governor Bullock almost equally and found no evidence on which to prosecute anyone.[13]

At Sandersville, Washington County, eighteen or twenty hooded men in January attacked the home of Major John C. Gallaher, a one-armed Confederate veteran, and carried him off. He escaped from the band and was found the next morning badly wounded. Gallaher was a newcomer in town; it had been discovered that he deserted a wife and children in Tennessee and was cohabiting with a woman he had picked up in Alabama.[14] In March a much larger group, estimated at 200 or more, invaded the town and lynched a Negro who had just been jailed on suspicion of arson. Judge Twiggs, whose home was in Sandersville, reported to Governor Bullock the impossibility of coping with these crimes by ordinary legal procedure: "The *same people* who are called upon to administer & vindicate the law, are the *same people* who violate it."[15] Nevertheless the unexpected happened in June, when one James Oxford, an acknowledged Ku Klux, was convicted of murder and sentenced to be hanged. Oxford had once before been released by his confederates from the Hancock County jail at Sparta, where he had been confined for another murder. It was generally believed that the Klan could have prevented his conviction at Sandersville if it had wanted to. Fearing another forcible release and having such recent evidence of the leakiness of the Sandersville jail, Judge Twiggs sent him to Milledgeville for safekeeping. But there another crowd collected and turned him loose in short order. They were under good discipline and reportedly had gathered from five counties at a rendezvous in Wilkinson County before going on to Milledgeville.[16] It was almost a matter of course for citizens to claim that the disguised parties came from a distance, and in the case of the larger raids this was likely true. After the Oxford affair the people of Washington County held a public meeting in which they condemned the actions of disguised parties and threatened to punish them with fire and sword if they continued; the county was quiet thereafter.[17]

In next-door Wilkinson County, however, the Klan burst forth in unprecedented activity at this time. (A contemporary pamphlet refers to the local Ku Klux here as the Constitutional Union Guard, the only instance I have seen of this designation outside of North Carolina.) Many blacks, including an old woman, were whipped, and several were killed, including the white Republican sheriff. The wife of Sheriff Mat Deason was mentally deranged and spent her life alternately at home and in the asylum. Her husband had taken up with a Negro woman twelve years before, living with her much of the time and fathering five children by her. When the Ku Klux interested themselves in this case Deason threatened to kill anyone who molested his family. It turned out otherwise, for in August Deason was shot and bludgeoned to death in a nocturnal surprise attack. His body and that of his Negro consort were tied up with bars of iron and dumped into a creek.[18]

Equally notable was the Wilkinson Klan's resort to castration as an instrument of social control. At least three black men were treated in this manner, one of them fatally, apparently on suspicion of involvement with white women. In the case of Bill Brigan "they tied him down on a log and took a buggy-trace to him, and whipped one of his seed entirely out and the other very nearly out."[19] Henry Lowther lived to report his treatment to the Congressional committee. One night in August the Klan called at his home and (as he was in hiding) warned his wife that he had five days to leave. Lowther had been an active Republican; he ascribed the threat partially to that and partially to the fact that he had prospered in a modest way at his trade and had sued some whites for money they owed him. In addition, however, he had been tending the land of a white woman whose reputation was not of the best; there was good reason to believe that his attentions were more than horticultural. In any event some Negro friends organized a company to protect him against attack. When Captain Eli Cummins, a lawyer and reputedly the local Klan chieftain, heard about this he contrived to have Lowther and fifteen other blacks arrested and jailed on the frivolous charge of conspiring to attack another Negro. All of the prisoners except Lowther were released almost immediately, but Cummins came to him in jail and offered him a choice: death or castration. Cummins also inquired whether he would put up a fight when "they" came to take him from jail that night. At 2 A.M. about 180 Ku Klux—as Lowther says—took him from jail and into a swamp two miles away. Here they repeated the alternatives, Lowther choosing castration. They performed the operation on the spot and then turned him loose, telling him to see a doctor and to leave the county as soon as he was able. In this condition, only half clothed on a cold night, Lowther set out on foot for the doctor's house more than two miles distant. He stopped at every house along the way, asking for help. It was 3 A.M., and every building seemed to be full of white men, up and about, but they refused to heed his appeals and told him to move along. When he reached the doctor's home there was no response at all, for that gentleman (a brother of Captain Cummins) had apparently been on the raid and had not yet returned; there were many who believed that he had performed the operation himself. At this point Lowther fainted and lay on the ground for a time until he recovered consciousness and made his way to a Negro home, where he got help. Whites later tried to persuade him that he had not reached the doctor's house, but Negro women who followed the trail of blood he made from house to house assured him otherwise. During his convalescence Lowther created a tremendous anxiety among the whites that he might try to prosecute his attackers. After three weeks he went to Macon and there filed charges. As soon as they discovered his whereabouts the Klan sent five men after him, so he went on to Atlanta and safety. Later the story was circulated that Lowther had been attacked for having violated the chastity of his stepdaughter.[20]

The Wilkinson Klan continued to ride, and many other Negroes fled the county. Most of the county officials either resigned or renounced the Republican party.[21] In September 1872 disguised bands were again marauding through the countryside, flogging Negroes who were organizing Republican clubs in that year's Presidential campaign.[22]

In the northwestern counties plagued with Ku Klux depredations, by far the worst were Floyd and Chattooga. The Klan had been active here in 1870, and dens were apparently organized in each militia district. It was the general view that Ku Klux membership here too had deteriorated since the early days and had become less political. The "respectable men" who had organized the Klan had largely fallen away, leaving it to younger poor whites who suffered more acutely from Negrophobia. Nevertheless, some well-to-do men—more in Rome and other towns than the planters whose labor force was being disrupted—continued to sympathize with and support Ku Klux activity if they did not actively participate in it. When Klansmen got into difficulties with the law most Conservatives tried to shield them, regardless of whether they approved the specific cases of marauding involved.[23]

A Union army colonel from Pennsylvania named Waltemire had settled down as a planter in Floyd County after the war. As a Democrat and a man of means who studiously avoided controversy, he was accepted and even highly regarded by Conservative society. But this did not exempt him, and particularly his Negro hands, from Ku Klux attention. On the night of December 26, 1870, about thirty disguised men raided his plantation, whipping two Negro men and an old woman and raping two or three girls. Waltemire was very closemouthed about the affair afterward, but in addition they apparently took a gun from him and made him dance for them; soon afterward he moved off the plantation.[24]

The night of February 6 may not have been typical for one Ku Klux band, but it was better documented than most. Of the twenty or so members, some at least came over from Cherokee County, Alabama, for the night's prowl. One of the first persons they visited was Thomas M. Drennon, a blacksmith and wagonmaker living three miles west of Rome. Drennon was one of the many white Republicans in this region who was afraid to vote that ticket because of the terror. When he denied being a Radical (under threats of a whipping if he answered otherwise) the Klansmen left him and moved on in the direction of town. They stopped next at the house of a Negro, Jordan Ware, whom they beat severely and robbed of a watch and gun. Ware had the reputation of being a good worker, but subsequent neighborhood gossip (broadcast in the Conservative press) had it that he was overly assertive and had addressed a passing white woman as "wife." The real sources of resentment were probably a certain local political influence and the fact that he rented a small farm and appeared to be prospering. The Klansmen then went on to the home of Joe Kennedy, another Negro. They shot and wounded him and beat his wife. The latter was a mulatto girl who apparently had been the mistress of one of the Klansmen; they were raided because of their marriage.[25]

About midnight the Klansmen rode into town. They committed no further violence, but they did stop the editor of the Rome *Courier* on the street. Editor B. F. Sawyer was an ardent Ku Klux apologist, but that did not prevent them from making him too dance for their amusement. This episode caused some good-natured banter between Sawyer and his journalistic rival, Henry W. Grady, who had become editor of the Rome *Commercial,* which carried a circumstantial account of the affair in its next issue. According to Sawyer this account told almost too much of the event not to have been written by an eyewitness.

We suspected all the while that we were exerting ourselves to please the ghostly crew, that we knew the form and recognized the snigger of the little fellow in the spotted shirt, who rode the little mule, and since no one but those engaged knew what transpired, we are now convinced that our suspicions were correct, and that the tail end of the Ku-Klux was no one else than our facetious young friend, Henry W. Grady.

Grady denied the identification—which would connect him implicitly with the Ware and Kennedy attacks as well—saying that Sawyer "was excited, and besides he always shuts his eyes when he whistles." His editorial remarks on other occasions do nothing to remove the suspicion that Grady was a member of the Klan.[26]

As early as January a number of planters and leading citizens around Rome were ready to speak out against the terror. The county grand jury in that month took the almost unprecedented step of condemning the actions of disguised bands. Their supposed purpose was to correct evils in the community, the grand jury said, but since legal officials existed to combat these evils

it follows as a clear proposition that those disguised bands are acting not only without lawful authority, but are actually offenders themselves against the laws of the land. . . . They are calculated to intimidate and frighten the ignorant, weak and helpless; to disturb the peace and quiet of the community; to render uneasy and dissatisfied the laboring population; to drive the laboring class from the country to the towns, and thus unsettle and seriously injure the farming interest, besides increasing the chances of pauperism in our towns.

Moreover, the element of disguise made it possible for malicious persons to commit the grossest crimes with impunity, the innocent suffering along with the guilty. The statement ended by calling on the members of all such organizations to disband and all good citizens to discountenance them and banish them from the county.

It was immediately apparent that the grand jury had stepped out of line. It was denounced by both of the local newspapers. Editor Sawyer of the *Courier* (who had not yet performed in the street for the Ku Klux) proclaimed the indictment "a magnificent tissue of bosh, uncalled for by the exigencies of the times, unfounded on fact, utterly worthless for the good it was doubtless intended to do and highly reprehensible and damaging to the interest, the prosperity and the reputation of the county." Sawyer said that he yielded to no one in his love for law and order, "but that our county is infested with such an element of mischief as this report avers, we do not believe. Its records are as free from crime as are any of the records of the most loyal county in New England." A week later a second grand jury echoed the *Courier* in denying any widespread lawlessness and repudiating the action of its predecessor. Critics accused the first grand jury of furnishing ammunition to Congressional investigators and thus encouraging federal intervention; it had defamed the good name of the county and committed near-treason.[27]

The *Courier* and other Conservatives were on the horns of the familiar dilemma. They knew as well as the grand jurors that crimes had been committed and things were getting out of hand. But they recoiled in fear and anger from any move that might bring retaliation or punishment of the offenders. Too many people were implicated in the terrorism for that. Editor Sawyer publicly regretted the Klan's entrance into Rome in February, for reasons deeper than his own personal discomfiture. He went much further, in fact: "Neither the interest of our people or the vindication of our peace and order requires their existence, and we unhesitatingly condemn their organization." When a Negro was murdered across the line in Chattooga County a few days later, the *Courier* pretended that malicious persons might have committed the crime in the guise of Ku Klux. "The time has passed for the Ku Klux," it repeated, and called respectfully on the people of Chattooga to disband the organization.[28]

Grady's *Commercial* took the same tack. In February it advised

those of its friends who have any connection whatever with secret organizations, *to remain perfectly quiet and orderly, for the present at any rate.* Let there be no suspicion of disorder or lawlessness; let there be no parading of disguised men, no stopping of innocent men and forcing them to dance; this is all child's play and foolishness. . . . The exciting elections have all passed; the good cause has triumphed; the enemies of Georgia are beat to the dust. . . . Then let the harsh asperities that were necessary during the "reign of terror" pass away like a dream.

"The eyes of the continent are on us," Grady continued; "a half dozen murders" in northwest Georgia during the next six months would be worth a hundred thousand Republican votes across the nation in 1872. But Grady called for no disbandment: *"Remember, brothers, that the strength and power of any secret organization rests in the attribute of mystery and hidden force, and in the fact that upon the thousand hills of our country a legion of brave hearts that are throbbing quietly can be called together by a tiny signal, and when the work is done, can melt away into shadowy nothing."* Only "if an inexorable necessity calls for action" should the Klan resume activity, and then it should "act promptly, with decision, and do nothing more than is absolutely necessary."[29]

But when Governor Bullock issued a proclamation reciting the atrocities on Colonel Waltemire's plantation and those of February 6, and offering rewards for the apprehension of their perpetrators, the *Courier* leaped to the Klan's defense.

We do not know anything about the whipping of the negro [Jordan Ware], but venture the assertion that if he was whipped at all, every lick he got was well deserved. . . . As to the outrages committed upon the premises of Colonel Waltemire, we cannot speak. We only know that so far as the maltreatment of Colonel Waltemire is concerned, that the charge is an arrant lie. We have never yet known a gentleman of Colonel Waltemire's address, worth, and character, to be interfered with by these horrid Ku-Klux, bad as they are. We only conjecture that if the outrages upon the dusky dames were perpetrated at all, they were done by some miserable radical scoundrels. . . .

Governor Bullock's reward money was drawn from the pockets "of a people whom he hates, and delights to slander and oppress." Months later Sawyer admitted to the Congressional committee that he knew little or nothing about the facts in these cases when he wrote his editorial. As to the Negroes whipped and raped on Waltemire's plantation: "I was not interested about them; I was more particularly interested about him, because he was a gentleman I very much admired and respected."[30] Outside attacks upon the Klan had led him to whitewash the organization he himself had gingerly opposed just before, and in subsequent issues to make substantially false denials of the outrages listed in Governor Bullock's proclamations.[31]

Some Klansmen may have heeded the calls to lie low, but others continued to ride, committing at least one more murder in Floyd County.[32] When efforts were made to arrest and indict them for various depredations on Negroes, it was almost impossible to make any progress. Suspects went into hiding and were shielded by the community; witnesses were afraid to testify before the grand jury, which returned only one indictment, and that grudgingly. Newspapers held up the accused as high-spirited boys out on a frolic who had done no real harm; their prosecutors were hounding them to gratify petty malice and to collect the governor's reward money. When a federal grand jury in Atlanta indicted one group which had escaped local prosecution the *Courier* threatened vengeance on the persons responsible. A deputy sheriff who was instrumental in this case received a Ku Klux warning which he later traced to a justice of the peace.[33]

Conditions were much the same in Chattooga County, next door. Klans were organized throughout the county and operated in close conjunction with dens in Cherokee County, Alabama. When an Alabama member was jailed for a minor offense at Tryon Factory, Chattooga County, early in the year members of the Chattooga and Cherokee Klans attacked the jail and released him.[34] Negro tenants on the plantation of Wesley Shropshire were raided so often that they threatened to move to Rome. Shropshire, a man of seventy-one, was himself vulnerable to Ku Klux persecution. Although a large slaveholder and longtime Democratic legislator before the war, he had become a Unionist, later served in the constitutional convention of 1868, and voted Republican in that year. He prevailed on the Negroes to stay and encouraged them to build a school for their children on the plantation. He also erected a school for white children half a mile away. Before the Negro school was completed the Klan returned and warned the blacks to stop. To reinforce the point they whipped the Negro teacher and left a note for Shropshire threatening to whip him too if he did not abandon the project. The Negroes stopped work on the building but established their school in a Negro church nearby. The Ku Klux returned again and burned the church. A story circulated through the community afterward that the Negroes themselves had burned the building because of disputes among themselves as to where the school should be located; another rationalization was that the Negro and white schools were too close together. But in fact the white school and the burned church were a mile apart and there had been no such dispute among the blacks. Although two Negroes were whipped in later raids, the blacks remained, built a new church, and established their school in it without further disturbance.[35] Raiding continued in the county at least until October, and as many as 200 Negroes may have fled into Rome in consequence.

Early in February Chattooga Klansmen became apprehensive that the Negroes were organizing to resist them. Two members went to the plantation of Robert S. Foster and pretended to be federal soldiers recruiting members for an anti-Ku Klux band. When one of the Negro hands there appeared to show some interest in the project, they killed him. Foster and his three sons (one of them a deputy sheriff in Floyd County) were themselves repeatedly molested by the Ku Klux when they made valiant but fruitless efforts to prosecute the suspected murderers.[36]

Despite this failure Chattooga was one of the few Southern counties where local officials were able to bring Klansmen to justice in the state courts. The case involved three young men, poor and illiterate, who robbed guns and a watch from some Negroes. One of the trio was the same Klansman who had recently been rescued from the jail at Tryon Factory, and another had participated in the Rome foray of February 6. The court-appointed defense counsel represented the best legal talent available in the district. The defendants probably would have escaped conviction if the local Klan organization had exerted itself to help them. According to defense counsel and the Democratic press, they were simply drunken boys on a frolic, and in fact they probably committed the depredations on their own initiative. But after they were sentenced in March to seven years in prison for robbery, Conservatives turned the affair to good account politically. The story went out, and was echoed through the country, that these convicted predators had turned out to be ex-Union soldiers and Republicans. The statement was almost certainly false, but it provided further evidence for those who cared to believe it that Republicans were responsible for most of the so-called Ku Klux outrages in the South.[37] Democrats also made much of the $7,000 in reward money which the prosecutors collected. They had all along characterized the governor's policy of offering rewards for the apprehension and conviction of Ku Klux as a gigantic Republican swindle—a means of enriching the party faithful at the expense of the taxpayers of Georgia. In the present case, however—the only one in which rewards were ever paid—the money went to the sheriff and two ex-sheriffs, all Democrats. They in turn gave $750 to the prosecuting attorney, a Republican. Later both the *Commercial* and the *Courier* in Rome retracted their charges of corruption and conceded that the money had been rightfully paid.[38]

Much less publicized was a case reported from nearby Bartow County, where three Klansmen were sentenced to life imprisonment in August for killing a Negro while going in a disguised company in June.[39] The Klan was relatively inactive in this county, and public opinion probably was less intimidated by it.

There was considerable Klan activity in the extreme northwest counties, just below Chattanooga, Tennessee. Beginning in 1870 in Gordon and Murray counties, Negroes were hanged or lynched, and there was much whipping and general harassment of Republicans of both races.[40] Tiny Dade County, in the corner between Tennessee and Alabama, boasted three Ku Klux dens under a Grand Giant.[41] One night a band of seventy-five commandeered a train on the Chattanooga and Alabama Railroad and took it on a two-hour trip. During the journey several Klansmen walked the length of the train with drawn pistols, apparently looking for someone whom they didn't find. At one station they took the telegraph operator from his office and made him stand on the platform in full sight of the frightened passengers while they whipped him thirty or forty lashes. His offense had been to declare after an earlier raid that he would die before the damned Ku Klux should ever whip him. After smashing his telegraph instruments and cutting the wires, they boarded the train and moved on. At another stop they took two Negro men and their wives from their homes and whipped them while the passengers listened to the victims' screams. When the night's business was done, the Ku Klux forced the train to back up to the Tennessee line, where they got off.[42]

Internal revenue agents in north Georgia identified the Klan primarily with moonshining operations. The federal assessor for that region testified that there were "at least a thousand little illicit copper-stills running in the district" in 1870–71, probably more than in any other district of the country. Most of these distillers were lawbreakers in other respects too, he said, such as horse thieves and peddlers or manufacturers of untaxed tobacco. They banded together to facilitate these operations and for mutual protection. Most of the evidence of a linkage between moonshining and the Ku Klux arises in about five counties of the northeast. Several Negroes from Walton County, already mentioned, testified that the major reason for raids upon them was apparently to frighten them into silence concerning illicit stills which Klansmen operated.[43]

White County, farther north, was one of those regions where revenue officers were afraid to go without a military escort. One of them had been murdered there by Klansmen in November 1870, when he was on the verge of arresting them for moonshining. When the Klan discovered that a Negro woman, Mary Brown, could identify the killers they first warned her to keep quiet and then tried to drive her off. Before dawn on May 21 they descended in force. She and her husband were both dragged from the house, stripped, beaten, and hanged briefly with chains around their necks. Some of the raiders (including the county's leading lawyer) took her off a short distance and questioned her closely concerning her knowledge of the murder. Then all of the female members of the household, including Mrs. Brown's mother and small daughter, were forced to disrobe and lie in the road while the Klansmen pranced around poking them with sticks and squealing—"the same as if they were stable horses just brought out." After an hour they departed with a warning to the Browns to leave the county. Republicans of both races were targets of Klan attack for political reasons as well. In July white Unionists organized a patrol of their own to ambush the Ku Klux as they went out on raids. One such ambuscade ended the raiding, although the arrival of troops soon afterward may have been the deterrent. As in many other Southern hill counties, the Klan was an instrument of feuding between wartime Confederates and Unionists, the latter being fewer in number, poorer economically, and less well organized.[44]

The evidence concerning Klan membership in Georgia in 1871 is similar to that in other states. Among witnesses before the Congressional committee, there was substantial agreement that the membership had deteriorated since 1868. Although men of property and standing were occasionally still active in the order—especially where political objectives remained to be achieved—it had become more and more a poor white organization. This was reflected in the accounts of men who were known or strongly suspected of night riding, and in the kind of persons arrested.[45] Many persons offered this explanation to account for the Klan's brutality. But in view of the brutality which had marked its course almost from the beginning, this defense of upper-class gentility is hard to accept. In Georgia too upper-class Conservatives had sanctioned terrorism when it served their own ends, but now that these were largely achieved they saw it increasingly as a cause of economic and social dislocation and as an invitation to greater federal intervention.

Benjamin H. Hill illustrated the problem of many Conservatives in his testimony before the Congressional committee. A furious opponent of Radicalism and all its works in 1868, he was presently moving to as moderate a position as it was safe for an ambitious Georgia Democrat to occupy. He now advocated a New Departure: the South must accept the Reconstruction acts and amendments with Negro suffrage, and it must put an end to Ku Kluxism or suffer continuing Northern control and punishment. The best men in the South recognize that outrages have taken place, Hill declared, and truly deplore them. Those who deny their existence are simply pandering to sectional prejudices for the sake of political advancement.

Yet Hill's testimony was filled with statements designed to soften these admissions and whitewash the terror which he well knew to exist. There was no general Ku Klux organization in Georgia, he asserted; both the Klan and the outrages it committed were local and sporadic. They were not political in motivation, although he conceded that the Klan had occasionally been used for this purpose. Republicans and Negroes were guilty of at least equal atrocities, he continued. A majority of Ku Klux were probably Republicans in some counties, he said, pointing to the three men who had been convicted in Chattooga County. Pursuing this fantasy a step further, he declared that Republicans had actually banded together to kill their fellow Republicans; the murdering of Democrats would not have aroused Northern opinion to the point of renewing federal intervention in Georgia. Hill professed not to know of any case in the state in which terrorism had made witnesses afraid to testify. Yet he himself had recently defended accused Klansmen in Jackson County, knew intimately the character of the terror there, and was doing what he could to cover it and protect its perpetrators. In behalf of the local Klan and the Conservative establishment there, he had promised J. R. Holliday that raiding would stop if Holliday ceased prosecuting the men whom he had battled through his house.[46]

Although Alexander H. Stephens had already pointed the way for Hill by rebuking Democratic newspapers which denied the Klan's existence, the precedent was not widely followed, and Stephens himself did nothing visible to suppress or discourage Ku Klux activity.[47] For Conservatives every social, political, and personal consideration dictated a continued defense or palliation—or silence at the very least—concerning the monster which had been set in motion three years before. And there were still many whites—perhaps a majority—who regarded the Klan as a beneficent and valuable institution.[48] The Savannah *Republican* (despite its name a Democratic organ) stood almost alone among the Democratic press when it declared in January: "These secret bands of marauders and assassins are a disgrace to any civilized country, and it is hoped some plan may yet be devised of ridding the country of their presence."[49] Such views were restricted, in public anyway, almost entirely to the Republican press, and it depended upon the Republicans to devise any effective plan to combat the evil.

Governor Bullock was continually besieged with letters and personal visits from victims of Ku Klux attacks, many of them Negroes, and from Republican politicians and others who lived in the areas of Klan activity. Where specific details of lawlessness were given, the information was taken down and sent to the respective superior court judges. They were instructed to present it to the grand juries as evidence on which to base prosecutions. Partly as a result of such prodding, scores of Klansmen were arrested in various counties, and some were indicted by grand juries. The Atlanta *New Era,* the chief Republican organ in the state, pleaded in vain with Democratic newspapers to report outrages fully and fairly, and with juries to indict or try cases without regard to the race or politics of victims. The actual convictions were apparently limited to the three isolated cases mentioned in Washington, Bartow, and Chattooga counties. These cases are extraordinary for the very fact of their existence, but they reflected no trend and had little if any effect.[50] The governor's policy of offering rewards to encourage prosecutions led to little besides Democratic charges of raiding the treasury.

Most of Bullock's errors were on the side of moderation. He refused to transfer a suspected Ku Klux prisoner from the Walker County jail, where there was fear of his being forcibly released, on the ground that the transfer would brand the whole county as lawless and embitter public opinion. He was also opposed to sending troops there, and in general he used soldiers more sparingly than in the past. Although he had successfully urged the restoration of federal control in 1868, he advocated no third reconstruction of Georgia in 1871, and even opposed the federal Ku Klux bill pending in Congress that spring. According to the *New Era*, which probably spoke for him, the responsibility for enforcing law and order still lay with the states; additional federal legislation was unnecessary and would irritate sores that should be left to heal themselves. When the Ku Klux bill became law Bullock made no objection to federal prosecutions under it, but he and the *New Era* continued to plead with local officials to head off this extremity by prosecuting offenders themselves.[51]

This moderation had no discernible effect on Georgia Conservatives. When Bullock and the *New Era* called attention to continuing outrages they were accused of slandering the state for political effect. They were like birds fouling their own nest, said the Atlanta *Constitution,* which declared that Georgia had no more disorders than other communities. When the Congressional investigating committee visited the state in October the *Constitution* denounced it as a political inquisition and falsified the nature of its findings, all the while disavowing any sympathy for lawlessness or the Ku Klux Klan.[52] The Democratic legislature, elected almost a year earlier, assembled in November and passed a resolution to the same effect. It promised to assist both the state and the federal courts in investigating and punishing any outrages that might have been committed. But since the legislature had denied the Klan's existence as a political organization and cast doubt on the evidence of outrages already gathered, the resolution meant very little.[53]

Meanwhile, as the legislators prepared to assemble, the air was full of reports that they intended to impeach the governor and replace him with a deserving Democrat. They had the votes to do so, and Bullock tried to outwit them by resigning before they met and turning over the governorship to the president of the senate, who was next in succession. Until the new legislature convened, this official was Benjamin F. Conley, a Republican. Bullock expected legal harassment even out of office and therefore left the state before his resignation was announced at the end of October. His flight gave color to the worst accusations which had been made against him, chiefly involving financial corruption, and was probably a tactical blunder. Although the legislature was never able to substantiate its charges of corruption and he was acquitted when he came back to stand trial in 1878, Bullock's name was blackened unnecessarily. Conley assumed office, but the legislature was not to be cheated of victory. It called a special gubernatorial election in December which the Republicans refused to contest, denying its legality. Democratic control of the state was so well assured by now that the Republicans could not have won in any event, and a Democratic governor, James M. Smith, was seated in Conley's place. Republican impotence was so fully apparent by this time that the transition had little effect on the Ku Klux Klan or state efforts to combat it. Raiding all but vanished toward the end of the year, largely because of its previous successes and the efforts of the federal government.

North Carolina: Rebels vs. Unionists in Rutherford

In North Carolina Klan activity continued into 1871 as Governor Holden was undergoing impeachment and removal for his attempts to stop it. The greatest disorder at that point was in five contiguous counties—Chatham, Harnett, Moore, Johnston, and Wake—in the middle of the state. One prominent target was a railway construction camp in Chatham. Some of the workers were Yankees, and the contractor in charge, William R. Howle, was a Republican. Also the camp contained a few females who bore a dubious relationship to the work at hand. Howle was threatened several times during the fall of 1870, and most of his Negro hands were driven off. He was denied credit by a local merchant who even had him arrested briefly on a trumped-up charge, and a magistrate confessed his inability to afford him any protection. Late in April forty or fifty Ku Klux raided the camp, whipped several men and women, and subjected an eighteen-year-old girl to other indignities. Howle went to Raleigh, obtained a commission as a deputy United States marshal, and returned to arrest three of his attackers. But he dared not spend his nights there, and his railway construction was completely broken up. As a result he forfeited his contract with a loss of $2,200 and went into bankruptcy.[1]

Several white farmers and planters of this vicinity also suffered attack for kindnesses to Negroes or for voting the Republican ticket. An elderly man who had distributed land among his former slaves was whipped at

least once and forced to walk home five miles naked in the cold after the
Ku Klux cut off his clothes with knives. A neighbor and his wife, who had
given an acre of land for a Negro school, were forced to burn the building
while the Klan looked on.

The greatest sufferers were the blacks, who were subjected to repeated
raids and beatings. Many slept in the woods that winter, and others moved
to Raleigh.[2] Still others fought back. Around Christmastime 1870, Essic
Harris of Chatham County fought off Klansmen who attacked his cabin.
The battle lasted for at least half an hour as the Klan ignored pleas by
Harris's landlord to leave him alone. They finally left only after Harris
wounded two of them. He too was wounded, but his wife and children
inside the house miraculously escaped injury. Another black man in
Harnett County reportedly killed a raider in a similar attack.[3]

More dangerous to the Klan were signs of Negro organization throughout the region. This seems at first to have been aimed at providing
collective defense against attack. When Klansmen learned of it they
increased their own activity, especially in confiscating Negroes' guns. This
presumably underlay the attack on Essic Harris; they had already broken
into his home and those of several neighbors, seizing guns a week or two
earlier. But the black organization soon turned to arson as a means of
retaliation. In December and January several barns and other outbuildings
went up in flames. Their owners were usually (but not invariably) suspected of complicity in Klan activity. As usual, the local authorities lost no
time in looking into these instances of Negro crime, and they soon
uncovered evidence of a secret oath-bound society. A number of blacks
were arrested and brought to trial in January 1871. Several were convicted
and sentenced to prison terms in the Chatham superior court, with Republican Judge Albion W. Tourgée presiding.[4]

The Democratic press continued to regard the enforcement of laws
against Klan terrorism as more outrageous than the terrorism itself. Here
too Democrats professed, on little or no evidence, to believe that many of
the Ku Klux outrages had been committed by Republicans in order to
hasten the sending of troops. Josiah Turner's Raleigh *Sentinel* declared that
anyone who favored the federal Ku Klux Act or North Carolina's Shoffner
Act would not hesitate to whip a woman for political effect. The *Sentinel*
denied that Ku Klux had any greater right to whip their fellow citizens than
President Grant had to send troops, but when local boys were arrested for
this offense by federal authorities they were regarded as martyrs. Well-to-
do Conservatives outdid one another in advancing bond money for the
accused.[5]

Outrages were also reported from several of the western mountain
counties;[6] but the Klan's main center of operations in 1871 came to be the

counties of Rutherford, Cleveland, Gaston, and Lincoln, west of Charlotte. These counties were adjacent to the worst Klan region of South Carolina, and there was much correspondence across the state and county lines. Of the four counties, Cleveland and Rutherford were by far the worst. They were overwhelmingly rural and isolated, Rutherford in particular. Its county seat of Rutherfordton was a village of fewer than 500, thirty-six miles from the nearest railway station and eighty miles from a telegraph office. The terrain in both counties ranged from hilly to mountainous; it was a land of small farmers and few Negroes. The Democrats dominated Cleveland with many votes to spare, but in Rutherford they were outnumbered by a large Unionist, white Republican element. The latter, combining politically with the few Negroes, were usually able to carry the county safely in a fair election. There had been great conflict here between Confederates and Unionists during the war, with the latter organizing into secret societies such as the Red Strings and the Heroes of America. After the war much of the bitterness persisted. Despite individual exceptions, the white Republicans were primarily poor farmers located in the least promising parts of the county. Thus where the partisan hatreds of the times were not compounded with the usual ingredient of race conflict, an artistocrat-poor white antipathy took its place. After the war Negroes and white Republicans organized into Union Leagues, and many ex-Confederates countered with the Ku Klux Klan. The Union Leagues had disappeared by 1871, but the Klan remained and in fact reached its pinnacle in numbers and operations early that year. Many Negroes suffered from Ku Klux depredations in both counties, but the majority of sufferers were white Republicans.[7]

The Ku Klux organization in most of these counties dated back to 1868; outrages began the next year and became progressively worse, reaching major proportions in 1870. The organization came later to Rutherford, probably late in 1869. In Cleveland, Lincoln, and Gaston the Klan appears to have begun under upper-class auspices. It resulted not only from the usual Conservative fears of the Union League and actual or potential Negro criminality, but also from the Republican state militia law of 1868 which added still another dimension to the specter of organized and armed Negroes taking over the community and running amuck.[8] The leadership in Cleveland included four of the county's leading attorneys and Democratic politicians: Colonel Leroy McAfee (chief of the county), Colonel H. D. Lee, H. D. Cabiness, and Captain Plato Durham. Another leader was Sheriff B. F. Logan.[9] McAfee was a leader in the Holden impeachment proceedings in 1870–71. He was also the uncle and boyhood idol of novelist Thomas Dixon, whose book The Clansman and other writings helped envelope the Klan in mythical glory a generation later.[10]

Upper-class leadership, where it existed, was reflected in greater organization and conceivably greater discipline among the members, although the latter point is dubious. The Democrats of Rutherford County, unlike those of Cleveland, Gaston, and Lincoln, were weak and disarrayed because of the Republican ascendancy there. This doubtless explains why the Klan came later, and spontaneously from below rather than from above. One den, perhaps the first, was organized in the winter of 1869–70 by a local man who brought it from Gaston. Others were formed during the next year by men who had been initiated into the order across the line in South Carolina, where many of the farmers went to sell their produce. The result was a haphazard growth of independent dens which acted as they pleased, often without constitution or bylaws or the faintest trace of authority from above. This condition was prevalent in some degree everywhere in the South, but it greatly alarmed the leadership in Cleveland County at a time when they were trying to control the excesses of their own followers. In the spring of 1871 they came over and tried to reorganize the Rutherford Klans, initiating many new members and installing Randolph A. Shotwell as the first county chief with instructions to bring the groups under control. Polk County, to the west, was in somewhat the same condition, and his authority extended there too.[11]

Probably no one could have performed that office, judging by its failures elsewhere, but Shotwell was hardly the man to inspire confidence of success. He was subject to the "softening influence of rather frequent potations," to use his phrase, and in general displayed an unstable personality. A young Confederate veteran embittered by the war and its aftermath, he was filled with hatred for Radicals and black men. After the excitement of wartime, he explained in a later memoir, he found village life dull and joined the Klan at an early date for the excitement it offered, as well as the feeling that he was working for a cause. He was well educated for the time and place and had mastered the vitriolic prose style which often passed for journalistic writing. In 1868 Shotwell began the *Vindicator,* a rickety Democratic weekly in Rutherfordton, which he ran on a shoestring until the shadow of bankruptcy forced him to sell it late that year. He then went to Asheville and edited a paper there; but after being wounded in a street fight with the United States district attorney, whom he had attacked for prosecuting Ku Klux cases, he returned to Rutherfordton. He ostensibly read law, but he was actually at loose ends and ran up whiskey bills with a group of equally aimless friends, to the mortification of his father, the Presbyterian minister.

Shotwell was an inefficient Klan chieftain. Although he was popular enough in his own circle, he had little acquaintance and no rapport with the illiterate country boys who made up most of the Klan's rank and file. His dissipations were so time-consuming that he seldom left town, and matters drifted. New dens sprang up, took on new members indiscriminately, and began night riding without his knowledge and with no regard to his authority. From his own later account, it is doubtful that he disapproved very strongly of the activity they were engaged in; certainly he made little effort to stop them.[12]

So far as they claimed any higher allegiance, the Klansmen in this part of the state belonged (at least by 1871) to the Invisible Empire, the same order that existed in adjacent South Carolina. The organization was divided into dens, and the names and duties of den officials correspond closely to those established in the Tennessee Prescript. Disguises varied, some wearing white and others red. The total membership in Cleveland County was 600 to 800; in Rutherford there were eight or more dens with at least 300 members.[13] The members belonged to every economic and social category, although small farmers and their sons predominated. This was another moonshining region, and members often used the Klan to further such activity. Many joined the order unwillingly. In some cases they were forced to affiliate because they had learned too much about it. In other cases they were ordered to choose between the Klan and the Republican party; the Klansmen refused to tolerate any "milk-and-cider men." Many, including some Republicans, joined for purposes of protection, promising to forswear the Republican party but with the understanding that they would take no part in Klan operations. They thereby bought immunity for themselves and their families in much the same fashion as weaker men attached themselves to feudal lords in the Middle Ages, to acquire security against the prevailing disorder.[14] Occasionally there were echoes of the familiar Conservative charge that Republicans put on disguises and raided their enemies in the guise of Ku Klux, but such cases were rare if they occurred at all.[15]

Klan raids were supposed to be ordered in advance by a committee of the local den, and this often happened in practice, but there were also unauthorized raids. Frequently another den (sometimes in an adjoining county or South Carolina) was called upon to do the work. As usual, this was probably truer of bigger raids than the smaller ones, but the fact that fewer victims here were Negroes may have made this practice more widespread than elsewhere; white men were more apt to prosecute their assailants if they recognized them. The most disordered parts of Rutherford County were the eastern and southern portions, adjoining Cleveland County and Spartanburg County, South Carolina. North Carolinians played an important role in Ku Klux activity beyond the state line, and their services were repaid in kind.

In Rutherford drunkenness was not confined to the county chief, and a great proportion of the raiding was stimulated with bootleg whiskey.[16] Under the circumstances it is surprising that, in Rutherford at least, the Klan committed no murders; several were reported in Cleveland. A few Negro girls were reportedly raped, but nearly all of the assaults were beatings—"Birch-bark on the bare backs," as Shotwell put it. Politics certainly played a part in these attacks; nearly all of the victims were Republicans and many were hated as former Leaguers or Red Strings, but as usual most attacks were attributed to personal transgressions or feuds. Personal and political feuds ran so deeply that they sundered families, and occasionally brother attacked brother. Apart from white Republicans and Negroes, the victims included women of easy virtue and white men accused of wife beating or concubinage. One of those whipped as a Unionist and Republican was John Nodine, an aged veteran of the War of 1812. Others were beaten for reporting illicit stills or talking too much about the Klan. Some victims were robbed, and Negroes especially were forced to surrender guns. Two Negro schools and a church were burned, as well as a black man's newly built house. Among the Negroes particularly, most of the outrages were probably never reported because of fear of worse to come.[17]

Despite their numerical advantage, Republicans in Rutherford County were at much the same disadvantage as those elsewhere. They made little effort to match the Ku Klux, either in organization or in violence. But their numbers emboldened local officials to take greater action against offenders than was customary in Klan-ridden counties. The first arrests they made were not followed by swift convictions, but they scared the Klan leadership into taking steps of its own to reorganize and repress violence. Actions by Congress to investigate the Klan and to enact laws against it were probably factors also.

Hence Messrs. McAfee, Lee, Cabiness, and Durham came over to Rutherfordton during court week late in March and conferred with local Democrats on the need to suppress unauthorized raiding. The upshot of this meeting was the effort to reorganize under Randolph Shotwell. During this visit Cabiness initiated scores of new members who were hopefully of higher caliber and more amenable to discipline than the current rank and file. In later weeks Shotwell made at least halfhearted efforts to go out and do the same in the countryside. On at least one occasion Plato Durham heard in advance of a projected raid in Rutherford County. With Cleveland Sheriff B. F. Logan and several others, he went to a meeting of the den involved and pleaded with them to desist, but in vain. The effort to reorganize and impose moderation from above was clearly failing.[18]

The raid in question was made on one Aaron Biggerstaff less than two weeks after Shotwell's installation and without his knowledge. Biggerstaff was an elderly man, an overly loud Unionist who was accused of having helped Federal soldiers seize horses from his Confederate neighbors during the war. He had also helped Union army prisoners to escape. On top of this, early in 1870 he had helped track a Ku Klux band to the home of his half brother (a member) after one of the first Klan raids in the county. Biggerstaff and his friends fired into the brother's house, for which he was later convicted of forcible trespass. On the night of April 8, 1871, about forty Klansmen raided Biggerstaff's home, whipping both him and his married daughter. The old man recognized some of his attackers and had them arrested. A preliminary hearing was scheduled to be held before a United States commissioner in Shelby, the Cleveland County seat, in May. Biggerstaff and his family set out for Shelby, intending to testify against the prisoners. Communications being what they were, it was an overnight trip, and at nightfall they set up camp along the roadside. The Klan had been following them. It suddenly swooped down and gave Biggerstaff another beating, with a warning to return home. For the time being he did as he was told, but he moved into Rutherfordton for safety and then submitted another list of names, including his half brother's, to the authorities. Some of the men he named were arrested by a United States marshal and a detachment of soldiers who came from Raleigh for the purpose, and others managed to escape.[19]

The Klan had already threatened to invade the town and assassinate several of the Republican leaders. The latter therefore began keeping a nocturnal armed watch which lasted for the greater part of May. Conservatives ridiculed them, complaining that it gave the town a bad name and was bad for business. The Republicans finally disbanded after local Democrats assured them individually and by formal resolution of the county convention that they were in no danger. In fact the convention, with dozens of Klansmen and Randolph Shotwell as secretary, pledged itself to assist the authorities in stopping outrages and bringing offenders to punishment.[20] Less than two weeks later, on the night of June 11, close to a hundred Klansmen invaded the town in the largest raid the county ever saw.

Their exact intentions were never clearly established and were in fact the subject of rather drunken dissension among themselves. In general they intended to silence Aaron Biggerstaff and to kill or intimidate the entire Republican county establishment. The Republican leaders had rendered themselves doubly obnoxious in recent weeks by exposing the Klan terror to the world and by doing everything they could to suppress the order and bring its members to justice. They had sent appeals to Washington and followed them up by testifying before Congressional committees; they had appealed to the governor and the President for troops; and they had instituted proceedings against some of the terrorists in both the state and the federal courts.

Unquestionably the foremost Republican in the county and the focal point of Conservative wrath was superior court judge George W. Logan. Logan had emerged during the war as the leading Unionist in this part of the state and was elected as such to the Confederate Congress. After the war no one was more eloquent than he in class appeals against the Conservative aristocracy or more effective in welding together the Republican organization which won control of the county in 1868. Democrats hated Logan with a passion, denouncing him as an ignorant demagogue, totally unfit by character or education to hold the office of judge. The leading lawyers of his circuit (nearly all Democrats) tried to secure his removal on the ground of incompetence. Logan was a demogogue, but the other charge is harder to substantiate. The lawyers claimed that he was too ignorant of the law to pass judgment on it, yet in 1869, soon after his elevation to the bench, the governor was asked to relieve him temporarily at the Rutherford and Polk court terms because he had earlier been employed as counsel in nearly three-fourths of the cases then on the docket. Much of the animus against him must be written off as politically inspired. Logan had been a target of Klan hostility for some time, and on one occasion he delayed holding the Cleveland court term because of threats on his life. At the same time he took the lead in efforts to procure troops for these counties and to prosecute suspected Klansmen. Randolph Shotwell even stretched a point by crediting a letter of Logan's, which was read on the Senate floor, with causing the passage of the federal Ku Klux Act.[21]

After Logan, the most outspoken opponents of the Klan were J. B. Carpenter, superior court clerk and editor of the Rutherford *Star,* and state legislator James M. Justice. Carpenter in particular had done yeoman work, carrying Logan's letter to Washington and testifying before the Ku Klux investigating committee. (In fact his presence there on June 11 likely spared him from attack that night.) The *Star* had consistently attacked the Ku Klux since their first appearance, and it was the only Republican organ in that part of the state. Justice had instituted legal proceedings against several Klansmen, and the Ku Klux understood early in June that he and Carpenter had the names of 200 members whom they proposed to arrest and prosecute in the next few weeks. This prospect drove the Klan to action.[22]

One of their first stops on the night of June 11 was the home of James Justice. He was awakened by a volley of gunshots and the sound of men breaking down his door with an ax. The Klansmen burst in and beat him into unconsciousness. They dragged him outside and down the street, all the while shouting and firing their guns. (Shotwell says they had repeatedly consulted their hip flasks on their way into town.) The main body went off toward the Rutherford *Star* office, leaving ten or twelve men in charge of Justice. He soon regained consciousness and was walked to a place just outside town where the Ku Klux had dismounted and left their horses. His captors held him here, repeatedly threatening his life and declaring that they intended "to rid this country of this damned, infamous, nigger government." They would hang the Republican leaders, they said, just as the latter were trying to hang the leading Klansmen. This persisted for half an hour, punctuated by the sounds of continual shooting and shouting in town, until the main body rejoined them.

The raid was badly planned and executed, owing in part to the general intoxication and lack of discipline. They made such a commotion getting Justice out that Biggerstaff and his daughter escaped before the Klan got around to searching the old hotel where they had been staying. They were also looking for Judge Logan and did not discover until now that he was holding court in another county. They found the office of the *Star* easily enough, however, and made a shambles of it. Then they quarreled over what to do with Justice, their only prisoner. Some wanted to dispatch him on the spot lest he identify them later. The leader told Justice that his death had already been decreed, but that he was reluctant to carry it out. Instead he tried to bargain for information: the whereabouts of Biggerstaff and Logan and the names of Klan informants who had talked to the Republicans. (One of the informants, a member whose sister the Klan had whipped, was already known, and they whipped him too that night.) In the end they released Justice and rode off after making him promise to support "the Southern cause" and take no part in the approaching political campaign.

Justice continued his political activity, nevertheless, and he redoubled his efforts to punish Klan terrorists. About half of the men had come from a distance; some belonged to the Horse Creek den in Spartanburg County and the leader identified himself as a South Carolinian. But others were local men whom Justice thought he recognized. He subsequently had about a dozen of them arrested, including Randolph Shotwell and his brother. Shotwell repeatedly denied taking part in the raid or even knowing of it beforehand. But he acknowledged later that worried men had been urging him to make such a raid ever since the arrests began. Other Klansmen testified under oath that Shotwell had organized the raid with intentions to kill Justice and Biggerstaff and break up the *Star* office. The Klan accomplished nothing by the Rutherfordton raid; rather it hastened arrests and the Klan's own destruction.[23]

The legislature had stripped Governor Caldwell of any power to employ militia effectively against the terrorists. And he had the example of

Governor Holden before him. Therefore, as Judge Logan and others reported outrages to him from Rutherford, Cleveland, and other counties early in the year, he passed them on to President Grant and the local Army command, asking that troops be sent. A detachment did go to Rutherford in April, after the first Biggerstaff raid. It made fifteen arrests and then withdrew, taking the prisoners to Shelby, where they were scheduled to appear until the second raid occurred.[24] After the Rutherfordton raid, and at the request of men of both parties, Caldwell sent the state attorney general and other legal officers there to investigate all recent outrages and prosecute offenders. He was prepared to call a special court term to sit for six months if necessary. Troops were sent back at the same time to help out and also to make arrests for illicit distilling.[25]

Until the soldiers and Governor Caldwell's emissaries arrived, the Klan continued to prowl around town making threats. A man was scared off one night just as he was on the point of firing into a window of Justice's residence. As soon as the soldiers arrived, the Ku Klux scattered or lay low. A large number—presumably those who had the most to fear—fled the county and escaped arrest. Scores of others came in (either voluntarily or under arrest) and made sworn statements concerning their knowledge of the organization and its activities. For many who had been unwilling Klansmen this afforded the first safe opportunity to get out. Their statements provided additional evidence against others, who were arrested in turn if they had not fled. Many prisoners were released on bond, but those charged with the most serious offenses (including Randolph Shotwell) were lodged in the county jail. The *Star* (now back in operation) jubilantly referred to this establishment as the Democratic Hotel. The arrests proceeded, often a few at a time, from mid-June through the remainder of the year and into 1872. Within a few weeks close to one hundred men had been bound over for trial.

The governor's original intention was to try these men in the state superior court. But a decision was soon made to proceed instead under the federal Enforcement Acts, and Caldwell's envoys left after a week. Most of the arrests were made, therefore, under the direction of the United States commissioner, Nathan Scoggins. Logan, Carpenter, Justice, and the other local Republican officials—the Klan's erstwhile victims—gave him their full and enthusiastic cooperation. In fact a New York *Herald* correspondent and the Army commandant in Raleigh, Major C. H. Morgan, neither of whom had an ax to grind, both mentioned after visits that an air of vindictiveness and revenge seemed to animate the prosecution. For this reason Morgan advised against a plan by Logan and Justice to organize a local militia company for protection against further Ku Klux incursions. Republicans received a shipment of fifty carbines to replace weapons which the Klan had previously confiscated from them. However jubilant the Republicans were in striking back at the terrorists, there is no good evidence that the prisoners or anyone else was seriously mistreated. The Rutherford Klan gave out far more violence and brutality than it ever received.

Republican fears of a Klan resurgence were not totally groundless. In July a party of Klansmen raided the McDowell County jail at Marion and released some of their colleagues who had been sent there owing to overcrowding at Rutherfordton. There were persistent reports that they planned a second major raid on Rutherfordton for the same purpose. Shotwell himself advised against this, and the prospect of a clash with federal troops prevented it from coming to pass. But to guard further against the possibility and to relieve the overcrowding, Shotwell and the other prisoners were transferred to Raleigh in August. When they went on trial there in September it was the first mass trial of Southern Ku Klux to occur under the federal Enforcement Acts, and it drew corresponding attention around the country.[26] Shotwell was convicted, sentenced to six years at hard labor, and fined $5,000. With several others he was sent to the federal penitentiary at Albany, New York, where he stayed for two years until pardoned by President Grant.[27]

Only two Democratic newspapers in the state, the Raleigh *Telegram* and the Salisbury *Old North State,* had conspicuously opposed the Klan all along; the others took their lead from Josiah Turner's Raleigh *Sentinel.* Thus they tended to minimize Ku Klux organization, attributing those outrages they could not overlook altogether to spontaneous groups who had no general significance. The idea of a broader Klan organization, especially if it was politically motivated, was dreamed up by the Republicans for their own gain. Editors also blamed Republicans for much of the raiding, but this rested more on faith than on evidence. When they did admit the Klan's existence they defended it as a bulwark of law and order against Negro crime. An old man told James Justice: "If it was not for them we would not be sitting here by this fire this morning, for the negroes would take it away from us. . . . The negroes are working well, and the fear of the Ku-Klux keeps them about right and proper."[28]

The *Vindicator* in Rutherfordton sometimes treated Ku Klux raids with a levity reminiscent of the early Klan days, as in the case of Aaron Biggerstaff: "On Saturday night, at about the hour when graveyards yawn and restless spirits walk the earth, a ghostly procession of men in disguise surrounded [his] home, and very unceremoniously proceeded to apply the rod to . . . father Aaron."[29] After the Rutherfordton raid had destroyed the press of its local competitor, the *Vindicator* reluctantly admitted that the Klan existed thereabouts and mildly condemned it. Local Democrats did the same and sometimes more vehemently in private.[30] However, the Raleigh *Sentinel* felt differently: "We think the radicals whipped Justice and destroyed the Rutherfordton *Star"*; real Ku Klux could not possibly have gone into that Republican town, captured the "king of the leaguers," and carried him off a prisoner. Furthermore, Justice had been handled very gently compared with such men as John W. Stephens and Wyatt Outlaw, whom the Klan had wished to punish. (The *Sentinel* forgot that it had accused the Republicans of murdering both Stephens and Outlaw.) "The success of the radical party depends on the continuation of the outrages upon negroes and worthless whites like Justice and Carpenter. If nobody will beat them they will beat themselves. If no one will destroy their press they will do it themselves." An Asheville editor suggested that the raid had been devised by Carpenter as a means of getting a new press from the bounty of sympathetic Republicans in the North.[31]

When the arrests began, the Democratic press let out the same anguished howls of persecution and tyranny as greeted Holden's militia campaign the year before. Now for the first time the Shelby *Banner* saw a reign of terror in next-door Rutherford. "Logan, Scoggins & Co., successors to Holden, Kirk, & Co.," were engaged in a despotic campaign which victimized

helpless women and children, the aged and infirm, as well as the strong and athletic. . . . Honest citizens dare not speak their honest political sentiments. To be politically opposed to these petty tyrants, is a passport to the black hole, the Rutherfordton jail, in which the best people of the country are . . . crowded almost to suffocation, begging EVEN FOR WATER, like famished children. The young men of the country, who are as innocent of crime as a new born babe, are leaving for other parts, rather than summit [*sic*] to the oppression of these people.

Vicious and ignorant vagabonds of both races were now wreaking vengeance after they had been properly chastised for their own crimes.[32] The *Vindicator* carried an article on the Ku Klux confessions that were coming in every day. It reported falsely that none of the persons confessing (Conservatives in this section called them "pukers") knew of any outrages committed or had participated in any. This information was copied by the *Sentinel* and thus distributed throughout the state. Many tears were shed, therefore, over the plight of poor farmers being separated from their families and crops and dragged, first to Rutherfordton and later to Raleigh, to face the long and expensive ordeal of standing trial for crimes they had not committed. Most of the defense costs were borne as usual by wealthy Conservatives who supplied some of the best lawyers in the state. Some Conservatives, including original Klansmen like David Schenck of Lincoln County, were ready to admit privately that some of these members deserved what they got, but very little of this appeared in the Conservative press. And even these men were still inclined to look upon the whole proceeding as political persecution.[33]

Meanwhile Commissioner Scoggins continued issuing arrest warrants and holding preliminary hearings. In October he moved over to Cleveland County and in November to Lincoln County. Colonel McAfee, the Cleveland Klan chief, was one of those arrested, and Sheriff Logan was reportedly among those who fled. The arrests in these and other counties extended at least into February 1872.[34] The effect of these arrests, and even more of the confessions arising from them, was to divide and embitter the Klansmen against one another. The diaries and correspondence of Randolph Shotwell and David Schenck are filled with anathemas hurled not only against their Republican "persecutors" but against "traitorous and lying" Klansmen who had testified against them, accusing them of activities in which they claimed to have taken no part, or indeed had tried to prevent.[35] Later, in the federal penitentiary, Shotwell and others would return the favor by incriminating some of those who were still at large.[36] On Christmas day the Cleveland County Klan (perhaps after another reorganization) tried to stage a parade in Shelby, but it was broken up by the Army lieutenant in command.[37] In general, Klan demoralization was so great that its activity came to a halt in North Carolina by the beginning of 1872.

CHAPTER 22

South Carolina: Outside York County

After the Klan played such a prominent part in the South Carolina Presidential campaign of 1868, Governor Robert K. Scott forcefully condemned the organization in his next legislative message. If the people of South Carolina did not curb the Klan, he warned, it might lead to counterorganization and civil war.[1] On the surface it looked as if his warning had been heeded. Violence subsided markedly during the next two years—more than in any other state except Virginia. Nevertheless, sporadic flurries of Klan activity in many upcountry counties were a subject of recurrent concern to the state government. Early in 1869 the legislature enacted a new militia law and empowered the governor to buy 2,000 stands of arms. Until the militia was organized and ready for service he was authorized to raise a company of 100 or more men and send them wherever they were needed.[2] That summer 300 Winchester rifles were dispatched to small militia companies which had been organized in Edgefield and Abbeville counties following a recurrence of violence there.[3]

Similar developments in York ultimately made that county the most conspicuous theater of Klan activity in the South. In October 1869 Klansmen there whipped a Negro, William Wright, and burned his house. When the owner of the house, a white man, complained to Columbia six state constables came up, organized a militia company of seventy men, and equipped them with more of the state's Winchester rifles. Nearly all the recruits were Negroes, but they elected a white man, John R. Faris, as their captain. The constables found it almost impossible to procure evidence against the marauders, but Wright identified one Abraham Sapoch as one of his assailants and had him arrested. In the face of strong evidence against him, Sapoch was discharged after producing an alibi; he in turn had a warrant issued for Wright, charging him with perjury and false arrest. Eventually Wright was convicted and sentenced to the penitentiary. Similarly the county grand jury, while admitting that persons had been outraged by armed bands, found no evidence to incriminate anyone. Instead it presented the militia company (which had done nothing) as a public nuisance. The Yorkville *Enquirer,* the local Democratic newspaper, initially criticized the Ku Klux depredations in mild terms, but it too found that the organizing and arming of Negro militia was a far greater outrage and source of danger to the community. Denying the existence of any secret organization save the Union League, it concluded that the militia was a political device intended to carry the county for the Republicans in the October 1870 elections.[4]

During the spring and summer of 1870 continuing scattered outrages led the state government to organize and equip other militia companies in several upcountry counties. The more this was done the more Conservatives fell prey to the old fear of a Negro uprising. At the same time they denied or ignored the outrages which preceded this organization and, like the Yorkville *Enquirer,* regarded the militia as a Republican means of taking the fall elections by storm. Some Democrats requested Scott's permission to organize companies of their own at state expense for protection against the imagined black peril. The governor refused, seeing them as the real source of danger and his own militia as a defensive force. Although state law forbade the organization of private companies, many whites did so anyway, as they had in 1868. Confederate Generals Wade Hampton and Matthew C. Butler encouraged this movement, Butler himself organizing a company in Edgefield.[5]

The extent of Conservative organization and the danger of a major confrontation were revealed by an incident in Laurens County in September. A disturbance occurred at the little town of Clinton between local Negroes and whites. Each side feared an aggressive move by the other and called for reinforcements. Within a few hours at least 300 Negroes assembled at the county seat of Laurensville, nine miles away. At the same time 1,000 or more armed whites converged on both towns, many of them coming from surrounding counties. They were organized in companies under a single command, and they proceeded to take over the towns and all their approaches. At Laurensville a wagonload of new Winchester rifles and ammunition was quickly issued to the assembling whites. At this point sane heads prevailed on both sides and the crisis passed with little or no bloodshed. The authorities feared this was but a prelude to a massive effort by the Conservatives themselves to take the coming state elections by storm.[6] Each side regarded itself as on the defensive, and violence actually diminished in the upcountry with the approach of the election on October 19.

Conservatives went all out to win this election, which involved the governorship and control of the entire state government. Given the state's large Negro majority, they realized the futility of contesting the Radicals on a straight party basis, which would have pitted Negroes against whites as in 1868. Instead they formed a coalition with disaffected Republicans of both races under the name of the Union Reform party. This was the only peaceful and legitimate way in which they could hope to win over enough Negro voters to carry the state and return to power. To make their ticket more attractive to Negro voters, they nominated a highly regarded Republican, Richard B. Carpenter, for governor and a number of black men for local offices. Despite the Reform party's endorsement of Negro suffrage and legal rights, there was no disguising the fact that most of its backers were white supremacy Democrats. The freedmen again cast their ballots all but unanimously for the Republican ticket headed by Governor Scott. He was re-elected by a vote of 85,071 to 51,537, which closely approximated the Negro and white voter registration.[7]

The election passed quietly in most places, but not in Laurens, which had become a racial and political powderkeg. Two days before the election hundreds of armed whites again converged on Laurensville and began patrolling the streets. This time too they may have feared a Negro riot, but many of the younger men were eager for a fight and intended to start it themselves. Their major concern was whether a company of federal troops which had been stationed there would intervene promptly enough to prevent them beforehand or catch them afterward. The troops were required as always to act on orders from the sheriff, and quite possibly he would be unwilling or afraid to call on them. On election day there was little disturbance in Laurensville, but at Clinton the whites attacked the polling place and drove off a state constable named Tyler, who was stationed there as an observer. Tyler at once came to Laurensville and mustered in the Negro militia company. Immediately the whites organized in formation opposite them, ready to charge. At this point the federal soldiers appeared and their commander persuaded both sides to disperse and the Negroes (but not the whites) to put up their arms. That night most of the outsiders of both races left town. The troops also departed the next morning in obedience to previous orders.

The riot broke out within hours of their leaving. Whether planned or not, it was precipitated by a fight between a local Conservative and a constable. A crowd gathered and someone fired a shot. Now more whites rushed to the scene and began firing at every Negro in sight. The Negroes fled, ending the melee. But the alarm had gone out, and hundreds of mounted whites were soon on their way into town again, often traveling in companies and under orders from superior officers. They kept coming for the next day or two, 2,500 or more, a large proportion from adjacent counties; General Butler said later that he had sent a company from Edgefield when a messenger arrived reporting that the Negroes in Laurens "were out of line." For two days there ensued a more or less systematic hunt for prominent Negroes and white Republicans, who either went into hiding or fled the county. About a dozen men were killed, most of them blacks and all Republicans; two of the victims were Negro legislator Wade Perrin and the newly elected probate judge, a white man.[8]

Conservatives around the state were frustrated and furious over the outcome of the election. There was not only anger at the blacks, but a near-hysterical feeling that they had thrown down the gauntlet to the whites. "We [regard] the solid black vote cast against the nominees of the Reform party as a declaration of war by the negro race against the white race, by ignorance against intelligence, by poverty against actual or potential wealth," declared the Charleston *Daily News,* ordinarily a voice of sanity. It was now the duty of white men to organize and arm themselves in the name of "decency, purity and political freedom." Other newspapers echoed this appeal.[9]

Some basis for white fears was afforded by Negro reactions to the Laurens riot. In Columbia, within a half hour after hearing the news, two Negro militia companies mustered in, fully armed and equipped, ready to march to Laurens as soon as they received the governor's order. This was not forthcoming, and Scott finally prevailed on them to disband after they had spent part of the night firing off guns in the streets and threatening bloody vengeance on their white oppressors.

It was against this background that the state executive committee of the Union Reform party met in Columbia in November, together with other leading Conservatives. At that meeting they authorized the creation of a statewide semisecret organization which they called the Council of Safety. The purpose was ostensibly defensive—to protect the outnumbered white population against the menace of a Negro rising. A constitution was drawn up, printed in pamphlet form, and distributed to leading men around the state in January 1871. Local councils were then set up in several counties, but the panic which inspired the organization gradually abated, and so did interest in the Council of Safety.[10]

On the other hand, the October election was followed by an upsurge of

Ku Klux organization and violence that soon dwarfed the terrorism of 1868. Night riding and outrages on Negroes took place in most of the upper counties, but earlier centers of terrorist activity like Abbeville, Edgefield, and Laurens remained relatively peaceful. The worst counties now were Spartanburg, York, Union, and Chester. Throughout this region Klan membership increased; by the spring of 1871 it came to embrace most of the adult white males in Spartanburg and York at least, and completely dominated public opinion.

There was no visible statewide Ku Klux organization, although there is hazy evidence of a common pattern of activity in many counties. Klan organizations in a number of them, not always contiguous, engaged in a nearly simultaneous effort during the spring of 1871 to intimidate local Republican officeholders into resigning. There is also evidence of an inter-county organization in the upcountry and extending into North Carolina, perhaps under the nominal leadership of J. Banks Lyle, the Spartanburg County chief. On one occasion a Grand Klan met in that county, composed of delegates from Spartanburg, York, Union, and Chester as well as some from North Carolina.[11] In general, however, similarities in Klan opera-tions were probably coincidental as they were throughout the South. Such cooperation as took place across county and state lines was fairly local in character and resulted more from appeals for help in individual cases than a continuing higher organization to enforce such appeals.

There were probably several county-wide Klan organizations headed by county chiefs. In Spartanburg and York these chiefs were powerful and active enough to have been generally known. Captain J. Banks Lyle of Spartanburg County was a Confederate veteran, state legislator, and principal of a male academy at Limestone Springs, near the North Carolina line. The chief in York County was Major James W. Avery, who had held the position since 1868. He was a planter and the proprietor of one of the county's largest stores, in Yorkville. Both men exercised active leadership; they planned and occasionally took part in raids, and were accessory to murders if they did not personally commit them. Despite the relatively high degree of organization, the secrecy and undercover nature of Klan opera-tions eroded and eventually destroyed Klan discipline in these counties as everywhere else. The leaders' objectives were largely political—to disarm and destroy the black militia, drive Republican officials from power, and bludgeon Republican voters into quiescence. They were not averse to punishing a suspected Negro rapist or murderer, but they had little interest in the regulation of petty misconduct among the blacks or the settling of personal grievances. Nevertheless, it was just such operations which domi-nated Klan activity by the rank and file. In the leaders' estimation this activity did more harm than good, by threatening to invoke the wrath of the federal government. Arrests and prosecutions would topple the whole organization and expose leaders as well as followers to the full penalties of the law. The purpose of the Grand Klan meeting referred to above was to forbid further raiding without its own order and to establish penalties for violations. This decree had little or no effect, and Avery in particular spent much of his time and energy in 1871 trying to stop or slow down the terror which he had helped to begin.

Here too the Klan drew its membership from every rank and class of white society—obviously so where it embraced the greater part of the adult white male population. The highest leaders were drawn from the more or less educated planter and professional class, while the rank and file represented every element from wealthy planters' sons to illiterate poor whites. Den chiefs were often little more educated, mature, or responsible than their followers, which explains much of the raiding that occurred. But, as elsewhere, much of the night riding was conducted on a free-lance basis by men or boys who were all but totally lacking in any sense of responsibility. Their intellectual and cultural horizon scarcely extended beyond the county line. Born into a society which regarded the black man as less than human and possessing no rights which they were bound to respect, a society which had flaunted its intolerance of any dissent on racial and sectional matters, and where the accustomed leaders themselves initiated violent proscription, these country boys lacked any conception of the moral enormity or the fateful consequences of the crimes they committed. As between the upper and lower classes, it would be difficult to assign the greater guilt for the atrocities which took place in the name of white supremacy.[12]

Some Klan operations extended as far into the low country as the counties of Clarendon and Sumter. Here rural stores were subjected to nocturnal attack and forced to close, in some cases because they were suspected of receiving stolen cotton from freedmen. One merchant was attacked after having rented land and advanced supplies to men of both races, enabling them to set up for themselves instead of remaining as hired laborers. Another was raided after he refused any more credit to men who did not repay him, but continued to extend it to Negroes who did. Blacks were whipped and occasionally murdered. Although political charges were not invariably brought against them, the victims of both races were almost invariably Republicans. The Klan in these counties appears to have been under greater upper-class control than elsewhere, and it dropped from sight in April 1871 after public notice that the leadership would punish any counterfeit Ku Klux activity.[13]

Similar activity was reported from Lancaster and Fairfield counties, farther inland. In Fairfield more than a hundred disguised Klansmen rode into Winnsboro one night in April with a bugler at their head and left a notice at the newspaper office demanding the resignation of most of the county officials.[14] This action was obviously part of a wider campaign because similar notices were served in a number of counties at about the same time.[15] A Negro county commissioner was assassinated in Clarendon,[16] and another in Newberry was attacked and wounded by a disguised party who raided his home. He in turn seriously wounded one of his assailants, a tavern loafer named Faulkner, who was captured and arrested. Faulkner showed signs of telling all he knew about the Klan, and after his release on bail, a party of white men followed him to Edgefield and murdered him.[17] The general charge against these county officials was that they were incompetent or corrupt. Many resigned under this pressure, and at least one (in Newberry) was legally prosecuted for malfeasance in office.

Chester County, north of Columbia, was one of those in which Ku Klux activity became most common after the 1870 elections. Night riding and the attendant outrages occurred all over the county but were most common in the western part, where plantations were largest and the Negro population greatest. Many blacks regularly slept out in the woods at night, but others determined to fight back. The obvious means of resistance lay in the militia companies which had been organized and armed for just this purpose. In February 1871 one of these companies, under a Negro captain, Jim Woods, began to picket the roads at night, sometimes turning back white men whose business they were unsure of. On the night of March 4 they repulsed a Ku Klux attack on Captain Woods's house, wounding one of the attackers and capturing some disguises. The next night they drove off a larger Klan assault. Fearing still worse to come, they mustered in the following morning, about eighty strong, and began marching toward the town of Chester, the county seat, to get reinforcements and more ammunition. Apparently they expected a massive white turnout against them, for they hoped to get help from another militia company in town and sent out runners as far as Union and Newberry counties to summon additional men. On reaching Chester they stacked their arms, stationed pickets, and obtained more ammunition from John C. Riester, a white Republican leader and the major in command of the county militia. The sheriff ordered them to disperse and return home, but they refused to do so, arguing that their purpose was wholly defensive.

The white men in town believed otherwise and proceeded to organize for their own defense. They sent messages as far as North Carolina calling for reinforcements to put down an impending Negro rising. During the night there was an exchange of gunfire between a small group of whites and a squad of militia. Around dawn the whites advanced in a body toward the railway depot, where they found the militia drawn up in line of battle to meet them. Stopping to parlay, they persuaded the blacks to agree to leave town and return home. But instead the Negroes went to a church five miles away, stationed themselves in a strong defensive position, and again sent out runners for rations and reinforcements. Their fear was that if they dispersed as the whites demanded, they would render themselves helpless in case of any white attack.

By this time hundreds of white men were converging on the county from all directions, responding to appeals and reports that grew more exaggerated the farther they spread. Many of those who responded—perhaps all of them—were Klansmen out of disguise. Some came down by train from Rock Hill, Charlotte, and Cleveland County, North Carolina; others came up from Winnsboro and points south. One contingent of fifty or sixty, coming toward Chester from the west, had to pass by the militia camp and found that they had blockaded the road. The blacks themselves opened fire, using trees and rocks for cover. The whites, led by Colonel Joseph F. Gist of Union, returned the fire and drove the militiamen back with a flank attack. The Negroes lacked the training, leadership, and morale to contest the field for very long against seasoned Confederate veterans. They retreated for three-quarters of a mile in fairly good order, occasionally turning and firing, but then broke and ran in all directions. The largest group, about twenty in number, headed northward toward York County, where a small federal garrison was posted. News of their coming preceded them and coincided with a local panic among whites there arising from similar causes. The York County sheriff went out with a posse, intercepted the militiamen, and took them into protective custody for a short time. They were then released and returned to their homes.

The "Chester riot" scared almost everyone. Major Riester went down to Columbia and returned with a company of federal infantry which was soon augmented by additional troops. A few days later Governor Scott sent up an officer to disarm the local militia companies. Riester wound up his affairs in Chester and left the county permanently, to the cheers of his Conservative neighbors. With the militia rendered powerless, the Ku Klux continued raiding in the countryside without any real hindrance either from it or from the federal garrison in town.[18]

The Klan was even more active in Union County to the west. In November 1870 it murdered a white Republican justice of the peace whose home was a political rallying place for Negroes. Soon afterward the recently elected probate judge was whipped. Several Negroes were murdered, and scores of them were beaten or otherwise outraged; some 200 fled the county in consequence.

It was a group of Negro militiamen again who indirectly precipitated the Klan's greatest feat, perhaps the most massive Ku Klux raid anywhere in the South. On the last night of 1870 a squad of militia was traveling along a country road, apparently on its way to guard the home of a white Republican who had been threatened. On the way they encountered one Mat Stevens, a one-armed Confederate veteran who peddled bootleg whiskey and was presently taking a barrel of it into Union, the county seat. The militia stopped him and demanded some of his freight. When he refused, several of the blacks took him into the woods and murdered him. This crime seemed to confirm all of the mounting white fears and hatred of the militia. The next day crowds of armed white men scoured the town and county, visiting the homes of militiamen, confiscating guns, and making several arrests. Sometimes this was done in an orderly fashion and sometimes not. At one house in town the blacks refused to admit them and a gun battle broke out, resulting in one death on either side. Eventually about a dozen Negroes were jailed, most of them for suspected complicity in the Stevens murder. For several days afterward there were fears that the blacks would try to release them forcibly, and a heavy guard was posted around the jail. To allay fears further, Governor Scott sent up an officer who completed the disarmament of the militia and took the guns back to Columbia.

On the night of January 4, forty or fifty disguised Klansmen rode into town and went to the jail. That building was constructed of stone with narrow windows, somewhat resembling a medieval fortress. With any sizable defense it was probably impregnable against attackers who lacked artillery. But none of the town patrol were at the jail that night; they were at the hotel instead, and the Klansmen ordered them to stay there. When the sheriff refused to surrender the keys at their demand he was overpowered. The Ku Klux broke into the jail and removed five prisoners whom they had most reason to believe were involved in Stevens' murder. They took those men out of town to a place in the woods and made them step forward one at a time to be shot by a firing squad. Two of the blacks were killed on the spot; the other three were wounded and left for dead but subsequently were rearrested.

At a public meeting the next day the townspeople requested that federal troops be sent for. Pending their arrival the town guard was to protect the remaining prisoners and police the town. The Negroes joined in this operation, and a measure of harmony was temporarily restored. But no troops came, and the guard was eventually discontinued. A month later the prisoners were still afraid that the Klan might return and finish the work it had bungled the first time. Accordingly some of them obtained a court order transferring them to Columbia for safekeeping. A new sheriff had taken office by this time. He was a weak man, much under the influence of a Conservative deputy whom the white community had insisted he take on as *de facto* sheriff. The deputy immediately found a technical flaw (real or imaginary) in the court order and showed it to most of the local lawyers for their opinion. These men believed that the transfer was a Radical trick to cheat justice by getting the prisoners to Columbia and then releasing them. The sheriff delayed obeying the order for several days, intending (as he later said) to take the prisoners to Columbia on February 13.

On the night of the twelfth the town was again invaded, this time by an army of at least 500 men, masked and gowned. They stationed guards along the streets who warned everyone to stay indoors, turn off his lights, and keep away from the windows. Operating with full military discipline, responding to whistle signals rather than voiced command, the main body surrounded the jail and demanded the keys. The jailer (who was later charged with participating in the earlier lynching) was reportedly overpowered, and the attackers intimidated his wife into giving them the keys. After ten Negro prisoners were removed a whistle was blown; the pickets came in, fell into ranks, and the whole party marched off with the black men in tow. The next morning eight bodies were discovered a mile and a half from town; two were hanging from a hickory tree and six were tied to trunks of other trees, their bodies riddled with bullets. The last two prisoners escaped; they were later apprehended, tried, convicted of the murder of Stevens, and executed.

In both raids the Ku Klux had come to Union from the north. Although the prisoners had identified some of their attackers the first time as local men, the great majority in the second raid probably came from Spartanburg and York counties; a few may have come from North Carolina. Troops were belatedly sent to Union, but Ku Klux bands continued to raid Negroes in the countryside for several months to come. Here too the Klan leadership tried to restrain such activity with published newspaper warnings against "counterfeit Ku Klux." Meanwhile all the Republican county officials were driven from office and replaced with Democrats. Republican leaders who would not repudiate their party had to stay in Columbia. As a refugee Negro legislator put it, the Union County Republican party "is scattered and beaten and run out. They are just like scattered sheep. . . . They have no leaders up there—no leaders."[19]

The presence of incompetent or illiterate Republican officials was one of the most frequent excuses given for Ku Klux activity in South Carolina. The speciousness of this argument is indicated by conditions in Spartanburg County. In terms of Klan organization and violence, this was one of the two worst counties in the state, yet it had a large white majority and Democrats had not needed the Klan's intercession to win most of the county offices. Night riding occurred all over the county, but the worst section was around Limestone Springs, the home of county chief J. Banks

Lyle. This region was adjacent to Rutherford County, North Carolina, and Klansmen on both sides of the line crossed over frequently, as in the Rutherfordton raid of June 1871. For many weeks Ku Klux raids were a regular Saturday night affair. Hundreds of Negroes and white Republicans (of whom there was a considerable number in that part of the county) regularly slept out in the woods and swamps during the winter and spring of 1870–71.

One of the first Ku Klux raids occurred just before the October 1870 election; the Republican election managers for Limestone Springs Township were visited by a party of forty or fifty men and warned not to hold an election. One of the managers, after being forced to drop his pants and submit to a whipping, was presented with the posteriors of a Negro man and woman (another election manager and his wife) and told to kiss them since he was such a believer in nigger equality. He avoided a further order to have sexual relations with the woman. The Klansmen forced him to march back and forth in double-quick time and then required the two men to whip each other. The Klansmen themselves whipped all three and used a knife to cut off a portion of the Negro man's left ear. One of the Ku Klux involved in this raid was a teacher at Limestone College (Captain Lyle's institution) who wore his academic robe and did not bother to disguise himself.

Several men were subsequently arrested for this raid. One of them, an elderly man who had apparently led the band, was himself forced to walk back and forth double quick, until he fainted. Democrats were furious at this breach of conduct and found it a far greater outrage than Ku Klux activity which might have preceded it. When the Spartanburg *Republican* printed a graphic account of the raid the Democratic paper in Union excoriated it for journalistic indecency; the outrage (if it occurred at all) must have been done by the Republicans themselves, it said. Soon afterward the prisoners were released on bond, and no further action was taken against them in state courts. On the other hand, the persons responsible for arresting them were hunted down and whipped by the Klan.

Although local government was controlled by the Democrats in Spartanburg, the Klan was distinctly political in much of its activity. In October it broke up the Union Leagues and intimidated voters in at least two election districts. Captain Lyle, having closed the polls altogether in his own district with the raid already described, brought twenty-five men to a neighboring polling place on election day and remained there during the day threatening death and destruction to Republicans. Subsequently, in raid after raid Klansmen declared that they intended to whip out every Negro and white Radical until nigger government was banished from the land. Republicans of both races were required to recant their party affiliation publicly lest they receive more severe treatment than they already had. John Genobles, a sixty-nine-year-old farmer, was whipped and told to make a public renunciation from the courthouse steps; he did so on the next sales day, when country people were in town in largest numbers. When he finished his statement some of the more prominent Democrats in town came up to shake his hand and welcome him to the fold. Other recipients of this Klan order elected to publish notices in the *Carolina Spartan,* the local Democratic newspaper. Such notices were fairly common during the winter and spring.

Two recipients of Klan attention were planters of impeccable antecedents who had followed former Governor J. L. Orr into the Republican party in 1870. In doing so they followed the old injunction to join them if you can't beat them. One of the two, Dr. John Winsmith, was awakened one night in March by about forty Klansmen in his yard. He met them with two single-shot pistols and proceeded to walk out among them shooting, cavalier style. He did little damage to the Ku Klux, who took cover, but they wounded him in seven places. They left, however, and did not bother him again. Winsmith's political associate, General B. F. Bates, chose a different course. Wishing to avoid such a confrontation himself, he took a leaf from the book of some of his humbler white Republican neighbors and joined the Klan. Then he organized a den composed exclusively of Republicans for purposes of self-protection. When this den refused an order from above to go on a raid they were themselves raided and Bates killed one of the attackers.

As always, raids were made for nonpolitical reasons too, although the victims were virtually all Republicans. The white election manager was also whipped for holding a Negro Sunday school and expanding it into a two-day-a-week affair. Some Negroes were whipped because they had displaced poor whites as tenant farmers. Others were attacked for giving up farm labor for better-paying jobs on a railway construction gang. Many were accused of committing crimes or social misdemeanors. A seventy-year-old man charged with stealing watermelons was shot down as he opened his door for the Ku Klux. Another black man, being whipped because he had voted the Republican ticket and gone to work on the railroad, overheard a white neighbor who was in the party whisper to the spokesman of the band, "Tell Isham when he comes to a white man's house to pull off his hat." A Negro woman was raided and beaten after she had declined to do domestic work for a white family. The Klan was also used to protect moonshining activity. Although the Negro militia were also offered here as a pretext for Klan activity, the local militia never fully organized. Most of their guns were never distributed, and all of them were eventually recalled to Columbia.

In November 1870 twenty to fifty Klansmen rode into the town of Spartanburg to demand the release of a white man who had been jailed on suspicion of killing a Negro. The sheriff threatened to shoot anyone who tried to break into the jail, and they eventually left empty-handed. After this, local Republicans clubbed together for mutual protection and slept at one another's houses in rotation. This lasted until the arrival of troops in March. Raiding continued in the countryside well into the summer of 1871, and rural Republicans sought refuge in the town, so far as they could find means of support there.

When a Congressional investigating subcommittee came to Spartanburg in July it was given an itemized list of 227 persons who had been outraged since the preceding fall; at least two persons were murdered by the Klan in that time. Most victims were Negroes, and half lived in Limestone Springs Township. The list was certainly incomplete, for many attacks were never reported. Informed witnesses guessed that a full total would be 400 to 500. Many of the victims were women and children.

The crime wave soon reached a point where Conservative landowners feared it would drive off their Negro laborers altogether. No Democrat dared stand up openly and denounce the Ku Klux, but biracial public meetings began to be held in several townships, in which the blacks promised collectively to take no further part in politics and whites denounced lawlessness in general terms. The *Carolina Spartan* did its part by publishing these resolutions (as well as the continuing individual renunciations by white Republicans) and by impartially condemning both the Ku Klux and the Union League. The local Klan leadership may itself have sponsored these public meetings as it did in York County, but otherwise it seems to have taken less interest in moderating the terror than was true of other counties. The terror had proceeded too far to be checked by such feeble efforts, and it finally ended as a result of federal intervention.[20]

CHAPTER 23

South Carolina: York County and the Climax of Terror

Bad as conditions were in Spartanburg, York County to the east was worse. In no Southern county did the Klan organize more fully or take over more completely. In every subject of which it chose to take cognizance the Klan was supreme; but, as elsewhere, no one was supreme within the Klan. It became a juggernaut propelled forward by the size and irresponsible character of its membership and the terror it inspired in every person in the county, including its own members. Within a few months the county was reduced to a state of near-anarchy which no one dared to combat. In none of these characteristics was it unique, of course, except in degree. Because it was regarded in a sense as the final straw by the federal government, it received more national publicity and governmental attention than any other Southern county. If the history of the Ku Klux Klan properly begins at Pulaski, Tennessee, it ends most fittingly at Yorkville, South Carolina.

The village itself was (and still is) a pleasant country town with tree-shaded streets and attractive homes. Not yet overshadowed by the nearby mill town of Rock Hill, it was the commercial center and capital of a moderately prosperous agricultural county devoted to the raising of cereals and cotton. There were few large plantations but many of medium size along with smaller farms. The county was relatively isolated, but it had recently acquired railway connections north and south; Yorkville was the upper terminus of a line running southward to Chester and Columbia, while Rock Hill, eighteen miles east, was on a line between Charlotte and Columbia. There was no telegraph to Yorkville until September 1871. The county population of 25,000 was divided almost evenly between blacks and whites. Perhaps a majority of the latter and virtually all of the former were illiterate. Only in the hillier upper portion, near the King's Mountain Revolutionary battleground, did whites predominate heavily. A minority of these were Republicans, and given the even racial balance of the county, they held the balance of political power whenever there was a full and free election.

The ease with which this political balance could be upset was one reason for the Klan's early appearance in York. It was one of the first counties in the state to which the Ku Klux movement spread in the spring of 1868.[1] Klan activity seems to have been responsible for diminishing the Negro vote and giving the county to the Democrats in the Presidential election of November 1868. The Klan lapsed into inactivity until early in 1870, when a flurry of raiding led to the organization and arming of several Negro militia companies. Whites then stepped up their own extralegal organization, but there was little or no violence before the October state election, which the Republicans carried in this county by 500 votes.

As elsewhere in the state, the Klan organized and became active to an unprecedented degree after the results of that election were known. York resembled every other county in the character of its Klan membership; men of every class belonged to the order, and it was organized and led at least initially by men of standing. Not even Spartanburg rivaled the *extent* of its membership, however. It was later shown that by the spring of 1871, about 1,800 of the 2,300 adult white males in the county were sworn members of the Ku Klux Klan. This figure included some white Republicans, and even a few Negroes were induced to participate in raids, although they were never initiated. Many persons joined the order through fear of the consequences to themselves if they did not. A large proportion of the members took no active part in its operations, if only for reasons of age. The county contained at least forty-five dens, ranging upward in size from ten members apiece. Perhaps a dozen of the dens were in Yorkville itself. The mayor and both town constables were members, and the county chief, Major J. W. Avery, was a leading merchant. There is no question that he controlled many Klan operations, although the smaller raids were usually ordered by den chiefs if they were ordered at all.[2]

Raiding began again in October 1870 and gradually increased in frequency, with Negroes the primary victims.[3] This gained comparatively little attention outside the black community until the Tom Roundtree murder early in December. Fifty or sixty Klansmen (some local and some summoned from North Carolina) came to Roundtree's house at night, shot him, and cut his throat. It was later urged in extenuation of the crime that he had been a belligerent, "bad Negro," who threatened to kill all the neighboring whites; actually he seems to have been a leader among the Negroes of the vicinity and may have threatened to resist the Ku Klux. His death was ordered by a Klan council headed by William C. Black, a former legislator and well-to-do landowner of the neighborhood. When Round-tree's widow identified several of the attackers and had them arrested, Black organized their defense and helped produce alibis which brought — their release. The widow and her children were driven from their home and forced to subsist on charity from the Army garrison which later came to town. This was the only serious effort to bring Klansmen to book in the local courts for some time to come.[4]

The Negro response to the mounting outrages took two forms. The militia companies were reactivated; they marched about, sometimes firing their guns, to the alarm of many whites; occasionally they guarded roads and stopped white men to inquire their business. They uttered many threats of retaliation, but as organized bodies they committed little or no violence. Other Negroes, however, took up the torch and began waging a war of arson on the property of individual whites. At least a dozen farm buildings went up in flames during January and February 1871 as the result of Negro incendiarism; perhaps two dozen buildings were burned by summer. Conservatives blamed the fires on white Republican leaders who allegedly incited the blacks by their incendiary language. Especially guilty in this view were state comptroller general John L. Neagle, a resident of the county, and county treasurer Edward M. Rose. Both men might have advocated arson as a last desperate means of striking back at Klan terrorism, but this defensive aspect was not emphasized or recognized in Conservative accusations.[5]

The Klan responded with threats of further escalation. On January 22 it issued a public notice that in case of further fires it would execute ten leading Negroes and two white sympathizers of the vicinity. It also threatened to execute the officers of Negro militia companies which continued to picket the roads, and to punish any persons using incendiary language.[6]

Partially as a result of this notice, Negroes in and around Yorkville came in turn to fear a massive attack by the whites. Accordingly, a militia company posted itself in town, using as headquarters a former hotel owned by state senator William E. Rose, father of the county treasurer. The building also housed treasurer Rose's office and a barroom. The militia marched up and down the streets, drilled, and shot off their guns, and they may occasionally have jostled white people off the sidewalk as Conservatives indignantly claimed. Reportedly the blacks also threatened to burn the town. On the night of January 25 some shots were fired from the hotel building; soon afterward three gin houses, a mill, and a barn burst into flames in various directions out of town, and easily visible there. Whites were certain that the shots had been a signal from the younger Rose to Negro arsonists. Fearing that the town would go up next, whites sent out messengers into the countryside calling for help. Scores of armed men— many or most of them Klansmen—responded to the call. Some came from as far as Gaston County, North Carolina. A clash was averted only by invoking the usual formula: the armed blacks withdrew, leaving the armed whites to patrol the town for some nights until fears abated.[7]

A few days later Governor Scott confirmed this arrangement for the future by sending an officer to disarm the county's militia companies—the same tactic he used after the outbreaks in Union and Chester counties.[8] The guns were stored in several places around the county. On the night of February 10, forty or fifty Klansmen called at the home of Captain John R. Faris, whose company had been the first to organize a year earlier. The Ku Klux confiscated a number of Winchester rifles stored on the premises and rode off.[9] Similar raids occurred throughout the county, undoubtedly ordered by Major Avery. Sometimes it was done in disguise after dark and sometimes openly in the daytime. About seventy-five guns were taken from the railway station in Rock Hill, and the total number seized was close to 200. Some ammunition was stored at the probate judge's office in York-ville; one night the office was broken into and one of the boxes removed. (It was later revealed that the mayor of Yorkville led this party.) The sheriff immediately dispatched the remainder of the ammunition and what few guns he had left to Columbia. The Klan also made a general search of Negro homes around the county, confiscating weapons.[10] By these means the Klan rendered most Negroes defenseless and also rearmed itself for its own continuing operations with the latest and most effective weapons then in existence.

From November 1870 into September 1871 the Ku Klux were out night after night raiding Negro cabins, often following a regular weekly schedule. When the terror abated in one neighborhood, it shifted to another for a time and then returned. The whole county was affected. There is no way of knowing how many persons were outraged, for as always many or most of the victims were afraid to report attacks. The best estimate is that there were 11 murders, more than 600 cases of whipping, beating, and other kinds of aggravated assault, plus uncounted instances of lesser personal abuse and threats. A few victims were white, but the vast majority were blacks, including men, women, and children. In addition four or five Negro schools and churches were burned or torn down; one of them was rebuilt and destroyed four successive times. It was a record of sustained brutality which few places in the country ever matched.

Attacks were made for the usual variety of reasons, but many were specifically political. One black man (Charles Good) refused after a whipping to make the desired promise that he would vote the Democratic ticket henceforth, and was subsequently killed. Men of both races were required to publish notices in the Yorkville *Enquirer* renouncing their Republican affiliation. Virtually the entire male Negro population in some districts slept out in the woods during the winter, spring, and summer to avoid attack; the handful of Democratic Negroes were never molested, however. After troops arrived in Yorkville many blacks sought asylum with them, and some slept in the commandant's yard. He issued rations, cared for the wounded, and put some of them to work at jobs around the village, but there was far too little employment or money to support all of them. Many fled the county entirely, abandoning homes, crops, and belongings. Some plantations were wholly denuded of labor.[11]

The coming of federal soldiers followed another crisis in February. As with the whites of Union and Chester counties at this time, the people of Yorkville were again seized with the fear of Negro revolt. Since the Klan was then in full career, completing the governor's disarmament of the black population, the reason for this alarm is hard to find. But Major Avery again sent word to his Ku Klux confederates in North Carolina, who responded (mostly from Cleveland County) to the number of 275. No crisis materialized, and they soon returned home.[12] County treasurer E. M. Rose was regarded as the root of all evil in Yorkville, and he had to be got out of the way. Accordingly, the Klan planned a large raid for the night of February 26, with the primary objective of capturing Rose and putting him to death. Then, after the plans had been laid and word had gone out to members to assemble at the proper time and place, Avery and his colleagues were thunderstruck to hear that a company of federal troops had been sent for and were due to arrive on the day preceding the attack. They were expected to come up by train from Chester. Since the raid could not be advanced on such short notice, the Klan decided to delay the troops. On the night of February 25 two rails were torn up from the track about two miles out of town. There was no intention to derail the troop train, since the locomotive which was supposed to pull it had not yet left Yorkville to go down to Chester. Moreover, the job was done very neatly and ultimately required only half an hour to repair. But when the damage was discovered on the morning of the twenty-sixth, the railroad crew simply looked over the situation and returned to town for the rest of the day. They thereby postponed the soldiers' arrival until the twenty-seventh.[13]

Meanwhile, on the night of the twenty-sixth, about fifty Ku Klux rode into town shortly after midnight and headed for Rose's Hotel, where the Republican leader lived and kept his office. Rose had been tipped off in advance and escaped through a window before the Klan could reach him.

They broke into the office, demolished the furnishings, and scattered records, but made only superficial efforts to open a safe supposedly containing the county funds. They also destroyed the barroom in the same building, spilling out all the liquor they could not consume on the spot or conveniently carry with them. Then they went to the home of Thomas Wright, a Negro county commissioner, who also managed to evade them. When some blacks began firing at them from cover, the Klansmen decided to write off the evening and left town. The raid was not a complete failure, however. The next day Rose came out of hiding and took refuge with the newly arrived soldiers. After four or five days the commander, Captain John Christopher, sent him to Columbia disguised as a soldier and he never returned. More than $12,000 of county money disappeared with him. The official explanation was that the Ku Klux had taken it, but Rose almost certainly absconded with it, probably going to Canada.[14]

There were no further raids on Yorkville itself, but the arrival of troops made no difference in Klan raiding in the country; this became more frequent and bloody than before. In fact most of the Ku Klux murders appear to have taken place within two weeks after the soldiers' arrival. On the night of February 25, the same night that the railway tracks were torn up, Anderson Brown, a Negro suspected of arson, was taken from his home and shot to death. Within the week two more Negroes were shot, one for suspected arson and the other for allegedly living with two white women.[15]

On March 6 came the most celebrated murder, the hanging of Jim Williams, recently a militia captain. Conservatives later justified the crime by quoting threats that he allegedly had made to "kill from the cradle up," and by claiming that he was the leader of a band of Negro Ku Klux. Williams had spoken out openly and often against the Klan, but so far had done nothing further. Somehow he still had a dozen or more militia guns in his possession, however, and the Klan feared him as an organizer of Negro resistance. His murder was so important that forty or fifty men were delegated to perform it. The leader of the raid was later identified as Dr. J. Rufus Bratton, a physician. Most of the band had no idea of the purpose of the raid until it was well under way. On nearing Williams' home some were ordered to hold the horses at a distance while the rest approached the house on foot. They broke in, dragged Williams outside, and hanged him from a nearby tree, Bratton himself putting the noose around his neck. Before leaving, they affixed a note to his body saying, "Capt. Jim Williams on his big muster."[16]

The next day the coroner went out and held an inquest, the jury returning the standard verdict of death by persons unknown. To reach the body in the first place he had to pass through a crowd of fifty or sixty Negro militiamen, members of Williams' late company, who were milling around in mixed confusion and defiance. For two days they threatened to kill all the white men in the vicinity, and might have done so if they had found a leader. Local whites felt so alarmed that they sent to Major Avery for men to help protect them. Avery came with fifteen or twenty men who spent the night and then returned to Yorkville.[17]

The confusion of these events was compounded by the coincidental arrival in the same neighborhood of about twenty Chester County militiamen, fleeing northward from their recent clash with whites there. Hearing of their approach, Sheriff Glenn summoned a posse and went to meet them. The militiamen were arrested, disarmed, and taken to Yorkville jail for safekeeping. Later Captain Christopher took charge of them and, when the excitement blew over, sent them back home clandestinely, one by one.[18]

The Negroes did not descend upon Yorkville, but the Klan continued to ride. A band of twenty or thirty shot another black militiaman, Alex Leech, and threw his body in a creek. At the ensuing inquest a Negro witness refused to testify, saying that his life would pay for it if he did. The coroner and other white men standing around the room nudged each other and laughed, and the jury returned the usual verdict.[19] By contrast, when a number of blacks banded together under disguise and robbed a store they were arrested the next day, tried, convicted, and sent to jail.[20]

There were already signs of a mild reaction to the terror among many Conservatives. They wanted to get rid of lawlessness and violence if it could be done on their own terms. Republicans and Negroes rather than the Klan itself were generally blamed for Ku Klux barbarism; white men were not really culpable for their own violence in view of the provocations they had received from Negro militia, Negro arsonists, and Republican officeholders. The Yorkville *Enquirer,* the county's only newspaper, was a voice of moderation by the standards of the time and place. On February 9 it impartially condemned both Negro burnings and Klan outrages, although the Union League (which was suspected of fomenting arson) was singled out for greater abuse than the Klan. The editor told older whites "to advise the young men not to engage in whipping and murdering the colored people."[21] Such elementary advice required a certain courage in York County in February 1871. Two days later a biracial public meeting was held in the Clay Hill region of the county, where whipping and burning had been common. The meeting recognized that Ku Klux outrages had preceded Negro arson (a rare concession), and it condemned both. Moreover, some of the whites promised to protect the Negroes from further outrage in return for a pledge not to hold any more secret nocturnal meetings of the Union League.[22]

The reaction spread after the bloody days of late February and early March. The Klan leadership itself was largely responsible. They had now achieved all of their objectives with the disruption of the militia, the cowing of the Negroes generally, and the expulsion of the foremost Radical leader. Especially with a federal garrison in residence, they saw more danger than benefit in continued raiding. But the terror persisted despite their probable efforts to contain it within the organization. On March 9 they published a notice in the *Enquirer* warning against unauthorized threats in the name of the Ku Klux Klan. Nevertheless, it declared, "the intelligent, honest white people (the tax-payers) of this county shall rule it! We can no longer put up with negro rule, black bayonets, and a miserably degraded and thievish set of lawmakers . . . the scum of the earth, the scrapings of creation. We are pledged to stop it; we are determined to end it, even if we are 'forced, by force, to use force.' "[23] The same themes were echoed in a series of public meetings held around the county (apparently under Klan auspices) in March and early April. They all condemned lawlessness, but Ku Klux brutality was referred to only in the vaguest terms. Their resolutions went on at far greater length concerning the evils of Republican rule, Negro arson, and the outrageous conduct of Negro militia in marching about the countryside under arms. Some of the meetings were composed only of whites and others were biracial. Two Negro meetings were held in York-ville, but a few white men were in attendance, pulling the strings. The secretary of both meetings was Jim Williams' murderer, Dr. J. Rufus Bratton. Under his guidance two Uncle Toms at the first meeting told how Radical leaders had deceived them in the past; in the future they would forgo politics altogether. At the second meeting a resolution was offered asking the remaining Republican officeholders in the county to resign. One black man had the temerity to speak against the resolution, but when it came to a vote there was no dissenting voice. The *Enquirer* lent its editorial support in succeeding issues to the call for law and order, and condemned some of the raiding that followed. The number of outrages appears to have fallen off momentarily.[24]

Until this reaction set in, Klan terrorism had become increasingly — virulent. For this reason three additional companies of federal troops were brought to the state in March and distributed in York, Spartanburg, and Union counties. Coming from Kansas, the soldiers were part of the Seventh Cavalry regiment which General George Custer was to make famous at Little Big Horn five years later. In command of the units sent to South Carolina was Major Lewis M. Merrill, who brought one of the companies to Yorkville and established his headquarters there on March 26. He superseded Captain Christopher as commander of the local garrison, which consisted now of a company each of cavalry and infantry. The soldiers' camp lay at the outskirts of town, while Merrill rented Rose's Hotel as headquarters and took the former county treasurer's office for his own use.[25]

Merrill was described by a New York *Tribune* reporter as having "the head, face, and spectacles of a German professor, and the frame of an athlete."[26] He was to play as large a part as any man in the country in uprooting the Ku Klux Klan. More than any other officer stationed in the South, he took an active interest in learning about the Klan, trying to turn public opinion against it, and ultimately arresting and prosecuting its members. But in March 1871, as he explained later, Merrill arrived in South Carolina with no more knowledge of the Klan than most Americans were getting from the daily papers. Furthermore, he was inclined to regard most of the accounts of Southern outrages as grossly exaggerated. He retained this view even after General Alfred H. Terry (who had assumed command of the Department of the South after dealing with the Klan in Georgia) assured him that he would "find that the half has not been told you." In Yorkville the leading citizens hastened to confirm his impression that there was no general Ku Klux organization and that the sporadic cases of violence had about come to an end. They did not end, however, and Merrill soon discovered that an organization did exist which strongly affected the incidence of violence at any given time. "I am now of opinion," he told Congressional investigators in July, "that I never conceived of such a state of social disorganization being possible in any civilized community as exists in this county now."[27]

Within ten days of his arrival, the Klan commenced operations again and continued them off and on until September. The first raid involved a nonviolent visit by disguised men to the home of a white man who was suspected of harboring a few remaining militia guns. Merrill decided to make an example of this case and had several men arrested, but the evidence against them was flimsy and the case was thrown out of court.[28] On several successive Saturday nights Negroes were whipped and otherwise outraged by Ku Klux gangs. Merrill spoke with some of the victims; they talked to him freely in private but refused to testify publicly unless he guaranteed them protection or helped them leave the county afterward. As one outrage followed another he gradually accumulated a large body of evidence against members of the Klan, involving not only the continuing cases of violence but others that had occurred before his arrival. Within a month he had caught on to the ambivalent position of those respectable men in the community who had inaugurated the terror for their own purposes but were no longer able to control it.[29] Merrill's evidence availed him little, however, even when he found witnesses brave enough to testify. Like other Army officers before him, he experienced a sense of growing frustration at the legal restrictions which bound him to assist inert civil authorities only when they requested it. "It requires great patience and self control to keep ones [sic] hands off these infamous cowards, when absolute knowledge exists of who they are, and what they do, and what they propose to do."

Many Klansmen were so stupid, and had become so self-confident by this time, that they operated on a regular schedule and committed blunders that would have laid them open to easy capture if any attempts had been made. And in view of the reluctance of witnesses to testify and the readiness of courts to accept Klan alibis over the evidence of those who did, Merrill decided that the only way of convicting the criminals was to lie in wait for them and catch them in the act. He maintained excellent relations with Sheriff Glenn, whom he described as an honest man, disposed to do his duty, but bumbling and inefficient in following up leads. Glenn agreed to use cavalry detachments to lie in wait for Ku Klux bands, but when Merrill proposed a specific plan of this sort on one occasion the sheriff gave excuses and it had to be abandoned. Merrill judged later that if the plan had been carried out it probably would have succeeded. By the end of May he came to suspect that Glenn himself was implicated with the Klan. A Negro Ku Klux victim once reported his attackers to the sheriff, who merely advised him to run off to North Carolina; later the Klan returned and repeated to the man everything he had told the sheriff. In 1872 Glenn was indicted by federal authorities as a member of the Ku Klux Klan.

There were now federal laws in existence against the Ku Klux, but Merrill found no more satisfaction from federal officials in South Carolina than from state authorities. The nearest deputy United States marshal and the United States commissioner in Columbia both made themselves scarce when he tried to contact them. Merrill could have made arrests easily enough on his own, but there was no one to whom he could take prisoners with any likelihood of their being held for trial and prosecuted.[30]

One of the most unsavory attacks in Ku Klux history occurred in the midst of Merrill's investigations, on the night of May 5. The victim was Elias Hill, a Negro in the Clay Hill neighborhood northeast of Yorkville, where the Klan had continued raiding regardless of the pledges made in February. Hill had been paralyzed since the age of seven (he was now fifty) and remained dwarflike in appearance, with a normal head and torso but the limbs of a child. He was unable to walk, crawl, or even feed himself without help. He was a man of intelligence and great strength of character, however, who learned to read and write early in life from white children who dropped in at his cabin on their way home from school. Eventually he became a Baptist preacher and a leader of the Negro community. After the war he opened a school for Negro children. Whites accused him of inciting the blacks to arson and in general of being a troublemaker. Hill denied this but conceded that he had been active politically: "I believe the republican party advocates what is nearer the laws of God than any other party, and therefore I feel that it is right." His religion taught him not to hate the white people, he explained later, but his experience taught him to distrust and fear them. Half a dozen disguised Klansmen burst in on him at about midnight, carried him into the yard, and dumped him on the ground. Then they questioned him repeatedly about his activities, punctuating the conversation with threats on his life and occasional blows with their fists. They also administered several lashes with a buggy whip. Finally they left, with injunctions for Hill to mend his ways, renounce his party affiliation, and cancel his subscription to the Charleston *Republican*. Although Hill and his black neighbors had kept their earlier pledges and the Klan had not, neighboring whites sympathized with this attack and attempted to justify it.[31]

The Negroes in this region despaired of living peacefully in South Carolina. Hill thought of emigrating west, but the stories of Ku Klux atrocities in other states discouraged this. He wrote therefore to the American Colonization Society in Washington and received literature concerning its longstanding settlements in Liberia. In July at least sixty families made the decision to emigrate. A party of 136, led by Hill, left at the end of October. "The entire number," commented the *Enquirer,* "is made up of the most industrious negroes in that section of the county, many of whom, since their emancipation, have shown themselves to be thrifty and energetic, and not a few of them had accumulated money." By January 3, 1872, they reached Monrovia, where Hill wrote back glowingly of their reception and future prospects. They expected soon to move to a new settlement twenty miles in the interior (Arthington) where land was reputedly good and timber plentiful.[32]

Meanwhile, in the wake of continuing raids on Hill and others, Merrill tried to mobilize public opinion against the Klan, hoping to stop the terrorism even if he could not punish the men responsible. On May 13 he summoned fifteen or twenty leading citizens; some of these he knew to be Klansmen who had helped light a fire they would now like to put out. In this conference he described recent incidents in such graphic detail that his visitors were both impressed and distressed at the extent of his knowledge. Their reaction was heightened when he indicated further that he had enough evidence about a number of individual Klansmen to send them to jail if they were ever brought before an impartial jury. That day might not be far off, he added, saying that he daily expected notice of a Presidential suspension of habeas corpus freeing him to make arrests. However, the citizens might yet avert this by taking timely action to halt the violence.

Merrill's message was heeded, especially since it coincided with the interests of the Klan leaders themselves. This interview was followed, he soon discovered through spies, by three successive Klan meetings. The more conservative members eventually prevailed in their advice to cooperate with Merrill and renounce further raiding, at least for the time being. Accordingly these men (including Major Avery and Dr. Bratton) drew up a short statement condemning future acts of violence, but saying nothing about past activity. This was published in the *Enquirer* on May 25 with many signatures appended. Copies of the notice were then circulated throughout the county, where additional signatures were rapidly acquired. These were published in succeeding issues of the newspaper. By the middle of June several hundred names had been obtained, including those of many Klansmen. Some members were reluctant to sign, but they were encouraged if not ordered to do so by the leadership and were afraid to be conspicuous by their absence. Merrill by now was well informed of the Klan's internal proceedings. He knew that the leaders had no intention of disbanding and were ready to resume activity later if occasion should demand it. But for the present they were very fearful that continuing violence would lead to military arrests and their own ruin. The editor of the *Enquirer* was privy to these consultations and cooperated fully in the leaders' policy of discouraging further outrages.

Earlier in May, Merrill had received (with other military commanders in the South) more or less *pro forma* instructions to aid federal civil authorities in making arrests under the Enforcement Acts of 1870 and 1871. Under the circumstances, he telegraphed his superiors on the twenty-fifth, asking if he could not possibly make arrests and hold prisoners in the face of opposition by the civil authorities. Although he tried to keep the telegram secret, he soon discovered that it was the talk of the town and had provoked the third Klan meeting mentioned above. The nearest telegraph office was in Chester, and the operator there (like many others in Ku Klux areas) was discovered to be a member of the Klan. The same was true of the locomotive engineer on the train between Chester and Yorkville, who may well have brought the story back. Some Klansmen were in favor of resisting any military arrests by force. But it was decided not to try that, since the Army could always bring superior force to bear. Moreover, a lawyer advised that Merrill had no power to make arrests for crimes committed before the passage of the Ku Klux Act in April. Merrill's message did reinforce the leaders' efforts to stop further outrages, however. If the present crisis could only blow over, allowing the troops to leave by fall, the more violent brethren could then have their way again. Violence did decline once more, but knowing as much as he did, Merrill was not very optimistic for the future.[33]

In June some of the more irrepressible Klansmen thought to intimidate Merrill by sneaking up in the night and firing on the Army camp. He learned of this in advance and almost looked forward to the opportunity of shooting it out with them. But instead he let it be known around town that he had heard of the plan and knew some of the men involved. Dr. Bratton and others immediately came to Merrill asking for the names so that they might prevent the attack. He refused and the attack never came, but it served once more to alarm Klan leaders over the irresponsibility of some of their followers. The latter were given to understand again that they must stop even talking of such measures or take the consequences.[34]

In York County white public opinion was virtually synonymous with Klan opinion. Those citizens who voiced any criticism at all of the Ku Klux almost always added that it had done some good by making the blacks more polite and industrious. Those who remarked its effect in driving off black laborers did so in the privacy of their intimate acquaintance. No one dared oppose the Klan openly beyond the position of its own leadership, for fear of turning it on himself. But the sickness went deeper than this. Such criticism as was evoked was aimed more at the inexpediency than the wrongfulness or inhumanity of Klan activity. The greatest extenuation that can be made for the general public is that most people knew little of Klan operations beyond their own neighborhoods, and they tended to discredit much of what they heard. Conservatives here as elsewhere regarded Republican atrocity stories as politically inspired exaggerations if not outright lies, and the human mind has a great capacity to reject what it does not want to believe. As Merrill later put it, "Martyrs have always been scarce, and a large crop of them was hardly to be looked for where the average conscience of the community was either benumbed by passion or overpowered by force."[35]

On July 22 Yorkville was visited by a three-man Congressional subcommittee investigating the Ku Klux Klan. Several York County residents had already been summoned to testify before the parent committee in Washington. One of them, Major Avery, came to the capital, remained two or three days before being called to testify, and then fled precipitously to Canada. When called upon to return he failed to respond. Later he returned to Yorkville, only to leave again during the visit of the subcommittee.[36] Others, including Dr. Bratton, stayed home and testified, preferring the ultimate risks of perjury to the immediate discomforts of exile. Local white opinion was extremely hostile to the committee and not a little fearful of what it might uncover. This was a common phenomenon wherever these subcommittees traveled in the South. The local Klan met three nights before the committee's visit. It voted to kill any member who divulged information concerning the organization; some members even suggested waylaying the committee members after the hearings were over and seizing the testimony it gathered, but this was not adopted.[37] The subcommittee had already held hearings in Columbia, Union, and Spartanburg before coming to Yorkville. Here, as in those places, it examined witnesses of every rank and station, from Major Merrill and prominent Conservative leaders to the humblest black men who had felt the Ku Klux scourge. Many of the latter had been located and induced to come through the efforts of Alexander S. Wallace, the Republican Congressman from that district. He was a resident of York County, but for some time had been a virtual refugee in Washington. Wallace indeed came to be regarded by local citizens as the evil genius of the whole anti-Klan movement. Proceeding on the devil theory, they accused him almost single-handedly of fathering the federal Ku Klux Act, bringing the Congressional subcommittee to South Carolina, and poisoning the mind of the previously well-disposed Merrill toward the people of Yorkville.[38] Wallace now presented an unforgettable figure—a tall man dressed in Mephistophelean black topped by a stovepipe hat—as he conducted his business around town, everywhere braving the scowls and curses of his white constituents and followed by a mob of hooting children.

Wallace was the target in an embarrassing but revealing incident in the hotel dining room on the evening of the committee's arrival. The Congressmen had just sat down to dinner when a Mr. Barry, a member of the local gentry and a regular boarder, sat down opposite Wallace and demanded loudly if he were not Congressman Wallace. He was obviously in his cups, and everyone ignored him. Then Barry grabbed a cream pitcher nearby and, rising from his seat, attempted to throw its contents on Wallace. But the hotelkeeper, who was serving table, caught Barry's arm, with the result that most of the cream fell on Representative Job Stevenson of Ohio, sitting next to Wallace. Stevenson and Wallace stood up abruptly and reached for their pockets. The *Enquirer,* in reporting the event, assumed that they had reached for weapons rather than for handkerchiefs, which told something of local mores. Barry was removed from the room, and later he sent back his apologies to Stevenson. This closed the incident, but Barry was hailed as a hero for days afterward. The episode appeared to have been planned by Barry and his friends, some of them favoring hot coffee instead of cream.

The evening's climax was still to come. If local whites resented the committee's presence, the blacks hailed it as a harbinger of deliverance. After dinner the Republican members were serenaded in front of the hotel by a Negro band and a crowd of well-wishers, who were surrounded and heckled by a number of young white rowdies. As the crowd was breaking up to go home, a white constable (and Klansman) tried to arrest one of the black musicians on a charge of obstructing the sidewalk. The Negro resisted, and in the ensuing scuffle the constable shot him five times. Major Merrill intervened to prevent a riot and persuaded the blacks to disperse. He prevailed on the mayor (also a Klansman) to get the whites to do likewise. Whites universally praised the constable, and he was exonerated by the town council; the Negroes were convinced that he had tried to provoke a riot in which many of them would have been slaughtered.[39]

The subcommittee—the *Enquirer* referred to it as "the sub-Outrage Committee"—remained in town for six days before returning to Washington. The testimony it heard amply confirmed the evidence and opinions Merrill had been accumulating since his arrival. But one would never have suspected this from the *Enquirer*'s scanty and *ex parte* reports. They utterly disparaged all of the damaging evidence, so far as they noticed it at all, very rarely descending to specifics. Such rebuttal as the paper attempted consisted of the character assassination of one witness hostile to the Klan and shotgun allegations that all hostile witnesses had been obtained through bribery and military force.[40]

Conservatives made much of the decrease in terrorism prior to the committee's arrival, but it picked up again in August and continued into September. It never reached the level of the preceding spring, but it created no sense of assurance that the Army could withdraw safely. This impression was confirmed by the travesty of justice attending the local court term in September.

Merrill had no real hope that the authorities would do anything to Klansmen, no matter how much evidence they were handed. But he assembled a good deal of it anyway and held it in readiness for the grand jury. Judge William M. Thomas in his charge to that body mentioned the cloud of martial law hanging over their heads if they did not punish outrages themselves; he admonished the jury therefore "not to make this Court a 'white washing Committee.'" That statement, it turned out, was intended more for Washington than for the grand jury. Neither Thomas nor the prosecutor was eager to receive or act on Merrill's evidence. The prosecutor told Merrill in so many words that it was pointless to try to prosecute such cases as the Jim Williams murder or the treasury raid, in which prominent men had been involved. The same attitude prevailed among the grand jury, some of whom (it later appeared) had the most direct personal reasons for wanting to keep facts hidden. The jury asked to see evidence only of outrages committed since the Congressional subcommittee's visit. There was no visible reason for writing off the previous eight months' terror save the interest of the Ku Klux leadership in protecting itself. Judge Thomas admitted as much to Merrill, saying that investigation of the greater crimes committed before July would only stir up public feeling unnecessarily. When Merrill turned over the limited data requested, involving ten or twelve cases, the jury spent four days in suppressing rather than investigating it. In fact, as Merrill pointed out later, it required more ingenuity to evade the evidence of crime than to find it out. Klansmen dominated the jury and overruled or browbeat the minority who wanted to discharge their duty. At least two jurors had themselves been accessory to Ku Klux murders. The grand jury's report was a tissue of half-truths and evasions. Several Klansmen were indicted for minor legal infractions, but the only case that was labeled a major Ku Klux outrage involved an assault by two Negroes on a third.[41]

By this time the state government in Columbia had also proved totally inadequate to cope with the terror. Governor Scott had taken a hard line between the elections of 1868 and 1870, when terrorism was sporadic and comparatively minimal. But as violence mushroomed after October 1870, partly in reaction to the militia he had organized to control it, the governor virtually gave up the contest. He retained the state constabulary, originally contemplated as a temporary measure in 1868, but the handful of constables he could send to any given county were simply overwhelmed by the magnitude of their assignment. Scott and some of his supporters put great reliance—at least publicly—on federal soldiers, and in November 1870 he sent a special envoy to Washington to plead for the retention of some troops who had been ordered to Georgia.[42] But at this late date the limitations on their effectiveness were well known. The extent to which Scott emphasized the value of soldiers was the measure of his own desperation.

Many Republicans called for far stronger medicine than the governor was dispensing. The Columbia *Union* advised the people to organize vigilance committees and "shoot down, on sight, the first disguised man who is seen prowling about."[43] The legislature, under the prodding of Negro members, came close to breaking with the governor altogether over what they regarded as his negligence in protecting the lives and interests of upcountry Republicans. In January 1871 the two houses passed a joint resolution inquiring pointedly why a sufficient military force had not been sent to those counties and why outlaws had not been brought to justice.[44] Less officially, many members demanded that Scott proclaim martial law, using the militia already organized there. A few even spoke of impeachment.

The governor's position was unenviable. The only militia he had available, or could possibly raise with any assurance that they would obey him and not the Ku Klux Klan, were Negroes. To invest black militia with the power of martial law would invite a race war which the blacks and the state government were in no position to win. One Democrat who offered to raise a white militia company under state authority admitted frankly that in any campaign to enforce the laws he would follow his race regardless of orders. With other Republican moderates, Scott saw the federal government as the only agency capable of suppressing the terror, and he wrote for more troops to station in the worst counties. He had supporters in the legislature too. After acrimonious debate, it voted down a martial law bill and instead adopted resolutions calling upon the President and Congress to send massive federal aid as the only alternative to anarchy. It was in answer to these appeals that additional troops were sent to the state in March under Major Merrill and posted in Union, Spartanburg, and York counties. This was done at the personal order of President Grant after delegations from South Carolina had gone to acquaint him verbally with conditions in the state. The President declared rather expansively that he would send ten regiments if necessary; but if a Democrat was elected President in 1872, he added, one of his first acts would be to withdraw these troops, and every Republican in South Carolina would be well advised to follow them out of the state.[45]

At the same time, conscious of his own weakness, the governor did everything he could to appease Conservative hostility, short of turning over the state to them. He sounded much like them in public statements minimizing the degree of the terror—which belied his real belief. In January he not only resisted Republican cries for martial law but sent agents to disarm the Negro militia already in existence in Union County after the Mat Stevens murder and the first Klan lynching there. In February he did the same in York County after the near-explosion between whites and Negro militia in Yorkville. In March he did the same in Chester following the white-militia skirmish there. On March 13 he held a five-hour conference with seventeen of the state's leading Conservatives, hoping to enlist their support of law and order. Although the talk was described as courteous, those gentlemen made it plain that they regarded themselves as holding the top cards. They attacked every aspect of the Republican state administration, especially the fact that they paid most of the taxes while Negroes supposedly drew most of the benefits. The greatest outrage to which the upper counties had been subjected in their estimation was the presence of armed Negro militiamen. They resolutely denied the existence of a Ku Klux organization, although they deprecated whatever lawlessness was too plain to deny or ignore. Any effort to put down disorders by invoking martial law, they said, would probably cost the head of the man who proclaimed it. The only real remedy for disorder was to alter the state government. Scott was unprepared to go that far, but in an effort to buy their support of law and order he agreed once more not to invoke martial law, to withdraw all militia guns still outstanding, and to remove from office all of the local justices of the peace and election managers who had given displeasure, replacing them with Conservatives. The opposition leaders seemed pleased, and they promised in turn to use their influence against lawlessness.[46]

Conservatives in private frequently registered shock and fear at continuing outrages, but these sentiments were seldom uttered publicly.[47] The Charleston *Daily News* remained one of the few strong Democratic voices in the South for stamping out Ku Kluxism by force if necessary. It too opposed martial law, but supported the governor and the use of federal troops in the upcountry.[48] Most Conservatives sympathized with the Klan in varying measure. "Until I am allowed to have a voice, either directly or indirectly in the State government . . . ," General Matthew C. Butler told the Congressional investigating committee, "I, for one, do not intend to raise my hand against [Klan violence]." His attitude toward the disorders, he said, was one of "passive indifference." Others were still ready to defend the Klan as a positive good.[49] Conservatives held a much-heralded Taxpayers' Convention at Columbia in May, in which they deplored lawlessness in stereotyped phrases but devoted most of their energy to indicting the state administration once more for corruption and inefficiency.[50]

As Ku Klux outrages continued, many Conservatives also grew more apprehensive of retaliatory violence by the blacks. This was the probable reason for an increase in the number of white military companies, although some observers saw the mobilization as a step toward overturning the state government by force. A Charlestonian told a New York *Herald* correspondent early in May:

> We have all round us negro national guards armed and equipped by the Legislature and Governor at our expense. . . . Regiment after regiment is organized with nigger colonels. The Lieutenant Governor of our State is a nigger; there are seventy-four niggers in the State Legislature who cannot read or write. . . . We are taxed until we can't draw breath, and . . . you . . . ask me what our boys are forming rifle clubs so suddenly for?

If any effort was made to use black militia against the white men of South Carolina, he declared, "in my calculation the niggers will go to the wall."[51]

Governor Scott had done nothing to arouse and everything to appease such white fears of the militia. He repeatedly portrayed the Conservative leadership of the state as desiring an end to acts of terrorism, giving them the benefit of the doubt. For that very reason he remained under fire from many Republicans. Some members of the legislature were refugees in Columbia, unable to return to their homes. They and the state's two Senators in Washington were charging Scott with weakness and even cowardice in surrendering to the forces of terrorism.[52]

Congressional passage of the Ku Klux Act in April gave Scott another federal straw to grasp at. He now looked forward to a Presidential order empowering the soldiers to make arrests—the same kind of order Merrill was seeking in Yorkville. In July, no arrests having taken place, he tried to stimulate them by offering rewards for each person apprehended with proof sufficient to convict. But Scott still decried talk of martial law, even by the federal government. When the President suspended habeas corpus in nine counties in October, Scott privately concurred in the measure beforehand and publicly regretted it afterward. This was the ultimate expression of futility, and with the action of the York County grand jury it demonstrated the necessity of decisive federal intervention.[53]

Part VI

THE FEDERAL GOVERNMENT
AND THE KU KLUX KLAN,
1870–1872

CHAPTER 24

Congress Legislates, Then Investigates

As soon as it spread from Tennessee in the spring of 1868, the Ku Klux conspiracy no longer lay within the power of most states to control. It was a sectional attempt to nullify the policy of Reconstruction which Congress had initiated in 1867, and Congress had to help put it down. If the Radical Republicans had really controlled that body, as outraged Conservatives thought they did, forceful measures would have been taken much sooner than they were. But most Republicans had been pushed into Congressional Reconstruction in the first place and begrudged every extension of federal power which it demanded. Within the traditional federal system, the crimes of the Ku Klux Klan were offenses against state and local law; the central government lacked jurisdiction over murder, assault, robbery, and trespass, and but for the Klan most Republicans would have kept it that way. They eventually did what they had to do in 1870 and 1871, but only after hundreds of Southern Republicans had lost their lives and thousands had suffered lacerated backs and broken bodies or had been driven from their homes and property. The bloody shirt had to be waved for three years before Congress moved itself to significant activity in behalf of elementary law and order.

The executive branch was more helpful, at least after Grant's inauguration in March 1869. Unlike the Johnson administration, which refused requests of Arkansas and Florida for arms to equip their militia, federal authorities now became receptive to such appeals. The North and South Carolina militia both received substantial armament from the federal government.[1]

The federal government's greatest contribution to suppressing Klan terrorism before 1871 lay in its use of the Army. The President had some discretion in this respect as commander in chief, but his powers were circumscribed by laws, some going back to 1795. Andrew Johnson of course had no connection with the Ku Klux Klan and little if any sympathy with it as an organization. So far as Congress had left him free to use the Army by 1868, he sent troops to the places where they seemed to be most urgently needed. Most of the responsibility in assigning troops lay with General Grant, the commanding general. Neither in that post before March 1869 nor as President afterward did Grant take the lead in deciding Reconstruction policies. Inexperienced and uncomfortable in matters political, he leaned over backward to avoid comparisons with Caesar, Cromwell, or Napoleon, and used the Army only in accordance with the most conservative construction of existing laws. Not until 1871 did Grant's growing self-confidence and growing exasperation with the Ku Klux terror permit him to take a more active course. Even then he relied as much as possible on Congress and his Cabinet, and adhered to the letter of the law in his role of commander in chief.

During the months prior to the readmission of the newly reconstructed states, when the Army exercised paramount authority, it arrested quite a few suspected Klansmen. But they seldom faced trial and punishment. The only means of providing a fair trial, given the corruption of civil justice, was to do it by military commission. Again the conservatism of the federal government—its unwillingness to depart from traditional civil procedure and incur the charge of military despotism—served as a barrier to justice. Most Army commanders were unwilling or afraid to order military trials in time of peace where the civil courts were open. Trying civilians by military commission was as alien to their experience and normal convictions of right as it was to the civilian population. Under the circumstances, moreover, it was so fraught with political hazards as to make them doubly reluctant. Most of the commanders in the South genuinely detested the Ku Klux Klan and sympathized with its victims. They were as angered as anyone by the countless evidences of terrorism around them, and they longed in private for the power to rectify it. But seldom was their outrage so great as to brave the storm of abuse they received from Conservatives, or to run the risk of destroying their careers, by ordering military trials. (They reaped a harvest of Conservative abuse anyway, while accomplishing comparatively little.) Most Ku Klux prisoners were either released or turned over to the local civil authorities, who in turn released them. When the latter happened, commanders were not above venting private anger at rebel society, rebel justice, and the incompetence of civil officials. This became easier still when civilian control was restored and they no longer had responsibility.

Thereafter the Army was restricted to aiding the civil authorities when they requested it. Governors in every state repeatedly asked for soldiers to be stationed in troubled localities, and their requests were usually heeded so far as troops were available. The number of these shiftings mounted into the hundreds. Governors usually made these requests on the basis of local appeals, sometimes from sheriffs and others in authority. But very few sheriffs actually used the soldiers to help them make arrests; the few Klansmen so taken were invariably turned loose by one means or another. The presence of soldiers was not totally useless, however. They occasionally interposed to prevent riots, and their presence often deterred raiding in the immediate localities where they were posted, if not in the surrounding countryside. If troops had not been available—as events after 1875 indicated—the Ku Klux Klan and its allies would have toppled state governments and taken over by force throughout the South.

When Congress was finally moved to action in 1870, it was thinking of the coming fall elections as much as the personal plight of Southern Republicans. The Fifteenth Amendment had just confirmed and extended Negro suffrage and empowered Congress to enforce it by appropriate legislation. The Enforcement Act of May 31, 1870, was concerned primarily with the bribery or intimidation of voters, which it made a federal offense, punishable in federal courts. But Section 6 made it a felony for two or more persons to conspire together or go in disguise with intent to deprive someone of *any* right or privilege of citizenship, or to punish him afterward for having exercised it. And if anyone, in violating these provisions, committed any other crime he was subject to the same penalties provided for that offense by the state in which it was committed. The President, finally, was empowered to use the armed forces of the United States to apprehend violators.[2]

Eventually Section 6 of this law provided the basis for many if not most of the federal indictments brought against members of the Ku Klux Klan. In 1870, however, federal authorities—at least those outside Kentucky—made almost no effort to enforce the law against the Klan. They obviously hoped that its mere presence on the statute books would serve as a deterrent to further terrorism. There were reports or rumors from time to time during the year that the administration was preparing to enforce the law, but nothing of the sort materialized.[3] The new law's effect upon the Klan in 1870 was wholly negligible. Voter intimidation took place on a large enough scale to reverse the will of the majority in Alabama, Georgia,

and perhaps other states, as well as in countless smaller localities throughout the South. President Grant called attention to this in his annual
message of December 5, but he had done almost nothing to encourage the
enforcement of the law.[4]

The first efforts that were made (outside of Kentucky) were the work of
a very few federal officials in Alabama and North Carolina. In February
1871 District Attorney John A. Minnis tried to prosecute several Klansmen from Coosa County, Alabama, who had whipped and shot several
Negroes after demanding to know how they had voted in the recent election. But when he got the suspects before the grand jury it professed to be
unsure of their identity and discharged them.[5] In April he was unable to
convince the United States commissioner that the beating received by a
Macon County Negro had resulted from the victim's voting; here too the
suspects he had arrested were released.[6] In a third case in June, a commissioner discharged suspected Klansmen after they produced alibis.[7] In
North Carolina, United States Deputy Marshal Joseph G. Hester (who
would be active in ferreting out Ku Klux for the next two years) arrested
several Klansmen in February after they had attacked the home of Essic
Harris in Chatham County. They all produced alibis, however, and were
discharged.[8] These cases constituted substantially the only efforts made to
apply the Enforcement Act against the Klan before April 1871, when
Congress passed a new law.

This measure was the result of a growing public demand. The President
and members of Congress were being deluged with reports of Southern
outrages, along with increasingly insistent appeals from Southern Republicans for help. After Grant's reference to the matter in his annual message,
the Senate requested him to furnish whatever information he had received.
He responded in January with two messages and a variety of supporting
documents indicating in general the unhappy state of affairs which the Ku
Klux terror had brought to pass in the South.[9] On January 19 the Senate
appointed a committee to investigate further. The existing Congress was
about to expire, and since much of the information furnished by the President related to North Carolina, it was decided to limit the investigation to
that state. The committee, headed by Senator John Scott of Pennsylvania,
was continued by the new 42d Congress and made its report on March 10. It
interviewed fifty-two witnesses, including men of both races and parties, in
and out of public office, Army officers and members of the Ku Klux Klan.
Most of the evidence related to Alamance and Caswell counties, where the
Klan had reigned supreme a year earlier and considerable inside information was now available; there was less about Cleveland, Rutherford, and
neighboring counties where the terrorism was in full swing at that very
time. Within the limits it had set for itself, the committee found out a great

deal concerning the organization, membership, and activities of the Constitutional Union Guard, the White Brotherhood, and the Invisible Empire in North Carolina. The majority report concluded that these organizations were primarily political in character, using intimidation, whipping, and murder in behalf of the Democratic party. It also found that they bound their members to commit crime and then were able in every case to prevent their apprehension and punishment. Despite its overemphasis on political matters, the report was fair and substantially accurate. The committee made no recommendations, but its detailed findings did much, however belatedly, to confirm and amplify Congressional understanding of the Ku Klux conspiracy.[10]

Reports of outrages continued to flow into Washington while the committee held its hearings. Especially urgent were the appeals from South Carolina, where Governor Scott and the legislature were crying for more troops. Grant raised the subject at a Cabinet meeting in February and said he was ready to send up to two regiments there from Texas if necessary. In reality he sent sixteen companies in March, including those under Major Merrill.[11] On February 28 Congress passed a second Enforcement Act, tightening federal controls over election procedures, but it had little relevance to the Ku Klux Klan. After the 41st Congress expired on March 4 its successor would not ordinarily have met until December. But many Republicans wanted the President to call it into session immediately to deal with the Ku Klux terror, which was finally being recognized in its true proportions. The fact that the administration already had ample power to proceed against the Klan seems to have escaped public attention in the clamor for tough new legislation. Some party leaders, including Grant, feared that a special session might provoke unwanted efforts to lower the tariff, but the Southern question prevailed and the new Congress met.

A joint Republican caucus agreed to support a stringent anti-Klan bill which had been drafted by Benjamin F. Butler of Massachusetts, one of the Radical leaders in the House. This measure would empower the President to suspend habeas corpus and to remove state officials when there was reason to doubt the validity of their election; United States marshals were also given the power to purge disloyal members from federal juries. The Senate passed this measure according to plan, but in the House a number of Republican moderates, led by James A. Garfield and James G. Blaine, broke ranks and joined the Democrats to defeat it. The bill's sponsors were furious. As Republicans hurled recriminations at one another it looked for a time as if no measure at all would pass. Finally Grant went to the Capitol himself on March 23 to confer with party leaders. He told them that he had been importuned for weeks to ask Congress for a law increasing his powers to combat Southern terrorism; but he had hesitated to do so for fear of being called a military despot. The Congressional leaders replied that no such law could be passed under the present circumstances unless he came out openly and asked for it; better ask now, said one, than have to use the power illegally when disorders mounted before the 1872 election.[12] On that, Grant called for pen and paper and wrote out the desired message on the spot. Without going into detail, he called for whatever additional power Congress judged necessary to "secure life, liberty, and property and the enforcement of law" throughout the country. If desirable, he added, Congress might want to provide for the measure's expiration at the end of the next session.[13]

The next day, following an interview with the attorney general of South Carolina, Grant issued a proclamation reciting the conditions in that state and commanding the members of "unlawful combinations" there to disperse and return to their homes within twenty days.[14] Existing laws required the President to issue such a proclamation before he used the Army to suppress insurrection or lawlessness. Such a proclamation was long overdue, but even now Grant seems to have contemplated no extraordinary use of troops in South Carolina or elsewhere. If it increased the apprehension of some Southern Ku Klux leaders, their followers continued to ride, all but oblivious to the Presidential proclamation.

Republican leaders in Congress soon produced a new Ku Klux bill, drafted by Representative Samuel Shellabarger of Ohio. This was almost as far-reaching as Butler's bill, but the men who had balked before were whipped into line and the measure became law on April 20. The Ku Klux Act sought to enforce the Fourteenth Amendment. It was now a federal offense to "conspire together, or go in disguise upon the public highway, or upon the premises of another for the purpose . . . of depriving any person or any class of persons of the equal protection of the laws, or of equal privileges or immunities under the laws," or to hinder state authorities from affording equal protection of the laws to all citizens. The penalties included fines of $500 to $5,000 or imprisonment or both, and liability to civil damage suits by aggrieved parties. Moreover, the President was empowered to use the armed forces as a last resort to suppress combinations of men violating these civil rights. The most controversial section, which was to expire at the end of the next regular session in 1872, empowered him to suspend the writ of habeas corpus. There was no provision for military trials, however; sooner or later any persons arrested by military order had to be turned over to the federal civil authorities. The act also provided for an oath to purge federal juries of Klansmen or their fellow travelers.[15] The law went further than its 1870 predecessor in several respects—most notably the habeas corpus provision—but it added comparatively little to the government's existing powers to cope with the Klan legally.

The Ku Klux bill was almost wholly a party measure, both North and South, with the Democrats opposing and Republicans favoring it. Horace Greeley's New York *Tribune* had been calling for such a measure since the beginning of the year, noting successive outrages as they occurred. "Mississippi is a healthy State for Mayors," one editorial exclaimed in March.

Mayor Crane of Jackson was shot by a murderer who goes unpunished. Mayor Sturgis of Meridian was expelled because he happened to be born in the North. And now Mayor Lacey of Aberdeen has been abducted by Ku-Klux [actually he was driven away too], probably because he was once an officer of the United States Army. Yet there are men in Congress who wish to spend a few months in inquiring whether loyal men at the South really need protection.[16]

Some of the Republican support was unenthusiastic, and a few party members in both sections opposed it altogether. Conservative Republicans were almost as unhappy as Democrats with the law's extension of federal power and joined the Democrats in depreciating the nature and extent of Ku Klux outrages. They were also lukewarm about conferring civil and political rights on Negroes in the first place; the welfare of both the country and the party, they felt, lay in conciliating the Southern whites and leaving the blacks alone.[17] Both Governor Bullock and the Atlanta *New Era* opposed the law, holding that the Georgia courts could suppress the Ku Klux if only they would.[18] Governor Alcorn of Mississippi held the same position, but the chief Republican organ in that state, the Jackson *Pilot,* disagreed. It eventually joined the Ames faction which had long demanded federal action against the Klan.[19]

Congressional Democrats issued an address to the people immediately after the law's passage. Not only did it place too much power in the hands of the President, they said, it was a mischievous attempt to stir up partisan and sectional strife in behalf of the Republican party.[20] Democrats concentrated on the habeas corpus provision, denouncing it as an instrument of military despotism. Representative Fernando Wood, former Calhoun supporter and wartime Copperhead in New York, said the law made Grant a dictator with the power to rule by martial law.[21] Representative S. S. (Sunset) Cox of New York even rose to the defense of the Ku Klux Klan. Praising the order more lavishly than any Southern Democrat dared to do at this point, he compared it with the Italian Carbonari, the German Tugenbund, and the Irish Fenians as a champion of popular liberty.[22]

The New York *Herald,* which usually hovered between the two parties as a matter of policy, joined the Democrats on this issue. Like them it minimized whatever Southern terrorism it did not deny altogether. Similar crimes occurred in the North, it said, and Southern Negroes were repeatedly guilty of murder, arson, and rape. The *Herald* repeatedly quoted from an impromptu speech of General Sherman in New Orleans, in which he said, "I probably have as good means of information as most persons in regard to what is called the Ku Klux, and am perfectly satisfied that the thing is greatly over-estimated; and if the Ku Klux bills were kept out of Congress and the army kept at their legitimate duties, there are enough good and true men in all Southern states to put down all Ku Klux or other bands of marauders."[23]

Sherman, the *Herald,* and Northern Democrats might be excused on grounds of ignorance, while a few Southern Republicans tried to appease forces stronger than they. To some extent Southern Democrats also lacked knowledge of what went on around them; they were subjected to a great deal of deliberate misinformation. But in considerable degree they knew what the Klan was about and regarded its cause as their own. As in slavery days, what the outside world saw as evidence of barbarism they saw as the defense of civilization. The Ku Klux Act roused many of them to the very heights of righteous wrath. Every member of Congress who voted for the law "was in his secret soul a perjured traitor," wrote the editor of the Rome (Georgia) *Courier,* who was hand in glove with the local Klan.[24] According to the Jackson, Mississippi, *Clarion* the object of the "unconstitutional and hideously despotic" measure was "to supercede [*sic*] State authority with the government of the bayonet and of marshal [*sic*] law." It was "predicated on no other foundation than the malice and cowardly hatred of its authors for the white inhabitants of the South, and their desire to retain power at the cost of principle and honor."[25] Josiah Turner's Raleigh *Sentinel,* in the state which had been most thoroughly investigated, said the bill's purpose was to enable Grant to "declare the State in insurrection and, by military terror, carry the [1872] election."[26] To Representative James M. Leach of North Carolina, the Ku Klux bill was itself the greatest of all Southern outrages—"an outrage upon the Constitution, an outrage upon liberty and free government, an outrage upon the good name of a noble State and a law-loving people. . . ." The only deprivation of rights Leach could descry in the Old North State was that imposed by "the Governor and his hireling soldiery last summer."[27]

Allowing for some exaggeration, these statements probably expressed the views of most white Southerners. But to some degree they were the products of convention and wounded sectional pride. Southern Conservatives resented the bloody shirt as they had resented the abolitionist indictment of slavery. That the accusations might be true was inadmissible, if only because such an admission constituted treason to the South and the white race. Thus it became almost as dangerous publicly to credit Ku Klux atrocities as it had been to speak out for abolition a decade before. Like Southern opposition to slavery, much potential opposition to the Klan existed but it was stifled or driven underground; the same was true of Democratic sentiment in favor of the Ku Klux Act. A Republican judge in western Alabama said that many Conservatives there applauded the measure as the only feasible means of restoring order to that troubled region, but they applauded privately.[28]

Two weeks after signing the act Grant issued a second proclamation, on May 3, calling on citizens to obey the new law and officials to enforce it. For his own part, he said, he was ready to invoke his fullest powers under the law to secure all citizens in the peaceful enjoyment of their constitutional rights. The tone of the proclamation was more conciliatory than threatening, however.[29] Having asked for the law as a distasteful duty, the President was even more reluctant to invoke its military provisions. Doubtless he hoped as he had with the other measure in 1870 that the mere existence of the law would scare the Ku Klux into desisting; in which case he would let bygones be bygones. Failing that, a few legal prosecutions might do the trick. (In any event the new law could not be applied *ex post facto* to crimes committed before its passage; any prosecutions for earlier crime would have to come under the act of 1870.) Having issued his proclamation, the President went to Long Branch, New Jersey, for the summer, leaving his subordinates to handle the details.[30]

His reluctance to invoke the new law was matched by their own; it was a political hot potato which no one wanted to touch. The War and the Justice departments, usually jealous of their own prerogatives, each believed that the other should initiate proceedings.[31] At length, on May 17, the Secretary of War and the Attorney General met and decided to implement it simultaneously. The first problem was to secure evidence against Klansmen as the basis for arrests and prosecutions.[32] Early in June the President, who kept in touch with events by mail and telegraph, authorized the employment of detectives for this purpose. A number were hired during the summer and went to work in several states under the direction of H. C. Whitley of New York, the head of the secret service. Often pretending to be businessmen or laborers seeking economic opportunities, they soon uncovered a mass of detailed evidence concerning Klan activities and the identity of those responsible.[33] In July the Justice Department sent out instructions, under a cloak of secrecy, for its officials in the South to begin prosecutions.[34] Two special prosecutors were appointed for this purpose in Georgia, perhaps because the United States attorney there was not regarded as zealous or competent enough to proceed on his own.[35] At long last the work of bringing Klansmen to book was under way.

Meanwhile, Congress had embarked on a searching investigation of the

Ku Klux Klan, one of the largest investigations in Congressional history up to that time. In March it had created a joint committee of seven Senators and fourteen Representatives, which organized on April 20, the day the Ku Klux Act became law. Its full title was the Joint Select Committee to Inquire into the Condition of Affairs in the Late Insurrectionary States.[36] Senator John Scott of Pennsylvania, who had headed the recent North Carolina investigation, was again chosen as chairman. The committee was authorized to form subcommittees to take testimony not only in Washington but throughout the South during the coming recess; it was to report its findings and recommendations after Congress reassembled in December. Since the Ku Klux Act was in process of becoming law when the committee was created, and the first steps toward enforcement were being taken as it began to hold hearings in May, the Committee's purpose is not entirely clear. Democrats charged that it was simply a political fishing expedition, designed to manufacture outrage stories for the 1872 Presidential campaign. The Republicans of course were perfectly willing to use outrage stories for this purpose, even if they did not have to manufacture them. There was also ground for thinking that an investigation might show the need for further legislation. Most importantly, Republicans probably saw the investigation as confirming the necessity of the Ku Klux Act and of the still more controversial task of enforcing it which likely lay ahead. The Democratic minority felt the equally pressing need to discredit the entire undertaking. Given these motivations, it is no wonder that political bias repeatedly appeared in the committee's proceedings; what is more significant is the fact that the committee produced a vast fund of solid information about the Ku Klux Klan and virtually every aspect of Southern life. Its witnesses reflected every shade of racial and political opinion. The twelve volumes of testimony it compiled constitute perhaps the richest single source of Southern history for this period, and the main source of information for the present study.

The hearings opened in Washington in May and continued, with a month's break, until September. At the same time, in June and July, a subcommittee of three visited South Carolina, the state where conditions appeared to be most serious. In the fall other subcommittees were sent to hold hearings in North Carolina, Georgia, Florida, Tennessee, Alabama, and Mississippi. Only minimal efforts were made to gather evidence from Louisiana, Arkansas, Texas, Virginia, and Tennessee, where the Klan had virtually disappeared by 1871; Kentucky was excluded as a state not "lately in insurrection." As in South Carolina, the subcommittees visited several of the main theaters of Klan activity, including Livingston, Alabama, and Columbus and Macon, Mississippi. Both parties were represented in all of the subcommittees' activities. Republicans were eager to explore as much of the Ku Klux conspiracy as they could and sometimes gave it a more political bearing than the evidence warranted. The Democrats, on the other hand, were concerned to minimize the Klan and especially its political bearings, preferring to expose Republican malfeasance instead. Majority and minority members located prospective witnesses through their respective party leaders in the states and localities involved, men like Congressman Wallace of South Carolina. Every witness, whether he was summoned by the Republican or Democratic members, was subject to cross-examination by the other. When the Republicans called a particularly informative or persuasive witness the minority tried to locate someone who could offset him. A Democratic member, for instance, wrote to General James H. Clanton, the Democratic state chairman in Alabama, sending copies of the testimony of several witnesses from that state who had recently testified in Washington, and asked for the names of other "witnesses to disprove the statements of those fellows."[37] In the nature of the case the Republicans contributed far more to the nation's understanding of the Ku Klux terror; the Democrats' contribution in that respect was often by inadvertence.

The committee's hearings were public, and much of the evidence was quoted or summarized in the press. In a few of the places visited by subcommittees the Klan was still active and it sometimes tried to intimidate or punish witnesses. A substantial number belonging to both races and parties were in fact intimidated, as their testimony made evident. But even the testimony of witnesses who obviously told less than the whole truth was useful, for it helped inadvertently to expose further the state of affairs which had called the committee into being. A few Klansmen who were summoned to testify, like James W. Avery of Yorkville, South Carolina, refused to appear and even fled to parts unknown. William L. Saunders, the scholarly reputed Grand Dragon of North Carolina, came to Washington and then left without testifying. He returned after a second summons, but refused to answer many of the questions on grounds of self-incrimination.[38] Such cases were rare, however; witnesses were guaranteed immunity from prosecution for what they said, except in case of perjury. Most of the Klansmen followed the example of Generals Forrest and John B. Gordon and told as much of the truth as they felt expedient; beyond that they resorted to poor memory, evasion, distortion, or outright perjury. Although Saunders and one or two others were threatened with contempt proceedings, no witnesses were ever legally called to account for their testimony.[39] Some few Negroes were subsequently raided by the Ku Klux, however, as a result of evidence they had given.

A word should be said about the credibility of witnesses on both sides. Sometimes Republican and Democratic witnesses were diametrically opposed concerning the very existence of outrages in a given state or locality. Any reader of the testimony must sympathize with the New York *Herald* reporter, writing from Rutherfordton, North Carolina, in May:

There is probably no country in the world in which it is harder to obtain accurate and reliable information, whether as to actual occurrences or even as to the political sentiments of the people than in these Southern States. I am pretty sure that I could get more truth out of an interview by pantomimic signs with a Carib Indian or King Thakombau or the Gaekwar of Baroda than out of a Southern carpet-bagger or scallawag or a Southern conservative or a Southern out-and-out dyed-in-the-wool unterrified democrat. Ask these latter in turn about something which has come directly under their eyes or is clearly within the compass of their experience and you will get diametrically opposite testimony from them all. Each will flatly contradict the other two, and you will get to the end of your investigation with a very decided belief that as the Apostle Paul has said in Holy Scripture, "All men (excepting yourself) are liars."

Witnesses often differed concerning the existence of a Ku Klux organization and who belonged to it or encouraged it. Conservatives at the time, like their sons and daughters who wrote Reconstruction histories a generation later, tended to make their case for the Klan by simply ignoring or lightly dismissing the testimony of Negro witnesses who had been the victims of Ku Klux attack: They were ignorant as posts and habitual liars who would say anything for money or personal gain; it was preposterous and insulting to accept their word against that of educated white men, including governors, senators, newspaper editors, legal luminaries, and Confederate heroes. What the Conservatives omitted to mention or failed to recognize was that their own witnesses had at least as great an ax to grind as the Republican witnesses had. So far as the latter were politically motivated, they wanted federal intervention in order to restore peaceful elections and majority rule. Troops were not wanted to carry elections by storm, nor did they do so. On the other hand, some Conservative witnesses were out to save their own personal or political skins, and virtually all were out to defend a white supremacy which was menaced by majority rule. Furthermore, the cavalier dismissal of eyewitness testimony violates one of the primary canons of historical method and the rules of evidence. The testimony of hundreds of witnesses made it amply clear that a reign of terror existed in much of the South and that the Conservative community tolerated and encouraged it. The testimony of Conservative witnesses showed also how they tried to cover it up.

The Democratic press did everything it could to discredit the investigation. Since witnesses received $2 per diem and a mileage allowance, those hostile to the Klan were accused of testifying for money and their characters were blackened by shotgun accusations or innuendo. Northern Democratic papers were almost as conspicuous as Southern in this regard. A correspondent of the New York *World,* for instance, wrote concerning the subcommittee's visit to Spartanburg, South Carolina, in July: "They found everything in readiness for them when they came. The highways and byways had been scoured, and many a vagabond negro, allured by the offer of $2 per day, exhibited himself marked with stripes which in many cases no doubt was done years ago at the pillory for crime. The evidence so far has not been important only as it discloses the miserable failure of the State Government." (In fact it fully documented the reign of terror in that county and exposed as the state government's major failure its inability to suppress Klan violence.) Congressman Wallace, the reporter continued,

is here to do the dirty work. He and such kindred cattle have the ear of the committee, and are doing all in their power to prejudice the committee against the people. The greatest proof of their forbearance is that they suffer such scoundrels to go unhung. It is said that the committee are getting very tired of their work; they are disgusted at the idea of being sent hundreds of miles to hear "Old Wives' Tales," and to listen with gravity to long recitations of family feuds and neighborhood difficulties.[40]

The Atlanta *Constitution* and the Rome *Courier* compared the committee to the Spanish Inquisition. But according to the *Constitution,* all the bribed and perjured witnesses it was able to assemble failed to establish the existence of a general Ku Klux organization in Georgia. "The only thing of the kind, a local affair, was shown to have in its membership two Radical revenue assessors." This story was pure invention, along with a reference to sickening revelations of Negro crime. The editor also stretched the truth considerably in saying that most outrages had been connected with illicit stills and were utterly outside politics.[41] Statements of this nature were so contrary to fact that they had to reflect deliberate distortion. The Southern Democratic press in particular was almost as concerned to suppress the truth about the investigation as about the Klan itself.

In December the hearings concluded and the subcommittees returned to Washington to compile their report. As finally submitted in February 1872, the majority and minority reports filled a volume of 632 pages; the accompanying testimony filled twelve more volumes.

The Democratic minority of course found no evidence of a general conspiracy to resist the laws; the disorders it conceded to exist were the wholly natural reactions of a liberty-loving people to Radical Reconstruction policies. "Had there been no wanton oppression in the South, there would have been no Ku-Kluxism. Had there been no rule of the tyrannical, corrupt, carpet-bagger or scalawag . . . there would have been no secret organizations. From the oppression and corruption of the one sprang the vice and outrage of the other."[42] Despite statements to this effect, the minority paradoxically denied that the violence arising from Republican policies was politically inspired. It was simply circumstance that those who took up arms to resist oppression were Democrats. The minority report even undertook to defend the Ku Klux of Mississippi in their revolt against the "gigantic school system" foisted on them by the Radicals. This was nothing more than a "system of robbery . . . to get enough radical schoolmasters into each county to control and manage the negroes." The oppressed white taxpayers

gave [the teachers] all sorts of notices to leave, hoping to intimidate them, and thus, without collision, rid themselves of their burdens; failing in that in several instances they banded together, disguised so . . . as to avoid detection and escape punishment, and whipped the schoolmasters. . . . That is all, or nearly all, there is, or ever was, of Ku-Kluxism in Mississippi anywhere. There was no politics in it. . . .[43]

Northern Democrats seldom evidenced embarrassment at having to defend or cover up the Ku Klux Klan. In large measure they shared its racial and political assumptions, and to all intents and purposes they joined the conspiracy. The racism underlying their position was well summarized by Representative Philadelph Van Trump of Ohio, one of the ablest minority members of the committee:

It was an oft-quoted political apothegm, long prior to the war, that no government could exist "half slave and half free." The paraphrase of that proposition is equally true, that no government can long exist "half black and half white." If the republican party . . . are so absorbed in the idea of this newly discovered political divinity in the negro, that they cannot comprehend its social repugnance or its political dangers; or, knowing it, have the wanton, wicked, and criminal purpose of disregarding its consequences,

then constitutional liberty on this continent was in grave danger. One race must rule and the other be ruled. The inevitable result of Radical Reconstruction, he said, would be race war and the triumph of the superior white race. For the blacks he saw only exodus or extinction.[44]

The majority report came much closer to the truth regarding the Ku Klux Klan and its place in Southern life. The Republicans exaggerated the degree and extent of Klan organization, along with its political character. But their view of a widespread Ku Klux conspiracy was much better founded than the Democrats' complete denial. The majority tended to blame the Southern Democratic leadership too broadly for initiating terrorism in the first place and credited them with more power than they actually possessed to stop it later, but the placement of responsibility in general was not far from the mark.[45] The Republican members admitted with considerable candor that corruption and malfeasance had existed in the governments of South Carolina and other states, but they found little evidence to link this with the nocturnal depredations of the Klan. The Klan arose before malfeasance had had a chance to develop; it existed in Mississippi, where corruption was not seriously alleged, but no longer existed in Louisiana, where corruption was rampant. Moreover, the guilty persons were almost never the ones attacked, the great majority of victims being helpless black men who were attacked for exercising their political and legal rights.[46] The Republicans did not credit, because they did not understand, the Negro insurrection panic which Southern whites recurrently experienced; to the majority it was enough to dismiss this as a cause of the Ku Klux Klan by pointing to the absence of evidence that the blacks ever contemplated such an insurrection. In the same vein, the majority report defended the Union Leagues as legitimate political organizations which engaged in no criminal activity; therefore any hostility to them could have only a partisan political motivation. And so far as apologists explained the Klan as a means of punishing Negro crime, the majority pointed out that the courts had almost no difficulty punishing such cases.[47] By this reasoning the majority narrowed itself down to a mixture of political and racial explanations for the Klan. Any Reconstruction policy, it said, would have been rejected by Southern whites "so long as it embraced the liberation, the civil and political elevation, of the negro."[48] Most of them were convinced that the two races could never cooperate on a basis of equality.[49] The Ku Klux movement, therefore, was at base an effort to deprive the Negro of his rights and to overthrow the Republican party which had extended and sought to maintain those rights. All in all, this was a tolerably accurate assessment.

The majority report was firm but remarkably lacking in vindictiveness. (In this respect it compared favorably with the minority report.) "The strong feeling which led to rebellion and sustained brave men, however mistaken, in resisting the Government which demanded their submission to its authority, the sincerity of whose belief was attested by their enormous sacrifice of life and treasure—this feeling cannot be expected to subside at once, nor in years." It required forty years for disaffection to grow into rebellion, and Northerners should not be surprised that the South had not become fully reconciled again in less than ten. Peaceful and law-abiding citizens should be encouraged in the South. "But while we invoke this forbearance and conciliation, fully recognizing that from far the largest part of the southern people a reluctant obedience is all that is to be hoped for, let it be understood that less than obedience the Government cannot accept." There can be no toleration of those "who permit the remnants of rebellious feeling, the antagonisms of race, or the bitterness of political partisanships to degrade the soldiers of Lee and Johnston into the cowardly midnight prowlers and assassins who scourge and kill the poor and defenseless." If the black man votes solidly with the Republican party, Ku Klux oppression is well calculated to keep him there. "If he is ignorant, he will not be educated by burning his school-houses and exiling his teachers; if he is wicked, he will not be made better by banishing to Liberia his religious teachers. If the resuscitation of the State is desired by his labor, neither will be secured by a persecution which depopulates townships and prevents the introduction of new labor and of capital."[50]

By the time the committee submitted its report, federal prosecutions were well under way to bring Klansmen to justice. The majority applauded these efforts and recommended that they continue. The only recommendation on which both the majority and the minority agreed was the desirability of removing the disabilities which debarred ex-Confederates from holding office.[51] That was subsequently provided by law in 1872.

CHAPTER 25

Arrests and Prosecutions, 1871–1872

At least one federal official in the South now went ahead with Ku Klux prosecutions without waiting for special word from Washington. The United States attorney for northern Mississippi, G. Wiley Wells, set to work in the middle of May, shortly after the Ku Klux Act had been passed. Most of the indictments he obtained from the grand jury were necessarily based on the Enforcement Act of 1870, since the new law could not be applied retroactively. Wells secured almost 200 indictments by early September. He found, as other prosecutors did in the weeks ahead, that federal grand juries were more willing to indict in Ku Klux cases than local grand juries had been. They were drawn from a larger area and were therefore less subject to local pressure, including threats of retaliation. Moreover, the process of selecting federal grand jurors was designed to eliminate Ku Klux members and sympathizers as far as possible. The indictments Wells obtained, together with the impact of the Ku Klux Act's passage, measurably slowed down Klan activity in Mississippi. The accompanying arrests were made in several northeastern counties where the Klan had been active, with soldiers usually accompanying the federal marshal or his deputies.

Twenty prisoners charged with murdering a Negro, Alec Page, on a Ku Klux raid in Monroe County immediately sued for their release on a writ of habeas corpus. At the ensuing hearing before Judge Robert A. Hill in

Oxford, which opened on June 28, the two leading defense counsel were L. Q. C. Lamar, one of the foremost Conservatives in the state and later Secretary of the Interior and Supreme Court justice, and General Samuel J. Gholson, widely acknowledged as the Klan chieftain in the defendants' home county. This hearing was the first federal court case involving the Ku Klux Klan, and it won corresponding publicity. This did not abate when, at one point in the proceedings, Lamar knocked down the United States marshal as he was attempting to enforce order in the courtroom. The government presented ample evidence to justify holding the men for trial. Judge Hill dismissed their petition, therefore, and required them to stand trial at the next court term in December. But pending that time the Klansmen were released on bond. When they returned home to Aberdeen they were greeted as returning heroes, with a welcoming crowd at the depot and the firing of cannon. Their legal expenses were paid by popular subscription.[1]

When the federal government at last indicated a determination to punish Ku Klux offenders a very few local officials joined in. Sheriff H. C. Powers of Oktibbeha County, Mississippi, went to the federal authorities and got arrest warrants for several Klansmen who had harassed Starkville storekeeper McLachlan earlier in the year. Seven or eight men were arrested and bound over for trial in this case; one forfeited his bond and ran off. Federal marshals later made other arrests with the help of soldiers. Colonel H. L. Muldrow, the Klan's chief organizer in Starkville and later a Congressman, served as defense counsel for many of the prisoners. None was ever punished, for the various trials were postponed from one term to another and eventually were dropped.[2]

The first actual trials of Ku Klux were those in North Carolina arising from the two Biggerstaff raids and the Rutherfordton raid of June 11. Commissioner Nathan Scoggins began hearing cases late in June, after the soldiers arrived and started making arrests in Rutherford County. At least forty persons were bound over, indicted by the grand jury, and put on trial in the United States circuit court at Raleigh in September. Here too most of the prosecutions were based on the act of 1870. Some of the defendants had been involved in more than one raid, and after conviction for one offense they pleaded guilty to others. There were forty-nine convictions in all, half of them following pleas of guilty, together with several acquittals. District Attorney D. H. Starbuck happily reported the results to Washington: "As these were the first convictions of Ku Klux in any U. States Courts, I feel we are entitled to the gratitude & thanks of law abiding people everywhere & especially of the Republican or Union Party of this nation which it was the purpose of this daring conspiracy to destroy." The convictions extended not only to men who were guilty of violence, Starbuck noted, but to sixteen others who were proved only to be members of the Klan. The prosecution argued successfully (if too broadly) that the purpose of the order itself was to destroy the freedom of elections through intimidation, and therefore every member became party to a conspiracy in violation of the law. Starbuck believed this to be a vital precedent and one which would effectively suppress the organization. But as it turned out, the federal courts became so clogged with Ku Klux cases involving serious crime that the trial even of those was seriously jeopardized. The men convicted at Raleigh were sentenced to varying fines and prison terms, with those receiving longer sentences (like Randolph Shotwell) being sent to the federal penitentiary in Albany, New York.[3]

Federal prosecution of the Ku Klux Klan centered in South Carolina. It was here alone that the military provisions of the Ku Klux Act were brought to bear. The men most responsible for setting this in motion were Major Lewis Merrill and Senator John Scott, the chairman of the Congressional investigating committee. Scott had been actively concerned to suppress the Klan since presiding over the North Carolina investigation early in the year. He was instrumental in having the detectives employed in June, and he subsequently headed the Congressional subcommittee which visited South Carolina. There he conferred with Merrill and others who confirmed his feeling that strong measures were urgently needed to stem the terror. After returning to Washington he continued to hear from informants in South Carolina about recurring Klan violence. Toward the end of August Scott relayed these reports to the President at Long Branch; he recommended military action, accompanied if necessary by a suspension of habeas corpus under the Ku Klux Act.

Grant was sufficiently disturbed by Scott's information to abandon his summer retreat and return to Washington, where he arrived unexpectedly on the last day of the month. He immediately conferred with Scott, who showed him the reports from Merrill and others. After a lengthy interview Grant was convinced and leaned strongly toward implementing Scott's recommendation. But then he reportedly visited one Cabinet member after another to seek further advice or confirmation of this view. The next day, September 1, he met the Cabinet collectively. They were less convinced than he of the necessity or desirability of military action and urged caution. Before issuing another proclamation commanding the Klan to disperse (which the Ku Klux Act required preliminary to suspending habeas corpus) it was decided to send the Attorney General to South Carolina to investigate conditions in person.[4]

Unlike Senator Scott, the Cabinet apparently still hoped to break up the Klan in South Carolina and elsewhere by normal legal process, using the Army only to help the civil authorities make arrests when they asked for it.

The suspension of habeas corpus was generally regarded as an ultimate weapon akin to martial law, with which it was usually confused. This view exaggerated its nature and effectiveness. Whatever the psychological impact of suspending habeas corpus might be because of this misconception, its only legal effect would be to enable federal authorities to hold prisoners without the usual evidence required before they stood trial.[5] But the authorities (especially in South Carolina) had been compiling evidence for months, and prosecutions were being successfully carried through without this power in Mississippi and North Carolina. The major legal justification for suspending habeas corpus—and it had some merit—was that it enabled the authorities to make mass arrests in greater numbers than would have been possible if each one had had to be backed immediately with formal charges defensible in court. In some counties the number of Ku Klux criminals made this normally necessary procedural safeguard impossible and undesirable. But, with or without habeas corpus, what was most desperately needed now and for a long time past was active effort to prosecute offenders, even if some got away.

Attorney General Amos T. Akerman was himself a Southerner by long adoption—a native of New Hampshire and a Dartmouth graduate who had moved to Elberton, Georgia, in the 1840's. After a somewhat reluctant wartime support of the Confederacy, he accepted Congressional Reconstruction and then helped organize the Republican party in Georgia.[6] He entered the Cabinet in June 1870, soon after the passage of the first Enforcement Act, and may well have been overruled in efforts to enforce that law at the outset.[7] Akerman was the only member of the Cabinet who had ever been in personal danger from the Ku Klux, and he did not take them lightly. In private correspondence he made it clear that he wanted very much to proceed against the Klan legally, breaking it up as an organization and punishing its most criminal members.[8]

With this in mind Akerman visited Raleigh, North Carolina, in mid-September, where he helped supervise the prosecutions then under way.[9] From Raleigh he proceeded according to instructions to Yorkville, South Carolina. Here he conferred with Major Merrill and carefully went through the evidence accumulated by that officer and neglected by the recent county grand jury. Coinciding with his visit, and probably because of it, the federal marshal now began making arrests in York County, using troops.[10] At the same time Akerman became convinced that it was necessary to invoke the President's fullest powers in South Carolina, suspending the writ of habeas corpus. (He also gained a very favorable impression of Merrill, later reporting to General Terry that he was the perfect man for the job there: "resolute, collected, bold and prudent, with a good legal head, very discriminating between truth and falsehood, very indignant at wrong, and yet master of his indignation; the safer because incredulous at the outset, and, therefore, disposed to scrutinize reports the more keenly. He has performed a difficult service with admirable success.") Accordingly Akerman went next to Louisville, conferred there with General Terry, and then met the President (who was en route to Washington from Chicago) at Dayton, Ohio. Grant apparently agreed to his recommendation, and on October 10 the Attorney General returned to South Carolina. From Yorkville he telegraphed Grant that matters were in proper shape for the President to move ahead.[11]

The preliminary proclamation appeared on October 12. It called attention to the continuing "unlawful combinations and conspiracies" in nine up-country counties and commanded the persons involved to disperse within five days and surrender their arms and disguises.[12] This was a matter of form which no one expected the Ku Klux to obey, although some of the leading Klansmen in York County, including Major Avery, had already taken flight at the time of Akerman's arrival and the first arrests. On October 17 came the second proclamation, suspending the writ of habeas corpus for persons arrested under the Ku Klux Act in the counties of Spartanburg, York, Marion, Chester, Laurens, Newberry, Fairfield, Lancaster, and Chesterfield.[13] In the last three counties Klan activity had been comparatively minimal, and Marion County was actually included by mistake. In preparing the proclamations from a draft which Akerman had written out in advance, Justice Department personnel apparently read "Marion" for "Union," which was the county intended. When the error was discovered new proclamations were issued revoking the suspension in Marion County and applying it to Union.[14]

Mass arrests began on October 19, after the arrival of three more companies of soldiers. Akerman remained in Yorkville until October 27, helping to supervise the arrests and laying the groundwork for the prosecutions to follow. The arrests were confined at first to York and Spartanburg counties and amounted to about one hundred by the time of Akerman's departure. They were made by the United States marshal for South Carolina and his deputies, assisted by soldiers from Major Merrill's command. The latter were distributed at a number of points in advance so as to make the first arrests simultaneously and with as little prior warning as possible. (The marshal, Louis E. Johnson, was a son of Reverdy Johnson, the Maryland lawyer and statesman who would soon act as chief defense counsel when the prisoners came to trial in Columbia.) It was Major Merrill, however, who played the key role in deploying forces, supplying evidence to justify the arrests, and taking depositions from the scores of Klansmen who took this opportunity to purge themselves through confession. "Day after day, for weeks," Merrill reported later, "men came in in such numbers that time to hear them confess and means to dispose of or take care of them both failed, and I was powerless to do anything more than secure the persons of those most deeply criminal, and send the rest to their homes on their personal parole to be forthcoming when called for. In some instances whole Klans, headed by their chief, came in and surrendered together."[15] Formal charges against the prisoners were delayed for several weeks because of the volume of arrests and confessions that had to be dealt with and because of the need for keeping evidence secret until all suspects had been rounded up. This was the major benefit conferred by the suspension of habeas corpus.

As in North Carolina, most of the "pukers" were innocent of major crimes, and in return for immunity or light treatment they gave information about others who were more deeply involved. By this means Merrill learned of five additional murders for the first time. In York County alone about 200 members fled the state, including the highest leaders. Dr. J. Rufus Bratton followed Major Avery to London, Ontario, where they were given asylum by Edward Manigault, a former Yorkville resident. In June 1872 Joseph G. Hester, the federal detective and deputy marshal from North Carolina, went to Detroit, where he engineered Bratton's capture in Canada, without the formalities of extradition. The doctor was brought across the border and taken back to Yorkville to stand trial. This action violated Canadian sovereignty, of course, and after diplomatic protests Bratton was returned there unpunished. Captain J. Banks Lyle, the legislator and Klan chief in Spartanburg County, also fled the state and was never prosecuted.[16]

The arrests continued through the remainder of the year and into 1872, and extended to several counties. By December 31, 1871, Merrill reported 195 persons imprisoned in York County alone for serious crimes, some of whom were later released on bail. In addition, about 100 from that county had evaded arrest by flight and at least 500 had voluntarily surrendered, given depositions, and been released.[17] The majority of Klansmen in the county, perhaps an additional thousand, were never disturbed; most of course were relatively innocent of crime. Nine prisoners were arrested by mistake and then released, usually within a few hours. One released prisoner was a thirteen-year-old boy, the son of a Klan chief who had initiated him into the order and taken him on a raid.

The whole process of arrests was made as efficiently and with as little physical force as the circumstances permitted. Despite Conservative charges of despotism and inhumanity, there was virtually no mistreatment of prisoners. Those kept under arrest were lodged in the county jail, a three-story brick structure. (In this community it was now dubbed the United States Hotel.) Conditions became crowded, but newspaper reporters and the prisoners themselves testified to their good treatment. They were allowed visitors every day, who showered them with additional food, flowers, and other delicacies, and they were frequently taken out under guard for walks in town. Since there were few white Republicans in the county, there was little of the fratricidal bitterness and desire for revenge found in Rutherfordton, North Carolina, a little earlier. If the Negroes found that revenge was sweet they did not parade their feelings.

It is hard to exaggerate the impact of the arrests on the community. The additional business brought to Yorkville by the presence of 400 soldiers was more than balanced by the demoralization of the county's white population, whose business virtually stopped. A New York *Tribune* correspondent reported the scene:

As I walked up the long street from the depot to the hotel, the place had the look of a town in war time recently captured by an invading army. There were soldiers everywhere. An infantry camp of clean, white tents, arranged in regular rows, with the alleys between prettily shaded with arbors of green boughs, stood in an oak grove near the station. A squad of cavalry rode by; blue coats strolled up and down the street and lounged about the doors of the stores, in which there seemed to be much talk and little traffic. Groups of countrymen in gray homespun stood upon the street corners and in the Court-House yard, engaged in low and excited talk. Other men who appeared, by their dress, villagers, could be seen through the open doors of lawyers' and doctors' offices, or standing in knots of three or four upon the sidewalks, absorbed in conversation on the one topic of the arrests. Everybody but the negroes and soldiers had the look of excitement and despondency always observable in the inhabitants of a conquered town, and the people I met eyed me suspiciously, as if they feared I might have come to empty some new vial of Government wrath upon their devoted heads.[18]

The same reporter noted, after comparing Ku Klux confessions and the evidence of atrocities with the comments of men on the street, that there seemed to be almost no public "sense of right and wrong, no appreciation of the heinousness of crimes committed upon helpless and unoffending people." Instead whites tended, at least in public, to confine their indignation to the "arbitrary arrests," tearing innocent men from their families or forcing them into flight to escape the tyranny. But the evidence of crime against those arrested, and the public exposure of criminality in general, was so overwhelming that it did not fail to register altogether. Some Conservatives privately assured Akerman, Merrill, and others that the government's activity was absolutely necessary to restore the community to decency. Many men privately welcomed the opportunity to assist in ending a terrorist conspiracy to which they had become (sooner or later) unwilling accessories. For some rank-and-file Klansmen this feeling was increased by resentment at many of their leaders, who had means to evade punishment for grosser crimes than they themselves were being arrested for. But these attitudes were almost never reflected publicly; the public reaction of the Democratic party was one of unrelieved outrage at federal tyranny. Six persons were arrested at their own request as witnesses, being afraid to testify unless it was made to appear that they had been compelled to do so.[19]

The same conditions and attitudes prevailed in varying degree wherever large-scale arrests took place. Small Army detachments were sent to Shelby, Rutherfordton, and other nearby points in North Carolina to pick up such refugees as Major Merrill indicated and convey them back to South Carolina.[20] Spartanburg County was the most nearly comparable to York. Hundreds of arrests produced more prisoners than the county jail would accommodate, and the upper floors of two stores were pressed into auxiliary service. The primary responsibility in making arrests and hearing confessions here was exercised by the federal civil officials; the local military commander furnished troops at their request but did not assume the initiative as Merrill did in Yorkville.[21] About 200 arrests were made in Union County by federal authorities.[22] In Chester County, by contrast, the sheriff and other local officials were stimulated by federal activity nearby to initiate arrests themselves. Federal authorities took up the task soon afterward and ultimately made about 150 arrests. This was just as well, for the county grand jury could find no evidence of Klan outrages and declared that the disorders cited in the President's proclamations were fictitious products of Republican malice.[23] There were also smaller-scale federal arrests later in Newberry and Laurens counties, with about forty persons in the latter arrested for participation in the election riot of October 1870.[24] In all of these counties scores or hundreds of Klansmen fled at the first arrests and thus escaped. There were almost no cases of forcible resistance. The arrests themselves occurred off and on from October 1871 into 1873, but the greatest number took place in the first few weeks. Governor Scott reported about 600 by November 28.[25] No arrests were made in Lancaster, Fairfield, and Chesterfield counties, where outrages had occurred but probably not in sufficient number to have justified their inclusion in the Presidential proclamations.

The number of prisoners, it turned out, was far too great for the courts to handle, and only the worst offenders were proceeded against with any seriousness. Attorney General Akerman instructed D. T. Corbin, the United States attorney for South Carolina, to classify the prisoners confidentially according to the degree of their criminality and whether they had been leaders or reluctant followers in the Ku Klux conspiracy. Less serious offenders were to be released on bail after making sworn confessions, with

a warning that they would be held accountable for their future behavior.[26]
Akerman hoped in this way at least to break up the organization for good
and end the violence. He was shocked at the depth and extent of the terror
as it was revealed to him in Yorkville; it far exceeded what he had experienced in his part of Georgia. "I doubt whether from the beginning of the
world until now," he wrote General Terry,

a community, nominally civilized, has been so fully under the domination of
systematic and organized depravity. If the people of the North really understood
it, there would be an outbreak of indignation unparalleled since April 1861.
. . . Though rejoiced at the suppression of Ku Kluxery, even in one neighborhood, I feel greatly saddened by this business. It has revealed a perversion of
moral sentiment among the Southern whites, which bodes ill to that part of the
country for this generation. Without a thorough moral renovation, society there
for many years will be—I can hardly bring myself to say savage, but certainly
very far from christian.[27]

A large proportion of the prosecutions in South Carolina too came under
the Enforcement Act of 1870 if only because the crimes had been committed before passage of the Ku Klux Act. In general the indictments were
drawn for conspiracy to injure or oppress citizens in the enjoyment of
various constitutional rights, including the right to bear arms where Ku
Klux seizure of guns was involved. Where murders were committed in the
process, the 1870 law permitted that as an additional count.[28]

The first cases came up for trial in the United States circuit court in
Columbia late in November. Some $10,000 was raised by public subscrip-
tion around the state to hire an illustrious panel of defense attorneys. They
were headed by Reverdy Johnson and Henry Stanbery, both former
Attorneys General of the United States and the latter a defense counsel in
Andrew Johnson's impeachment trial in 1868. The prosecution was headed
by United States Attorney Corbin and Daniel H. Chamberlain, the attorney
general and later governor of South Carolina. One of the two judges, Hugh
L. Bond, had presided at the recently concluded Ku Klux trials in Raleigh.
Out of 220 persons indicted at this court term, only 58 were brought
to trial, the rest being postponed; 53 pleaded guilty at the outset, leaving
only 5 to stand trial, all from York County. During the proceedings it was
made amply clear that the Klan had a political purpose and that it had engaged in a veritable orgy of brutality at the expense of largely unoffending
and defenseless Negroes in York County. The defense counsel themselves
were not quite prepared for the quantity and character of the evidence
brought against their clients. Reverdy Johnson was so moved by the revelations of cruelty that he got up at one point and delivered as eloquent an attack upon Ku Klux terrorism as had come from the mouth of any Republican. All five defendants were convicted. Together with those who pleaded

guilty, they were sentenced by Judge Bond to prison terms ranging from three months to five years and fines of $10 up to $1,000.[29]

Those with sentences of a year or longer were sent to join the North Carolinians in the Albany penitentiary. "A more forlorn, woe-begone, haggard-looking crew could scarcely be found," said the *New York Times* of the twenty-four prisoners who passed through that city on their way to Albany late in January. "With one or two exceptions, they bore upon their faces the stolid look of utter ignorance. . . . Only one or two could read or write. Their rough, haggard faces, ragged garments, and unkempt hair presented a singular spectacle. . . ." From this description, their prison treatment had deteriorated since their days in the Yorkville jail.[30]

South Carolina was the only state in which habeas corpus was suspended, and the attention of Washington and the nation was naturally centered upon it. But arrests and prosecutions proceeded in other states too along more conventional lines. In North Carolina federal civil authorities, aided by troops, continued making arrests around the state during and after the Raleigh trials. Klansmen in several counties flocked in to make confessions as soon as the arrests began in their vicinity. Most of this took place in Rutherford, Cleveland, Gaston, and Lincoln, the southwestern counties which had been the main theater of Klan activity earlier in the year; but J. G. Hester made a number of arrests in Sampson County in the east, and an Army detachment that went there late in November gathered more than 100 confessions in a week.[31] By that time a total of 763 indictments had been made in the state, including duplications for men charged with more than one offense. Of this number, 23 pleaded guilty, 24 were tried and convicted, 13 were acquitted, and 9 cases were dropped in a subsequent court term; the great majority still awaited trial at the end of the year.[32]

Hester had already gone in July to Caswell County, where he discovered more about the courthouse murder of state senator John W. Stephens in May 1870.[33] But no arrests followed either here or in adjacent Alamance, where Governor Holden's militia campaign had come to such an inconclusive end a year before.

Into this void stepped Judge Albion Tourgée of the North Carolina superior court, who had done all he could to prosecute Klansmen in 1869 and 1870. In December 1871 he took advantage of a dispute between two Alamance Klansmen to secure evidence and make arrests arising from the Wyatt Outlaw murder in Graham and several other crimes. Many of the men he sought were able to escape, but he prevailed on the county grand jury to indict sixty-three Klansmen for various felonies and eighteen (including former county chief Jacob A. Long) for the murder of Outlaw. Other less serious offenders Tourgée released on payment of court costs. Some of those arrested belonged to the best families in the county, and

Conservatives were thrown into consternation. "Our worst fears are realized," wrote one lawyer and White Brotherhood leader to elder statesman William A. Graham.[34] Tourgée was so encouraged by his success that he applied for Hester's services to uncover similar evidence in Orange County.[35] But the sequel proved once more how futile it was to seek prosecutions in the state courts. Within a month of his arrests and before the cases could come to trial, the Democratic legislature repealed the law on which the felony indictments were based. They could hardly repeal the law against murder, but Conservatives introduced another bill to grant amnesty for all crimes committed in behalf of secret societies. They made a great show of bipartisanship by including the Union League, but Republicans were unimpressed and opposed the measure bitterly. (The League had not sponsored crimes, and the few Negroes who committed Klan-like offenses had long since been punished in Judge Tourgée's court.) Passage of the amnesty measure was delayed until 1873, but the Alamance prisoners never came to trial at all.[36]

The Justice Department began investigating Klan activity in Georgia in July 1871. Neither the federal district attorney nor any other official there initiated large-scale prosecutions. In fact District Attorney John D. Pope dragged his feet in prosecuting the cases that others brought before him. Such initiative as was displayed was on the part of two special attorneys, J. H. Caldwell and J. E. Bryant, who were appointed in the summer to investigate and work up cases.[37] When H. C. Whitley, the head of the secret service, offered to go all-out against the Georgia Klan if he was given a company of cavalry, his proposal was apparently shelved.[38] Attorney General Akerman defended his South Carolina policy to fellow Republicans of Georgia, but he indicated no urgency in applying the same measures there.[39] Governor Bullock and the Atlanta *New Era* had always been lukewarm toward federal enforcement, and in October they were still pleading with Georgians to forestall it by suppressing the Ku Klux themselves.[40] The arrests which began in that month, therefore, were by no means as numerous as in the Carolinas. The officer making many of them was Deputy Marshal James Skiles, who took squads of soldiers to several north Georgia counties in the latter part of the year, arrested groups of a dozen or so Klansmen, and brought them to Atlanta. In a few cases he was aided by sheriffs and other local officials, but that was the exception rather than the rule. In Gwinnett County (where the sheriff helped to arrest several men for burning the courthouse) local justices of the peace were afraid to issue arrest warrants because of prior threats. Moreover, Skiles had to release four prisoners when a Democratic leader threatened otherwise to have him mobbed.[41] In Dade County he himself was arrested for false imprisonment.[42]

District Attorney Pope urged the federal grand jury in Atlanta to indict many of the prisoners, but the lack of enthusiasm in that body at least equaled his own. The process of grand jury selection in Georgia favored the appointment of a large number of Democrats. It did return about thirty Ku Klux indictments in October, but in other cases where Pope thought the evidence was strong it refused to act. In several instances continuing terrorism frightened key witnesses into not testifying. Some of those who were indicted had not yet been arrested, and some never were. No cases were scheduled for trial before March 1872. Meanwhile defendants secured some of the foremost legal talent in the state, like Ben Hill, to defend them, often with outside financial support.[43]

Still less was done in Florida, where Jackson County ranked as one of the most terror-ridden communities in the South. Republican leaders urged the President in November to proclaim martial law or suspend habeas corpus in that county, if nothing else was done. They claimed that eleven more political murders had taken place there since the assassination of J. Q. Dickinson in April, and there had been 179 unpunished murders since the end of the war.[44] Habeas corpus was not suspended, but a small detachment of troops went to Marianna on December 7 to make arrests. Four days later they apprehended James Coker, the local Klan chief and ringleader in the terror, and took him to Tallahassee. At the December federal court term fourteen cases came up for trial under the Enforcement Acts, resulting in only one conviction and one acquittal. Two cases were dropped, and the rest, including Coker's, were held over until 1872; at that time his case too was dropped. On the other hand, violence virtually ended in Florida by the end of 1871. This included Jackson County, where the Republicans were thus enabled to win a special legislative election in December.[45]

In Alabama District Attorney John A. Minnis had been one of the first federal officials to prosecute Klansmen. In October, after hearing from Sheriff F. M. Treadway of the virtual guerrilla warfare between Unionists and Klansmen in Fayette County, Minnis went there to make arrests. Most of the suspects got word of his coming and fled, but he arrested two men and took them to Huntsville to stand trial. United States marshals arrested Klansmen in other counties as well. By the end of the year federal grand juries had indicted about 130 persons in the state, but no trials had been held because of a shortage of personnel to prepare the cases. Meanwhile arrests, flights, and confessions continued, and Klan violence ground almost to a halt.[46]

In Mississippi too the arrests which began in the early summer increased thereafter. Almost 200 indictments were handed down by the end of the year, but the only cases ready for trial at the December court term were twenty-eight men from Monroe County, most of whom had lost their bid for release in the Oxford hearing in June. When they finally came to trial all pleaded guilty. Despite the fact that they had committed murder, they were given suspended sentences.[47]

The thin flow of arrests and prosecutions in Kentucky has already been mentioned.[48] Elsewhere in the South there was little or no attempt to prosecute Klansmen under the Enforcement Acts in 1871. In most of the remaining states the Klan had disappeared by this time, and in some it had passed on before those acts became law.

In the states where prosecutions *were* seriously undertaken, officials were concerned at the tremendous load of business they entailed. The number of federal prosecutors, judges, and clerks simply was not adequate to the task. Dockets became overloaded, and there were unconscionable delays in bringing cases to a close. None had greater cause to bemoan the situation than Attorney General Akerman and District Attorney Corbin in South Carolina, where the greatest traffic jam occurred. Only in York County had there been anything like a thorough campaign of arrests and prosecutions by the end of the year; it was not yet finished there, and cases had hardly begun in the other counties. Even restricting prosecutions to the most serious offenders was producing more cases than the courts could handle, unless Congress provided for additional personnel and longer court terms. If Congress did not provide this help, the two officials warned, most of the cases would lapse and the guilty would continue to punish the innocent as heretofore.[49]

Akerman resigned as Attorney General at the end of 1871, to be replaced by former senator George H. Williams of Oregon. His reasons were not announced, and the speculation ranged from personality clashes with his Cabinet colleagues to the political expediency of having a West Coast man in the Cabinet. But Akerman may well have resigned (as some believed) over an apparent refusal by the administration to back a more vigorous policy against the Klan.[50] In any event, no special provisions were made of the magnitude he and Corbin favored.

When the Congressional investigating committee submitted its report in February 1872, the Republican majority seconded the call for expanding the judiciary in the states affected. It also requested another year's extension of the President's power to suspend habeas corpus, which was due to expire with Congress' adjournment in the summer.[51] Senator Scott reported a bill for this purpose which passed the Senate, but it died in the House.[52] President Grant had used this power in South Carolina with the greatest reluctance, and he refused pleas to use it in Florida and elsewhere. Probably this made little difference except for its psychological impact. Even in South Carolina the suspension had not prevented hundreds of

Klansmen from fleeing arrest; whatever usefulness it had in facilitating large-scale arrests had by now largely disappeared. Much graver was the failure of Congress to enlarge the judiciary and thus facilitate prosecutions.

The federal courts continued to try Ku Klux cases in 1872 in most of the states where they had taken place the year before. But everywhere the number of cases concluded was pitifully small compared with the number of indictments. Even the latter fell off as prosecutors and grand juries recognized the unlikelihood of ever bringing them to trial. In South Carolina the April court term at Charleston produced only thirty-six more convictions, together with one acquittal.[53] Major Merrill remained at Yorkville throughout the year, making arrests in decreasing numbers; other officials did the same in other counties. By summer rumors became current that he was about to be superseded, that arrests and prosecutions were about to stop, and that those persons already convicted would be pardoned. Merrill, Corbin, and many others were worried by these reports, fearing a resurgence of the Klan spirit if not of Klan outrages in consequence. Attorney General Williams denied any change of policy and ordered them to proceed as before. But when they asked for a special court term in August to help clear the backlog of cases, none was provided.[54] By November Corbin had about a thousand indictments pending. In desperation he was forced to recommend that, even among the accused murderers, only the most serious offenders be tried. At the ensuing court term in Columbia that month, only a few cases were heard, resulting in nine convictions.[55]

Conditions were only a little less aggravated in other states. Arrests continued to take place in diminishing number throughout 1872, with substantial numbers of indictments following, but very few cases were tried. Well over a thousand indictments were pending in North Carolina by the end of 1872, with about the same proportion of trials and convictions as in South Carolina.[56] In Alabama, Georgia, and Florida the numbers of arrests and indictments were much smaller, with correspondingly less excuse for the small number of cases completed.[57] By July 1872 there were sixty-five Klansmen in the Albany penitentiary,[58] and a much greater number were serving shorter sentences in various Southern prisons.

Federal authorities in Mississippi seem to have avoided the problem of congested dockets in a unique fashion. In the northern district of that state alone, 325 cases were reported as disposed of in 1872, resulting in 262 convictions.[59] The judge and district attorney apparently expedited business and secured convictions by promising suspended sentences in return for pleas of guilty. (This was likely the case with the twenty-eight Monroe County Klansmen who pleaded guilty and received suspended sentences in December 1871.) By this means Klansmen escaped punishment for their past crimes but the court left hanging over their heads the possibility of imposing sentence if they resumed their activities. Whatever the justice of this policy it seemed to be equally effective in discouraging further Klan activity. It was also designed in all likelihood to extend the hand of conciliation to the outraged Conservatives.

Democratic reactions to the arrests and prosecutions were almost uniformly hostile everywhere. As usual there were some Conservatives who privately admitted the propriety or even necessity of the policy, but few cared to commit this treason in public. Even the Charleston *Daily News* discovered that the Klan outrages which it had consistently condemned in South Carolina were "either fabrications or gross perversions of the truth." There was no Ku Kluxing in York County, it said; and when men fled their homes to avoid military arrest it meant only that they were fleeing from despotism. The arrests had been procured by mercenary witnesses and would be followed by farcical trials as in North Carolina.[60] The same changes were rung with variations throughout the South. Conservative journals and Conservative witnesses before the Congressional committee expatiated upon the reign of terror accompanying the federal arrests, although they had seen none arising from Klan activity. When individuals were arrested for committing specific outrages, there was commonly so much solicitude to proclaim the innocence of the suspects that there was none left to inquire who did commit the crimes and how they might be apprehended.[61]

Very little violence attended the arrests in any state, but much was made of little. Soldiers entering a house near Starkville, Mississippi, to arrest a suspected Klansman found a person lying in bed with the covers over his head. They pulled the covers down far enough to discover that it was a woman and then left. But as the story spread in the next few days, she had been all but sexually assaulted. Citizens prevailed on a United States commissioner to issue arrest warrants for the deputy marshal and soldiers, and demanded that Sheriff Powers organize them as a posse. He refused and managed only with difficulty to prevent them from galloping off to capture the Yankees as the latter returned to their post. Later the marshal and soldiers returned voluntarily to submit to arrest, but the furor had died out and no action was taken. The Klansman whom they initially sought and arrested subsequently ran off and forfeited his bond.[62]

The restraint of the Yorkville *Enquirer* in describing arrests was rather exceptional. Its neighbor, the *Carolina Spartan,* having denied the Klan's existence in Spartanburg County, was naturally incensed to hear about the misdeeds of troops who went to the boys' academy at Limestone Springs to arrest its principal. That gentleman, county chief J. Banks Lyle, having departed before their arrival, the soldiers reportedly broke down doors, rode their horses onto his front lawn, and even appropriated the boys' breakfast. Like other South Carolina papers, the *Spartan* mourned the crops lost, the business disrupted, and the families separated by these causeless and malicious arrests or by the flights to evade them.[63]

Some of those arrested everywhere were among the "very best men in the community," and it was taken for granted that they were morally incapable of committing the crimes imputed to them—if the crimes had been committed at all.[64] When prisoners confessed publicly and circumstantially to having witnessed or participated in crimes of the grossest brutality, they were not to be believed; their very appearance stamped them as ignorant, confused, and not above lying to procure their release.[65]

The prosecutions which followed were equally outrageous, although some newspapers found that the failure to prosecute some of the prisoners or their early release was an equal sign of federal turpitude, showing the causelessness of their original arrest. The Raleigh *Sentinel* admitted that some of the men convicted there were probably guilty, but it resented every step taken to ascertain that fact.[66] Prosecution witnesses were subjected to a sustained character assassination; not infrequently they were threatened with physical retaliation or legal prosecution in the local courts: "The parties who were so indecently zealous before our last [county] Grand Juries, to get bills against the silly boys in Livingston District, for their drunken frolick, have at last succeeded [with] the United States Grand Jury at Atlanta," noted the Rome *Courier,* referring to a masked attack on some Negroes. "And now the young men who so thoughtlessly engaged in that unfortunate frolic, will have to be outcasts and fugitives in a strange land, or brave the horrors of a Northern prison." Whether "their persecutors" were moved by malice or cupidity, "they are every one known, and the honest people of Floyd County will not soon forget them."[67] Federal officials occasionally had as much difficulty persuading witnesses to testify, and protecting them afterward, as state authorities had had.

The trials themselves were a miscarriage of justice, Conservatives generally agreed, even if they did nail a few guilty men. The Enforcement Acts were unconstitutional, the offenses alleged had nothing to do with politics or civil rights if they occurred at all, the witnesses were perjured, the juries packed, and the judges biased. Judge Bond, who sat and passed sentence in the most publicized trials in Raleigh and Columbia, was singled out for particular abuse. The Rome *Courier,* which had compared the Congressional investigation with the Spanish Inquisition, found the closest parallel here to be with Judge Jeffries and the Bloody Assizes of King James II.[68]

And President Grant's greatest personal anxiety was confirmed: "Grant is a dictator, declares martial law when it suits his pleasure," announced the Raleigh *Sentinel.* "Grant is master—the people his slaves. . . . Now, instead of civil law, we have kuklux acts, martial law, the despotism of the bayonets. . . . "[69] Even if he were not this bad and had good intentions, said the New York *Herald* (which never really made up its mind on the question), he still had to learn that he was no longer a wartime general in the field.[70]

As with earlier state activity to check the Klan, the degree of Democratic outrage over federal arrests and prosecutions was the measure of their effectiveness. Night riding and outrages by disguised bands continued to be reported in several states from December 1871 into October 1872, perhaps increasing somewhat with the advent of the fall Presidential election.[71] But these cases were isolated and relatively few in number. Despite this sporadic activity and a few reports of Klan reorganization in northern Mississippi and elsewhere, the federal government had broken the back of the Ku Klux Klans throughout most of the South.[72] The campaign of 1872 was more peaceful than any since the advent of Radical Reconstruction. Such violence and intimidation as occurred—and it was considerable, especially in Georgia and Louisiana—was undertaken without disguise and probably with a minimum of continuing organization.

It was obvious well before the election that the government was moderating the enforcement campaign which it had entered upon so reluctantly a year before. Perfectly good cases were being abandoned or shelved indefinitely because the courts could not handle them, and Congress refused to take any further action. Klan activity had fallen off to the point where extraordinary legal efforts no longer seemed necessary to preserve order or to ensure a peaceful election. For practicing Republican politicians the freedom of elections had always rivaled abstract justice as a motive in determining attitudes and policies toward the Klan. When Ku Klux terrorists had threatened to take elections by storm, they hesitantly adopted a hard line. With that necessity gone, there was no point in risking a negative public reaction by pushing the matter further.

Attorney General Williams instructed federal officials throughout 1872 to continue prosecuting those cases involving murder. But beginning in August the administration coupled this with a selective pardoning policy. The credit for initiating this new turn belonged to Gerrit Smith, the old abolitionist. Smith visited the Albany penitentiary in July, talked with many of the Ku Klux prisoners, and then wrote a letter to Grant characterizing most of them as ignorant men who had been duped into joining the organization; several of them, he said, deserved pardons. When this letter was referred to Attorney General Williams he sent Whitley, the secret service chief, to Albany to investigate and make a recommendation regarding clemency. Whitley interviewed about forty prisoners incognito and heard the same things they had told Smith. No matter that only the guiltiest

Klansmen had been prosecuted in the first place, and only the worst of those had been convicted and sent to Albany; clemency was in the air. Whitley did what was doubtless expected of him and recommended pardons for a substantial number of the inmates.[73]

The first of these were granted soon afterward, but sparingly.[74] Whitley's report was published, and it loosed a flood of petitions from friends, relatives, and other interested persons in behalf of individual prisoners. Each case was referred for comment to the district attorney and other officials who had prosecuted it in the first place. Corbin and Merrill in South Carolina were among those who recommended clemency in some cases, but they strenuously advised against it in others and urged that prosecutions continue in the serious cases which had not yet come to trial. The greatest efforts to secure pardons, Merrill noted in September, were almost invariably in behalf of Klansmen who had money and influence, and some of these were the guiltiest members of the organization. Given the orgy of crime which had set these prosecutions in motion, he said, great clemency had already been shown in the very selectivity of the prosecutions. Local Conservatives still regarded Klansmen as heroes and martyrs; when Dr. Bratton was brought back from Canada in June, the best people in the community rushed to greet him and offer their support. They regarded every sign of mercy as an indication of weakness and became more defiant of the government. Merrill was all the less inclined to extend mercy to Klansmen, he said, as it seemed to threaten a renewal of terrorism against hundreds of innocent people, including witnesses. Just two days before he wrote this letter, in September, he reported, a white man had had his throat slit from ear to ear and lay near death, largely because he had been a prosecution witness in the recent trials.[75]

For the time being at least, this view prevailed in Washington too. When former Governor Scott and his new successor, Franklin J. Moses, urged an end to prosecutions and a general pardon of those already convicted in South Carolina, the Attorney General joined Corbin and Merrill in opposition. Each case must be judged on its own merits, he said.[76] In his annual message in December, the President, just triumphantly re-elected, said he was willing to grant clemency in worthy cases in order to tranquilize public opinion; but he was still determined to enforce the laws vigorously as long as combinations and conspiracies of armed men continued to disturb the peace.[77]

Nevertheless, prosecutions continued to fall off and pardons to mount early in 1873. The Klan did not revive in any strength, but its members and fellow travelers remained vocal in their threats of retribution against Republicans.[78] Klan outrages continued to occur sporadically, sometimes leading to new arrests and prosecutions.[79] In January J. G. Hester called, apparently in vain, for troops to help him arrest some men whom he had linked with the Stephens murder in Yanceyville, North Carolina, while Alamance County Klansmen, emboldened by both federal and state amnesty measures, engaged in another flurry of raiding.[80]

In February 1873 the South Carolina legislature belatedly voted $35,000 to pay the rewards of $200 apiece offered by Governor Scott in July 1871 for the arrest of Klansmen with evidence to convict. As now implemented, there was little to justify this measure. A claims commission appointed by the governor began by awarding $500 apiece to themselves and then divided the remainder among half a dozen men, most of them federal officials who had received their regular salaries while making arrests in the line of duty. The chief result of this affair was to substantiate in many minds the Conservative smears of the whole enforcement campaign and some of the men who were most directly involved in it. Major Merrill received more than half of the total—$20,700—and assigned $5,000 of it to a man whose service allegedly consisted in lobbying the bill through the legislature. Merrill was plagued by this for the rest of his life. He left South Carolina in June 1873 and, after two extended sick leaves, retired from the service in 1886. When his promotion to lieutenant colonel was recommended at that time, Southern Senators were able to block it for four years, at least in part because he had accepted money for performing services in the line of duty.[81]

By April, Attorney General Williams was ordering federal district attorneys in the Carolinas to suspend further prosecution of cases already indicted, but to prosecute new cases as they arose. "All that is desired," he advised, "is that Ku Klux and other similar combinations of persons, shall be abandoned, and the rights of all persons respected; and when this is done obviously there will be little need for proceeding any further with criminal prosecutions" under the Enforcement Acts.[82] Men who had fled to evade arrest, moreover, were informed in July that they were free to return home unless their crimes fell into a small category of offenses so aggravated that they could not be overlooked.[83] The number of pardons granted by the President grew correspondingly. Despite an adverse recommendation by District Attorney Starbuck in North Carolina, Randolph Shotwell was pardoned in August and returned home to Rutherfordton.[84] Not only were most of the prosecutions suspended, but in the latter part of 1873 and in 1874 they were formally dropped; this was done in 1,091 cases in South Carolina alone.[85] New cases continued to be prosecuted in the federal courts for several years as they arose, and resulted in a number of convictions. But the number was small and continued to fall.[86] Pardons continued to be granted, even to the most serious offenders, until 1875. By that year virtually all but the most recent offenders had either served out their sentences or received pardons.

In 1876 the Supreme Court emasculated the Enforcement Acts by ruling that the federal government could protect civil rights only against their abridgment by states, not individuals.[87] Moreover, public opinion was either apathetic or hostile by that time toward vigorous enforcement. The North had become tired of the necessity of enforcing order and fair elections, of protecting the Negro freedman from his white neighbors, by the use of federal troops. What passed for enlightened opinion cried out to leave the South alone, and when President Rutherford B. Hayes reached the White House in 1877 he pledged to do just that. Reconstruction had come to an end.

— After 1877, when the Democrats recaptured South Carolina, a mutual agreement was made by state and federal officials to drop all legal charges of a political nature. Owing to the intercession of Wade Hampton with President Hayes, Dr. Bratton was finally permitted to return to Yorkville from his five-year exile in London, Ontario.[88]

— The federal government's enforcement campaign broke the back of the Ku Klux Klans, even if it failed to end them absolutely. On the other hand, it failed lamentably to bring more than a few Klansmen to justice after one of the most far-flung and persistent crime waves in American history. Southern violence now assumed other forms, almost as lethal, probably more effective, and certainly more lasting than the Ku Klux Klan.

Epilogue: Apotheosis and Rebirth

No simple generalization can sum up the effects or accomplishments of the Ku Klux Klan. Certainly it did not end Reconstruction, as some of its admirers came to believe in later years. It cannot even be credited with overthrowing Republican control in any Southern state, although it was a contributory factor in all of them. Its contribution was greatest in Georgia, where the Klan played a distinct if subsidiary role in the victorious white supremacy campaign of 1870. It directly or indirectly influenced the Democratic victories in Alabama and North Carolina the same year, although Republicans were able to elect governors in both of these states in 1872. Within most states, the Klan was clearly instrumental in breaking up the Union League and local Republican organization in many counties. It also helped to perpetuate the social and economic subservience of those Negroes in its sphere of operations whom it did not kill or drive away altogether.

Perhaps the Klan's most important effect—politically and otherwise— was to weaken Negro and Republican morale. The fact that it could get by with anything drastically reduced their will and capacity to sustain themselves. It became clear that local and state governments were powerless to cope with the Klan or in general to preserve the lives, property, and security of private citizens. Total reliance, therefore, had to be on Washington, where attitudes and responses were governed by Northern public opinion.

The perennial disorders in Dixie eventually brought a profound weariness with the Southern and Negro questions. The Northern public was tired of crusading. It was tired of using troops to buttress governments which could not stand alone. By 1874 it wanted peace and a return to normalcy more than it wanted to preserve equal rights for Negroes or majority rule in the South. As this became evident, Conservative expectations rose proportionately. Once the federal arrests and prosecutions fell off in 1873, it became ever clearer that terrorism was the surest and quickest road to victory in the South.

Every year brought the downfall of additional Republican state governments. This was not the work of scattered Ku Klux bands who continued to prowl in several states, but of open white paramilitary organization and wholesale intimidation backed up on occasion by mob violence and more or less inspired rioting. By these means Alabama was captured in 1874 and Mississippi in 1875. The culmination was in 1876–77, when Rutherford B. Hayes agreed to the conquest of South Carolina, Louisiana, and Florida in return for Southern Democratic acquiescence in his election to the Presidency.

Even friends of the Ku Klux Klan regretted the continuing legacy of violence which it appeared to leave behind, long after Reconstruction. The Klan may not have been responsible for the high incidence of lynching which persisted for decades; this might well have occurred anyway. Nor was it responsible for the race riots which continued into the twentieth century. But there were occasional outbreaks of night riding in later years by men who obviously drew inspiration from the Klan. One such group was the Whitecaps, who organized in southwestern Mississippi in 1892–93 and again ten years later to drive Negro tenants off of lands which had been taken away from whites by foreclosure.[1] Another consisted of tobacco farmers in western Kentucky who waged the "Black Patch War" between 1904 and 1910, trying to enforce by intimidation and violence a policy of curtailed production in order to raise commodity prices.

Simultaneous with these movements, there was a very marked tendency all around the country to repudiate the notion of racial equality in favor of a rejuvenated white supremacy. The two decades beginning in 1890 brought the rights and privileges of American Negroes to their lowest ebb since Emancipation. With few exceptions, white men North and South came to the conclusion that if black men were not congenitally inferior, at least they were lower on the evolutionary ladder; full equality was something to be realized only in the dim future, if ever. This attitude sanctioned overseas imperialism and suggested that we had a "civilizing mission" among our "little brown brothers" in the Philippines and elsewhere. It could not help but lead to a re-evaluation of the preceding era of Reconstruction, when national policy had run in a different direction. Thus Congress repealed and the Supreme Court nullified a great part of the Reconstruction legislation in behalf of the Negro. More particularly, the nation as a whole acquiesced in the wholesale disfranchisement of black men in the South by a series of legal tricks circumventing the Fifteenth Amendment, and the enactment of segregation or Jim Crow laws which evaded the Fourteenth.

It is not surprising that in these years the "Lost Cause" of the Confederacy achieved a popularity among Southerners which it probably never attained between 1861 and 1865. Equally noble in retrospect was the gallant fight that Southerners had waged against Yankee and Negro oppression in the dark days after 1865. The Ku Klux Klan was glorified as the savior of white civilization—and Northerners for the most part agreed. The Klan legend came to a head in 1905. Walter Lynwood Fleming reissued the old book by Lester and Wilson in that year, adding a long and appreciative introduction of his own. But the primary cause of the Klan cult was the appearance of Thomas Dixon's romantic novel *The Clansman.* In this book, as in his simultaneous nonfiction article on the Klan in the *Metropolitan Magazine,* Dixon overlooked or brushed aside the ugly realities of Ku Klux activity. His Knights were white-robed Galahads who rode in silent procession, burned crosses, and descended to physical violence only under extreme provocation and with the noblest motives.[2] Dixon's novel evoked a minor stream of reminiscence by old Klansmen, who found themselves a center of admiring attention from newspaper reporters, young historians, and Daughters of the Confederacy. Like Dixon, they generally presented a selective (and occasionally fictitious) account of their motives and exploits a generation earlier. Their view of the Klan was accepted by scholars as well as the general public. It made such rapid progress, of course, because it harmonized so well with contemporary views on race and Reconstruction. The climax came in 1915 when D. W. Griffith perpetuated *The Clansman* in film with his path-breaking motion picture *The Birth of a Nation.* Public fascination with the new entertainment vehicle merged readily with public acceptance of its central theme. The Klan seemingly had won eternal salvation despite its sins.

One of its fervent admirers was William J. Simmons of Atlanta, whose father had belonged to the order and who therefore had heard about it throughout his boyhood. In 1900, at the age of twenty, Simmons had a sudden nocturnal vision of white-robed Klansmen passing across the wall of his room; thereupon, as he later recalled, he made a solemn vow to "found a fraternal organization which would be a memorial to the Ku Klux Klan." In 1915, doubtless moved further by *The Birth of a Nation,* he did found such an organization and led a group of men to the top of Stone

Mountain, where they burned a cross on Thanksgiving night. With this act of mistaken symbolism the second Ku Klux Klan was born.

During the First World War the new Klan won attention as a super-patriotic organization. In the early 1920's it mushroomed to national proportions, far exceeding the membership and geographical extent of the Reconstruction Klan. The new order shared the Negrophobia of the old, but its list of hates and fears reached also to Catholics, Jews, immigrants, radicals, organized labor, and other groups who posed an imagined threat to individuals in every part of the country. In addition, the new Klan developed into a financial racket among its promoters, some of whom became rich in consequence. This had not happened during Reconstruction. But the new Klan, as a vigilante organization practicing intimidation and violence on those it opposed, and wielding tremendous political power in behalf of intolerance and proscription, bore a striking resemblance to its predecessor. The distinctions between them are less than many people—deprecating the new but celebrating the old—have wanted to believe.[3]

The postwar wave of fear and intolerance which the Klan rode to prominence after 1920—producing also the Red scare, labor repression, immigration restriction, and anti-evolution laws—noticeably abated by the late 1920's. Klan membership and influence fell proportionately. They remained at a low ebb through the 1930's and 1940's, until called to new life by the civil rights movement and especially the desegregation decisions of the 1950's. These gave the Klan a new lease on life, but the order has fragmented seriously in recent years and some of its leaders have gone to jail. It continues as a fringe group of the radical right, once again primarily in the South, but shorn of the power and prestige which it once shared with its spiritual ancestor.

Source Notes

INTRODUCTION: RADICAL RECONSTRUCTION: THE RELUCTANT REVOLUTION

1. "The Central Theme of Southern History," *American Historical Review,* XXXIV (Oct. 1928), 30–43.
2. Walter Lynwood Fleming (ed.), *Documentary History of Reconstruction,* 2 vols. (Cleveland, 1906–7), I, 229.
3. Myrta Lockett Avary (ed.), *Recollections of Alexander H. Stephens* (N.Y., 1910), p. 207.
4. George Washington Cable, *The Negro Question,* ed. by Arlin Turner (N.Y., 1958), pp. 140, 171–73.
5. *Report of the Joint Select Committee to Inquire into the Condition of Affairs in the Late Insurrectionary States,* 13 vols. (Washington, 1872), *House Reports,* 42d Congress, 2d sess., No. 22 (cited hereafter as *KKK Report*), Georgia, p. 528.
6. See on this point Joel Williamson, *After Slavery: The Negro in South Carolina During Reconstruction, 1861–1877* (Chapel Hill, N.C., 1965), pp. 241–46.
7. For a discussion of the status of free Negroes before the war, see Theodore Brantner Wilson, *The Black Codes of the South* (University, Ala., 1965), pp. 30–41.
8. Cable, *The Negro Question,* pp. 138–39.
9. *Senate Executive Documents,* 39th Congress, 1st sess., No. 2, pp. 19–20.

10. *KKK Report,* Alabama, pp. 93, 456; Georgia, p. 32, for statements on the assumed right to continue whipping Negroes and the frequency of the practice.

11. *Ibid.,* Mississippi, p. 305.

12. See August Meier and Elliott M. Rudwick, *From Plantation to Ghetto: An Interpretive History of American Negroes* (N.Y., 1966), p. 134.

13. Whitelaw Reid, *After the War: A Tour of the Southern States, 1865–1866,* reprint ed. (N.Y., 1965), p. 59.

14. *KKK Report,* Florida, pp. 106–7. For statements of the Negro desire for land, and the difficulties and hazards of obtaining it, see *ibid.,* Georgia, pp. 524, 701–2, 861; John Richard Dennett, *The South as It Is: 1865–1866,* reprint ed. (N.Y., 1965), pp. 344–45; William Watson Davis, *The Civil War and Reconstruction in Florida* (N.Y., 1913), p. 592.

15. Charles Stearns, *The Black Man of the South, and the Rebels* (N.Y., 1872), pp. 326–58, 364.

16. *KKK Report,* South Carolina, p. 1236; Alabama, p. 1525; Robert Somers, *The Southern States Since the War, 1870–1871* (N.Y., 1871), pp. 17, 30, 60, 65, 75–76, 146–47, 280. Carl Schurz, in *Senate Executive Documents,* 39th Congress, 1st sess., No. 2, pp. 30–31.

17. Schurz, in *Senate Executive Documents,* 39th Congress, 1st sess., No. 2, pp. 28–31; *KKK Report,* Alabama, pp. 856, 1318, 1836; Georgia, pp. 125, 243, 270, 320.

18. *Senate Executive Documents,* 39th Congress, 1st sess., No. 2, p. 32; *KKK Report,* Alabama, p. 1836; South Carolina, p. 15.

19. *KKK Report,* South Carolina, p. 239; Alabama, p. 1318; Georgia, p. 756. For a modern discussion of this view, see John Dollard, *Caste and Class in a Southern Town,* 3d ed. (Garden City, N.Y., 1949), p. 294.

20. See Somers, *Southern States Since the War,* p. 65.

21. See *KKK Report,* Georgia, p. 270; Davis, *Civil War and Reconstruction in Florida,* p. 594; Williamson, *After Slavery,* pp. 322–25.

22. For expressions of this view, see Fleming, *Documentary History of Reconstruction,* I, 84–85; II, 273; *KKK Report,* North Carolina, p. 318; Georgia, pp. 74, 757; Alabama, p. 550.

23. Dollard, *Caste and Class in a Southern Town,* pp. 125–26.

24. *KKK Report,* Georgia, p. 756. See also testimony of Gen. John B. Gordon, *ibid.,* pp. 305, 307–8.

25. *Ibid.,* Alabama, pp. 426–27, 552, 1801–2; South Carolina, p. 1222; Georgia, pp. 305, 524, 805; Mississippi, p. 559; Williamson, *After Slavery,* pp. 213–18; Vernon L. Wharton, *The Negro in Mississippi, 1865–1890* (Chapel Hill, N.C., 1947), pp. 243–46.

26. David Macrae, *The Americans at Home: Pen and Ink Sketches of American Men, Manners and Institutions,* reprint ed. (N.Y., 1952), pp. 296–97.

27. *KKK Report,* Georgia, p. 529.

28. *Ibid.,* p. 124. Historian Claude Bowers sensationalized the matter even further with the announcement in his account of the period that "Rape is

the foul daughter of Reconstruction." *The Tragic Era: The Revolution after Lincoln* (Boston, 1929), pp. 307–8.

29. June 25, 1868.
30. *Senate Executive Documents*, 39th Congress, 1st sess., no. 2, pp. 31–32. For a later discussion, see again Dollard, *Caste and Class in a Southern Town*, pp. 287, 319–20.
31. Clement Eaton, *Freedom of Thought in the Old South* (N.Y., 1940), pp. 89–116; Harvey Wish, "The Slave Insurrection Panic of 1856," *Journal of Southern History*, V (May 1939), 206–22.
32. Dennett, *The South as It Is*, pp. 176, 190, 269, 275–76; *KKK Report, Alabama*, pp. 1318–22; Wharton, *The Negro in Mississippi*, pp. 218–19; Williamson, *After Slavery*, pp. 249–52.
33. Louis F. Post, "A 'Carpetbagger' in South Carolina," *Journal of Negro History*, X (1925), pp. 63–64. See also Gunnar Myrdal, *An American Dilemma*, 2 vols. (N.Y., 1944), I, 40–42.
34. Dollard, *Caste and Class in a Southern Town*, p. 385, gives a more recent expression of this attitude.
35. For Lincoln's Reconstruction policies, see Herman Belz, *Reconstructing the Union: Theory and Policy during the Civil War* (Ithaca, N.Y., 1969), and William B. Hesseltine, *Lincoln's Plan of Reconstruction* (Tuscaloosa, Ala., 1960).
36. The best and fullest accounts of Reconstruction under Johnson are Eric McKitrick, *Andrew Johnson and Reconstruction* (Chicago, 1960); La-Wanda Cox and John H. Cox, *Politics, Principle, and Prejudice, 1865–1866* (N.Y., 1963); and W. R. Brock, *An American Crisis: Congress and Reconstruction, 1865–1867* (London, 1963).
37. The fullest account of the Black Codes is Wilson, *The Black Codes of the South*, already cited.
38. See George R. Bentley, *A History of the Freedmen's Bureau* (Philadelphia, 1955); John A. Carpenter, *Sword and Olive Branch: Oliver Otis Howard* (Pittsburgh, 1964); Martin Abbott, *The Freedmen's Bureau in South Carolina, 1865–1872* (Chapel Hill, N.C., 1967); John Cox and LaWanda Cox, "General O. O. Howard and the Misrepresented Bureau," *Journal of Southern History*, XIX (Nov. 1953), 427–56.
39. See C. Vann Woodward, *The Burden of Southern History* (Baton Rouge, 1960), pp. 75–96, and Woodward's "Seeds of Failure in Radical Race Policy," *American Philosophical Society Proceedings*, CX, 1 (Feb. 18, 1966), 1–9, both of which discuss the motivations of Republican policy and perhaps overemphasize Northern racism. The fullest account of the Fifteenth Amendment, William Gillette's *The Right to Vote* (Baltimore, 1965), may overemphasize Republican grasping for Negro votes. More favorable to the party in this matter is LaWanda Cox and John H. Cox, "Negro Suffrage and Republican Politics: The Problem of Motivation in Reconstruction Historiography," *Journal of Southern History*, XXXIII (Aug. 1967), 303–30.

40. See statements to this effect by Governors Parsons and Lindsay of Alabama, one a Republican and the other a Democrat, in *KKK Report, Alabama,* pp. 88–89, 203.

41. See Albion W. Tourgée, *The Invisible Empire,* part II of his *A Fool's Errand, by One of the Fools* (N.Y., 1880), p. 498; Lewis H. Blair, *A Southern Prophecy,* ed. by C. Vann Woodward (Boston, 1964), pp. 70–71.

42. See Wharton, *The Negro in Mississippi,* pp. 167–72, 179; Williamson, *After Slavery,* pp. 376–81; Samuel D. Smith, *The Negro in Congress, 1870–1901* (Chapel Hill, N.C., 1940).

43. Ames to James W. Garner, Lowell, Mass., Jan. 17, 1900, in James W. Garner Papers, Mississippi Department of Archives and History.

44. See Richard N. Current, "Carpetbaggers Reconsidered," in David H. Pinkney and Theodore Ropp (eds.), *A Festschrift for Frederick B. Artz* (Durham, N.C., 1964), pp. 139–57; and Current's *Three Carpetbag Governors* (Baton Rouge, 1967).

45. See Allen W. Trelease, "Who Were the Scalawags?" *Journal of Southern History,* XXIX (Nov. 1963), 445–68. Cf. David Donald, "The Scalawag in Mississippi Reconstruction," *Journal of Southern History,* X (Nov. 1944), 447–60, and Otto H. Olsen, "Reconsidering the Scalawags," *Civil War History,* XII (Dec. 1966), 304–20. See also the exchange of letters of Donald and the present writer in *Journal of Southern History,* XXX (May 1964), 253–57.

46. See Lillian A. Pereyra, *James Lusk Alcorn, Persistent Whig* (Baton Rouge, 1966); Williamson, *After Slavery,* pp. 374–75.

47. July 2, 1870.

48. Jack B. Scroggs, "Carpetbagger Constitutional Reform in the South Atlantic States, 1867–1868," *Journal of Southern History,* XXVII (Nov. 1961), 475–93; Wharton, *The Negro in Mississippi.*

49. For discussions of corruption, see Wharton, *The Negro in Mississippi,* p. 179; Roger W. Shugg, *Origins of Class Struggle in Louisiana* (Baton Rouge, 1939), pp. 226–27; Current, *Three Carpetbag Governors;* Williamson, *After Slavery,* pp. 382–405.

50. For excerpts from the League's ritual, constitution, and bylaws, see *KKK Report,* South Carolina, pp. 950–53. A statement by a Negro member of the responsibilities and activities of members in Alabama appears in *ibid.,* Alabama, p. 685. A contemporary Republican defense of the League, emphasizing its moderating role, appears in a speech by Senator John Pool of North Carolina, in *Congressional Globe,* 42d Congress, 1st sess., Appendix, p. 102. For examples of contemporary Democratic attitudes toward the League, see *KKK Report,* Alabama, pp. 229, 357, 818, 1678–82, 1687–91, 1803, 1811; North Carolina, pp. 304 ff.; South Carolina, pp. 1200–1; Georgia, pp. 274–75. The League is in need of a historian, but it has been treated in summary fashion by almost every historian of the Reconstruction period. For the older, hostile view, see Walter Lynwood Fleming, *The Sequel of Appomattox* (New Haven, 1919), pp. 190–94. For more recent and favorable views, see Wharton, *The Negro*

in Mississippi, pp. 165–66; Otto H. Olsen, *Carpetbagger's Crusade: The Life of Albion Winegar Tourgée* (Baltimore, 1965), pp. 83–84.

51. Cf. C. Vann Woodward, *The Strange Career of Jim Crow*, 2d rev. ed. (N.Y., 1966); Charles E. Wynes, *Race Relations in Virginia, 1870–1902* (Charlottesville, 1961), esp. chap. 5; Williamson, *After Slavery*, chap. 10; Wharton, *The Negro in Mississippi*, p. 175.

52. See Henry Lee Swint, *The Northern Teacher in the South, 1862–1870* (Nashville, 1941), esp. pp. 35–36; Wharton, *The Negro in Mississippi*, pp. 244–45; Williamson, *After Slavery*, pp. 219–33; Francis B. Simkins and Robert H. Woody, *South Carolina during Reconstruction* (Chapel Hill, N.C., 1932), pp. 434–43; Alfred H. Kelly, "The Congressional Controversy over School Segregation, 1867–1875," *American Historical Review*, LXIV (1959), 537–63.

53. See Wharton, *The Negro in Mississippi*, p. 175.

54. See Carter Goodrich, "Public Aid to Railroads in the Reconstruction South," *Political Science Quarterly*, LXXI (1956), 407–42.

55. Scroggs, "Carpetbagger Constitutional Reform," pp. 479–80; John C. Reed, "What I Know of the Ku Klux Klan," *Uncle Remus's Magazine*, I, 8 (Jan. 1908), 24.

56. See Carpenter, *Sword and Olive Branch*, pp. 106–7, 114; Bentley, *History of the Freedmen's Bureau*, pp. 89–102, 144–46; LaWanda Cox, "The Promise of Land for the Freedmen," *Mississippi Valley Historical Review*, XLV (Dec. 1958), 413–40; Williamson, *After Slavery*, pp. 142–56; Wharton, *The Negro in Mississippi*, pp. 60–61.

57. *KKK Report*, Committee Report, pp. 228–30. See also Wharton, *The Negro in Mississippi*, pp. 170–71, 177–79.

58. However, South Carolina and perhaps other states deliberately raised assessed valuations for the dual purpose of increasing revenue and forcing owners of unused lands to sell, thus enhancing the program of land redistribution. Williamson, *After Slavery*, pp. 151–52.

59. See *KKK Report*, Georgia, p. 861; Committee Report, p. 91; Fleming (ed.), *Documentary History of Reconstruction*, II, 343.

60. *KKK Report*, Committee Report, pp. 2, 92; *Congressional Globe*, 42d Congress, 1st sess., Appendix, p. 28.

61. James E. Sefton, *The United States Army and Reconstruction, 1865–1877* (Baton Rouge, 1967), pp. 261–62.

62. The fullest discussion of this question, which differs in some respects from my own in the following chapters, is Otis A. Singletary, *Negro Militia and Reconstruction* (Austin, Tex., 1957).

63. Fleming (ed.), *Documentary History of Reconstruction*, I, 455–56.

64. Feb. 8, 1868.

65. *KKK Report*, Alabama, p. 244.

66. See T. Harry Williams, "An Analysis of Some Reconstruction Attitudes," *Journal of Southern History*, XII (Nov. 1946), 475–80, and his *Romance and Realism in Southern Politics* (Athens, Ga., 1961), pp. 22–26. The hatreds engendered in this period endured for generations, and historian

J. G. de Roulhac Hamilton of North Carolina was able to write in all seriousness in 1914 that "no free people ever labored under more galling oppression or more grievous misrule." *Reconstruction in North Carolina* (N.Y., 1914), p. 454. See also Walter Lynwood Fleming, *Civil War and Reconstruction in Alabama* (N.Y., 1905), pp. 655–57.

67. See Otto H. Olsen, "The Ku Klux Klan: A Study in Reconstruction Politics and Propaganda," *North Carolina Historical Review*, XXXIX (Summer 1962), 351–52.

68. See *KKK Report*, Georgia, p. 284.

69. *The True Believer* (N.Y., 1951), p. 86.

70. Letter of H. C. Luce, April 12, 1871, in N.Y. *Daily Tribune*, April 25, 1871. See Swint, *Northern Teacher in the South*, esp. pp. 136, 141; Wharton, *The Negro in Mississippi*, pp. 244–46; Fleming, *Civil War and Reconstruction in Alabama*, pp. 628–29. For ante-bellum attitudes toward public education, see Eaton, *Freedom of Thought in the Old South*, pp. 66–77; John Hope Franklin, *The Militant South*, reprint ed. (Boston, 1964), pp. 129–30.

71. See Francis B. Simkins, "The Ku Klux Klan in South Carolina, 1868–1871," *Journal of Negro History*, XII (1927), 629–30; Davis, *Civil War and Reconstruction in Florida*, pp. 587–90.

72. New Orleans *Times*, July 28, 1868.

73. Macrae, *The Americans at Home*, pp. 296–97.

74. This point concerning Republican conservatism in matters of federalism and civil liberties is well made by Alfred H. Kelly in Harold M. Hyman (ed.), *New Frontiers of the American Reconstruction* (Urbana, Ill., 1966), pp. 41–57.

75. Reid, *After the War*, p. 288.

76. St. Martinville *Courier of the Teche*, Sept. 19, 1868, quoted in *House Miscellaneous Documents*, 41st Congress, 2d sess., No. 154, pt. 2, p. 320. Nevertheless the attempt to woo Negro votes was probably carried furthest in Louisiana. See T. Harry Williams, "The Louisiana Unification Movement of 1873," *Journal of Southern History*, XI (Aug. 1945), 349–69, and his "Analysis of Some Reconstruction Attitudes," pp. 475–86.

77. Quoted in Montgomery *Alabama State Journal*, Oct. 1, 1868.

78. Quoted in Avery Craven, *The Growth of Southern Nationalism, 1848–1861* (Baton Rouge, 1953), pp. 394–95.

79. See W. J. Cash, *The Mind of the South*, reprint ed. (N.Y., 1954), pp. 55–56, 85, 99–100; Franklin, *The Militant South*, esp. pp. 24–25, 33, 44–62, 72–77; Clement Eaton, "Mob Violence in the Old South," *Mississippi Valley Historical Review*, XXIX (1942), 351–70; Eaton, *Freedom of Thought in the Old South*, esp. pp. 63, 194–95; Daniel R. Hundley, *Social Relations in Our Southern States* (N.Y., 1860), chap. 6. For the slave patrol, see Fleming, *Civil War and Reconstruction in Alabama*, pp. 657–58.

80. Dennett, *The South as It Is*, p. 300.

81. See Wharton, *The Negro in Mississippi*, pp. 216–17, for a good description

of these conditions in Mississippi, and Davis, *Civil War and Reconstruction in Florida,* pp. 590–91, 601–4, for Florida. Concerning liquor and the carrying of arms, see *KKK Report,* Alabama, pp. 433, 1318. Concerning general Southern lawlessness from 1866 to 1871, see Ellis P. Oberholtzer, *A History of the United States since the Civil War,* 5 vols. (N.Y., 1917–37), II, 362–68.

82. Cash, *Mind of the South,* pp. 123–24, 127.

83. Richard C. Beckett, "Some Effects of Military Reconstruction in Monroe County," *Mississippi Historical Society Publications,* VIII (1904), p. 179.

84. See the discussion of later but comparable segregation attitudes in Dollard, *Caste and Class in a Southern Town,* pp. 319–20, and Myrdal, *An American Dilemma,* I, xcviii–xcix.

85. John A. Carpenter, "Atrocities in the Reconstruction Period," *Journal of Negro History,* XLVII (Oct. 1962), 236–44. See also Joe M. Richardson, *The Negro in the Reconstruction of Florida, 1865–1877* (Tallahassee, 1965), pp. 161–64.

86. Singletary, *Negro Militia and Reconstruction,* pp. 5–6; W. McKee Evans, *Ballots and Fence Rails: Reconstruction on the Lower Cape Fear* (Chapel Hill, N.C., 1967), pp. 68 ff., 130 ff.

87. *KKK Report,* Alabama, p. 263.

88. St. Martinville *Courier of the Teche,* Oct. 30, 1868, quoted in *House Miscellaneous Documents,* 41st Congress, 2d sess., No. 154, pt. 2, p. 320.

89. *KKK Report,* Florida, p. 94.

90. Some of the ante-bellum vigilantes had operated in disguise. See *ibid.,* Alabama, p. 347.

91. *House Executive Documents,* 39th Congress, 1st sess., No. 70, pp. 202–8 (quotation from p. 202).

92. *Ibid.,* 39th Congress, 2d sess., No. 1, p. 746.

93. For information about these predecessors of the Klan, see *ibid.,* pp. 58, 63–64, 67–68, 748; *ibid.,* 40th Congress, 2d sess., No. 1, II, pt. 1, pp. 201 ff., 664–88; Fleming, *Civil War and Reconstruction in Alabama,* pp. 658–60; Richardson, *Negro in the Reconstruction of Florida,* pp. 161–64; Dennett, *The South as It Is,* pp. 308–9, regarding secret societies in New Orleans.

94. *KKK Report,* Alabama, p. 489.

95. This point evoked a surprising amount of disagreement, even among historians writing about Reconstruction years later. A former Georgia Klansman, John C. Reed, took sharp exception in 1908 to those who continued to deny the Klan's political intent; its major purpose as he had known it as a county leader and organizer in eastern Georgia was strictly political—to overthrow Radical Republican rule. "What I Know of the Ku Klux Klan," *Uncle Remus's Magazine,* I, 8 (Jan. 1908), 24.

96. By far the fullest and fairest discussion of the causes of the Ku Klux Klan then or later was the report of the Republican majority of a Congressional joint committee which investigated the Klan in 1871. It is marred by an overemphasis on the Klan's political motivations, but that factor was

unquestionably central. The majority were fair in their condemnation of Radical corruption and malfeasance. The Democratic minority report, on the other hand, was a whitewash of the Klan which shared most of the latter's racist preconceptions. Most of the later historians who have gone into this question in any detail choose to follow the Democratic apologists and write off the majority report as a purely partisan document. See *KKK Report,* Committee Report, esp. pp. 80–99, and the discussion of the committee's work in Chapter 24 below. For an exception to the generalization about later historians, see Simkins, "The Ku Klux Klan in South Carolina," pp. 629–37.

97. Hoffer, *The True Believer,* p. 93.

CHAPTER 1: THE BIRTH AND TRANSFORMATION OF THE KU KLUX KLAN, 1866–1867

1. The Klan has almost as many birthdays as historians. Capt. John C. Lester, one of the original six members, wrote the first full account of the Klan's origins in collaboration with Rev. D. L. Wilson, who moved to Pulaski in 1880 and had never been a member but knew some of them well. See J. C. Lester and D. L. Wilson, *Ku Klux Klan, Its Origin, Growth, and Disbandment* (Nashville, 1884), and especially the edition by Walter Lynwood Fleming (N.Y., 1905), p. 53. Although Lester and Wilson placed the birthdate in May 1866, Wilson placed the founding in June in a magazine article of his own, written in the same year: "The Ku Klux Klan, Its Growth and Disbandment," *Century Magazine,* XXVIII (n.s. VI) (1884), 399. Maj. James R. Crowe, another of the founders, writing some forty years after the event, placed it in the fall or winter of 1865–66. J. R. Crowe to W. L. Fleming, Sheffield, Ala., May 22, 1905 and April 15, 1906, in Fleming Papers, New York Public Library; Laura (Martin) Rose, *The Ku Klux Klan or Invisible Empire* (New Orleans, 1914), p. 20. John B. Kennedy, a third founder, writing in 1912, recalled it as being late in December 1865. Kennedy to Mrs. John Sifford, Lawrenceburg, Tenn., Sept. 28, 1912, in Camden, Ark., *Beacon, ca.* Oct. 1912 (copy in Arkansas History Commission clipping file, No. 2.2667). Susan Lawrence Davis, in her unreliable *Authentic History, Ku Klux Klan, 1865–1877* (N.Y., 1924), p. 6, places the date with characteristic precision as December 24, 1865. And Stanley Horn, in his *Invisible Empire: The Story of the Ku Klux Klan, 1866–1871* (Boston, 1939), p. 9, long the standard work on the Klan, apparently follows her in making it "an evening late in December 1865." A person with some knowledge of the matter wrote in the New York *Herald* in April 1868 that the order had originated in Giles County, Tennessee (of which Pulaski is the county seat), in August 1866. (Quoted in Yorkville, (S.C.) *Enquirer,* April 23, 1868.) The best evidence for June is that the Klan held a first anniversary parade in Pulaski on June 5, 1867.

2. Lester and Wilson, *Ku Klux Klan,* Fleming ed., pp. 55, 60; William E. Mockler, "The Source of *'Ku Klux,'* " *Names,* III (March 1955), 15–17.
3. The fullest, indeed almost the only, firsthand account of the Klan's founding and early organization and activity is the book by Lester and Wilson. The Fleming edition is more useful than the original because of the editor's additional information. See pp. 19–22, 50–67. See also Richmond *Enquirer & Examiner,* April 30, 1868 (containing a letter by an anonymous founder), copied in the Pulaski *Citizen,* May 22, 1868; Rose, *The Ku Klux Klan,* pp. 20–21. The most accurate later account is in Horn, *Invisible Empire,* pp. 8–17.
4. Richmond *Enquirer & Examiner,* April 30, 1868, copied in Pulaski *Citizen,* May 22, 1868.
5. See Lester and Wilson, *Ku Klux Klan,* Fleming ed., pp. 22, 67, 80, 90; letters of Crowe and Kennedy in Rose, *The Ku Klux Klan,* pp. 20–24, and in Arkansas History Commission clipping file, No. 2.2667. Walter Lynwood Fleming, the distinguished Southern historian of the early twentieth century who did much to codify and refurbish the Southern myth about the horrors of Reconstruction and the glories of white resistance to it, took a much more affirmative position on the Klan and its operations than did Lester and Wilson or the writer of the 1868 letter. In bringing out his new edition of the Lester and Wilson book in 1905 he felt obliged to criticize their apologetic tone as unrealistic and improper, given the supposed evils of the day and the absence of more peaceful means to combat them. See pp. 18–19.
6. The fullest account of these developments is in Thomas B. Alexander, *Political Reconstruction in Tennessee* (Nashville, 1950), chaps. 1–9.
7. Tennessee reports for 1866, Synopses of Reports of Assistant Commissioners, Freedmen's Bureau Records, Record Group 105, National Archives (hereafter abbreviated as RG 105, NA). For further examples, see Nashville *Press and Times,* Jan. 26, April 19, 1866.
8. Nashville *Press and Times,* July 12, 1866.
9. Alexander, *Political Reconstruction in Tennessee,* p. 179.
10. Quoted in report of J. R. Lewis, Nashville, for Aug. 1866, Tennessee Monthly Reports, Freedmen's Bureau Records, RG 105, NA.
11. Pulaski *Citizen,* Aug. 10, 1866.
12. Gen. F. D. Sewall, inspection report on Kentucky and Tennessee, Sept. 17, 1866, Synopses of Reports of Assistant Commissioners; report of Capt. Michael Walsh, Nashville, for Sept. 1866, Tennessee Monthly Reports, Freedmen's Bureau Records, RG 105, NA.
13. Tennessee reports for Dec. 1866 to April 1867, Synopses of Reports of Assistant Commissioners; reports of Capt. Michael Walsh, Nashville, for Nov. 1866 to March 1867, Tennessee Monthly Reports, Freedmen's Bureau Records, RG 105, NA; Pulaski *Citizen,* Feb. 22, May 3, 1867.
14. Lester and Wilson, for example, claim that the Klan was much talked about in Pulaski in July and August 1866, with the local paper carrying some notice of it in every issue. Fleming ed., p. 68. But the first

communication from the Klan appeared in the *Citizen* near the end of March 1867, and there had been no mention of it before.

15. Lester and Wilson speak of a rapid and extensive growth inside and outside the state at this time, sparked by a feeling that the Klan had some serious mission to perform. Their dating is probably wrong here too, this growth taking place in the spring of 1867 and afterward. Fleming ed., pp. 68–72.

16. *KKK Report,* Alabama, p. 660. Many Southerners would deny that the Klan was a political organization, even when it patently was; but this man, testifying before a Congressional investigating committee, was perfectly frank in discussing the Klan's later political activities.

17. Lester and Wilson, *Ku Klux Klan,* Fleming ed., pp. 73–74.

18. *Ibid.,* pp. 83–84; Richmond *Enquirer & Examiner,* April 30, 1868, copied in Pulaski *Citizen,* May 22, 1868.

19. Nashville *Press and Times,* March 5, 1867; also in Robert H. White (ed.), *Messages of the Governors of Tennessee,* 6 vols. (Nashville, 1952–   ), V, 553–55.

20. Brownlow to Stanton, Feb. 26, 1867; same to Thomas, March 1, 1867, Governors' Correspondence (letterbook), Tennessee State Library and Archives.

21. Pulaski *Citizen,* April 12, June 28, 1867.

22. *Invisible Empire,* p. 33.

23. For sketches of these two men, see Horn, *Invisible Empire,* p. 113; John Allison (ed.), *Notable Men of Tennessee* (Atlanta, 1905), I, 101–2; II, 51–52.

24. Lester and Wilson say it was in early summer; others specify April or May. *Ku Klux Klan,* Fleming ed., p. 84; Rose, *The Ku Klux Klan,* p. 40.

25. The Prescript is printed in Horn, *Invisible Empire,* pp. 381–93, in *KKK Report,* Miscellaneous Testimony, pp. 35–41, and in Lester and Wilson, *Ku Klux Klan,* Fleming ed., pp. 135–50. For background and discussion of the Nashville meeting and its work, see Lester and Wilson, *Ku Klux Klan,* Fleming ed., pp. 84–90; Alexander, *Political Reconstruction in Tennessee,* pp. 179–80; John B. Kennedy to Mrs. John Sifford, Lawrenceburg, Tenn., Sept. 28, 1912, in Camden, Ark., *Beacon, ca.* Oct. 1912 (copy in Arkansas History Commission clipping file, No. 2.2667); Horn, *Invisible Empire,* pp. 32–41.

26. The Empire was now defined as including all of the ex-Confederate states by name, plus Maryland, Kentucky, and Missouri.

27. Printed in Horn, *Invisible Empire,* pp. 395–409, and Lester and Wilson, *Ku Klux Klan,* Fleming ed., pp. 153–76. Both Prescripts were printed in small pamphlet form after their adoption. They were distributed to Klan officials across the South, the original version being sent initially without notice or explanation from Memphis to the Grand Cyclops of each den. This version apparently had a wider circulation than the revision. It was apparently produced in a small printshop, for the printer ran out of asterisks and printer's daggers before the end. The revised Prescript was

secretly printed (as the first may have been) in the office of the Pulaski *Citizen,* which lay across a narrow passageway from General Gordon's law office. Most surviving Klansmen in Fleming's day were aware of only one of the versions, and Lester and Wilson, among others, have confused them. Prescripts and any other Klan documents were almost universally destroyed when dens disbanded, and copies of both Prescripts are very rare today. See Fleming's Introduction to his edition of Lester and Wilson, pp. 37–41. For details of printing, see statement of Laps D. McCord, in "Ku Klux Klan," *American Historical Magazine,* V (Jan. 1900), 4–5, relative to the revised Prescript, and Stanley Horn's description, presumably of the original version, in *Invisible Empire,* p. 33.

28. Another myth which enjoyed a limited circulation later, if not at the time, was that General Robert E. Lee was offered the position but declined it on grounds of health, at the same time giving the organization his blessing. See, for example, Andrew Lytle, *Bedford Forrest and His Critter Company,* rev. ed. (N.Y., 1960), p. 383. Lee abstained completely from political life and almost as completely from any expression of political opinion after the war. From what we know of his views he would probably have repudiated even the limited activity contemplated by the Klan's leadership in 1867.

29. Some writers locate the earlier organizational meeting also in Room 10. There is no way of knowing whether this represents coincidence or confusion; it is conceivable that the two events were simultaneous. See John W. Morton, *The Artillery of Nathan Bedford Forrest's Cavalry* (Nashville and Dallas, 1909), pp. 338, 343–45; Thomas Dixon, "The Story of [the] Ku Klux Klan," *Metropolitan Magazine,* XXII (Sept. 1905), 657–69; Forrest's testimony in *KKK Report,* Miscellaneous Testimony, pp. 3–41; Robert S. Henry, *"First with the Most" Forrest* (N.Y., 1944), pp. 444–48; Horn, *Invisible Empire,* pp. 313–16; Nash K. Burger and John K. Bettersworth, *South of Appomattox* (N.Y., 1959), p. 134. It is possible that Forrest's initiation took place as late as November 1867. The Nashville *Republican Banner* on November 19 announced his arrival in the city the previous day for the first time since the war. The newspaper indicates that other Confederate military leaders happened to converge on Nashville at the same time: Admiral Raphael Semmes, General Kirby Smith, General John C. Brown of Pulaski—and Father Abram J. Ryan, whose reported Klan connection will be discussed later. *Republican Banner,* Nov. 19–22, 1867.

30. For wholesale ascriptions of membership in the Klan by famous personages, see Davis, *Authentic History, Ku Klux Klan.*

31. *Ibid.,* pp. 103–4; *Brownlow's Knoxville Whig,* June 24, 1868; Little Rock *Daily Arkansas Gazette,* Sept. 16, 1868.

32. See Robert L. Duncan, *Reluctant General: The Life and Times of Albert Pike* (N.Y., 1961), pp. 267–68; Greenville, Tex., *Messenger,* Oct. 2, 1930, in Ku Klux Klan clipping file, Tennessee State Library; Davis, *Authentic History, Ku Klux Klan,* pp. 271–77.

33. Charles Albert Snodgrass, *The History of Freemasonry in Tennessee, 1789–1943* (Nashville, 1944), pp. 137, 308; Allison (ed.), *Notable Men of Tennessee*, II, 52.

34. See *KKK Report*, South Carolina, pp. 281, 333, 347–48; Alabama, p. 1560.

35. *Ibid.*, South Carolina, pp. 1269–70, 1277.

36. Horn, *Invisible Empire*, p. 113.

37. Morton, *Artillery of Nathan Bedford Forrest's Cavalry*, p. 345.

38. Horn, *Invisible Empire*, p. 85.

39. *Ibid.*, p. 113; Lester and Wilson, *Ku Klux Klan*, Fleming ed., p. 27.

40. Meriwether to W. L. Fleming, St. Louis, Sept. 30, 1909, Fleming Papers, New York Public Library.

41. *KKK Report*, Alabama, p. 892.

42. *Ibid.*, Miscellaneous Testimony, pp. 4–35; Burger and Bettersworth, *South of Appomattox*, pp. 130–41.

43. Pulaski *Citizen*, June 7, 1867. Some later writers, including Lester and Wilson (*Ku Klux Klan*, Fleming ed., pp. 91–92), mistakenly refer to a parade in Pulaski on July 4, 1867. However, the Klan staged parades in many Tennessee towns, including Pulaski, on July 4, 1868.

44. Pulaski *Citizen*, May 24, June 14, 1867.

45. [William Thomas Richardson], *Historic Pulaski, Birthplace of the Ku Klux Klan* . . . ([Nashville], 1913), p. 7.

46. Report of George E. Judd, Pulaski, for July 1867, Nashville Sub-district, Letters Received; reports of Michael Walsh, Nashville, for April to July 1867, Tennessee Monthly Reports; reports of Gen. W. P. Carlin, Nashville, for April to July 1867, Synopses of Reports of Assistant Commissioners, 1867–1869, Freedmen's Bureau Records, RG 105, NA; Pulaski *Citizen*, June 28, July 26, 1867; Thomas B. Alexander, "Kukluxism in Tennessee, 1865–1869," *Tennessee Historical Quarterly*, VIII (1949), 200–1; Alexander, *Political Reconstruction in Tennessee*, pp. 180–81.

47. See Nashville *Republican Banner*, May 29, 1867 ff.; Pulaski *Citizen*, June 7, 14, July 26, 1867.

48. *KKK Report*, Committee Report, p. 81.

49. Report of George E. Judd, Pulaski, for Aug. 1867, Nashville Sub-district, Letters Received, Freedmen's Bureau Records, RG 105, NA.

50. Pulaski *Citizen*, Aug. 23, 1867.

51. *Ibid.*, Aug. 30, Sept. 6, 13, 1867; George E. Judd to Capt. Michael Walsh, Pulaski, Sept. 5, 1867, Nashville Sub-district, Letters Received; Report of Capt. Michael Walsh, Sept. 16, 1867, Tennessee Inspection Reports, 1865–1869, Freedmen's Bureau Records, RG 105, NA.

52. Quoted in report of Gen. W. P. Carlin, Nashville, for Dec. 1867, Reports of Assistant Commissioners, Retained Copies, Freedmen's Bureau Records, RG 105, NA.

53. Philip M. Hamer (ed.), *Tennessee: A History, 1673–1932*, 4 vols. (N.Y., 1933), II, 636.

54. Nashville *Republican Banner*, Dec. 13, 1867.

55. *Ibid.*, Dec. 28, 1867.

56. *KKK Report,* Miscellaneous Testimony, pp. 6, 22–24. A Tennessee newspaper notice, reprinted in the *Congressional Globe,* was headed "K.K.K. Pale Face Shrouded Division XVI." *Congressional Globe,* 42d Congress, 1st sess., Appendix, p. 287.
57. Pulaski *Citizen,* March 6, 1868.
58. Nashville *Republican Banner,* March 12, Oct. 18, 1868, Jan. 22, 1869.
59. See also Horn, *Invisible Empire,* pp. 346–48.
60. *Daily Memphis Avalanche,* March 20, 1868; *Brownlow's Knoxville Whig,* July 8, 1868; Nashville *Press and Times,* Aug. 4, 1868; Alexander, *Political Reconstruction in Tennessee,* p. 183.

CHAPTER 2: EXPANSION AND VIOLENCE IN TENNESSEE, 1868

1. Reports of Gen. W. P. Carlin, Nashville, Jan.–July 1868, Synopses of Reports of Assistant Commissioners, 1867–1869; letters from H. A. Eastman, Columbia, Jan. 25, June 6, 13, 1868, Nashville Sub-district, Letters Received; Report of Capt. George E. Judd, Nashville, for May 1868, Tennessee Monthly Reports, Freedmen's Bureau Records, RG 105, NA; *House Executive Documents,* 40th Congress, 2d sess., No. 329, pp. 33, 36, 40–42; Tennessee *House Journal,* Extra Session, 1868, p. 209; Tennessee General Assembly, Senate, Committee on Military Affairs, *Report of Evidence Taken before the Military Committee in Relation to Outrages Committed by the Ku Klux Klan in Middle and West Tennessee. . . .* (Nashville, 1868); Nashville *Press and Times,* Jan. 28, March 11, 14, April 13, 14, 18, June 15, 23, July 29, Aug. 3, 1868; New York *Daily Tribune,* July 20, 1868.
2. Nashville *Republican Banner,* March 5, 7, 1868; Pulaski *Citizen,* March 6, 1868; Stanley F. Horn, *Invisible Empire: The Story of the Ku Klux Klan, 1866–1871* (Boston, 1939), pp. 81–82.
3. Letter of H. A. Eastman, Columbia, June 6, 1868, Nashville Sub-district, Letters Received, Freedmen's Bureau Records, RG 105, NA.
4. H. A. Eastman to Capt. G. E. Judd, Columbia, July 16, 1868, Nashville Sub-district, Special Reports, Freedmen's Bureau Records, RG 105, NA; Nashville *Republican Banner,* July 14, 18, 1868.
5. Eastman report, July 16, 1868, *ibid.;* Tennessee *House Journal,* Extra Session, 1868, p. 206.
6. *House Executive Documents,* 40th Congress, 2d sess., No. 329, pp. 48–51. The Grand Giant's order was copied in other papers, including the Pulaski *Citizen* (June 26, 1868), no doubt partially with an eye to its further provision that no Klansmen from another county might enter Maury without high-level authorization. The order is also reprinted in Horn, *Invisible Empire,* pp. 364–65.
7. Report of Capt. Michael Walsh, Nashville, Jan. 11, 1868, enclosed with letter of Gen. W. P. Carlin to Gen. O. O. Howard, Nashville, Jan. 15,

1868, in Assistant Adjutant General, Letters Received, Freedmen's Bureau Records, RG 105, NA; Nashville *Republican Banner,* Jan. 9, 11, 1868.

8. Pulaski *Citizen,* Feb. 14, 1868.

9. *House Executive Documents,* 40th Congress, 2d sess., No. 329, p. 40; Tennessee Assembly, Committee on Military Affairs, *Report of Evidence,* pp. 5–6, 40–41, 47, 64; Pulaski *Citizen,* May 1, July 3, 1868; reports of C. R. Simpson, Pulaski, for April, June 1868, Tennessee Monthly Reports, Freedmen's Bureau Records, RG 105, NA.

10. Pulaski *Citizen,* July 3, 1868.

11. *Ibid.,* July 10, 1868; J. C. Lester and D. L. Wilson, *Ku Klux Klan,* ed. by Walter L. Fleming (N.Y. and Washington, 1905), pp. 92–95. Lester and Wilson mistakenly date the parade on July 4, 1867, instead of 1868.

12. Pulaski *Citizen,* April 3, July 10, 1868; report of C. R. Simpson, Pulaski, for July 1868 (identifying the victim as Miller Brick), Tennessee Monthly Reports, Freedmen's Bureau Records, RG 105, NA; Tennessee *House Journal,* Extra Session, 1868, pp. 201–3, 209.

13. Report of Gen. W. P. Carlin, Nashville, for Jan. 1868, Reports of Assistant Commissioners, Retained Copies (Tenn.), Freedmen's Bureau Records, RG 105, NA; Horn, *Invisible Empire,* p. 348.

14. *House Executive Documents,* 40th Congress, 2d sess., No. 329, p. 37.

15. Nashville *Press and Times,* Jan. 31, 1868.

16. *House Miscellaneous Documents,* 41st Congress, 2d sess., No. 53, pp. 214–15.

17. *Ibid.,* p. 196; *House Executive Documents,* 40th Congress, 2d sess., No. 329, pp. 45–47; Report of Gen. W. P. Carlin, Nashville, for June 1868, in Synopses of Reports of Assistant Commissioners, 1867–1869, Freedmen's Bureau Records, RG 105, NA.

18. Tennessee *House Journal,* Extra Session, 1868, pp. 186, 195.

19. *House Miscellaneous Documents,* 41st Congress, 2d sess., No. 53, p. 46.

20. *House Executive Documents,* 40th Congress, 2d sess., No. 329, p. 43.

21. Pulaski *Citizen,* July 10, 1868; *House Miscellaneous Documents,* 41st Congress, 2d sess., No. 53, pp. 261–62.

22. Pulaski *Citizen,* March 13, 1868; Nashville *Republican Banner,* Feb. 29, 1868.

23. Nashville *Republican Banner,* July 7, 1868; Pulaski *Citizen,* July 10, 1868. There was also some synchronized parading on a night in June by Klan units in Lincoln and Marshall counties. Nashville *Press and Times,* June 17, 1868.

24. Nashville *Press and Times,* March 6, 7, 1868. Cf. Horn, *Invisible Empire,* pp. 98–99.

25. *House Executive Documents,* 40th Congress, 2d sess., No. 329, p. 37.

26. *Daily Memphis Avalanche,* March 11, 12, 1868; Horn, *Invisible Empire,* pp. 92–95.

27. *Daily Memphis Avalanche,* March 19, 1868.

28. Memphis *Evening Post,* July 13, 1868; N.Y. *Daily Tribune,* July 21, 1868;

Little Rock *Morning Republican,* Aug. 3, 1868; Horn, *Invisible Empire,* p. 96.

29. *Daily Memphis Avalanche,* April 1, 7, 8, 9, 1868 (the last issue quoting the *Appeal*); Memphis *Daily Post,* April 7, 8, 15, May 1, 1868; Nashville *Press and Times,* March 26, 1868 (quoting the *Bulletin*).

30. Nashville *Press and Times,* March 19, 20, 1868.

31. *House Executive Documents,* 40th Congress, 3d sess., No. 1, III, pt. 1, pp. 182–86.

32. For further evidence of Ku Klux activity in Tennessee between January and July 1868, see Tennessee Assembly, Committee on Military Affairs, *Report of Evidence, passim;* reports of agents, sub-assistant commissioners, and the assistant commissioner of the Freedmen's Bureau, in the Freedmen's Bureau Records, RG 105, NA; Thomas B. Alexander, *Political Reconstruction in Tennessee* (Nashville, 1950), pp. 184–87; Horn, *Invisible Empire,* chap. 4.

33. Pulaski *Citizen,* Feb. 21, 1868, copied from Franklin *Review.*

34. Nashville *Republican Banner,* July 17, 1868, as copied in Pulaski *Citizen,* July 24, 1868. Lester and Wilson (*Ku Klux Klan,* Fleming ed., pp. 109–11) mistakenly place this document in the fall of 1868. Horn (reprinting it in his *Invisible Empire,* pp. 366–67) follows suit.

35. *KKK Report,* Miscellaneous Testimony, p. 34; cf. *ibid.,* p. 6.

36. Memphis *Appeal,* Aug. 13, 1868, quoted in Pulaski *Citizen,* Aug. 21, 1868.

37. Tennessee *House Journal,* Extra Session, 1868, pp. 208–9.

38. James W. Patton, *Unionism and Reconstruction in Tennessee, 1860–1869* (Chapel Hill, N.C., 1934), p. 189.

39. *House Executive Documents,* 40th Congress, 3d sess., No. 1, III, pt. 1, pp. 144–48; Robert H. White (ed.), *Messages of the Governors of Tennessee,* 6 vols. (Nashville, 1952–   ), V, 608–11; Patton, *Unionism and Reconstruction in Tennessee,* pp. 189–90; Thomas B. Alexander, "Kukluxism in Tennessee, 1865–1869," *Tennessee Historical Quarterly,* VIII (1949), 207.

40. White (ed.), *Messages of the Governors of Tennessee,* V, 613–14.

41. Tennessee Assembly, Committee on Military Affairs, *Report of Evidence;* Tennessee *House Journal,* Extra Session, 1868, pp. 185–222.

42. *Acts of the State of Tennessee,* Special Session, 1868, pp. 18–25.

43. Report of G. E. Judd, Nashville, for July 1868, Tennessee Monthly Reports; report of Gen. W. P. Carlin, Nashville, for July 1868, Synopses of Reports of Assistant Commissioners, 1867–1869, Freedmen's Bureau Records, RG 105, NA.

44. See Nashville *Republican Banner,* Sept. 12, 1868, for a typical Conservative reaction to the militia law.

45. E. Merton Coulter, *William G. Brownlow, Fighting Parson of the Southern Highlands* (Chapel Hill, N.C., 1937), p. 358.

46. Pulaski *Citizen,* Aug. 7, 1868; Coulter, *Brownlow,* p. 360.

47. *House Executive Documents,* 40th Congress, 3d sess., No. 1, III, pt. 1, pp. xxx, 146–48; Nashville *Press and Times,* Sept. 16, 19, Oct. 31, 1868;

Pulaski *Citizen,* Aug. 7, 1868; White (ed.), *Messages of the Governors of Tennessee,* V, 633; Patton, *Unionism and Reconstruction in Tennessee,* p. 198; Alexander, *Political Reconstruction in Tennessee,* p. 187. Cf. the very different interpretation of these events in Coulter, *Brownlow,* pp. 361–65.

48. Nashville *Press and Times,* Sept. 17, 1868.
49. This interview was published all over the country. In a reflective moment a few days later Forrest retracted the more self-incriminating statements, claiming to have been misrepresented, but the retraction came from an access of discretion rather than any change of attitude or policy; he had made the same threat before a public meeting in Memphis more than two weeks earlier, but without the specific references to the Klan. *KKK Report,* Miscellaneous Testimony, pp. 4–6, 32–35 (reprinted in Horn, *Invisible Empire,* pp. 410–16); Pulaski *Citizen,* Aug. 14, 1868.
50. Pulaski *Citizen,* Aug. 7, 1868.
51. Tennessee *House Journal,* Extra Session, 1868, pp. 213–15; reports of Gen. W. P. Carlin, Nashville, for Aug., Sept., 1868, Synopses of Reports of Assistant Commissioners, 1867–1869, Freedmen's Bureau Records, RG 105, NA.

CHAPTER 3: ORGANIZATION AND EXPANSION

1. *KKK Report,* Miscellaneous Testimony, pp. 9, 26–27.
2. Nash K. Burger and John K. Bettersworth, *South of Appomattox* (N.Y., 1959), p. 130.
3. W. D. Wood, "The Ku Klux Klan," *Texas State Historical Association Quarterly,* IX (April 1906), 266.
4. See *KKK Report,* Alabama, p. 395; William A. Dunning, *Reconstruction, Political and Economic, 1865–1877* (N.Y. and London, 1907), pp. 122–23; Walter Lynwood Fleming, *The Sequel of Appomattox* (New Haven, 1919), pp. 258–59; Walter Lynwood Fleming, *Civil War and Reconstruction in Alabama* (N.Y., 1905), p. 668; J. G. de Roulhac Hamilton, *Reconstruction in North Carolina* (N.Y., 1914), pp. 463–64; Stanley F. Horn, *Invisible Empire: The Story of the Ku Klux Klan, 1866–1871* (Boston, 1939), pp. 69, 361–72.
5. *KKK Report,* Mississippi, 323.
6. Charles Stearns, *The Black Man of the South, and the Rebels* (N.Y., 1872), pp. 424–26, 429. Ralph L. Peek says that violence in Florida "was executed by the 'better sort' of white people, i.e., as distinguished from the 'cracker' class, or poorer element. The younger men of the upper class made the night rides, waged a campaign of intimidation by beatings, floggings, and murders. . . ." In this, he says, they were encouraged by the upper class generally. "Lawlessness in Florida, 1868–1871," *Florida Historical Quarterly,* XL (Oct. 1961), 184.

7. John Hope Franklin, *Reconstruction: After the Civil War* (Chicago, 1961), p. 161.
8. Charles W. Ramsdell, *Reconstruction in Texas* (N.Y., 1910), p. 233.
9. Fleming, *Civil War and Reconstruction in Alabama*, pp. 674–76; Albion W. Tourgée, *The Invisible Empire*, part II of his *A Fool's Errand, by One of the Fools* (N.Y., 1880), pp. 419–23. Tourgée conveniently quotes a large number of eyewitness descriptions of Ku Klux disguises which were given by persons from several states before the Congressional investigating committee of 1871. See also Horn, *Invisible Empire*, pp. 58–66. In 1925 the obituary of Mrs. Sylina Bland Montgomery, who had just died at the age of ninety, credited her with making the first Ku Klux uniform worn in Memphis. This was given to General Forrest, so the story goes, and he was so pleased with her handiwork that she was asked to make many more; she did so night after night. See Memphis *News & Scimitar*, Aug. 10, 1925.
10. Tuscaloosa *Independent Monitor*, April 1, 1868.
11. *Montgomery Mail*, quoted in Columbus, Ga., *Daily Sun*, March 21, 1868.
12. Little Rock *Morning Republican*, May 13, 1868.
13. Wood, "The Ku Klux Klan," pp. 264–65.
14. Nashville *Republican Banner*, Feb. 16, 1868, copied in Batesville *North Arkansas Times*, April 18, 1868.
15. Two Northern-born Republicans who believed that the freedmen were taken in were Margaret Newbold (Thorpe) Stokes ("Life in Virginia, By a 'Yankee Teacher,' . . . ," ed. by Richard L. Morton, *Virginia Magazine of History and Biography*, LXIV [April 1956], 202–3) and Charles Stearns (*Black Man of the South*, pp. 422–23). Among the rare accounts by Klansmen who claim themselves to have hoodwinked superstitious Negroes, see Wood, "The Ku Klux Klan," p. 267; confession of Capt. John G. Lea of Caswell County, N.C., in Greensboro (N.C.) *Daily News*, Oct. 2, 1935. In the latter case, see also Myrta Avary, *Dixie After the War, Social Conditions, 1865–1877* (N.Y., 1906), p. 277, and statement of William G. Garland, 1869, in William W. Holden Papers, Duke University.
16. *House Miscellaneous Documents*, 41st Congress, 2d sess., No. 154, pt. 1, pp. 153–54; see also p. 531.
17. *KKK Report*, Georgia, p. 468.
18. See *ibid.*, Alabama, 863; *House Miscellaneous Documents*, 41st Congress, 2d sess., No. 154, pt. 1, p. 401.
19. *House Miscellaneous Documents*, 41st Congress, 2d sess., No. 154, pt. 2, p. 163.
20. For a fuller discussion of this question with similar conclusions, see Grady McWhiney and Francis B. Simkins, "The Ghostly Legend of the Ku-Klux Klan," *Negro History Bulletin*, XIV (1951), 110–12. For examples of historians accepting and perpetuating the myth, see Fleming, *Sequel of Appomattox*, pp. 254–57; his *Civil War and Reconstruction in Alabama*, pp. 676–77; Julia Kendel, "Reconstruction in Lafayette County,"

Mississippi Historical Society Publications, XIII (1913), 240; Horn, *Invisible Empire*, pp. 18–20.

21. Nashville *Republican Banner*, March 29, April 7, 1868.
22. Pulaski *Citizen*, April 24, 1868.
23. See E. Merton Coulter, *The South During Reconstruction* (Baton Rouge, 1947), pp. 168–69; Horn, *Invisible Empire*, chap. 15.
24. Quoted in Pulaski *Citizen*, Sept. 4, 1868.
25. Austin, Tex., *Tri-Weekly State Gazette*, Feb. 15, 1869; Horn, *Invisible Empire*, pp. 337–38.
26. Quoted in Yorkville (S.C.) *Enquirer*, April 16, 1868.
27. Copied in Charleston, S.C., *Republican*, March 29, 1871.
28. Quoted in *House Miscellaneous Documents*, 41st Congress, 2d sess., No. 154, pt. 2, p. 32.
29. Quoted in Raleigh *Daily Standard*, April 11, 1868.
30. Richmond *Enquirer & Examiner*, April 30, 1868, as copied in Pulaski *Citizen*, May 22, 1868.
31. Quoted in Yorkville (S.C.) *Enquirer*, April 23, 1868.
32. Quoted in Pulaski *Citizen*, April 17, 1868.
33. Walter Lynwood Fleming explains the lack of Klan activity in heavily Negro counties by saying that the freedmen were most obedient and best behaved in these areas. J. C. Lester and D. L. Wilson, *Ku Klux Klan*, ed. by W. L. Fleming (N.Y., 1905), p. 23. Actually they had things more nearly their own way here, politically if not economically, and whites found themselves in no danger physically or otherwise.
34. This is based on inclusion of all the ex-Confederate states except Virginia, where the Klan hardly existed at all, but adding Kentucky, where it operated longer than anywhere else.

CHAPTER 4: THE SOUTH ATLANTIC STATES

1. New York *Herald*, April 13, 1868; Little Rock *Morning Republican*, April 18, 1868.
2. Quoted in Raleigh *Daily Standard*, April 11, 1868.
3. Margaret Newbold (Thorpe) Stokes, "Life in Virginia, By a 'Yankee Teacher,' . . . ," ed. by Richard L. Morton, *Virginia Magazine of History and Biography*, LXIV (April 1956), 202–3.
4. Reports of W. A. McNulty, Culpeper Court House; F. W. Haskell, Heathsville; J. F. Wilson, Lynchburg; C. S. Schaeffer, Christiansburg; John A. McDonnell, Winchester; (?) Hall, Woodstock; Morton Harens, Warrenton; W. S. Chase, Manassas, for April 1868, Virginia Operations Reports; Report of Gen. O. Brown, Richmond, for April 1868, Synopses of Reports of Assistant Commissioners, 1867–1869, Freedmen's Bureau Records, RG 105, NA.
5. New Orleans *Republican*, June 20, 1868; *New York Times*, March 1, 1869. See also Luther C. Tibbets, *Spirit of the South* (Washington, 1869),

wherein the author reports receiving Ku Klux warnings in Spotsylvania County in July and August 1868.

6. On the other hand, Kentucky experienced even less of Reconstruction or Republican control than Virginia, and the Klan received little or no encouragement from Democratic state leaders there, yet it flourished at the grass roots in some counties for years. All of this serves to reiterate the essentially local character of the Ku Klux Klan.

7. *KKK Report,* North Carolina, p. 324.

8. *Ibid.,* South Carolina, p. 1862.

9. J. J. Martin to Gov. W. W. Holden, Martin's Lime Kiln, Oct. 23, 1870, in Holden Papers, Duke University (reprinted anonymously in *Senate Reports,* 42d Congress, 1st sess., No. 1, p. lxiii); *ibid.,* p. 117.

10. *Ibid.,* p. iv. See statements to this effect by an Arkansas Klansman, in Powell Clayton, *The Aftermath of the Civil War, in Arkansas* (N.Y., 1915), p. 85, and by a North Carolinian, in *Trial of William W. Holden, Governor of North Carolina . . . ,* 3 vols. (Raleigh, 1871), p. 1603.

11. William W. Holden, *Third Annual Message . . . Nov. 1870* (Raleigh, 1870), Appendix, pp. 86–89; *Senate Reports,* 42d Congress, 1st sess., No. 1, p. lxi; *Trial of William W. Holden,* pp. 1581, 1589–90, 1640, 2022, 2227, 2233, 2236, 2251.

12. *Trial of William W. Holden,* pp. 1589, 1603.

13. *Ibid.,* p. 1971; J. G. de Roulhac Hamilton, *Reconstruction in North Carolina* (N.Y., 1914), pp. 457–58.

14. *Trial of William W. Holden,* p. 2227.

15. See Hamilton, *Reconstruction in North Carolina,* pp. 454–57.

16. See biographical sketch by Collier Cobb, in Samuel A. Ashe (ed.), *Biographical History of North Carolina,* 8 vols. (Greensboro, 1905–17), IV, 381–89.

17. Hamilton, *Reconstruction in North Carolina,* p. 461; *KKK Report,* Committee Report, pp. 354–61.

18. Hamilton, *Reconstruction in North Carolina,* p. 459.

19. W. McKee Evans, *Ballots and Fence Rails: Reconstruction on the Lower Cape Fear* (Chapel Hill, N.C., 1967), pp. 98–102; Raleigh *Daily Standard,* March 26, April 20, 1868.

20. Raleigh *Daily Standard,* April 15, 22, 1868; H. C. Thompson to Benjamin S. Hedrick, Chapel Hill, April 3, 1868, and same to "Sister," April 14, 1868, in Benjamin S. Hedrick Papers, Duke University.

21. Raleigh *Daily Standard,* March, 25, April 11, 1868.

22. Raleigh *Sentinel,* April 30, 1868.

23. Yorkville *Enquirer,* March 5, 1868.

24. Charleston *Daily News,* March 24, 1868; Columbia *Phoenix,* March 26, 1868.

25. Quoted in Columbia *Phoenix,* April 15, 1868.

26. Yorkville *Enquirer,* April 2, 1868.

27. Charleston *Daily News,* May 7, 1868.

28. Francis B. Simkins, "The Ku Klux Klan in South Carolina, 1868–1871,"

Journal of Negro History, XII (1927), 608; *Evidence Taken by the Committee of Investigation of the Third Congressional District under Authority of the General Assembly of . . . South Carolina, Regular Session 1868–1869* (Columbia, 1870), p. 656; *House Miscellaneous Documents,* 41st Congress, 1st sess., No. 17, pp. 16, 36, 44.

29. J. K. Chambers to Iredell Jones and Thomas May, June 28, 1868; and "Head Quarters—General Order No. 1" (*ca.* Oct. 1868), in Iredell Jones Papers, South Caroliniana Library, University of South Carolina.

30. [William Thomas Richardson], *Historic Pulaski, Birthplace of the Ku Klux Klan* . . . ([Nashville], 1913), pp. 7–8.

31. Report of W. F. DeKnight, Abbeville, for June 1868, Reports of Operations, South Carolina; letters of DeKnight, Abbeville, June 9, 10, 1868, South Carolina, Assistant Commissioner, Letters Received; Reports of Assistant Commissioner for South Carolina, June–Sept. 1868, Synopses of Reports of Assistant Commissioners, 1867–1869, Freedmen's Bureau Records, RG 105, NA.

32. Yorkville *Enquirer,* Sept. 10, 1868.

33. *Acts of the General Assembly of . . . South Carolina,* Special Session, 1868, p. 16.

34. *KKK Report,* Georgia, pp. 432–33; Allen P. Tankersley, *John B. Gordon: A Study in Gallantry* (Atlanta, 1955), pp. 247–48; Alan Conway, *The Reconstruction of Georgia* (Minneapolis, 1966), p. 171.

35. *KKK Report,* Georgia, pp. 308–42.

36. J. E. Bryant to Atty. Gen. A. T. Akerman, Augusta, Ga., Sept. 11, 1871; same to same, Washington, Oct. 31, 1871, Justice Dept., Source-Chronological File, Georgia, RG 60, NA.

37. John C. Reed, "What I Know of the Ku Klux Klan," *Uncle Remus's Magazine,* I, 8 (Jan. 1908), 24–26.

38. C. Mildred Thompson, *Reconstruction in Georgia . . . 1865–1872* (N.Y., 1915), pp. 376–77, 380, 389.

39. *KKK Report,* Georgia, pp. 184, 186–88, 317, 431–34, 451–53, 532–35, 770, 782, 784–85, 969, 1035–36; Columbus *Daily Sun,* March 24, April 1, 7, 1868; *Radical Rule: Military Outrage in Georgia; Arrest of Columbus Prisoners with Facts Connected with Their Imprisonment and Release* (Louisville, Ky., 1868), pp. 3–5; Capt. William Mills to Brig. Gen. C. C. Sibley, Columbus, Ga., March 31, 1868, Headquarters of the Army, Letters Received, 1868–1869, RG 108, NA. General Forrest was reportedly in Columbus on the day of the murder, along with a number of other prominent Democrats. *KKK Report,* Georgia, 534. Albion Tourgée, the North Carolina Republican leader, judge, and later novelist, wrote (under the pseudonym Wenckar) after the murder that he had known Ashburn as a member of General Rosecrans' wartime staff and found much more to admire than to blame in him. Raleigh *Daily Standard,* April 10, 1868.

40. Columbus *Daily Sun,* April 1, 1868.

41. Capt. William Mills to Lieut. J. E. Hosmer, A.A.G., Columbus, Ga.,

March 31, 1868, Headquarters of the Army, Letters Received, 1868–1869, RG 108, NA.

42. *Radical Rule: Military Outrage in Georgia . . . ;* Atlanta *Constitution,* June 30, 1868 ff., containing proceedings of the military court; Augusta *Daily Chronicle and Sentinel,* Sept. 18, 1868, containing Gen. Meade's official report on the affair; *KKK Report,* Georgia, pp. 184, 317–18, 533, 782–84. Columbus Democrats seemed able to control the county thereafter without the Klan, despite a slight Negro population majority. This was a skill which Georgia Democrats mastered early.

43. Edward McPherson, *Political History of the United States during the Period of Reconstruction,* 2d ed. (Washington, 1871), pp. 320–21. Meade also asked General Grant for another regiment of soldiers in case this appeal was not sufficient. Meade to Grant, Atlanta, April 5, 1868, Headquarters of the Army, Telegrams Received, 1868–1869; same to same, April 4, 1868, Headquarters of the Army, Letters Received, 1868–1869, RG 108, NA.

44. Columbus *Daily Sun,* April 3, 1868; Nashville *Republican Banner,* April 9, 1868.

45. Atlanta *Daily New Era,* April 10, 1868 ff.; Jack B. Scroggs, "Southern Reconstruction: A Radical View," *Journal of Southern History,* XXIV (Nov. 1958), 415.

46. Charles Stearns, *The Black Man of the South, and the Rebels* (N.Y., 1872), pp. 421–22; *KKK Report,* Georgia, pp. 736–38; letter of M. S. Whalen, Augusta, July 14, 1868, in Georgia, Assistant Commissioner, Register of Letters Received, Freedmen's Bureau Records, RG 105, NA.

47. Gov. Rufus B. Bullock to Gen. Meade, April 29, 1868, Bullock Correspondence, Georgia Archives; Eugene Davis (governor's secretary) to E. S. Griffin, Aug. 28, 1868, Executive Dept. Letterbooks, Georgia Archives.

48. *KKK Report,* Florida, pp. 156 ff. (Young Men's Democratic Club constitution on pp. 157–58), 226 ff., 265–66, 293 ff.; William Watson Davis, *The Civil War and Reconstruction in Florida* (N.Y., 1913), pp. 561–64; Ralph L. Peek, "Aftermath of Military Reconstruction, 1868–1869," *Florida Historical Quarterly,* XLIII (Oct. 1964), 131–32; Ralph L. Peek, "Lawlessness in Florida, 1868–1871," *ibid.,* XL (Oct. 1961), 184–85.

49. Joe M. Richardson, *The Negro in the Reconstruction of Florida, 1865–1877* (Tallahassee, 1965), pp. 165–68.

CHAPTER 5: ALABAMA, MISSISSIPPI, AND KENTUCKY

1. For Montgomery: Columbus, Ga., *Daily Sun,* March 21, 1868; for Talladega: Montgomery *Daily State Sentinel,* April 4, 1868; for Mobile: Little Rock *Daily Arkansas Gazette,* April 11, 1868.

2. *KKK Report,* Alabama, p. 1790.

3. Montgomery *Advertiser,* June 12, 1906.

4. Statement of J. H. Alston, Tuskegee, April 4, 1868, enclosed in letter of

Gen. O. L. Shepherd to A.A.G., Montgomery, April 6, 1868, Office of Assistant Adjutant General, Letters Received, 1868, Freedmen's Bureau Records, RG 105, NA; *KKK Report,* Alabama, especially Alston's testimony, pp. 1016 ff.

5. *KKK Report,* Alabama, pp. 745–46.
6. Montgomery *Daily State Sentinel,* Jan. 6, Feb. 12, 1868.
7. *Ibid.,* March 7, 1868 ff.
8. *Ibid.,* March 23, 1868; Huntsville *Advocate,* April 7, 1868; *KKK Report,* Alabama, pp. 135, 431–32, 443, 660–62, 833–35, 892, 919; Walter Lynwood Fleming, *Civil War and Reconstruction in Alabama* (N.Y., 1905), pp. 661–67, 677.
9. Fleming, *Civil War and Reconstruction in Alabama,* p. 669.
10. *House Reports,* 43d Congress, 2d sess., No. 262, pp. 882–83.
11. Ms. of Dr. G. P. L. Reid, Marion, Ala., *ca.* 1905 (undated), in Walter Lynwood Fleming Papers, New York Public Library; Fleming, *Civil War and Reconstruction in Alabama,* pp. 669–70, 673; William Garrott Brown, *The Lower South in American History* (N.Y., 1902), pp. 209–15. Brown does not give the name of his informant or the county involved in his detailed account, but he himself was a native of Perry County and probably derived his information from Dr. Reid.
12. Thomas Chalmers McCorvey, *Alabama Historical Sketches,* ed. by George Burke Johnston (Charlottesville, Va., 1960), pp. 170–73.
13. The KWC apparently existed there in 1871, however, releasing one of its members from the local jail. *KKK Report,* Miscellaneous Testimony, pp. 18–19.
14. John L. Hunnicutt, *Reconstruction in West Alabama: The Memoirs of John L. Hunnicutt,* ed. by William Stanley Hoole (Tuscaloosa, 1959), pp. 51–58.
15. William E. W. Yerby, *History of Greensboro, Alabama, from Its Earliest Settlement* (Montgomery, 1908), p. 62; report of C. A. Gale, Greensboro, for March 1868, Alabama Monthly Reports, Freedmen's Bureau Records, RG 105, NA.
16. Report of A. S. Bennett, Demopolis, for March 1868, Alabama Monthly Reports; letter of C. A. Gale, Greensboro, April 9, 1868, in Demopolis, Ala., Sub-district, Letters Received book, Freedmen's Bureau Records, RG 105, NA; Tuscaloosa *Independent Monitor,* April 1, 1868; *KKK Report,* Alabama, p. 1278. The Ku Klux Klan was occasionally and incidentally anti-Semitic, but the Jewish population in the rural and small-town South was so tiny that this was nowhere a central concern.
17. Report of A. S. Bennett, Demopolis, for March 1868, in Alabama Monthly Reports, Freedmen's Bureau Records, RG 105, NA.
18. *KKK Report,* Alabama, p. 274; Stanley F. Horn, *Invisible Empire: The Story of the Ku Klux Klan, 1866–1871* (Boston, 1939), pp. 120–21.
19. For Wilcox: Washington *Daily Morning Chronicle,* April 15, 1868; Marengo: Report of C. W. Pierce, Demopolis, for April 1868, Alabama Monthly Reports, Freedmen's Bureau Records, RG 105, NA; Pickens:

Hunnicutt, *Reconstruction in West Alabama,* pp. 45–46, 80; Sumter: Daniel Price to Maj. C. W. Pierce, Livingston, April 13, May 1, 1868, Demopolis, Ala., Sub-district, Letters Received, Freedmen's Bureau Records, RG 105, NA.

20. Tuscaloosa *Independent Monitor,* April 21, 1868; Ryland Randolph, Autobiographical Episodes, John W. DuBose Papers, Alabama Archives.
21. Tuscaloosa *Independent Monitor,* Dec. 4, 1867.
22. *Ibid.,* Dec. 4, 1867, Jan. 1, 1868; Ryland Randolph to W. L. Fleming, Cornelia, St. Clair County, Ala., Aug. 21, 27, 1901, in W. L. Fleming Papers, New York Public Library; Fleming, *Civil War and Reconstruction in Alabama,* pp. 677–78; John W. DuBose, *Alabama's Tragic Decade: Ten Years of Alabama, 1865–1874,* ed. by James K. Greer (Birmingham, 1940), pp. 210, 242; Randolph, Autobiographical Episodes, DuBose Papers.
23. Tuscaloosa *Independent Monitor,* March 18, 1868.
24. Montgomery *Daily State Sentinel,* March 31, 1868.
25. Randolph to Fleming, Cornelia, St. Clair County, Ala., Aug. 21, 1901, W. L. Fleming Papers.
26. Randolph, Autobiographical Episodes, DuBose Papers.
27. Tuscaloosa *Independent Monitor,* April 28, May 5, 1868.
28. *Monitor,* as reported in Richmond *Enquirer & Examiner,* May 29, 1868.
29. Randolph, Autobiographical Episodes, DuBose Papers; Tuscaloosa *Independent Monitor,* May 26, July 28, 1868.
30. Tuscaloosa *Independent Monitor,* June 23, 1868.
31. *Ibid.,* Aug. 18, 25, Sept. 1, 1868.
32. *Ibid.,* Sept. 1, 1868. The cartoon is reproduced in Fleming, *Civil War and Reconstruction in Alabama,* p. 612. See Sarah Van V. Woolfolk, "The Political Cartoons of the Tuskaloosa *Independent Monitor* and Tuskaloosa *Blade,* 1867–1873," *Alabama Historical Quarterly,* XXVII (Fall and Winter 1965), 140–65.
33. Montgomery *Mail,* Sept. 26, 1868, quoted in Montgomery *Alabama State Journal,* same date.
34. See H. M. Somerville to Robert McKee, Tuscaloosa, Oct. 3, 1868, Robert McKee Papers, Alabama Archives.
35. D. Woodruff to Gov. W. H. Smith, Tuscaloosa, Aug. 12, 1868; S. S. Plowman to same, Moore's Bridge, Tuscaloosa County, July 12, 1868, Governors' Correspondence, Alabama Archives.
36. *KKK Report,* Georgia, p. 506; F. M. Goodfellow to D. C. Rugg, Decatur, Ala., Aug. 16, 1868, Huntsville, Ala., Sub-district, Letters Received book, Freedmen's Bureau Records, RG 105, NA; Decatur *Republican,* Aug. 12, 1868, as quoted in New Orleans *Republican,* Aug. 20, 1868; J. J. Hinds to Gov. Smith, Washington, D.C., Aug. 16, 1868, in Governors' Correspondence, Alabama Archives.
37. J. M. Hinds to Gov. Smith, Decatur, Aug. 1, 1868, in Governors' Correspondence, Alabama Archives.

38. C. P. Simmons to Gov. Smith, Tuscumbia, Sept. 3, 1868, and J. M. Rogers to same, Florence, Aug. 12, 1868, in Governors' Correspondence, Alabama Archives.
39. General Orders No. 11, enclosed in letter of Gen. O. L. Shepherd to A.A.G., Montgomery, April 6, 1868, in Office of Assistant Adjutant General, Letters Received, Freedmen's Bureau Records, RG 105, NA; also in Montgomery *Daily State Sentinel,* April 6, 1868, and other newspapers.
40. Letters to Gov. Smith from J. M. Rogers, Florence, Aug. 12, Residents of Morgan County, Rasham's Gap, Aug. 14, and J. J. Hinds, Washington, D.C., Aug. 16, 1868, in Governors' Correspondence, Alabama Archives.
41. Otis A. Singletary, in his useful monograph, *Negro Militia and Reconstruction* (Austin, Tex., 1957, esp. pp. 145–47), criticizes the failure of Southern governors generally to use Negro militia, citing this consideration as one of the reasons they used, but he presents no argument to lessen its validity.
42. *KKK Report,* Mississippi, pp. 232, 586; Memphis *Daily Post,* April 9, 1868; Julia Kendel, "Reconstruction in Lafayette County," *Mississippi Historical Society Publications,* XIII (1913), 239; Ernest Franklin Puckett, "Reconstruction in Monroe County," *ibid.,* XI (1910), 128; Irby C. Nichols, "Reconstruction in De Soto County," *ibid.,* XI (1910), 310.
43. Vicksburg *Weekly Republican,* April 14, 1868; Washington *Daily Morning Chronicle,* March 25, 1868; *Daily Memphis Avalanche,* March 26, 1868; Memphis *Daily Post,* March 23, 1868.
44. *KKK Report,* Mississippi, pp. 212–17, 223; Fred M. Witty, "Reconstruction in Carroll and Montgomery Counties," *Mississippi Historical Society Publications,* X (1909), 129–31; Nannie Lacey, "Reconstruction in Leake County," *ibid.,* XI (1911), 284.
45. Jackson *Daily Clarion,* April 7, 22, 28, June 3, 1868.
46. Memphis *Daily Post,* April 23, 1868; Memphis *Evening Post,* May 25, 1868; *KKK Report,* Mississippi, pp. 16, 299, 303; Lacey, "Reconstruction in Leake County," p. 284; John W. Kyle, "Reconstruction in Panola County," *Mississippi Historical Society Publications,* XIII (1913), 51–53; Forrest Cooper, "Reconstruction in Scott County," *ibid.,* 111, 127–28; Kendel, "Reconstruction in Lafayette County," *ibid.,* 230, 239, 248; Julia C. Brown, "Reconstruction in Yalobusha and Grenada Counties," *ibid.,* XII (1912), 235; Ruth Watkins, "Reconstruction in Marshall County," *ibid.,* 160, 163, 178–80, 200; Witty, "Reconstruction in Carroll and Montgomery Counties," *ibid.,* X (1909), 129–32; F. Z. Browne, "Reconstruction in Oktibbeha County," *ibid.,* XIII (1913), 281, 283; E. C. Coleman, Jr., "Reconstruction in Attala County," *ibid.,* X (1910), 156–60; Albert T. Morgan, *Yazoo, or The Picket Line of Freedom in the South* (Washington, 1884), pp. 160, 206; Henry C. Warmoth, *War, Politics and Reconstruction* (N.Y., 1930), pp. 71–72; Jackson *Tri-Weekly Clarion,* March 9, 11, 1868; Vicksburg *Weekly Republican,* May, June 1868, *passim,* Dec. 6, 1868; New Orleans *Republican,* July 25,

1868; *House Miscellaneous Documents,* 40th Congress, 3d sess., No. 53, pp. 97, 206–7, 215.

47. Watkins, "Reconstruction in Marshall County," pp. 163, 178; Jackson *Semi-Weekly Clarion,* Sept. 25, Oct. 3, 6, 1871.

48. See E. Merton Coulter, *The Civil War and Readjustment in Kentucky* (Chapel Hill, N.C., 1926), pp. 359–64.

49. Kentucky reports for April, June 1868, Synopses of Reports of Assistant Commissioners, 1867–1869, Freedmen's Bureau Records, RG 105, NA; *House Executive Documents,* 40th Congress, 2d sess., No. 329, p. 19.

50. New Orleans *Republican,* May 24, 1868.

51. Frankfort *Commonwealth,* July 10, Aug. 21, 28, 1868. See also *Senate Miscellaneous Documents,* 42d Congress, 1st sess., No. 49.

52. Eugenia D. Potts to Arthur Potts, Lancaster, Ky., July 13, 1868, William I and II Potts Papers, Duke University. See also Kentucky reports for June to September 1868, Synopses of Reports of Assistant Commissioners, 1867–1869, Freedmen's Bureau Records, RG 105, NA.

53. Kentucky reports for Aug., Sept. 1868, *ibid.*

54. N.Y. *Daily Tribune,* Aug. 28, 1868.

55. *Ibid.,* June 18, 29, July 4, Sept. 8, 1868; Frankfort *Commonwealth,* July 10, Sept. 11, 1868; Kentucky reports for June, Aug., Sept. 1868, Synopses of Reports of Assistant Commissioners, 1867–1869, Freedmen's Bureau Records, RG 105, NA.

CHAPTER 6: THE TRANS-MISSISSIPPI STATES

1. A KWC ritual (headed "C.K." or "C.R.," however) in the Breda Family Papers, Dept. of Archives and Manuscripts, Louisiana State University, states that the society was organized on May 22, 1867. See also Allie Bayne Windham Webb, "Organization and Activities of the Knights of the White Camelia in Louisiana, 1867–1869," Louisiana Academy of Sciences, *Proceedings,* XVII (1954), 110–14; John R. Ficklen, *History of Reconstruction in Louisiana (Through 1868)* (Baltimore, 1910), pp. 215–18; *House Miscellaneous Documents,* 41st Congress, 2d sess., No. 154, pt. 1, pp. 517, 556 (where members identify DeBlanc as from St. Martin Parish), 575; pt. 2, pp. 84, 87.

2. The Archives Division of the University of Texas Library contains a typescript copy of a KWC ritual, indicating that it was "adopted at a General Convention of the Order, June 4, 1868," and that it was published in New Orleans that year. Another so headed is with the manuscripts of Dr. G. P. L. Reid of Marion, Ala., in the W. L. Fleming Papers, New York Public Library. This was perhaps a revised ritual, like the revised Ku Klux Klan Prescript of 1868.

3. *House Miscellaneous Documents,* 41st Congress, 2d sess., No. 154, pt. 1, p. 572; pt. 2, pp. 84, 237–42, 342, 414–15, 726.

4. See New Orleans *Times,* March 27, 1868 ff.

5. The initial question put by a member to a stranger to determine whether he belonged to the order was "Are you free?" A former member commented, "It was the most awkwardly constructed arrangement possible. To go up to a white man, not knowing whether he was a member of the order or not, and ask him, 'Are you free?' would be very likely to get you into a difficulty. Possibly the first intimation you received that he was not a member would be to get knocked down." *House Miscellaneous Documents,* 41st Congress, 2d sess., No. 154, pt. 1, p. 733.

6. Louisiana General Assembly, *Report of the Joint Committee . . . on the Conduct of the State Elections and the Condition of Peace and Order in the State; Session of 1869* (New Orleans, 1869), pp. 258–61; Walter Lynwood Fleming (ed.), *Documentary History of Reconstruction,* 2 vols. (Cleveland, 1906–7), II, 350–53. The Department of Archives and Manuscripts, Louisiana State University, has a copy of the ritual in French, which came from Ascension Parish.

7. Walter Lynwood Fleming (ed.), *Documents Relating to Reconstruction* (Morgantown, W. Va., 1904), No. 1, pp. 8–20; *House Miscellaneous Documents,* 41st Congress, 2d sess., No. 154, pt. 1, p. 727; pt. 2, pp. 84–87, 230–33, 339.

8. Shreveport *South-Western,* April 1, 8, 15, 1868; New Orleans *Times,* March 27, 31, April 1, 2, 9, 12, 14, 15, 1868; Louisiana General Assembly, *Report of the Joint Committee . . . 1869,* p. 186; *House Miscellaneous Documents,* 41st Congress, 2d sess., No. 154, pt. 2, pp. 22–23.

9. Louisiana General Assembly, *Report of the Joint Committee . . . on the Conduct of the Late Elections, and the Condition of Peace and Order in the State* (New Orleans, 1868), pp. 20–21; *Report of the Joint Committee . . . 1869,* pp. 142, 292–93; *House Miscellaneous Documents,* 41st Congress, 2d sess., No. 154, pt. 2, p. 155; New Orleans *Republican,* April 18, 1868.

10. New Orleans *Republican,* April 22, 24, 25, 26, 1868; Washington *Morning Chronicle,* May 2, 1868; W. L. Miefitt (sp. ?) to H. C. Warmoth, Shreveport, April 29, 1868, Warmoth Papers, Southern Historical Collection, University of North Carolina.

11. See Shreveport *South-Western,* May 6, 1868; New Orleans *Republican,* April 28, May 6, 10, 15, June 10, 1868.

12. *House Miscellaneous Documents,* 41st Congress, 2d sess., No. 154, pt. 2, pp. 13, 17–18, 362, 388.

13. New Orleans *Republican,* May 10, July 17, 18, 21, 22, 25, 1868; Louisiana reports for May, July, and August 1868, Synopses of Reports of Assistant Commissioners, 1867–1869, Freedmen's Bureau Records, RG 105, NA; Louisiana General Assembly, *Report of the Joint Committee* (1868), pp. 17, 21–23, 29–31, 59–63; *House Miscellaneous Documents,* 41st Congress, 2d sess., No. 154, pt. 1, pp. 328–30; pt. 2, pp. 398–99, 405, 407. For Richland Parish, see M. Liddell to St. John R. Liddell, Buccleuch, July 29, Aug. 17, 1868, Liddell Family Papers, Department of Archives and Manuscripts, Louisiana State University.

14. New Orleans *Republican,* June 28, July 2, 1868; Louisiana General Assembly, *Report of the Joint Committee . . . 1869,* p. 155.
15. New Orleans *Republican,* May 15, 22, 23, June 5, 6, 17, July 12, 26, 1868; Louisiana General Assembly, *Report of the Joint Committee* (1868), pp. 19–20, 48–49.
16. Notice, dated April 27, 1868, Warmoth Papers, Southern Historical Collection, University of North Carolina.
17. New Orleans *Republican,* July 1, 1868; New Orleans *Times,* July 8, 1868.
18. New Orleans *Republican,* July 26, 28, Aug. 2, 5, 1868.
19. See Henry C. Warmoth, *War, Politics and Reconstruction: Stormy Days in Louisiana* (N.Y., 1930), p. 72; *House Miscellaneous Documents,* 41st Congress, 2d sess., No. 154, pt. 2, pp. 22–24.
20. New Orleans *Times,* May 16, Aug. 7, 9, 13, 1868; *Picayune,* quoted in Batesville *North Arkansas Times,* June 6, 1868.
21. Shreveport *South-Western,* April 1, 22, May 6, 27, July 22, Aug. 5, 1868.
22. *Ibid.,* Nov. 18, 1868.
23. *Acts Passed by the General Assembly of . . . Louisiana,* 1868, pp. 44–46.
24. *House Executive Documents,* 40th Congress, 3d sess., No. 1, III, pt. 1, pp. xix–xx; *Louisiana Senate Journal,* Executive Session, 1868, pp. 5, 51; New Orleans *Republican,* July 31, 1868; *American Annual Cyclopaedia,* 1868, p. 438.
25. Little Rock *Daily Arkansas Gazette,* March 18, 1868.
26. Little Rock *Morning Republican,* April 3, 6, 1868.
27. Batesville *North Arkansas Times,* April 4, 11, 1868.
28. *Ibid.,* April 18, 1868.
29. Little Rock *Daily Arkansas Gazette,* May 15, 16, 1868.
30. Orval T. Driggs, Jr., "The Issues of the Powell Clayton Regime, 1868–1871," *Arkansas Historical Quarterly,* VIII (1949), 16.
31. Little Rock *Daily Arkansas Gazette,* May 24, 1868.
32. Arkansas report for April 1868 (dated May 25), Synopses of Reports of Assistant Commissioners, 1867–1869, Freedmen's Bureau Records, RG 105, NA.
33. Powell Clayton, *The Aftermath of the Civil War in Arkansas* (N.Y., 1915), pp. 74–78, 83; *KKK Report,* Miscellaneous Testimony, pp. 362–75, 381. See also John M. Harrell, *The Brooks and Baxter War: A History of the Reconstruction Period in Arkansas* (St. Louis, 1893), pp. 61–62, 69. Harrell believes that the organization in Arkansas was spontaneous and organized from below.
34. Clayton, *Aftermath,* pp. 59–60, 83; Robert J. Brown, "Arkansas Led Ku-Klux Klan," undated typescript ms., Arkansas History Commission. The Klan assembled several hundred men on a few occasions later in 1868, but none of these mobilizations was aimed at Little Rock. Klan performance against the state militia was inglorious in every case. See Chapter 10 below.
35. Harrell, *Brooks and Baxter War,* p. 70; New Orleans *Republican,* Nov. 10, 1868.

36. Little Rock *Morning Republican,* June 10, 1868.
37. *Ibid.,* Aug. 28, Sept. 5, 7, 11, 1868; W. Beasley to Gov. Clayton, Lamerline (?), Ark., Aug. 29, 1868, Governors' Letters Received (letterbook), Arkansas History Commission.
38. *KKK Report,* Miscellaneous Testimony, p. 332; Memphis *Evening Post,* Aug. 29, 1868; Little Rock *Morning Republican,* Aug. 31, Sept. 5, 1868.
39. *KKK Report,* Miscellaneous Testimony, p. 328.
40. *Ibid.*
41. Clayton, *Aftermath,* pp. 79–80, 88–89.
42. Arkansas report for April 1868 (dated May 25), Synopses of Reports of Assistant Commissioners, 1867–1869, Freedmen's Bureau Records, RG 105, NA.
43. Little Rock *Morning Republican,* May 16, July 18, 1868.
44. *Ibid.,* April 20, 1868.
45. *Ibid.,* July 3, 4, 1868.
46. Arkansas General Assembly, *Acts, Resolutions and Memorials,* April–July 1868, pp. 44–50; Little Rock *Morning Republican,* Aug. 27, 1868.
47. *American Annual Cyclopaedia,* 1868, p. 39.
48. Letters to Gov. Clayton from D. P. Upham and Wm. P. Anderson, Augusta, Aug. 31, 1868, Governors' Letters Received (letterbook), Arkansas History Commission.
49. *Journal of the Reconstruction Convention . . . Austin, Texas . . . 1868,* 2 vols. (Austin, 1870), I, 193–203, 501–2.
50. *Ibid.,* I, 504.
51. Report of Charles Schmidt, Sumpter [*sic*], Tex., for April 1868, Texas Monthly Reports, Freedmen's Bureau Records, RG 105, NA.
52. *House Executive Documents,* 42d Congress, 2d sess., No. 268, p. 49. See also the letterbooks of Governor Elisha Pease for March 1868 to Feb. 1869, Governors' Correspondence, Archives Division, Texas State Library, for evidence of the persistence of these conditions.
53. New Orleans *Republican,* Jan. 11, 19, 1868.
54. Marshall, Tex., *Weekly Harrison Flag,* April 10, 17, 24, 1868. See also Shreveport, La., *South-Western,* April 22, 1868.
55. Reports for April 1868 from Charles Schmidt, Sumter; DeWitt C. Brown, Paris; Louis W. Stevenson, Columbus, Texas Monthly Reports; report of N. H. Randlett, Millican, July 1868, Synopses of Reports of Assistant Commissioners, 1867–1869; letters of J. A. Wright, Palestine, April 22, 1868, and Charles F. Rand, Clarksville, May 10, 1868, in Texas, Assistant Commissioner, Letters Received, Freedmen's Bureau Records, RG 105, NA; *Weekly Austin Republican,* April 22, 1868 ff.; *Tri-Weekly Austin Republican,* May 2, 1868; Marshall *Weekly Harrison Flag,* April 24, 1868; New Orleans *Republican,* June 4, 1868; New York *Daily Tribune,* June 29, 1868.
56. For accounts of this kind of activity, see W. D. Wood, "The Ku Klux Klan," *Texas State Historical Association Quarterly,* IX (April 1906), 266–67; Marshall *Weekly Harrison Flag,* April 24, 1868.

57. Charles F. Rand to Lieut. J. P. Richardson, Clarksville, May 10, 1868, Texas, Assistant Commissioner, Letters Received, Freedmen's Bureau Records, RG 105, NA.
58. Leonie R. Weyland and Houston Wade, *An Early History of Fayette County* (La Grange, Tex., 1936), pp. 265–66.
59. Report of N. H. Randlett, Millican, July 1868, in Synopses of Reports of Assistant Commissioners, 1867–1869, Freedmen's Bureau Records, RG 105, NA.
60. Letter of Capt. T. M. K. Smith, Marshall, June 24, 1868, Texas, Assistant Commissioner, Letters Received, Freedmen's Bureau Records, RG 105, NA.
61. Report of Capt. T. M. K. Smith, Marshall, for July 1868, Texas Monthly Reports, Freedmen's Bureau Records, RG 105, NA.
62. *Daily Austin Republican,* Aug. 1, 4, 1868; Marshall *Texas Republican,* Aug. 7, 1868.
63. For information about the town and its decline, see Winnie Mims Dean, *Jefferson, Texas, Queen of the Cypress* (Dallas, 1953), pp. 3–4; S. S. McKay, "Social Conditions in Texas in the Eighteen Seventies," West Texas Historical Association, *Yearbook,* XIV (1938), 39–40; *New York Times,* Feb. 12, 1869.
64. New York *Daily Tribune,* July 13, 1869.
65. *Daily Memphis Avalanche,* Feb. 22, 1868.
66. For the founding of the *Ultra Ku Klux,* see Marshall *Weekly Harrison Flag,* May 1, 1868.
67. *Journal of the Reconstruction Convention,* I, 197.
68. *Daily Austin Republican,* July 7, 31, 1868; Marshall *Weekly Harrison Flag,* July 9, 1868.
69. Quoted in Marshall *Texas Republican,* Aug. 14, 1868.
70. *Daily Austin Republican,* July 22, 31, 1868.
71. Pease to Gen. J. J. Reynolds, July 23, 1868, Governors' Correspondence (letterbook), Archives Division, Texas State Library.
72. James E. Sefton, *The United States Army and Reconstruction, 1865–1877* (Baton Rouge, 1967), pp. 261–62; Robert W. Shook, "The Federal Military in Texas, 1865–1870," *Texas Military History,* VI (Spring 1967), 19–20.
73. New York *Daily Tribune,* Aug. 13, 1868; D. Campbell to C. Caldwell, Jefferson, Sept. 3, 1868 (copy), and same to Gov. Pease, Sept. 5, 1868, Governors' Correspondence, Archives Division, Texas State Library.
74. New York *Daily Tribune,* Aug. 13, 1868; Marshall *Texas Republican,* Sept. 25, 1868.
75. Wood, "The Ku Klux Klan," p. 266.
76. Weyland and Wade, *Early History of Fayette County,* p. 265.
77. Houston *Union,* Aug. 28, Sept. 9, 1869; William C. Nunn, *Texas Under the Carpetbaggers* (Austin, 1961), p. 252. A man at Georgetown, near Austin, possessed a copy of the KWC ritual, but if he ever organized a

Council there, no evidence of it survives. Ritual in George Rouser Papers, Archives Division, Texas State Library.

78. George Templeton Strong, *Diary,* ed. by Allan Nevins and Milton Halsey Thomas, 4 vols. (N.Y., 1952), IV, 202.

79. New York *Herald,* April 8, 1868.

CHAPTER 7: THE SOUTHEAST AND KENTUCKY

1. Kirk H. Porter and Donald B. Johnson (eds.), *National Party Platforms, 1840–1956* (Urbana, Ill., 1956), pp. 37, 39.

2. The Klan idea even made a brief appearance in northern New Jersey in September. Republicans in Essex and Hudson counties received notices in regular Ku Klux form (some of them printed) threatening death if they did not leave the state. State militiamen were favorite targets of these missives, and one lieutenant was assaulted in Kearny by persons who left a Ku Klux notice at the scene of the attack. Nashville, Tenn., *Press and Times,* Sept. 23, 1868; Montgomery *Alabama State Journal,* Sept. 29, 1868; *Daily Austin* (Tex.) *Republican,* Oct. 2, 1868, quoting Newark *Daily Advertiser,* Sept. 21, 1868.

3. For references to organization at this time in Cleveland, Gaston, and Lincoln counties, west of Charlotte, see *KKK Report,* North Carolina, pp. 208, 215–16, 317–18, 363–64, 383–84; David Schenck Diary, Sept. 30, 1871, Southern Historical Collection, University of North Carolina. For Guilford and Alamance, see William W. Holden, *Third Annual Message . . . Nov. 1870* (Raleigh, 1870), Appendix, pp. 86–88; *Trial of William W. Holden, Governor of North Carolina . . . ,* 3 vols. (Raleigh, 1871), pp. 722, 724, 1568–70, 1684, 1806–7, 1945, 1958–60, 1966–69, 1985; *Senate Reports,* 42d Congress, 1st sess., No. 1, pp. 256–58, 306. For Sampson County, see Lieut. J. S. McEwan to Atty. Gen. Akerman, Nov. 24, 28, 1871, Justice Department Source-Chronological File, Eastern North Carolina, RG 60, NA.

4. For Stokes and Wake, see *Senate Reports,* 42d Congress, 1st sess., No. 1, pp. lxiii, 72; for Moore, Raleigh *Daily Standard,* May 27, 1870; for Granville, *ibid.,* Oct. 15, 30, 1868.

5. *KKK Report,* North Carolina, pp. 44–45, 50.

6. Silas L. Curtis *et al.* to Gov. Holden, Oct. 11, 1868, Governors' Correspondence, North Carolina Archives.

7. Raleigh *Daily Standard,* Oct. 14, 1868. For the activities around Oxford, see *ibid.,* Oct. 15, 30, 1868, and Silas L. Curtis *et al.* to Gov. Holden, Oct. 11, 1868, Governors' Correspondence, North Carolina Archives.

8. Correspondence between Gov. Holden and Gen. Nelson A. Miles, in N.Y. *Herald,* Oct. 12, 1868.

9. Holden, *Third Annual Message,* p. 12; *ibid.,* Appendix, pp. 1–5.

10. *House Miscellaneous Documents,* 41st Congress, 1st sess., No. 18, pp.

31–34, 41–44; *ibid.,* 41st Congress, 2d sess., No. 17, pt. 2, pp. 44, 46; *KKK Report,* South Carolina, pp. 50, 1256–60, 1338–41.

11. Herbert Shapiro, "The Ku Klux Klan during Reconstruction: The South Carolina Episode," *Journal of Negro History,* XLIX (Jan. 1964), 36–37; *House Miscellaneous Documents,* 41st Congress, 1st sess., No. 17, pp. 16–22, 27–28, 33–34, 37, 40, 45, 47, 49, 51–52, 54, 57; *ibid.,* 2d sess., No. 17, pt. 2, pp. 4–9, 12–16, 22–25, 28–45; *ibid.,* 41st Congress, 1st sess., No. 18, pp. 25, 31–34, 48; *KKK Report,* South Carolina, pp. 1256–60, 1325, 1338–41; South Carolina reports for Sept. and Nov. 1868, Synopses of Reports of Assistant Commissioners, 1867–1869; W. F. De-Knight to Lieut. William Stone, Abbeville, Nov. 6, 1868, in South Carolina, Assistant Commissioner, Letters Received, Freedmen's Bureau Records, RG 105, NA; New York *Daily Tribune,* May 8, 1871; Yorkville (S.C.) *Enquirer,* Feb. 18, 1869; South Carolina General Assembly, *Evidence Taken by the Committee of Investigation of the Third Congressional District . . . 1868–1869* (Columbia, 1870), *passim.*

12. See Joel Williamson, *After Slavery: The Negro in South Carolina During Reconstruction, 1861–1877* (Chapel Hill, N.C., 1965), *passim.*

13. *House Miscellaneous Documents,* 41st Congress, 1st sess., No. 18, pp. 31–34; also in *KKK Report,* South Carolina, pp. 1257–60. The Democrats later professed to believe that Republicans themselves had hired the killing in order to incense the Negroes against the whites. See *KKK Report,* South Carolina, p. 109. Explanations of this sort were a favorite ploy which often misled people at a distance, and sometimes the more gullible closer at hand.

14. Shapiro, "The Ku Klux Klan during Reconstruction," pp. 35–36.

15. Chief Constable John B. Hubbard to W. H. Griffin, Oct. 22, 29, Nov. 2, 1869, Chief Constable's Letterbook, 1868, South Carolina Archives.

16. *Acts of the General Assembly of the State of South Carolina, Passed at the Special Session of 1868,* pp. 85–86.

17. *KKK Report,* South Carolina, pp. 1254–55.

18. *House Miscellaneous Documents,* 41st Congress, 2d sess., No. 17, pt. 2, p. 46.

19. House and Senate Resolution, Sept. 26, 1868, in Governors' Letters, South Carolina Archives; report of Col. J. R. Edie, Columbia, for year ending Sept. 30, 1868, Synopses of Reports of Assistant Commissioners, 1867–1869, Freedmen's Bureau Records, RG 105, NA; *House Miscellaneous Documents,* 41st Congress, 2d sess., No. 17, pt. 2, p. 46; Annual Message of Nov. 28, 1871 (printed copy), p. 25, in Legislative System, Messages, Gov. R. K. Scott, South Carolina Archives.

20. *Evidence Taken by the Committee of Investigation, passim; KKK Report,* South Carolina, pp. 13, 1943, 1955, 1959–60; *House Miscellaneous Documents,* 41st Congress, 2d sess., No. 17, pt. 2, pp. 32, 37–43, 46; *ibid.,* 41st Congress, 1st sess., No. 18, p. 26; *ibid.,* No. 17, pp. 18, 22, 37, 50, 52–53, 54, 57; Shapiro, "The Ku Klux Klan during Reconstruction," pp. 37–39. Members of the Abbeville Democratic clubs denied any

improper actions by those organizations. They also claimed to believe that the Klan had no existence there at all, and that if it did exist it had no connection with the Democratic clubs. *House Miscellaneous Documents,* 41st Congress, 1st sess., No. 35, pp. 29–39. But apart from the evidence of William K. Tolbert, the Randolph assassin, to the contrary, it is hard to believe that the two movements could be engaged in such similar work in the same communities without some connection. Cf. Francis B. Simkins, "The Ku Klux Klan in South Carolina, 1868–1871," *Journal of Negro History,* XII (1927), 611.

21. Charleston *Daily News,* Oct. 20, 21, 1868.

22. For Schley County, see Rev. H. W. Pierson, *A Letter to Hon. Charles Sumner; "Statements" of Outrages upon Freedmen in Georgia and Account of My Expulsion from Andersonville, Ga.* (Washington, 1870); for Jones County, *Senate Miscellaneous Documents,* 40th Congress, 3d sess., No. 52, p. 83; for Jasper County, *KKK Report,* Georgia, p. 607; for Cherokee County, *ibid.,* pp. 666–67.

23. *House Miscellaneous Documents,* 40th Congress, 3d sess., No. 52, p. 41. See also Jack B. Scroggs, "Southern Reconstruction: A Radical View," *Journal of Southern History,* XXIV (Nov. 1958), p. 421.

24. Theodore B. Fitz-Simons, Jr., "The Camilla Riot," *Georgia Historical Quarterly,* XXXV (June 1951), 116–25; Alan Conway, *The Reconstruction of Georgia* (Minneapolis, 1966), pp. 168–70.

25. John C. Reed, "What I Know of the Ku Klux Klan," *Uncle Remus's Magazine,* I, 8 (Jan. 1908), 26.

26. Entry of letter from Joe McWhorter, Lexington, Ga., Sept. 30, 1868, in Georgia, Assistant Commissioner, Register of Letters Received, Freedmen's Bureau Records, RG 105, NA.

27. *House Miscellaneous Documents,* 40th Congress, 3d sess., No. 52, pp. 28, 59–60, 79–82; *KKK Report,* Georgia, pp. 210–11; R. C. Anthony to M. Frank Gallagher, Warrenton, Ga., Oct. 27, 1868, Warrenton, Georgia, Letters Sent book; entry of letter of John H. Sullivan, Greensboro, Ga., Oct. 29, 1868, in Georgia, Assistant Commissioner, Register of Letters Received, Freedmen's Bureau Records, RG 105, NA.

28. *Acts of the General Assembly of the State of Georgia . . . Called Session . . . 1868,* p. 183; Orders of Sept. 14 and Oct. 9, 1868, Executive Minutes, 1866–1870, Georgia Archives. For an account of Norris's travail in Warren County, see Chapter 14.

29. Reed, "What I Know of the Ku Klux Klan," *Uncle Remus's Magazine,* I, 9 (Feb. 1908), p. 20; John C. Reed to Walter L. Fleming, Atlanta, Aug. 1, 1906, in W. L. Fleming Papers, New York Public Library; *KKK Report,* Georgia, p. 738.

30. *KKK Report,* Georgia, pp. 454–59; *ibid.,* Committee Report, p. 249; Conway, *The Reconstruction of Georgia,* pp. 173–77; C. Mildred Thompson, *Reconstruction in Georgia, Economic, Social, Political, 1865–1872* (N.Y., 1915), pp. 362, 375–76, 389.

31. *House Executive Documents,* 40th Congress, 3d sess., No. 1, III, pt. 1, p. 1042; W. S. Simkins, "Why the Ku Klux Klan," *The Alcalde,* IV (June 19, 1916), 740–43, 747.

32. *KKK Report,* Florida, pp. 263, 268.

33. Ralph L. Peek, "Aftermath of Military Reconstruction, 1868–1869," *Florida Historical Quarterly,* XLIII (Oct. 1964), 130, 133.

34. William Watson Davis, *The Civil War and Reconstruction in Florida* (N.Y., 1913), pp. 540–41.

35. *Florida Assembly Journal,* 1870, p. 20, quoted in Peek, "Aftermath of Military Reconstruction," p. 130.

36. T. W. Gregory, *Reconstruction and the Ku Klux Klan: A Paper Read Before the Arkansas and Texas Bar Associations . . . 1906* (n.p., n.d.), pp. 16–17; Simkins, "Why the Ku Klux Klan," pp. 746–47; *New York Times,* Nov. 7, 1868; Peek, "Aftermath of Military Reconstruction," pp. 134–35; *KKK Report,* Florida, pp. 122, 124, 167.

37. Letters to Gov. Smith from R. Blair, Tuscaloosa, Sept. 14, 1868; Sheriff T. P. Lewis, Tuscaloosa, Dec. 13, 1868; and J. J. Giers, Tuscaloosa, Dec. 14, 1868, Governors' Correspondence, Alabama Archives; Tuscaloosa *Independent Monitor,* Nov. 24, 1868; *KKK Report,* Alabama, pp. 1750, 1767–68, 1851–52, 1969–71, 1980–82, 2000, 2002–4.

38. Letter of Capt. G. M. Brayton, Selma, Ala., Nov. 7, 1868, Third Military District, Letters Received, RG 98, NA.

39. J. L. Stelzig to R. A. Wilson, Livingston, Ala., Oct. 2, 6, ? (undated letter), 8 (two letters), 1868; Adam Kenard to Gov. Smith (telegram), Bennetts, Ala., Oct. 5, 1868; Daniel Price to Gov. Smith, Livingston, Oct. 7, 1868; J. L. Stelzig to Gov. Smith, Livingston, Oct. 7, 1868; R. A. Wilson to Gov. Smith, Demopolis, Ala., Oct. 16, 1868; Gerard Choutteau to Gov. Smith, Ramsey Station, Ala., Nov. 14, 1868, in Governors' Correspondence, Alabama Archives; John L. Stelzig to R. A. Wilson, Livingston, Oct. 8, 1868, in Demopolis, Ala., Letters Received, Freedmen's Bureau Records, RG 105, NA; *KKK Report,* Alabama, pp. 1804–7. In July, Price had been freer in advising Negroes generally to retaliate against violence if they could not get justice in the courts, but there is no evidence that he ever called for specific acts of violence. See Livingston *Journal,* Sept. 24, 1869.

40. *KKK Report,* Alabama, pp. 475, 477–78, 486, 742–43, 754, 770.

41. J. Ronayne to Secretary of State Charles Miller, Huntsville, Oct. 15, 1868; G. A. Smith to Lieut. Gov. A. J. Applegate, Courtland, Ala., Sept. 16, 1868; W. B. Figures to Gov. Smith, Huntsville, Oct. 20, 1868; Neander H. Rice to Gov. Smith, Florence, Ala., Oct. 30, 1868, in Governors' Correspondence, Alabama Archives; Nashville *Press and Times,* Oct. 19, 1868; *KKK Report,* Alabama, pp. 680–82, 686, 813–15, 919, 921, 927–28, 935, 942–44, 1196; Huntsville *Advocate,* Sept. 22, 1868, quoted in Montgomery *Alabama State Journal,* Sept. 28, 1868.

42. Nashville *Press and Times,* Oct. 31, 1868.

43. New York *Daily Tribune,* Sept. 22, 1868.

44. *KKK Report,* Alabama, pp. 660–61, 933–34.

45. *Ibid.,* p. 723; W. B. Figures to Gov. Smith, Huntsville, Oct. 20, 1868, Governors' Correspondence, Alabama Archives. Compare the reverent account of the Klan around Athens in Susan Lawrence Davis, *Authentic History, Ku Klux Klan, 1865–1877* (N.Y., 1924).

46. Nashville *Press and Times,* Oct. 19, 1868; letters of J. Ronayne, Huntsville, Oct. 15, 1868, and W. B. Figures, Huntsville, Oct. 20, 1868, in Governors' Correspondence, Alabama Archives.

47. B. Lentz to Gov. Smith, Elk River, Ala., Nov. 1, 1868, in Governors' Correspondence, Alabama Archives.

48. John H. Wager to Col. E. Beecher, Athens, Oct. 14, 1868, in Athens, Ala., Letters Sent book, 1868–69, Freedmen's Bureau Records, RG 105, NA.

49. W. B. Figures to Gov. Smith, Huntsville, Oct. 20, 1868, Governors' Correspondence, Alabama Archives.

50. Huntsville *Advocate,* Nov. 3, 1868; *KKK Report,* Alabama, pp. 599, 602, 614, 618, 785–86, 818–21, 834, 849, 854, 873–75, 900–2, 910; Stanley F. Horn, *Invisible Empire: The Story of the Ku Klux Klan, 1866–1871* (Boston, 1939), pp. 131–35.

51. Walter Lynwood Fleming, *Civil War and Reconstruction in Alabama* (N.Y., 1905), pp. 694–95. See the governor's later explanation of his policy, in *Alabama House Journal,* 1869–1870, pp. 10–13.

52. *Alabama Senate Journal,* 1868, pp. 248–49.

53. For the resolution of Nov. 14, 1868 creating the joint investigating committee, see *Acts of the Sessions of July, September and November, 1868, of the General Assembly of Alabama . . . ,* p. 593. For the report, see Alabama General Assembly, *Report of Joint Committee on Outrages* (Montgomery, 1868), esp. pp. 3–6.

54. *Acts of . . . 1868,* pp. 444–46, 452–54.

55. See *House Miscellaneous Documents,* 40th Congress, 3d sess., No. 53, pp. 55, 144–45; Little Rock *Morning Republican,* Sept. 10, 1868; Memphis *Evening Post,* Sept. 25, 1868; Irby C. Nichols, "Reconstruction in De Soto County," *Mississippi Historical Society Publications,* XI (1910), 311; Albert T. Morgan, *Yazoo, or the Picket Line of Freedom in the South* (Washington, 1884), pp. 236, 243–44, 246, 261; *KKK Report,* Mississippi, p. 262.

56. New York *Daily Tribune,* Oct. 31, 1868, Dec. 31, 1870; *House Executive Documents,* 40th Congress, 3d sess., No. 1, III, pt. 1, pp. 187, 1056–57; Kentucky reports for Sept. to Nov. 1868, Synopses of Reports of Assistant Commissioners, 1867–1869, Freedmen's Bureau Records, RG 105, NA; *Senate Executive Documents,* 41st Congress, 3d sess., No. 46; *New York Times,* June 26, 1869; Nashville *Press and Times,* Sept. 23, 1868 (regarding Henderson); Frankfort *Commonwealth,* Nov. 13, 1868. Cf. Louisville *Courier-Journal,* Nov. 16, 24, 1868.

57. *Senate Reports,* 42d Congress, 1st sess., No. 1, p. li.

58. *New York Times,* Aug. 4, 1869.

59. New York *Daily Tribune,* Oct. 31, 1868; *Senate Miscellaneous Documents,* 42d Congress, 1st sess., No. 49.
60. *New York Times,* Aug. 4, 1869.
61. Kentucky report for Sept. 1868, Synopses of Reports of Assistant Commissioners, 1867–1869, Freedmen's Bureau Records, RG 105, NA; Frankfort *Commonwealth,* Oct. 16, 23, 1868.
62. New York *Daily Tribune,* Dec. 25, 1868.
63. Gov. Harrison Reed, Tallahassee, Fla., Sept. 2, 1868, and Wm. E. Chandler and Wm. Claflin, New York City, Sept. 10, 1868, to Gov. Smith, Governors' Correspondence, Alabama Archives.
64. Thomas L. Tullock to Gov. Smith, Washington, Oct. 22, 1868, Governors' Correspondence, Alabama Archives.

CHAPTER 8: LOUISIANA

1. *House Miscellaneous Documents,* 41st Congress, 1st sess., No. 12, pp. 12–15, 19; *ibid.,* 41st Congress, 2d sess., No. 154, pt. 1, pp. 404–6, 443–46, 450–51, 549–50, 554–55, 560, 564, 568, 572–73, 634, 670; Louisiana General Assembly, *Report of the Joint Committee . . . on the Conduct of the State Elections and the Condition of Peace and Order in the State, Session of 1869* (New Orleans, 1869), pp. 9–11, 95–98, 104, 109, 189, 204; Henry Clay Warmoth, *War, Politics and Reconstruction: Stormy Days in Louisiana* (N.Y., 1930), pp. 67–70.
2. *House Miscellaneous Documents,* 41st Congress, 2d sess., No. 154, pt. 1, pp. 413, 462, 517–18, 570, 601, 667–68.
3. Estimates of casualties varied from 20 to more than 200, but Democratic newspapers and a later Republican legislative investigation both tended to favor a figure near 200. *Ibid.,* p. 416; New Orleans *Republican,* Oct. 3, 5, 8, 12, 1868; *Report of the Joint Committee . . . 1869,* pp. 14, 73–94; Warmoth, *War, Politics and Reconstruction,* p. 67.
4. *House Miscellaneous Documents,* 41st Congress, 2d sess., No. 154, pt. 1, pp. 275–78, 282–83, 349.
5. New Orleans *Republican,* Nov. 19, 1868; *Report of the Joint Committee . . . 1869,* p. 148.
6. *House Miscellaneous Documents,* 41st Congress, 2d sess., No. 154, pt. 1, pp. 284–85, 470, 525–26; *ibid.,* pt. 2, pp. 48–49.
7. *Ibid.,* pt. 1, pp. 147, 149, 605, 607, 662–63.
8. For the Caddo and Bossier murders, see *Report of the Joint Committee . . . 1869,* pp. 15–17, 121–24, 133 ff. For information on Klan activity in this part of the state, see *ibid.,* pp. 153, 155, 172, 176, 281–82; *House Miscellaneous Documents,* 41st Congress, 1st sess., No. 16, p. 7; *ibid.,* 2d sess., No. 154, pt. 1, pp. 69, 75, 144–45, 153–54, 199, 210–11, 216, 293–94 311, 328–30, 364–365, 478–79, 527, 531, 589–91, 607–8, 678, 700, 716, 718–19, 726–31; pt. 2, pp. 13, 17–18, 22–23, 26–28, 66–67, 154–55, 162–63, 168–69, 362, 364, 388, 390, 396, 400–1, 405,

407–9, 496–97; Shreveport *South-Western*, Jan. 6, Feb. 17, 1869; New Orleans *Republican*, Nov. 17, Dec. 26, 1868.

9. For Washington Parish, see *House Miscellaneous Documents*, 41st Congress, 1st sess., No. 13, pp. 23–24; *ibid.*, 2d sess., No. 154, pt. 1, pp. 223, 308, 370, 394, 397–98, 400–1; *Report of the Joint Committee . . . 1869*, pp. 130–31. For St. Tammany, see *House Miscellaneous Documents*, 41st Congress, 1st sess., No. 13, p. 42; *Report of the Joint Committee . . . 1869*, pp. 151–52; New Orleans *Republican*, Oct. 15, 1868.

10. For St. Helena, see *House Miscellaneous Documents*, 41st Congress, 1st sess., No. 13, pp. 20, 27; *ibid.*, 2d sess., No. 154, pt. 1, pp. 83, 85, 90–91, 95, 97–99, 225–26, 238, 295–301, 401; *ibid.*, pt. 2, pp. 104–6; *Report of the Joint Committee . . . 1869*, pp. 193–202.

11. *Report of the Joint Committee . . . 1869*, p. 265; *House Miscellaneous Documents*, 41st Congress, 2d sess., No. 154, pt. 2, pp. 84–87, 320–45.

12. New Orleans *Republican*, Sept. 23, 26, 1868.

13. *Report of the Joint Committee . . . 1869*, pp. 18, 111 ff.

14. Minutes of meeting, Sept. 29, 1868, Wharton Family Papers, Department of Archives and Manuscripts, Louisiana State University.

15. *House Miscellaneous Documents*, 41st Congress, 2d sess., No. 154, pt. 2, pp. 331–33; John M. Bonner to his mother, New Orleans, Oct. 13, 1868, Bonner Family Papers, Department of Archives and Manuscripts, Louisiana State University.

16. *Report of the Joint Committee . . . 1869*, p. 263; *House Miscellaneous Documents*, 41st Congress, 2d sess., No. 154, pt. 2, pp. 87, 527–29.

17. *Report of the Joint Committee . . . 1869*, pp. 17, 23, 47–61, 263–68.

18. *Ibid.*, pp. 11–13, 23–25, 213 ff., 266; report of Gen. Rousseau in New Orleans *Times*, Dec. 4, 1868. See correction of details regarding the number of blacks and whites on the police force, in the issue of Dec. 13, 1868. See also Warmoth, *War, Politics and Reconstruction*, pp. 76–78; New Orleans *Republican*, Oct. 27–31, Nov. 5, 1868; *House Miscellaneous Documents*, 41st Congress, 2d sess., No. 154, pt. 2, pp. 516–17. Prior to the outbreak it was announced in KWC Councils that members could go to one or more gun shops owned by members and take what guns they needed, charging them to the order. *Report of the Joint Committee . . . 1869*, p. 267. Members of the KWC later denied steadfastly that they were anything but a peaceful defensive order, or that they had influenced the outcome of the election in any way. See *House Miscellaneous Documents*, 41st Congress, 2d sess., No. 154, pt. 2, pp. 235, 237, 273, 279, 286, 296, 339–43.

19. Louisiana report for Oct. 1868, Synopses of Reports of Assistant Commissioners, 1867–1869, Freedmen's Bureau Records, RG 105, NA.

20. *KKK Report*, Committee Report, pp. 251–52.

21. *House Miscellaneous Documents*, 41st Congress, 2d sess., No. 154, pt. 2, pp. 313–17.

22. See *ibid.*, pp. 319–20; New Orleans *Times*, Nov. 21, 1868.

23. *Report of the Joint Committee . . . 1869*, pp. 19, 26, 301–21; New Orleans *Republican*, Oct. 31, Nov. 2, 3, 1868; report of Gen. Rousseau in New Orleans *Times*, Dec. 4, 1868; Warmoth, *War, Politics and Reconstruction*, pp. 78–79; *House Miscellaneous Documents*, 41st Congress, 2d sess., No. 154, pt. 1, Appendix, p. xxvi; pt. 2, p. 521; *KKK Report*, Committee Report, p. 250.
24. *Report of the Joint Committee . . . 1869*, esp. pp. 268–69; New Orleans *Republican*, Dec. 2, 1868; Allie Bayne Windham Webb, "Organization and Activities of the Knights of the White Camelia in Louisiana, 1867–1869," Louisiana Academy of Sciences, *Proceedings*, XVII (1954), pp. 115–17.
25. See the partial membership list and the preamble to its constitution, in Walter Lynwood Fleming (ed.), *Documents Relating to Reconstruction* (Morgantown, W. Va., 1904), nos. 4–5, pp. 59–60.
26. After the 1868 election Democratic leaders sometimes tried to discourage violence which no longer served their purposes. When a disguised band pillaged a plantation and murdered three Negroes in De Soto Parish late in December the local Democratic newspaper condemned the action and a special public meeting was held for the same purpose. Shreveport *South-Western*, Jan. 6, Feb. 17, 1869. For evidence of an extensive Ku Klux organization localized around Colfax late in 1871, see *New York Times*, Dec. 7, 1871.

CHAPTER 9: TEXAS: THE KNIGHTS OF THE RISING SUN

1. *Journal of the Reconstruction Convention . . . Austin, Texas . . . 1868*, 2 vols. (Austin, 1870), II, 108–9, 113–14, 125–26, 132–33; Houston *Union*, Sept. 30, Nov. 5, 1868, Jan. 2, 15, 1869; *Daily Austin Republican*, Sept. 21, Oct. 22, 1868.
2. Letters to Gov. Pease from H. C. Pedigo, Sumter, Tex., Sept. 11, 1868; Anonymous, Sumpter [*sic*], Nov. 12, 1868; S. Hackworth, [Washington County, *ca.* Nov. 1868]; and J. A. Wright, Palestine, Tex., Jan. 13, 1869, Governors' Correspondence, Archives Division, Texas State Library.
3. Quoted in report of Secretary of War for 1868, *House Executive Documents*, 40th Congress, 3d sess., No. 1, III, pt. 1, pp. 704–5.
4. Reprinted in Montgomery *Alabama State Journal*, Jan. 30, 1869.
5. Gov. Elisha Pease to Gen. J. J. Reynolds, Sept. 22, 1868, Pease letterbooks, Governors' Correspondence, Archives Division, Texas State Library.
6. See Marshall *Texas Republican*, Aug. 28, 1868.
7. New York *Daily Tribune*, Sept. 18, 1868; James E. Sefton, *The United States Army and Reconstruction, 1865–1877* (Baton Rouge, 1967), pp. 191–92. For references to Ku Klux demonstrations and warnings in Ellis and Van Zandt counties, see Marshall *Texas Republican*, Sept. 25, Oct. 9, 1868.
8. Marshall *Texas Republican*, Dec. 4, 1868.

9. *Ibid.,* Sept. 11, Oct. 9, 1868; J. H. Fowler to Gov. Pease, [Paris, Tex.], Sept. 19, 1868, Governors' Correspondence, Archives Division, Texas State Library; résumé of letter of Col. D. C. Brown to Gen. J. J. Reynolds, Paris, Oct. 28, 1868, in Texas, Assistant Commissioner, Register of Letters Received, 1867–69; report of Brown for Oct. 1868, Texas Monthly Reports, Freedmen's Bureau Records, RG 105, NA.

10. Report of Lieut. E. C. Henshaw, Marshall, Tex., for Nov. 1868, Texas Monthly Reports, Freedmen's Bureau Records, RG 105, NA.

11. Report of Lieut. H. Sweeney, Jefferson, Tex., for Oct. 1868, in Texas Monthly Reports, Freedmen's Bureau Records, RG 105, NA; Judge C. Caldwell to Gov. Pease, Jefferson, Sept. 30, 1868, Governors' Correspondence, Archives Division, Texas State Library; New Orleans *Republican,* quoted in Shreveport *South-Western,* Dec. 2, 1868. The marauding extended into Davis (now Cass) County, immediately to the north, where seven Negroes were killed in a raid on a single plantation in October. Marshall *Texas Republican,* Oct. 23, 1868; Gov. Pease to Gen. J. J. Reynolds, Sept. 10, 1868, Governor Pease letterbooks, Governors' Correspondence, Archives Division, Texas State Library.

12. Maj. James Curtis to Gen. J. J. Reynolds, Jefferson, Sept. 19, 1868, in Texas, Assistant Commissioner, Letters Received, Freedmen's Bureau Records, RG 105, NA.

13. Marshall *Texas Republican,* Sept. 25, 1868.

14. This account, including the quotations, is based primarily upon an article by the former Bureau agent, in the New York *Daily Tribune,* July 31, 1869. See also Gen. George P. Buell to Lieut. L. V. Caziarc, Jefferson, Feb. 10, 1869, in Fifth Military District, Post of Jefferson, Tex., vol. 331: Letters Sent, 1868–1869, RG 98, NA; transcript of testimony before later military court, in clippings from the Jefferson *Times,* in Records of the House Select Committee on Reconstruction: Texas, No. 641, RG 233, NA; New Orleans *Republican,* Oct. 12, 24, 28, 1868; *Daily Austin Republican,* Oct. 23, 1868; Houston *Union,* May 10, 1869.

15. New Orleans *Republican,* Oct. 12, 13, 24, 1868; *Daily Austin Republican,* Oct. 23, 1868; Houston *Union,* May 10, 1869; D. Campbell to Gov. Pease, New Orleans, Nov. 3, 1868, Governors' Correspondence, Archives Division, Texas State Library; testimony of Richard Figures before military court, June 2, 1869, in clippings from Jefferson *Times,* in Records of House Select Committee on Reconstruction: Texas, No. 641, RG 233, NA.

16. The files of the Jefferson *Times* for this period are apparently lost, but its accounts were copied by the Marshall *Texas Republican* (Oct. 16, 30, Nov. 13, 1868, Jan. 15, 1869), a Democratic paper despite its name, which added similar remarks of its own, and by the *Daily Austin Republican* (Nov. 25, 1868), which was Republican in affiliation.

17. C. T. Garland of Jefferson, for instance, declared in a speech in May 1869 that the real grievance against Smith was that he associated with Negroes and induced them to join the Republican party. "I can produce

a thousand witnesses, if necessary, to swear that Smith invariably exhorted them to be good and law-abiding citizens." Houston *Union,* May 24, 1869; see also *ibid.,* Feb. 5, May 10, 1869.

18. Judge Caldwell was given similar treatment after his escape from Jefferson. Democratic papers began circulating a story that he arrived in Houston in January 1869 in a state of intoxication. While drunk, they said, he went to the home of one of the first families, interrupting a dinner party, and demanded "a girl and a bed." On being ejected, he went to a saloon where he insulted a stranger and received a beating in return. Houston *Times,* Jan. 20, 1869, copied in Shreveport *South-Western,* Feb. 10, 1869. To this the editor of the *Republican* in Austin could only reply that he knew Caldwell well, that he never saw him take more than a glass of beer, and that so far as he knew, Caldwell's personal character was above reproach; if the story was true, he continued, he had no excuse for Caldwell, but before believing it he required better authority than the editor of the Houston *Times. Weekly Austin Republican,* Feb. 3, 1869. Like the imputations of communism in later times, it was easier to make such accusations than it was to refute them even when they were false.

19. *Daily Austin Republican,* Oct. 21, 1868.

20. For the soldier tipping off a friend of Mabry's, see Winnie Mims Dean, *Jefferson, Texas, Queen of the Cypress* (Dallas, 1953), p. 34.

21. Marshall *Texas Republican,* Nov. 6, Dec. 11, 1868, Jan. 15, Feb. 26, March 26, April 2, 23, May 21, 28, 1869; New York *Daily Tribune,* July 13, 31, 1869; Shreveport *South-Western,* March 10, April 7, May 26, June 2, 1869; Houston *Union,* March 3, Sept. 14, Oct. 28, 30, Nov. 6, 1869; clippings from Jefferson *Times* on the trial proceedings, in Records of the House Select Committee on Reconstruction: Texas, No. 641, RG 233, NA; Capt. James B. Brown to Lieut. C. E. Morse, Jefferson, Nov. 4, 10, 24, Dec. 8, 11, 12, 1868; Gen. George P. Buell to Asst. Adj. Gen. of Fifth Military District, Jefferson, Dec. 24, Dec. 25 (telegram), 1868, Jan. 14, 15, 20, Feb. 10, 19, April 5, 1869, in Fifth Military District, vol. 331: Post of Jefferson, Tex., Letters Sent, 1868–1869; same to same, Jefferson, March 9, 19, 1869; [Buell] to Judge Duval, April 24, 1869; Lieut. B. F. Grafton to Thomas Smith, Jefferson, June 21, 1869; Buell to Capt. C. E. Morse, July 1, Aug. 16, Oct. 31, 1869, Jan. 18, 1870; same to Col. H. C. Wood, June 29, 1869; orders of Oct. 8, 22, 1869, in Records of Post of Jefferson, Tex.: Letters Sent book, 1869–1870; summary of letter of R. W. Loughery to [Buell], Jefferson, March 6, 1869, in Fifth Military District, vol. 343: Post of Jefferson, Tex.: Register of Letters Received, 1869–1870, RG 98, NA.

22. See Boyd W. Johnson, "Cullen Montgomery Baker: The Arkansas-Texas Desperado," *Arkansas Historical Quarterly,* XXV (Autumn 1966), 229–39.

23. The total number of troops stationed in Texas in this period actually decreased somewhat. See Robert W. Shook, "The Federal Military in Texas, 1865–1870," *Texas Military History,* VI (Spring 1967), 20, 48–51.

24. *New York Times,* Oct. 25, 1868.

25. Résumé of letter of Lieut. H. Sweeney, Dec. 14, 1868, in Texas, Assistant Commissioner, Letters Received, Freedmen's Bureau Records, RG 105, NA.

26. Sefton, *The United States Army and Reconstruction,* pp. 192–93.

27. For references to Klan activity in 1869, 1870, and 1871, see *Weekly Austin Republican,* Feb. 17, Oct. 6, 1869; *State Journal Appendix Containing Official Report of the Debates and Proceedings of the Twelfth Legislature,* vol. I (Austin, 1870), pp. 27, 82 ff.; Gov. E. J. Davis to Gen. J. J. Reynolds, April 9, 1870, and to C. D. Morris, Dec. 7, 1870, in Executive Record Books, Correspondence Series, Archives Division, Texas State Library; William C. Nunn, *Texas Under the Carpetbaggers* (Austin, 1961), pp. 248–52; *KKK Report,* Committee Report, p. 211; *House Executive Documents,* 42d Congress, 2d sess., No. 268, p. 48.

28. *Texas Senate Journal,* First Session, 1870, pp. 14–15.

29. H. P. N. Gammel (comp.), *The Laws of Texas, 1822–1897,* 10 vols. (Austin, 1898), VI, 185–86, 190, 193–95; VII, 21–23.

30. See *KKK Report,* Committee Report, p. 210; *ibid.,* Miscellaneous Testimony, p. 355; *House Executive Documents,* 42d Congress, 2d sess., No. 268, pp. 47–49; Ann Patton Baenziger, "The Texas State Police During Reconstruction: A Reexamination," *Southwestern Historical Quarterly,* LXXII (April 1969), 470–91.

CHAPTER 10: THE ARKANSAS MILITIA VS. THE KU KLUX KLAN

1. Gen. C. H. Smith to Gen. L. H. Rousseau, Little Rock, Nov. 3, 1868, copy in Governors' Letters Received (letterbook), Arkansas History Commission.

2. See Chapter 6.

3. Memphis *Evening Post,* Dec. 19, 1868.

4. *KKK Report,* Miscellaneous Testimony, p. 331; (?) F. White to Gov. Clayton, Helena, Ark., Sept. 19, 1868, Governors' Letters Received (letterbook), Arkansas History Commission; Little Rock *Morning Republican,* Sept. 18, Dec. 25, 1868.

5. Little Rock *Morning Republican,* Oct. 16, 1868, Feb. 16, 1869; Powell Clayton, *The Aftermath of the Civil War in Arkansas* (N.Y., 1915), p. 117. Dollar was accused (at least posthumously) of abandoning his family and living with a Negro woman. John M. Harrell, *The Brooks and Baxter War: A History of the Reconstruction Period in Arkansas* (St. Louis, 1893), p. 87.

6. *KKK Report,* Miscellaneous Testimony, p. 327; Little Rock *Morning Republican,* Feb. 12, 16, 1869; New York *Daily Tribune,* Nov. 14, 1868; William M. Harrison to Gov. Clayton, Monticello, Nov. 19, 1868, Governors' Letters Received (letterbook), Arkansas History Commission.

For comparable Ku Klux activities in Union, Bradley, Ashley, Columbia, and Ouachita counties, see Little Rock *Morning Republican*, Sept. 22, Oct. 17, 22, Nov. 25, 1868, Jan. 22, 1869; *KKK Report*, Miscellaneous Testimony, p. 329; Walter Hodges to Gov. Clayton, Camden, Sept. 22, 1868, Governors' Letters Received (letterbook), Arkansas History Commission. Cf. J. H. Atkinson (ed.), "Clayton and Catterson Rob Columbia County," *Arkansas Historical Quarterly*, XXI (Summer 1962), 153–55.

7. *KKK Report*, Miscellaneous Testimony, pp. 330–31; Little Rock *Morning Republican*, Jan. 22, 1869.

8. *KKK Report*, Miscellaneous Testimony, pp. 329–30; letters to Gov. Clayton from A. D. Hawkins, Rocky Comfort, Ark., Oct. 26, 1868, and Gen. C. H. Smith, Little Rock, Oct. 30, 1868, Governors' Letters Received (letterbook), Arkansas History Commission; Little Rock *Morning Republican*, Jan. 22, 1869. For reports of Klan murders and threats in Hempstead County, see Little Rock *Morning Republican*, Sept. 11, 1868.

9. *KKK Report*, Miscellaneous Testimony, pp. 331–32. See also Little Rock *Morning Republican*, Oct. 20, 1868, and other letters from Steel, Oct. 19, 1868, Jan. 13, March 4, 1869, in Governors' Letters Received (letterbook), Arkansas History Commission.

10. Little Rock *Morning Republican*, Oct. 20, Dec. 28, 1868.

11. Sheriff Spear later said that Mason was on his way to register voters, while other persons said he was acting as a law officer at the time.

12. If this was the force expansively referred to by General Shaver in his later reminiscence, it was certainly not poised to attack Little Rock as he said.

13. Democratic and Republican sources differ in both their selection and their interpretation of these facts. The chief Democratic accounts are to be found in the Batesville *North Arkansas Times*, Sept. 26, Oct. 3, 10, 1868, and in Harrell, *The Brooks and Baxter War*, pp. 73–77. The main Republican accounts are William Monks's reminiscences in his *History of Southern Missouri and Northern Arkansas* (West Plains, Mo., 1907), pp. 207–14, and the Little Rock *Morning Republican*, Oct. 6, 22, 1868. See also *KKK Report*, Miscellaneous Testimony, pp. 328, 331; letters to Gov. Clayton from Sheriff William E. Spear, Salem, Ark., Oct. 5, 1868; County Clerk Wiley King, Salem, Oct. 8, 1868; and John Creagan, Jacksonport, Ark., Oct. 4, 1868, Governors' Letters Received (letterbook), Arkansas History Commission; and telegrams to Clayton from Sheriff John J. Palmer et al., Batesville, Ark., Sept. 29, 1868, and Judge Elisha Baxter, Batesville, Oct. 1, 1868, in "Brooks and Baxter War Telegrams" scrapbook, Arkansas History Commission.

14. Letters to Gov. Clayton from John Creagan, Jacksonport, Ark., Oct. 4, 12, 23, Nov. 4, 1868; Capt. Wm. Briam, Jacksonport, Nov. 6, 1868; and D. P. Upham, Augusta, Ark., Oct. 4, 1868, in Governors' Letters Received (letterbook), Arkansas History Commission; *KKK Report*, Miscellaneous Testimony, pp. 330, 332; Little Rock *Morning Republican*, Nov. 7, Dec. 25, 1868.

15. Letters to Gov. Clayton from Capt. E. M. Main, Marion, Ark., Oct. 5,

1868; Gen. C. H. Smith, Little Rock, Oct. 29, 1868; and Senator E. G. Barker, Little Rock, Nov. 12, 1868, Governors' Letters Received (letterbook), Arkansas History Commission; Memphis *Evening Post,* Oct. 28, 1868; *Arkansas House Journal,* 1868–1869, p. 42; Clayton, *Aftermath of the Civil War in Arkansas,* pp. 135–37.

16. Little Rock *Morning Republican,* Nov. 25, 1868. Hinds's murderers were not discovered and may not have been Klansmen, but his death was part of the general terror in which the Klan took the leading part. Perhaps mention should also be made of Republican Congressman Thomas Haughey of Alabama, who was assassinated in the courthouse at Decatur, Alabama, in 1870, a year after his term in Congress had expired.

17. Memphis *Evening Post,* Jan. 28, 1869.

18. See Little Rock *Daily Arkansas Gazette,* Sept. 20, 1868; Little Rock *Morning Republican,* Sept. 22, 1868; Clayton, *Aftermath of the Civil War in Arkansas,* pp. 88 ff.

19. Clayton, *Aftermath of the Civil War in Arkansas,* pp. 57–58, 61–63, 74–87; *KKK Report,* Miscellaneous Testimony, pp. 362–90.

20. Little Rock *Morning Republican,* Sept. 28, 1868; governor's proclamation of Oct. 26, 1868, printed in Batesville *North Arkansas Times,* Oct. 31, 1868.

21. See summarized letters of Clayton to Gen. C. H. Smith, Aug. 18, 1868, and of Gen. Thomas H. Neill to Gen. Smith, New Orleans, Sept. 8, Oct. 7, 1868, in Fourth Military District Records, vol. 65: Letters Received, Commandant, District of Arkansas, 1868–1869, RG 98, NA.

22. Memphis *Avalanche,* as quoted in Memphis *Evening Post,* Oct. 8, 14, 1868, and Little Rock *Daily Arkansas Gazette,* Oct. 14, 1868.

23. Memphis *Avalanche,* as quoted in Memphis *Evening Post,* Oct. 17, 1868. See the account of James L. Hodges of the purchase of the arms, and of Capt. Houston concerning their capture, in Arkansas, *Report of the State Auditor, 1868* (Little Rock, 1868), pp. 7–11. Houston's report was originally submitted in a letter to Gov. Clayton, Memphis, Oct. 17, 1868, which is copied in the Governors' Letters Received (letterbook), Arkansas History Commission. Clayton reported on the incident and the prior efforts to secure arms in his message to the legislature of Nov. 24, 1868, printed in Little Rock *Morning Republican,* Nov. 25, 1868. He gave a later account in his *Aftermath of the Civil War in Arkansas,* pp. 106–8. See also newspaper accounts and comments in Little Rock *Morning Republican,* Oct. 5, 16, 17, 20, 1868; Batesville *North Arkansas Times,* Oct. 24, 1868; New York *Daily Tribune,* Oct. 29, 31, Nov. 2, 1868; and the account in Stanley F. Horn, *Invisible Empire: The Story of the Ku Klux Klan, 1866–1871* (Boston, 1939), pp. 248–52.

24. Clayton, *Aftermath of the Civil War in Arkansas,* pp. 108–9; Howard K. Beale (ed.), *Diary of Gideon Welles,* 3 vols. (N.Y., 1960), III, 460–62. Welles also repeated a Democratic newspaper canard that Clayton and one or more cronies had bought the guns as a speculation, intending to resell them to the state at a personal profit. The legislature had never appropriated

money for the weapons, but Clayton was confident that it would do so when it reassembled in November. Meanwhile he and several other men pledged their personal credit to reimburse the purchasing agent in the unlikely event that it refused. There seems to be no basis for the charge of profiteering. See his legislative message of Nov. 24, 1868, in Little Rock *Morning Republican*, Nov. 25, 1868.

25. Printed in Little Rock *Morning Republican*, Oct. 16, 1868.

26. See W. Dean Burnham, *Presidential Ballots, 1836–1892* (Baltimore, 1955), p. 896.

27. Printed in Little Rock *Daily Arkansas Gazette*, Nov. 6, 1868; Harrell, *The Brooks and Baxter War*, pp. 66–67.

28. See Little Rock *Morning Republican*, Nov. 19, 1868; Gen. C. H. Smith to Gov. Clayton, Little Rock, Oct. 30, 1868; copy of same to Gen. L. H. Rousseau, Little Rock, Nov. 3, 1868, Governors' Letters Received (letterbook), Arkansas History Commission; Smith's report to the Freedmen's Bureau for the last three months of 1868, in Synopses of Reports of Assistant Commissioners, 1867–1869, Freedmen's Bureau Records, RG 105, NA; and Smith to Gen. Thomas H. Neill, Nov. 3, 1868, Jan. 7, 1869, Fourth Military District Records, vol. 64: Commander, District of Arkansas, Letters Sent, 1868–1869, RG 98, NA.

29. Clayton, *Aftermath of the Civil War in Arkansas*, pp. 61, 63, 104–5; Little Rock *Morning Republican*, Nov. 25, 1868 (including his legislative message of the previous day); Clayton's letter to sheriffs and other officials, in *New York Times*, Nov. 18, 1868; Harrell, *The Brooks and Baxter War*, pp. 66–67.

30. The legislature was almost unanimously Republican in composition, owing to Democratic abstention during the state election earlier in the year. Replies Clayton received from legislators in answer to his communication of November 1 are preserved in the Governors' Letters Received (letterbook), Arkansas History Commission. Some opposed his policy altogether, but most were generally in approval.

31. Many years later Clayton explained that he had not dictated or approved this letter and regarded it as indiscreet, but that it accurately expressed his views nevertheless. *Aftermath of the Civil War in Arkansas*, pp. 290–91. See also Little Rock *Morning Republican*, Nov. 24, 25, 28, Dec. 7, 14–19, 1868, Jan. 20, 21, 1869; *New York Times*, Jan. 8, Feb. 1, 1869.

32. General Orders no. 8, in Little Rock *Morning Republican*, Nov. 17, 1868.

33. Clayton, *Aftermath of the Civil War in Arkansas*, pp. 108–11.

34. Report of Gen. Horace Porter, in *New York Times*, Jan. 8, 1869.

35. See Boyd W. Johnson, "Cullen Montgomery Baker: The Arkansas-Texas Desperado," *Arkansas Historical Quarterly*, XXV (Autumn 1966), pp. 229–39.

36. The governor subsequently ordered all militia detachments passing through counties not under martial law to report their presence as soon as possible to the sheriffs. Any bodies of men claiming to be militia who could not

show proper orders were subject to arrest. Little Rock *Daily Arkansas Gazette,* Jan. 17, 1869.

37. Republican and Democratic accounts of the Catterson campaign varied widely and cannot be fully reconciled. Both tended to omit certain events unfavorable to their respective views, and the interpretations were even more diverse. For Republican versions, see Clayton, *Aftermath of the Civil War in Arkansas,* pp. 111–16; Little Rock *Morning Republican,* Nov. 24, Dec. 2, 3, 17, 1868, Jan. 15, 22, 1869. See also letters to the governor from Catterson and Judge J. H. Willson of Sevier County, Nov. 27 to Dec. 16, 1868, in Governors' Letters Received (letterbook), Arkansas History Commission. Democratic accounts appeared in Little Rock *Daily Arkansas Gazette,* Jan. 3, 14–16, 1869; Washington (Ark.) *Telegraph,* Nov. 18, 1868, as quoted in Memphis *Appeal,* Nov. 29, 1868 (or Pulaski [Tenn.] *Citizen,* Dec. 4, 1868); Virginia Buxton (ed.), "Clayton's Militia in Sevier and Howard Counties," *Arkansas Historical Quarterly,* XX (Winter 1961), 344–50; J. H. Atkinson (ed.), "Clayton and Catterson Rob Columbia County," *ibid.,* XXI (Summer 1962), 155–57; Harrell, *The Brooks and Baxter War,* pp. 85–89, including Clayton's order regarding arrest and punishment.

38. Harrell, *The Brooks and Baxter War,* p. 86; Little Rock *Morning Republican,* Dec. 3, 17, 1868, Jan. 12, Feb. 5, 1869; Maj. R. L. Archer to Gov. Clayton, Magnolia, Ark., Dec. 26, 1868, Governors' Letters Received (letterbook), Arkansas History Commission.

39. For the southeastern campaign, see Clayton, *Aftermath of the Civil War in Arkansas,* pp. 116–18; Little Rock *Daily Arkansas Gazette,* Jan. 6, 7, 1869; Little Rock *Morning Republican,* Dec. 25, 1868; Harrell, *The Brooks and Baxter War,* pp. 86–87; letters to Gov. Clayton from Col. Mallory, Monticello, Dec. 6, 1868; Judge W. W. Hughey, Warren, Bradley County, Dec. 8, 1868; and Judge Will Harrison, Monticello, Jan. 23, 1869, in Governors' Letters Received (letterbook), Arkansas History Commission.

40. Clayton, *Aftermath of the Civil War in Arkansas,* pp. 144–63, 186; Little Rock *Morning Republican,* Dec. 7, 16, 1868; *KKK Report, Miscellaneous Testimony,* pp. 326–27 (including the quotation); letters to Clayton from Capt. J. L. Matthews, Capt. John Gibbons, and others in Conway County, Dec. 4–21, 1868, and from Gen. C. H. Smith, Little Rock, Jan. 15, 1869, Governors' Letters Received (letterbook), Arkansas History Commission; New York *Daily Tribune,* Dec. 10, 21, 22, 28, 1868, Jan. 4, 1869.

41. Letters to Gov. Clayton from John J. Cole, Searcy, Nov. 30, 1868; D. P. Upham, Batesville, Nov. 25, 1868; Sheriff W. W. Nisbett, Jonesboro, Nov. 16, Dec. 2, 1868; Sheriff R. L. Landers of Izard County, Nov. 25, Dec. 4, 1868, Governors' Letters Received (letterbook), Arkansas History Commission.

42. For the widely varying accounts of the operations in Woodruff County, see Clayton, *Aftermath of the Civil War in Arkansas,* pp. 119–25; Little Rock *Morning Republican,* Dec. 15 (including the governor's message to

the legislature), 21, 22, 25, 1868; Little Rock *Daily Arkansas Gazette,*
Jan. 17, 1869; Memphis *Evening Post,* Jan. 25, Feb. 5, 9, 1869;
telegrams to Gov. Clayton from Gen. Upham, Augusta, Dec. 19, 1868,
and to Adj. Gen. Danforth from Capt. J. H. Rosa, Augusta, Jan. 8, 1869,
in "Brooks and Baxter War Telegrams" scrapbook, Arkansas History
Commission; letters to Clayton from Upham, Augusta, Dec. 9, 15, 18,
1868, and undated letter (received Dec. 31, 1868) accompanied by
resolutions of citizens of Woodruff County, in Governors' Letters Received
(letterbook), Arkansas History Commission; Harrell, *The Brooks and
Baxter War,* pp. 80–84; Margaret T. Rose, "Clayton's Aftermath of the
Civil War in Arkansas," *Arkansas Historical Association Publications,* IV
(1917), 59, 64–65.
43. Telegrams from Adj. Gen. Danforth to Gov. Clayton, Augusta, Jan. 20,
1869; Lieut. Col. E. M. Main to Danforth, Marion, Ark., Feb. 15, 1869;
and Lieut. Col. Wm. Monks to Gov. Clayton, Jacksonport, Ark., Feb. 23,
1869, in "Brooks and Baxter War Telegrams" scrapbook, Arkansas History
Commission; Monks, *History of Southern Missouri and Northern Arkansas,*
pp. 221–26; Little Rock *Morning Republican,* Feb. 17, 1869.
44. Clayton, *Aftermath of the Civil War in Arkansas,* pp. 126–30, 134–37,
142–43, 163, 181–82 (including the quotation about Clarence Collier);
KKK Report, Miscellaneous Testimony, p. 329; letters to Gov. Clayton
from Col. J. L. Watson [Crittenden County], Jan. 3, 15, 1869; Gen.
Gideon J. Pillow, Memphis, Jan. 20, 1869; Gen. D. P. Upham, n.p.,
Jan. 25, 1869; Maj. E. M. Main, Marion, Feb. 26, 1869, Governors'
Letters Received (letterbook), Arkansas History Commission; *Arkansas
House Journal,* 1868–1869, pp. 42, 407–8, 732–33; *Arkansas Senate
Journal,* 1868–1869, pp. 709–10; J. B. Heiskell to Gov. D. C. Senter,
Memphis, March 5, 1869, in Governors' Correspondence, Tennessee State
Library and Archives; L. B. Eaton to Gen. John Eaton, Memphis, March
7, 1869, in John Eaton Papers, University of Tennessee; Nashville *Press
and Times,* Jan. 25, Feb. 20, 1869; Memphis *Evening Post,* Oct. 28,
Nov. 28, Dec. 15, 23, 1868, March 2, 3, 10, 11, April 8, 1869;
Little Rock *Morning Republican,* Nov. 30, Dec. 22, 23, 31, 1868, Jan.
4–8, 11–13, 18, 20–21, 27–29, Feb. 1, 4, 6, 13, 15, March 3, 6, 8, 11,
15–16, 23, 25, 1869; Memphis *Appeal,* quoted in Little Rock *Daily
Arkansas Gazette,* Jan. 6, 9, 10, March 30, 1869; New York *Daily
Tribune,* July 21, 1869; *New York Times,* Jan. 19, March, 7, July 21,
1869.
45. *Arkansas House Journal,* 1868–1869, pp. 227, 408; *ibid.,* 1871, p. 39;
KKK Report, Committee Report, p. 186.
46. See Little Rock *Morning Republican,* Jan. 27, 1869; Judge W. L. Brown
to Gov. Clayton, Georgetown, Ark., May 4, 1869, Governors' Letters
Received (letterbook), Arkansas History Commission.
47. See Little Rock *Morning Republican,* Jan. 12–13, 16, March 23, 1869;
Clayton, *Aftermath of the Civil War in Arkansas,* pp. 204–6.
48. Nashville *Press and Times,* Jan. 23, 1869.

49. Memphis *Appeal,* Dec. 31, 1868, quoted in Little Rock *Daily Arkansas Gazette,* Jan. 6, 1869.
50. In later years the most jaundiced Democratic view became accepted as historical truth. See, for example, Harrell, *The Brooks and Baxter War,* and Thomas S. Staples, *Reconstruction in Arkansas, 1862–1874* (N.Y., 1923), pp. 294–302. With the more favorable recent view of Radical Reconstruction as a whole, this hostility has abated somewhat. See the brief but more balanced discussion in Orval T. Driggs, Jr., "The Issues of the Powell Clayton Regime, 1868–1871," *Arkansas Historical Quarterly,* VIII (1949), 22–28.
51. Clayton, *Aftermath of the Civil War in Arkansas,* pp. 132–33, 202–4; *New York Times,* Jan. 8, 1869 (for Porter's report); New York *Daily Tribune,* Dec. 22, 23, 28, 1868; letters to Gov. Clayton from Senator B. F. Rice, Washington, Nov. 23, 26, 1868, Governors' Letters Received (letterbook), Arkansas History Commission; report of state senate committee to investigate militia outrages, in *Arkansas Senate Journal,* 1868–1869, pp. 709–11; telegrams to Gov. Clayton from Senator B. F. Rice *et al.,* Washington, Jan. 16, 1869, and Representatives James T. Elliott and Logan H. Roots, Washington, Jan. 22, 1869, in "Brooks and Baxter War Telegrams" scrapbook, Arkansas History Commission. In his *Aftermath of the Civil War in Arkansas,* pp. 197–202, Clayton quotes effectively from Democratic newspapers around the state in 1869–70, which commented upon the unparalleled prosperity and good order prevailing in their regions. This was in the wake of his militia campaign, although they seldom if ever made that connection.
52. Quoted in Little Rock *Morning Republican,* Feb. 1, 1869.
53. New Orleans *Republican,* Nov. 10, 13, 1868.
54. *Congressional Globe,* 42d Congress, 1st sess., Appendix, p. 200.
55. *Acts, Resolutions and Memorials of the General Assembly of the State of Arkansas,* Session of November 1868, pp. 63–69; Charles Nordhoff, *The Cotton States in the Spring and Summer of 1875* (N.Y., 1876), p. 35; Staples, *Reconstruction in Arkansas,* p. 306; Little Rock *Morning Republican,* April 3, 1869 (for the Klan resignations).

CHAPTER 11: TENNESSEE: ABORTIVE MARTIAL LAW AND DISBANDMENT

1. *House Miscellaneous Documents,* 41st Congress, 2d sess., No. 53, pp. 180–84, 216–18, 227–28, 240–41; Pulaski *Citizen,* Nov. 6, 13, 1868.
2. For Lincoln County, see *House Miscellaneous Documents,* 41st Congress, 2d sess., No. 53, pp. 24, 33–35, 162, 164, 166–70, 176–77, 252. In September Klansmen in Lincoln County attacked a Negro house in which arms were reportedly being stored. The freedmen inside resisted, killing one Klansman. The attackers then withdrew, but later returned, captured one of the blacks, and hanged him. Pulaski *Citizen,* Sept. 11, 1868. For

the Klan activity in Franklin County, see *House Miscellaneous Documents,* 41st Congress, 2d sess., No. 53, pp. 76, 82, 138, 140–41, 143, 145, 149, 151–52, 155. For Coffee County, *ibid.,* pp. 6, 8, 10, 17, 229–30, 234–36. For Bedford County, *ibid.,* p. 255. For Marshall County, *ibid.,* pp. 43, 47, 49, 52, 55–56, 58, 244–46, 256. For Rutherford County, *ibid.,* pp. 192, 194, 196, 213–16. For Overton County, Nashville *Press and Times,* Jan. 10, 1869. The Memphis *Evening Post* also carried a number of articles concerning Ku Klux activity in middle and west Tennessee both before and after the election.

3. Nashville *Press and Times,* Nov. 10, 1868.

4. *House Miscellaneous Documents,* 41st Congress, 2d sess., No. 143, p. 58; New York *Daily Tribune,* Nov. 2, 4, 1868; Memphis *Evening Post,* Oct. and Nov. 1868, *passim.* See also Nashville *Telegram,* Sept. 18, 1868, as quoted in *Daily Austin* (Tex.) *Republican,* Sept. 30, 1868; Nashville *Press and Times,* Oct. 31, Nov. 10, 1868. Cf. Thomas B. Alexander, *Political Reconstruction in Tennessee* (Nashville, 1950), pp. 189–91.

5. Alexander, *Political Reconstruction in Tennessee,* pp. 191–94. See also *Congressional Globe,* 41st Congress, 3d sess., Appendix, p. 214. Cf. E. Merton Coulter, *William G. Brownlow, Fighting Parson of the Southern Highlands* (Chapel Hill, N.C., 1937), p. 366.

6. Memphis *Evening Post,* Nov. 1868–Jan. 1869, *passim,* esp. issue of Dec. 2, 1868; Memphis *Avalanche,* quoted in Nashville *Press and Times,* Jan. 18, 1869.

7. *House Miscellaneous Documents,* 41st Congress, 2d sess., No. 53, pp. 232–33, 235–36; Nashville *Press and Times,* Jan. 14, 1869.

8. *House Miscellaneous Documents,* 41st Congress, 2d sess., No. 53, p. 261; Memphis *Post,* Jan. 6, 1869, as quoted in Montgomery *Alabama State Journal,* Jan. 11, 1869; Nashville *Press and Times,* Jan. 9, 14, 1869; Little Rock *Morning Republican,* Jan. 12, 1869.

9. Nashville *Press and Times,* Jan. 10, 12, 15, 27, 1869. The authority for the Ku Klux execution of its own member is Gen. G. G. Dibrell, the Grand Titan of that congressional district. See Nashville *Republican Banner,* Jan. 17, 1869. For other references to Klan activity in middle Tennessee from November 1868 through January 1869, see *House Miscellaneous Documents,* 41st Congress, 2d sess., No. 53, pp. 18, 22, 30, 35, 54, 81, 84, 152, 158, 162, 252, 256; Nashville *Press and Times,* Jan. 19, 20, 27, 1869.

10. The published details of this episode are sketchy and inconsistent. For contemporary or near-contemporary accounts, see Nashville *Press and Times,* Jan. 13, 14, 1869; Nashville *Republican Banner,* Jan. 14, 15, Feb. 27, 1869; *KKK Report,* Georgia, pp. 748–49. For a much later reminiscence by a Klansman who claimed to have tipped off his brethren about Barmore, see Nashville *Banner,* May 3, 1936. See also the full but undocumented account in Stanley F. Horn, *Invisible Empire: The Story of the Ku Klux Klan, 1866–1871* (Boston, 1939), pp. 108–12.

11. Report of F. H. Reeves, Columbia, for Dec. 1868, Tennessee Monthly

Reports, Freedmen's Bureau Records, RG 105, NA; *House Miscellaneous Documents*, 41st Congress, 2d sess., No. 53, pp. 180, 182–85, 216, 219, 240–41; *Brownlow's Knoxville Whig*, Dec. 16, 1868; Pulaski *Citizen*, Dec. 11, 1868; Nashville *Republican Banner*, Dec. 22, 29, 1868. The Fayetteville *Observer*, also a Klan supporter, now changed its position the same way. See issue of Dec. 10, 1868. The resentment and fear of Klan excesses by its erstwhile sympathizers and leaders are also reflected in Lester and Wilson's later treatment of this period. See J. C. Lester and D. L. Wilson, *Ku Klux Klan*, ed. by W. L. Fleming (N.Y., 1905), pp. 100 ff.

12. Nashville *Republican Banner*, Jan. 15, 1869, quoted in Nashville *Press and Times*, Jan. 16, 1869.

13. *American Annual Cyclopaedia*, 1869, p. 661 (for the Shelbyville statement); Nashville *Republican Banner*, Jan. 17, 26, 1869; Nashville *Press and Times*, Jan. 22, 1869; *House Miscellaneous Documents*, 41st Congress, 2d sess., No. 53, p. 231.

14. The order is reproduced in Susan Lawrence Davis, *Authentic History, Ku Klux Klan, 1865–1877* (N.Y., 1924), pp. 125–27, where the author misdates the document and misunderstands its meaning. It carries the heading "Dismal Era, 4th Green Day, Last Hour, C.A.R.N." According to the Prescript this is translated as 12 o'clock on the fourth Monday of January 1869. That day fell on January 25. See Horn, *Invisible Empire*, pp. 37, 40, 356–57, 409. See also Thomas B. Alexander, "Kukluxism in Tennessee, 1865–1869," *Tennessee Historical Quarterly*, VIII (1949), 217–18, or his *Political Reconstruction in Tennessee*, pp. 197–98.

15. *Acts of the State of Tennessee*, 1868–1869, pp. 14–15; Nashville *Press and Times*, Jan. 16, 1869.

16. Nashville *Press and Times*, Jan. 26, 1869.

17. Quoted in Nashville *Press and Times*, Jan. 18, 1869.

18. Nashville *Republican Banner*, Jan. 26, 1869; Nashville *Press and Times*, Jan. 26, 1869; *House Miscellaneous Documents*, 41st Congress, 2d sess., No. 53, pp. 252–53.

19. Republican legislators testified to a marked improvement in many counties by mid-February. Nashville *Press and Times*, Feb. 18, 1869.

20. *KKK Report*, Committee Report, p. 460 (for Brownlow's proclamation). His reasoning is set forth by a Knoxville correspondent in the *New York Times*, Jan. 31, 1869. The counties involved were Overton, Jackson, Maury, Giles, Marshall, Lawrence, Gibson, Madison, and Haywood. On the basis of surviving evidence, several others would have been at least as appropriate as Jackson, Lawrence, and Madison. There was no explanation why these counties rather than others were singled out.

21. Nashville *Republican Banner*, Feb. 25, 1869. Cf. the discussion in James W. Patton, *Unionism and Reconstruction in Tennessee, 1860–1869* (Chapel Hill, N.C., 1934), pp. 199–200; Alexander, *Political Reconstruction in Tennessee*, pp. 195–97; Coulter, *William G. Brownlow*, pp. 366–67, 372–73; Alrutheus A. Taylor, *The Negro in Tennessee, 1865–1880*

(Washington, 1941), p. 99. Alexander may overestimate the importance of Detective Barmore's activities and of his death in influencing Brownlow to invoke martial law.

22. Nashville *Republican Banner,* Feb. 28, March 4, 9, 18, 1869. The five companies sent to Jackson and Overton counties were commanded by Major George W. Kirk of Jonesboro, who would receive national attention a year later as commander of Governor W. W. Holden's North Carolina militia.

23. March 12, 1869.

24. Hugh F. Ewing *et al.* to Gov. Senter, Nashville, Feb. 25, 1869, Governors' Correspondence, Tennessee State Library and Archives. See also letters from J. C. Walker, Sheriff David H. Parsons, and A. Cox on Feb. 25 and 26.

25. Typescript copy of letter from O. H. Crebbs to James R. Crowe, Columbus, Tex., Feb. 18, 1888, in W. L. Fleming Papers, New York Public Library; Nashville *Press and Times,* May 19, 1869. See also *House Miscellaneous Documents,* 41st Congress, 2d sess., No. 53, pp. 242–43. There was a similar exodus in Overton County. See Nashville *Press and Times,* March 16, 1869.

26. Nashville *Republican Banner,* March 2, 3, 9, 27, April 1, 1869; Pulaski *Citizen,* March 19, April 23, 30, 1869; Nashville *Press and Times,* March 24, May 6, 1869; petitions of A. B. Charpic *et al.,* Pulaski, April 12, and T. J. Harrison *et al.,* Giles County, June 16, 1869; letters to Gov. Senter from A. B. Charpic [Pulaski?], June 17, 1869; Maj. J. K. Clingan [?], Humboldt, May 15, 1869; Sheriff H. A. Morse, Trenton, May 15, 1869, Governors' Correspondence, Tennessee State Library and Archives.

27. According to a Republican in Gibson County, the militia arrested a Ku Klux there in May, no civil official being willing to do so. But when he was brought to trial for brutally attacking a Negro, the magistrate acquitted him despite plain and positive evidence of his guilt. W. H. Stilwell to Gen. John Eaton, Humboldt, May 17, 1869, John Eaton Papers, University of Tennessee. See also Stilwell's letter of May 10, 1869 to [Horace] Andrews, in same collection.

28. See J. A. Sharp, "The Downfall of the Radicals in Tennessee," *East Tennessee Historical Society Publications,* V (1933), pp. 107–24.

29. *KKK Report,* Miscellaneous Testimony, pp. 6–7, 11–12, 15–16, 29–30.

30. See Robert S. Henry, *"First with the Most" Forrest* (N.Y., 1944), pp. 450, 535 n.

31. Memphis *Evening Post,* March 2, 3, 20, 1869.

32. Lester and Wilson, *Ku Klux Klan,* Fleming ed., pp. 129–31; D. L. Wilson, "The Ku Klux Klan, Its Growth and Disbandment," *Century Magazine,* XXVIII (n.s. VI) (1884), p. 410.

33. Minor Meriwether to W. L. Fleming, St. Louis, Sept. 30, 1909, W. L. Fleming Papers, New York Public Library.

34. Interview with Judge J. P. Young, former secretary of a Memphis den,

cited in Henry, *"First with the Most" Forrest,* pp. 448–49. The novelist Thomas Dixon, deriving his information from Capt. John W. Morton, the Nashville Klansman who supposedly initiated Forrest into the order in 1867, wrote that Forrest disbanded the Klan in 1870, but there is no other support for this view. See John W. Morton, *The Artillery of Nathan Bedford Forrest's Cavalry* (Nashville and Dallas, 1909), Appendix, p. 345. Dixon describes, presumably also on Morton's authority, a final massive Klan parade in Nashville which followed the dissolution order. Other witnesses or participants described this parade many years later, but none gave any indication of its date. See Morton, *Artillery of Forrest's Cavalry,* Appendix, pp. 345–46; Nashville *Banner,* Aug. 26, 1934, May 3, 1936; Winchester, Tenn., *Chronicle,* Jan. 14, 1932; Horn, *Invisible Empire,* pp. 99–100.

35. See discussions of the disbandment in Horn, *Invisible Empire,* pp. 356–62, and Alexander, "Kukluxism in Tennessee," pp. 217–19.

36. Letters from Sheriff J. S. Webb, Murfreesboro, Aug. 28, 1869, and T. M. McKinley, Gallatin, Sept. 1, 1869, Governors' Correspondence, Tennessee State Library and Archives; Pulaski *Citizen,* Sept. 3, 1869; New York *Daily Tribune,* Aug. 27, Sept. 1, 2, 4, 1869.

37. Wilson County *Herald,* quoted in New York *Daily Tribune* and Pulaski *Citizen,* both of Sept. 17, 1869.

38. Letters of J. C. Reavis, Dresden, Sept. 12, and Louis M. Williams, Newbern, Sept. 14, 1869, Governors' Correspondence, Tennessee State Library and Archives.

39. Pulaski *Citizen,* Dec. 24, 1869.

CHAPTER 12: NORTH CAROLINA: THE TERROR IN ALAMANCE

1. *Senate Reports,* 42d Congress, 1st sess., No. 1 (hereafter abbreviated *SR*), pp. lxi, ci, civ, cvii, 239.

2. *Ibid.,* pp. lx, 239–40, 242–44, 248; Gen. Edward W. Hinks to Gov. Holden, Goldsboro, Feb. 18, 1869; Stephen Lasetter to Gen. Hickman [Hinks], Feb. 19, 1869; Judge S. W. Watts to Gov. Holden, Oxford, Aug. 14, 1869, Governors' Correspondence, North Carolina Archives.

3. Gen. Edw. W. Hinks to Gov. Holden, Goldsboro, Feb. 18, 1869, Governors' Correspondence, North Carolina Archives; *SR,* pp. cvi–cix, 241–42, 396.

4. *Ibid.,* pp. civ, 243; New Bern *Times,* copied in Raleigh *Daily Standard,* Sept. 8, 1869; Raleigh *Daily Standard,* Sept. 9, 1869.

5. *SR,* pp. lx, cii, 239.

6. *Ibid.,* pp. lx–lxi, ci, 98, 241–44, 249, 373; letters to Gov. Holden from D. D. Colgrove, Trenton, N.C., May 29, 1869; Jno. G. Colgrove, Morganton, N.C., June 5, 1869; Judge C. R. Thomas, New Bern, May

31, 1869 (letter and telegram), Governors' Corespondence, North Carolina Archives; Raleigh *Daily Standard,* June 3, 1869.

7. *SR,* pp. 100–2.

8. *Ibid.,* pp. cii, 240.

9. *Ibid.,* pp. 98, 100–2; Adjutant General's Report for 1868–1869, Document No. 10 in North Carolina *Executive and Legislative Documents,* 1869–1870, p. 2; Adjutant General's report, Jan. 26, 1871, Document No. 24, *ibid.,* 1870–1871, p. 2; Raleigh *Daily Standard,* June 5, 1869; William W. Holden, *Memoirs* (Durham, N.C., 1911), p. 125 (in which he erroneously states that he sent the militia to Lenoir County); letters to Gov. Holden from M. L. Shepard, Trenton, June 28, 1869; Lieut. Col. R. T. Berry, New Bern, Aug. 17, 1869 (telegram); L. D. Wilkie, Jones County, Oct. 18, 1869, Governors' Correspondence, North Carolina Archives.

10. *SR,* pp. xcvi–cix, 92–96, 241; letters to Gov. Holden from Jno. P. Sherard, Goldsboro, Oct. 28, 1869; Wm. J. Clarke, Kinston, Nov. 3, 1869, Governors' Correspondence, North Carolina Archives; Holden, *Memoirs,* p. 125; Holden, *Third Annual Message . . . Nov. 1870* (Raleigh, 1870), pp. 7–10, 13, 17 (in which he erroneously dates the Lenoir arrests in June instead of August); New Bern *Times,* quoted in Raleigh *Daily Standard,* Aug. 26, 27, 1869.

11. Raleigh *Sentinel,* April 29, Nov. 2, 1869.

12. Raleigh *Daily Standard,* June 3, 5, 18, Sept. 9, 1869.

13. *Ibid.,* May 27, 1870.

14. Holden, *Third Annual Message,* Appendix, pp. 86–87; testimony of James E. Boyd, Aug. 31, 1870, Ku Klux Klan Papers, Duke University; *SR,* pp. 7, 22, 257, 267; R. H. Wray to A. W. Tourgée, Reidsville, Dec. 9, 1868, Albion W. Tourgée Papers, microfilm, Southern Historical Collection, University of North Carolina.

15. Testimony of Capt. Eli S. Euliss and James E. Boyd, Aug. 31, 1870, Ku Klux Klan Papers, Duke University; *Trial of William W. Holden, Governor of North Carolina,* 3 vols. (Raleigh, 1871), pp. 1640, 1767–69, 1772, 1952, 1966–68, 1971, 1985–87, 2022, 2233, 2236, 2238, 2240, 2251, 2255; *SR,* pp. 7, 257, 259, 261, 263, 306–7; Holden, *Third Annual Message,* Appendix, pp. 88–89.

16. Lieut. F. W. Liedtke to Col. Jacob F. Chur, Company Shops, N.C., Nov. 15, 1868, Graham, N.C., Letters Sent book, 1868, Freedmen's Bureau Records, RG 105, NA.

17. *SR,* pp. lxv, lxvi, 341–49; *Trial of William W. Holden,* pp. 1311 ff., 1601, 1998–99, 2002–3, 2239–40; Holden, *Third Annual Message,* Appendix, p. 89; *Congressional Globe,* 42d Congress, 1st sess., Appendix, pp. 34–35. For the controversy regarding Holt's alleged transgressions, see Raleigh *Sentinel,* March 25, 1869; Raleigh *Daily Standard,* April 7, 1869.

18. *Trial of William W. Holden,* p. 2001.

19. *Ibid.,* pp. 625–26, 1192–99, 1201 ff., 1856–58, 2001, 2003–4, 2237–38 2243–45; *SR,* pp. lxvi, lxvii, 8, 30, 32. Jacob Long later claimed that the raid was designed to break up a Negro police force which the

Republican municipal government had formed. *Trial of William W. Holden,* pp. 2237, 2245–46. But this body, consisting of four Negroes and one white, was apparently created after the raid and because of it. *Ibid.,* pp. 1895–97.

20. *Trial of William W. Holden,* pp. 1427 ff.; *SR,* p. lxvi.

21. *SR,* pp. lxvi, 33, 43; H. A. Badham to Gov. Holden, Graham, March 23, 1869, Governors' Correspondence, North Carolina Archives.

22. *Trial of William W. Holden,* pp. 1883–86, 1900–1, 2052–53, 2056; *SR,* p. 31.

23. *Trial of William W. Holden,* pp. 1897–98; Raleigh *Sentinel,* March 30, 1869; letters to Gov. Holden from Henry M. Ray *et al.,* Graham, March 22, 1869, and H. A. Badham, Graham, March 22 (two letters), 23, 1869, Governors' Correspondence, North Carolina Archives.

24. Raleigh *Daily Standard,* March 24, 1869.

25. Capt. R. L. Bosher to Gov. Holden, Graham, March 28, 1869, Governors' Correspondence, North Carolina Archives.

26. *Public and Private Laws of North Carolina,* 1868–1869, p. 613.

27. *Trial of William W. Holden,* p. 31.

28. Raleigh *Sentinel,* March 25, 30, 1869.

29. William Campbell to Gov. Holden, Company Shops, April 14, 1869, Governors' Correspondence, North Carolina Archives.

30. Letters to Gov. Holden from Thos. A. Ragland *et al.,* Wentworth, N.C., May 12, 1869; Scales & Scales *et al.,* Wentworth, May 27, 1869, Governors' Correspondence, North Carolina Archives; letters to A. W. Tourgée from Thomas Settle, Wentworth, May 12, 1869; Gov. Holden, Raleigh, May 20, 1869, Albion W. Tourgée Papers, microfilm, Southern Historical Collection, University of North Carolina; Raleigh *Daily Standard,* May 14, 1869.

31. *SR,* pp. 85–87, 125; A. W. Tourgée to Gov. Holden, Greensboro, July 3, 1869, Governors' Correspondence, North Carolina Archives; Thos. A. Ragland *et al.* to Justice Thomas Settle, Wentworth, July 13, 1869, and Settle to Gov. Holden, Wentworth, July 28, 1869, W. W. Holden Papers, Duke University; Raleigh *Daily Standard,* Aug. 19, Sept. 28, 1869.

32. H. C. Thompson to [Benjamin S. Hedrick ?], Chapel Hill, July 26, 1869, B. S. Hedrick Papers, Duke University.

33. *SR,* pp. 41–43, 45–46, 191–93, 195; Holden, *Third Annual Message,* Appendix, pp. 27–28, 89; *KKK Report,* North Carolina, pp. 2–4, 8; *Trial of William W. Holden,* pp. 1793 ff., 1840 ff., 1848 ff., 1853 ff.; E. McCroray to Gov. Holden, Hillsboro, Feb. 13, 1871, W. W. Holden Papers, Duke University.

34. *KKK Report,* North Carolina, pp. 8–9.

35. Copied in Raleigh *Daily Standard,* Sept. 16, 1869.

36. James B. Mason to Gov. Holden, Chapel Hill, Sept. 22, 1869, Governors' Correspondence, North Carolina Archives; Mason to Holden, Chapel Hill, Jan. 10, 1871, W. W. Holden Papers, Duke University; J. G. de

Roulhac Hamilton, *Reconstruction in North Carolina* (N.Y., 1914), p. 484.

37. Raleigh *Daily Standard*, Oct. 5, 30, 1869.
38. *Trial of William W. Holden*, pp. 1793 ff.
39. See the laudatory treatment in J. G. de Roulhac Hamilton, "Civil War and Reconstruction in Orange County," in Hugh T. Lefler and Paul W. Wager (eds.), *Orange County, 1752–1952* (Chapel Hill, N.C., 1953), pp. 116–19.
40. Holden, *Third Annual Message*, Appendix, p. 33.
41. *SR*, pp. 415–19.
42. Holden, *Third Annual Message*, Appendix, p. 32; *KKK Report*, North Carolina, pp. 363–65, 373–75, 377–78, 383–92, 398–400; anonymous undated letter, probably from Gaston County Klan leader Calvin E. Grier, to Capt. R. A. Shotwell, Nathan Shotwell Papers, Southern Historical Collection, University of North Carolina; David Schenck Diary, Dec. 18, 1869, in Southern Historical Collection, University of North Carolina.
43. Otto H. Olsen, "The Ku Klux Klan: A Study in Reconstruction Politics and Propaganda," *North Carolina Historical Review*, XXXIX (Summer, 1962), p. 345.
44. *SR*, p. 83; *Trial of William W. Holden*, pp. 1773, 1860, 2040–41.
45. Testimony of James E. Boyd, Aug. 31, 1870, Ku Klux Klan Papers, Duke University.
46. For this incident, see *Trial of William W. Holden*, pp. 644, 1813, 1823, 1901, 2039; *SR*, pp. 80, 264–65, 347–48. For examples of Democratic use of it to ascribe other outrages to Negroes, see Hillsborough *Recorder*, March 16, 1870, and Raleigh *Sentinel*, April 22, 1870.
47. *Trial of William W. Holden*, pp. 1769–70.
48. Confession of William Patton, Aug. 2, 1870, Governors' Correspondence, North Carolina Archives.
49. See statements, chiefly of former members, in *SR*, pp. lix, 7, 20, 161–65, 257–58, 264–65, 272, 284–85, 292–93, 297, 299, 309, 320; Holden, *Third Annual Message*, Appendix, p. 86; *Trial of William W. Holden*, pp. 691–92, 697, 713, 724, 1003–4, 1205 ff., 1271, 1530, 1558, 1640–41, 1684, 1771, 1807, 1809, 1993, 2015, 2227, 2234. For the meditated attack on Albright and efforts to prevent it, see *SR*, pp. lvi, 7, 80–81, 83–84, 142–43, 287, 294, 313–14; *Trial of William W. Holden*, pp. 1408–9, 1773.
50. See statements of members in W. W. Holden Papers, Duke University; also in *SR*, pp. lvi–lix, lxi, 19, 263; *Trial of William W. Holden*, pp. 713, 1220 ff., 2000–1. Regarding CUG membership, see *ibid.*, pp. 1987, 2162–63.
51. For references to the White Brotherhood, see Holden, *Third Annual Message*, Appendix, pp. 87–89; *SR*, pp. 9, 17, 20, 36, 257–58, 261–63, 267; *Trial of William W. Holden*, pp. 1287–88, 1534, 1581, 1583, 1586, 1588, 1945, 1948–50, 1952, 1994, 2022, 2162–64, 2236–38, 2249–50. For the CUG, see *ibid.*, pp. 1971–75, 1985–87.

52. *SR*, pp. lxvii, 17–18, 22–24, 286; *Trial of William W. Holden*, pp. 1253–54, 1553, 1771.
53. *Trial of William W. Holden*, pp. 1390 ff.; *SR*, p. lxvi.
54. *Trial of William W. Holden*, pp. 1397 ff., 1513 ff.
55. *Ibid.*, pp. 1445 ff.; *SR*, p. lxvi.
56. *SR*, pp. lxv, 144 ff.; *Trial of William W. Holden*, pp. 596–97, 655–56, 1522–23, 1786–87; H. C. Vogell to Gen. O. O. Howard, Raleigh, Dec. 14, 1869, and A. B. Corliss to Gov. Holden, Company Shops, Nov. 29, 30, 1869, Governors' Correspondence, North Carolina Archives; Raleigh *Daily Standard*, Jan. 12, 1870.
57. For this raid, see *Trial of William W. Holden*, pp. 1375 ff., 1381 ff., 1387 ff.
58. *Ibid.*, pp. 1355 ff.; *SR*, p. cxiii.
59. *Trial of William W. Holden*, pp. 2008–9; *SR*, p. lxvi.
60. *Trial of William W. Holden*, pp. 1167 ff., 1454 ff.
61. *Ibid.*, pp. 1404 ff.
62. Raleigh *Sentinel*, Dec. 18, 1869.
63. Confession of Eli Euliss, Aug. 16, 1870, Governors' Correspondence, North Carolina Archives; *SR*, pp. lix, 7–8, 25–26, 143; *Trial of William W. Holden*, pp. 632, 1526–29, 1531–34, 1591–92, 1600, 1975–78, 1988–89; Holden, *Third Annual Message*, Appendix, pp. 89–90; Holden, *Memoirs*, p. 168.
64. *Trial of William W. Holden*, pp. 993–95, 1609–10, 1642, 1647–48; Raleigh *Sentinel*, Jan. 12, 1870.
65. *Trial of William W. Holden*, pp. 1645, 1684.
66. *SR*, p. lix.
67. *SR*, pp. 81, 83; *Trial of William W. Holden*, pp. 1781–82, 1883–86, 1888.
68. *Trial of William W. Holden*, p. 1201.
69. *SR*, pp. 23, 30–31, 37–38, 40, 83, 264–65, 268, 343, 347–49, 420; confessions of Eli Euliss, Aug. 16, 1870, and F. U. Blanchard, Aug. 17, 1870, Governors' Correspondence, North Carolina Archives; *Trial of William W. Holden*, pp. 642–45, 651–56, 659, 1812–13, 1822–24, 1838–39, 1883–86, 2039–40, 2042; H. A. Badham *et al.* to Gov. Holden, Graham, Feb. 28, 1870, W. W. Holden Papers, Duke University.
70. *SR*, pp. lxv–lxvii, cxiii, 18–19, 21–22, 31–32, 78, 80, 252, 260–61, 266, 270, 357; Holden, *Third Annual Message*, Appendix, p. 90; *Trial of William W. Holden*, pp. 1184 ff., 1192 ff., 1199, 1241 ff., 1363 ff., 1591, 1855–57, 1944, 1963, 2244–45, 2250; Olsen, "The Ku Klux Klan," pp. 354–56. For an example of the posthumous slanders of Outlaw, see the account of the murder in the Greensboro *Patriot*, March 3, 1870.
71. *SR*, pp. lxv, cxii, 22, 35, 254, 290–91; Holden, *Third Annual Message*, Appendix, p. 90; *Trial of William W. Holden*, pp. 520–21, 699, 1301 ff., 1422–23; Raleigh *Daily Standard*, March 31, 1870; Raleigh *Sentinel*, March 21, 1870.
72. See *SR*, pp. 22, 78.

73. W. A. Patterson to Holden, Rock Creek, Alamance County, March 14, 1870, Governors' Correspondence, North Carolina Archives.

74. *Trial of William W. Holden,* pp. 996–98, 1003, 1648; *SR,* pp. xci–xcii, 255.

75. See letters to Holden from A. D. Ramseur, Ramseur's Mills, Catawba County, Nov. 23, 1869; J. N. Shaver, Sweet Home, Iredell County, Jan. 10, 1870; H. C. Vogell, Raleigh, Jan. 29, 1870 (enclosing letter to Vogell from Edward Payson Hall, Philadelphia, Pa., Jan. 27, 1870); Luke Blackmer, Salisbury, Feb. 4, 1870, Governors' Correspondence, North Carolina Archives. See also the letters of inquiry from Holden to the sheriffs of those counties, in Holden, *Third Annual Message,* Appendix, pp. 40–41, and their replies, from S. A. Kelly, Mocksville, Feb. 5, 1870; Wm. A. Walton, Salisbury, Feb. 7, 1870; and W. F. Wasson, Statesville, Feb. 8, 1870, Governors' Correspondence, North Carolina Archives.

76. David S. Barrett to Gov. Holden, Carthage, N.C., April 8, 1870, Governors' Correspondence, North Carolina Archives.

77. See anonymous undated statement regarding Wayne and Sampson counties, in W. W. Holden Papers, Duke University; Lieut. J. S. McEwan to Atty. Gen. Akerman, Westbrook Twp., Sampson County, Nov. 24, 28, 1871, in Justice Department, Source-Chronological File, Eastern North Carolina, RG 60, NA.

78. *SR,* pp. 27–29, 72, 76–77; Raleigh *Daily Standard,* April 14, 20, 22, 23, 1870.

79. Raleigh *Daily Standard,* Oct. 21, Dec. 22, 1869; Holden, *Third Annual Message,* Appendix, pp. 37–40; *KKK Report,* North Carolina, pp. 86 ff.; *SR,* pp. 386–87; "A True Republican" to Gov. Holden, Chatham County, Feb. 3, 1870, Governors' Correspondence, North Carolina Archives; A. W. Tourgée to Holden, Pittsboro, N.C., May 17, 1870, Governors' Letterbooks No. 61, North Carolina Archives.

80. Anonymous letter to S. S. Ashley, Chapel Hill, Dec. 1, 1869, Governors' Correspondence, North Carolina Archives.

81. *SR,* p. 408; Holden, *Third Annual Message,* Appendix, p. 51.

82. See Raleigh *Sentinel,* June 16, July 27, Sept. 17, 27, 28, Oct. 14, 1869.

83. Raleigh *Daily Standard,* Oct. 21, 1869.

84. Raleigh *Sentinel,* March 16, 1870; Col. Joseph C. Webb to W. L. Saunders, Texas, Sept. 21, 1874, W. L. Saunders Papers, Southern Historical Collection, University of North Carolina.

85. Raleigh *Daily Standard,* Oct. 15, 1869.

CHAPTER 13: NORTH CAROLINA: THE KIRK-HOLDEN WAR, 1870

1. As quoted in Greensboro *Patriot,* Oct. 28, 1869.

2. See William W. Holden, *Third Annual Message . . . Nov. 1870* (Raleigh, 1870), Appendix, p. 56; Raleigh *Daily Standard,* Sept. 23, 1869, May 9, 23, 1870.

3. *Trial of William W. Holden, Governor of North Carolina,* 3 vols. (Raleigh, 1871), pp. 34–35.

4. Messages of November 16 and December 16, 1869, Documents Nos. 1 (pp. 9–11) and 20, North Carolina *Executive and Legislative Documents, 1869–1870; Public Laws of the State of North Carolina . . . 1869–70,* pp. 64–66.

5. See the remarks of Republican state senator G. W. Welker in the debate on the bill, Raleigh *Daily Standard,* Jan. 26, 1870, and of Judges Daniel R. Russell and George W. Brooks in *SR,* pp. 179–80, 276.

6. See *New York Times,* March 24, 1870.

7. Raleigh *Daily Standard,* Oct. 19, Dec. 28, 1869.

8. *SR,* p. xciv; *Trial of William W. Holden,* pp. 166–67; Raleigh *Daily Standard,* April 1, 8, 1870; P. R. Harden to Gov. Holden, Graham, April 18, 1870, Governors' Correspondence, North Carolina Archives.

9. For the correspondence pertaining to the disposition and function of these troops, see Post of Raleigh, Letters Sent book, 1868–1870, March 2–26, 1870, RG 98, NA. See also *SR,* pp. xci–xciii, cxiii–cxiv.

10. For the employment of detectives, see Holden to Tod R. Caldwell, Feb. 23, 1870, in Governors' Letterbooks No. 61, North Carolina Archives.

11. *SR,* pp. 386–87; Holden, *Third Annual Message,* p. 17; N. A. Ramsey to Holden, Pittsboro, May 23, 1870, Governors' Correspondence, North Carolina Archives.

12. *KKK Report,* North Carolina, pp. 1–2, 5–7, 12; J. G. de Roulhac Hamilton, "Civil War and Reconstruction in Orange County," in Hugh T. Lefler and Paul W. Wager (eds.), *Orange County, 1752–1952* (Chapel Hill, N.C., 1953), pp. 119–20; Holden, *Third Annual Message,* Appendix, pp. 41–47; Pride Jones to Holden, Hillsboro, March 21, 1870, Governors' Correspondence, North Carolina Archives; Jones to Holden, April 19, and Holden to Jones, April 22, 1870, Governors' Letterbooks No. 61, North Carolina Archives.

13. Holden, *Third Annual Message,* Appendix, pp. 51–55.

14. *Trial of William W. Holden,* pp. 1143–44, 2075 ff., 2085 ff., 2097 ff., 2129–30, 2146 ff., 2149 ff., 2176 ff.; letters to Holden from John W. Stephens, Yanceyville, May 2, 16, 1870; T. J. Foster *et al.,* n.p., [*ca.* May 2, 1870]; Samuel Allen, Yanceyville, May 14, 1870, Governors' Correspondence, North Carolina Archives; Raleigh *Daily Standard,* May 6, 1870; *SR,* pp. 47 ff.; Wilson Carey to Holden, Yanceyville, Nov. 3, 1870, W. W. Holden Papers, Duke University.

15. *Trial of William W. Holden,* pp. 1479 ff.

16. Greensboro *Patriot,* Feb. 10, 1870.

17. *Ibid.;* Senator John Pool to Gov. Holden, Washington, June 22, 1870, W. W. Holden Papers, Duke University.

18. Letters to Gov. Holden from John W. Stephens, Yanceyville, May 2, 16, 1870; T. J. Foster *et al.,* n.p., [*ca.* May 2, 1870]; Samuel Allen, Yanceyville, May 14, 1870, Governors' Correspondence, North Carolina

Archives; Raleigh *Daily Standard,* May 6, 1870; *Trial of William W. Holden,* pp. 1144, 2152, 2159–60.

19. J. W. Stephens to Holden, Yanceyville, Aug. 29, 1868, Governors' Correspondence, North Carolina Archives.

20. J. W. Stephens to Holden, Yanceyville, June 20, 1868, W. W. Holden Papers, North Carolina Archives.

21. Holden, *Third Annual Message,* Appendix, p. 54.

22. For the controversy over his character and activities, see *Trial of William W. Holden,* pp. 814, 829, 879, 2212; Holden, *Third Annual Message,* Appendix, pp. 101–3, 119; *SR,* pp. 372, 400–1; J. G. de Roulhac Hamilton, *Reconstruction in North Carolina* (N.Y., 1914), p. 473; Otto H. Olsen, "The Ku Klux Klan: A Study in Reconstruction Politics and Propaganda," *North Carolina Historical Review,* XXXIX (Summer 1962), 356–58; Frank Nash, "John Walter Stephens," in Samuel A. Ashe (ed.), *Biographical History of North Carolina,* 8 vols. (Greensboro, 1905–17), IV, 417–20; Andrew J. Stedman, *Murder and Mystery, History of the Life and Death of John W. Stephens* ([Greensboro, 1870]), pp. 6–18; Luther Montrose Carlton, "The Assassination of John Walter Stephens," Trinity College Historical Society, *Annual Publication of Historical Papers, 1898,* vol. II, pp. 2–5; Tom Henderson, "Murder of 'Chicken' Stephens," *The State,* VI (March 25, 1939), p. 9; Greensboro *Daily News,* Oct. 2, 1935.

23. The same courthouse still stands in Yanceyville, and the murder room serves as an office. In front of the building stands the only historical marker I have seen in the South commemorating a Ku Klux attack. For accounts of the assassination, see Holden, *Third Annual Message,* Appendix, pp. 97–99, 101–2, 121; *Trial of William W. Holden,* pp. 829–30, 864, 2125–28; Stedman, *Murder and Mystery,* pp. 20 ff.; *SR,* p. 142; statement of Capt. John G. Lea in Greensboro *Daily News,* Oct. 2, 1935; report of J. G. Hester, July 22, 1871, enclosed with letter to A. J. Falls, Greensboro, July 25, 1871, Justice Department Source-Chronological File, Eastern North Carolina, RG 60, NA.

24. Raleigh *Sentinel,* May 26, June 1, 2, 27, July 4, 1870; Stedman, *Murder and Mystery,* pp. 37–39; Holden, *Third Annual Message,* Appendix, pp. 103 ff.; *SR,* pp. 399–401, 406; Greensboro *Patriot,* May 26, 1870; Hillsborough *Recorder,* June 1, 1870. For accounts of the chicken affair, in which Stephens apparently killed two of a neighbor's fowl which strayed into his barn, see Raleigh *Daily Standard,* May 26, 1870; Rockingham County court records, February term 1865, in Graham, N.C., Letters Sent book, 1868, Freedmen's Bureau Records, RG 105, NA; Stedman, *Murder and Mystery,* pp. 9–10; Carlton, "The Assassination of John Walter Stephens," pp. 2–4. This matter would have been inconsequential if Democrats had not attempted to ruin his career by tagging him Chicken Stephens.

25. See *Trial of William W. Holden,* pp. 765–66, 789–92, 828, 1605, 1832–33, 1836, 2133–39, 2141–46; Raleigh *Sentinel,* May 26, June 6, 1870;

Hillsborough *Recorder,* June 1, 1870; Holden, *Third Annual Message,* Appendix, pp. 97–99, 121, 132; undated statement [1870] by Joseph Ben Shaw, Governors' Correspondence, North Carolina Archives; Olsen, "The Ku Klux Klan," pp. 358–59; Carlton, "The Assassination of John Walter Stephens," p. 11; Henderson, "Murder of 'Chicken' Stephens," pp. 19, 24; statement of Capt. John G. Lea, Greensboro *Daily News,* Oct. 2, 1935; *New York Times,* Feb. 26, 1873; see also *New York Times,* June 29, 1872.

26. Telegram from Holden to Senators Pool and Abbott, May 25, 1870, Governors' Letterbooks No. 61, North Carolina Archives; *Trial of William W. Holden,* pp. 38–39; Raleigh *Daily Standard,* June 1, 10, 1870.

27. Hamilton, *Reconstruction in North Carolina,* pp. 496–99, 503–6; testimony of R. C. Badger and Isaac J. Young concerning the June meeting in Raleigh, in Raleigh *Sentinel,* April 8, 10, 1871; speeches of Senator John Pool, in *Congressional Globe,* 42d Congress, 1st sess., pp. 604–7, 664; *ibid.,* Appendix, p. 108; letters to Gov. Holden from Wm. J. Clarke, Washington, June 18, 1870, and W. R. Albright, Graham, June 28, 1870, Governors' Correspondence, North Carolina Archives; Raleigh *Daily Standard,* July 2, 14, 21, 1870; *Trial of William W. Holden,* pp. 40–41, 139, 233, 1746–50, 1902–3; *SR,* pp. 5, 153, 273–74, 276.

28. Hamilton, *Reconstruction in North Carolina,* pp. 499–501, 504–5, 515–16; *Trial of William W. Holden,* pp. 40–42, 283.

29. *Congressional Globe,* 42d Congress, 1st sess., p. 606; *Trial of William W. Holden,* pp. 50, 119, 584–85, 587, 591, 601–10, 665, 702–4, 714–17, 719, 741 ff., 773–75, 900–1; *SR,* pp. lxxx, 5, 11, 65, 67, 169, 312; William W. Holden, *Memoirs* (Durham, N.C., 1911), p. 124.

30. *SR,* pp. lxxvii, 166–67, 403–4; letters to Gov. Holden from Republicans in western North Carolina, June 1870, Governors' Correspondence, North Carolina Archives; Rutherfordton Rutherford *Star,* July 30, 1870; Hillsborough *Recorder,* July 20, 1870; New York *Daily Tribune,* July 27, Aug. 5, 1870; *Trial of William W. Holden,* pp. 750–51, 1504, 1506, 2057, 2059, 2063; *Congressional Globe,* 42d Congress, 1st sess., p. 605.

31. *Congressional Globe,* 42d Congress, 1st sess., p. 605; *Trial of William W. Holden,* pp. 607–8, 741 ff., 854, 874; *SR,* pp. 5, 15–16, 153, 156, 255, 405; New York *Daily Tribune,* Aug. 5, 1870; Raleigh *Daily Standard,* July 29, 1870; statement of Capt. John G. Lea, Greensboro *Daily News,* Oct. 2, 1935. Regarding the Turner arrest, see *Congressional Globe,* 42d Congress, 1st sess., p. 605; *Trial of William W. Holden,* pp. 44–45, 894–913, 968, 974, 1003 (owing to mispagination this is the second p. 1003, following p. 1004); *SR,* pp. 8, 21, 157, 349 ff., 370–71; Holden, *Memoirs,* p. 164; Holden, *Third Annual Message,* Appendix, p. 90. R. T. Berry identified Bergen as the responsible party and reported Bergen's reason for ordering it. See Berry to Holden, New Bern, Nov. 28, 1870, W. W. Holden Papers, Duke University.

32. *Congressional Globe,* 42d Congress, 1st sess., p. 605; *Trial of William W. Holden,* pp. 42, 611–12, 614–16, 661–63, 673–75, 702–3, 714–17, 719,

773–75, 795, 972–74, 977, 981, 1147, 1729 ff., 1741, 1810–11, 2168, 2360; *SR*, pp. 6, 11–12, 16, 150–53, 157, 255, 311–13, 315, 320–22.

33. *SR*, pp. 38, 80–81, 294, 297, 313; *Trial of William W. Holden*, pp. 1905, 1913, 1924.

34. Raleigh *Daily Standard*, July 30, Aug. 1, 18, 1870. For the statement by Boyd and other leaders, see *SR*, pp. lv–lvi; for further information about Boyd's case, see *SR*, pp. 7–8, 17–26, 82, 299–300; *Trial of William W. Holden*, pp. 1615–25, 1633–35; Boyd's testimony, Aug. 31, 1870, Ku Klux Klan Papers, Duke University; statement of Capt. John G. Lea, Greensboro *Daily News*, Oct. 2, 1935. The statements and confessions were placed on file in Raleigh. Many were subsequently published (together with later testimony by the same persons) by state and federal agencies investigating the Klan. See the large number of confessions, July and August 1870, in Governors' Correspondence, North Carolina Archives; Ku Klux Klan Papers and W. W. Holden Papers, Duke University; and published confessions in *SR*, *Trial of William W. Holden*, and the Appendix to Holden's *Third Annual Message*.

35. *SR*, pp. 2, 20–21, 24, 80–83, 295; *Trial of William W. Holden*, p. 2251.

36. Boyd to Holden, Graham, Aug. 1, 1870, Governors' Correspondence, North Carolina Archives.

37. *KKK Report*, North Carolina, pp. 377, 396.

38. Raleigh *Sentinel*, July 29, 30, Sept. 10, 1870; *SR*, pp. 19, 364–66; *Trial of William W. Holden*, p. 2028; James E. Boyd to Judge Thomas Settle, Graham, Dec. 24, 1872, Thomas Settle Papers, Southern Historical Collection, University of North Carolina. Boyd became a Republican and many years later was appointed a federal district judge by President McKinley.

39. Greensboro *Patriot*, March 10, July 21, 1870.

40. For the exchange between Holden and Pearson, see Holden, *Third Annual Message*, Appendix, pp. 60–62, 64–76, 79; William H. Battle, *A Report of the Proceedings in the Habeas Corpus Cases . . .* (Raleigh, 1870), pp. 49–59; *SR*, p. 12. See the interview of a New York *Tribune* correspondent with Pearson, in New York *Daily Tribune*, Aug. 3, 1870.

41. *Trial of William W. Holden*, p. 233; *SR*, p. 155.

42. For the federal proceedings and the circumstances surrounding them, see Holden, *Third Annual Message*, Appendix, pp. 80–82; *SR*, pp. xlv, 5, 12–13, 16, 38, 80–81, 273–75; letters of Holden to Pearson, Aug. 15, 1870, and to Kirk, Aug. 18, 1870, Governors' Letterbooks No. 61, North Carolina Archives; Battle, *Habeas Corpus Cases*, pp. 67 ff.

43. Holden, *Third Annual Message*, Appendix, pp. 91–285.

44. See *Trial of William W. Holden*, pp. 765–66; *SR*, p. 2.

45. Holden, *Third Annual Message*, Appendix, p. 286; William R. Albright *et al.* to Holden, Nov. 1870, Governors' Correspondence, North Carolina Archives; *SR*, pp. 9, 80, 83, 420.

46. *SR*, pp. 5–6, 13–14, 16.

47. *Congressional Globe*, 42d Congress, 1st sess., p. 607.

48. *SR,* p. 21; New York *Daily Tribune,* Aug. 3, 1870; testimony of James E. Boyd, Aug. 31, 1870, Ku Klux Klan Papers, Duke University; *Congressional Globe,* 42d Congress, 1st sess., Appendix, p. 108.
49. *SR,* pp. 9–10, 20, 26, 38–39; Olsen, "The Ku Klux Klan," p. 360; Raleigh *Daily Standard,* Aug. 12, 1870; *Trial of William W. Holden,* pp. 1790–92.
50. Holden, *Third Annual Message,* p. 19.
51. E. Cobb *et al.* to Holden, Lincolnton, May 11, 1870; Col. James H. Marsh to Holden, Lincolnton, May 17, 1870; Holden to W. P. Bynum, May 17, 1870; Bynum to Holden, Lincolnton, May 20, 1870, Governors' Correspondence, North Carolina Archives. See also the David Schenck Diary, June 16, 1870, Southern Historical Collection, University of North Carolina.
52. *SR,* pp. 52–54; Rutherford *Star,* Dec. 10, 17, 1870; Judge George W. Logan to Gov. Caldwell, Rutherfordton, Dec. 27, 1870, Governors' Letterbooks, No. 62, North Carolina Archives; Hamilton, *Reconstruction in North Carolina,* p. 506.
53. *SR,* pp. xvii–xix, xxvii–xxviii, 76, 388–89, 391, 408; *KKK Report,* North Carolina, pp. 13–16, 31 ff., 51 ff., 72 ff., 86 ff.
54. See the evaluation by Senator Pool, in *Congressional Globe,* 42d Congress, 1st sess., pp. 604–7; *ibid.,* Appendix, p. 108.
55. *Trial of William W. Holden,* p. 1; *SR,* pp. liv, 8, 20–21; Thomas Dixon, "The Story of the Ku Klux Klan," *Metropolitan Magazine,* XXII (Sept. 1905), 664.
56. *Trial of William W. Holden,* pp. 1–2, 9–18, 2539–60; *Congressional Globe,* 42d Congress, 1st sess., Appendix, p. 109; New York *Daily Tribune,* March 23, 1871; *New York Times,* Aug. 2, Dec. 28, 1870, March 17, 24, 1871; copy of letter from Holden to L. P. Olds, Washington, D.C. [1871], W. W. Holden Papers, Duke University; Cortez A. M. Ewing, "Two Reconstruction Impeachments," *North Carolina Historical Review,* XV (1938), pp. 204, 216–25.
57. *Public Laws of North Carolina,* 1870–1871, pp. 47, 200, 202.

CHAPTER 14: GEORGIA AND FLORIDA: WARREN COUNTY AND THE CONSERVATIVE CONQUEST OF GEORGIA

1. *KKK Report,* Georgia, pp. 193–96, 267–68.
2. *Ibid.,* pp. 690–91, 1022, 1028, 1165–68, 1198–1204, 1209.
3. *Ibid.,* pp. 195, 211, 217.
4. *House Miscellaneous Documents,* 40th Congress, 3d sess., No. 52, pp. 29, 78–79; R. C. Anthony to M. Frank Gallagher, Warrrenton, Ga., Sept. 7, Oct. 27, 1868, Warrenton, Ga., Letters Sent book; letter from Anthony, Oct. 9, 1868, in Georgia, Assistant Commissioner, Letters Received, Freedmen's Bureau Records, RG 105, NA; New York *Daily Tribune,* June 21, 1869.

5. Letters from R. C. Anthony, Warrenton, Nov. 1, 12, 1868, and Lieut. H. Catley, Augusta, Dec. 4, 1868, Georgia, Assistant Commissioner, Letters Received, Freedmen's Bureau Records, RG 105, NA; *House Miscellaneous Documents,* 40th Congress, 3d sess., No. 52, pp. 28, 79, 81–82; New York *Daily Tribune,* Nov. 21, 1868.

6. *House Miscellaneous Documents,* 40th Congress, 3d sess., No. 52, pp. 79–80; letters from R. C. Anthony, Nov. 2, 22, 1868 (the former with enclosed affidavit of Perry Jeffers, Jr., Nov. 10, 1868), Georgia, Assistant Commissioner, Letters Received, Freedmen's Bureau Records, RG 105, NA; *KKK Report,* Georgia, pp. 209–11, 220, 1018, 1029, 1108.

7. R. C. Anthony to Col. J. R. Lewis, Warrenton, Nov. 10, 1868, Warrenton, Ga., Letters Sent book; letters from Anthony, Warrenton, Nov. 3, 7, 19, 1868; from Sheriff J. C. Norris, Warrenton, Nov. 25, 1868; and report of Maj. H. F. Brownson, Atlanta, Dec. 2, 1868, in Georgia, Assistant Commissioner, Letters Received; Lieut. H. Catley to A.A.G., Augusta, Nov. 30, Dec. 3, 1868, in Augusta, Ga., Sub-assistant Commissioner, Letters Sent book, Freedmen's Bureau Records, RG 105, NA; Gov. Bullock to Gen. Meade, Nov. 17, 1868, and Eugene Davis (governor's secretary) to Sheriff Norris, Nov. 18, 1868, in Executive Department Letterbooks, Georgia Archives; *House Miscellaneous Documents,* 40th Congress, 3d sess., No. 52, p. 81; *Senate Reports,* 42d Congress, 1st sess., No. 1, p. liii; *KKK Report,* Georgia, p. 1029.

8. *KKK Report,* Georgia, pp. 196–97; statement of Reuben Neal, July 7, 1869, No. 1155 S 69, Records of the Adjutant General's Office, RG 94, NA; R. C. Anthony to A.A.G., Warrenton, Aug. 21, 1868, in Warrenton, Ga., Letters Sent book, Freedmen's Bureau Records, RG 105, NA.

9. *KKK Report,* Georgia, pp. 197–98, 220–21, 266–67, 287, 289, 770, 1022, 1024, 1164–65, 1168–69; R. C. Anthony to A.A.G., Warrenton, Aug. 21, 1868, in Warrenton, Ga., Letters Sent book, Freedmen's Bureau Records, RG 105, NA; Augusta *Chronicle and Sentinel,* March 13, 14, 1869; *Daily Atlanta Intelligencer,* March 23, 1869; Atlanta *Daily New Era,* Dec. 14, 1871. Dr. R. M. Hall was later identified as Grand Giant of the Warren County Klan, but his name does not figure prominently in its activities. J. E. Bryant to Atty. Gen. Akerman, Washington, Oct. 31, 1871, Justice Department Source-Chronological File, Georgia, RG 60, NA.

10. *KKK Report,* Georgia, pp. 197–201, 282–83, 789, 1024–25, 1161–64, 1169–71; Augusta *Chronicle and Sentinel,* March 14, 16, 1869.

11. *KKK Report,* Georgia, pp. 193, 201, 221.

12. New York *Daily Tribune,* March 17, 1869.

13. See Augusta *Chronicle and Sentinel,* April 14, 1869.

14. *KKK Report, Georgia,* pp. 207–8, 231, 737, 1019–21, 1023, 1025–26, 1029, 1150–51; Augusta *Chronicle and Sentinel,* May 12, Dec. 29, 30, 1869; letter of Joseph Adkins, Warrenton, April 18, 1868, in Augusta, Ga., Sub-assistant Commissioner, Letters Received book, Freedmen's Bureau Records, RG 105, NA.

15. Augusta *Chronicle and Sentinel,* May 12, June 11, 1869; Shreveport, La.,

South-Western, June 9, 1869; New York *Daily Tribune,* May 14, 1869; *New York Times,* May 30, June 3, 6, 8, 11, 1869; report of Capt. N. B. Hull, Warrenton, June 4, 1869, No. 354 A 69; extract of confidential conversation between Curran Battle and Gov. Bullock, June 20, 1869, No. 1155 S 69, in Records of the Adjutant General's Office, RG 94, NA; *KKK Report,* Georgia, pp. 268–69, 737, 742–43, 770, 1025, 1030, 1033, 1151, 1158, 1210–11.

16. *KKK Report,* Georgia, p. 1019; *New York Times,* June 11, 1869.

17. Correspondence of May 13, 21, June 4–8, 19, 1869, in Post of Warrenton, Ga., Letters Sent book, 1869–1871, RG 98, NA; *KKK Report,* Georgia, pp. 201, 221–22, 1104–5, 1107–8; Augusta *Chronicle and Sentinel,* May 22, June 9, 10, 12, 1869; letters of Eugene Davis and Gov. Bullock to Gen. Terry, June 2, 3, 1869, in Executive Department Letterbooks, Georgia Archives; order from Gov. Bullock to Atty. Gen. Farrow, June 9, 1869, in Executive Minutes, 1866–1870, Georgia Archives; report of Atty. Gen. Farrow, June 19, 1869, and letter of John Neal to Gov. Bullock, Warren County, June 17, 1869, No. 1155 S 69, Records of the Adjutant General's Office, RG 94, NA.

18. Extract of confidential conversation between Curran Battle and Gov. Bullock, June 20, 1869, No. 1155 S 69, Records of the Adjutant General's Office, RG 94, NA.

19. Grand jury presentment, Oct. 8, 1869, in Warren County Superior Court Records (microfilm), Georgia Archives; Augusta *Chronicle and Sentinel,* Oct. 14, 17, 1869.

20. *Acts of the General Assembly of the State of Georgia . . . 1869,* pp. 204–5.

21. *KKK Report,* Georgia, pp. 696–705, 1113–14, 1117. 'For other references to Ku Klux activity in that part of the state in 1869, see *ibid.,* pp. 351, 692–96, 731–33, 864–65, 954 ff.; *Senate Reports,* 42d Congress, 1st sess., No. 1, p. xli; Augusta *Chronicle and Sentinel,* Oct. 10, 1869; *Congressional Globe,* 41st Congress, 2d sess., Appendix, p. 30; proclamation of Gov. Bullock, Nov. 29, 1869, offering rewards for the arrest of persons suspected of specified crimes, in Executive Minutes, 1866–1870, Georgia Archives.

22. Gov. Bullock to Gen. Terry, June 23, 1869, No. 1155 S 69, in Records of the Adjutant General's Office, RG 94, NA.

23. *Senate Executive Documents,* 41st Congress, 2d sess., No. 3, pp. 2–3.

24. Gen. Alfred H. Terry to A.A.G., Military Division of the South, June 11, 1871, enclosed with letter of President Grant, Sept. 1, 1871, in Justice Department, Attorney General's Office, Letters Received from the President, RG 60, NA; *Daily Atlanta Intelligencer,* Jan. 13, 26, 1870; Atlanta *Daily New Era,* Jan. 16, 27, 1870.

25. Augusta *Chronicle and Sentinel,* Jan. 20, 22, Feb. 3, May 5, 1870; letters of Maj. F. H. Torbett, Warrenton, Ga., Jan. 14, 16, 18, 23, 24, 28, 1870, in Post of Warrenton, Ga., Letters Sent book, 1869–1871, RG 98, NA.

26. *KKK Report,* Georgia, pp. 204–6, 230, 268, 283, 1027; Atlanta *Daily New Era,* Aug. 10, 1871.
27. Augusta *Chronicle and Sentinel,* March 31, 1870.
28. Maj. F. H. Torbett to Maj. Jacob Kline, Warrenton, April 21, 22, 1870; Torbett to Maj. J. H. Taylor, Warrenton, Sept. 29, 1870, Post of Warrenton, Ga., Letters Sent book, 1869–1871, RG 98, NA; *KKK Report,* Georgia, pp. 201–5, 223–29, 232–33, 1028, 1031, 1034, 1105–10, 1116; Augusta *Chronicle and Sentinel,* May 5, 1870; Atlanta *Daily New Era,* May 6, 7, 1870, Aug. 10, 1871; pardon from Gov. Bullock of John C. Norris, March 31, 1871, in Warren County Superior Court Records (microfilm), Georgia Archives.
29. Atlanta *Daily New Era,* Aug. 19, 1870; *Atlanta Constitution,* Oct. 8, 1870, April 15, 1871; *KKK Report,* Georgia, pp. 206–7.
30. *KKK Report,* Georgia, pp. 1–17 (Richardson quotation on p. 13), 235–43, 351, 360, 420, 460–62, 739, 873, 925–26, 1116; Gov. Bullock to Gen. Terry, July 19, 1870; R. H. Atkinson (governor's secretary) to Judge H. D. D. Twiggs, Nov. 21, 1870; Bullock to Judge Twiggs and to sheriff of Washington County, Dec. 6, 1870, Executive Department Letterbooks, Georgia Archives.
31. *KKK Report,* Georgia, p. 1103.
32. Rome *Weekly Courier,* Jan. 14, 21, 1870.
33. For Chattooga County, see *ibid.,* Jan. 21, 28, March 4, April 1, 1870; *KKK Report,* Georgia, pp. 61–64, 93–95, 105–6, 129, 136, 512, 914, 917, 950–52. For references to limited Klan activity in 1870 in Cherokee, Haralson, and Floyd counties, respectively, see *ibid.,* pp. 390 ff., 472 ff., 917–18; for Walker and Whitfield counties, see Atlanta *Daily New Era,* Feb. 12, 1870; *KKK Report,* Georgia, pp. 567 ff., 576 ff., 1002 ff.
34. *KKK Report,* Georgia, p. 1116; Gov. Bullock to Gen. Terry, July 19, 1870; same to Judge Twiggs and to Sheriff of Washington County, Dec. 6, 1870; same to Gen. Terry and to Sheriff A. H. Hewitt, Oct. 5, 1870; R. H. Atkinson to Judge Twiggs, Nov. 21, 1870; Bullock to Col. J. H. Taylor, Dec. 16, 1870, Executive Department Letterbooks, Georgia Archives; *Daily Atlanta Intelligencer,* May 7, 1870.
35. Bullock to Terry, Nov. 5, 1870, Executive Department Letterbooks, Georgia Archives.
36. For references to the conduct of the campaign and election around the state, see Rufus B. Bullock, *Address . . . to the People of Georgia, October, 1872* (n.p., n.d.), p. 46; *KKK Report,* Georgia, pp. 14, 23, 65, 70, 75, 80–81, 213, 252 ff., 435, 516 ff., 607 ff., 697–99, 714, 873, 875, 925, 948–49, 954 ff., 974 ff., 1037, 1040; New York *Daily Tribune,* June 9, 1871; Atlanta *Daily New Era,* Dec. 20, 1870; *Daily Atlanta Intelligencer,* Dec. 28, 1870; John C. Reed, "What I Know of the Ku Klux Klan," *Uncle Remus's Magazine,* XXIII, 5 (July 1908), 16–17; 6 (Aug. 1908), 35–38; Charles Stearns, *The Black Man of the South, and the Rebels* (N.Y., 1872), pp. 287 ff.
37. Reed, "What I Know of the Ku Klux Klan," *Uncle Remus's Magazine,*

XXIII, 6 (Aug. 1908), p. 38; John C. Reed, *The Brothers' War* (Boston, 1905), p. xiii.

38. *KKK Report,* Florida, pp. 114 ff., 125 ff., 159–64, 176 ff., 221, 226 ff., 260 ff., 267 ff., 293 ff., 307 ff.; William Watson Davis, *The Civil War and Reconstruction in Florida* (N.Y., 1913), pp. 579–83; Joe M. Richardson, *The Negro in the Reconstruction of Florida, 1865–1877* (Tallahassee, 1965), pp. 166–68.

39. *KKK Report,* Florida, p. 174.

40. *Ibid.,* pp. 109 ff., 136 ff., 144 ff., 184 ff., 222; Ralph L. Peek, "Lawlessness in Florida, 1868–1871," *Florida Historical Quarterly,* XL (Oct. 1961), 172–73, 178.

41. *KKK Report,* Florida, pp. 100, 144 ff., 205–6, 281 ff.; Davis, *Civil War and Reconstruction in Florida,* p. 568.

42. *KKK Report,* Florida, p. 94.

43. *Ibid.,* pp. 78–82, 110, 140, 145, 150, 188–92, 207, 289–91; Davis, *Civil War and Reconstruction in Florida,* pp. 568–77; Peek, "Lawlessness in Florida," pp. 176–80.

44. Davis, *Civil War and Reconstruction in Florida,* pp. 577–79; *KKK Report,* Florida, pp. 205, 215; Peek, "Lawlessness in Florida," pp. 181–82.

45. *KKK Report,* Florida, pp. 109 ff., 144 ff., 283–84; *Congressional Globe,* 42d Congress, 1st sess., p. 654.

46. Ralph L. Peek, "Election of 1870 and the End of Reconstruction in Florida," *Florida Historical Quarterly,* XLV (April 1967), 353–65; *KKK Report,* Florida, pp. 76 ff., 103 ff., 125 ff., 225, 236, 260 ff., 291–93, 307 ff.; W. S. Simkins, "Why the Ku Klux Klan," *The Alcalde,* IV (June 19, 1916), 743–45.

CHAPTER 15: ALABAMA: TERRORISM IN THE WESTERN BLACK BELT

1. *Alabama Senate Journal,* 1868, pp. 248–49; *Acts of the Sessions of July, September and November, 1868, of the General Assembly of Alabama* . . . , p. 593; Alabama General Assembly, *Report of Joint Committee on Outrages* (Montgomery, 1868), pp. 3–6.

2. *Acts* . . . *of Alabama,* 1868, pp. 444–46, 452–54, 521.

3. *KKK Report,* Alabama, pp. 172, 493, 1854–55. Cf. Walter Lynwood Fleming, *Civil War and Reconstruction in Alabama* (N.Y., 1905), pp. 695–97.

4. Fleming, *Civil War and Reconstruction in Alabama,* pp. 690–91; *KKK Report,* Alabama, pp. 165, 171, 661, 715, 725, 785.

5. Gerard Choutteau to Gov. Smith, Ramsey Station, Sumter County, Nov. 14, 1868; John L. Stelzig to same, Livingston, Dec. 10, 1868; Daniel Price to R. A. Wilson, Livingston, Dec. 11, 1868; R. A. Wilson to Col. Beecher, Demopolis, Dec. 12, 1868; Choutteau to Gov. Smith, Livingston, May 17, June 1, 1869; E. W. Smith to same, Livingston, June 4, July 3,

1869; A. W. Dillard to same, Gainesville, June 5, 1869; R. Chapman to same, Livingston, June 6, 1869, in Governors' Correspondence, Alabama Archives; D. L. Dalton (governor's secretary) to Choutteau, May 20, 1869; same to A. W. Dillard and Reuben Chapman, June 9, 1869; same to R. Chapman and E. W. Smith, June 15, 1869, Governors' Letterbooks, Alabama Archives; *KKK Report*, Alabama, pp. 1668 ff.

6. Letters to Gov. Smith from George W. Houston, Livingston, Aug. 13, 1869, and Sheriff A. W. Dillard, Livingston, Aug. 14, 1869, Governors' Correspondence, Alabama Archives; *KKK Report*, Alabama, pp. 998–1002, 1574–76, 1673–74; Livingston *Journal*, Aug. 20, 1869.

7. Livingston *Journal*, Aug. 20, 27, 1869.

8. *Ibid.*, Aug. 20, 27, Sept. 10, 17, 1869.

9. *KKK Report*, Alabama, pp. 1001, 1675, 1798 ff.; Livingston *Journal*, Aug. 20, Sept. 3, 1869.

10. Livingston *Journal*, Aug. 20, 1869; Gov. John M. Palmer to Gov. Smith, Springfield, Ill., Oct. 4, 1869, Oct. 31, 1870, Governors' Correspondence, Alabama Archives; D. L. Dalton to Gov. Palmer, Oct. 11, 1869, Governors' Letterbooks, Alabama Archives.

11. Letters of D. L. Dalton to George W. Houston and Sheriff of Sumter County, Aug. 16, 1869; to Gen. A. H. Terry, Aug. 18, 1869; to J. A. Abrahams and Sheriff Dillard, Aug. 19, 1869; and to Charles Hays, Oct. 20, 1869, Governors' Letterbooks, Alabama Archives; Livingston *Journal*, Oct. 1, 1869.

12. Livingston *Journal*, Sept. 24, 1869.

13. *Ibid.*, Oct. 1, 1869.

14. *KKK Report*, Alabama, pp. 1576–77, 1605–6, 1945.

15. Livingston *Journal*, June 24, 1870.

16. Charles Hays to Gov. Smith, Washington, June 24, 1870; Sheriff A. E. Moore to D. L. Dalton, Livingston, June 25, 1870, Governors' Correspondence, Alabama Archives.

17. Letters to Gov. Smith from Sheriff A. E. Moore, Belmont, Aug. 1, 1870 (telegram); W. B. Jones, Demopolis, Aug. 4, 1870 (telegram); Pierce Burton, Demopolis, Aug. 4, 1870, Governors' Correspondence, Alabama Archives; Gov. Smith to Sheriff Moore, Aug. 1, 1870 (telegram), and to Pierce Burton, Aug. 2, 1870 (telegram), Governors' Letterbooks, Alabama Archives; Livingston *Journal*, Aug. 5, 1870; *KKK Report*, Alabama, pp. 1452, 1565 ff., 1666–67.

18. *KKK Report*, Alabama, pp. 1772–74, 1780, 1812, 1835–37; D. H. Trabb to Gov. Smith, Livingston, Aug. 12, 1870 (telegram), Governors' Correspondence, Alabama Archives; Livingston *Journal*, Aug. 19, Sept. 2, 1870; Montgomery *Alabama State Journal*, Aug. 24, 27, 1870.

19. Livingston *Journal*, Aug. 26, 1870; *KKK Report*, Alabama, pp. 345, 349, 1578–79, 1606–7, 1773–74, 1807, 1944.

20. Livingston *Journal*, Aug. 26, 1870.

21. *Ibid.*, Aug. 26, Sept. 2, 1870; *KKK Report*, Alabama, p. 1773.

22. Livingston *Journal*, Sept. 2, 16, 30, 1870. Cf. *KKK Report*, Alabama, p. 1774.
23. *KKK Report*, Alabama, p. 1191; James Martin *et al.* to Gov. Smith, Union, Greene County, May 25, 1869; Charles Hays to same, Aug. 4, 7, 1869, Governors' Correspondence, Alabama Archives.
24. *KKK Report*, Alabama, pp. 352, 528–30, 555, 1191, 1212–17, 1234, 1241, 1789, 1842–43; letters to Gov. Smith from Maggie Davis, Eutaw, April 1, 1870; W. B. Jones, Demopolis, April 3, 1870; A. A. Smith, Eutaw, April 7, May 20, 1870; "Republican," Eutaw, April 9, 1870; Gen. S. W. Crawford, Huntsville, April 11, 1870 (telegram); William Miller, Mobile, April 14, 15, May 9, 1870; Judge A. R. Davis, Eutaw, April 16, 1870; Gen. A. H. Terry, Atlanta, April 21, 1870 (telegram); J. A. Minnis, Eutaw, May 5, 1870, Governors' Correspondence, Alabama Archives; report of J. A. Minnis, Eutaw, May 20, 1870; letter (copy) of G. Cleaveland to William Miller, Eutaw, April 2, 1870, with letter of Miller to Gov. Smith, Mobile, May 3, 1870; Samuel B. Brown to Gov. Smith, Eutaw, June 25, 1870, in special Ku Klux Klan folder with 1870 correspondence, Governors' Correspondence, Alabama Archives; D. L. Dalton to Gov. Smith, April 4, 1870; Gov. Smith to Gen. Crawford, April 4, 1870; Smith to Gen. Terry, April 6, 19, 1870, in Governors' Letterbooks, Alabama Archives; H. C. Whitley to Atty. Gen. Akerman, New York, Sept. 29, 1871, in "Reconstruction in the South, 1871–1879" (microfilm), O. W. Holmes Devise, Justice Department Records, RG 60, NA.
25. *Monitor*, Feb. 23, 1869.
26. *Ibid.*, Feb. 16, March 16, 1869.
27. Fleming, *Civil War and Reconstruction in Alabama*, pp. 611–15; *KKK Report*, Alabama, pp. 111–14, 425–27; James B. Sellers, *History of the University of Alabama*, vol. I (University, Ala., 1953), pp. 298 ff.; Stanley F. Horn, *Invisible Empire: The Story of the Ku Klux Klan, 1866–1871* (Boston, 1939), pp. 128–31.
28. *KKK Report*, Alabama, p. 426; *Monitor*, Jan. 5, 26, March 2, April 6, 13, 1869.
29. *Monitor*, Jan. 5, 1869.
30. *Ibid.*, March 2, 1869.
31. Ryland Randolph, Autobiographical Episodes, in John W. DuBose Papers, Alabama Archives; Tuscaloosa *Independent Monitor*, April 5, May 3, 10, July 26, 1870; letters to Gov. Smith from G. A. Smith, Santa Fe, N.M., April 16, 1870; Sheriff J. J. Pegues, Tuscaloosa, April 28, 1870 (telegram, with accompanying copy of letter from William A. Smith, Decatur, Ill., May 17, 1870); Cornelia Bibb Vaughan, Tuscaloosa, April 20, 1870, Governors' Correspondence, Alabama Archives; Gov. Smith to Mrs. Vaughan, April 24, 1870, and to Sheriff Pegues, April 28, 1870 (telegram), in Governors' Letterbooks, Alabama Archives; Fleming, *Civil War and Reconstruction in Alabama*, p. 614; Livingston *Journal*, May 6, 1870; *KKK Report*, Alabama, p. 1979.

32. *KKK Report,* Alabama, pp. 417–18, 423; Fleming, *Civil War and Reconstruction in Alabama,* pp. 614–16.
33. Colored Citizens of Tuscaloosa to Gov. Smith, April 22, 1869; Sheriff T. P. Lewis to same, Tuscaloosa, May 5, 1869, in Governors' Correspondence, Alabama Archives; Montgomery *Alabama State Journal,* April 29, May 13, 1869; *Monitor,* April 27, 1869.
34. *Monitor,* May 25, 1869; Montgomery *Alabama State Journal,* May 13, 22, 24, 1869; S. A. M. Wood to Gov. Smith, Tuscaloosa, May 5, 1869; same to D. L. Dalton, May 20, 29, 1869; J. C. Loomis to Gov. Smith, Tuscaloosa, May 11, 1869; C. L. Williams to Smith, Tuscaloosa, May 13, June 2, 1869; J. J. Pegues to D. L. Dalton, Tuscaloosa, May 14, 1869; Gov. Smith to D. L. Dalton, Wedowee, Ala., May 20, 1869; Judge William Miller to Dalton, Tuscaloosa, May 22, 1869; D. Woodruff to Dalton, Tuscaloosa, May 26, June 4, 1869, in Governors' Correspondence, Alabama Archives; D. L. Dalton to J. C. Loomis, May 17, 1869, in Governors' Letterbooks, Alabama Archives.
35. D. Woodruff to D. L. Dalton, Tuscaloosa, June 4, July 16, 1869; J. D. F. Richards to Gov. Smith, Tuscaloosa, June 10, 1869; Richards to Judge Peck, June 12, 1869; Richards to D. L. Dalton, June 21, 1869; Jacob Miller to Gov. Smith, Oragona, Ala., June 14, 20, July 3, Aug. 24, 1869; same to same, Fayette County, July 12, 1869; Sheriff J. J. Pegues to Dalton, Tuscaloosa, June 22, 1869, in Governors' Correspondence, Alabama Archives; letters of Dalton to J. D. F. Richards, June 16, 1869; to J. J. Pegues, June 17, 24, 25, 1869; to Jacob Miller, June 25, 1869, in Governors' Letterbooks, Alabama Archives; *Senate Reports,* 42d Congress, 1st sess., No. 1, pp. xl, xlix.
36. *Monitor,* June 22, Sept. 14, 21, 1869; *KKK Report,* Alabama, p. 1992.
37. Gen. A. H. Terry to Gov. Smith, Atlanta, Jan. 22, 1870, with extract of Gen. Crawford's report of Jan. 14, in Governors' Correspondence, Alabama Archives; Gov. Smith to Gen. Terry, Jan. 24, 1870, in Governors' Letterbooks, Alabama Archives.
38. Montgomery *Alabama State Journal,* Sept. 20, Oct. 13, 1869.
39. *Monitor,* March 15, 22, 1870.
40. Anonymous letter to Gov. Smith from Tuscaloosa County, May 1, 1870; Sheriff J. J. Pegues to Gov. Smith, Tuscaloosa, May 9, 1870, in Governors' Correspondence, Alabama Archives; Montgomery *Alabama State Journal,* May 22, 1870. For references to scattered Klan activity in other counties of western and southern Alabama during 1869 and early 1870, see Sheriff W. L. Guin to Gov. Smith, Vernon, Ala., Dec. 20, 1869; Judge W. T. Blackford to Charles Miller, Greensboro, Ala., May 13, 1869; Daniel Wheeler to Gov. Smith, Fort Deposit, Ala., Feb. 10, 1870; Jacob Fisher to Gov. Smith, Bladen Springs, Ala., June 1, 1869; Ben Lane Posey to Gov. Smith, Mobile, June 12, 1869; affidavit of Jesse H. Booth, Autauga County, Dec. 8, 1869 (in special Ku Klux Klan folder with 1870 correspondence), in Governors' Correspondence, Alabama Archives; D. L. Dalton to Sheriff of Conecuh County, Aug. 30, 1869, in Governors' Letterbooks, Alabama Archives; *KKK Report,* Alabama, p. 1762.

CHAPTER 16: ALABAMA: THE NORTHERN COUNTIES, AND THE 1870 CAMPAIGN

1. See Neander H. Rice to Gov. Smith, Florence, March 1, 1869, Governors' Correspondence, Alabama Archives; *KKK Report,* Alabama, pp. 715, 785, 787.
2. *KKK Report,* Alabama, pp. 140–41, 147, 431–33, 443–44, 462 ff., 477, 486, 598–600, 624, 640, 649–50, 781, 783, 892, 919–21, 935, 942–43, 946–48, 975, 1170, 1197, 1212, 1755–61, 1768–69. Cf. Walter Lynwood Fleming, *Civil War and Reconstruction in Alabama* (N.Y., 1905), pp. 628–29.
3. Neander H. Rice to Gov. Smith, Florence, Nov. 23, 1868, Governors' Correspondence, Alabama Archives.
4. Letters to Gov. Smith from James M. Warren, Hillsboro, Ala., June 15, 1869, and Sheriff Wm. H. Lentz, Athens, July 15, 1869, Governors' Correspondence, Alabama Archives; *KKK Report,* Alabama, pp. 1196–97. A year later some of the most prominent men in Lawrence County pledged their support to Negroes who had just beaten off a Ku Klux attack and had reason to fear a return visit. *KKK Report,* Alabama, pp. 1223–28; letters to Gov. Smith from John H. Wager, Huntsville, Aug. 16, 1870; (?) Allen, Huntsville [Aug. 16, 1870]; T. C. Brannon, Oakville P.O., Aug. 29, 1870, Governors' Correspondence, Alabama Archives.
5. Gov. Smith to Hamilton Fish, April 28, 1869, Governors' Letterbooks, Alabama Archives. For specific accounts of Klan activity in this region generally from late 1868 through the summer of 1869, see *KKK Report,* Alabama, 475–76, 487, 927–33, 993–97, 1170, 1185–87, 1193, 1199–1200, 1203–4, 1212, 1762; and the Governors' Correspondence, Alabama Archives.
6. *House Miscellaneous Documents,* 40th Congress, 3d sess., No. 23; W. B. Figures to Gov. Smith, Huntsville, Jan. 5, 1869, Governors' Correspondence, Alabama Archives; Montgomery *Alabama State Journal,* Jan. 13, 14, 1869.
7. *KKK Report,* Alabama, pp. 857–69, 934, 1164, 1185–87, 1194 ff.; Montgomery *Alabama State Journal,* Jan. 13, 14, July 31, 1869; letters to Gov. Smith from James D. Weir, Huntsville, May 15, 1869; D. C. Humphreys, June 12, July 26, 27, 1869; Judge Lewis M. Douglas, Huntsville, July 26, 1869 (with accompanying statement of James Sandford); Wade McDonald, Huntsville, July 26, 1869; William B. Figures, Huntsville, July 26, 30, 1869; Eph. Latham, Huntsville, July 27, 1869; A. S. Lakin, Huntsville, July 27, 1869; John H. Wager, Huntsville, July 31, Aug. 1, 1869; Joseph P. Doyle, Huntsville, Aug. 1, 1869 (telegram); Thomas M. Green, Huntsville, Aug. 1, 1869; Lewis M. Douglas *et al.* to D. L. Dalton, Huntsville, July 31, 1869 (telegram), Governors' Correspondence, Alabama Archives; telegrams of D. L. Dalton to Lewis M. Douglas, Aug. 1,

1869, and to Sheriff Doyle, Aug. 2, 1869, Governors' Letterbooks, Alabama Archives.

8. See Gen. A. H. Terry to Gov. Smith, Atlanta, Aug. 29, 1869, Governors' Correspondence, Alabama Archives; D. L. Dalton to Gen. Terry, Aug. 25, 27, 1869, Governors' Letterbooks, Alabama Archives.

9. See letters to G. L. Meigs, April 9, 1869; to sheriffs of Jackson and Marshall counties, Feb. 13, 1869; to sheriff of Jackson County, May 1, 1869; to sheriff of Sumter County, Aug. 16, 1869, Governors' Letterbooks, Alabama Archives.

10. *KKK Report,* Alabama, pp. 936, 1193; John A. Determan *et al.* to Gov. Smith, Jacksonville, Aug. 7, 1869.

11. Letters to Gov. Smith from Sol Clayton, Lebanon, May 28, 1869, and W. J. Haralson and G. W. Malone, Lebanon, Aug. 16, 1869, Governors' Correspondence, Alabama Archives; D. L. Dalton to Gen. Terry, Aug. 25, 1869, Governors' Letterbooks, Alabama Archives.

12. *Alabama House Journal,* 1869–1870, pp. 7–13. See also D. L. Dalton to Charles Hays, Aug. 12, 1869, Governors' Letterbooks, Alabama Archives.

13. D. L. Dalton to gentlemen of Jacksonville, Aug. 12, 1869, Governors' Letterbooks, Alabama Archives.

14. *KKK Report,* Alabama, pp. 728–34, 738, 742–43, 745, 748–54, 770, 774–76, 1207–10; F. W. White to Gov. Smith, Blount County, April 23, June 8, 1870, Governors' Correspondence, Alabama Archives.

15. *KKK Report,* Alabama, pp. 778–79, 942–44.

16. *Ibid.,* p. 1170.

17. *Ibid.,* pp. 132, 610–11, 777–80, 1170, 1211, 1233–34, 1241; letters to Gov. Smith from Sheriff H. G. Thomas, Decatur, March 18, April 28, 1870; Gen. S. W. Crawford, Huntsville, April 6, 1870; S. S. Stinson, April 29, 1870; anonymous letter, DesArc, Ark., June 16, 1870, Governors' Correspondence, Alabama Archives; Gov. Smith to Sheriff H. G. Thomas, April 11, 1870, Governors' Letterbooks, Alabama Archives.

18. See *KKK Report,* Alabama, p. 1046; letters to Gov. Smith from Ashley C. Wood *et al.,* Talladega, April 23, 1870, and H. C. Sanford, Spring Garden, May 9, 1870, Governors' Correspondence, Alabama Archives.

19. *KKK Report,* Alabama, pp. 1017–23, 1059–62.

20. *Ibid.,* p. 1212; Gen. S. W. Crawford to Gov. Smith, Huntsville, March 21, April 6, 1870 (the former in special Ku Klux Klan folder with 1870 correspondence), Governors' Correspondence, Alabama Archives.

21. Montgomery *Alabama State Journal,* April 12, 1870; Gov. Smith to Senator Willard Warner, April 14, 1870 (telegram), and to D. C. Humphreys and D. P. Lewis, April 20, 1870, Governors' Letterbooks, Alabama Archives.

22. J. A. Minnis to Gov. Smith, Eutaw, May 5, 1870, Governors' Correspondence, Alabama Archives; Gov. Smith to President Grant, July 23, 1870, Governors' Letterbooks, Alabama Archives.

23. Letters to Gov. Smith from J. F. Morton, Vernon, April 26, 1870, and from Morton, Dublin, Ala., May 4, 1870; Sheriff F. M. Treadway,

Fayetteville, Oct. 1870 (all in special Ku Klux Klan folder with 1870 correspondence); J. F. Morton, Dublin, June 10, 1870; Sheriff F. M. Treadway, Fayette C.H., Oct. 31, 1870; H. M. Morton, Dublin, Nov. 3, 1870, Governors' Correspondence, Alabama Archives; Gov. Smith to J. F. Morton, May 13, 1870; to H. M. Morton, June 21, 1870, Governors' Letterbooks, Alabama Archives; J. A. Minnis to Atty. Gen. Akerman, Montgomery, Sept. 8, Oct. 13, 1871, Justice Department Source-Chronological File, Northern Alabama, RG 60, NA; *KKK Report,* Alabama, pp. 547, 559–60, 1229–30, 1762–63.

24. Thomas D. Foster to Gen. S. W. Crawford, Jacksonville, March 14, 1870; letters to Gov. Smith from W. P. Crook *et al.,* Jacksonville, May 13, 1870; James F. DeCamp, Patona, June 29, 1870; Thomas M. Peters, Patona, Sept. 20, 1870, Governors' Correspondence, Alabama Archives; *KKK Report,* Alabama, p. 485.

25. *KKK Report,* Alabama, pp. 77–79, 428–29, 445–46, 462–73, 481–85, 1173, 1235–38. Among the Klansmen involved were a den from Jacksonville and one from Ladiga, towns some miles away. H. C. Whitley to Atty. Gen. Williams, New York, Jan. 1872, "Reconstruction in the South, 1871–1879" (microfilm), O. W. Holmes Devise, Justice Department Records, RG 60, NA.

26. *KKK Report,* Alabama, pp. 77–79, 462–72, 481–85.

27. Montgomery *Alabama State Journal,* April 5, 1871; *New York Times,* Dec. 23, 1871.

28. *KKK Report,* Alabama, pp. 421, 494–95.

29. *Ibid.,* pp. 223, 1017–39, 1059–70, 1093–97, 1104–12, 1240.

30. *Ibid.,* p. 421; see also p. 1836.

31. Charles Hays to Senator Willard Warner, Myrtle Hall, Sept. 15, 1870, and to Gov. Smith, same place and date; Samuel B. Brown to Gov. Smith, Eutaw, Sept. 15, 19, 1870 (all in special Ku Klux Klan folder with 1870 correspondence); letters to Gov. Smith from Hays, Eutaw, Sept. 18, 1870, and from William Miller, Mobile, Sept. 19, 1870, Governors' Correspondence, Alabama Archives.

32. *KKK Report,* Alabama, pp. 1725, 1738–39; Livingston *Journal,* Dec. 15, 1871.

33. *Congressional Globe,* 41st Congress, 3d sess., Appendix, p. 111; *KKK Report,* Alabama, pp. 81, 1836. See also the bland account in the Livingston *Journal,* Oct. 28, 1870.

34. *Congressional Globe,* 41st Congress, 3d sess., p. 573; *ibid.,* Appendix, p. 111; *KKK Report,* Alabama, pp. 4–5, 10, 14–15, 27–29, 44–45, 80–81, 221, 261–62, 268–71, 278–79, 284, 296–97, 301–3, 307–10, 317, 319; Eutaw *Whig & Observer,* quoted in Livingston *Journal,* Oct. 28, 1870; Montgomery *Alabama State Journal,* Nov. 2, 1870.

35. James E. Sefton, *The United States Army and Reconstruction, 1865–1877* (Baton Rouge, 1967), pp. 232–33.

36. For election figures, see New York *Tribune, Tribune Almanac,* 1871, and W. Dean Burnham, *Presidential Ballots, 1836–1892* (Baltimore, 1955).

See also *Congressional Globe,* 42d Congress, 1st sess., Appendix, p. 269; *KKK Report,* Alabama, pp. 101, 223, 239, 252–53, 1618–19, 1624–26, 1725, 1774, 1822; Livingston *Journal,* Nov. 11, 18, 1870, Dec. 15, 1871.
37. Tuscaloosa *Independent Monitor,* Nov. 15, 1870.
38. *KKK Report,* Alabama, p. 223; Montgomery *Alabama State Journal,* July 29, 1871; *New York Times,* Dec. 23, 1871; Fleming, *Civil War and Reconstruction in Alabama,* pp. 750–52.

CHAPTER 17: MISSISSIPPI, TENNESSEE, AND KENTUCKY

1. John W. Kyle, "Reconstruction in Panola County," *Mississippi Historical Society Publications,* XIII (1913), 51–54; Lem L. Griffin to Gov. Adelbert Ames, Memphis, Feb. 7, 1869, Governors' Correspondence, Mississippi Archives; Memphis *Evening Post,* Feb. 18, March 23, 1869; Nashville *Press and Times,* Feb. 20, 1869; Jackson *Tri-Weekly Clarion,* March 30, April 13, 1869; *KKK Report,* Mississippi, pp. 782–83. See also Julia Kendel, "Reconstruction in Lafayette County," *Mississippi Historical Society Publications,* XIII (1913), 239–44, for Klan action and organization in a neighboring county.
2. Jackson *Weekly Mississippi Pilot,* March 12, 1870. See also Memphis *Evening Post,* March 26, 1869; Jackson *Semi-Weekly Clarion,* April 11, 1871.
3. Jackson *Semi-Weekly Clarion,* March 8, 1870; Jackson *Weekly Mississippi Pilot,* Nov. 19, 26, 1870; *KKK Report,* Mississippi, pp. 24, 46, 74–75, 114, 165–66.
4. Samuel A. Agnew Diary, Jan. 6, 1869, Southern Historical Collection, University of North Carolina.
5. Jackson *Weekly Mississippi Pilot,* Nov. 19, 1870.
6. For references to Klan activity in 1869–70 in Chickasaw County, see *KKK Report,* Mississippi, pp. 332, 437, 1029; for Monroe County, *ibid.,* pp. 268–69, 298, 358–59, 786, 803 ff., 1146–47; for Lowndes County, *ibid.,* pp. 423, 718, 724; for Noxubee County, *ibid.,* pp. 224–25, 228, 425–26, 469–73, 478, 571; for Winston County, *ibid.,* pp. 432, 544 ff.; for Lauderdale County, *ibid.,* pp. 24, 46, 74–75. See also Ruth Watkins, "Reconstruction in Newton County," *Mississippi Historical Society Publications,* XI (1910), 219–21.
7. For Kemper County, see Capt. James Kelly to Maj. John Eagan, Lauderdale, Miss., May 19, 1869; same to Lieut. W. Atwood, July 3, 1869; deposition of Fanny Payton, June 16, 1869; extract of John McRae to Lieut. J. O. Shelby, DeKalb, Miss., May 29, 1869, in Post of Lauderdale, Miss., Letters Sent, 1868–1869, vol. 92, Fourth Military District Records, RG 98, NA; *KKK Report,* Mississippi, pp. 247, 249–52, 256–58, 261. For references to the inability to secure conviction of criminals, see *KKK Report,* Mississippi, pp. 24, 75, 268–69, 358–59, 362, 423, 721, 803 ff.

8. James W. Garner, *Reconstruction in Mississippi* (N.Y., 1901), pp. 342–43; *Laws of the State of Mississippi,* 1870, pp. 89–92, 132–43, 607–8.

9. Quoted in Garner, *Reconstruction in Mississippi,* p. 345 n.; see also Vernon L. Wharton, *The Negro in Mississippi, 1865–1890* (Chapel Hill, N.C., 1947), pp. 220–21.

10. Jackson *Semi-Weekly Clarion,* April 1, 8, 12, 1870.

11. Ms. biography of Alcorn by his daughter, in James L. Alcorn Papers, Mississippi Archives; Garner, *Reconstruction in Mississippi,* p. 343; Lillian A. Pereyra, *James Lusk Alcorn, Persistent Whig* (Baton Rouge, 1966), pp. 134–35; *Congressional Globe,* 42d Congress, 2d sess., Appendix, pp. 406, 408.

12. Frankfort (Ky.) *Commonwealth,* Dec. 31, 1869; New York *Daily Tribune,* Feb. 8, March 16, 1870.

13. *Acts of the State of Tennessee,* 1869–1870, pp. 67–68, 97, 131–32, 353–55; *American Annual Cyclopaedia,* 1870, pp. 706–7; New York *Daily Tribune,* Feb. 8, March 16, 19, 22, 25, 1870; *Congressional Globe,* 41st Congress, 2d sess., Appendix, pp. 294–303, 420–23; 42d Congress, 1st sess., Appendix, pp. 308–9; Alrutheus A. Taylor, *The Negro in Tennessee, 1865–1880* (Washington, 1941), pp. 100–1.

14. New York *Daily Tribune,* Nov. 1, 7, 1870; Atlanta *Daily New Era,* Nov. 11, 1870; *Senate Executive Documents,* 41st Congress, 3d session, No. 22; *Congressional Globe,* 41st Congress, 3d sess., Appendix, pp. 214, 226.

15. Taylor, *The Negro in Tennessee,* p. 101; *Congressional Globe,* 42d Congress, 1st sess., p. 445; Louisville *Courier-Journal,* March 10, 1871.

16. Louisville *Courier-Journal,* June 2, 1871.

17. Atlanta *Daily New Era,* May 9, 1871, citing Nashville *Union and American,* May 6, 1871.

18. Louisville *Courier-Journal,* Oct. 4, 5, 1871; *New York Times,* Oct. 7, 1871.

19. Frankfort *Commonwealth,* Jan. 22, March 19, 26, April 2, 9, June 25, July 9, 1869; Louisville *Courier-Journal,* Jan. 13, Feb. 4, June 23, 1869.

20. Louisville *Courier-Journal,* April 3, 1869.

21. *Ibid.,* March 12, 1869; Frankfort *Commonwealth,* July 2, 1869.

22. Louisville *Courier-Journal,* July 2, Aug. 29, 30, Sept. 3, 17, 1869; Frankfort *Commonwealth,* Aug. 13, 27, Sept. 3, 10, Oct. 15, 1869; report of Adjutant General, Nov. 30, 1869, in *Kentucky Legislative Documents,* 1869, No. 15, pp. 5–6, 10.

23. Frankfort *Commonwealth,* Oct. 29, Nov. 19, Dec. 17, 1869, Jan. 7, Feb. 4, 11, 18, 25, 1870; Louisville *Courier-Journal,* Feb. 12, 1870.

24. G. W. Daniel *et al.* to President Grant, Booneville, Ky. [*ca.* Jan. 1, 1870], in Adjutant General's Office Records, No. 1155 S 69, RG 94, NA. The Louisville *Courier-Journal* and especially the Republican Frankfort *Commonwealth* carried frequent accounts in this period of Klan or regulator outrages around the state.

25. *Courier-Journal,* Jan. 17, March 14, April 2, Dec. 13, 1870.

26. Frankfort *Commonwealth,* May 20, 1870.

27. See *ibid.,* Aug. 5, 1870.
28. See Louisville *Courier-Journal,* May 28, 1870; Frankfort *Commonwealth,* June 17, Aug. 12, 1870.
29. Printed in Louisville *Courier-Journal,* Aug. 17, 1870.
30. *Frankfort Commonwealth,* Aug. 12, Dec. 9, 1870; report of Adjutant General, Nov. 30, 1870, in *Kentucky Legislative Documents,* 1870, No. 9, pp. 9, 11–12; governor's message, Jan. 5, 1871, in *Kentucky House Journal,* 1871, pp. 15–17.
31. See Frankfort *Commonwealth,* Sept. 30, Nov. 11, Dec. 9, 1870.
32. Louisville *Courier-Journal,* Sept. 30, 1870; Frankfort *Commonwealth,* Oct. 7, 1870.
33. Quoted in Louisville *Courier-Journal,* Sept. 19, 1870.
34. Quoted in Frankfort *Commonwealth,* Sept. 16, 1870; see also issue of Sept. 30.
35. Louisville *Courier-Journal,* Nov. 25, 26, 1870.
36. *Ibid.,* Nov. 28, Dec. 9, 13, 1870.

CHAPTER 18: MISSISSIPPI: THE CAMPAIGN AGAINST SCHOOLS

1. *KKK Report,* Mississippi, pp. 226, 230, 233–34, 238, 259, 269–70, 278, 281, 475–76, 809, 814, 1089, 1152–54. Regarding Mayor Lacey, see Richard C. Beckett, "Some Effects of Military Reconstruction in Monroe County," *Mississippi Historical Society Publications,* VIII (1904), p. 185.
2. *KKK Report,* Mississippi, pp. 332–33, 364, 678, 1074–75; Jackson *Daily Mississippi Pilot,* Dec. 26, 29, 1871.
3. *KKK Report,* Mississippi, pp. 233, 235, 238–39, 278, 330, 335–36, 363, 470–71, 473–74, 482 ff., 672, 720, 1086–87, 1152, 1154–55.
4. See *ibid.,* pp. 224–26, 231, 277, 330, 336, 417, 420, 423, 482 ff., 643–45, 664, 672, 676–77, 702, 710, 989–91, 1143–44, 1153.
5. *Ibid.,* pp. 54–55, 283–84, 333, 357–58, 436, 702, 710, 989 ff., 1103, 1154; F. Z. Browne, "Reconstruction in Oktibbeha County," *Mississippi Historical Society Publications,* XIII (1913), pp. 281, 283–85, 288.
6. *KKK Report,* Mississippi, p. 6–20, 23–53, 63–82, 96–164, 168–211, 220–22, 254; *ibid.,* Alabama, pp. 1049, 1436–37, 1599, 1601; *Congressional Globe,* 42d Congress, 1st sess., pp. 196–97; *ibid.,* Appendix, pp. 129, 278; Livingston (Ala.) *Journal,* Feb. 10–March 3, 1871.
7. Stanley F. Horn, *Invisible Empire: The Story of the Ku Klux Klan, 1866–1871* (Boston, 1939), p. 151.
8. *KKK Report,* Committee Report, pp. 73–77, 377–78; *ibid.,* Mississippi, pp. 76, 82–83, 86, 226, 260–61, 265, 271–77, 281–85, 325–33, 340, 353, 367, 371, 418–22, 434, 477–48, 492 ff., 502, 571–72, 590, 601, 640, 649–50, 693–95, 720, 1080–82, 1150; *Mississippi Senate Journal,* 1872, Appendix, pp. 181–87, 246–47, 252, 264; Vernon L. Wharton, *The Negro in Mississippi, 1865–1890* (Chapel Hill, N.C., 1947), pp.

244–45; Beckett, "Some Effects of Military Reconstruction in Monroe County," pp. 179–80.

9. *KKK Report,* Mississippi, pp. 82–95, 461–65, 1039–94, 1100–3, 1108–10, 1152, 1159; Jackson *Semi-Weekly Clarion,* May 26, 1871; Horn, *Invisible Empire,* pp. 152–55.

10. See *KKK Report,* Mississippi, pp. 236, 243–44, 274–76, 296, 339, 350, 358, 365–66, 424–25, 435, 507–8, 590, 592, 1029, 1099, 1139, 1159; G. J. Leftwich, "Reconstruction in Monroe County," *Mississippi Historical Society Publications,* IX (1906), p. 69.

11. *KKK Report,* Mississippi, pp. 262–63, 265, 461, 1026–27, 1139, 1154, 1159; Leftwich, "Reconstruction in Monroe County," p. 65; Ernest Franklin Puckett, "Reconstruction in Monroe County," *Mississippi Historical Society Publications,* XI (1910), p. 128; William C. Harris, *Presidential Reconstruction in Mississippi* (Baton Rouge, 1967), pp. 118–19, 123.

12. *KKK Report,* Mississippi, pp. 279–80, 293, 775, 808–13.

13. *Ibid.,* pp. 295, 865–66; Jackson *Semi-Weekly Clarion,* May 2, 1871.

14. Quoted in New York *Daily Tribune,* March 28, 1871.

15. Columbus *Index,* quoted in Jackson *Daily Mississippi Pilot,* May 22, 1871.

16. Jackson *Semi-Weekly Clarion,* March 21, 28, 1871.

17. See *KKK Report,* Mississippi, pp. 640, 648–49, 721, 1102.

18. E. P. Jacobson to Atty. Gen. Akerman, Jackson, Aug. 7, 1871, Justice Department Source-Chronological File, Southern Mississippi, RG 60, NA.

19. *KKK Report,* Mississippi, pp. 91, 252–53, 258–59, 1089–93, 1107; Ruth Watkins, "Reconstruction in Newton County," *Mississippi Historical Society Publications,* XI (1910), pp. 220–21; testimony of Elijah Smith and others, in Ku Klux Klan and Election Conditions in Mississippi, "Reconstruction in the South, 1871–1879" (microfilm), O. W. Holmes Devise, Justice Department Records, RG 60, NA.

20. *KKK Report,* Mississippi, pp. 241, 476–77, 500.

21. *Ibid.,* pp. 500–1, 677–79, 1017–20, 1062–63, 1089–92.

22. *Ibid.,* pp. 258, 1067, 1138.

23. Lillian A. Pereyra, *James Lusk Alcorn, Persistent Whig* (Baton Rouge, 1966), pp. 135, 137–41; *Congressional Globe,* 42d Congress, 1st sess., p. 196; *ibid.,* Appendix, pp. 266, 277; *ibid.,* 2d sess., Appendix, pp. 405–6, 408; *KKK Report,* Mississippi, pp. 239, 444; New York *Daily Tribune,* March 25, 1871; Jackson *Semi-Weekly Clarion,* March 21, April 7, 25, 1871; *New York Times,* May 15, 1871.

CHAPTER 19: ALABAMA, FLORIDA, AND KENTUCKY

1. *KKK Report,* Alabama, pp. 333, 1327–30, 1436–37, 1565 ff., 1618, 1724, 1868 ff., 1940 ff., 1953–54; Livingston *Journal,* Dec. 16, 23, 1870; copy of anonymous letter to Congressman Charles Hays, Haysville, Ala., April 8, 1871, with letter of Congressman Joseph H. Sloss to Gov. Lindsay,

Washington, April 12, 1871, Governors' Correspondence, Alabama Archives.

2. *KKK Report,* Alabama, pp. 1649–60, 1728–33, 1874–75, 1916, 1923 ff., 1928–29, 1933 ff.; letters to Gov. Lindsay from Judge L. R. Smith, Mobile, April 13, 1871, and Mt. Sterling, Nov. 17, 1871, Feb. 9, 1872; cf. letter of J. P. Evans, Bladon Springs, Dec. 2, 1871, Governors' Correspondence, Alabama Archives.

3. *KKK Report,* Alabama, pp. 1993–2007.

4. *Ibid.,* pp. 1048–54, 1324–27, 1330–33, 1433–36, 1440.

5. *Ibid.,* pp. 333, 1778, 1916; Montgomery *Alabama State Journal,* March 7, 1871; Livingston *Journal,* Feb. 24, 1871; L. R. Smith to Gov. Lindsay, Mobile, April 13, 1871, Mt. Sterling, Nov. 17, 1871, Governors' Correspondence, Alabama Archives.

6. *KKK Report,* Alabama, pp. 1283, 1778, 1916; L. R. Smith to Gov. Lindsay, Mobile, April 13, 1871, Governors' Correspondence, Alabama Archives.

7. *Congressional Globe,* 41st Congress, 3d sess., Appendix, p. 111; Montgomery *Alabama State Journal,* Feb. 5, 1871; *KKK Report,* Alabama, p. 1052.

8. Blackford did not specifically identify Forrest as his informant regarding the Klan, but taking the two men's testimony together, it could hardly have been anyone else. *KKK Report,* Miscellaneous Testimony, pp. 16–19; *ibid.,* Alabama, pp. 1271 ff., 1475–98, 1503, 1518 ff.; letters to Gov. William H. Smith from W. T. Blackford, Greensboro, Sept. 12, Dec. 20, 1868; James J. Garrett, Greensboro, Oct. 19, 1868; B. L. Whalen and J. E. Love, Greensboro, Dec. 19, 1868, Governors' Correspondence, Alabama Archives.

9. *KKK Report,* Alabama, pp. 728, 733, 770, 919–20, 945–48, 1746–47, 1754, 1757–58, 1764; *Congressional Globe,* 42d Congress, 1st sess., p. 156; Montgomery *Alabama State Journal,* May 19, 1871; H. C. Whitley to Atty. Gen. Akerman, New York, Sept. 29, 1871, Jan. 1872; "Reconstruction in the South, 1871–1879" (microfilm), O. W. Holmes Devise, Justice Department Records, RG 60, NA.

10. *KKK Report,* Alabama, pp. 547–48, 559–60, 1763; New York *Daily Tribune,* June 28, 1871; Joseph H. Sloss to John A. Steele, Washington, Feb. 23, 1871, Governors' Correspondence, Alabama Archives; J. A. Minnis to Atty. Gen. Akerman, Montgomery, Sept. 8, Oct. 13, 1871, Justice Department Source-Chronological File, Northern Alabama, RG 60, NA.

11. *New York Times,* Jan. 25, 1871; Montgomery *Alabama State Journal,* Feb. 4, May 24, June 3, 14, 1871; *KKK Report,* Alabama, pp. 533–34, 537–38, 1006–15, 1125–29, 1132, 1136–39; John A. Minnis to Atty. Gen. Williams, Montgomery, June 25, 1872, Justice Department Source-Chronological File, Middle Alabama, RG 60, NA.

12. See *KKK Report,* Alabama, pp. 728, 783, 919, 921, 935, 947, 1007,

1015, 1126–27, 1139, 1857; Montgomery *Alabama State Journal,* May 19, June 3, 1871.

13. Quoted in Montgomery *Alabama State Journal,* Feb. 22, 1871.

14. *Ibid.,* June 6, 1871; Susan Lawrence Davis, *Authentic History, Ku Klux Klan, 1865–1877* (N.Y., 1924), pp. 155–58; Stanley F. Horn, *Invisible Empire: The Story of the Ku Klux Klan, 1866–1871* (Boston, 1939), pp. 142–44.

15. *KKK Report,* Alabama, pp. 1853–54, 1868 ff., 1940 ff.

16. *Ibid.,* p. 262.

17. Montgomery *Alabama State Journal,* May 24, 1871.

18. *KKK Report,* Alabama, pp. 229, 240–41, 533–34.

19. Montgomery *Alabama State Journal,* May 28, June 1, 3, 1871; *KKK Report,* Alabama, pp. 329–30. For more general evidence on this subject, see *ibid.,* pp. 108, 260–61, 265, 274, 332–34, 344, 534, 551, 725, 781, 787, 1137, 1174–75, 1519–20, 1606, 1618, 1757, 1760–62, 1854; Livingston *Journal,* March 10, Nov. 17, 1871; Montgomery *Alabama State Journal,* April 26, 28, May 19, June 14, 1871; Judge L. R. Smith to Gov. Lindsay, Mt. Sterling, Feb. 9, 1872, Governors' Correspondence, Alabama Archives; J. A. Minnis to Atty. Gen. Akerman, Montgomery, Sept. 8, Oct. 13, 1871, Justice Department Source-Chronological File, Northern Alabama, RG 60, NA.

20. *KKK Report,* Alabama, p. 175; *New York Times,* Jan. 25, 1871; *Alabama Senate Journal,* 1870–1871, p. 76. See also *ibid.,* 1871–1872, pp. 8–9.

21. Joseph H. Sloss to John A. Steele, Washington, Feb. 23, 1871, and to Gov. Lindsay, Washington, April 12, 1871, Governors' Correspondence, Alabama Archives; *KKK Report,* Alabama, pp. 1176–77.

22. *KKK Report,* Florida, pp. 267–72.

23. *Ibid.,* pp. 260–67.

24. For activities in Clay and Baker counties, see *ibid.,* pp. 54–75.

25. *New York Times,* April 17, 1871; Ralph L. Peek, "Lawlessness in Florida, 1868–1871," *Florida Historical Quarterly,* XL (Oct. 1961), 181–83; William Watson Davis, *The Civil War and Reconstruction in Florida* (N.Y., 1913), pp. 583–84; *KKK Report,* Florida, pp. 77–81, 83–86, 90–93, 144 ff., 206–7, 221–22, 274–79, 303–5.

26. *KKK Report,* Florida, pp. 77, 83, 90–91, 93, 144 ff., 165–66, 184–91, 272–79; E. M. Cheney to President Grant, Jacksonville, Nov. 18, 1871, with affidavit of Negro residents of Jackson County, Nov. 16, 1871, Justice Department Source-Chronological File, Southern Florida, RG 60, NA; Ralph L. Peek, "Curbing of Voter Intimidation in Florida, 1871," *Florida Historical Quarterly,* XLIII (April 1965), 346.

27. Frankfort *Commonwealth,* Jan. 13, 20, 27, 1871. For an inside account of the Klan in this region, extending for several years after 1871, see Jesse Fears, *Confession of Richard H. Shuck, A Member of the Owen and Henry County Marauders of the State of Kentucky* (Frankfort, 1877).

28. *Congressional Globe,* 42d Congress, 1st sess., p. 238; *ibid.,* Appendix, p. 145; *Kentucky House Journal,* 1871, pp. 271–72.

29. Louisville *Courier-Journal,* March 5, 31, 1871; *New York Times,* March 7, 1871.

30. Frankfort *Commonwealth,* March 3, 1871; Louisville *Courier-Journal,* Feb. 27, 28, 1871.

31. *Kentucky House Journal,* 1871, pp. 15–17.

32. *Ibid.,* pp. 270–71, reprinted in *Congressional Globe,* 42d Congress, 1st sess., p. 239.

33. Lexington *Gazette* and Hopkinsville *New Era* quoted in Frankfort *Commonwealth,* Feb. 10, April 14, 1871, respectively. See Louisville *Courier-Journal* throughout this period, but especially the reply to its critics on March 6, 1871.

34. See charge of Judge Pryor of Frankfort after the Ku Klux raid there, in New York *Daily Tribune,* March 7, 1871, and of Judge Bruce in Shelbyville, in *Courier-Journal,* March 20, 1871, reprinted in *Congressional Globe,* 42d Congress, 1st sess., p. 237.

35. *Courier-Journal,* March 24, 1871, reprinted in *Congressional Globe,* 42d Congress, 1st sess., p. 350. The *New York Times* (April 26, 1871) believed that the legislature's failure to act was the result of physical intimidation by the Klan, which had shown that it could enter Frankfort at will. The senators who voted for the bill received no special attention from the Klan, however.

36. *Congressional Globe,* 42d Congress, 1st sess., p. 164.

37. Louisville *Courier-Journal,* March 23, 1871.

38. *Senate Miscellaneous Documents,* 42d Congress, 1st sess., No. 49.

39. Frankfort *Commonwealth,* March 31, 1871. See also the letter of a Kentuckian in the New York *Daily Tribune,* March 28, 1871.

40. Quoted in *Congressional Globe,* 42d Congress, 1st sess., Appendix, p. 286.

41. See *Courier-Journal,* March 24, 29, April 1, 1871.

42. Frankfort *Commonwealth,* April 21, May 5, 1871; Louisville *Courier-Journal,* April 11, 29, June 2, 1871.

43. Louisville *Courier-Journal,* April 1, 6, 1871.

44. Frankfort *Commonwealth,* May 12, July 21, 1871; Louisville *Courier-Journal,* July 22, 23, 25, 1871.

45. Frankfort *Commonwealth,* Feb. 17, 1871; Louisville *Courier-Journal,* Feb. 18, 1871.

46. See Frankfort *Commonwealth,* Jan. 20, 27, July 28, Aug. 25, 1871; Louisville *Courier-Journal,* March 29, 30, July 21, 23, 25, Aug. 4, 5, 7, 22, 1871; *New York Times,* Aug. 25, 1871.

47. Frankfort *Commonwealth,* Aug. 11, Sept. 29, 1871; *New York Times,* Aug. 9, 1871; Louisville *Courier-Journal,* Sept. 24, 26, 29, 1871.

48. Frankfort *Commonwealth,* Nov. 3, 1871.

49. See *ibid.,* Sept. 22, 29, Oct. 13, Nov. 3, 1871; Louisville *Courier-Journal,* Sept. 21, 1871.

50. Message of Dec. 4, 1871, reprinted in *Congressional Globe,* 42d Congress, 2d sess., p. 598.

CHAPTER 20: GEORGIA

1. See Atlanta *Daily New Era,* Feb. 25, July 16, 1871; Gov. Bullock to Judge A. D. Harvey, March 14, 1871, Executive Department Letterbooks, Georgia Archives.
2. *KKK Report,* Georgia, pp. 611, 1039–40.
3. *Ibid.,* pp. 697–99.
4. *Ibid.,* pp. 363 ff., 372, 407–11, 411 ff. 472 ff., 544 ff., 551–52, 555–59, 1008–17.
5. *Ibid.,* p. 402.
6. *Ibid.,* p. 864.
7. *Ibid.,* pp. 414 ff., 460–61, 746, 753 ff.; Atlanta *Daily New Era,* Oct. 24, 1871.
8. *KKK Report,* Georgia, pp. 350–52, 517. For further information about Klan activity in Gwinnett, Walton, and Jackson, see pp. 350–55, 400–2, 414–19, 423–25, 462 ff., 465 ff., 468 ff., 481–82, 516–18, 520 ff., 602–5, 649, 710, 713–14, 745–47, 751, 864, 866–67.
9. For Clarke, Burke, and Columbia counties, see *KKK Report,* Georgia, pp. 9, 13, 1096; Charles Stearns, *The Black Man of the South, and the Rebels* (N.Y., 1872), pp. 409–10.
10. *KKK Report,* Georgia, pp. 926, 931.
11. *Ibid.,* pp. 668–71.
12. *Ibid.,* pp. 653, 655–62, 664–65, 867 ff., 1060–61.
13. *Ibid.,* p. 1043; Atlanta *Daily New Era,* Jan. 19, Feb. 25, 1871.
14. Judge H. D. D. Twiggs to Gov. Bullock, Sandersville, Jan. 5, 1871, Governors' Correspondence, Georgia Archives; *Daily Atlanta Intelligencer,* Jan. 8, 1871; *KKK Report,* Georgia, p. 1044.
15. Judge H. D. D. Twiggs to Gov. Bullock, Sandersville, March 29, 1871, Governors' Correspondence, Georgia Archives; *KKK Report,* Georgia, p. 1044.
16. J. E. Bryant to Atty. Gen. Akerman, Washington, D.C., Oct. 31, 1871, Justice Department Source-Chronological File, Georgia, RG 60, NA; *KKK Report,* Georgia, p. 1051.
17. *KKK Report,* Georgia, p. 1045.
18. *Ibid.,* pp. 359–60, 362–63; *The Nation's Peril: Twelve Years' Experience in the South* (N.Y., 1872), pp. 41–46; J. E. Bryant to Atty. Gen. Akerman, Washington, D.C., Oct. 31, 1871, Justice Department Source-Chronological File, Georgia, RG 60, NA.
19. Bryant to Akerman, *ibid.; KKK Report,* Georgia, p. 359.
20. Bryant to Akerman, *ibid.; KKK Report,* Georgia, pp. 356–63, 426, 431, 973.
21. *KKK Report,* Georgia, p. 360; R. H. Atkinson (governor's secretary) to

G. W. Payne, Nov. 2, 1871, Executive Department Letterbooks, Georgia Archives; Charles Hooks to President Grant, Atlanta, Nov. 20, 1871, in Justice Department, Attorney General's Office, Letters Received from the President, RG 60, NA.

22. *New York Times,* Sept. 26, 1872.
23. See the similar analysis by an Atlanta correspondent in the New York *Daily Tribune,* June 14, 1871.
24. *KKK Report,* Georgia, pp. 884–86, 900, 914, 949–50, 952–53.
25. *Ibid.,* pp. 44–45, 74–75, 403–6, 884, 920, 1000.
26. Sawyer later denied that he had been forced to dance, but the denial seems hard to square with his statement at the time. See *KKK Report,* Georgia, pp. 46, 74, 85, 625, 636, 882, 884–85, 892; Rome *Weekly Courier,* Feb. 10, Aug. 18, 1871. Grady had started out as associate editor of the *Courier* in September 1869, but left it for the *Commercial* in 1870.
27. Rome *Weekly Courier,* Jan. 27, Feb. 3, 1871; *KKK Report,* Georgia, pp. 625, 879–80.
28. Rome *Weekly Courier,* Feb. 10, 17, 1871.
29. *KKK Report,* Georgia, p. 886.
30. *Ibid.,* pp. 883–86.
31. *Ibid.,* p. 887; Rome *Weekly Courier,* March 3, 1871.
32. Proclamation of Gov. Bullock, May 17, 1871, in Atlanta *Daily New Era,* May 23, 1871; *KKK Report,* Georgia, p. 75.
33. *KKK Report,* Georgia, pp. 77, 625, 673–75, 677, 887, 893–94, 902, 1001.
34. *Ibid.,* pp. 20, 1000, 1002.
35. *Ibid.,* pp. 41–42, 298, 914, 1100–1, 1103.
36. *Ibid.,* pp. 21–22, 76–77, 672, 1070 ff., 1079.
37. *Ibid.,* 20, 24, 106, 326, 786–87, 1000, 1002; Rome *Weekly Courier,* March 17, 1871. See also Atlanta *Constitution,* March 16, 1871, and Columbia, S.C., *Daily Phoenix,* April 5, 1871, regarding the alleged Republican affiliation of the culprits.
38. *KKK Report,* Georgia, pp. 23, 32, 39–41, 293, 948, 999–1001, 1078; Gov. Bullock to C. P. Forsyth, March 20, 1871, Executive Department Letterbooks, Georgia Archives; Rome *Weekly Courier,* April 14, 21, 1871.
39. Atlanta *Daily New Era,* Aug. 15, 1871.
40. *KKK Report,* Georgia, pp. 567–80, 1002 ff.; proclamation of Gov. Bullock, May 17, 1871, in Atlanta *Daily New Era,* May 23, 1871. See also the correspondence of Bullock and D. C. Sutton of Walker County in same issue.
41. Atlanta *Daily New Era,* Dec. 17, 1871.
42. *KKK Report,* Georgia, pp. 744–45.
43. For evidence about Walton, Gwinnett, and Jackson counties, see *ibid.,* pp. 401, 462 ff., 465 ff., 468 ff., 749, 864, 1126–27.
44. *Ibid.,* pp. 372, 375–77, 386–90, 497–515, 908 ff., 1171–75. For similar, if less aggravated, conditions in Habersham County, next door, see pp. 484–89, 493–95.

45. See *ibid.*, pp. 24, 26–27, 352, 420, 476, 625, 680, 1072, 1080.

46. *Ibid.*, pp. 422–23, 753–55, 771, 773, 786–90.

47. See *New York Times*, April 28, 1871; Atlanta *Daily New Era,* May 3, 1871. The Augusta *Constitutionalist* issued a long editorial in November attacking present manifestations of Klan violence, but not the organization in its first inception. It felt obliged to base much of its criticism on the ground that federal bayonets would return otherwise. See *KKK Report,* Georgia, pp. 1216–17.

48. See *KKK Report,* Georgia, pp. 24, 27, 41, 92–93, 99, 110, 352, 420, 422–23, 436–37, 1135; Stearns, *Black Man of the South,* pp. 416–17.

49. Savannah *Republican,* Jan. 6, 1871, quoted in *Daily Atlanta Intelligencer,* Jan. 8, 1871.

50. See Atlanta *Daily New Era,* April 9, May 3, 1871.

51. *Ibid.,* April 20, May 9, 23, 25, Oct. 17, 20, 22, 1871.

52. Atlanta *Constitution,* Nov. 8, 9, 1871.

53. *KKK Report,* Georgia, pp. 1214–15.

CHAPTER 21: NORTH CAROLINA: REBELS VS. UNIONISTS IN RUTHERFORD

1. *KKK Report,* North Carolina, pp. 37–38, 51 ff., 65 ff., 83–85.

2. *SR,* pp. 72, 387; *KKK Report,* North Carolina, pp. 31 ff., 86 ff.

3. *KKK Report,* North Carolina, pp. 15, 31 ff., 86 ff.; Gov. Caldwell to Coroner of Harnett County, May 10, 1871, Governors' Letterbooks No. 62, North Carolina Archives.

4. *SR,* pp. 76, 388, 391; *ibid.,* pt. 2, pp. 39–48; *KKK Report,* North Carolina, pp. 15, 50, 83, 85, 93, 100.

5. *SR.,* p. 388; *KKK Report,* North Carolina, pp. 13 ff.; Raleigh *Sentinel,* May 10, 13, 1871.

6. *KKK Report,* North Carolina, pp. 138; *SR,* pp. 118–19; (Rutherfordton) Rutherford *Star,* May 6, 1871.

7. See the characterizations of Rutherford County in New York *Herald,* June 13, 1871: Randolph Abbott Shotwell, *Papers,* ed. by J. G. de Roulhac Hamilton, 3 vols. (Raleigh, 1929–36), II, 280–82, 285–300, 387; Clarence W. Griffin, *History of Old Tryon and Rutherford Counties, North Carolina, 1730–1936* (Asheville, N.C., 1937), p. 336. For the relationship between the Union League and the Ku Klux Klan in Cleveland County, see *KKK Report,* North Carolina, p. 317.

8. *KKK Report,* North Carolina, p. 317. See also David Schenck Diary, Sept. 30, 1871, Southern Historical Collection, University of North Carolina.

9. *KKK Report,* North Carolina, pp. 30–31, 175, 203, 316–18, 321–24, 506; Rutherford *Star,* Nov. 11, 18, 1871; Shotwell, *Papers,* II, 280, 348; Lieut. J. S. McEwan to Atty. Gen. Akerman, Washington, D.C., Oct. 18, 1871, Justice Department Source-Chronological File, Eastern North Carolina, RG 60, NA.

10. See Dixon, "The Story of the Ku Klux Klan," *Metropolitan Magazine,* XXII (Sept. 1905), 664.

11. *KKK Report,* North Carolina, pp. 110–11, 147, 207, 215–16, 223, 228–29; Shotwell, *Papers,* II, 279, 344, 347–49. Dixon indicates that McAfee tried to disband the Klan in Cleveland County after Holden's overthrow. "Story of the Ku Klux Klan," p. 666.

12. Shotwell, *Papers,* II, 300–6, 310, 321, 344–51, 370–80, 397–98, 401–6. This memoir is full of inconsistencies, as in the time of Shotwell's first affiliation with the Klan. He is highly defensive throughout, despite disarming candor about some of his personal weaknesses. His disavowals of participation in Klan violence, especially the Rutherfordton raid of June 11, 1871, are contradicted by several outside sources. See also Rutherford *Star,* July 2, 16, 1870.

13. *KKK Report,* North Carolina, pp. 173–74, 203–4, 209, 216–17, 221, 321, 426; *SR,* pp. 127, 187; Shotwell, *Papers,* II, 370; Judge J. M. Cloud to Gov. Caldwell, Salisbury, July 12, 1871, Governors' Correspondence, North Carolina Archives.

14. *KKK Report,* North Carolina, pp. 115, 119, 123–25, 146–48, 185, 207, 212, 222, 234, 427, 552–54; Shotwell *Papers,* II, 345. Only outside pressure seems to explain the membership, attested by two confessed members, of United States Commissioner Nathan Scoggins, a Republican who took an active and even zealous part in bringing Klansmen to book later in 1871. See Lieut. J. S. McEwan to Atty. Gen. Akerman, Washington, D.C., Oct. 18, 1871, Justice Department Source-Chronological File, Eastern North Carolina, RG 60, NA.

15. See Shotwell, *Papers,* II, 345–46.

16. *Ibid.,* pp. 344–46, 366–67, 372, 396, 407, 425.

17. *Ibid.,* pp. 344–46: *KKK Report,* North Carolina, pp. 16, 19 ff., 102 ff., 148, 204–5, 208–9, 211, 214, 427, 437, 443; *SR,* pp. 127–29, 186–87; Gov. Caldwell to President Grant, April 20, 1871, Governors' Letterbooks No. 62, North Carolina Archives; *Congressional Globe,* 42d Congress, 1st sess., p. 656; Rutherford *Star,* Feb. 11, March 25, April 29, May 6, 1871.

18. Shotwell, *Papers,* II, 346–51, 395: *KKK Report,* North Carolina, pp. 326–28, 378, 425–26; Rutherford *Star,* April 8, 1871. For the growing alarm of Conservatives in general at increasing violence in the state, see New York *Daily Tribune,* Feb. 21, 1871.

19. *KKK Report,* North Carolina, pp. 16, 18–19, 20 ff., 111–14, 170–72, 188 ff., 211, 305–7, 367–68, 453 ff.; Rutherford *Star,* May 27, 1871; Judge G. W. Logan to Gov. Caldwell, Rutherfordton, April 9, 1871, Governors' Letterbooks No. 62, North Carolina Archives; Shotwell, *Papers,* II, 351–52, 356–69.

20. *KKK Report,* North Carolina, pp. 102 ff., 178–79; Shotwell, *Papers,* II, 385: Rutherford *Star,* May 6, 1871; text of convention resolution in Raleigh *Sentinel,* June 3, 1871; J. B. Carpenter *et al.* to Gov. Caldwell, Rutherfordton, May 14, 1871, Governors' Correspondence, North Carolina Archives.

21. L. F. Churchill and G. M. Whiteside to Gov. Holden, Rutherfordton, Aug. 11, 1869, Governors' Correspondence, North Carolina Archives; David Schenck Diary, 1871, *passim*, Southern Historical Collection, University of North Carolina; *SR*, p. 186; Shotwell, *Papers*, II, 281–82, 293–94, 337–42, 351–55, 361; *KKK Report*, North Carolina, pp. 102 ff., 145, 153–54; Rutherford *Star*, May 6, Aug. 19, 1871.

22. See letters from Logan and Carpenter to Gov. Caldwell, Dec. 27, 1870 to May 14, 1871, Governors' Correspondence and Governors' Letterbooks No. 62, North Carolina Archives; Congressional testimony of Logan and Carpenter in *SR*, pp. 186–88, and in *KKK Report*, North Carolina, pp. 19 ff.; Rutherford *Star*, April 29, 1871; Shotwell, *Papers*, II, 388–96; New York *Herald*, May 22, 1871.

23. *KKK Report*, North Carolina, pp. 102 ff., 205–7, 309, 328, 428–33, 448–49; Shotwell, *Papers*, II, 384, 386–97, 400–1, 406–27, 430–31; III, 30; Raleigh *Sentinel*, Sept. 5, 1871; *New York Times*, Nov. 11, 1871; Rutherford *Star*, June 24, 28, 1871; letters to Gov. Caldwell from James M. Justice, Rutherfordton, June 12, 1871, and Judge J. M. Cloud, Salisbury, July 12, 1871, Governors' Correspondence, North Carolina Archives.

24. Gov. Caldwell to Judge G. W. Logan, Jan. 5, 1871, and to President Grant, April 20, 1871, Governors' Letterbooks No. 62, North Carolina Archives; Maj. C. H. Morgan to Adj. Gen., Department of the East, Raleigh, May 17, 1871, in Post of Raleigh, Letters Sent book, 1869–1872, RG 98, NA.

25. Gov. Caldwell to Judge J. M. Cloud, June 15, 1871, Governors' Letterbooks No. 62, North Carolina Archives; Maj. C. H. Morgan to Adj. Gen., Department of the East, Raleigh, June 17 (two letters), July 8, 1871; Morgan to Capt. V. K. Hart, Raleigh, June 25, 1871, in Post of Raleigh, Letters Sent book, 1869–1872, RG 98, NA; Rutherford *Star*, June 24, 28, 1871.

26. Maj. C. H. Morgan to A. A. G., Department of the East, Raleigh, July 8, 14, Aug. 11, 25, 1871; Morgan to Capt. V. K. Hart, Raleigh, Aug. 3, 9, 23, 1871, in Post of Raleigh, Letters Sent book, 1869–1872, RG 98, NA; letters to Gov. Caldwell from Judge G. W. Logan, Rutherfordton, July 5, Aug. 7, 1871; Rutherford County Commissioners, Rutherfordton, July 5, 1871; Judge J. M. Cloud, Salisbury, July 12, 1871; Nathan Scoggins, Rutherfordton, July 19, 21, 1871, Governors' Correspondence, North Carolina Archives; Rutherford *Star*, July 8, 22, 29, Aug. 5, 12, 19, 1871; *KKK Report*, North Carolina, pp. 162, 175–76, 209–10, 214–15, 232–35.

27. Shotwell, *Papers*, III, 55, 430–31.

28. *KKK Report*, North Carolina, pp. 137, 142–45, 248–49, 271; *SR*, p. 126; Raleigh *Sentinel*, May 1, 23, 1871.

29. Quoted in Rutherford *Star*, April 22, 1871.

30. *KKK Report*, North Carolina, p. 142; Rutherford *Star*, June 28, 1871.

31. *KKK Report*, North Carolina, pp. 142–43: Raleigh *Sentinel*, June 21, 1871; Rutherford *Star*, June 28, 1871. As Justice pointed out, Republicans needed no additional political capital in that county. "We are as strongly republi-

can as we care to be, if our people were allowed to vote." When an election was held in August on the question of summoning a new state constitutional convention, Rutherford County was opposed (the Republican position) by two to one.

32. Quoted in Yorkville (S.C.) *Enquirer,* Aug. 24, 1871.
33. *KKK Report,* North Carolina, pp. 142–44, 182, 271–72, 379–80; David Schenck Diary, Sept. 30, Oct. 29, 1871, Southern Historical Collection, University of North Carolina; Judge J. M. Cloud to Gov. Caldwell, Salisbury, July 12, 1871, Governors' Correspondence, North Carolina Archives.
34. Rutherford *Star,* Oct. 28, Nov. 4, 11, 18, 1871, Feb. 10, 1872; David Schenck Diary, Sept. 4, 30, Oct. 23, 28, Dec. (no day specified) 1871, Feb. 5, 1872, Southern Historical Collection, University of North Carolina.
35. See David Schenck Diary, Sept. 4, 1871 to Feb. 5, 1872, Southern Historical Collection, University of North Carolina; Shotwell, *Papers,* II, 349–51, 404; Randolph Shotwell to Nathan Shotwell, Rutherfordton jail, n.d., Nathan Shotwell Papers, Southern Historical Collection, University of North Carolina.
36. Lieut. J. S. McEwan to Atty. Gen. Akerman, Washington, D.C., Oct. 18, 1871, Justice Department Source-Chronological File, Eastern North Carolina, RG 60, NA.
37. *KKK Report,* North Carolina, pp. 591–92.

CHAPTER 22: SOUTH CAROLINA: OUTSIDE YORK COUNTY

1. Message of Nov. 27, 1868, in Legislative System, Messages, South Carolina Archives.
2. *Acts and Joint Resolutions of the General Assembly of the State of South Carolina . . . 1868–1869,* pp. 215–19, 285, 287.
3. *Message of Robert K. Scott, Governor of South Carolina . . . November, 1869* (Columbia, 1869), pp. 356–57. For Klan activity in Lancaster County in December 1868, see *South Carolina House Journal,* 1868–69, pp. 110–11, 653–54; for Spartanburg County in December 1869, see letters to Gov. Scott from A. P. Turner, Spartanburg, Dec. 23, 1869, and William M. Fleming, Spartanburg, Dec. 26, 1869, Governors' Letters, South Carolina Archives; for Sumter County in late 1869 and early 1870, see New York *Daily Tribune,* Nov. 15, 1869, and Charleston *Daily Republican,* Feb. 19, 1870.
4. Yorkville *Enquirer,* Feb. 3, 10, 24, April 7, May 5, 1870, Jan. 19, 1871; Charleston *Daily Republican,* April 2, 1870; *House Miscellaneous Documents,* 41st Congress, 2d sess., No. 17, pt. 2, pp. 37–38, 46; *KKK Report,* South Carolina, pp. 1487, 1508, 1552–56.
5. *KKK Report,* South Carolina, pp. 1202–3, 1225: Yorkville *Enquirer,* Sept. 15, 1870; R. H. Woody, "The South Carolina Election of 1870," *North Carolina Historical Review,* VIII (1931), 177–79.

6. Report of Deputy Constable H. A. Wilson to Chief Constable John B. Hubbard, and letter of Hubbard to Gov. Scott, both of Sept. 21, 1870, in Executive Papers, South Carolina Archives; *KKK Report*, South Carolina, pp. 1304–5, 1329–30.

7. See Woody, "South Carolina Election of 1870," *passim.*

8. *KKK Report*, South Carolina, pp. 76–78, 330–49, 1144–55, 1208–9, 1305 ff., 1326 ff.; William Watts Ball, *The State that Forgot* (Indianapolis, 1932), pp. 151–54; John A. Leland, *A Voice from South Carolina* (Charleston, 1879), pp. 51 ff., 63–64.

9. See extracts quoted in Gov. Scott's Annual Message of Nov. 28, 1871, pp. 25–26, in Legislative System, Messages, South Carolina Archives.

10. *KKK Report*, South Carolina, pp. 23–25, 102–5, 122. There may have been a relationship in some counties between the Council of Safety and a resurgence of the Ku Klux Klan following the election. See *ibid.*, p. 1291.

11. *Ibid.*, p. 1613; New York *Daily Tribune*, Nov. 24, 1871.

12. See the characteristics of Klan organization, membership, and operations in *New York Times*, Nov. 11, 1871; New York *Daily Tribune*, Nov. 24, 25, 1871; and *KKK Report*, South Carolina, *passim.* Information by members about Lyle and Avery is contained in *KKK Report*, South Carolina, *passim,* and in Lieut. J. S. McEwan to Atty. Gen. Akerman, Washington, Oct. 18, 1871, Justice Department Source-Chronological File, Eastern North Carolina, RG 60, NA. See also the discussions in Francis B. Simkins, "The Ku Klux Klan in South Carolina, 1868–1871," *Journal of Negro History*, XII (1927), 613–21; *KKK Report*, Committee Report, pp. 28–51; Herbert Shapiro, "The Ku Klux Klan during Reconstruction: The South Carolina Episode," *Journal of Negro History*, XLIX (Jan. 1964), 48–51.

13. *KKK Report*, South Carolina, pp. 41–48, 124, 274–88; Sumter *Watchman,* quoted in Columbia *Daily Phoenix*, April 29, 1871.

14. For Lancaster, see *New York Times*, April 15, 1871. For Fairfield, *KKK Report*, South Carolina, pp. 316–25; Yorkville *Enquirer*, May 4, 1871; Columbia *Daily Phoenix*, May 2, 1871; New York *Herald*, May 12, 1871; New York *Daily Tribune*, May 22, 1871. For a similar descent upon Orangeburg in August, see Columbia *Daily Phoenix*, Aug. 25, 27, 1871.

15. For Williamsburg and Darlington counties, see Atlanta *Daily New Era*, May 28, 1871. For Union County, *KKK Report*, South Carolina, pp. 987–88, 1096 ff.

16. *KKK Report*, South Carolina, pp. 283, 286–87.

17. New York *Daily Tribune*, May 22, 26, 1871; *KKK Report*, South Carolina, pp. 72–73, 139–44, 327–29.

18. Yorkville *Enquirer*, March 9, 16, 30, 1871; *KKK Report*, South Carolina, pp. 39–41, 1028–29, 1035, 1041–50, 1428–43, 1450–53, 1580–90; New York *Daily Tribune*, April 28, 1871.

19. *KKK Report*, South Carolina, pp. 28, 32, 64–68, 74–75, 80, 98, 802–4, 962–1009, 1017–23, 1029–31, 1062, 1069 ff., 1091–94, 1112–14, 1121–23, 1126, 1128–31, 1136–42, 1155–57, 1159–62; *Reports and Resolutions of the General Assembly of the State of South Carolina*, 1870–1871, pp.

906–8; letter of Judge William M. Thomas in Charleston *Daily News,* quoted in Spartanburg *Carolina Spartan,* March 9, 1871; Yorkville *Enquirer,* Jan. 12, 19, Feb. 16, 23, Nov. 2, 1871; letter of Sheriff J. Rice Rogers in Columbia *Daily Phoenix,* Jan. 14, 1871; *South Carolina House Journal,* 1870–1871, pp. 420–23; testimony of Sheriff Philip Dunn before legislative investigating committee, Feb. 15, 1871, in Penal System, Sheriffs, Union County, 1867–1870, South Carolina Archives; John S. Reynolds, *Reconstruction in South Carolina, 1865–1877* (Columbia, 1905), p. 186.

20. Spartanburg *Carolina Spartan,* Nov. 24, Dec. 1, 8, 15, 1870; Spartanburg *Republican,* quoted in (Rutherfordton, N.C.) Rutherford *Star,* April 22, 1871; New York *Daily Tribune,* May 12, 1871; William M. Fleming to Atty. Gen. Akerman, Spartanburg, Nov. 7, 1871, Justice Department Source-Chronological File, South Carolina, RG 60, NA; *KKK Report,* South Carolina, pp. 26–36, 99–100, 184–202, 245–46, 296–315, 349–446, 520–701, 722–62, 797–806, 843–948, 197–284.

CHAPTER 23: SOUTH CAROLINA: YORK COUNTY AND THE CLIMAX OF TERROR

1. See Chapter 4.
2. *KKK Report,* South Carolina, pp. 206, 1363–64, 1374, 1484, 1603, 1681, 1691, 1693, 1706, 1725, 1924, 1938; Cincinnati *Commercial,* quoted in Yorkville *Enquirer,* Nov. 16, 1871; New York *Daily Tribune,* Nov. 7, 14, 16, 1871; New York *Herald,* Dec. 1, 1871; Maj. Lewis Merrill to Maj. J. H. Taylor, Yorkville, May 4, June 9, 1871, and to Gen. A. H. Terry, Nov. 6, 1871, Post of Yorkville, S.C., Letters Sent, 1871–1872, RG 98, NA.
3. New York *Daily Tribune,* Nov. 14, 1871; *KKK Report,* South Carolina, p. 1730.
4. *KKK Report,* South Carolina, pp. 210–11, 702, 718, 1472, 1544 ff.; Maj. Lewis Merrill to Atty. Gen. Williams, Yorkville, Sept. 30, 1872, Justice Department, Source-Chronological File, South Carolina, RG 60, NA; New York *Daily Tribune,* Nov. 16, 1871.
5. New York *Herald,* Dec. 1, 1871; Yorkville *Enquirer,* Feb. 2, 23, March 16, April 6, 1871; New York *Daily Tribune,* Nov. 14, 1871; *KKK Report,* South Carolina, pp. 207–8, 217–19, 707, 710–11, 1358–59, 1469, 1471–72, 1540, 1730.
6. Columbia *Daily Phoenix,* Feb. 1, 1871.
7. New York *Herald,* Dec. 1, 1871; *KKK Report,* South Carolina, pp. 207, 706–7, 1295, 1298, 1371, 1469–70, 1730–31; Yorkville *Enquirer,* Feb. 2, 1871; Lieut. J. S. McEwan to Atty. Gen. Akerman, Washington, Oct. 18, 1871, Justice Department Source-Chronological File, Eastern North Carolina, RG 60, NA.
8. *KKK Report,* South Carolina, pp. 215, 225, 711.
9. Yorkville *Enquirer,* Feb. 16, 1871.
10. *KKK Report,* South Carolina, pp. 215, 1366, 1369–70, 1471; New York *Daily Tribune,* Nov. 14, 1871; Yorkville *Enquirer,* Feb. 23, 1871; Maj.

Lewis Merrill to A.A.G., Department of the South, June 9, Aug. 28, 1871, Post of Yorkville, S.C., Letters Sent, 1871–1872, RG 98, NA.

11. *KKK Report,* South Carolina, pp. 213, 215, 223, 1409, 1465, 1472, 1474–75, 1480, 1483, 1485, 1602, 1761, 1842; New York *Herald,* Dec. 1, 1871; New York *Daily Tribune,* Nov. 14, 1871; letters of Maj. Lewis Merrill to A.A.G., Department of the South, May 4 to Sept. 17, 1871, Post of Yorkville, S.C., Letters Sent, 1871–1872, RG 98, NA.

12. *KKK Report,* South Carolina, pp. 1288–97.

13. *Ibid.,* pp. 1346, 1375, 1465–67; Yorkville *Enquirer,* March 2, 1871, quoted in Columbia *Daily Phoenix,* March 3, 1871.

14. *KKK Report,* South Carolina, pp. 704–8, 1273, 1289–91, 1348, 1366–67, 1470–71, 1557, 1563, 1611–12; New York *Herald,* Dec. 1, 1871; Yorkville *Enquirer,* March 2, 1871, quoted in Columbia *Daily Phoenix,* March 3, 1871; *Enquirer,* March 9, 16, 1871; *Phoenix,* March 12, 1871. The report of a legislative investigation of the money's disappearance was apparently a deliberate whitewash of Rose, based on the false statement that the safe had actually been opened during the raid. See *Reports and Resolutions of the General Assembly of the State of South Carolina,* 1872–1872, p. 988; *Acts and Joint Resolutions of the General Assembly of the State of South Carolina . . . 1871–'72,* p. 287.

15. Columbia *Daily Phoenix,* March 3, 12 1871; New York *Herald,* Dec. 1, 1871; *KKK Report,* South Carolina, pp. 211, 703, 1472.

16. Williams was also known as Jim Rainey. *KKK Report,* South Carolina, pp. 212, 1364–65, 1472, 1712–41, 1758 ff., 1795–99; Columbia *Daily Phoenix,* March 12, 1871; *Congressional Globe,* 42d Congress, 2d sess., pp. 3583–84; New York *Daily Tribune,* Nov. 16, 1871.

17. *KKK Report, South Carolina,* pp. 709–10; Columbia *Daily Phoenix,* March 14, 1871.

18. Letters of Capt. John Christopher to Gov. Scott and Sheriff Glenn, Yorkville, March 8, 9, 1870 [*sic,* 1871] printed in *Congressional Globe,* 42d Congress, 1st sess., p. 391; Christopher to Gov. Scott, Yorkville, March 15, 1871, in Military Affairs, Letters, South Carolina Archives; Columbia *Daily Phoenix,* March 14, 1871; Yorkville *Enquirer,* March 16, 1871.

19. *KKK Report,* South Carolina, p. 1472; Maj. Lewis Merrill to A.A.G., Department of the South, June 10, 1871, Post of Yorkville, S.C., Letters Sent, 1871–1872, RG 98, NA.

20. *KKK Report,* South Carolina, pp. 208–9, 219.

21. Quoted in *ibid.,* pp. 1540–41.

22. *Ibid.,* pp. 1361–62, 1410; Yorkville *Enquirer,* Feb. 16, 1871.

23. Yorkville *Enquirer,* March 9, 1871, copied in *KKK Report,* South Carolina, pp. 1347–48.

24. Yorkville *Enquirer,* March 16, 23, 30, April 6, 20, 1871; *KKK Report,* South Carolina, pp. 1352–54, 1541–43; Capt. John Christopher to Gov. Scott, Yorkville, March 17, 1871, in Military Affairs, Letters, South Carolina Archives.

25. Yorkville *Enquirer,* March 30, 1871; Maj. Merrill to A.A.G., Department

of the South, April 21, 1871, Post of Yorkville, S.C., Letters Sent, 1871–1872, RG 98, NA.

26. New York *Daily Tribune,* Nov. 13, 1871.
27. *KKK Report,* South Carolina, p. 1482; Merrill to A.A.G., Department of the South, May 4, 1871, Post of Yorkville, S.C., Letters Sent, 1871–1872, RG 98, NA.
28. Merrill to A.A.G., Department of the South, May 4, 1871, Post of Yorkville, S.C., Letters Sent, 1871–1872, RG 98, NA; Yorkville *Enquirer,* April 20, 1871.
29. Major Avery inserted a notice in the *Enquirer* on May 4 which was at once an exhortation to Klansmen and an advertisement for his own store. Headlined "Governor Scott's Militia," it said: "The Governor having disarmed and disbanded his Militia, and removed the most objectionable of the Trial Justices, it is certainly the duty of every white man in the county, to do all in his power to preserve the peace and keep down all disturbances; so that every man, woman and child may come in safety, and see my large and elegant stock of Goods, just purchased in the Northern markets, very low for cash, and to be sold at correspondingly low rates for the money and the money only. Absolutely no credit."
30. Merrill to A.A.G., Department of the South, May 4, 19, 26, June 9, 1871, Post of Yorkville, S.C., Letters Sent, 1871–1872, RG 98, NA; *KKK Report,* South Carolina, pp. 1564–65, 1572–73, 1600. For Glenn's indictment, see U.S. Attorney D. T. Corbin to Atty. Gen. Williams, Charleston, June 29, 1872, Justice Department Source-Chronological File, South Carolina, RG 60, NA.
31. *KKK Report,* South Carolina, pp. 1406 ff., 1477; *Congressional Globe,* 42d Congress, 2d sess., pp. 3580–81.
32. *KKK Report,* pp. 1410–12; Yorkville *Enquirer,* July 20, Nov. 2, 1871, Feb. 22, 1872.
33. *KKK Report,* South Carolina, pp. 222, 713, 1497–1503, 1521; Yorkville *Enquirer,* May 18–June 15, 1871; Merrill to A.A.G., Department of the South, May 19–June 9, 1871, Post of Yorkville, S.C., Letters Sent, 1871–1872, RG 98, NA. The decrying of violence did not extend to the Klan's efforts to drive the last remaining Republican officeholders from power. A disguised party visited the home of a trial justice in the Fort Mills district in May; they missed him, but a few days later some of the local citizens, out of disguise, pressured him into resigning by threats of further visitations. Columbia *Union,* May 22, 1871, quoted in Atlanta *Daily New Era,* May 24, 1871; Yorkville *Enquirer,* May 25, June 1, 1871.
34. Merrill to A.A.G., Department of the South, June 10, July 17, 1871, Post of Yorkville, S.C., Letters Sent, 1871–1872, RG 98, NA; *KKK Report,* South Carolina, pp. 714, 1481, 1503–4.
35. *KKK Report,* South Carolina, pp. 1482, 1519–20, 1532, 1603, 1605–6; New York *Daily Tribune,* Nov. 14, 1871; Merrill to A.A.G., Department of the South, May 4, Aug. 3, 1871, Post of Yorkville, S.C., Letters Sent, 1871–1872, RG 98, NA.

36. New York *Daily Tribune,* Nov. 7, 1871.
37. H. C. Whitley to Atty. Gen. Akerman, New York, Sept. 29, 1871, in "Reconstruction in the South, 1871–1879" (microfilm), O. W. Holmes Devise, Justice Department Records, RG 60, NA.
38. New York *Herald,* Dec. 1, 1871.
39. Yorkville *Enquirer,* July 27, Aug. 3, 1871; *New York Times,* July 30, 1871; *KKK Report,* South Carolina, pp. 1533–34; Merrill to A.A.G., Department of the South, Aug. 3, 1871, Post of Yorkville, S.C., Letters Sent, 1871–1872, RG 98, NA.
40. Yorkville *Enquirer,* July 27, Aug. 3, 1871.
41. Merrill to A.A.G., Department of the South, Aug. 3–Sept. 17, 1871, Post of Yorkville S.C., Letters Sent, 1871–1872, RG 98, NA; New York *Herald,* Dec. 1, 1871; Yorkville *Enquirer,* Sept. 28, Oct. 5, 1871; *KKK Report,* South Carolina, pp. 1600–2, 1607–12.
42. New York *Daily Tribune,* Nov. 8, 1870.
43. Quoted in Charleston *Daily News,* Jan. 9, 1871.
44. *Reports and Resolutions of the General Assembly of the State of South Carolina,* 1870–71, p. 1249.
45. Gov. Scott's messages of Jan. 16 and Nov. 28, 1871, in Legislative System, Messages, South Carolina Archives; Charleston *Daily Republican,* Jan. 13, 19, 20, 26, 1871; *Senate Executive Documents,* 41st Congress, 3d sess., No. 28; *Reports and Resolutions of the General Assembly of the State of South Carolina,* 1870–1871, pp. 905–8, 1254, 1422–23; John S. Reynolds, *Reconstruction in South Carolina, 1865–1877* (Columbia, 1905), p. 186; Gov. Scott to President Grant, Columbia, March 9, 1871 (telegram); State Atty. Gen. D. H. Chamberlain to Atty. Gen. Akerman, Columbia, March 16, 1871, Justice Department Source-Chronological File, South Carolina, RG 60, NA; Atty. Gen. Akerman to Gov. Scott, March 11, 1871, Attorney General, Letters Sent books, RG 60, NA; New York *Daily Tribune,* March 22, 1871.
46. *New York Times,* March 22, 1871; Gov. Scott's message of Nov. 28, 1871, pp. 30–31, in Legislative System, Messages, South Carolina Archives; *KKK Report,* South Carolina, p. 107; Charleston *Republican,* quoted in New York *Daily Tribune,* March 20, 1871; Herbert Shapiro, "The Ku Klux Klan during Reconstruction: The South Carolina Episode," *Journal of Negro History,* XLIX (Jan. 1964), 44–45. Scott reported later that out of 7,845 stands of arms originally issued to the militia, he was unable to recover 1,467, most of which had apparently fallen into the hands of the Ku Klux. *Special Message of His Excellency Robert K. Scott . . . in Reply to Charges Made Against Him* (Columbia, 1872), pp. 18–19.
47. New York *Daily Tribune,* May 22, 1871; New York *Herald,* June 5, Oct. 19, 1871.
48. Charleston *Daily News,* Jan. 31, Feb. 15, 18, 20, 1871. The Barnwell *Sentinel* (where the Klan had never become violent) refused to publish a Ku Klux notice to a local official to resign and repudiated all such efforts. Quoted in Columbia *Daily Phoenix,* June 6, 1871.

49. *KKK Report,* South Carolina, pp. 1191, 1204; Shapiro, "The Ku Klux Klan," pp. 51–53; New York *Daily Tribune,* May 2, 1871.
50. *KKK Report,* South Carolina, pp. 472 ff.
51. New York *Herald,* May 4, 1871; New York *Daily Tribune,* May 22, 1871.
52. New York *Daily Tribune,* March 15, May 26, 1871.
53. *New York Times,* April 25, 1871; New York *Herald,* May 27, June 5, Oct. 19, 1871; Atty. Gen. Akerman to Gen. A. H. Terry, Washington, Nov. 18, 1871, Akerman Letterbooks, University of Virginia; Reynolds, *Reconstruction in South Carolina,* p. 216.

CHAPTER 24: CONGRESS LEGISLATES, THEN INVESTIGATES

1. Otis A. Singletary, *Negro Militia and Reconstruction* (Austin, Tex., 1957), pp. 28–29.
2. United States *Statutes at Large,* XVI, 140–43; William Watson Davis, "The Federal Enforcement Acts," in *Studies in Southern History and Politics Inscribed to William Archibald Dunning* (N.Y., 1914), pp. 209–15. The most recent study of the federal enforcement policy is Everette Swinney, "Enforcing the Fifteenth Amendment, 1870–1877," *Journal of Southern History,* XXVIII (May 1962), 202–18. See also Edwin C. Woolley, "Grant's Southern Policy," in *Studies in Southern History and Politics,* pp. 179–201.
3. See Raleigh *Daily Standard,* July 27, 1870; Louisville *Courier-Journal,* Nov. 26, 1870.
4. James D. Richardson (ed.), *A Compilation of the Messages and Papers of the Presidents,* 10 vols. (Washington, 1898), VII, 96.
5. *KKK Report,* Alabama, p. 533.
6. Montgomery *Alabama State Journal,* April 26–28, 1871.
7. *Ibid.,* June 14, 1871; *KKK Report,* Alabama, pp. 537–38, 1008.
8. *Senate Reports,* 42d Congress, 1st sess., No. 1, p. 388; *KKK Report,* North Carolina, pp. 15–16, 32–34, 93–95.
9. *Senate Executive Documents,* 41st Congress, 3d sess., No. 16, pts. 1, 2.
10. The testimony and report are published in *Senate Reports,* 42d Congress, 1st sess., No. 1 (abbreviated *SR* in chapters above devoted to North Carolina).
11. Hamilton Fish diary, Feb. 24, 1871, quoted in Allan Nevins, *Hamilton Fish: The Inner History of the Grant Administration* (N.Y., 1936), pp. 601–2.
12. George F. Hoar, *Autobiography of Seventy Years,* 2 vols. (N.Y., 1903), I, 204–6.
13. Richardson, *Messages and Papers of the Presidents,* VII, 127–28.
14. *Ibid.,* pp. 132–33.
15. *Statutes at Large,* XVII, 13–15. My discussion of the events leading to the passage of the act follows that of William B. Hesseltine, *Ulysses S. Grant, Politician* (N.Y., 1935), pp. 241–46.

16. New York *Daily Tribune*, March 17, 1871.
17. See Carl Schurz, *Reminiscences*, 3 vols. (N.Y., 1908), II, 277–79; III, 330–33.
18. Louisville *Courier-Journal*, May 2, 1871; Atlanta *Daily New Era*, May 25, 1871.
19. Jackson *Daily Mississippi Pilot*, March 17, 1871.
20. Hesseltine, *Ulysses S. Grant*, p. 246.
21. *Congressional Globe*, 42d Congress, 1st sess., Appendix, p. 74. As a matter of fact, few persons, friends or foes, bothered to inquire very far into the actual meaning or usefulness of the habeas corpus provision. "Martial law" was a striking phrase, and it proved to be more useful for partisan argument on both sides than the actual habeas corpus power would be in suppressing the Klan.
22. *Congressional Globe*, 42d Congress, 1st sess., p. 453.
23. New York *Herald*, May 2, 5, 1871.
24. *KKK Report*, Georgia, p. 889.
25. Jackson *Semi-Weekly Clarion*, April 14, 1871.
26. Raleigh *Sentinel*, May 10, 1871.
27. *Congressional Globe*, 42d Congress, 1st sess., p. 480.
28. *KKK Report*, Alabama, p. 108.
29. Richardson, *Messages and Papers of the Presidents*, VII, 134–35.
30. Hesseltine, *Ulysses S. Grant*, p. 259.
31. Washington dispatch of May 4, in Jackson *Daily Mississippi Pilot*, May 5, 1871.
32. New York *Herald*, May 18, June 23, 1871.
33. Senator John Scott to President Grant, Washington, June 8, 1871, with Grant's endorsement of June 9; O. E. Babcock (President's secretary) to Atty. Gen. Akerman, June 15, 1871, in Attorney General's Office, Letters Received from the President; Atty. Gen. Akerman to Col. H. C. Whitley, June 28, 1871, in Attorney General, Letters Sent books, RG 60, NA. For accounts of the detectives' operations and findings, see Whitley to Atty. Gen. Akerman, New York, Sept. 29, 1871 ff., in "Reconstruction in the South, 1871–1879" (microfilm), O. W. Holmes Devise, Justice Department Records, RG 60, NA.
34. D. T. Corbin to Atty. Gen. Akerman, Philadelphia, July 18, 1871 (telegram), Justice Department Source-Chronological File, South Carolina, RG 60, NA; New York *Herald*, July 27, 1871.
35. Letters to Atty. Gen. Akerman from J. E. Bryant, Augusta, Ga., Aug. 1, Sept. 11, 1871, and J. H. Caldwell, Gainesville, Ga., Aug. 4, 1871, Justice Department Source-Chronological File, Georgia, RG 60, NA; *KKK Report*, Georgia, p. 425.
36. An account of its organization and procedure is contained in its final report, *KKK Report*, Committee Report, pp. 1–2.
37. Unsigned copy of letter, May 20, 1871, Robert McKee Papers, Alabama Archives. See also *KKK Report*, Georgia, p. 438.
38. *KKK Report*, North Carolina, pp. 354 ff.

39. Forrest later reportedly admitted to friends that he had engaged in some gentlemanly lying. Nash K. Burger and John K. Bettersworth, *South of Appomattox* (N.Y., 1959), p. 140.
40. Quoted in Columbia *Daily Phoenix,* July 21, 1871. See also a similar article from the Union (S.C.) *Times,* reprinted in the *Phoenix,* July 16, 1871.
41. Atlanta *Constitution,* Nov. 9, 1871; Rome (Ga.) *Courier,* Oct. 24, Nov. 17, 1871, the former article quoted in *KKK Report,* Georgia, p. 674; see also *ibid.,* p. 891.
42. *KKK Report,* Committee Report, pp. 292, 422, 508.
43. *Ibid.,* pp. 377–78; see also p. 513.
44. *Ibid.,* pp. 516–17.
45. See *ibid.,* p. 51.
46. See *ibid.,* pp. 85–93, 124–25.
47. *Ibid.,* p. 84.
48. *Ibid.,* p. 86.
49. *Ibid.,* pp. 95–97.
50. *Ibid.,* pp. 98–99.
51. *Ibid.,* pp. 99–100, 509.

CHAPTER 25: ARRESTS AND PROSECUTIONS, 1871–1872

1. *KKK Report,* Mississippi, pp. 234, 239–40, 278–79, 287, 362, 381, 934–36, 1148–49; *New York Times,* Sept. 9, 1871. The proceedings of the Oxford hearings are reprinted in *KKK Report,* Mississippi, pp. 936–87.
2. *KKK Report,* Mississippi, pp. 996–97; F. Z. Browne, "Reconstruction in Oktibbeha County," *Mississippi Historical Society Publications,* XIII (1913), 283–85, 288.
3. D. H. Starbuck to Acting Atty. Gen. B. H. Bristow, Salem, N.C., Oct. 5, 1871, Justice Department Source-Chronological File, Western North Carolina, RG 60, NA; *KKK Report,* North Carolina, pp. 417, 453, 469.
4. New York *Herald,* Sept. 1, 2, 1871; Louisville *Courier-Journal,* Sept. 3, 9, 10, 1871; President Grant to Atty. Gen. Ackerman, Sept. 1, 1871, with letters of Gen. A. H. Terry (Louisville, June 11, 1871) and Senator John Scott (Washington, Sept. 1, 1871), in Attorney General's Office, Letters Received from the President, RG 60, NA; *New York Times,* Oct. 31, 1871.
5. Representative Luke Poland of Vermont, a Republican member of the investigating committee, was one of the few persons who made this point clear. See *Congressional Globe,* 42d Congress, 2d sess., Appendix, p. 495.
6. *New York Times,* June 17, 1870.
7. See Raleigh *Daily Standard,* July 27, 1870.
8. See his letters to U.S. Attorney E. P. Jacobson, Aug. 18, 1871, and Judge R. A. Hill, Sept. 12, 1871, Akerman Letterbooks, University of Virginia.

9. New York *Herald,* Sept. 16, 1871. Early in October, when reports reached Washington that efforts were being made in North Carolina to suspend sentences and postpone further trials, the Justice Department ordered officials there to press forward. Acting Atty. Gen. Bristow to D. H. Starbuck, Oct. 2, 1871 (telegram and letter), in Attorney General's Office, Instruction Books, RG 60, NA.

10. U.S. Marshal L. E. Johnson to Atty. Gen. Akerman, Columbia, Oct. 7, 1871 (telegram), Justice Department Source-Chronological File, South Carolina, RG 60, NA; Yorkville *Enquirer,* Sept. 28, 1871; Maj. Lewis Merrill to A.A.G., Department of the South, Oct. 3, 1871, Post of Yorkville, S.C., Letters Sent, 1871–1872, RG 98, NA.

11. For Akerman's travels and activity, see *New York Times,* Oct. 31, 1871; New York *Herald,* Dec. 1, 1871; *KKK Report,* South Carolina, p. 1602; James D. Richardson (ed.), *A Compilation of the Messages and Papers of the Presidents,* 10 vols. (Washington, 1898), VII, 163–64; Akerman to Gen. A. H. Terry, Washington, Nov. 18, 1871, Akerman Letterbooks, University of Virginia.

12. Richardson, *Messages and Papers of the Presidents,* VII, 135–36.

13. *Ibid.,* pp. 136–37.

14. *Ibid.,* pp. 138–41; Acting Atty. Gen. Bristow to Akerman, Oct. 21, 1871 (telegram), in Attorney General's Office, book of Letters Sent to Executive and Legislative Departments, RG 60, NA.

15. *KKK Report,* South Carolina, p. 1602.

16. For Bratton's case, see *Congressional Globe,* 42d Congress, 2d sess., pp. 3583–84; John S. Reynolds, *Reconstruction in South Carolina, 1865–1877* (Columbia, 1905), p. 201; Maj. Lewis Merrill to D. T. Corbin, Yorkville, June 11, 1872 (telegram), Post of Yorkville, S.C., Post Endorsement Book, RG 98, NA; Fred Landon, "The Kidnapping of Dr. Rufus Bratton," *Journal of Negro History,* X (July 1925), 330–33; U.S. Marshal R. M. Wallace to Atty. Gen. Williams, Charleston, July 5, 1872, and Merrill to Adjutant General, Yorkville, July 11, 1872 (cipher telegram), Justice Department Source-Chronological File, South Carolina, RG 60, NA; Louis F. Post, "A 'Carpetbagger' in South Carolina," *Journal of Negro History,* X (1925), 61–62; Atty. Gen. Williams to Merrill, July 13, 1872, in Attorney General's Office, Letters Sent books, RG 60, NA. For Avery's flight, see New York *Daily Tribune,* Nov. 7, 1871; Merrill to Atty. Gen. Akerman, Yorkville, Nov. 13, Dec. 7, 1871, Justice Department Source-Chronological File, South Carolina, RG 60, NA.

17. The prisoners represented the same economic and social spectrum as the Klan membership. It was reported to U.S. Commissioner of Education John Eaton in November that, of the 115 prisoners then in jail at Yorkville, nine could read but not write and eleven were unable to either read or write. The last figure would have been larger if most of those who had been drawn into the order through ignorance had not been released almost at once. Lieut. J. Aspinwall to Eaton, Nov. 30, 1871, Post of Yorkville, S.C., Letters Sent, 1871–1872, RG 98, NA.

18. New York *Daily Tribune,* Nov. 13, 1871.
19. For accounts of the York County arrests and their immediate sequel, see *New York Times,* Oct. 31, 1871; New York *Herald,* Dec. 1, 1871; *KKK Report,* South Carolina, pp. 1602–5; Post, "A 'Carpetbagger' in South Carolina," pp. 43–44; Maj. Lewis Merrill to Gen. A. H. Terry, Nov. 6, 1871, Post of Yorkville, S.C., Letters Sent, 1871–1872, RG 98, NA; Yorkville *Enquirer,* Oct. 19, 26, Nov. 2, 9, 16, 23, 1871 (the issue of Nov. 16 containing a long descriptive article by a correspondent of the Cincinnati *Commercial*); New York *Daily Tribune,* Nov. 13, 14, 1871. For Conservative attacks on the arrests, see Columbia *Daily Phoenix,* Oct. 24, 1871; New York *Herald,* Dec. 1, 1871; Reynolds, *Reconstruction in South Carolina,* pp. 198–99. John A. Leland, who was himself arrested for Klan activity in Laurens County, several years later characterized Merrill as a "brute" who "degraded the uniform he wore, by such acts of cruelty and tyranny towards unprotected and helpless families, as the lowest Ku-Klux would have blushed to have acknowledged against the most obnoxious negro." The major, Leland explained, was motivated by "an inordinate greed for [reward] money, and a Nero-like delight in human torture." Leland, *A Voice from South Carolina* (Charleston, 1879), pp. 87–88, 133. The Yorkville *Enquirer*'s accounts of the arrests were very moderate and factual, and spoke highly of the prisoners' treatment.
20. See correspondence of Oct. 23–28, Dec. 23, 1871, in Post of Yorkville, S.C., Letters Received book, 1871–1872; Letters Received, 1871–1876; and Telegrams Sent and Received, 1871–1874; see also Maj. C. H. Morgan to Merrill, March 2, 1872, Post of Raleigh, N.C., Letters Sent book, 1871–1872, all in RG 98, NA. See also President Grant to Atty. Gen. Akerman, Dec. 4, 1871, with accompanying petition, in Attorney General's Office, Letters Received from the President, RG 60, NA.
21. New York *Daily Tribune,* Nov. 24, 1871; U. S. Marshal L. E. Johnson to Atty. Gen. Akerman, Spartanburg, Nov. 4, 1871, Justice Department Source-Chronological File, South Carolina, RG 60, NA; Spartanburg *Carolina Spartan,* Oct. 19, Nov. 9, 30, 1871; Reynolds, *Reconstruction in South Carolina,* p. 199.
22. Union (S.C.) *Times,* Oct. 26, 1871, quoted in Spartanburg *Carolina Spartan,* Nov. 2, 1871; Reynolds, *Reconstruction in South Carolina,* p. 199.
23. Chester *Reporter,* Oct. 26, 1871, quoted in Yorkville *Enquirer,* Nov. 2, 1871; *Cincinnati Commercial,* quoted in *ibid.,* Nov. 16, 1871; Maj. W. Harvey Brown to Atty. Gen. Williams, Atlanta, June 29, 1873, Justice Department Source-Chronological File, Georgia, RG 60, NA; Reynolds, *Reconstruction in South Carolina,* p. 200.
24. Reynolds, *Reconstruction in South Carolina,* p. 200. For a highly colored account of the Laurens arrests in March and April 1872 by one of those arrested, see Leland, *A Voice from South Carolina,* pp. 90–99. Leland's wrath at being arrested was tempered by his subsequent prison experience in Columbia and Charleston. With the other prisoners he was regarded

as a martyr by white society, and he enjoyed their lavish attention and hospitality as well as the service of an old family retainer during his month's confinement. See *ibid.*, pp. 101–32.

25. Annual message, Nov. 28, 1871, p. 31, in Legislative System, Messages, South Carolina Archives. See also D. T. Corbin to Atty. Gen. Akerman, Yorkville, Nov. 13, 1871, Justice Department Source-Chronological File, South Carolina, RG 60, NA; Atty. Gen. Akerman's annual report, in *New York Times,* Jan. 16, 1872.

26. Akerman to Corbin, Nov. 10, 1871, Attorney General's Office, Instruction Books, RG 60, NA. See also Akerman to B. D. Silliman, Nov. 9, 1871, Akerman Letterbooks, University of Virginia.

27. Akerman to Gen. Terry, Washington, Nov. 18, 1871, Akerman Letterbooks, University of Virginia.

28. D. T. Corbin to Akerman, Yorkville, Nov. 13, 1871, Justice Department Source-Chronological File, South Carolina, RG 60, NA; *House Executive Documents,* 42d Congress, 2d sess., no. 268, pp. 5–17.

29. The trial proceedings are printed in *KKK Report,* South Carolina, pp. 1615–1990. See also New York *Herald,* Dec. 25, 1871; *House Executive Documents,* 42d Congress, 2d sess., No. 268, pp. 5–19; Reynolds, *Reconstruction in South Carolina,* pp. 202–13. Toward the end of his trial one of the defendants, Dr. Edward T. Avery, was permitted by one of his lawyers to run away. He returned home many months later and was rearrested, but sentence was never passed and his only formal punishment consisted in forfeiting his $3,000 bond. He was pardoned in March 1874. Disbarment proceedings were instituted against his attorney, but they later were dropped. See *KKK Report,* South Carolina, pp. 1963, 1966, 1975–82; Atty. Gen. Williams to D. T. Corbin, April 23, May 1, 1873, in Attorney General's Office, Instruction Books; Corbin to Williams, Charleston, March 28, 1874, Justice Department Source-Chronological File, South Carolina, RG 60, NA; Justice Department Pardon Records, D-505, RG 204, NA; Reynolds, *Reconstruction in South Carolina,* pp. 208–10; Douglas Summers Brown, *A City Without Cobwebs: A History of Rock Hill, South Carolina* (Columbia, 1953), pp. 148–51.

30. *New York Times,* Jan. 27, 1872, quoted in *KKK Report,* Committee Report, p. 514. The Charleston *Daily News* (Jan. 24, 1872) similarly described their appearance there a few days earlier, as quoted in Yorkville *Enquirer,* Feb. 1, 1872.

31. See (Rutherfordton) Rutherford *Star,* Oct. 28, 1871 ff.; Raleigh *Carolina Era,* Nov. 4, 1871 ff.; David Schenck Diary, Sept. 30, 1871 ff., Southern Historical Collection, University of North Carolina; H. C. Whitley to Atty. Gen. Williams, New York, Jan. 1872 (n.d.), in "Reconstruction in the South, 1871–1879" (microfilm), O. W. Holmes Devise, Justice Department Records, RG 60, NA; Lieut. J. S. McEwan to Atty. Gen. Akerman, Westbrook Twp., Sampson County, N.C., Nov. 24, 28, 1871, Justice Department Source-Chronological File, Eastern North Carolina, RG 60, NA; Maj. C. H. Morgan to Adjutant General, Department of the

South, Nov. 25, Dec. 2, 11, 1871, Post of Raleigh, N.C., Letters Sent book, 1871–1872, RG 98, NA.

32. *KKK Report,* North Carolina, p. 415.
33. Report of J. G. Hester, July 22, 1871, with letter to A. J. Falls, Greensboro, July 25, 1871, Justice Department Source-Chronological File, Eastern North Carolina, RG 60, NA.
34. George F. Bason to Graham, Graham, N.C., Dec. 18, 19, 1871, William A. Graham Papers, Southern Historical Collection, University of North Carolina.
35. Tourgée to Gov. Caldwell, Greensboro, Dec. 29, 1871, Governors' Correspondence, North Carolina Archives; Atty. Gen. Williams to H. C. Whitley, Jan. 17, 1872, in Attorney General's Office, Letters Sent Books, RG 60, NA.
36. Otto H. Olsen, *Carpetbagger's Crusade: The Life of Albion Winegar Tourgée* (Baltimore, 1965), pp. 184–86; Olsen, "The Ku Klux Klan: A Study in Reconstruction Politics and Propaganda," *North Carolina Historical Review,* XXXIX (Summer 1962), 361–62.
37. See letters of Caldwell and Bryant to Atty. Gen. Akerman, Aug. 1, 4, Sept. 11, Oct. 31, 1871, Justice Department Source-Chronological File, Georgia, RG 60, NA.
38. Whitley to Atty. Gen. Akerman, Oct. 12, 1871, Justice Department Source-Chronological File, Southern New York, RG 60, NA.
39. See Akerman's letters to Foster Blodgett, H. P. Farrow, and James Atkins, Nov. 8, 25, 29, 1871, Akerman Letterbooks, University of Virginia.
40. Atlanta *Daily New Era,* Oct. 17, 20, 22, 1871.
41. *KKK Report,* Georgia, pp. 745–46, 749.
42. Atlanta *Daily New Era,* Dec. 8, 22, 1871.
43. *KKK Report,* Georgia, pp. 368 ff., 422–23, 509, 545, 673, 753–54; H. C. Whitley to Atty. Gen. Williams, Jan. (n.d.), Aug. 15, 1872, in "Reconstruction in the South, 1871–1879" (microfilm), O. W. Holmes Devise, Justice Department Records, RG 60, NA.
44. President Grant to Atty. Gen. Akerman, Dec. 11, 13, 1871, with letters of Representative Horace Maynard and Senator Abijah Gilbert, Attorney General's Office, Letters Received from the President, RG 60, NA; New York *Herald,* Dec. 12, 1871.
45. Ralph L. Peek, "Curbing of Voter Intimidation in Florida, 1871," *Florida Historical Quarterly,* XLIII (April 1965), 346; William Watson Davis, *The Civil War and Reconstruction in Florida* (N.Y., 1913), p. 585; *Senate Executive Documents,* 42d Congress, 3d sess., No. 32, p. 24.
46. Minnis to Atty. Gen. Akerman, Sept. 8, Oct. 13, Dec. 1, 28, 1871, Jan. 24, 1872, Justice Department Source-Chronological File, Northern Alabama, RG 60, NA; *KKK Report,* Alabama, pp. 320, 552–53; Montgomery *Alabama State Journal,* Dec. 10, 1871.
47. *House Executive Documents,* 42d Congress, 2d sess., No. 268, pp. 34–41;

James W. Garner, *Reconstruction in Mississippi* (N.Y., 1901), pp. 352–53.

48. See Chapter 19.

49. D. T. Corbin to the Attorney General, Jan. 5, Feb. 20, July 22, 1872, Justice Department Source-Chronological File, South Carolina, RG 60, NA; Akerman's annual report for 1871, in *New York Times*, Jan. 16, 1872.

50. See William B. Hesseltine, *Ulysses S. Grant, Politician* (N.Y., 1935), p. 262; New York *Herald*, Dec. 5, 1871.

51. *KKK Report*, Committee Report, pp. 99–100.

52. Congressional Globe, 42d Congress, 2d sess., pp. 3579, 3727, 3931, 4323.

53. *Senate Executive Documents*, 42d Congress, 3d sess., No. 32, p. 11.

54. See the report of a Republican convention at Spartanburg, June 28, 1872, in Executive Papers (Gov. Scott), South Carolina Archives; Maj. Merrill to Adjutant General, Yorkville, July 11, 1872 (cipher telegram), and D. T. Corbin to Atty. Gen. Williams, Charleston, July 22, 1872, Justice Department Source-Chronological File, South Carolina, RG 60, NA; Atty. Gen. Williams to Merrill, July 13, 1872, in Attorney General's Office, Letters Sent Books, RG 60, NA; report of Maj. Merrill, Sept. 23, 1872, in *House Executive Documents*, 42d Congress, 3d sess., No. 1, pp. 89–91.

55. D. T. Corbin to Atty. Gen. Williams, Charleston, Nov. 2, 1872, Justice Department Source-Chronological File, South Carolina, RG 60 NA; Reynolds, *Reconstruction in South Carolina*, pp. 214–15.

56. *House Executive Documents*, 42d Congress, 2d sess., No. 268, pp. 4, 20–29; *Senate Executive Documents*, 42d Congress, 3d sess., No. 32, p. 10; *New York Times*, July 6, 1872.

57. See John A. Minnis to Attorney General, Montgomery, Ala., Dec. 1, 28, 1871, Jan. 24, June 21, 25, 1872, Justice Department Source-Chronological File, Middle Alabama, RG 60, NA; Walter Lynwood Fleming, *Civil War and Reconstruction in Alabama* (N.Y., 1905), pp. 706–7; Davis, *Civil War and Reconstruction in Florida*, pp. 585–86.

58. See Atty. Gen. Williams to H. C. Whitley, Aug. 2, 1872, in Attorney General's Office, Letters Sent Books, RG 60, NA.

59. *Senate Executive Documents*, 42d Congress, 3d sess., No. 32, p. 11. See also *House Executive Documents*, 42d Congress, 2d sess., No. 268, pp. 31–41.

60. See issues of Oct. 6, 7, 26, Nov. 6, 1871.

61. See Montgomery, Ala., *Advertiser*, quoted in Montgomery *Alabama State Journal*, April 28, 1871.

62. *KKK Report*, Mississippi, pp. 997–1000.

63. See issues of Oct. 19, Nov. 9, 1871.

64. See Union (S.C.) *Times*, Oct. 26, 1871, quoted in Spartanburg *Carolina Spartan*, Nov. 2, 1871; New York *Herald*, Oct. 26, 1871; Columbia *Daily Phoenix*, Nov. 9, 25, 1871.

65. See the account of a Charleston *Daily News* correspondent at Spartanburg, quoted in Columbia *Daily Phoenix*, Nov. 2, 1871.

66. See issue of Oct. 5, 1871.

67. Rome *Weekly Courier,* Oct. 27, 1871. See also *KKK Report,* Mississippi, pp. 473, 1160.
68. Rome *Weekly Courier,* Sept. 29, 1871. See also Columbia *Daily Phoenix,* Jan. 6, 10, 1872; Raleigh *Sentinel,* Oct. 5, 1871; Spartanburg *Carolina Spartan,* Jan. 11, 1872.
69. Raleigh *Sentinel,* Oct. 21, 1871.
70. New York *Herald,* Oct. 21, 1871; cf. issue of Oct. 18, 1871.
71. See *Congressional Globe,* 42d Congress, 2d sess., p. 598; letters to Gov. Scott from S. E. Lane, Oro, Chesterfield County, Sept. 30, 1872, and Col. Lewis Merrill, Yorkville, Oct. 6, 1872, in Executive Papers, South Carolina Archives; Leon B. Richardson, *William E. Chandler, Republican* (N.Y., 1940), pp. 159–60; Fleming, *Civil War and Reconstruction in Alabama,* p. 706; *New York Times,* Oct. 5, 17, 1872; G. Wiley Wells to Atty. Gen. Williams, Holly Springs, Miss., April 2, 18, 1872, Justice Department Source-Chronological File, Northern Mississippi, RG 60, NA.
72. For evidence of Klan reorganizations, as well as the decline of violence, see H. C. Whitley to Atty. Gen. Williams, New York, Aug. 15, Sept. 15, 1872, in "Reconstruction in the South, 1871–1879" (microfilm), O. W. Holmes Devise, Justice Department Records, RG 60, NA.
73. Atty. Gen. Williams to Whitley, Aug. 2, 1872, in Attorney General's Office, Letters Sent Books, RG 60, NA; Whitley's report, Aug. 9, 1872, in *New York Times,* Aug. 14, 1872.
74. See Justice Department Pardon Records, D-296 and D-338, RG 204, NA.
75. Letters to Atty. Gen. Williams from Col. Lewis Merrill, Yorkville, Sept. 30, 1872, and D. T. Corbin, Charleston, Nov. 2, 1872, Justice Department Source-Chronological File, South Carolina, RG 60, NA. See also Justice Department Pardon Records, D-110 and D-301, RG 204, NA.
76. Corbin to Williams, Charleston, Nov. 2, 1872, Justice Department Source-Chronological File, South Carolina, RG 60, NA; letters from Williams to Alexander H. Stephens, Sept. 16, 1872, and to Robert Scott, Dec. 5, 1872, in Attorney General's Office, Letters Sent Books, RG 60, NA.
77. Richardson, *Messages and Papers of the Presidents,* VII, 199.
78. See petition of Union County Republicans, Feb. 20, 1873, and letter of Gov. F. J. Moses to Senators T. J. Robertson and J. J. Patterson, March 7, 1873, in Military Affairs, Petitions, South Carolina Archives.
79. See G. Wiley Wells to Atty. Gen. Williams, Holly Springs, Miss., April 5, 1873, Justice Department Source-Chronological File, Northern Mississippi, RG 60, NA.
80. J. G. Hester to Atty. Gen. Williams, Greensboro, N.C., Jan. 13, 1873, Justice Department Source-Chronological File, Western North Carolina, RG 60, NA; *New York Times,* Feb. 26, 27, 1873.
81. Reynolds, *Reconstruction in South Carolina,* pp. 216–17; George W. Cullum, *Biographical Register of the Officers and Graduates of the U.S. Military Academy . . . 1802–1890,* 3d ed., 7 vols. (Boston and N.Y., 1891–1920) II, 624–25; see also Maj. W. Harvey Brown to Atty. Gen.

Williams, Atlanta, June 29, 1873, Justice Department Source-Chronological File, Georgia, RG 60, NA; Leland, *A Voice from South Carolina*, pp. 87–88, 133–34.

82. Williams to James M. Blount, April 15, 1873, in Attorney General's Office, Letters Sent Books; see also Williams to V. S. Lusk, June 21, 1873, in Attorney General's Office, Instruction Books, RG 60, NA.

83. Williams to Messrs. Porter, Kershaw, *et al.*, July 31, 1873, in Attorney General's Office, Letters Sent Books, RG 60, NA (printed in *New York Times*, Aug. 1, 1873).

84. *New York Times*, Sept. 22, 1873; Justice Department Pardon Records, D-349, RG 204, NA; see also D-110, concerning Samuel G. Brown of York County, S.C.

85. Francis B. Simkins, "The Ku Klux Klan in South Carolina, 1868–1871," *Journal of Negro History*, XII (1927), 646; D. T. Corbin to Atty. Gen. Williams, Charleston, March 28, 1874, Justice Department Source-Chronological File, South Carolina, RG 60, NA. On the other hand, Williams set detectives to work in September 1873 to expose Klan activity in Kentucky. Williams to H. C. Whitley, Sept. 4, 1873, in Attorney General's Office, Letters Sent Books, RG 60, NA. A month later, in the superior court of Johnston County, North Carolina, a white man and a Negro were convicted of murdering a Negro while in disguise, and were sentenced to hang. *New York Times*, Oct. 2, 1873.

86. William Watson Davis lists the following numbers of cases brought under the Enforcement Acts and disposed of in one way or another by the federal courts:

Year	Total Cases	Southern Cases
1871	314	263
1872	856	832
1873	1,304	1,271
1874	966	954
1875	234	221

After 1875 the number was always less than 200 per year, with only 25 Southern cases in 1878. However, a few cases arose annually until 1897. Out of a total of 7,372 cases, 5,172 in the South, between 1870 and 1897, there were 1,423 convictions, 903 acquittals, and 5,046 dropped or dismissed. The geographical distribution was: South Carolina 1,519, Mississippi 1,172, North Carolina 623, Tennessee 509, Texas 203, Alabama 219, Florida 181, Maryland 162, Louisiana 161, Kentucky 120, Virginia 79, Georgia 75, Arkansas 55. William Watson Davis, "The Federal Enforcement Acts," in *Studies in Southern History and Politics Inscribed to William Archibald Dunning* (N.Y., 1914), p. 224. See also Everette Swinney, "Enforcing the Fifteenth Amendment, 1870–1877," *Journal of Southern History*, XXVIII (May 1962), 205–9. Cf. his contrasting figures

(p. 217) for cases instituted in each state, 1870–1877: South Carolina 1,387, Mississippi 1,175, North Carolina 559, Tennessee 214, Alabama 134, Kentucky 116, Georgia 73, Maryland 56, Florida 41, Texas 29, West Virginia 27, Virginia 16, Louisiana 4, Arkansas 3, and Missouri 3.

87. *U.S.* v. *Reese,* 92 U.S. 214; *U.S.* v. *Cruikshank,* 92 U.S. 542.

88. Hampton M. Jarrell, *Wade Hampton and the Negro: The Road Not Taken* (Columbia, 1949), pp. 175–86.

EPILOGUE: APOTHEOSIS AND REBIRTH

1. See William F. Holmes, "Whitecapping: Agrarian Violence in Mississippi, 1902–1906," *Journal of Southern History,* XXXV (May 1969), 165–85.

2. See the recent biography by Raymond Allen Cook, *Fire from the Flint: The Amazing Careers of Thomas Dixon* (Winston-Salem, N.C., 1968).

3. The best general account of the second Ku Klux Klan is David M. Chalmers, *Hooded Americanism: The First Century of the Ku Klux Klan, 1865–1965* (Garden City, N.Y., 1965). But see also the more specialized treatments in Charles C. Alexander, *The Ku Klux Klan in the Southwest* (Lexington, Ky., 1965); Kenneth T. Jackson, *The Ku Klux Klan in the City, 1915–1930* (N.Y., 1967); and Arnold S. Rice, *The Ku Klux Klan in American Politics* (Washington, 1962).

Bibliographical Essay

This essay is intended to supplement rather than duplicate the specific citations. I have not attempted to list here all of the materials that I found to be of some use, especially in matters peripheral to the Klan.

When I began this study I expected one of my major sources to be "inside accounts" of membership, organization, and activity, written by Klansmen privately at the time and publicly in later years. I soon discovered, however, that contemporary inside evidence about the Klan probably never did exist in any significant quantity, except as it was evoked by Congressional and other investigations, and certainly it does not exist now in any quantity except as published testimony. Much of the information which had to be transmitted within the organization was conveyed orally, and what had to be written was sooner or later destroyed. In fact I found only one document of this sort, the general orders of the chief of York County, South Carolina, in the fall of 1868, in the Iredell Jones Papers, South Caroliniana Library, University of South Carolina. Moreover, I found only two significant contemporaneous accounts of the Klan written privately by members. Both were in diary or journal form and were from the same part of North Carolina: David Schenck's manuscript diary, in the Southern Historical Collection, University of North Carolina, Chapel Hill, and Randolph Abbott Shotwell, *Papers,* ed. by J. G. de Roulhac Hamilton, 3 vols. (Raleigh, 1929–36). Both of these members denied taking part in raids, and their accounts dealt more with organization, attitudes, and the trauma of federal prosecution.

Later reminiscences turned up in greater number, dating especially from about 1905, but neither their number nor their quality matched my expectations. The first and foremost of these is John C. Lester and David L. Wilson's *Ku Klux Klan, Its Origin, Growth, and Disbandment* (Nashville, 1884), reissued with a long introduction by Walter Lynwood Fleming (N.Y., 1905). The book is valuable primarily for its inside view of the Klan's origins around Pulaski. Even here it is fragmentary and occasionally inaccurate; these lapses become more frequent the further it gets away from that time and place. There are only two other reminiscenses of much value, John C. Reed's "What I Know of the Ku Klux Klan," which appeared in ten installments in *Uncle Remus's Magazine* between January and November 1908, dealing with the author's experiences as Klan chief in Oglethorpe County, Georgia; and W. S. Simkins' "Why the Ku Klux Klan," *The Alcalde,* IV (June 19, 1916), 735–48, concerned with Simkins' experiences in Jefferson County, Florida. (Both of these periodicals are scarce; I found the former at the Library of Congress and the latter at the Texas State Library.) The remainder were ephemeral, often vague, and occasionally incredible. I am certain that others of this genre exist which I have not found—buried in newspapers and private correspondence, unknown as yet to any periodical or manuscript guide—but their value is problematical.

Original expectations were borne out fully in the value of the thirteen-volume report of the Congressional investigating committee of 1871. This is by far the most important single source of information concerning the Klan, as the frequency of my citations throughout the book (*KKK Report*) suggests. I describe it at some length in Chapter 24. It can be found either as *Senate Reports,* 42d Congress, 2d sess., No. 41 (serial 1484–96), or *House Reports,* 42d Congress, 2d sess., No. 22 (serial 1529–41).

The Klan was a subject of smaller and more localized Congressional investigations as well, and the testimony evoked by these inquiries is also of great value. For the most part they dealt with other times or places than those covered in the main investigation, and the testimony complements rather than duplicates the large report. One of these inquiries is the Senate investigation of early 1871, which concentrated primarily on Alamance and Caswell counties, North Carolina. The testimony and report (abbreviated *SR* in the North Carolina chapters) are found in *Senate Reports,* 42d Congress, 1st sess., No. 1. The Joint Committee on Reconstruction took important testimony about Klan activity in Georgia and Mississippi late in 1868, which appears in *House Miscellaneous Documents,* 40th Congress, 3d sess., No. 52 and No. 53, respectively (serial 1385). There is also an abundance of testimony arising from investigations of contested Congressional elections in 1868. In several cases Republican candidates alleged terrorist tactics by the opposition, and both sides produced witnesses who dealt with this question in detail, sometimes giving extensive information about the Klan. This testimony appears in the *House Miscellaneous Documents,* as follows: 41st Congress, 1st sess., Nos. 12–13 (serial 1402), contested elections in Louisiana; *ibid.,* Nos. 17, 18, 35 (serial 1402), three districts in South Carolina; 41st Congress, 2d sess., No. 17, p. 2 (serial 1431), South Carolina again; *ibid.,* Nos. 53, 143 (serial 1433), two districts in Tennessee; and *ibid.,* No. 154 (serial 1435), Louisiana again.

The *Congressional Globe* is also a useful source of information, for Congressional proceedings and opinion and also for the occasional documents which it reproduces. These range from governors' messages through newspaper editorials to letters from constituents.

Several states conducted legislative investigations of their own into the Klan, with resultant reports of varying size and value. One of the shortest, least valuable, and hardest to find (I located it at the Library of Congress, but not in Alabama) is Alabama General Assembly, *Report of [the] Joint Committee on Outrages* (Montgomery, 1868). More important were the *Report of the Joint Committee of the General Assembly of Louisiana on the Conduct of the Late Elections, and the Condition of Peace and Order in the State* (New Orleans, 1868), and its sequel, *Report of the Joint Committee . . . on the Conduct of the State Elections . . . Session of 1869* (New Orleans, 1869). The latter of these is the larger and more valuable; a *Supplemental Report* (New Orleans, 1869) essentially duplicates it. Of comparable importance is *Evidence Taken by the Committee of Investigation of the Third Congressional District under Authority of the General Assembly of the State of South Carolina, Regular Session 1868–1869* (Columbia, 1870), sometimes referred to as the Crews committee report; it was also published as *Report on the Evidence and the Evidence Taken . . .* (Columbia, 1870). See finally, in this connection, Tennessee Senate Committee on Military Affairs, *Report of Evidence Taken before the Military Committee in Relation to Outrages Committed by the Ku Klux Klan in Middle and West Tennessee. Submitted . . . 2nd Day of September, 1868* (Nashville, 1868). It was long customary to scoff at these reports or dismiss them as biased, as with the Congressional documents, but under the usual rules of historical evidence they must be taken seriously.

Other categories of state documents also reflect the concern created by the Klan and the kinds of action which states took to combat it. An obvious example is the session laws of each Southern state from 1868 to 1871, and occasionally beyond. Few state officials made reference in their annual reports to the Klan or their own efforts to deal with it, but adjutant generals sometimes reported on militia activity, and the auditor general of Arkansas reported on the efforts to get militia guns in 1868. These reports usually are found in published annual volumes of state documents. State legislative journals are sometimes valuable, not only for legislative proceedings relative to the Klan, but for their inclusion of the governors' messages. Legislative debates concerning the Klan in several states are occasionally found in newspapers like the Little Rock *Republican*. Two of the most important sources for Klan activity in North Carolina are the *Third Annual Message of W. W. Holden . . . Nov. 1870* (Raleigh, 1870), containing many prior documents in a large appendix, and the massive record of his impeachment, the *Trial of William W. Holden, Governor of North Carolina*, 3 vols. (Raleigh, 1871). Also valuable for Texas is the *Journal of the Reconstruction Convention, Which Met at Austin, Texas, June 1, A.D., 1868*, 2 vols. (Austin, 1870), containing the report of its Committee on Lawlessness and Violence.

Much information about the Klan, and especially about governmental efforts to cope with it, is found in the unpublished archives of both the federal and the state governments. Within the National Archives there are several categories of records which bear upon the Klan and its suppression. First and foremost are the Freedmen's Bureau records (Record Group 105), which are very full until 1869, when the bureau was substantially phased out of existence. I found especially valuable the monthly reports, and synopses thereof, of the assistant commissioner for each state (these also served as a rough index to local agents' records); the monthly reports of local agents and sub-assistant commissioners in the areas where the Klan was active; and the correspondence of these various officials. Several other agencies of the War Department, more specifically military in character, also yield valuable records. These include the Adjutant General's Office records (RG 94), much of which are now on microfilm; the letters and telegrams received by the Headquarters of the Army (RG 108); and the records of various military posts throughout the South (in RG 98), of which the most valuable for me were Raleigh and Rutherfordton, North Carolina; Yorkville, South Carolina; Warrenton, Georgia; and Jefferson, Texas. The Justice Department records (RG 60) also contain a great amount of material bearing on the Klan. This is included in the instruction books and the various categories of correspondence of the Attorney General, and especially in the Source-Chronological Files for the respective court districts. Much of the Attorney General's correspondence is also available now on microfilm.

By far the most valuable state archival materials pertaining to the Klan are the respective governors' correspondence. This varied tremendously in quantity and quality from one state to another, and especially from one governor to another. Some executives regarded their correspondence as private property and either destroyed it or took it with them when they left office; there was no general rule on the subject. Much the fullest and most valuable files were those of Governor William H. Smith of Alabama. I am afraid that his favor to me in this respect is ill repaid in the text of this book. Other states in which the governors' correspondence is relatively full during the Klan years are Arkansas, Georgia, North Carolina, and Texas. The correspondence usually consists of letters received and letterbooks containing copies of outgoing communications. The other states yielded comparatively little. Other categories of unpublished state documents were much less valuable, but I should mention the Military Affairs File and the Chief Constable's letterbooks in the South Carolina Archives.

There are not many published documents or records of a private or unofficial character bearing on the Klan. Walter Lynwood Fleming's *Documentary History of Reconstruction,* 2 vols. (Cleveland, 1906–7; reprinted 1966) and his *Documents Relating to Reconstruction* (Morgantown, W. Va., 1904) contain some materials pertaining to the Klan and similar organizations. James D. Richardson's *A Compilation of the Messages and Papers of the Presidents,* 10 vols. (Washington, 1898), is the source of President Grant's messages and proclamations relating to the Klan. Albion W. Tourgée's *The Invisible Empire,* published with the second edition of his novel *A Fool's Errand* (N.Y., 1880), contains a wide sampling of documentary materials on the Klan drawn from other sources, chiefly the *KKK Report.* Governor Powell Clayton's *The Aftermath of the Civil War in Arkansas* (N.Y., 1915) is a gold mine of information about the Klan and especially its suppression in that state. By comparison, Henry Clay Warmoth's *War, Politics and Reconstruction: Stormy Days in Louisiana* (N.Y., 1930) and William W. Holden's *Memoirs* (Durham, N.C., 1911) are thin concerning the Klan. Other, more localized records or documents are cited in footnotes.

As my footnote citations attest, contemporary newspapers provided a vast amount of information about every aspect of the Ku Klux conspiracy. They provided not only news of specific events but editorial opinion and a feel for the dynamics of the whole Ku Klux movement. The number of newspaper files from that period which survive, either in the original or in microfilm, is very large, and it was necessary to make a sampling. For Northern and national coverage I chose the New York *Tribune,* the New York *Herald,* and the *New York Times.* The *Times Index* is invaluable, serving as a rough chronological guide to stories in other newspapers as well. Within the South, I tried to pick at least one major Democratic and Republican organ in each state, plus local papers (usually weeklies) in counties where the Klan was especially active. As explained in Chapter 3, both Democratic and Republican papers were invaluable, often for quite different reasons. The most valuable Republican papers were Governor Holden's Raleigh *Standard,* the Rutherfordton, N.C., Rutherford *Star,* the Charleston *Republican,* the Atlanta *New Era,* the Jacksonville *Florida Union,* the Montgomery *Alabama State Journal,* the Jackson *Mississippi Pilot,* the Nashville *Press and Times,* the Memphis *Post,* the Frankfort *Commonwealth,* the Little Rock *Republican,* the New Orleans *Republican,* and the Austin *Republican.* The most useful Democratic papers were the Richmond *Enquirer & Examiner,* the Raleigh *Sentinel,* The Yorkville (S.C.) *Enquirer,* the Columbia *Phoenix,* the Charleston *Daily News,* the Atlanta *Intelligencer* and Atlanta *Constitution,* the Rome *Courier,* the Augusta *Chronicle and Sentinel,* the Livingston (Ala.) *Journal,* the Tuscaloosa *Independent Monitor,* the Nashville *Republican Banner,* the Pulaski *Citizen,* the Memphis *Avalanche,* the Louisville *Courier-Journal,* the Little Rock *Arkansas Gazette,* the Batesville *North Arkansas Times,* the New Orleans *Times,* the Shreveport *South-Western,* the Marshall, Tex., *Harrison Flag* and *Texas Republican,* and the Austin *Tri-Weekly State Gazette.* Other newspapers yielded additional information, but owing to the general practice of copying articles from one another, a much longer list would bring rapidly diminishing returns.

With the exception of Lester and Wilson's book, which is primarily a firsthand account, most of the earlier histories of the Ku Klux Klan—those published in either book or article form up to the 1920's—are virtually worthless. I have used and cited several of them for limited purposes, but their greatest interest and value lie in their own attitudes and interpretations as a subject in itself, rather than for the light they shed on the Klan. They are primarily noteworthy as documents in the continuing historiography of the Klan. Most were written by amateurs with little regard for the evaluation of historical evidence. For the most part they are uncritical panegyrics to the Klan and its racist objectives, some treating it with humor and others with almost religious veneration. Of the whole group, probably the most worthwhile is historian William Garrott Brown's "The Ku Klux Movement," *Atlantic,* LXXXVII (1901), 634–44, and reprinted as Chapter 4 of his *The Lower South in American History* (N.Y., 1902). No scholarly history of the Klan was ever published in this period, although Walter Lynwood Fleming intended for a time to write one and collected some materials for it. These are in his papers in the New York Public Library.

Among the scholarly histories of Reconstruction which appeared early in the twentieth century, the Klan received somewhat more professional attention, although general attitudes were similar. These works varied in the quality of their treatment of the Klan just as they varied in over-all quality. Walter Lynwood Fleming knew more about the organization and its kinfolk than anyone else and wrote more about them. However, he exceeded most of the rest in his degree of Negrophobia. See his *Civil War and Reconstruction in Alabama* (N.Y., 1905); "The Ku Klux Testimony Relating to Alabama," *Gulf States Historical Magazine,* II (1903), 155–60; and *The Sequel of Appomattox* (New Haven, 1919). J. G. de Roulhac Hamilton, *Reconstruction in North Carolina* (N.Y., 1914), is quite comparable with Fleming. John S. Reynolds, *Reconstruction in South Carolina* (Columbia, 1905), is even more bitter about Reconstruction, but the book has bits of information which are hard to find anywhere else. More balanced are the discussions in C. Mildred Thompson, *Reconstruction in Georgia, Economic, Social, Political, 1865–1872* (N.Y., 1915); William Watson Davis, *The Civil War and Reconstruction in Florida* (N.Y., 1913); James W. Garner, *Reconstruction in Mississippi* (N.Y., 1901); and E. Merton Coulter, *The Civil War and Readjustment in Kentucky* (Chapel Hill, N.C., 1926). The other state histories of Reconstruction dating from this period have very little to say about the Klan. However, special mention should be made of a long series of county studies of Reconstruction in Mississippi, appearing soon after the turn of the century in the *Mississippi Historical Society Publications.* These articles share most of the drawbacks already noted, including amateurishness, but many of them contain useful local information that would be altogether lacking without them. Also worthy of mention are W. D. Wood's "The Ku Klux Klan," *Texas State Historical Association Quarterly,* IX (April 1906), 262–68, which relates to Texas, and John M. Harrell's *The Brooks and Baxter War: A History of the Reconstruction Period in Arkansas* (St. Louis, 1893), which contains much information presented from a pro-Klan point of view.

Since the 1920's, and particularly since 1950, the character of Reconstruction historiography has markedly changed. Carpetbaggers and scalawags have become less villainous and Negroes more capable than before, and the Klan's reputation has plummeted downward. This tendency was not yet very noticeable when Stanley F. Horn brought out his *Invisible Empire: The Story of the Ku Klux Klan 1866–1871* (Boston, 1939). This, the fullest history of the order to date, takes the traditional pro-Klan view and therefore differs sharply from my own interpretation. It contains no documentation, which diminishes its scholarly value, but I have nevertheless found it valuable for some elusive matters concerning the Klan in Tennessee which have not appeared elsewhere. Outside of Tennessee, it is based on readily available published sources. The only other work which attempts to cover the Reconstruction Klan in any detail is William P. Randel, *The Ku Klux Klan, A Century of Infamy* (Philadelphia and N.Y.,

1965). Despite its more modern viewpoint, it is also lacking in documentation and is careless of detail.

The following works, not confined to a single state, are also of value for what they say directly or tangentially about the Klan or related topics: John A. Carpenter, "Atrocities in the Reconstruction Period," *Journal of Negro History,* XLVII (Oct. 1962), 234–47, which helps provide the context of my study; William Watson Davis, "The Federal Enforcement Acts," and Edwin C. Woolley, "Grant's Southern Policy," both in *Studies in Southern History and Politics Inscribed to William Archibald Dunning* (N.Y., 1914); Grady McWhiney and Francis B. Simkins, "The Ghostly Legend of the Ku-Klux Klan," *Negro History Bulletin,* XIV (1951), 109–12, which scotches the myth of superstitious Negro fear of Klan ghosts; James E. Sefton, *The United States Army and Reconstruction, 1865–1877* (Baton Rouge, 1967), the fullest account of its subject; Otis A. Singletary, *Negro Militia and Reconstruction* (Austin, 1957); and Everette Swinney, "Enforcing the Fifteenth Amendment, 1870–1877," *Journal of Southern History,* XXVIII (May, 1962), 202–18.

Specialized state studies of the same kind include: Orval T. Driggs, Jr., "The Issues of the Powell Clayton Regime, 1868–1871," *Arkansas Historical Quarterly,* VIII (1949), 1–75; four exceptionally valuable articles by Ralph L. Peek on Florida, all in the *Florida Historical Quarterly,* "Aftermath of Military Reconstruction, 1868–1869," XLIII (Oct. 1964), 123–41; "Curbing of Voter Intimidation in Florida, 1871," XLIII (April 1965), 333–48; "Election of 1870 and the End of Reconstruction in Florida," XLV (April 1967), 352–68; and "Lawlessness in Florida, 1868–1871," XL (Oct. 1961), 164–85; Joe M. Richardson's equally fine *The Negro in the Reconstruction of Florida, 1865–1877* (Tallahassee, 1965); Alan Conway, *The Reconstruction of Georgia* (Minneapolis, 1966); Allie Bayne Windham Webb, "Organization and Activities of the Knights of the White Camelia in Louisiana, 1867–1869," Louisiana Academy of Sciences, *Proceedings,* XVII (1954), 110–18; Vernon L. Wharton's path-breaking *The Negro in Mississippi, 1865–1890* (Chapel Hill, N.C., 1947); Lillian A. Pereyra, *James Lusk Alcorn, Persistent Whig* (Baton Rouge, 1966); W. McKee Evans, *Ballots and Fence Rails: Reconstruction on the Lower Cape Fear* (Chapel Hill, N.C., 1967), one of the best books written on Southern Reconstruction; Otto H. Olsen's two valuable studies of North Carolina, *Carpetbagger's Crusade: The Life of Albion Winegar Tourgée* (Baltimore, 1965), and "The Ku Klux Klan: A Study in Reconstruction Politics and Propaganda," *North Carolina Historical Review,* XXXIX (Summer 1962), 340–62, which I have followed in some places and which my own research substantiates in others; Herbert Shapiro, "The Ku Klux Klan during Reconstruction: The South Carolina

Episode," *Journal of Negro History,* XLIX (Jan. 1964), 34–55, similarly very helpful; Francis B. Simkins' still useful "The Ku Klux Klan in South Carolina, 1868–1871," *Journal of Negro History,* XII (1927), 606–47; Robert H. Woody, "The South Carolina Election of 1870," *North Carolina Historical Review,* VIII (1931), 168–86; Simkins and Woody's joint *South Carolina During Reconstruction* (Chapel Hill, N.C., 1932), which was probably the first major work of Reconstruction revisionism; Joel Williamson's important *After Slavery: The Negro in South Carolina During Reconstruction, 1861–1877* (Chapel Hill, N.C., 1965); Thomas B. Alexander's two studies, "Kukluxism in Tennessee, 1865–1869," *Tennessee Historical Quarterly,* VIII (1949), 195–219, and *Political Reconstruction in Tennessee* (Nashville, 1950), both very useful despite a more favorable view of the Klan than my own; E. Merton Coulter's hostile view of *William G. Brownlow, Fighting Parson of the Southern Highlands* (Chapel Hill, N.C., 1937); James W. Patton, *Unionism and Reconstruction in Tennessee* (Chapel Hill, N.C., 1934); and Robert W. Shook, "The Federal Military in Texas, 1865–1870," *Texas Military History,* VI (Spring 1967), 3–53.

Index

533